THE BEGINNINGS
OF NATIONAL POLITICS

THE BEGINNINGS
OF NATIONAL
POLITICS

An Interpretive History
of the Continental Congress

JACK N. RAKOVE

Alfred A. Knopf *New York* *1979*

Copyright © 1979 by Jack N. Rakove

All rights reserved under International and Pan-American Copy-
right Conventions. Published in the United States by Alfred A.
Knopf, Inc., New York, and simultaneously in Canada by Random
House of Canada Limited, Toronto. Distributed by Random
House, Inc., New York.

Library of Congress Cataloging in Publication Data

Rakove, Jack N. 1947–
The beginnings of national politics.

Bibliography: p.
Includes Index.
1. United States—Politics and government—Revolu-
tion, 1775–1783. 2. United States. Continental
Congress. 3. United States—Politics and government—
1783–1789. I. Title
E210.R34   1979   973.3′12   79-10227
ISBN 0-394-42370-4

Manufactured in the United States of America

FIRST EDITION

For my parents

Contents

Acknowledgments

————————◌◌◌————————

TO Bernard Bailyn I owe not only my conversion to the study of early American history but the intellectual excitement of working with a teacher whose standards, expectations, and example have constantly stimulated my own efforts. I am equally grateful to Wallace MacCaffrey for first instructing me in the responsibilities of scholarship and teaching. Pauline Maier's early and continuing interest in my work has meant much more to me than she has probably realized. More recently Richard D. Brown, Ronald P. Formisano, Michael Kammen, William Stinchcombe, Clarence Ver Steeg, Stephen S. Webb, and my Colgate colleague Harry Payne have all offered useful advice and, what is perhaps more important, encouragement. Jane Garrett's patience and confidence and Ellen G. Mastromonaco's assistance were also deeply appreciated.

Financial support from the Graduate School of Arts and Sciences at Harvard University, the National Endowment for the Humanities, and the Research Council and the Humanities Faculty Development Fund of Colgate University have defrayed the costs of research and typing. Danielle Koenig was a calm and efficient typist. I cannot thank by name all of the archivists and librarians who assisted me in the course of my research, but I am particularly grateful to Nathaniel Bunker and Michael Cotter of Widener Library and to Martha Cordova of Colgate. Paul H. Smith and Gerard Gawalt provided useful advice about manuscript sources at an earlier stage of this project.

xi

I have dedicated this book to my parents, both of whom contributed directly to its making. From my father I learned that the study of American politics begins with an attempt to understand the distinctive attitudes of American politicians. My mother, a woman of remarkable energy, spent the better part of a summer typing the original version of this book. But those were hardly their most important contributions. My wife, Helen, gave up a promising career as my research "partner" to pursue her own profession, but without her support, patience, and occasional exercise of discipline, this book could not have been written. Our son, Robert, was content to lie on the floor of my study while I was revising the chapters on the late 1770's, but by the early 1780's he was struggling to get at the typewriter. Perhaps he was trying to save me from whatever errors I have missed, which of course are my responsibility alone.

—J.N.R.

Preface

————————————∾————————————

TWO momentous meetings at Philadelphia frame the subject of this book: the First Continental Congress of 1774 and
the Constitutional Convention of 1787. Few contemporaries
would have been greatly surprised had either meeting ended in
failure or had the union that the Congress embodied dissolved at
any of several critical points in between. Nor were the members
of Congress ever able to ignore the precarious foundation of their
authority. The creation of an effective national government was
thus one of the most difficult and persistent tasks that the Revolutionaries confronted, and it was a problem whose dimensions
seemed to change with the course of events. In the early years
of the Revolution, union depended largely on the delegates' ability to frame a broadly acceptable strategy of resistance. By the
late 1770's and early 1780's, it meant devising expedients to sustain a tottering war effort and the morale of a tired populace.
After independence was secured, the continued existence of a
federal union came to require a thorough and incisive reexami-
nation of the major principles of American republicanism.

Seen from this perspective, the history of the Continental
Congress poses two major problems. One requires asking, quite
simply, how Congress first acquired and then sought to maintain
its authority. What assumptions, considerations, and conditions
shaped the exercise of congressional power during each of the
major phases of its existence? Because the authority of Congress
ultimately rested on the success of its measures, this question

leads naturally toward an analysis of why certain policies were adopted and how decisions were reached. The second major problem involves asking how members of Congress and other American leaders attempted to resolve the difficult theoretical questions that inevitably arose in the course of creating a federal system of government. What was the original American under-standing of the nature of federalism, and how was it affected by the experience of managing a revolution? These are the questions this book attempts to answer.

Modern historians of the Congress have approached these problems by emphasizing the factional character of its politics and the ideological differences that distinguished rival groups of delegates.* In the writings of Merrill Jensen, these divisions seem comparatively simple. Jensen describes a clear and persistent conflict between radicals and conservatives, the former favoring independence and the creation of sovereign republican govern-ments in the states, the latter initially desiring reconciliation with Britain and, when that failed, working for the establishment of a strong national government capable of preserving their élite status and property. The radicals prevailed in 1776 and 1777, with the drafting of the Declaration of Independence and its constitu-tional equivalent, the Articles of Confederation. But the conser-vatives, after an energetic but unsuccessful resurgence in the early 1780's, finally secured a decisive advantage with the calling of the Constitutional Convention.† Jensen's general argument

---

*An important exception is, of course, Edmund C. Burnett, whose eight-volume edition of *Letters of Members of the Continental Congress* (Washington, D.C., 1921–36) provided the foundation for modern scholarship on the Congress. Despite its shortcomings, Burnett's *Letters* was a marvelous work of historical editing. His own history of *The Continental Congress* (New York, 1941) is, how-ever, disappointing; though perhaps definitive as a narrative, it avoids interpreta-tion and analysis and thus has had little appreciable effect on historical scholar-ship. A new and greatly expanded edition of the delegates' correspondence is now being published under the auspices of the Library of Congress—Paul H. Smith, *et al.*, eds., *Letters of Delegates to Congress, 1774–1789* (Washington, D.C., 1976–).

†This interpretation is most forcibly expressed in Jensen's two books, *The Articles of Confederation: An Interpretation of the Social-Constitutional History of the American Revolution, 1774–1781* (Madison, Wisc., 1941), and *The New Na-tion: A History of the United States During the Confederation, 1781–1789* (New York, 1950).

has been further developed by E. James Ferguson in his definitive study of Revolutionary finance.*

H. James Henderson has recently offered a more complex interpretation of congressional partisanship, based in large measure on the methods of roll-call analysis. Henderson argues that recognizable factions existed throughout the history of Congress, and that sectional differences were the most important source of division. An equally distinctive feature of Henderson's interpretation, however, is that it explains these conflicts in ideological terms. Disagreements over policies and institutions thus reflected the divergent meanings and goals that different groups found in the Revolution itself.† It is in this sense that Henderson's analysis can be compared to the work of Jensen and his students. For while the two interpretations differ in their treatment of the dynamics of faction, they see policymaking within Congress in similar terms. Coherent factions were vying for power—indeed for control of the Revolution—and the specific decisions that Congress reached reflected their respective strengths at particular points.

Because it conforms to modern conceptions of political behavior, such an approach may at first seem attractive in its realism; whether it accurately describes how Congress actually reached decisions is, however, another question. Without denying that significant divisions often did exist within Congress, this book offers a different interpretation of its politics. It argues that major decisions of Congress owed much less to partisan conflict than other historians have concluded. Other considerations usu-

*E. James Ferguson, *The Power of the Purse: A History of American Public Finance, 1776–1790* (Chapel Hill, N.C., 1961).

†H. James Henderson, *Party Politics in the Continental Congress* (New York, 1974). Henderson's use of the concept of ideology is critical to his argument that congressional voting blocs were not merely clusters of like-minded men but cohesive legislative parties. For reasons that will become clear in the text, I remain unconvinced that these voting blocs constituted legislative parties in any meaningful sense of the term. My understanding of this question has been sharpened by Ronald P. Formisano's critique of recent literature on the first American party system: "Deferential-Participant Politics: The Early Republic's Political Culture, 1789–1840," *American Political Science Review*, 68 (1974), 473–87; and see also Jack R. Pole's review of Jackson T. Main, *Political Parties Before the Constitution* (Chapel Hill, N.C., 1973), in the *American Historical Review*, 78 (1973), 1527.

ally proved more important: the extent to which external events limited available alternatives, the delegates' shared assumptions about the requirements of resistance, and their sensitivity to the preservation of Congress's authority. A realistic analysis of congressional politics must begin, I would argue, by reconstructing what courses of action the delegates actually perceived were available to them. I have therefore sought to be faithful to the flow of events, to ask what was proposed and when, to delineate what was actually at stake in specific decisions, and to avoid (or at least minimize) the use of key words—radical, conservative, nationalist, parochialist—that characterize positions without accurately describing them. To view the situation of Congress from this perspective is to recognize that American leaders encountered a series of perplexing and difficult problems, rooted in the distinctive character of the Revolution and the dislocations it produced. Novel issues, intractable problems, unattractive options, partial solutions: these were the usual determinants of Revolutionary policymaking, as the Handlins argued long ago.*

This conception of the character of congressional politics also has important implications for our understanding of the Articles of Confederation and of the ambitions of the delegates themselves. This book supports what is sometimes called the "nationalist" interpretation of the origins of American union. It argues that the framers of the Articles intended to vest certain sovereign powers in Congress and to subordinate the states to its decisions. But more important, it also attempts to treat the development of early federalist thinking historically: to show, that is, that the problem of federalism was at first not carefully examined, that basic issues were neither clearly posed nor well understood, and that pragmatic considerations continually impeded the progress of constitutional thought. An understanding of the burdensome and even tedious aspects of running a revolutionary war raises similar questions about the delegates' ambitions and political motives. These men were not professional politicians in

---

*Oscar and Mary F. Handlin, "Radicals and Conservatives in New England After Independence," *New England Quarterly,* 17 (1944), 343–55, and "Revolutionary Economic Policy in Massachusetts," *William and Mary Quarterly,* 3d ser., 4 (1947), 3–26. The implications of the Handlins' work extend, of course, beyond Massachusetts. For an equally incisive discussion of the problem of characterizing positions as radical or conservative, see Cecilia Kenyon, "Republicanism and Radicalism in the American Revolution," *ibid.,* 19 (1962), 153–82.

the modern sense of the term, and not surprisingly, few of them found attendance at Congress either enjoyable or rewarding. Most were anxious to return home as soon as they respectably could. An examination of their complaints, attitudes, and careers suggests that—at least at this level of politics—few delegates consciously saw themselves competing for power or struggling to control the Revolution.

To clarify the major lines of interpretation, this book is divided into four parts. Part One examines the strategy of opposition to Great Britain as it developed between the early 1770's, when a few American leaders began to think about the idea of an intercolonial congress, and the ratification of the French alliance in 1778. The events of these years require careful examination because they defined the major assumptions and lessons that governed the conduct of national politics. Part Two traces the framing of the Articles of Confederation and describes the problems and conditions that shaped congressional administration of the war before the Articles were ratified in 1781. Part Three examines the crises that marked the final years of the war, when partisan animosities, major issues of foreign policy, and the specter of a financial and logistical catastrophe first called into question the apparent lessons of the mid-1770's. Finally, Part Four reviews the progressive deterioration of congressional authority after 1783 and traces the evolving strategy of reform that led to the Constitutional Convention of 1787. The book ends with an explanation of the conditions that enabled the Convention to transcend the limited and static boundaries within which previous discussions of the problems of union had been confined, and thus to transform the entire structure and character of national politics. To go further—to analyze the Convention's deliberations, the ratification debates of 1787–88, and the politics of the First Congress—would require a second volume.

Part One

RESISTANCE
AND
REVOLUTION

CHAPTER I

Resistance Without Union, 1770-1774

A LTHOUGH great revolutions do not spring from transient causes, they are often launched amid conditions of confusion, uncertainty, and surprise. Under these circumstances, even aspiring rebels and seasoned politicians find it difficult to lay careful plans or anticipate events. In 1773, when the idea of an American congress was first proposed, the leaders of colonial resistance to British policies were casting about for ways to end the "political Lethargy" of the preceding three years. Their tentative speculations about reviving intercolonial cooperation scarcely foreshadowed the popular mobilization that would take place in 1774 or the astounding authority the First Continental Congress would acquire. The discussions of 1773 thus reveal as much about the obstacles American leaders faced as the solutions later events would provide. They suggest, too, how barely skeletal a framework for intercolonial politics existed before the Coercive Acts transformed the course of American resistance and simplified the tasks confronting the delegates who assembled at Philadelphia in September 1774. Yet lessons and memories drawn from the seemingly fallow years of the early 1770's lingered. The decisions of the First Congress reflected not only the clarification of issues that took place during the summer of 1774, but also the mood of uncertainty and lassitude that had characterized the earlier years of the decade.

The Fallow Years

EARLY in the spring of 1770, Parliament repealed all the Town-shend duties except that on tea. The new ministry of Lord North hoped that colonial opposition could not survive a substantial repeal of the ill-conceived duties levied in 1767. Eager to resume normal commercial operations and suspicious of the rumored duplicity of competitors in other ports, American merchants demanded an end to the non-importation of British goods. By early fall the colonial boycott so laboriously pieced together in 1768 and 1769 had virtually collapsed, leaving in its place an atmosphere of mutual recrimination between town and country, rival cities, and even regions. Local efforts to prevent the drinking of dutied tea continued, with mixed success, but prospects for maintaining a cohesive intercolonial opposition to imperial policy had seemingly evaporated.[1]

To the comparatively small number of colonial politicians who consciously continued to identify themselves as leaders of resistance, repeal did little to weaken the darker suspicions of British intentions aroused during the struggles of the 1760's. Indeed the retention of the tea duty, like the Declaratory Act of 1766, signaled the government's refusal to accept American interpretations of the great constitutional questions. So long as Parliament claimed a right to levy taxes and enact laws binding the colonists, future disputes seemed likely. Moreover, other government measures not requiring parliamentary action might still be seen as part of a systematic effort to subvert American liberties. If the ministry planned no frontal assault against the rights of all the colonies, dangerous forays might be launched against individual provinces. Such, for example, was the plan to provide crown salaries for Massachusetts officials. "Here is displayed another part of that pernicious plan of government laid down for America," Francis Dana informed Henry Marchant. " 'Tis opening in this Province, but it will be extended thro out the Continent"; and once carried to completion, it would reduce the colonists "to a state too humiliating and abject to be endured by a people whose ideas of Political Freedom are no better than a Hottentot's."[2]

If their convictions were no less compelling than before, however, the strategy of resistance that emerged after 1770 was tentative, even passive. American leaders lamented the absence of any obvious bonds of union and cooperation but could at first imagine no effective remedies. The acrimony accompanying the breakdown of non-importation seemed to pose powerful obstacles to new activity, particularly when the problems encountered even in organizing a boycott were recalled. As Arthur Lee observed from London in February 1773, "the late experience of mutual faithlessness, with the disunited state which is the consequence of it, renders the probability of our harmonizing, in any mode of effectual opposition, extremely small."[3] The local committees that had been formed to enforce non-importation had disbanded, and in their absence intercolonial political contacts were substantially reduced. Even the character of correspondence seemed to have changed. In the late 1760's, organized committees of Sons of Liberty, consciously striving to maintain a unified resistance, had created what were in effect quasi-official channels of communication. By contrast the political correspondence of the early 1770's was essentially a private exchange of mutual exhortations and news of British politics: it did little more than allow men of similar views to share information and speculation as often or infrequently as they liked. Their absorption with British politics reflected a conviction that the next phase of the struggle could be launched only from London, that the initiative lay again with the government "at home."

The difficulty colonial leaders experienced simply in maintaining regular communication with each other and reliable sources of information in England was one measure of the prevailing political inertia. Convinced that resistance would again be necessary but stymied by the visible decline of popular interest in politics, they groped for ways to revive a modicum of cohesion. As early as January 1771 Arthur Lee began preaching the need to establish a regular network of correspondence. Eight months later Samuel Adams responded to Lee's hint with a genteel vision of American corresponding societies—modeled after the English Society of Supporters of the Bill of Rights—which would appoint deputies to an annual convention and correspond with allies in London. But, Adams abruptly apologized, "This is a sudden thought and drops undigested from my pen. It would be an arduous task for any man to attempt to awaken a sufficient Number in the colonies to so grand an undertaking." Evidently he decided the task was too arduous. Another year passed before the creation of the Boston Committee of Correspondence, and that committee, once organized, confined its activities to Massachusetts.[4]

In 1773, at the suggestion of the Virginia Burgesses, the provincial assemblies established standing committees of correspondence. But in fact those committees conducted little correspondence before the crisis of 1774. Samuel Adams and Richard Henry Lee did not begin corresponding until 1773, and as late as December of that year Charles Thomson could still suggest that "a correspondence might be opened and kept up between the politicians and principal men in the several governments."[5] Surviving letters suggest that hardly more than a score of men scattered throughout the continent were actively involved in this network. Many of the key actors of the Revolution remained outside its limited range, including such figures as Washington, John Jay, James Duane, Henry Laurens, and Robert Morris.

Ideologically committed as the surviving radical leaders clearly were, it would nevertheless be wrong to think of them as a revolutionary cadre waiting to exploit some new crisis to seize power. Only in Massachusetts, where the administration of Thomas Hutchinson provided a convenient target, did the old issues of the 1760's still dominate provincial politics. Imperial questions also provoked less serious controversies in South Carolina, Maryland, and New York. But elsewhere other issues were quick to reassert themselves: familiar contests over patronage and place, the allocation of new lands, or the extension of effective government to the frontier.

Nor were most radical leaders intensely committed to political life for its own sake. Only the still-elusive figure of Samuel Adams suggests a recognizable revolutionary "type"; and not because Adams was already bent on American independence—a dubious claim—but rather because his ascetic devotion to the mundane tasks of political organization set him apart even from his closest colleagues. Other former leaders of resistance welcomed the opportunity to lay political concerns aside. John Dickinson "has been lost to the cause of Liberty ever since his Letters were well received," William Shippen, Jr., complained in 1770; and when Samuel Adams pressed Dickinson to write in support of the Massachusetts General Court's running debate with Hutchinson, the famous "Pennsylvania Farmer" declined.[6]

For American radicals as for colonial officeholders in general, politics remained an avocation, not a career: a way for merchants and planters to acquire public prestige to complement private wealth, for lawyers to gain celebrity and thus clients, for village notables to confirm their superior status, or for land speculators to develop useful connections. Most of their time was still spent tending to private affairs, and they preferred it that way. They had yet to be seduced, as Hannah Arendt has shrewdly observed, by the "charms" of "the acts and deeds which liberation demanded from them . . . the speech-making and decision-taking, the oratory and the business, the thinking and the persuading, and the actual doing which proved necessary" to carry the Revolution through "to its logical conclusion: independent government and the foundation of a new body politic."[7]

Given the character of their own attitude toward politics, they were not surprised that popular interest in the imperial questions of the 1760's had visibly slackened in the absence of palpable threats to colonial liberties. Yet they also sensed that a substantial portion of the general public had not entirely forgotten the concerns vented during the agitation of the 1760's. Writing to Arthur Lee shortly after the collapse of non-importation, John Dickinson struck a curiously sanguine note in describing prospects for future resistance. "My countrymen have been provoked," he remarked,

but not quite enough. Thanks to the excellent spirit of administration, I doubt not but proper measures will be pursued for provoking them still more. Some future oppression will render them more attentive to what is offered to them; and the calm friend of freedom, who faithfully watches and calls out on a new danger, will be more regarded than if he endeavours to repeat the alarm on an attack that is thought to have been in some measure repelled. I do not despair.

In this letter, Dickinson succinctly outlined the model of behavior that other opposition leaders would find most attractive during the years immediately ahead. Sensible that popular opinion could be mobilized only by some new crisis, believing that in 1770 they had reached and exhausted the limits of their ability to alter the course of events, they settled down for a period of watching and waiting—and writing. Because popular indifference or apostasy—drinking dutied tea, for example—could create embarrassing precedents, the principles of resistance had to be kept

alive even when colonial rights were not directly threatened.
Celebrating the repeal of the Stamp Act, commemorating the
Boston Massacre, publishing exhortatory newspaper essays, and
observing other rituals could not change the basic political situa-
tion, but they were still necessary. The great dilemma, Charles
Thomson noted, was that:

An ill timed resistance may ruin the cause, and a supine passive acquiescence damp the spirit of liberty. Experience evinces that unsuccessful
attempts strengthen the power, they are meant to controul; and on the
other hand, how difficult it is to rouse a people whose spirits are broken
with oppression and who are long accustomed to servile obedience. The
greater care, therefore, is necessary to keep awake the sense of liberty,
and at the same time not to hazard a breach, until proper measures are
concerted to insure success.

Arthur Lee's favorite adage—*Fortiter in re, suaviter in modo**—
remained the watchword of opposition.[8]
   But what precisely were radical leaders waiting for? None
would challenge Dickinson's belief that the principles of opposition had to be preserved "till Time shall ripen the Period for
asserting more successfully the Liberties of these Colonies; that
thereby they may be kept on the Watch to seize the happy
opportunity, whenever it offers."[9] But the difficulty of foreseeing
when and how that opportunity would arise further complicated
the task of forming a coherent plan of opposition. Nevertheless,
colonial leaders were free to indulge their imaginations by con-
structing alternative scenarios for the future course of imperial
politics. Their speculations reveal something of the uncertainty
that continued to cloud their thinking well into 1774. Although
it took little foresight to recognize that American independence
could prove the eventual result of a progressive deterioration of
imperial relations, there is scant direct evidence to suggest that
colonial leaders were actively contemplating this possibility.
Constitutional reform within the empire remained the only legitimate goal, and each of the scenarios they envisioned was directed toward the establishment of American liberties within
that context.
   Considerations of demography inspired the most pacific of
these lines of development. Balancing their confident visions of

*Which can be loosely translated as "Firm in principles, prudent in means."

an ever-expanding, ever more prosperous America against a
Hogarthian image of English corruption and degeneracy, some
colonial leaders concluded that, in every measurable index of
social progress, the colonies were ultimately destined to overtake
the mother country. The reapportionment of political rights
would naturally follow America's growing wealth and, it was
implied, Britain's increasing dependence on colonial resources.
Understandably ignorant of the profound transformation of British society that was itself beginning in the late eighteenth century, some colonial politicians readily believed that a strategy of
avoiding conflict would not only favor their cause but ultimately
prove decisive. Few found this policy more attractive than Benjamin Franklin and Arthur Lee, the two men whose letters from
London provided American whigs with their most important
sources of political intelligence, and their Boston correspondent
Thomas Cushing, the speaker of the Massachusetts House. "Our
natural increase in wealth and population, will in a course of
years, effectually settle this dispute in our favor," Cushing observed in 1773, while continued controversy over the extent of
Parliament's authority might produce "a rupture fatal to both
countries." Like Franklin, Cushing hoped the government
would have the wisdom to retract its odious system of colonial
regulations, thereby allowing the tired constitutional questions
"to fall asleep" and Britain to regain the affection of its colonies.[10]
     Other occasions might arise, however, to enable the colonies
to exploit their natural advantages more directly. Any grave
international situation that led a beleaguered Britain to seek
American assistance would allow the colonies to demand formal
recognition of their disputed rights. In the early 1770's, then,
colonial leaders followed every rumor of a European crisis, and
although no war materialized, the evidence of recent history
made it reasonable to suppose that one must eventually occur.
The longer one was delayed, of course, the more valuable would
American assistance become. And whenever war did finally
break out, Charles Thomson noted in 1773, "Then will be the
time for the American legislatures, with modesty & firmness, to
recapitulate their wrongs, explain their grievances and assert
their rights." But what if, even then, Britain balked at confirming
American liberties and adopted coercive measures against the
colonies instead? American ends would still be served. For either, as Franklin predicted, "such compulsory attempts will con-

tribute to unite and strengthen us," or, as Arthur Lee observed, British embroilment in Europe would undercut "any military operation against us." Moreover this scenario had a valuable sanction in English constitutional history, which showed, Franklin noted, that "in similar situations of the subjects here, redress would seldom be obtained but by withholding aids when the sovereign was in distress."[11]

Both of these scenarios—of demographic growth or international crisis—had an indefinite quality about them; neither implied that a resumption of the struggles of the 1760's was imminent. But one other line of development also seemed imaginable. Some overt, blatant act of the British government might suddenly precipitate a radical change in the existing static situation, enraging the people at large and giving radical leaders a new opportunity to regain political influence and mobilize a more cohesive opposition. In 1771 and 1772 this, too, seemed remote, but events in 1773 made such a scenario more plausible.

One common assumption united each of these attempts to foresee the future course of imperial politics: that colonial leaders could themselves do little to alter the state of politics. They had either to react to events abroad or else wait until the passage of time and the development of American society provided new solutions to old problems. What is striking about their speculations, then, is the essential tone of passivity that runs through them. In the early 1770's, the task of organizing an active, viable intercolonial resistance movement posed almost insuperable obstacles. In the absence of a galvanizing crisis on which they could capitalize, effective political organization seemed inconceivable.

The Idea of a Congress

EVENTS in the New Year of 1773 gave these speculations a clearer focus and also fostered the first serious discussions of the idea of convening an American congress. On January 5, the royal commission appointed to investigate the burning of the schooner *Gaspée* off the Rhode Island coast held its first meeting in Newport. On the next day, not far to the north, Governor Thomas Hutchinson opened the new session of the Massachusetts General Court with a closely reasoned defense of the indivisible sovereignty of Parliament. Empowered to return any suspects it identified to Britain for trial, the *Gaspée* Commission constituted an apparent encroachment on the civil liberties of individuals— although its failure to discover the culprits partly defused the threat it posed. By contrast, while Hutchinson's speech itself raised no immediate dangers, its implications were more ominous. Responding to the inflammatory attacks his Boston enemies had launched against his acceptance of a crown salary and a similar proposal for paying the salaries of provincial judges, Hutchinson naïvely hoped to undermine their influence by a thorough refutation of their constitutional arguments. He was also convinced that his opponents intended to convert their recent activities into a campaign to revive intercolonial opposition to the government, a specter that reinforced the need to demonstrate the absurdity of their position. Ironically, it was Hutchinson's response to the threat he perceived that gave Samuel Adams and his colleagues the opportunity they had been waiting for.[12]

Whether the plans of the Boston radicals were initially as ambitious and well laid as Hutchinson assumed is questionable. When a group of Rhode Island politicians wrote to ask how their colony should oppose the *Gaspée* Commission, the tentative advice Samuel Adams offered was remarkably cautious.[13] And while Hutchinson's address sparked an extended public debate with the General Court, Adams and Cushing were careful to inform their correspondents that the assembly had been reluctant to issue any reply. "The Silence of the other Assemblies of late upon every Subject that concerns the joynt Interest of the Colonies," Adams wrote John Dickinson, "rendered it somewhat difficult to determine what to say with Propriety." Although such an apology might have been somewhat disingenuous, the Massachusetts leaders did fear that other colonies might accuse them of precipitating a needless, harmful controversy—a legitimate concern that would influence their actions well into 1775.[14]

Both the circumstances and substance of this debate—a haughty, ambitious governor, disseminating dangerous doctrines —minimized this danger, however, and the Boston leaders were not slow to appreciate its other potential uses. Simple republication of the relevant documents would help awaken public opinion throughout the continent. But more important, the debate might provide an opportunity for erecting new mechanisms of intercolonial cooperation. In its first reply to Hutchinson, the

Massachusetts House dangled a hint that it might be necessary to call a congress to determine where to draw "the line of distinction between the supreme authority of Parliament, and the total independence of the colonies."[15] In March, responding to news of the *Gaspée* Commission, the Virginia House of Burgesses called for the appointment of standing provincial committees of correspondence, a proposal that encouraged further consideration of the idea of a congress. And in April, Cushing and Adams respectively raised the question in separate letters to Franklin and Lee.[16]

In the early months of 1773, neither Franklin nor Lee would have favored such a suggestion. Franklin was still attached to the notion of avoiding open conflict, while Lee worried that "The northern colonies are precipitating matters too much." In June, Lee warned Samuel Adams that "the open measure of a congress" might provoke Britain to retaliate before the colonies had realized their natural strength. Within a fortnight, however, Lee changed his mind, and in early July, Franklin, too, endorsed the idea. Both men argued, in effect, that the government would not voluntarily grant the constitutional concessions American whigs desired. "Some degree of compulsion" was necessary, Lee noted, while Franklin suggested that the government would prove more receptive to proposals issued by a congress held in peacetime than by one called to exploit Britain's insecurity in the event of war. For the first time, both men seemed willing to support American initiatives that they recognized might well "bring the dispute to a crisis."[17]

With these endorsements in hand, the Boston leaders apparently gave the idea of a congress renewed consideration. By late August, Hutchinson had been informed that Adams and his collaborators had written to other colonies to suggest the convening of a congress.[18] One month later the case for a congress was carefully explored in an essay published in the *Boston Gazette* and subsequently reprinted in other colonies. Despite the efforts of statesmen in Britain and America, "Observation" wrote, "no plan of union is yet agreed on between them, the dispute continues, and every thing floats in uncertainty." Given this state of affairs, the author proposed

That a congress of American states be assembled as soon as possible, draw up a Bill of Rights and publish it to the world; choose an ambassador to reside at the British court to act for the united colonies; appoint where the congress shall annually meet, and how it may be summoned upon any extraordinary occasion, what farther steps necessary to be taken, &c.

Hutchinson read this piece and found his year-long suspicions confirmed, though he also suggested that the agitation for a congress—the measure he deemed "most likely to rekindle a general flame in the Colonies"—reflected the dejection he professed to observe in "the leaders of the Party."[19]

Yet suggestive as these references seem, what ultimately remains more striking is that colonial leaders failed to move toward the creation of a congress even though a promising opportunity for such an innovation soon arose. For during these same autumn weeks Americans were learning of the government's new plan to grant the East India Company a tea monopoly in the colonies, a decision that logically could have provided the occasion for converting these scattered hints of intercolonial union into a movement for a congress. Yet such a movement did not take place; nor apparently was it even seriously considered. The opposition to the Tea Act of 1773 was effective but not innovative. Its tactics were essentially a reversion to the non-importation movement of 1768–70. Decisions to obstruct the landing and sale of the tea were made autonomously by local meetings and committees. Correspondence among major commercial centers and between seaports and the countryside increased, but the provincial committees of correspondence, so enthusiastically formed during the preceding months, remained empty vessels, neither directing nor coordinating resistance.[20]

Nevertheless, at the turn of the critical year of 1774 radical leaders could view the prospects for resistance with greater optimism than had been possible a year before. Virginia's response to the *Gaspée* Commission, the skillful exploitation of the debate between Hutchinson and the General Court, the subsequent clamor over the publication of Hutchinson's private letters, and the rapid mobilization of opposition to the Tea Act: all of these developments demonstrated that colonial resistance had discovered a new and surprising cohesion. Somewhat ironically, however, these events also served to distract radical leaders from examining the problem of American union more carefully. In the political vocabulary of 1773, union was still largely defined in terms of reaching fundamental agreement on principles, not of creating new mechanisms or institutions of coordination.[21]

Nor could agreement over principles by itself define a program of resistance or eliminate the substantial uncertainty that still colored patriot thinking. Many of the underlying assumptions of the early 1770's remained intact. A constitutional reconciliation with Britain, achieved either through the negotiation of an American "Bill of Rights" or a repeal of the objectionable measures enacted since 1763, was still the only legitimate goal of opposition. But political speculations retained an indefinite and naïve character. A restoration of the harmony of 1771–72 was entirely conceivable. If Thomas Hutchinson could be removed from office, the potentially explosive situation in Massachusetts could be defused—which was what Franklin had intended by transmitting the governor's letters to the Boston radicals. In many ways, too, colonial leaders were content to let the initiative again pass over to the government. If the ministry acted wisely and gauged colonial popular opinion correctly, it might also avoid new provocations, even in the wake of the Boston Tea Party. Despite the quickened anxieties recent events had evoked, the private political correspondence of this period betrays little sense of imminent crisis.[22]

So, in perhaps the most detailed assessment of American prospects composed during these months, Charles Thomson could still advocate a strategy of moderate protest and delay. The assemblies should again submit well-reasoned petitions, Thomson wrote the Boston Committee, while politicians in each province "opened" a correspondence. Meanwhile the colonial militias should be strengthened, and "young men of fortune" encouraged to "enter into foreign service, to visit foreign courts, and to establish acquaintances and connexions abroad." Some of the colonies, Thomson concluded, "are in their infancy and can yield no support to the common cause; others are guided by men of doubtful, some by men of timid dispositions; and the greatest part not sufficiently roused or animated."[23] As late as April 1774 the major interest of radical leaders seemed to center on William Goddard's scheme for an American post office, a measure not without constitutional implications but scarcely a bridge to revolution.[24]

Even in Massachusetts no one could be sure what the coming months would bring, and a certain degree of caution still seemed advisable. After preparing a circular letter urging the formation of a common intercolonial front of opposition, the Boston Committee of Correspondence decided to restrict the official distribution of this proposal to Massachusetts. The committee's provincial counterpart issued a circular letter largely confined to repeating vague exhortations of the need for union. In the early months of 1774 opinions about the government's response to the Tea Party varied widely. Although the radical physician Thomas Young hinted that "our next attack will be upon the Customs House," others thought that Hutchinson's imminent departure for England might usher in a period of relative peace. Elbridge Gerry wrote thoughtfully about the need for military training as a long-term aid to resistance.[25] In April, a scant five weeks before news of the Boston Port Act reached the colonies, John Adams could still assess the likely course of Anglo-American politics and find himself

of the same opinion that I have been for many Years, that there is not Spirit enough on Either side to bring the Question to a compleat Decision—and that We shall oscilate like a Pendulum and fluctuate like the Ocean, for many Years to come, and never obtain a compleat Redress of American Grievances, nor submit to an absolute Establishment of Parliamentary Authority[,] but be trimming between both as we have been for ten Years past, for more Years to come than you and I shall live. Our Children, may see Revolutions, and be concerned and active in effecting them of which we can form no conception.

Adams had studied imperial politics for a decade, and his skeptical opinion was entirely consistent with the rhythm of the events he had observed.[26]

Nevertheless, from the events of 1773 the Boston leaders apparently drew one conclusion that would have critical consequences in 1774. The success of spontaneously organized local movements to prevent the sale of East India tea demonstrated that an intercolonial boycott could be effectively mounted whenever a suitable opportunity arose and without prior consultations in a congress. Occasional references to a congress were still made, notably in John Hancock's commemoration of the Boston Massacre. Yet it is perhaps equally significant that when Samuel Adams sent a copy of this speech to John Dickinson, he failed even to mention, much less endorse, the measure Hancock had described as "the most effectual method of establishing such an

Union as the present posture of our affairs requires."²⁷ As their
strategy in the weeks immediately following the arrival of the
Boston Port Act revealed, Adams and his colleagues were inclined to gamble that rural Massachusetts and the other colonies
could be induced to join an immediate commercial boycott without the prior convening of a congress. Thus while in 1773 the idea
of calling a congress had been considered a radical, even provocative step, in the crisis of 1774 it could be proposed and accepted
as a comparatively restrained response to overt British coercion
—a shift in perspective that helps to explain how the First Congress acquired such substantial power so rapidly.

The Structure of Politics

To radical leaders in the early 1770's, then, colonial union was
preeminently a problem of politics, not of government. Concerned with maintaining popular support, recognizing that the
real initiative in imperial affairs rested with Britain, their absorption in tactical problems diverted them from giving sustained
consideration to the form and shape some future union might
take. They could have had little interest in the various plans for
unifying the colonies that periodically circulated through the
winding corridors of the imperial bureaucracy. Nothing was
wrong with the colonial constitutions, they thought, that could
not be cured by curtailing the influence of the ministry in England and the unwarranted powers claimed by Parliament or exercised by imperial lackeys in America. Such a prescription left
them unconcerned about longer range problems of intercolonial
government.

Thus in fact it was not the leaders of resistance who thought
longest and hardest about the inherent problems of unifying and
integrating thirteen distinct provinces. Their concerns were
political. It was instead imperial officials and latent loyalists
who believed that the turbulence of American politics was a
function of the weakness of government, and a problem whose
solution required subordinating individual provinces and parochial interests to a set of common policies, unifying institutions,
and external controls. And little in their experience suggested
that the colonists could efficiently govern their own provinces,

much less cooperate in managing the affairs of some continental confederacy.

In retrospect, of course, British policymakers obviously committed one of their gravest errors when they converted this image of colonial political immaturity into an argument for the likely success of a policy of repression. They simply failed to anticipate the extent to which the logic of resistance generated a nationalist impulse sufficiently powerful to carry the Americans through the critical first stages of revolution. Yet in the context of the early 1770's, when the conditions favoring the creation of a viable American union seemed less potent than the obstacles the colonists would have to overcome, their skepticism was certainly justifiable. For what is most striking about the structure of American politics on the eve of independence is the apparent absence of several prerequisites for the establishment of what would become, in effect, a national government.

There were, in the first place, no readily available or immediately appealing models capable of outlining what form an American confederation should take. The theoretical definitions of confederations found in familiar Enlightenment treatises on international law and politics were merely suggestive, not instructive. And the thrust of the previous decade's debate over the authority of Parliament left potentially nagging problems about the extent of provincial autonomy. Although a congress composed of representatives elected by each of the colonies would obviate the principal objection the colonists had levied against Parliament, the apportionment of power between some central agency and its constituencies might well prove troublesome. Yet there is little evidence to suggest that any leader of resistance gave these matters serious thought before 1774. In December 1771, it is true, "American Solon" had announced his intention "to write a system of government, and civil policy, for the united provinces in America," which would be "ready for them whenever necessity shall oblige them to set up a government of their own." But when the fruits of his labors were published, they consisted of two meager proposals, one for establishing "a *states general*"—not further defined—the other for opening free trade with Europe.[28]

Visible signs of the basis for serious political conflict both within and between colonies posed a second potential problem.

The same developments that radical leaders pointed to as evidence of the colonies' future strength—expanding areas of settlement, new sources of immigration, favorable demographic conditions, growing commerce—also produced major social dislocations that inevitably had disruptive political consequences. In the Carolinas and Pennsylvania, the failure to extend effective and honest government to newly settled interior areas generated political tensions between the frontier and seaboard. The ethnic and religious diversity of the middle colonies was already creating a social basis for political divisions, anticipating patterns of popular alignment that would become dominant in the mass politics of the next century.[29] Elsewhere the increasing complexity of colonial economies generated a different sort of social foundation for political competition—as in the conflicts between commercializing towns and subsistence farming communities in Massachusetts and Connecticut, or the rivalries between trading ports in Maryland and Rhode Island. And it required little foresight to recognize potential sources of conflict between colonies over various issues: the control and settlement of the vast American interior; disputed provincial boundaries; ethnic, religious, and cultural differences; sectional loyalties already reflecting the presence or absence of slave labor; or the fears the smaller colonies harbored against the purported aggrandizing designs of their larger neighbors.

Although the colonies did share some rough attributes in common, to a remarkable degree they remained distinctive communities, each possessing a special set of demographic, economic, and political characteristics. And, like members of other colonial societies, the cultural identity of the American colonists was defined less by their relations with their neighbors than by their conception of the metropolitan culture. When Americans looked outside their colonial borders, it was still London that drew their attention, not Hartford or Annapolis, Philadelphia or Charlestown—much less Marblehead, a fishing port whose population of five thousand made it the sixth largest town in America at the time of the Stamp Act.[30] And if the decade before independence witnessed the emergence of signs of a new American self-consciousness, this sense of national identity was itself a product of the resistance movement, and thus to a large extent dependent on the stimulus of imperial policy.[31] The imperatives of opposing Great Britain would naturally encourage the colonists to repudiate the standards of the parent culture and even temporarily suppress many of the problems that jeopardized American unity; but they could not remove the deeper strains and differences that distinguished thirteen provincial societies.

As a social fabric of national integration had yet to be pieced together, so too the informal political mechanisms necessary to allow a confederation to function efficiently remained to be invented. The rudimentary correspondence of the early 1770's provided only the barest foundation for coordinating policymaking and administration among the various levels of politics. The mere apportionment of responsibility among federal, provincial, and local agencies of resistance would not by itself reveal *how* power and influence were to be exercised. Nor was it even clear who would compose a national political élite. The leaders of colonial resistance were, after all, provincial politicians. When Samuel Adams left Boston to attend the First Continental Congress, it was his first trip outside his native province, taken one month short of his fifty-second birthday. Moreover, capable as the "gentlemen freeholders," aspiring lawyers, and leisured merchants who composed the provincial governing classes were, their previous experience could scarcely prepare them for the novel responsibilities and demands the Revolution would impose. In the individual colonies, the displacement of loyalist officials opened up opportunities for politicians who had previously and enviously stood outside the narrow circle of favor. But at the national level of politics, where burdens would prove heavier and rewards less flattering, the problem would be to recruit a pool of officeholders where none had existed before.

During the early 1770's the active leaders of American resistance gave such questions little sustained thought, and only gradually in the years that followed would they become aware of the various theoretical and structural problems that the creation of a continental government entailed. Before 1774 their energies were directed instead simply toward keeping the idea of opposition alive. But in another sense the task of creating an American union was peculiarly a problem of maintaining a cohesive resistance by agreeing upon common goals and tactics. The early history of the American confederacy can be written only by explaining how common policies were fashioned and carried out, both within and without the chambers of the Continental Congress.

CHAPTER II

The Creation
of a Mandate

———————————— ⟨∿⟩ ————————————

C OPIES of the Boston Port Act, which ordered the closing of
the town's harbor until the East India Company was indem-
nified for its lost tea, began reaching American ports during the
second week of May 1774. Following weeks brought additional
parliamentary blows: the Massachusetts Government Act, which
drastically altered the structure of provincial government; the
Administration of Justice Act; the amended Quartering Act; and
the Quebec Act.[1] Their political implications were immediately
obvious. The time of watching and waiting was clearly over, but
a period of intricate political maneuvering necessarily followed
the first shock of surprise at the severity of the government's
actions. The eagerness with which Boston challenged the rest of
the continent to come to its support further complicated the
situation. At a town meeting on May 13, the Boston radicals had
pushed through a resolution demanding the immediate stoppage
of all American trade with Britain and the West Indies. This
proposal met stiff opposition elsewhere, and the idea of convening a congress quickly emerged as the logical alternative to the
Boston demand. The confusion that initially prevailed, though
intense, was brief. By late June the basic agenda for the First
Continental Congress, which was to meet in September, had
been outlined. During the rest of the summer a strong popular
mandate to abide by its determinations developed, bringing with

it a surprising degree of consensus about the policies the congress
should pursue.

The Calling of a Congress

RESISTANCE leaders in Massachusetts had a natural tendency to
equate the plight of their colony and its capital—"now suffering
in the common cause," to use the stock phrase of 1774—with the
common cause itself. Their anxiety generated much of the confusion that marked the early weeks of this new crisis. Invoking
precedents set during the opposition to the Townshend duties
and the Tea Act, the Boston town meeting directed its initial
appeals for an immediate comprehensive boycott to the other
principal American ports. There they were received by politicians who recalled the acrimonious collapse of non-importation
in 1770, and by merchants who were reluctant to join any boycott
until they had time to gain a clearer picture of events and, not
incidentally, to build up their stocks of imported goods. Had the
government chosen some milder response to the Boston Tea
Party, their private reluctance to support Boston could have
been more readily justified. The government's actions, however,
preempted that possibility, and discussion quickly turned to the
tactics, not the propriety of resistance.[2]

In New York and Philadelphia opposition to an abrupt stoppage of trade was so strong that active patriots instantly recognized that the calling of some sort of congress was the most
acceptable alternative. The New York radical Isaac Sears had
immediately raised the idea of non-importation, but by May 15,
even before receiving the Boston proposal, he and Alexander
McDougall urged the Boston Committee of Correspondence to
agree to a prior meeting of committees representing the major
ports. After another week of public agitation and closeted maneuvers, the newly formed Committee of Fifty-one formally proposed the meeting of a congress of provincial deputies, to frame
"some unanimous resolution . . . not only respecting your deplorable circumstances, but for the security of our common rights."[3]
Sears and McDougall held out the hope that New York would
eventually agree to a boycott, but the first reports to reach Boston from Philadelphia were even less encouraging. There, as
letters from both the Committee of Correspondence chosen on

May 20 and resistance leaders writing privately made clear, the opinion prevailed that any boycott must be "reserved as our last resource." The Philadelphia leaders argued not only that a boycott should be the work of a congress, but that commercial resistance should be postponed until after the congress had first tried more pacific measures. A boycott could not be mounted, Thomas Mifflin informed Samuel Adams, "without some previous Step [being] taken to obtain Redress." The deputies should go to congress carrying

Details of Grievances which they severally labour under with respect to trade &c—These Details to be digested at the Congress into a petition Remonstrance Bill of Rights or into such Form as may be thought most eligible—The Deputies met to nominate a certain Number of their Body to go to England and lay their Grievances at the Foot of the Throne &c &c; this to be the last Attempt to petition or remonstrate.

Charles Thomson repeated the same arguments a week later.[4]

Nor was the initial response in New England unequivocally favorable to Boston. Although a Providence town meeting of May 17 endorsed the Boston proposal in principle, it too stated a clear preference for a congress. Writing from Connecticut, Silas Deane also insisted on the prior convening of a conference of the committees of correspondence. When Samuel Adams argued in reply that such a conference "cannot be had speedily enough to answer for the present Emergency," Deane reiterated his objections to hasty measures, endorsed the recommendations of the New York Committee, and conceded only that a preliminary conference of the northern committees might be held first.[5]

By the end of the third week of May, then, the Boston Committee of Correspondence almost certainly knew that its proposed boycott would not go over easily, if at all, in Connecticut, New York, and Philadelphia. Taken aback by this opposition, the committee and its members shuffled awkwardly between issuing vague endorsements of a congress and more urgent pleas for a boycott. On May 21, for example, the committee wrote Providence that not one but two congresses—one of merchants, the other of *"American States"*—were necessary. But at the end of the month it was still arguing, in official letters to New York and Philadelphia, that an effective boycott could be mounted without the prior convening of a congress. And on June 8 the committee launched an ambitious campaign to bring the entire province of

Massachusetts into a Solemn League and Covenant to halt all commercial intercourse with Great Britain and the West Indies.[6]

Given the warnings against rash, unilateral actions that the committee had already received, its decision to promote the Solemn League seems rather puzzling. Why did the committee appea: willing to risk alienating the intercolonial support it had long s ight and now desperately desired? The surviving correspondence is not particularly revealing: motives have to be inferred from circumstances. Possibly the Boston leaders hoped to capitalize on the additional jolt just provided by the Massachusetts Government Act. Or perhaps they feared that a failure to organize quick and effective resistance within Massachusetts might encourage their local opponents to marshal support for a campaign to make restitution for the tea, and thus compromise their own efforts in the near future. The friendly address presented by a group of Boston merchants to the departing Thomas Hutchinson was already proving an embarrassment. To some extent the Solemn League may thus have been designed to overawe opposition within the town by enlisting support for strong measures from the rest of the province. But this risky initiative also had important continental implications. Moderates in other colonies might exploit signs of division or timidity in Massachusetts to argue against implementing any boycott and to push instead for the sort of bland and ineffectual measures being discussed in Philadelphia. Despite its local orientation, then, the Solemn League was probably intended to influence politics outside the province, by demonstrating not only that Massachusetts was united, but also that an effective boycott could be spontaneously fashioned by scattered communities acting without prior consultation. If Massachusetts set the example, the other colonies might well follow. But, conversely, if Massachusetts could not do so now, the others might refuse to do so later.[7]

Before the response of rural Massachusetts could be registered, however, additional letters from Deane and Thomson[8] and the first news from the southern colonies made it clear that compliance with the call for a congress could be delayed no longer. The Virginia assembly had been in session when news of the Port Act arrived. But the Burgesses had decided to complete their regular business before taking up the new crisis, and Governor Dunmore dissolved the legislature before a serious response to the Port Act could be considered. In two rump sessions on May

27 and 29, however, the members remaining in Williamsburg endorsed the "expediency" of a general congress and called a provincial convention to meet on August 1, though suggesting at the same time that no boycott should take place before these meetings were held. Political leaders in neighboring Maryland initially seemed more receptive than those of any other colony to the Boston proposal, but they, too, soon agreed that delay was necessary.[9]

During the second week of June the cumulative news from the southward evidently convinced the Massachusetts leaders, many of whom were then at Salem attending the General Court, that their accession to a congress must finally be announced. The presence of the loyalist Daniel Leonard on the committee appointed to report on the state of the province posed a minor obstacle to action. But after Samuel Adams had plied Leonard with "smooth & placid Observations" and Robert T. Paine enticed him to take several days off for a court appearance, the committee was able to deliver its report, which called for a congress to assemble at Philadelphia in early September. On June 17, behind doors locked to prevent the new governor, Thomas Gage, from dissolving the assembly, the General Court approved the committee's proposal, invited the other colonies to a congress, and elected five delegates for the province.[10]

During the weeks that followed, the Boston leaders were also forced to admit that the desultory progress of the Solemn League and Covenant would prevent their implementing a program of commercial resistance even at the provincial level. Sharing the reservations already voiced by merchants and politicians in other colonies, the towns of rural Massachusetts placed greater emphasis on the importance of union than the necessity for some immediate response. What troubled them was not the idea of nonconsumption, which in a general sense they approved, but its timing, its emphasis on immediate action when other colonies and common sense called for prudence. "It was the General opinion of the Meeting," the Palmer Committee of Correspondence noted,

That it was best to Omit Sineing a Non Importation agreement until the General Congress had met. And then without the Least Dout there will be some wise and Good Plan fixt: Whereby Every Government will Joyn with one heart and one Mind, which will give Life and Strength to a Non Importation agreement and will do more Execution than Swords,

Spears, or Guns. Then we may Set under our own Vines and figtrees and Eat the fruit of our own Industry and Not be obliged to Market the Best of our Toilsum Labour to pay for the Insipped Superfluities of our cruel and Impolitick Mother.

Even those towns that did sign the Covenant clearly regarded it as an interim agreement, to be altered or discarded as the congress might see fit.[11]

Thus the fate of their early responses to the Coercive Acts suggests that the Massachusetts radicals—veteran agitators as they were—had miscalculated twice, failing to anticipate the reactions not only of the other colonies but of their own province as well. Relying on the rapid and spontaneous mobilization of intercolonial opposition to the Tea Act of 1773 and on the deference the towns of Massachusetts had previously shown toward the leadership of the Boston Committee, they temporarily ignored the lessons inculcated in the early 1770's, when in the absence of effective cooperation colonial leaders had invested new meaning in the need for prudent and united action.

Yet throughout their early campaign, the Boston radicals retained two grounds for security. One was that the calling of a congress, a project they had themselves considered in 1773, was an alternative they could readily accept. The other was that the implications of this crisis were too blatant for the other colonies to ignore. Some of their correspondents, to be sure, admonished the Boston leaders for their adventurism. "Nothing can throw us into a pernicious confusion," John Dickinson pointedly reminded Josiah Quincy, "but one colony's breaking the line of opposition, by advancing too hastily before the rest." Nevertheless, politicians elsewhere were not inclined to criticize Boston too severely. It was, Silas Deane complained, "very wrong, totally and absolutely so," for Boston to act unilaterally, "directly contrary to every principle of good reason and sound policy." And yet, Deane added, "Their present distracted situation must atone for their errors, and we must do the best we can, for and with them."[12]

Moreover, despite their initial failure, the militant Boston initiatives had one further consequence. The first step in building a broad mandate for the coming congress was to portray it as a sensible, prudent alternative to more extreme measures. By raising the specter of an immediate renewal of commercial resistance and the potential revival of intercolonial animosities, the resolutions of the Boston town meeting inadvertently provided a natural foil against which popular support for a congress could grow. What in 1773 had seemed to be one of the most provocative measures the colonists could pursue now emerged as a rational, even restrained course of action. Ironically, in the flurry of their early reactions, both the radical leaders in Boston and their moderate counterparts elsewhere failed to grasp that the decision to invest one central body with the leadership of resistance was in itself the single most innovative step the colonists could take. For although the events of 1774 gave new force to the tactics and principles of opposition, both of these drew on precedents well established during the previous decade. But the reorganization of the structure of resistance under the auspices of a congress carried with it the prospect of making American opposition more cohesive and efficient than it had ever been before.

Mobilizing Popular Opinion

THE common agreement to defer major decisions to the forthcoming congress permitted a mild relaxation of the mood of crisis that had prevailed in the late spring. It brought no end to political maneuvers and discussions, however, but merely provided them with a new focus. By mid-June colonial leaders were busy defining the issues that the congress would have to consider and the measures it should pursue. Their efforts were complemented and reinforced by the wave of public meetings that were held throughout the colonies during the rest of the summer.

Two problems immediately seemed critical: the tone and content of the petition or declaration of rights the congress would predictably adopt, and the risks and benefits of a resumption of commercial resistance. The alternative courses of action seemed surprisingly clear. First, should the congress merely prepare a definitive statement of American rights, leaving the government to accept or reject these demands as it pleased; or should it strike a more conciliatory posture, propose concessions as well as grievances, and perhaps dispatch ambassadors to negotiate a settlement with the North ministry? Second, should the congress postpone adopting coercive measures until the fate of its petition were known; or should it petition and mount a boycott simultaneously, reinforcing its statement of principles with an effective show of force?

If Samuel Adams and his circle were the obvious advocates of the more militant strategy, John Dickinson and the moderate whig leaders of Philadelphia—Joseph Reed, Charles Thomson, George Clymer—quickly emerged as the most insistent proponents of a conciliatory approach. From the outset they argued that the congress should follow the least provocative course possible: avoiding a boycott, drafting a temperate petition, offering to confirm Parliament's right to regulate trade—even though, as Clymer admitted, they acknowledged the validity of "the opinion which old charters in many early transactions justify, that the absolute independence of the colonies from Parliament was intended." To some extent, the other Philadelphia leaders were carried along by the strength of Dickinson's commitment to reconciliation alone. Moreover, despite the aspersions that had recently been cast on his patriotism, the continental celebrity Dickinson had acquired through his *Letters from a Farmer in Pennsylvania* itself guaranteed that his views would have to be taken seriously, for he was one of only a handful of colonial leaders whose personal position could substantially affect public opinion. And Dickinson was "fixt in an Opinion of petitioning first," Thomas Mifflin informed Samuel Adams, "whilst many of his Friends & our people generally think it will be of no Use, but may ruin the Cause by an unnecessary Delay"—an early sign of the adversary role Dickinson would play during the next two years.[13]

Moderates like Dickinson were well aware that prospects for reconciliation would also depend on developments in Massachusetts. Discussions of the central issues of petitions and resistance thus presupposed that an uneasy truce could be maintained in that colony while the government was being permitted to reconsider its repressive legislation. But that presumption was itself questionable, and the colonists therefore faced a third broad problem. Should Massachusetts be permitted to resist the execution of the new acts, even at the risk of jeopardizing the chances for successful negotiations with the government? Open defiance of the Massachusetts Government Act might provoke armed conflict with British troops; but a passive acceptance of the new administration could create damaging constitutional precedents and suggest that the colonists were uncertain of their arguments or unwilling to carry resistance too far.

Before any of these questions could be answered, however, the delegates to the First Congress would need reliable knowledge of the state of public opinion. In the late spring the seaports had dominated the earliest reactions to the new crisis, effectively defining the issues that needed to be resolved. They were the first to learn of the Port Act and—given the threats that both Parliament and Boston posed to their commerce—the most immediately concerned. Having been more directly involved in earlier phases of opposition, the inhabitants of the larger towns were also better prepared to reorganize the extra-legal committees that constituted the apparatus of resistance. Although the precise composition of these committees could itself spark heated controversy—as in New York and Philadelphia, where merchants, artisans, and politicians continually jockeyed for influence—their appointment was relatively easy to arrange.

The first wave of reaction to the Coercive Acts thus flowed through and deepened older channels of communication and organization that had rested largely unused in the early 1770's. But beginning in early June, rural towns and counties in each of the colonies held meetings to draft their own resolutions, appoint committees of correspondence, and instruct their regular representatives or elect delegates to the forthcoming provincial conventions. Only in Massachusetts and some scattered towns in New England did the existence of standing committees of correspondence predate the passage of the Coercive Acts. Elsewhere these committees were being appointed either for the first time since the late 1760's or not at all, and were thus the products, not the instigators of crisis.[14]

We still know all too little about how these meetings were organized and conducted, how many people comprised the "respectable number" who always seemed to attend, or who composed the new committees. Nor can we measure whether those recruited into this expanding cadre were motivated by ideological convictions, personal ambitions, or (what seems more likely) some indefinite combination of the two. In the political context of 1774, these committees remained extra-legal rather than revolutionary institutions. Only where local notables were closely tied to the royal governors, as in New Hampshire or western Massachusetts, did they pose a challenge to local élites and power structures.[15] Even where the dissolution of colonial legislatures led to the calling of provincial conventions to elect delegates to congress, the intention was to circumvent the prerogative of the governors, not to undermine or overthrow the existing constitutions of government. The provincial conventions met briefly, elected and instructed delegates, and adjourned. So, too, the local committees had little to do: once having dispatched their resolves to newspapers and neighboring communities, they also lapsed into inactivity.

Yet the significance of these meetings and committees transcended their initially limited responsibilities in several ways. In the first place, they commonly echoed the call for a congress while pledging to accept and carry out whatever policies it ultimately adopted. To a large extent, this strikingly deferential posture reflected a natural uncertainty and caution affecting local leaders everywhere. The simple magnitude of this new crisis and the likelihood of further British reprisals left political leaders at every level reluctant to take initiatives whose consequences might well prove awesome. Necessarily exerting their influence through extra-legal committees, they were also anxious to secure as much external support for their local actions as they could possibly muster. Linking their own existence to the deliberations of a body being ritualistically hailed as "the collected wisdom of the continent" was an obvious way of enhancing their own precarious status and authority. The notion of "hanging together" rather than separately must have already become attractive.

The delegates concurrently being appointed to the congress shared this mood of uncertainty or, as John Adams put it, "unutterable Anxiety."[16] But from their perspective, the simple appearance of these committees, pledging to support whatever decisions the congress reached, must have been an important source of reassurance. It was enough to know that a latent apparatus of resistance was already in place, since its existence suggested that a thorough, comprehensive boycott was not only practicable but could be set into operation on relatively short notice. Yet the results of these local meetings had even wider implications. Provincial assemblies and conventions could appoint and instruct delegates, and give the approaching congress a certain formal sanction. But it was left to these local meetings to outline what actions the people at large expected and were willing to accept. A system of opinion taking based on the communication of spirited resolves consciously framed for public

consumption and rhetorical effect was obviously crude and potentially unreliable. That, after all, was what the experience of
the Boston Committee of Correspondence seemed to suggest:
despite its previous extensive correspondence with the towns,
the committee had somehow failed to detect the streak of political caution that undermined its campaign for the Solemn
League. By default, however, no other adequate registers of public opinion were available at either the provincial or intercolonial
level, and it seems reasonable to conclude that American leaders
monitored these proceedings closely. Printed weekly in the
newspapers, where they consumed whole columns of small print
and often left little room for the publication of polemical essays,
their cumulative influence was considerable.

These resolves did not resemble the provincial *cahiers* of
Revolutionary France. They were not, that is, a mélange of parochial grievances that had to be converted into a generalized
indictment of the existing regime before they justified political
upheaval. Among all these local resolutions there were, to be
sure, significant differences in emphasis, wording, and detail—in
part reflecting the desire of local politicians to define and restate
the issues in their own terms. Some raised matters of local concern, declaiming against gambling, horse racing, or the importation of slaves. Some enumerated articles to be exempted from
non-importation or debated the timing of non-exportation; and
others again recommended closing the courts or halting prosecu-
tions for debt while trade was stopped. County meetings in Virginia and New Jersey commonly reaffirmed their loyalty to the
crown, while those in Maryland did not. Virginians seemed particularly inclined to condemn the greed of the East India Company. New England towns urged their brethren to eschew all
private controversies and act with forbearing charity.

But such nuances were secondary to more basic points of
agreement. Taken collectively, these local resolutions created a
powerful corpus of popular opinion supporting resistance rather
than protest and militancy rather than concessions. Some meetings did stop short of endorsing commercial resistance or issuing
detailed statements on the major constitutional questions, contenting themselves instead with promises to obey whatever
recommendations the congress proposed. But such cautious resolutions were in a minority. Meetings that approved more detailed resolves agreed that Parliament had no right to tax the

colonies, violate their charters, or enact laws interfering with their "internal police." Their positions lay closer to the emerging theory of imperial federalism, which saw the crown as the only legitimate bond between colonies and mother country, than to the tenuous belief that some line could still be drawn between the powers Parliament could and could not exercise over America. The freeholders of Granville County, North Carolina, summarized this simplified notion of empire as succinctly as Thomas Jefferson or James Wilson were to do in their more polished essays:

Resolved, That the King at the head of his American Assemblies, constitutes a supreme Legislature in the respective Colonies, and that as Free men we can be bound by no law, but such as we assent to, either by ourselves, or our Representatives. . . . Resolved, That the executive power, constitutionally vested in the Crown and which presides equally over Great Britain and America, is a sufficient security for the due subordination of the Colonies without the Parliament's assuming powers of Legislation and Taxation which we enjoy distinct from, and in equal degree with them.[17]

This general repudiation of parliamentary authority and its recent abuse implied that the congress should not address the government as humble supplicants but issue an unequivocal, assertive declaration of colonial rights and grievances.

On the question of the tactics of opposition, the local resolutions also indicated that a resumption of commercial resistance, if carefully planned and uniformly enforced, was necessary. Various meetings expressed reservations on matters of detail: non-exportation was less popular than non-importation; some counties hoped to continue exporting their produce through late 1775; a few compiled shopping lists of goods to be exempted from a ban on imports. Doubts were also raised about the propriety of subjecting the West Indies to non-exportation. Lurking beneath the general approval of commercial resistance, then, were a number of troublesome details; but these merely reinforced the need to have a comprehensive plan framed for all the colonies.

Opposition to a boycott continued among clusters of interested merchants throughout the colonies, and some of the local meetings that failed to endorse commercial resistance may well have hoped it would not be adopted. But if they actually preferred to see the Philadelphia scheme of petitioning before stopping trade prevail, they failed to endorse it publicly, and their silence was telling. In effect, the division of expressible public sentiment did not lie between those who favored or opposed a boycott, those who denied or recognized parliamentary authority, or even between those who differed as to whether petitioning should precede or merely accompany resistance. Rather it seemed to lie between those who were prepared to take relatively advanced positions on issues and tactics, and those who would defer to the decision of congress. Loyalist writers who later argued that the congress had been appointed to "fall upon some scheme to accommodate the dispute . . . and mark out a line of government" between Parliament and the colonies were projecting their own hopes, not accurately describing the actual course of public debate.[18]

These local resolutions assume greater importance when compared to the more cautious instructions that the provincial assemblies and conventions gave their delegates. Had other sources of public opinion not been available, they alone would scarcely have provided a decisive mandate for the congress. The resolves of the New England colonies, Connecticut excepted, were the sparest. None of them pledged to abide by the decisions of the congress or even mentioned commercial resistance, although perhaps they simply assumed a boycott would occur and chose not to press the point openly. Six of the remaining eight colonies endorsed non-importation, and five of these six nonexportation, with varying degrees of enthusiasm. A Pennsylvania convention hastily called to exert pressure on the legal assembly supported a boycott, but argued almost plaintively that it should remain a last resort to be tried only after petitioning failed. Four of the five colonies pledging to obey the decisions of congress implied that their acquiescence might depend on their own delegates' concurrence in the measures adopted.[19] Thomas Jefferson thought this one of the "Defects in the Association" adopted by the Virginia convention in August. "We are to conform to such resolutions only of the Congress as our deputies assent to," he noted on his own copy of the Association, "which totally destroys that union of conduct in the several colonies which was the very purpose of calling a Congress."[20]

Nonetheless, though the provincial resolves could have been more forceful, they could also have been more restrained. As it was, only Pennsylvania and Connecticut offered to grant voluntary aids to the crown, while only three colonies instructed their delegates to press for renewed petitions to the crown and Parliament. On balance, then, the provincial instructions also contributed to the substantial discretionary authority congress would enjoy, while leaving the delegates free to rely on other evidence which suggested that a strong response to the Coercive Acts would prove generally acceptable.

Expectations

BEYOND the intricate problems of fashioning a strategy and apparatus of resistance, the congress would also have to frame a definitive statement of American rights and grievances. Although the colonists had little trouble identifying their basic complaints, the welter of claims arising from overlapping American appeals to colonial charters, traditional English liberties, and natural rights would have to be sorted out and coherently arranged. Moreover, the delegates would also have to decide how the government and people of Great Britain were to be approached: what diplomatic "signals" would best convey the delicate balance between American demands for a recognition of their rights and the complementary hope for a plan of reconciliation that would leave the empire intact?

Custom dictated that any petition should be composed "in a Language suited to the Ears of Princes," as John Randolph wrote, "and presented in a Manner in which Kings are usually addressed"—and politics required that it express fervent pledges of loyalty to crown and empire, if not to Parliament. "Although we are oppressed," one North Carolina county resolved,

we will still adhere to the civil Obligation exacting our allegiance to the best of Kings, as we entertain a most cordial affection to His Majesty's Person and can never wish to see the executive authority in other hands. Blessed with freedom, we will cheerfully knee the throne erected by our Fathers and kiss the sceptre they taught us to reverence.[21]

But humility, many whig writers believed, could be carried too far. American grievances should be plainly expressed, not coyly disguised; whatever cobwebs still cluttered British perceptions must at last be swept away. Thomas Jefferson sensed this clearly when he proposed that the congress submit "an humble and

dutiful address" to George III, but also one "penned in the language of truth, and devoid of those expressions of servility which
would persuade his majesty that we are asking favors and not
rights." Other writers suggested that the congress should simply
"lay our claims before the Nation and demand a ratification of
them," or wondered whether "a sensible, manly, brave Remonstrance from the People of America to the People of England
. . . would not be productive of better effects than any Petition
or Address to such a King, and such a Parliament?"[22] Indeed,
some questioned whether any petition should be sent at all. What
could the Americans now say that Parliament had not known
when it passed the Coercive Acts? As one Boston writer noted:
"It will, therefore, be vain and ridiculous, and may perhaps be
deemed disrespectful, for our Congress to offer a petition filled
with old, trite, threadbare matters and arguments, which had a
full discussion when the Acts passed." John Randolph agreed.
"The *Americans* may argue till Doomsday," he wrote, "but I fear
that they will find the Parliament deaf to their Reasoning, and
their Eloquence unavailing."[23]

Randolph's pessimism was a mark of his continuing loyalism,
but the candor of these other writers reflected the clarifying
impact of the Coercive Acts themselves. Plain speech was necessary because previously tangled constitutional issues had now
been reduced to a stark simplicity. For what the legislation of
1774 revealed was that in the British view there were no practical
or theoretical limits to the exercise of parliamentary sovereignty
over the colonies. The attempt to draw the elusive line between
the authority of Parliament and the rights of the colonies accordingly became fruitless. What might Parliament not do if it had
already abrogated the royal charter of Massachusetts, interfered
with the mechanics of administering justice, or, as in the Quebec
Act, arbitrarily altered provincial boundaries? And if the authority to regulate trade could be construed to justify closing an
American port entirely, was it safe to concede even that power
to Parliament?

Pursuing arguments developed over the previous decade to
a conclusion that was now both logical and expedient, whig
pamphleteers such as Jefferson, James Wilson, and James Iredell
worked out a definitive American position on the structure of the
empire. Implicitly drawing on the central points raised by the
Massachusetts General Court in its debates with Thomas Hutch-

inson, they sketched a theory of imperial federalism that would make the crown, in Jefferson's words, "the balance of a great, if a well poised empire." The proper "dependence of the Americans," Wilson concluded, lay in their being "subjects of the King of Great Britain" only; no obedience was owed to Parliament. The colonial assemblies, hitherto often described as parliaments in miniature, would be elevated to effective parity with the Parliament of Westminster. Parliament and the American assemblies would belong to one polity by virtue of their common but parallel relations to the crown. The proper legislative functions of each would run no further than the respective boundaries of the realm of Great Britain and the individual colonies.[24]

Denying that Parliament had any right to legislate for the colonies called into question the future status of the Navigation Acts, whose validity the colonies had nominally accepted for a century. Was Parliament to retain the power to regulate the channels of commerce? James Wilson, for one, argued that it should not. "Why may not this power be intrusted to the king," he asked, "as a part of the royal prerogative?"[25] Other whig writers suggested that a continued parliamentary exercise of this power could still be justified—but only in the form of a concession freely offered by the colonies as a practical basis for compromise, not as a matter of right. The determinative view of this issue was most carefully outlined in the Fairfax County (Virginia) Resolves, traditionally attributed to George Mason and George Washington. In the past, they noted, parliamentary regulation of trade "was thought just and reasonable," and so the Americans had "cheerfully acquiesced in It," even though it was "in some Degree repugnant to the Principles of the Constitution." If Parliament would now renounce its unconstitutional claims over the colonies, a renewal of this earlier concession could be negotiated.[26] Even then, a number of Americans believed that the navigation system required liberal revision and the removal of arbitrary restrictions on colonial exports and commerce. "Why," asked Thomson Mason, the author of a lengthy series of essays in the *Virginia Gazette*, "should not Britons on this have as good a right to extend their trade to every corner of the globe as those on the other side of the Atlantic?"[27]

Nowhere was the difficulty of arguing a contrary position more embarrassingly revealed than in John Dickinson's midsummer *Essay on the Constitutional Power of Great-Britain over the Colonies in America,* which marked a final attempt to discover the line between parliamentary authority and American liberty. Dickinson accepted the orthodox denial of Parliament's authority in matters of internal legislation and taxation. But, he argued,

As to the second head, a power of regulating our trade, our opinion is, that it is legally vested in parliament, not as a supreme legislature over these colonies, but as the supreme legislature and full representative of the parent state, and the only judge between her and her children in commercial interests, which the nature of the case in the progress of their growth admitted.

Demonstrating the validity of this assertion was another matter, however. Dickinson's supporting reasoning was neither elegant nor clear; his text, one commentator has observed, "disappears altogether in a sea of footnotes and footnotes to footnotes," and throughout he seemed more concerned with denying the familiar British rejoinder that "a power of regulation is a power of legislation, and a power of legislation, if constitutional, must be universal and supreme in the utmost sense of the words." After clumsily attempting to recount how Parliament had acquired its power over trade, Dickinson abruptly announced: "We will proceed on a concession, that the power of regulating trade is vested in Parliament."[28]

Why Dickinson hoped the government would now accept distinctions it had previously ridiculed remains uncertain. Nevertheless, he was not alone in arguing that the congress would have not only to catalogue grievances but to devise substantive proposals for accommodation. Other writers who were still prepared to defend the supremacy of Parliament—and who would thus not quibble over the regulation of trade—thought the road to compromise lay in finding some reliable mode of granting the aids and requisitions that Britain sought. The delegates should use their "united zeal and abilities in substituting some adequate, permanent, and effectual supply . . . in the place of uncertain, ineffectual requisitions," wrote the author of the pamphlet *A Letter from a Virginian.* And in South Carolina, William Henry Drayton proposed the solution of erecting "a HIGH COURT of ASSEMBLY of North America," to be elected, with the king's consent, by the colonial assemblies, and authorized to "grant general aids to the British Crown," apportion the quota to be paid by each colony, and pass certain general "Acts of Legislation" binding on all the provinces.[29]

The *Letter from a Virginian* was patently a loyalist pamphlet. Drayton was a trimming politician who had opposed non-importation in 1769, whose conversion to whig principles followed a stormy dispute over his seat on the provincial council, and who would still go only so far as to deny that Parliament could "legally exercise over the Colonies, any powers which it cannot exercise over Great Britain."[30] Like Dickinson, such writers could muster little popular support for their proposals; but at the very least the simple propagation of their ideas nurtured an expectation that the delegates would have to consider plans of accommodation. By the late summer of 1774, then, even tories and trimmers were willing to vest wide discretionary authority in the congress. Where some moderates questioned whether the delegates had been chosen with sufficient propriety to enable them to act for the continent, the *Letter from a Virginian* conceded that they were "chosen as freely as the Circumstances of the Times would admit; with less Cabal and Intrigue than is usually employed for a Seat in many of our legal provincial Assemblies, and without even the Suspicion of Venality"; they would be "the Oracles of our Country," whose "Opinions will have the Effect of Laws." Other loyalists made a virtue of necessity. Fearing that "incendiaries, scattering abroad the firebrands of faction," would further inflame a "populace, already intoxicated with a few magical wands," Thomas Bradbury Chandler asked "Whether full confidence ought not to be reposed in the wisdom, the prudence, and patriotic spirit of our representatives at the congress, who are generally men of property, and have much more to risque than most of their constituents?"[31]

In private and public writings alike, Americans spoke of the approaching congress in what can only be described as worshipful terms. "The Congress is the whole Secritt," wrote one merchant. "What they do, I have no doubt will answer, for I suppose never in any Part of the world ever appear'd so many bright Luminaries in all probability as will there." William Smith, the New York historian, called it "the grand Wittenagemoot," after the ancient Anglo-Saxon council of dignitaries. "Our whole dependence is in the wisdom, prudence and determination of the Congress," a Connecticut politician wrote, "the highest and most respectable Council that ever was (and perhaps that ever will be) in America, who will give laws to the whole Continent, laws like unto those of the Medes and Persians, which must not be altered, but must and I believe will be strictly and most religiously observ'd."[32]

This inclination to view the congress in such deferential terms inhibited speculation about the actual decisions it would reach, and too many uncertainties remained for contemporaries to be able to predict its outcome with any measure of confidence. Nevertheless, the events of the summer did shape the proceedings of the First Congress in several critical ways. In the first place, they provided the assembling delegates with a remarkably broad mandate. Relatively unhindered by restrictive instructions, empowered to canvass a wide range of issues, assured of popular support for their decisions, the delegates had almost effortlessly acquired the prerogative of defining the future course of resistance. At the same time the events, meetings, and discussions of these months did give advocates of a more militant strategy certain important advantages. Had the government been more discriminating in its choice of punishments for Massachusetts, the inherent difficulty of mobilizing an intercolonial consensus would have been greatly enhanced. But the impact and tenor of the Coercive Acts themselves narrowed the scope of potential differences among the leaders of American opposition—both those who had been active in earlier campaigns and those who were entering the movement for the first time—by creating a situation that seemed to demand a forthright response, expressed not merely in the renewal of commercial resistance but also in the preparation of unequivocal statements of colonial rights and grievances. And the apparent severity of this new crisis placed a further premium on the maintenance of unity for its own sake, a consideration that in coming months often induced both the more moderate and militant wings of resistance to cooperate in measures that neither entirely favored.

This emphasis on unity, consensus, and deference to the new congress—much of it couched in a patriotic rhetoric that sounds inherently suspect to modern ears—strikes a sharp contrast with much of what we know about the reality of local and intercolonial politics that summer. As political leaders outside Massachusetts had used the idea of a congress to circumvent Boston's impulsive demand for immediate retaliation, so, too, in some communities pleas for unity became the obvious tools of en-

trenched interests and local élites resisting challenges from
newly assertive groups. When, for example, a group of Philadelphia artisans urged the moderate city committee appointed in
mid-June to hold additional mass meetings, the committee replied that it had

a firm confidence that whatever the congress shall devise and recommend, will be adhered to not only by every province but by every city
and County and we hope by the individuals of each province. We think
it best therefore to refrain from all Meetings which may have tendency
to shew any diversity of Sentiments among ourselves. We are now hap-
pily united. We are all animated in the general cause and pursuing the
constitutional Mode for obtaining redress of our grievances. Let us
therefore wait the event of the Congress.

But such appeals were not merely defensive. Many Revolutionary leaders believed that no local issue was of the same order of
magnitude as the struggle with Britain.[33] Whatever expedient
uses such pleas might have had in specific localities, the emo-
tional energy invested in this patriotic rhetoric—which can be as
easily traced in private as in public writings—suggests that it was
not merely a superficial gloss concealing more interested or concrete motives or actions. It is plausible to assume, rather, that
elements of a revolutionary ideology had in fact penetrated more
deeply within the various levels of colonial society than even
contemporaries suspected. If anything, resistance leaders were
taken aback by the dimension of the popular response to the
Coercive Acts. "The Boston Port bill," Samuel Adams later recalled, "suddenly wrought a Union of the Colonies which could
not be brot about by the Industry of years in reasoning on the
necessity of it for the Common Safety."[34]
    It is, of course, possible that politicians like Adams failed to
identify and understand the complex and disparate motives, attitudes, and even anxieties that led thousands of colonists to participate in the early stages of rebellion. Perhaps the crisis of imperial authority was merely the occasion that individuals and
groups seized to pursue goals different from those motivating a
more articulate, ideologically aroused élite. In recent years, some
historians have suggested that this process of popular mobilization and the colonists' adoption of a distinctive political ideology
could have come only in response to a series of unsettling social
changes: an increasing stratification of society, subtle shifts in the

relations between classes, ambivalent attitudes toward the superiority of metropolitan culture, the emergence of new personality types shaped by demographic and economic forces, and other dislocating phenomena.[35]

All of these forces may have been somehow at work—although it must be observed that this argument remains largely conjectural and quite possibly unprovable. But in any event, there is little evidence to suggest that an awareness of these changes actually influenced the perceptions of Revolutionary leaders. They explained the scope and spontaneity of the general response to the Coercive Acts as a rational reaction to the manifest implications of this new turn in British policy and as an outgrowth of the larger political education of the past decade. The preservation of the rough consensus the British government had created naturally became one of the principal responsibilities of the delegates to the First Congress. Recent events certainly encouraged them to believe that their decisions would command widespread popular support. But the delegates could also not afford to forget how abruptly a seemingly unified movement had dissolved in 1770, and how difficult it had been to reorganize effective opposition thereafter.

CHAPTER III

The First
Continental Congress

———————————⟶⟵———————————

THE deliberations of the First Congress tested the true
meaning of the patriotic fervor and rhetoric unleashed over
the summer. They determined much of the course and character
that American resistance would assume during the next two
years, and they also shaped and refined many of the assumptions
that would subsequently influence the conduct of continental
politics over an even longer period. For these reasons and others,
the First Continental Congress came to be celebrated in early
Revolutionary mythology as a truly heroic assembly, a fitting
symbol of the sunshine patriotism of 1774.

Because its decisions clearly placed the colonies in a posture
of confrontation with Britain rather than accommodation, the
results of the First Congress have often been portrayed as a
victory for the more radical wing of the opposition movement,
usually identified with the so-called Adams-Lee junto—the two
Adamses of Massachusetts and Richard H. Lee of Virginia. This
group is presumed to have somehow manipulated events and
debates to foreclose the possibility of reconciliation and enhance
the likelihood of independence. The interpretation is highly mis-
leading. It distorts the actual results of the Congress and ignores
its striking success in formulating compromises and creating a
basic initial consensus that most members could conscientiously
support. Instead, it may be argued that their decisions reflected

not only common perceptions of the nature of the current crisis but a sensitivity to the peculiar status of Congress itself, an extra-legal body whose authority would obviously depend on its ability to maintain a broad range of popular support.

The Problem of Massachusetts

ON the morning of August 10, 1774, the Massachusetts delegates gathered at the house of Thomas Cushing to take their departure from Boston. Their leisurely nineteen-day journey was designed to allow them to confer with local leaders in Connecticut, New York, and New Jersey before reaching Philadelphia on the 29th, a week before the Congress opened. Other delegations were also anxious to discover more about the state of public opinion in other colonies and the views of their new colleagues. In some cases, suspicion reinforced curiosity. When, upon arriving at New York, the Connecticut delegates were rushed to a dinner being given for their Massachusetts and South Carolina counter-parts, Silas Deane took advantage of that moment when "the glass had circulated just long enough to raise the spirits of every-one just to that nice point which is above disguise or suspicion" to mingle with his hosts and explore their "real sentiments." Not surprisingly, Deane's doubts remained unconfirmed. Such occasions called for the kind of solemnity and ostentatious patriotism reflected in the toasts that John Adams recorded at an early dinner in Philadelphia: "May the collision of British flint and American steel produce that spark of liberty which shall illumine the latest posterity," "Unanimity to the Congress," and the like.[1]

At Philadelphia the delegates quickly plunged into a succes-sion of dinners and visits that facilitated a reasonably candid exchange of opinions and, as Deane discovered, a certain amount of indigestion. Early conviviality was necessary. Some of the delegates knew or had corresponded with each other, and nine had served together at the Stamp Act Congress, but most were strangers—a useful reminder of the essentially provincial charac-ter of American politics and politicians before 1774. The familiar sketches of the delegates that John Adams recorded in his diary —R. H. Lee, "very high" after drinking "Burgundy the whole afternoon" with John Dickinson; Edward Rutledge, "young, sprightly, but not deep"; Caesar Rodney, "the oddest looking man in the world," with a face "not bigger than a large apple" —testify not only to his flair for description but also to the fact that the emerging leaders of a revolution now almost a decade in the making remained largely unacquainted, and thus intent on forming first impressions of each other.[2] Adams was atypical only because his impressions were more striking and better preserved.

Visits, dinners, toasts, and the development of some sense of camaraderie were a vital part of the early days of the Congress. But its opening sessions were also marked by a mood of foreboding over events in Massachusetts. When the Bay Colony delegates set out for Philadelphia, they left behind them a province that seemed to be verging toward anarchy. In early August the new governor, Thomas Gage, began to implement the provisions of the Massachusetts Government Act. He provoked immediate resistance. The new provincial councillors were mobbed and hounded into resigning their royal commissions, much as the stamp collectors had been nine years ago. Angry crowds prevented courts from sitting, jurors refused to perform their duties, and town meetings continued to be held—all in defiance of the Government Act. Accounts of these proceedings were prominently featured in American newspapers while the delegates were en route to Philadelphia. Moreover, on September 6 (its second day of meeting) Congress learned that a party of royal troops had raided the Massachusetts arsenal at Charlestown five days earlier. Although the rumor that half a dozen colonists had been killed and Boston itself bombarded was eventually discredited, this was an intensely sobering episode—particularly when the response of rural New England became known. By all accounts the roads had been clogged with thousands of men who had quickly formed in their militia companies and marched to Boston's defense.[3] Civil war suddenly seemed imaginable. "This controversy will at last be decided by arms," Charles Carroll* predicted; " . . . the oppressions of the Bostonians & Gage's endeavours to enforce the new plan of government will hurry that distressed & provoked People into some violence, which may end in blood."[4]

These events undermined the assumptions that had previ-

---

*The Charles Carroll referred to throughout this book is Charles Carroll of Carrollton, not Charles Carroll the barrister.

ously sustained colonial moderates in their hopes that a stable truce could be maintained in Massachusetts until the Congress had had time to devise a suitable plan for reconciliation. Had the problem simply been to enable Boston to endure the economic consequences of the Port Act, the situation would have seemed less dangerous: the town's residents could be supported by the contributions that communities throughout the colonies were already making. But the delegates now had to consider how far Massachusetts could be authorized to go in resisting Gage's activities—recognizing, with memories of the Boston Massacre doubtless in mind, that incidents of armed conflict were easily foreseeable. On the other hand, a passive acceptance of the new regime not only seemed unjustified, given the illegality of the Government Act, but could also create constitutional precedents damaging to the general colonial position.

Thomas Gage thus unwittingly gave the Massachusetts delegates a new opportunity to influence the drift of opinion in the other colonies and Congress alike. After the failure of their earlier abortive initiatives, the Massachusetts leaders had reevaluated their alarmist tactics. At the prodding of Joseph Hawley, the leading whig of western Massachusetts, the delegates consciously adopted a posture of restraint, with apparent success. The New England delegates, Charles Carroll noted, "are as moderate as any—nay the most so." Next to the Virginians, Joseph Reed observed, "the Bostonians are mere Milksops." The pose was deliberate, John Adams confessed; he and his colleagues were "obliged to act with great delicacy and caution, to keep ourselves out of sight, and to feel pulses, and to sound the depths; to insinuate our sentiments, designs, and desires, by means of other persons, sometimes of one province, and sometimes of another."[5]

The Massachusetts delegates hoped to secure congressional support for resistance to the Government Act, and perhaps for the removal of British troops from Boston as well. Their plan for influencing Congress was worked out in an exchange of letters between Samuel Adams and his Boston collaborator Joseph Warren while the delegates were on their way to Philadelphia. Warren proposed that the delegates secure the adoption of resolutions denouncing the new provincial councillors. In reply, Adams evidently suggested that the desired resolutions should first be prepared by one of the Massachusetts county conventions that were soon to meet, then transmitted to the Congress for approval.[6] Gage's activities provided a perfect foil for this ploy. Thus when Paul Revere rode into Philadelphia on September 16, carrying with him a copy of the militant Suffolk County Resolves, the stage was set for the first serious test of congressional sentiment.

Although the original draft of the Suffolk Resolves was surprisingly restrained, the revised text that Revere carried and the Massachusetts delegates laid before Congress on the 17th was designed to express a forthright commitment to a program of resistance. The Resolves were prefaced by a stirring and, some thought, inflammatory preamble, replete with references to the dangers Massachusetts faced from "the arbitrary will of a licentious minister," "the parricide which points the dagger to our bosoms," and the "military executioners" who "thronged" Boston's streets. Such language was harsher, though only by degree, than other resolutions of 1774, and it shocked many who read it. Yet the substantive proposals following these rhetorical flourishes were quite carefully drawn, and it is their character that helps to explain why Congress unanimously endorsed the Suffolk Resolves and urged the people of Massachusetts to "persever[e] in the same firm and temperate conduct" the Resolves recommended.[7]

For neither as framed in Massachusetts nor ratified in Philadelphia were the Suffolk Resolves as belligerent or provocative as they have often been portrayed. Their central intent was to devise a plan of opposition that would enable the colony to defy the Government Act without alienating the support of the other colonies. To that end, the Resolves detailed a series of measures that would effectively circumvent and nullify the authority of the new administration but avoid any direct confrontation with Gage or his troops. Several provisions sought to obstruct the administration of justice by courts whose authority was now tainted. The people were asked to disregard the actions of judges holding commissions under the new act; jurors, sheriffs, and other judicial officers were promised support for refusing to execute their orders; and the prompt settlement of debts and the arbitration of other disputes were recommended as ways of avoiding recourse to legal remedies. Local tax collectors were advised to withhold their receipts from the provincial treasury, and the provincial councillors were urged to resign their commissions. The resolves thus fashioned a strategy of civil disobedience, but not passive resistance. Balancing a promise of restraint against a threat of force, the critical twelfth resolve stated

That during the present hostile appearances on the part of Great-Britain, notwithstanding the many insults and oppressions which we most sensibly resent, yet, nevertheless, from our affection to his majesty, which we have at all times evidenced, we are determined to act merely upon the defensive, so long as such conduct may be vindicated by reason and the principles of self-preservation, but no longer.[8]

Other provisions endorsed commercial resistance and military training.

Why did Congress unanimously ratify the Resolves? That question cannot be answered simply by invoking the loyalist delegate Joseph Galloway's later tribute to the "superior application" of Samuel Adams.[9] Given that Congress also voted to make this endorsement its first public act, it seems more plausible to conclude that the delegates were consciously issuing an early signal of their intentions and concern. They hoped both to forestall further disruptive acts in New England and to provide the American public and the British government with some indication of their sentiments. Gage was clearly warned that a continuation of his recent activities would only elicit further intercolonial support for Massachusetts—a warning he was now prepared to take to heart. In a more general vein, the government was warned that its attempt to isolate and punish Massachusetts was already doomed to failure.[10]

Even more important, by this act of ratification most delegates probably hoped to restrain the conduct of resistance in Massachusetts within the lines drawn by the Suffolk Resolves themselves. Only if Gage used force to carry out his policies would the people be justified in taking stronger measures; even then they remained bound to act "merely upon the defensive." Other measures that were already under discussion in Massachusetts—a unilateral resumption of legal government under the first or second royal charters, or offensive measures to drive the British from Boston—would not be tolerated. The intentions of Congress were finely drawn but unambiguous, as Samuel Adams was careful to inform Joseph Warren in late September. The Congress, Adams noted, have not yet come to final resolutions. It becomes them to be deliberate. I have been assured, in private conversation, with individuals, that, if you should be driven to the necessity of acting in the defence of your lives and liberty, you would be justified by their constituents, and openly supported by all the means in their power; but whether they will ever be prevailed upon to think it necessary for you to set up another form of government, I very much question. . . .

Invoking as always the vital necessity of union, Adams argued for patience and restraint. John Adams found it more difficult to overcome his exasperation with the cautious attitude of other delegations, but he too recognized the need to appease their anxieties. The delegates "Start at one Thought of taking up the old Charter," Adams wrote William Tudor. "They Shudder at the Prospect of Blood. Yet they are unanimously and unalterably against your Submission, to any of the Acts for a Single Moment." But, he complained, although "We hear, perpetually, the most figurative Panegyrics upon our Wisdom Fortitude and Temperance: The most fervent Exhortations to perseverance . . . nothing more is done."[11]

That Congress considered its endorsement of the Suffolk Resolves a moderate alternative to other imaginable measures became apparent when the situation of Massachusetts was reviewed in early October. On October 6 Paul Revere again rode into Philadelphia, this time to report that the British were erecting fortifications around Boston. Hoping to exploit Gage's miscues again, the Adamses and R. H. Lee introduced a new series of recommendations authorizing Massachusetts to go beyond the plan of resistance outlined in the Suffolk Resolves. This time, however, their proposals were not adopted. Congress rejected a motion offered by Lee advising the inhabitants of Boston to abandon their garrisoned town. It substituted a comparatively restrained letter of protest to Gage in place of a shrill composition of Samuel Adams's. And it refused to recommend measures designed to bring colonial militias to a heightened state of readiness or to permit Massachusetts to resume legal government under its own authority. Instead, Congress approved a set of resolutions reflecting the members' belief that they had done all they could to condone resistance in Massachusetts. The people of the Bay Colony were advised "to conduct themselves peaceably" toward Gage and his troops, "avoiding & discountenancing every viola-

tion of his Majesty's property, or any insult to his troops, and
. . . peaceably and firmly persever[ing] in the line they are now
conducting themselves, on the defensive."[12]

The delegates' willingness to supervise the course of resistance in Massachusetts created an important precedent for the
role Congress would play in the emerging Revolutionary polity.
By asking Congress to judge the legality of their provincial government, the Massachusetts leaders endowed that body with
authority they could never have conceded to Parliament. Its
responsibilities would not be confined simply to formulating a
common strategy of opposition to Britain; Congress would also
regulate the basic political changes that would take place in
every colony as the crisis deepened. Its reluctance to allow Massachusetts to resume the first charter thus mattered less than its
simple willingness to take that question under consideration—a
decision that Congress affirmed by rejecting a motion to leave
Massachusetts "to her own discretion with respect to government and justice, as well as defence."[13]

The Association

THE ominous developments in Massachusetts were not the most
important problem confronting Congress, but they were the
most urgent and they deeply influenced its subsequent actions.
After the astounding spontaneous mobilization of the New England militia, the notion that commercial resistance was too radical a measure to command popular support no longer seemed
credible. During the second fortnight of September, Congress
quickly moved to approve the rough outlines of a boycott. On
September 22 it issued its second public resolution, requesting
merchants to suspend further importations from Britain "until
the sense of the Congress" was made known. On the 26th and
27th the delegates debated the details of a boycott and unanimously resolved to halt the importation of British and Irish goods
after December 1. Several days later Congress approved another
resolution banning exports to Britain, Ireland, and the West Indies after September 10, 1775.[14]

The need to resume commercial resistance had ceased to be
an issue, either in Congress or "without doors." Even in the city

of New York, the absent delegate Philip Livingston reported, non-importation "will give no uneasiness . . . and a non-exportation to commence the middle of September next will be cheerfully acquiesced in."[15] With the apparent exception of Joseph Galloway, no delegate raised any serious objections against a boycott. Debate centered instead on predictable but intricate details concerning the timing and extent of the respective embargoes and the particular interests of individual colonies. The Virginia delegates had been instructed that non-exportation could not begin before August 1775, while the South Carolinians insisted on exempting their colony's staples, rice and indigo, from an embargo. After a further debate on October 6 devoted to reviewing the commercial interests of each colony, the task of framing a comprehensive agreement was referred to a committee. Their report, the proposed Association, was delivered October 12, debated and amended, and finally signed on the 20th.[16]

The central assumption underlying the Association was that the reputed value of colonial commerce left both the government and vital elements of the British economy vulnerable to American coercion. Non-importation would presumably produce unemployment and mercantile failures; non-exportation of southern commodities would reduce government revenues and so aggravate the finances of a nation burdened with a massive public debt. Delegates like Samuel Chase could thus assert that a total boycott of British and West Indian commerce "must produce a national bankruptcy, in a very short space of time."[17] Yet while most delegates still believed that economic coercion was the most promising mode of resistance, their confident attachment to this strategy was less valid than it had been in the 1760's. The ministry of Lord North had overcome the domestic political uncertainties that had weakened the resolve of its predecessors. Committed to its colonial policy and having anticipated the possibility of another colonial boycott, the ministry had also been strengthened by the results of the parliamentary elections it suddenly called for November 1774, which left it firmly in control of the House of Commons and comfortably insulated from the feeble protests of the "friends of America."[18]

The belief that economic coercion would give the colonists political leverage against the government was thus ill-founded. But regardless of its effect on Britain, the Association was destined to have a substantial impact on the character of colonial resistance. Its fourteen carefully drafted articles defined in elaborate detail the regulations and procedures under which the boycott would be enforced. Article 11 was crucial. It called for the election of committees of inspection "in every county, city, and town, by those who are qualified to vote for representatives in the legislature, whose business it shall be attentively to observe the conduct of all persons touching this association."[19] With one stroke, Congress thus formally sanctioned the extra-legal committees that had moved into the political vacuum of the summer, specified their duties, and reached out to impose its own control over these local forces.

Because its provisions were specific and authoritative, the Association absolved local leaders of the major policymaking responsibilities they had generally been reluctant to assume over the summer. At the same time, by empowering them "to establish such farther regulations as they think proper," it encouraged a certain measure of local initiative, designed not only to meet unforeseen contingencies but also to enhance the committees' sense of participation and patriotic morale. Nevertheless, Congress intended the committees to steer a narrow course. As in earlier boycotts, they were instructed to rely on the tactics of ostracism rather than coercion to secure uniform compliance— though their victims could properly complain that in practice this distinction was meaningless. The committees "should certainly take care not to exceed the powers which by the nature of their Institution were intended to be given them," Peyton Randolph, the president of the First Congress, wrote in February 1775. Even when dealing with "miscreants" who deliberately violated the Association, Randolph continued, "I have advised the gentlest methods in bringing them to a sense of their misconduct. Rigorous methods shou'd be avoided till obstinate opposition calls on us to take care that the public shall not suffer."[20]

More important than the substantive powers that the Association actually delegated to the local committees was the relation it established among the various levels of resistance. The delegates were deeply concerned with the problem of bestowing legitimacy on the entire apparatus of resistance, from town committees and provincial conventions to the Congress itself. By the very act of promulgating the Association, Congress imparted its own prestige and authority to local leaders whose own status was still uncertain. Local committees that had originally been instrumental in calling the Congress were now to be transformed, in a sense, into its administrative agencies, existing to implement its policies. At the same time, by calling for the election of new committees to replace those appointed under the irregular and hectic conditions of the summer, Congress arranged not only to give them a new mandate but to hold a referendum on its own policies as well. By extension, Congress too would be able to argue that its authority flowed from the express will of the people.

With its emphasis on marshaling popular support, the Association thus marked an important early step toward the eventual creation of avowedly republican governments. But in the context of 1774, that step was still only tentative. For one thing, Congress remained determined to limit the activities of popular committees to the tasks of resistance alone, not to make them vehicles for overthrowing legal government. More important, the persistently deferential attitude that the committees continued to hold toward Congress suggests that local leaders were not yet prepared to assert that popular support alone constituted a sufficient foundation for their authority. They remained grateful for congressional guidance. In the nebulous conditions of 1774 and 1775, power and legitimacy would continue to flow reciprocally between each of the levels of the emerging Revolutionary polity: down from the Congress as well as up from the people and their conventions.[21]

Rights and Grievances

THE comparative ease with which Congress framed its policies concerning Massachusetts and the Association suggests that these aspects of resistance proved less divisive than had earlier been anticipated. The most difficult questions confronting the delegates were those involving the rights and grievances the colonies should claim and the diplomatic posture Congress should adopt toward Great Britain. From the beginning, the delegates devoted most of their attention to these issues. On September 7, Congress appointed two large committees to draft the relevant reports: one of twenty-two members "to State the rights of the

Colonies in general . . . and the means most proper to be pursued for obtaining a restoration of them"; and another, made up of one delegate from each colony, to examine acts of Parliament relating to American trade and manufactures.[22]

By the fourth week of September, after the committees had delivered their reports, questions of the ends and means of resistance grew closely intertwined, complicating the task of hammering out positions that could receive common support. Anxious to balance the commitments to Massachusetts and commercial resistance with more conciliatory measures, moderates offered a series of proposals that enabled Congress to consider what sorts of compromises it was prepared to make to secure an accommodation. During the three weeks from September 24 to October 15, Congress shifted back and forth between discussions of resistance and accommodation, considering, in order, non-importation, the Galloway plan of union, non-exportation, the major provisions of a petition to the king, the changing situation around Boston, a declaration of rights, and finally the Association. As this rhythm of debate itself suggests, the advocates for one course could not proceed far without exciting the worst fears of their opponents. Yet the result of the ensuing divisions and maneuvers was a set of compromises on principles and tactics that virtually all of the members could support.

Of the various delegates composing the conciliatory wing of Congress, the most prominent was Joseph Galloway, speaker of the Pennsylvania assembly, sometime ally of Benjamin Franklin, and an eventual loyalist whose later apologias have occasionally misled historians. During the summer Galloway had maneuvered to retain control of his colony's delegation and succeeded in preventing John Dickinson, long his rival, from being elected to Congress—a myopic achievement, since Dickinson's presence would have greatly augmented the strength of those favoring accommodation over resistance. Casting himself in an iconoclastic role, Galloway drafted a plan for a new imperial constitution which, he believed, would offer a genuine basis for reconciliation and allow its author to cut through the delusive cant of opposition rhetoric. In Congress, however, Galloway proved an ineffective leader.[23] More important advocates of accommodation were James Duane and John Jay of New York, who supported Galloway but also offered conciliatory initiatives of their own. Prominent lawyers and thoroughgoing patricians, vaguely connected through their marriages into the Livingston clan (their wives were first cousins), Duane and Jay quickly emerged as the most articulate advocates of moderation. Supporting them were other members of the New York, Pennsylvania, and Maryland delegations—the nucleus of conciliatory strength during the next two years—as well as Edmund Pendleton of Virginia and John Rutledge of South Carolina.[24]

The first debate in the committee on rights revealed something of the problems congressional moderates would encounter in pressing the case for accommodation. The immediate issue was whether the colonies should invoke natural law as one of the foundations for their claims, as R. H. Lee argued, or rely instead on firmer legal and constitutional precedents, an approach Galloway, Duane, and John Rutledge favored because it might seem less provocative to the British government. The issue itself and the committee's endorsement of Lee's position are less significant than the concessions the moderates made while stating their case. For on the actual substance of American rights, Galloway and Duane espoused positions no less advanced than those taken by Lee or Roger Sherman. Indeed, Galloway went so far as to declare that "all the Acts of Parliament made since [the emigration of our Ancestors], are Violations of our Rights," and to admit that his "arguments tend to an independency of the Colonies."[25]

From the outset, then, moderates were forced to concede several critical points while striving to open some avenue of accommodation that a perceptive British government might recognize and respond to. This strategy was doubly difficult. It required convincing their colleagues not to insist on an absolute denial of parliamentary authority over the colonies, a position that the Coercive Acts had rendered not only less credible but almost illogical. And it presupposed that the government would in fact be able to ignore the more bellicose signals Congress would emit and concentrate instead on whatever finer hints of accommodation it might eventually incorporate in its statements and petitions.

The Galloway plan of union constituted the one attempt to escape these constraints, and its rejection confirmed the difficulty of transcending most delegates' conception of the basic issues separating Britain and America. Introduced on September 28 in a clear attempt to avert a decision on non-exportation, the Galloway plan envisioned the creation of an intercolonial legislature, elected by the provincial assemblies and empowered to enact legislation "for regulating and administering all the general police and affairs of the colonies" and, in wartime, to pass "bills for granting aid to the crown." Under the supervision of a royal legate, this "Grand Council" would become "an inferior and distinct branch of the British legislature." Parliament could still enact "general regulations" for the colonies, but the consent of both bodies would be necessary to validate all measures originating in either, with the exception of American grants of aid. After a candid debate on the 28th, Congress voted six colonies to five, with one divided, to defer its further consideration. The debate was probably never resumed. On October 22, Congress voted to expunge all references to the Galloway plan from its minutes.[26]

Galloway later equated the narrowness of the procedural vote of September 28 with the real division of opinion on the merits of the plan itself. Its rejection, he implied, was another perverse tribute to the guile of his opponents, a faction of "congregational and presbyterian republicans, or men of bankrupt fortunes," led by Samuel Adams, who were already committed to independence.[27]

Even without its jaundiced and self-serving qualities, this explanation is unconvincing. An unconcerted procedural vote on a novel topic is scarcely a reliable test of sentiments. The agenda of Congress itself warranted delay, since Galloway had interrupted the debate on commercial resistance. Perhaps more important, the fact that his plan was not reexamined during the following three weeks, when Congress *was* debating proposals for accommodation, suggests that it did not command wide support, and that the vote of the 28th did not reflect an even division of opinion on the proposal's substantive merits. A more satisfactory explanation of the reasons why Congress rejected Galloway's plan emerges when the results of the debates of the first fortnight of October are examined.[28]

On October 1, having approved non-exportation the day before, Congress unanimously resolved to prepare a petition to the king. The authors of this resolution remain unknown, but the valuable evidence in a recently discovered fragment of a diary kept by Silas Deane points toward James Duane and John Jay, since both men came prepared to propose specific instructions for the five-man committee appointed to draft the petition. Although Duane and Jay had spoken in support of Galloway's plan on the 28th, the conciliatory measures they now introduced differed substantially from his—suggesting, again, that Congress had not been overly receptive to the Pennsylvanian's proposal.

Deane's notes for October 1 begin with Jay's motion "that the proposal for paying for the Tea be added to the Instruction." Four delegates spoke in favor of this motion; nine opposed it, including Edward Rutledge, who three days earlier had called the Galloway plan "almost a perfect plan." The objections must have proved telling, for Jay's motion was unanimously rejected. Since it was well known that repeal of the Port Act required restitution being made for the tea destroyed in Boston Harbor, Congress had thus spurned the most obvious of conciliatory gestures.[29]

Duane promptly "made a Long speech & then a Motion" for another instruction to the committee. The resolution he introduced was designed to obviate the rationale used by the government to justify American taxation. After first reminding the king that the colonies "have always cheerfully complied with the royal Requisitions for raising Supplies of Men and Money," the resolution would then have had Congress express its confidence that the provincial assemblies would "readily concur in any plan consistent with constitutional liberty for drawing forth the united Councils aid and Strength of these Branches of his Majesty's Dominions whenever it shall be found necessary." Where the Galloway plan had presumed that the assemblies were too parochial to act responsibly, Duane's resolution stipulated that they could be trusted to recognize the legitimate needs of the empire.[30]

Duane met immediate opposition when R. H. Lee proposed to offer an amendment "to extend [the motion], To raising also, a Militia, & Arming them, for Our defense." The subversive intent of Lee's remarks was obvious, for as Silas Deane recorded, "Mr Duane resents it." His resentment doubtless increased on Monday the 3rd, when Lee formally introduced his amendment. Its text did not differ radically from Duane's until it came to consider the defense of America. Here, however, what Duane had intended as a conciliatory offer was converted into a thinly veiled warning of American defiance. Lee asserted that it was not only "quite unreasonable" for Britain to bear the expense of maintaining an army in America, but also "unnecessary and improper, as North America is able, willing, and under Providence, determined to defend, protect, and secure itself." Moreover, to demonstrate the truth of this assertion, Lee proposed that Congress advise the colonies to take appropriate measures to strengthen, discipline, and arm their militias.[31]

The ensuing debate evoked a frank discussion of military resistance. One of the Rutledges thought that the amendment amounted to "a Declaration of Warr, which if intended, no other Measure ought to be taken up," while Benjamin Harrison argued "that it will tend, only to irritate, whereas Our Business is to reconcile—that We are unable to defend Ourselves." Lee and Patrick Henry replied that the business of Congress included preparing America for defense and the failure of commercial resistance: "in that Case Arms are Necessary, & if then, it is Necessary Now," Henry noted. "Arms are a Resource to which We shall be forced, a Resource afforded Us by God & Nature, & why in the Name of both are We to hesitate providing them Now whilst in Our power?"

Despite this plea, the revised instruction approved later that day was far closer to Duane's original motion than Lee's amendment. For while it offered to defray the expenses of administering government and justice, Lee's bristling references to the militia were reduced to a milder statement asserting that the militia was adequate for colonial defense, "if put upon a proper footing"—which should be done immediately—"and that in case of war," the colonies would be ready to provide "any further forces that may be necessary." This revised motion "was carried Unanimously," Deane noted, although that may have meant only with the consent of each delegation, not of all the members.[32]

The next phase of debate, which took place between October 3 and 5, is the most difficult to reconstruct. It began with Thomas Lynch asking whether the "Regulations of Trade or Acts of Charles the Second should be considered as obligatory." But subsequent debate broadened the question, leaving Congress to discuss whether it should confine its protests to actions taken by Parliament since 1763—as the delegates had in fact temporarily resolved to do on September 24—or include earlier infringements of colonial liberties as well. A proliferation of motions and amendments and the terseness of Deane's notes complicate the analysis of this debate. Eventually the four New England colonies, Virginia, and North Carolina carried a resolution instructing the committee to propose a restoration of the situation that the colonies "were in at the close of the late war"—a position that left the status of the Navigation Acts still unresolved. The more conciliatory delegates seem to have opposed this resolution, perhaps because they believed it should go further and explicitly confirm the validity of legislation enacted before 1763. Or it is possible that they thought the colonies ultimately would have to challenge the earlier enactments, in which case a failure to present an explicit, comprehensive list of grievances now might only enhance British suspicions and hostility later.[33]

By restricting its list of grievances to the years since 1763, however, Congress left open the question that Thomas Lynch had initially posed: were the Navigation Acts to be regarded as legitimate, and if so, on what grounds? When Congress finally took up the declaration on rights a week later, this issue emerged as the only serious cause of division. Again it was James Duane who pushed most persistently for American concessions. "Mr. Duane has had his Heart sett upon asserting in our Bill of Rights, the Authority of Parliament to regulate the Trade of the Colonies," John Adams noted. "He is for grounding it on Compact, Acquiescence, Necessity, Protection, not merely on our Consent." And again, as a week earlier, Congress found itself almost evenly divided. An October 13 vote on the question of allowing Parliament to regulate trade produced a stalemate: five colonies on either side, Massachusetts and Rhode Island divided.[34]

When debate resumed the next day, the Declaration of Rights was formally approved. Eight of its ten key resolutions passed without a dissenting vote, but the critical fourth resolution did not. Its first provision, reserving to the provincial assemblies "a free and exclusive power of legislation . . . in all cases of taxation and internal polity, subject only to the negative of their sovereign," though far-reaching, generated little debate. The real problem and its compromised solution followed.

But, from the necessity of the case, and a regard to the mutual interest of both countries, we cheerfully consent to the operation of such acts of the British parliament, as are bona fide, restrained to the regulation of our external commerce, for the purpose of securing the commercial advantages of the whole empire to the mother country, and the commercial benefits of its respective members; excluding every idea of taxation, internal or external, for raising a revenue on the subjects in America, without their consent.

Although this text adopted significant phrases from resolutions Duane had earlier drafted, it fell short of providing the expansive justification for this concession that he desired. The apparent compromise followed the logic of the Fairfax Resolves. The colonies would grant Parliament authority to regulate trade, but do so only on the narrowest grounds of mutual interest and consent —"out of their mere grace & Favor," as Galloway later put it— avoiding any admission of parliamentary right. Whenever these interests ceased to be mutual, consent could presumably be revoked.[35]

The Declaration of Rights offered no further concessions. It confirmed the central constitutional claims American theorists had been elaborating for a decade, and thus left little room for compromise. Consistent with its resolution of October 5, Congress did eliminate from its list of grievances those measures that merely amended statutes enacted prior to 1763. This was merely a gesture, however. Only "an ardent desire, that harmony and mutual intercourse of affection may be restored" led the delegates to "pass over for the present" the numerous other "infringements and violations" of colonial liberties their researches had uncovered.[36]

With the Declaration of Rights approved, an increasingly restless Congress devoted its final days of meeting to completing action on the Association and to composing separate addresses to the king and to the peoples of America, Great Britain, and Quebec. The royal petition required considerable revision, and emerged finally as the work of John Dickinson, who had been belatedly elected to Congress on October 15. But the changes Dickinson made in the petition were rhetorical rather than substantive. The essential policies of the First Congress had been determined or confirmed during the first fortnight of October.[37]

The results of those debates demonstrated the inability of delegates such as Duane and Jay to commit Congress to an avowedly conciliatory policy. Restitution would not be made for the tea brewed in Boston Harbor. The inherent right of Parliament to regulate imperial affairs had not been recognized. And even the acknowledgment of the colonies' responsibility to help defray the costs of empire was couched in terms that would scarcely have encouraged a renewed British confidence in American loyalty. The address to the king merely offered to make "such provision" for meeting the expenses of government "as has been and shall be judged, by the legislatures . . . just and reasonable to their respective circumstances."[38]

The essential positions that the First Congress adopted were thus stringent. They affirmed the autonomy of the colonial legislatures and offered little in the way of compromise, but presupposed instead that the first concessions and conciliatory gestures had to come from Britain. And yet these decisions were not produced by the manipulative talents, chicanery, or coercion of any faction. The notes of debate kept by Deane and John Adams clearly demonstrate that congressional discussions were open, candid, and relatively free of rancor, and that pressures to compromise were strong. If anything, the deliberate pace of debate and the numerous dinners and visits held after hours provided ample opportunities for exploring alternatives and finding common ground—a concern that most members consciously shared. Worried that their constituents might grow impatient, some of the delegates wrote home to explain the delay in reaching decisions. "Unanimity being in our view of the last importance," the Connecticut delegates wrote to Governor Trumbull, "every one must be heard, even on those points or subjects, which are in themselves not of the last importance."[39]

What is perhaps even more striking about the First Congress is that the issues at dispute were surprisingly narrow and frequently concerned troublesome details rather than large questions. Only Galloway was recorded arguing against non-exportation; no one, not even Galloway, defended the claims of parliamentary supremacy that lay at the heart of the imperial crisis. The delegates thus managed to confine serious controversy to the overlapping problems of the validity of legislation enacted before 1763 and the basis on which Parliament might be allowed to continue regulating colonial trade. The limited scope of this debate is better appreciated when it is viewed from the perspective of London: even had Congress offered fuller concessions on these points, it would not have answered British objections that American ideas were outright constitutional heresy.

It is, then, the general substance of the positions Congress finally hammered out that also explains why the Galloway plan was unacceptable. By giving Parliament a veto over American legislation and creating a royal legate whose powers would dwarf those already possessed by the colonial governors, Galloway conceded too much. His plan violated the delegates' general conviction that responsibility for the current crisis lay not in the deficiencies of the colonial legislatures but rather in the excessive claims and ambitions of the ministry and Parliament.

The decisions of the First Congress were thus to shape the future course of events, not because the delegates were consciously aiming toward independence, but because they required the government to make the initial concessions necessary to launch serious negotiations. Nor did these decisions constitute victory for "radicals" and defeat for "conservatives." Neither John Adams nor Joseph Galloway, R. H. Lee nor James Duane, could be entirely pleased with the results: their favorite ideas, which marked the extremes of congressional thinking, had been strongly modified or rejected by their colleagues. By spurning proposals clearly pointing toward military preparations, by requiring Massachusetts to act "on the defensive," and by narrowing their list of grievances and toning down the language of their declarations, a majority of the delegates may well have believed that they were adopting a reasonably moderate policy of opposition. It was true that they had taken strong positions on questions of constitutional rights—positions they hoped would finally force the government to recognize the validity of American claims. They had fashioned a boycott that promised to be even more cohesive and effective than the campaigns of the 1760's. Above all, they had demonstrated that unified American resistance was possible. But Congress also declined to adopt more militant tactics that delegates such as John Adams and Patrick Henry thought were justifiable even in 1774.[40]

Nor were the decisions of 1774 merely a patchwork compromise covering irreconcilable positions. They defined a strategy of resistance and diplomacy with a logic and integrity of its own. The colonists would demonstrate their willingness to resist whatever actions Britain took, but seek to avoid actions that they deemed provocative. They would affirm essential constitutional arguments, but not insist that every facet of the imperial system be immediately adjusted to suit colonial convictions. Congressional moderates, while nursing their doubts, could thus believe that the program of the First Congress could constitute a feasible basis for reconciliation, *if* the government were indeed prepared to compromise and *if* a further deterioration of the situation in Massachusetts could be prevented. Whether the government would understand the signals Congress was emitting, or the rather fine distinctions it was making, posed more difficult questions.

CHAPTER IV

War and Politics,
1775–1776

————————————— ⌇ —————————————

A S one of its last acts, the First Congress had resolved that
another Congress should assemble on May 10, 1775, "unless
the redress of grievances, which we have desired, be obtained
before that time." Some of the delegates had "supposed," Samuel
Ward observed in December, "that if our Grievances were
redressed this Winter there would be no Necessity of another
Congress."[1] But events were to prove otherwise. In January the
British government chose to ignore the royal petition so pain-
stakingly prepared in October. In April came the electrifying
and dreaded news of the outbreak of hostilities in Massachusetts.
"The unnatural sheding the Blood of our dear Country men,"
one Connecticut leader noted, "seems to have had a wonderfull
Effect to unite all in great Resolution to defend & revenge innocent blood."[2] Three weeks later, most of the delegates to the
First Congress reassembled at Philadelphia to face a situation as
critical as anything they could have imagined the previous fall.

In 1775 as in 1774 external events and public opinion narrowed the range of options available to Congress while exerting
a powerful pressure to maintain some basis for compromise
within its chamber. Precisely because an escalation of resistance
seemed unavoidable, moderate delegates grew more determined to open some new avenue of accommodation or at least
to prevent any hardening of American positions. While failing to

modify the stringent diplomatic posture adopted in 1774, their efforts did create an uneasy compromise that left neither wing of Congress wholly satisfied but allowed both to continue to cooperate on framing more expedient measures. The events and decisions of 1775 thus indicate the restraints that considerations of policy and politics imposed on expressions of partisanship.

A Mandate Renewed

SLIGHTLY more than six months separated the adjournment of the First Continental Congress and the opening of the Second. The delay seemed generous even by eighteenth-century standards: the government had needed less time to frame and deliver its response to the Boston Tea Party. After seven restive weeks in Philadelphia, the delegates to the First Congress had been eager to return to their families. But continuing political obligations and anxieties were inescapable. The delegates could expect that they would have to report to their provincial constituents, play an active role in supervising the enforcement of the Association, and keep abreast of developments in New England and whatever intelligence was received from Britain. Perhaps more important, all but a handful of the delegates recognized that they would have to act to prevent the decisions of the Congress from being thwarted within their own provinces.

Publication of the various proceedings of the Congress abruptly ended the suspension of judgment that had lasted into the fall of 1774. *What Think Ye of the Congress Now?*, the loyalist pamphleteer Thomas Bradbury Chandler asked his readers, defining the great public question of the winter of 1774–75, and other avowed loyalists quickly began publishing pamphlets and essays denouncing both the policies and the authority of Congress. Although this sudden burst of protest from writers who had previously supported the calling of the Congress took various forms—from the relatively dispassionate "Massachusettensis" essays of Daniel Leonard to the ill-tempered accusations of Joseph Galloway—most loyalists agreed on the charges to be leveled against the Congress. Their polemical campaign had two immediate goals: to obstruct the implementation of the Association; and to induce one or more of the colonial legislatures to disavow the Congress and draft separate petitions that would hopefully encourage the government to initiate new conciliatory measures of its own.[3]

The loyalists' indictment of Congress reflected their gloomy assessments of the consequences its acts would predictably produce in Britain and were already having in America. The delegates had betrayed what loyalists now recalled, naïvely or disingenuously, to have been their original duty. Far from narrowing the breach between Britain and America by "mark[ing] out a line of government, that would sufficiently ascertain and establish the right of jurisdiction in the one, and secure the liberties of the other," Congress had demanded concessions Britain could never make and offered terms of accommodation too humiliating for the government to accept. Equally alarming, by vesting quasi-coercive powers in local committees of inspection, the Association had condoned the subversion of legal government. Effective power was rapidly slipping away from the provincial governments to extra-legal conventions and committees. The whigs seemed bent on destroying the very colonial constitutions they ostensibly wished to protect, while the petty but ugly forms of intimidation to which critics of the Association were already being exposed suggested that local zealots placed no greater value on the preservation of personal liberties.[4]

Denunciations of the policies of Congress inevitably led to challenges to its legitimacy as well. Given the circumstances of their election, whom did the delegates actually represent? Were they not, Samuel Seabury objected, "at best, but delegates of delegates," whose acts were scarcely binding on the people at large? No one "could have imagined," a New York legislator wrote, "had not experience convinced him, that a Congress could have supposed itself vested with a power to enact laws for the government of the whole continent . . . without previously consulting the several *colony legislatures.*" Even if the delegates could credibly claim some authority, Chandler asked, was it not true "that all that was done or projected by the Congress in the way of hostility against Great-Britain (and little was done or projected by them in any other way) was uncommissioned and unauthorised, and cannot be binding even upon their constituents?"[5]

Loyalist writers thus launched the first serious effort to define the source and nature of congressional authority, in the process drawing, with no little irony, on assumptions about representation and consent that American whigs had long applied against claims of parliamentary supremacy over the colonies. Their arguments were expedient, plausible, and ultimately irrelevant to the fluid political situation of early 1775. For although enforcement of the Association did encounter indifference or even outright hostility in various localities, evidence of widespread popular approval for the Congress seemed decisive. The apparent enthusiasm with which village and county meetings moved to ratify the Association and appoint committees of inspection provided convincing proof that Congress had renewed its mandate. Loyalist arguments were futile because, quite simply, the decisions of Congress had themselves come to constitute the dominant standards of political legitimacy. Men could still differ widely about the prospects for reconciliation or war, British concessions or colonial unity. But the First Congress had defined both the tactics and goals of resistance, and for individuals everywhere the immediate political choice lay between accepting or repudiating its authority. Allegiance to Congress had become the principal test of the right to participate in the emerging Revolutionary polity.[6]

There exists no better testimony to the astonishing power Congress had acquired than the hapless comments of the royal officials who were obliged to oppose it. The recommendations of Congress were "received implicitly," Governor Wentworth of New Hampshire reported. "So great is the present delusion, that most people receive them as matters of obedience, not of considerate examination, whereon they may exercise their own judgment." On Christmas Eve, 1774, Governor Dunmore of Virginia described the collapse of his government, now "entirely disregarded if not wholly overturned." Committees of inspection, supported by militia companies, were being appointed in every county, and were already busily monitoring "the conduct of every inhabitant without distinction . . . stigmatiz[ing] as they term it such as they find transgressing what they are now hardy enough to call the laws of the Congress," which, Dunmore added, "they talk of in a style of respect and treat with marks of reverence which they never bestowed on their legal Government or the laws proceeding from it."[7] Even justices of the peace were helping to carry out their directives.

Although Dunmore predicted that people would eventually come to their senses, loyalist leaders had little reason to be optimistic about their campaign to mobilize broad opposition to Congress. There were, of course, pockets of pro-loyalist sentiment scattered throughout the colonies. Yet drawing these disparate potential opponents of whig policies into a cohesive intercolonial movement proved difficult, not merely because (as historians have generally agreed) loyalists were inherently less well organized than their antagonists, but also because much popular "loyalism" was rooted in preexisting local conflicts whose sources were largely tangential to the major causes of the Anglo-American crisis. In the Carolina backcountry, much of rural New York, polyglot enclaves in the middle colonies, or areas where tenant farming was common, loyalty to crown and empire mattered less than hostility to local whig leaders generated by earlier conflicts, ethnic or religious animosities, or quarrels between landlords and tenants. At the provincial level of politics, the problems of overcoming or at least neutralizing this opposition would grow more difficult as prosecution of first the Association and then the war exacerbated these conflicts. But dangerous as such opposition could become, it failed to threaten the hegemony of Congress at the intercolonial level.[8]

A more serious threat to American union might come from the colonial assemblies. By December 1774 it seemed obvious, as James Duane noted, that "our different Assemblies will be called upon by Government" to state their own ideas of reconciliation. Still searching for some avenue of compromise, Duane was disposed to see where such initiatives might lead; and when, in early 1775, a majority of the New York assembly first refused to ratify the proceedings of the First Congress or elect delegates to the Second and then dispatched mild petitions to the king and Parliament, he defended their actions.[9] Similar attempts elsewhere, however, produced the embarrassing results that Governor Wentworth had foreseen when he predicted that "the respective Assemblies will embrace the first hour of their meeting formally to recognise all the proceedings of the Congress; and if they should superadd, it will not probably be less violent than the example, which will be their foundation." The Pennsylvania assembly rejected Joseph Galloway's arguments and voted against petitioning; the New Jersey representatives did approve a petition, but its language and requests were, as Governor William Franklin recognized, scarcely more conciliatory than those of Congress.[10] And when, in June 1775, Dunmore asked the Virginia House of Burgesses to consider the brief conciliatory proposal that Parliament had approved in February, the Burgesses adopted a set of resolutions repudiating not only the substance of the proposal but the propriety of its submission to individual assemblies rather than the Continental Congress. "For ourselves," they declared, "we have exhausted every mode of application which our invention could suggest as proper and promising."[11]

The net effect of these provincial developments was to confirm the broad policy prerogatives of the Congress. If anything, the apostate tendencies of New York, whose loyal legislators were rumored to be the objects of lucrative ministerial bribes, reiterated the necessity of maintaining a united front of opposition. And the eventual fate of the New York petitions, which the government never seriously considered, demonstrated anew what resistance leaders had believed all along. The real issues at stake in the imperial crisis had nothing to do with the form or tone of American petitions. The debilitated state of resistance in New York and the halting progress of public opinion in the other middle colonies would affect the timing of congressional decisions but not alter the deeper assumptions upon which they rested.[12]

Colonial moderates proved as sensitive to these considerations as anyone. "I am glad to find your Council and Assembly . . . behave so well," Joseph Reed wrote Charles Pettit, a New Jersey relation and political dependent, "for though I think the Congress proceeded on too high a scale, I know the designs of the Ministry, and the temper of the people of England so well, that I am confident nothing but a union in any scheme would relieve us from the oppressions they were meditating, and which the present measures were only designed to introduce."[13] Even more revealing was the equivocal path that James Duane followed during the months separating the First and Second Congresses: defending the actions of the New York legislature, proposing amendments to the implementation of the Association in New York that Alexander McDougall suspected were designed to "destroy it," suggesting that the colonial legislatures consider whatever diplomatic initiatives the government undertook, but finally accepting reelection to the Congress. Fearful of civil war and the aggrandizing ambitions of New England—natural attitudes for an Albany landowner and speculator—Duane could have easily followed his embittered friend Joseph Galloway into isolation, loyalism, and exile. Instead he eventually accepted the arguments of other moderates and remained active in the leadership of resistance. "You and I, I believe, thought much alike and were equally distressed on particular Points," the moderate Maryland delegate Thomas Johnson, Jr., had written to him in December 1774, "but as Things are now circumstanced if the Proceedings of the Congress come before the Assemblies I am afraid a Disapprobation of any Article might be of infinite Mischief to our Cause."[14]

Union remained the paramount good. "The great Point, *at present*, is to keep up the appearance of an unbroken Harmony in public measures," John Dickinson wrote in late January, "for fear of encouraging Great Britain to Hostilities, which, otherwise, she would avoid. When she has made her Choice, and it proves inimical, I hope every Man of Sense & Virtue in America will draw his Sword, without any Regard for the yet respectable Doctrine of Disunion."[15] Three months later, Dickinson reluctantly recognized that the conditions he dreaded had been fulfilled.

Policies Reconsidered

WHILE adherence to the Congress remained public orthodoxy, colonial leaders gave their private speculations free rein. As James Duane and Thomas Johnson had discussed the idea of allowing individual assemblies to receive government proposals, Samuel Adams and Thomas Cushing apparently disagreed over what response Congress should make if the government offered limited concessions. Cushing believed Congress could rest content with the "mere repeal of the obnoxious Acts"; Adams thought it should demand "the most solem ratification of an American Bill of Rights," a view that Arthur Lee also endorsed.[16] Other delegates raised different problems. Silas Deane discussed the utility of framing articles of confederation; Samuel Ward proposed that Congress meet annually, regardless of the outcome of the current crisis; Samuel Chase argued that the colonies should immediately initiate serious military preparations.[17] For the most part, however, the delegates remained more anxiously concerned to learn the government's response to the program of the First Congress. "We are all gaping for intelligence from the new parliament," Peyton Randolph wrote early in January. Some predicted that "we are to be treated as rebels and Enemies without any ceremony"; others that the acts would be repealed, "on condition that we pay for the tea and acknowledge the Superiority of Parliament." In that case, Randolph noted, "What is meant by superiority must be properly defined, otherwise they may as well persue their old plan."[18]

By the early spring of 1775, events in London and Massachusetts were clarifying the choices that would confront Congress when it reconvened at Philadelphia in May. Fresh from its success at the surprise parliamentary election of the fall, the ministry showed little interest in reconciliation. After a deceptive initial expression of interest, the petition of the First Congress was rudely ignored. The House of Lords decisively rejected a conciliatory bill offered by the Earl of Chatham. Although unresponsive to many American demands, Chatham's bill was far superior to the transparently inadequate alternative Parliament adopted instead, which merely suggested that it would suspend its power of taxation if the colonies made provision for the support of government. Massachusetts was declared to be in a state of rebellion, and additional acts were passed restraining the commerce of all the colonies save New York, North Carolina, and Georgia.[19]

More alarming than any of these developments was the long-dreaded outbreak of fighting in Massachusetts. Although pressure to launch offensive operations against the British troops in Boston had been building in the Bay Colony since early fall, its Provincial Congress had managed to keep the conduct of resistance within the guidelines endorsed by the Continental Congress. The affidavits that local officials scrupulously gathered from participants at Lexington and Concord—and that were quickly printed in colonial newspapers—left little doubt that responsibility for the onset of civil war lay squarely with Thomas Gage and, by implication, his superiors. Americans everywhere reacted accordingly. Popular demonstrations of patriotic fervor took on a military air that contrasted sharply with the more sober proceedings of 1774. En route to Philadelphia, the Massachusetts delegation encountered an endless series of enthusiastic receptions, replete with honor guards, militia companies drawn up for inspection in village squares, and cheering bystanders lining the highways. Approaching New York, the carriage of a flustered

John Hancock was met by "Persons appearing with proper Har-
nesses [who] insisted upon Taking out my Horses and Dragging
me into and through the City, a Circumstance I would not have
had Taken place upon any Consideration, not being fond of such
Parade." Their arrival at Philadelphia proved equally tumultu-
ous—and indicative of the progress of public opinion.[20]

Such popular manifestations of militant patriotism naturally
reinforced the assembling delegates' sense of urgency, but they
served another purpose as well. In 1775, as in 1774, these demonstrations provided the most forceful expressions of public opinion
that were available, and thus revealed that armed resistance to
Britain was not merely acceptable but generally expected. Nor
did the delegates' formal credentials and instructions impose any
meaningful restraint on their deliberations. Their wording was
sufficiently vague to fulfill Samuel Ward's wish that "being free
from all Restraints We may deliberate with Freedom, resolve
wisely & execute with Firmness whatever the Necessities of our
Country may require." Moreover, the paralysis that increasingly
affected legally constituted governments in most of the colonies
could only enhance the prestige and deference that Congress
already enjoyed. The reelection of virtually the entire membership of the First Congress was another mark of confidence. Fifty
of the sixty-five delegates attending this second session had
served in 1774, and their previously acquired sense of collegiality
facilitated candid debate. Confident of their authority, the delegates felt no compunctions about preserving the privacy of their
deliberations. An injunction to secrecy that Congress adopted on
May 11 was observed so scrupulously in their correspondence that
only the modern discovery of several key documents has made
it possible to reconstruct the critical debates that took place early
in the session.[21]

On May 16, after several days of preliminary formalities, Congress went into a committee of the whole to consider "the state
of America." As in 1774, discussions of the tactics of resistance,
prospects for reconciliation, and the precise rights the colonists
should claim inevitably overlapped. According to the brief notes
kept by Silas Deane, debate began with R. H. Lee introducing
"proposals for raising an army." These were seconded by Thomas
Lynch and John Rutledge. Rutledge evidently altered the intended thrust of the debate, however, by "insist[ing] that previously some other points must be settled, such as do We aim at

independancy? or do We only ask for a Restoration of Rights & putting of Us on Our old footing?" Robert R. Livingston endorsed Rutledge's objections against plunging into questions of means without reevaluating the goals of resistance. He was followed by John Adams, who apparently sought to show that such a review was not necessary by reiterating the essential position adopted in 1774: "independance on Parliament is absolutely to be averrd in the Americans, but a dependance on the Crown is what We own."[22]

At this point John Dickinson intervened. His prestige made him the natural leader of those members whose preference for conciliatory measures had been intensified by the outbreak of war. Elected to the First Congress too late to influence its major decisions, Dickinson returned determined to convince Congress to couple preparations for defense with forthright steps toward negotiations. His lengthy speech of the 16th began by admitting that "a Vigorous preparation for Warr" and "a Vigorous prosecution of it" were necessary. But then he returned to his old concern "to strike out still a further plan for a reconciliation if it is possible." He was "very timid," Deane noted, and "is for giving up intirely the Regulating of Trade, argues smoothly but Sophistically on the Subject and gives rather disgust."

Deane's last comment suggests that many members were reluctant to initiate a potentially wide-ranging debate on diplomacy before undertaking urgent military preparations. During the next week Congress apparently concentrated on the latter, considering reports of the capture of Ticonderoga by New England militia and requests from the New York delegates for advice on the defensive measures their colony should take in case British troops occupied New York City. But when Deane's notes of debates resumed on May 23, "the Question shall We Treat"— that is, negotiate with Britain—lay before Congress. In a second lengthy speech, Dickinson argued strongly for a comprehensive strategy embodying three major elements: "prepar[ing] with the utmost Diligence for War," submitting a second petition to the crown, and "sending Agents to England, to treat of an Accomodation." Dickinson clearly intended to create an environment and conditions that would enable candid negotiations to take place between the government and emissaries from Congress. Rather than submit a petition "That dwelt on our Rights"— already so forcefully asserted that "Repetition is needless"—Dickinson argued that the new text should instead stress the colonists' desire for "Relief from our Fears & Jealousies" and their continued attachment to king and empire. Similarly, the embassy Congress would send to England was to have substantive powers of negotiation: their instructions would specify "what Concessions and what Demands they are to make in every Event favourable or unfavourable that shall occurr." The most important concession Dickinson advocated was an unequivocal acknowledgment of Parliament's right to regulate imperial trade, but during the debate of the 23rd the possibility of making restitution for the tea destroyed at Boston was also broached.[23]

Opposition to Dickinson's proposals did not center on the question of a second petition, though some delegates, like John Adams, thought it redundant and embarrassing. Nor did the idea of *proposing* negotiations seem objectionable, for late on the 23rd a motion to include such an invitation in the royal petition "pass'd agreeable to all." But on the questions of modifying the positions of 1774 and dispatching envoys to England, Dickinson and his supporters met heavy criticism. On the 23rd, Patrick Henry had declared that "the Bill of rights must never be receded from," and when the next day Samuel Chase again raised "the old affair of the right of regulating Trade," an acrimonious debate followed. The Maryland delegates and Dickinson repeated their case for further concessions, and their impatient opponents, finding further debate on this subject pointless, were "severe" in reply. Dickinson was roundly attacked by Thomas Mifflin, Lee, and perhaps most revealingly by John Rutledge, who had cooperated with Duane and Galloway in 1774 but now delivered a stinging rebuke to Dickinson. Rutledge said he was "against any Concession whatever, that Lord North has given Us his Ultimatum with which We cannot agree—Treats Dickinsons plan with the utmost Contempt—and is so severe that *Chase* rises to explain himself." A further rejoinder by Thomas Stone of Maryland proved so "disagreeable that one half of the Congress withdraw."[24]

Two days later (May 26) Congress approved five resolutions comprising the best statement of general policy the committee of the whole could produce. One was an additional instruction to the New York Provincial Congress, urging them "to persevere the more vigorously in preparing for their defence, as it is very uncertain whether the earnest endeavours of the Congress to accomodate the unhappy difference between G. Britain and the colonies by conciliatory Measures will be successful." The remaining set of four resolutions marked the results of the debate begun by Lee's motion and Rutledge's questions of May 16. The first two resolutions invoked the various acts and events that had brought America "to a dangerous and critical situation," and concluded by recommending that "these colonies be immediately put into a state of defence." The third resolution repeated, however, that Congress wished for nothing more than "a restoration of the harmony formerly subsisting" between Britain and America, and authorized the preparation of a second petition to the king. The final resolution—the only one not to pass unanimously—proposed "that measures be entered into for opening a Negotiation" with the government, "and that this be made a part of the petition to the King."[25]

In their ambivalence, these resolutions embodied a tacit compromise that enabled both the militant and conciliatory wings of Congress to pursue the measures each believed necessary. The organization of military resistance—the task to which Congress now turned—was not itself at issue. The real problem was to fashion a diplomatic strategy appropriate to the changing conditions of 1775. In the face of British obstinacy and the outbreak of war, should Congress modify its positions of 1774 as a gesture toward accommodation, or reaffirm them to demonstrate its unshaken commitment to a full redress of American grievances? Militant delegates, though unable to prevent the preparation of a second petition, apparently succeeded in blocking any reduction of the demands of 1774. Conciliatory delegates would be allowed to draft the petition—Dickinson, Jay, and Thomas Johnson were a majority of the committee appointed for that task— but not to retreat from the positions Congress had already adopted. The committee was probably given some leeway to devise new ways of approaching the government, which would explain why Benjamin Franklin, recently returned from London but so far mysteriously silent within Congress, was named to it. Its ultimate failure to offer any innovative proposal "for opening a Negotiation" may well have reflected the pessimistic conclusions Franklin had drawn from the failure of his own diplomatic efforts in London during the preceding months.[26]

Three considerations determined the outcome of the debates of late May. The first was the effect that a reduction of American demands, arriving hard upon news of the first hostilities, would presumably have on the British government. If the ministry had already refused even to recognize a Congress representing a surprisingly united America, would it now offer concessions to a body that seemed to flinch at the prospect of war? That seemed unlikely. Conversely, John Adams noted, some delegates still hoped "that Ministry and Parliament, will immediately receed as soon as they hear of the Battle of Lexington, the Spirit of New York and Phyladelphia, the Permanency of the Union of the Colonies etc." In either event, a logical position for Congress to adopt involved reaffirming its own interest in negotiations without undercutting its bargaining position by premature concessions.[27]

The state of public opinion exerted a second influence on this debate. The mandate expressed in the wave of public meetings held to ratify and implement the proceedings of the First Congress was, if anything, more decisive than the one formed during the summer of 1774. Lexington and Concord had done nothing to shake this foundation of popular support; by all accounts, they had strengthened it. Moderate delegates could assert, correctly, that radical measures that seemed to tend toward independence remained generally unacceptable. But they could point to no groundswell of popular opinion favoring the adoption of more conciliatory gestures. More militant delegates could argue, on the other hand, that any signs of a congressional retreat would only play into the hands of loyalist writers, who could then suggest that Congress was either internally divided or uncertain of its own positions. By submitting a second petition, Congress could placate moderate elements of public opinion; by adhering to its earlier stands, it could continue to command the allegiance of those who already doubted the prospects for reconciliation.

Considerations of diplomacy and domestic politics thus cautioned the delegates against modifying the policies of 1774. But, in the third place, internal pressures also encouraged the two polar groups of delegates to strike some *modus vivendi* that would enable Congress to proceed with the pressing tasks of organizing an army. Conciliatory delegates continued to wonder whether even modest American concessions might not crack British intransigence. But unable to command majority support for their recommendations, they had no choice other than to accept policies whose consequences they foresaw but did not desire—particularly when they agreed, as Dickinson had admitted, that the colonies had to prove themselves willing to oppose force with force. Militant delegates operated under similar constraints. John Adams privately grumbled about the obstructionist tactics of Dickinson, the "certain great Fortune and piddling Genius" whose insistence on pursuing reconciliation, he complained in his famous intercepted letter, "has given a silly Cast to our whole Doings." Yet it was undeniably more important to pacify moderate members than cavalierly disregard their hopes. The dispatch of a second petition containing what Adams called "a delicate Proposal of Negociation" might be redundant at best, but the need to keep Dickinson and his allies actively engaged justified allowing them to pursue their favored scheme. "Discord and total Disunion," Adams realized, "would be the certain Effect of a resolute Refusal to petition and negociate."[28] No useful purpose would be served if the conciliatory faction left Congress: what was at stake was not a problem of wresting political control from one's opponents, but of fashioning policies that all factions could support. Correctly anticipating that events would progressively strengthen their position, the militant delegates could also expect a gradual narrowing of differences of opinion within Congress.

Two incidents involving the Massachusetts and New York delegations illustrate how these constraints worked. Early in June Congress received a letter from the Massachusetts Provincial Congress requesting its advice on the resumption of legal government, a step that the creation of a provincial army now made unavoidable, because "the sword should in all free states be subservient to the civil powers." Since the fall of 1774 the Massachusetts delegates had been kept well informed of their constituents' desire to restore legal government, either under the original charter of 1629 or (perhaps even more hopefully) through the framing of a new constitution. With this desire they privately sympathized. For Samuel Adams, however, the preeminent problem remained, as ever, to preserve "union" both within Congress and at home in his native province. Convinced that other delegates were still unwilling to authorize the writing of new constitutions—a step that clearly implied the repudiation of all forms of British authority, royal as well as parliamentary— Adams held to the formula he had outlined to Joseph Warren the previous September. Then he had argued that Governor Gage's

conduct could be used to justify a declaration vacating his commission, and that the second charter of 1691 could thereupon be
resumed, with the provincial council acting as both the upper
house of the legislature and the executive branch of government.
Although this proposal effectively nullified the Massachusetts
Government Act, it could fairly be considered the least offensive
way of coping with the problem of providing the Bay Colony
leaders with the legal trappings of authority they needed. For
Adams it had the additional virtue of precluding, at least temporarily, the bitter internal disputes that would predictably arise
whenever Massachusetts undertook the reformation of its government. Within a week of its receipt of the Massachusetts letter,
Congress adopted Adams's formula.[29]

Several weeks later the New York delegation also chose to
ignore the wishes of its constituents in the interest of preserving
congressional harmony. In late June the Provincial Congress
drafted its own plan of reconciliation, which was forwarded to
the delegation at Philadelphia in the hope that Congress might
be persuaded to adopt one or more of its provisions. Had this plan
arrived some weeks earlier, when Congress was actively debating reconciliation, the New York delegates, who were themselves committed to accommodation, might well have used it to
advantage. But to attempt to reopen that debate in July, after
Congress had effectively tabled those issues in order to concentrate on more pressing matters, was pointless. Forced to balance
the wishes of the Provincial Congress against the state of congressional politics, the New York delegates quickly decided not to
introduce their constituents' plan.[30]

Yet if both conciliatory and militant delegates alike were
obliged to defer to the realities of what might be called coalition
politics, their hopes and perhaps even their expectations continued to differ, and events could ultimately favor the arguments
of only one of these groups. During the opening weeks of the
Second Congress moderates had been able to extract some
concessions from their opponents. Although their most important proposals had been rejected, the committee drafting the
royal petition had been authorized to devise some plan for opening negotiations; and in a revealing decision of early June, Congress had prohibited any American expeditions against Canada,
which suggested a continuing intention of acting "on the defensive."[31]

But the carnage at Bunker Hill on June 17—a battle, like Lexington and Concord, clearly initiated by the British—seriously weakened the moderate position within Congress in two ways: by allowing militant delegates to argue that a forceful American response was justified, and by requiring conciliatory members to reaffirm their own commitment to resistance. Within days the resolution regarding operations against Canada had been reversed.[32] When John Dickinson was called upon to revise the Declaration on Taking Arms that George Washington was to read when he took command of the continental army, he produced a text that was more severe than Thomas Jefferson's original version. It was Dickinson's way of proving that he was no less patriotic than his colleagues.[33] And perhaps most important, when the second royal petition was finally approved on July 8, it failed to propose any new or specific format for initiating negotiations. The petition merely dropped the whole problem into the lap of George III, who was asked "to direct some mode, by which the united applications of your faithful colonists to the throne . . . may be improved into a happy and permanent reconciliation." The narrowly framed conciliatory proposal that Parliament had approved in February received even less polite treatment. Referred to the committee of the whole on May 26, it languished unconsidered until July 22, when four members were appointed to prepare a reply. Not until July 31, two days before it adjourned, did Congress approve Jefferson's biting rejection of this "unreasonable and insidious" proposition.[34]

The rapidity with which Congress set about reorganizing the conduct of American resistance provides further evidence of the limits that considerations of policy imposed on expressions of partisanship. It took only a week to approve the Massachusetts request for permission to resume legal government. On June 10 Congress passed a series of recommendations concerning the manufacture and collection of munitions. Four days later it approved the first resolutions creating a continental army. The next day Washington was appointed commanding general. A plan for staff appointments was adopted on June 16. Six days later Congress approved its first emission of bills of credit, and on the last day of the month it approved a comprehensive set of military regulations.[35] Each of these actions was destined to have momentous consequences. Despite its carefully delineated character, the Massachusetts resolution of June 9 created an important

precedent for the establishment of new governments throughout the colonies. The various military resolutions not only committed the colonies to matching Britain's escalation of the conflict, they also reinforced the government's conviction that
American opposition was essentially treasonous and could only
be overcome by a policy of repression. And the decision to resort
to currency finance helped to create a cluster of economic problems that would shape many of the critical political issues and
alignments of the first decade and a half of American independence. Yet with the possible exception of the maneuvers surrounding the appointment of Washington, there is little evidence that any of these issues generated serious divisions within
Congress.

The Prospect of Independence

PHILADELPHIA has never been a pleasant place to spend a summer, and by July most delegates were anxious to return home.
On August 2, after a session lasting exactly twelve weeks, Congress adjourned. At first glance it seems almost astonishing that
men responsible for directing a civil war should vote a recess of
five weeks. Only recently the delegates had contemplated moving to Hartford or Albany, where Congress would be able to
supervise its army more closely. Yet the delegates did feel burdened by the novel demands on their time and energy that
service at Congress was already imposing. Perhaps more important, they were aware of the difficulties the provincial conventions were encountering in carrying out the new responsibilities
thrust upon them with the outbreak of war. Local patriot leaders
and other observers were beginning to express doubts about the
abilities and sometimes the motives of provincial officials and
representatives, foreshadowing the complaints that would be
directed against the state legislatures after independence. For
the delegates, then, a late summer recess offered a useful opportunity to monitor local developments and to assist in the
implementation of the broad policy directives Congress had
issued.[36]

When Congress reconvened—a week late—on September 13,
it avoided the type of general debate about principles and goals
that John Rutledge and John Dickinson had initiated in May.

Congressional moderates made no new suggestions for accommodation. In mid-August Thomas Johnson had predicted that the second petition would be "rejected with contempt," and none of the news from England so much as hinted at a reversal in British policy.[37] As yet, any discussion of a declaration of independence remained recognizably premature. But the more militant members of Congress now anticipated that that subject would soon become debatable. In the early fall they began to propose measures clearly conceived as prerequisites to a decision on independence: the creation of legal governments in all the colonies, the framing of a confederation, and the opening of negotiations with potential European allies. Their attempts to place this agenda under consideration prompted much of the political skirmishing of the ensuing months. For despite their own deepening pessimism, moderates continued to nurse their hope that some sudden development—American success in Canada, shifts in British public opinion, a weakening of the government's resolve—would produce negotiations. They therefore opposed the adoption of policies and pregnant statements implying that Congress was abandoning its original goal of securing a redress of grievances that would leave the British empire intact. The tension that resulted from these conflicting views led to a continuation of the uneasy compromise that allowed Congress to proceed with measures of resistance while leaving more fundamental questions of policy unresolved.

But none of the delegates could ignore the discouraging signals Congress received during the fall of 1775 and winter of 1776, which provided the catalyst making a serious consideration of independence conceivable. Texts of the royal proclamation of August 23, which declared America to be in a state of rebellion, reached Philadelphia in late October. Little more than a week later came news that the king would take no official notice of the second petition. Despite these events, in early January 1776 James Duane could still explain his presence at Congress by noting, "If Parliament should offer reasonable Terms of Conciliation I should never forgive myself for being absent on so great and Interesting an Occasion. I am not without some hopes of a Just and honourable Peace." Two days later, copies of the bellicose royal speech opening the October session of Parliament were printed in Philadelphia. Here the king had described American leaders as "the authors and promoters of this desperate conspiracy." The petitions of Congress, he charged, had been "meant only to amuse" the government and to mislead an "unhappy and deluded multitude" of their fellow colonists, while the delegates meanwhile "were preparing for a general revolt . . . manifestly carried on for the purpose of establishing an independent empire."[38]

When texts of the Prohibitory Act, which subjected all American oceanic commerce to confiscation by the Royal Navy, were laid before Congress on February 27, the theoretical case against George III was essentially complete. Once the king had definitively removed the colonists from his protection—by waging war against them, outlawing them as rebels, and confiscating their property—he had forfeited all claims to their allegiance. By early 1776 it took little ingenuity to demonstrate that the colonies could now rightfully renounce their subjection to the mother country.[39] Precisely because this conclusion seemed self-evident, Congress spent little time pondering the principles and charges that Thomas Jefferson eventually enumerated in the Declaration of Independence. What did trouble the delegates were more pragmatic questions about the necessity, utility, and timing of a formal declaration. It was their concern with the hard political consequences of a decision for independence that governed the maneuvers leading up to the resolution of July 2, 1776.

One issue best revealed the conflicting factors that Congress had to resolve before a decision on independence could be reached: the question of whether the colonies should be authorized to create new legal governments to supplant the provincial congresses that held power in most of the colonies. The imperatives of war had drastically enlarged the duties of these bodies, which now constituted the effective government in every colony but Rhode Island and Connecticut (where the governors were popularly elected), Pennsylvania, and Massachusetts. Instead of merely supervising the Association, local leaders now had to organize and arm military units, gather munitions, raise taxes, and quash pockets of political dissent. Given the expanded scope of their activities, they were eager to acquire the trappings of legal authority; and because no royal governor could possibly sanction any of these measures, the establishment of new constitutions emerged as the obvious alternative to a continuation of the ambiguous interregnum of 1774–75. In early November 1775 Congress had authorized New Hampshire and South Carolina to establish governments; and it could be expected that other colonies would make similar requests within a matter of months.[40] At the same time, mounting popular enthusiasm for a thorough reformation of the corrupt old regime suggested that the fictions devised for Massachusetts might not provide a useful precedent elsewhere. A simple resumption of the existing legal governments, now purged of loyal executive officials, would not go far enough. By widening popular participation in politics through its apparatus of committees, mass meetings, and militia companies, the resistance movement had helped to foster a sudden zeal for republican government. Indeed, by early 1776 the attractions of republicanism, though still fearful to some, were themselves becoming an important stimulus to the growth of revolutionary sentiment.[41]

From the perspective of Congress, this pressure for the creation of new republican governments posed opportunities and problems alike. Although the provincial congresses were nominally superior to the Continental Congress in the sense that they formally elected and instructed their delegations, in practice and function they served as the subordinate administrative agencies of Congress itself. Insofar as their conversion into legal governments would enhance their authority, most delegates recognized that the efficiency of American resistance would be improved. Yet two further considerations led toward a different conclusion. One was the likelihood that a reconstruction of government, undertaken with avowedly republican intentions, would both distract attention from more urgent matters and disrupt the existing rough consensus on issues of resistance by bringing different individuals and social groups into active competition for control of the new regimes. Samuel Adams had quickly perceived that this process was at work in his native province, and his legalistic solution to the problem of government in Massachusetts marked an attempt to use the prestige of Congress to restrain the unruly tendencies of his countrymen.

Delegates from the middle colonies not only shared Adams's fear but, if anything, felt it more acutely. For the ethnic and religious diversity of these colonies, complicated in northern New York and Maryland by class antagonisms between landowners and tenants and in Pennsylvania by animosities between Philadelphia and the frontier, threatened to generate political conflicts that appeals to the common cause could well fail to contain.[42] Thorough élitists that many of the middle colonies' delegates were—and more realistic than their opponents within Congress when it came to assessing the difficulties America would have to overcome to secure its independence—they felt little personal enthusiasm for the wisdom of creating popular democracies in the midst of a revolutionary civil war.

So, too, congressional moderates found a second argument against any sweeping reconstruction of government in the effect it would have on the diplomacy of the Anglo-American conflict, muted and indirect as that had so far been. As both signal and symbol, a decision to replace the existing colonial charters with new constitutions unilaterally framed by the Americans would be tantamount to a declaration of independence. At the very least, it would contradict the position Congress had publicly adopted of desiring merely a return to the *status quo ante,* and thus greatly enlarge the scope of colonial demands. Beyond that, however, a unilateral reformation of government would implicitly renounce the role the crown had always played in the colonial constitutions, and with it the theory of imperial federalism Congress had previously accepted. The colonial charters could no longer be described as contracts between the king and his subjects settled in America. For moderate delegates, still intent on preventing a door to reconciliation from being finally sealed, this was no idle point of political theory.

As the arguments on this one issue suggest, Congress had to weigh the legitimate, pressing needs of resistance against the political impact that the adoption of certain measures would have either on policymakers in London or on public opinion in both America and Britain. Other problems evoked similar conflicts. Should Congress invite foreign merchants to enter American ports, bringing vital supplies in exchange for colonial commodities? Should it dissolve the non-exportation agreement and allow American merchants to export to the rest of the world, earning the hard currency that would be needed to support continental credit? At some point the economic hardships imposed by the Association and the material needs of the army would finally force America to defy the traditional restrictions of the British navigation system, which Congress still nominally accepted.[43] Other proposals suggested that Congress would have to concede the futility of maintaining its increasingly tenuous distinction between "offensive" and "defensive" modes of resistance. When R. H. Lee moved to halt the operations of the royal post office—a seemingly innocuous measure—Thomas Willing objected that this appeared to be "one of the offensive measures which are improper at this time," when the delegates still did not know "but there may be a negotiation." Samuel Adams had to reply weakly that this *was* "a defensive measure," since America's enemies were taking advantage of the royal post to disseminate information harmful to the common cause.[44] And when Congress debated a resolution authorizing privateering voyages against British shipping, John Jay argued that he "was for a War against such only of the British Nation as are our Enemies."[45]

What is striking about the debates on these and other issues, however, is that moderate delegates pursued a strategy of delay rather than outright opposition toward the militant proposals that were regularly advanced after each new jolt from the government. Their position was bolstered in the fall of 1775 when several provincial conventions and legislatures issued new instructions binding their delegations to oppose independence. Although none of these instructions materially enhanced the prospects for reconciliation or even suggested new concessions Congress could offer, they did allow delegates such as Dickinson, Duane, Jay, and Johnson to raise objections against any measure that seemed to be a harbinger of independence. Indeed, it seems likely that the passage of these new instructions was actively solicited and arranged by conciliatory delegates who foresaw the obstructive value they would have in future debates. This was clearly what happened in Pennsylvania, where John Dickinson was the probable author of the set of instructions that eventually constituted one of the final obstacles to a declaration of independence. "I think them ill timed, timorous and weak," wrote Samuel Chase, who had supported Dickinson's conciliatory proposals of late May; "they were not drawn by Men fit to conquer the World and rule her when she's wildest. . . . They suit the Palates of the persons instructed and were probably drawn by themselves."[46]

This strategy of delay remained tenable through the late winter of 1776, partly because even militant delegates recognized that a large body of public opinion was still unprepared for measures that smacked too strongly of independence. Yet the moderates knew that they were conducting a holding action at best. As events made the prospect of independence more likely, they

found themselves clinging to the stringent positions Congress
had previously adopted; they had no conciliatory initiatives left
to propose. The considerations that had militated against a reduction of the colonies' demands in May grew more powerful
with every passing month. By the late summer of 1775 moderates
such as Jay and Thomas Johnson justified their advocacy of delay
on grounds of expediency rather than by falsely magnifying the
prospects for accommodation. Writing in mid-August to defend
the submission of the second petition, Johnson argued that

we ought, in my opinion, to conduct ourselves so as to unite America and
divide Britain; this, as it appears to me, may most likely be effected by
doing rather more than less in the peaceable line, than would be required if our petition is rejected with contempt, which I think most
likely. Will not our friends in England be still more exasperated against
the Court? And will not our very moderate men on this side of the water
be compelled to own the necessity of opposing force by force? The
rejection of the New York petition was very serviceable to America.

Seven weeks later Johnson again defended the wisdom of a gradual escalation of resistance. In sixteen months, he reminded Congress on October 6, thirteen colonies "have been brought to an
Armed Opposition to the Claims of Great Britain. The line We
have pursued has been the Line We ought to have pursued: If
what we have done had been proposed two Years ago, 4 Colonies
would not have been for it."[47]

Despite their substantial doubts about the chances for American victory, most moderates felt few reservations about the policies Congress had adopted or the deeper justice of the common
cause. "For my part," the ambitious Philadelphia merchant and
newly elected delegate Robert Morris informed his trading partner Samuel Inglis,

I considered this Subject early & fixed on principle the part I should take
in the unhappy Contest. I sided with this Country because their claims
are founded in Justice and I wish every Friend to the American Cause
may act on the same principle [and] that every Tory would consider it
well before they act against it, but I doubt your Friends have only
thought the Power of Great Britain insurmountable & founded their
Conduct on that belief. This I believe to be the case with most of the
Tories in America.[48]

Writing to James Duane in mid-February, Robert R. Livingston
could grumble that "upon what ground we stand I have been too

long absent from Congress to say, or how far our views may be *enlarged.*" But only ten days later he admitted:

Whatever may be our object I am persuaded that it is time the people should be weaned from too warm an attachment to a nation who have lost the virtues on which it was originally grounded. It will be easy to return to their old prejudices (if necessary) when Britain offers such terms as we can safely close with. This I once expected from their justice, then hoped from their fears, & am now growing more indifferent about.[49]

The moderates' sense of priorities was revealed in an often re-peated saying that became something of a congressional motto: "That the Colonies may continue connected . . . with Britain, is our second Wish: Our first is, THAT AMERICA MAY BE FREE."[50] When Congress created two secret committees to conduct its foreign correspondence and make arrangements for the impor-tation of vital supplies, moderates dominated the membership of both committees. And when, in December 1775, the New Jersey assembly again debated the propriety of submitting its own peti-tion for reconciliation, it was Dickinson and Jay who led the congressional delegation sent to dissuade the legislators from weakening the American position. None of their critics in Con-gress could have objected to any of their remarks.[51]

CHAPTER V

Independence

———————————⟡———————————

C HARLES PETTIT, a New Jersey lawyer and public official, was one of the "many obscure 'patriots' whose involvement with events was," in Bernard Bailyn's words, "superficial and who simply drifted marginally one way instead of the other in response to immediate pressures." Earlier appointed to several provincial offices through the influence of his brother-in-law, Joseph Reed, he spent much of 1775 and 1776 worrying whether or when to resign from the collapsing administration of Governor William Franklin, meanwhile holding himself "ready to lay hold on any Occasion that may afford me an Object worthy of Pursuit." Made sensitive to every shift in the political wind by his own trimming, Pettit intuitively understood the problems Congress faced as it moved toward independence. By early spring he believed that a formal declaration had become a question more of timing than policy. "However determined the Congress may be to cut the Ligament," he wrote his patron,

it would certainly be attended with Danger to do it suddenly in this present State of Things. For however right and necessary the Measure may be the People at large must individually see and feel the Necessity and Propriety of it before they will give it such an Acquiescence as is necessary to ensure it success. An explicit Declaration of it now would probably raise up such a Schism as would be more dreadful than any outward Enemy. Whereas a few Months—perhaps a few Weeks may, like the Sun to ripening Fruit, make that pleasant and desirable which at present appears sour and disgusting. Besides they (the Congress) have no Occasion to be hasty in the Matter. They may, and I presume do take all their Measures on the same Plan without a Declaration as they would with it, and the Work will in Effect be accomplished before the Multitude perceive it is begun.

Although Pettit erred in presuming that all of the delegates had agreed on an actual "plan" for independence—an indication of how little was known outside Congress of its internal divisions—his analysis accurately identified several of the key considerations that shaped the decision of early July.[1]

Without compelling evidence of popular support, a declaration of independence would have been inconceivable. But changes in public opinion alone could not demonstrate that a decision was necessary or even useful. To the members of the Continental Congress, deeply conscious as they were of the magnitude of the revolution they were making, the question of independence was essentially a pragmatic problem of tactics. Its logic, necessity, and timing were intimately linked to a perplexing cluster of practical considerations. The delegates had to calculate what effects a formal declaration would have on American public opinion, on the British government and public, at the courts of potential European allies, and upon the authority and influence of Congress itself. And their understanding of how that decision was ultimately reached defined the major lessons they learned from this first phase of national politics.

The Decision for Independence

THOMAS PAINE'S *Common Sense* was published in Philadelphia on January 10, 1776, two days after the delegates had read the king's speech opening the October Parliament. "Had the spirit of prophecy directed the birth of this production," Paine later wrote of his pamphlet's fortuitous appearance, "it could not have brought it forth at a more reasonable juncture or at a more necessary time. The bloody-mindedness of the one shows the necessity of pursuing the doctrine of the other." Taken together, the king's insulting accusations and Paine's iconoclastic assault on monarchy and empire removed the last restraints inhibiting candid public discussion of independence.[2]

Like tens of thousands of their countrymen, the delegates

were captivated by the brilliance of Paine's performance and often annoyed by his more outrageous statements. Yet despite the novelty and force of its arguments and the innovative simplicity of its language, *Common Sense* probably had little direct impact on their thinking about independence.[3] Nor was the pragmatic rationale for independence much influenced by the grand principles that Thomas Jefferson would shortly incorporate in the other seminal document of 1776, the Declaration of July 4. From the perspective of the Continental Congress, a decision for total separation from Britain depended on more prosaic considerations, linked less to a justification of the right to revolution than to the immediate needs of American resistance. At the most general level, the delegates had to decide what useful purposes a formal declaration would actually serve. Certainly it would eliminate the last vestigial hopes for reconciliation. But how would it aid the conduct of American resistance? For most intents and purposes, the Americans were already acting as if they were an independent nation: waging war, creating new governments, issuing money, and enacting other expedient measures. If a declaration would enable Congress to do little it had not done before, should it be adopted at the risk of diminishing the broad popular support Congress had previously enjoyed? In the second place, the delegates had to consider whether independence could safely be declared before other preliminary measures had been adopted: the resumption of legal government in all the colonies, the framing of a confederation, and the opening of negotiations with potential European allies. Finally, Congress had to decide whether it should intervene in the public debate that the unlikely tandem of George III and Thomas Paine had managed to launch in early January.

It was this last question that initially commanded the attention of Congress. On January 9, a group of conciliatory delegates led by James Wilson moved that Congress should "expressly declare to their Constituents and the World their present Intentions respecting an Independency." In part, this proposal sprang from the personal pique and frustration that moderates felt upon reading the government's latest misrepresentation of colonial resistance as a "desperate conspiracy" bent on securing independence. They could not pretend to speak for the private hopes and ambitions of some of their colleagues, but they did know that Congress had repeatedly renounced any intention of seeking independence, and that only a deep personal commitment to reconciliation justified their own involvement in politics. Reasons of honor alone demanded a public refutation of the king's insults. Beyond such private motives, however, moderates shared two other fears. One was that any dramatic shift in public opinion would undermine their own debating position within Congress by demonstrating that independence had become acceptable—a process that might be retarded if Congress reiterated its hopes for an accommodation. The second fear was that gullible elements of the population might swallow the government's line. "It is much to be wished that People would read the Proceedings of the Congress," John Jay observed in a conclusion to a set of "Proofs that the Colonies Do Not Aim at Independence" that he culled from the congressional journals, "and consult their own Judgments and not suffer themselves to be *duped by Men who are paid for deceiving them.*" If that happened, the authority of Congress, and with it the cohesion of the common cause, might be jeopardized.[4]

After some debate, Congress followed earlier precedent by allowing a committee of moderates—Wilson, Dickinson, Duane, and William Hooper—to draft a suitable address. Their work was read before Congress on February 13, tabled, and never reconsidered. Literary defects contributed to this result: Richard Smith noted that it was "very long, badly written, and full against Independency." But these flaws do not fully explain its rejection, since the address could have been revised, and since it in fact concluded with a warning that "Though an independent empire is not our *wish* . . . it may be the fate of our countrymen and ourselves." The central defect of the address lay elsewhere, in its awkward attempt to straddle the widening gap between the original goals of resistance and the growing likelihood of independence. This problem had alarmed Samuel Adams when Wilson introduced his motion. "I thought Congress had already been explicit enough," Adams wrote, "and was apprehensive that we might get ourselves upon dangerous ground." What was the point, Adams and other critics must have argued, of rehearsing familiar arguments against American representation in Parliament, describing the events that had made militant resistance necessary, or recalling earlier disavowals of independence? Another such declaration would be not only redundant of previous statements but potentially embarrassing, since Congress might

soon have to begin preparing public opinion to accept independence as the logical, unavoidable outcome of the imperial crisis.[5]

By the same token, however, the still uncertain and divided
character of public opinion enabled moderates to prevent the
endorsement of resolutions indicating that Congress was actively
contemplating independence. In January Samuel Adams and
Benjamin Franklin were rebuffed when, in an attempt to capitalize on the king's speech, they proposed that Congress consider
the subject of confederation. And when, two months later,
George Wythe and R. H. Lee moved that the preamble to the
resolution approving privateering should indict the king "as the
Author of our Miseries instead of the Ministry," they too met
defeat on the ground "that this was effectually severing the King
from us forever."[6]

The result of these maneuvers was a tacit agreement that
Congress would not immediately intervene in the public debate
about independence that had been launched with the sensational impact of *Common Sense*. Militant delegates accepted this
policy because they anticipated that events would shortly provide conclusive support for their position. By late February the
New England delegates were being informed that their constituents were ready for independence. *Common Sense* "is read with
great avidity," William Tudor wrote John Adams. "The Doctrine
it holds up is calculated for the Climate of N. England and though
some timid *pidling* souls"—a dig at John Dickinson—"shrink at
the Idea, 99 in a 100 wish for a Declaration of Independence from
the Congress."[7] Reports of British attempts to recruit European
mercenaries and the predictable reaction to the Prohibitory Act
could only make Paine's doctrines more palatable elsewhere.

John Adams continually fretted about the harmful effects the
delaying tactics of congressional moderates might have on public
opinion; but Samuel Adams, who better understood the limits of
intercolonial politics, remained confident that the government
would ultimately demonstrate the necessity of independence. In
a remarkable and personally revealing letter written to Samuel
Cooper on the last day of April, Adams surveyed the general state
of public opinion and found cause for alarm only in the behavior
of New York, still "as unenlightened in the Nature & Importance
of our political Disputes as any one of the united Colonies."
Although he was disappointed, Adams confessed, that new governments and a confederation had not yet been established,

I bear it tollerably well. I am disposed to believe that everything is ordered for the best, and if I do not find myself chargeable with Neglect I am not greatly chagrind when things do not go on exactly according to my mind. Indeed I have the Happiness of believing that what I most earnestly wish for will in due time be effected. We cannot make Events. Our Business is wisely to improve them. There has been much to do to confirm doubting Friends & fortify the Timid. It requires time to bring honest Men to think & determine alike in important Matters. Mankind are governed more by their feelings than by reason. Events which excite those feelings will produce wonderfull Effects. The Boston Port bill suddenly wrought a Union of the Colonies which could not be brot about by the Industry of years in reasoning on the necessity of it for the Common Safety.

Since Lexington and Concord "one Event has brot another on," and now the extension of hostilities to the southern colonies left little doubt that all the colonies would soon think alike. One battle to the south, Adams concluded, "would do more towards a Declaration of Independency than a long chain of conclusive Arguments in a provincial Convention or the Continental Congress."[8]

In contrast to this tone of quiet assurance, moderates desperately clung to two flimsy signs that Britain might be either willing or possibly compelled to negotiate. One was a provision of the Prohibitory Act authorizing the crown to appoint peace commissioners.[9] No one knew whom the government might select, or when they would arrive in America, or with what powers and instructions; but in the absence of more definite intelligence it could at least be suggested that negotiations might ensue. This possibility was reinforced in mid-March when reports that the government had failed to arrange the hire of Russian mercenaries arrived almost simultaneously with news that the British had evacuated Boston. These developments suggested that the government might be unable to field a large army in time to mount an effective summer campaign. They also fed a more sinister fear that Britain might prefer to partition North America with France and Spain rather than wage a long and costly struggle to regain the colonies' allegiance.[10]

Moderates seized on these hopes because, by February 1776, most delegates agreed that clear evidence of a continuing British commitment to a policy of war and repression would force Congress to solicit foreign assistance, and that this in turn would require a declaration of independence to establish America's diplomatic credibility. For congressional thinking about independence was governed, more than anything else, by the intimate connection between the material needs of the American economy and war effort and considerations of foreign policy and diplomacy. Since the summer of 1775, Congress had been actively but inconclusively debating the nature of the assistance America might attract from Britain's traditional enemies, France and Spain, and from European neutrals. Few questions were more perplexing. Sources of foreign intelligence were few and unreliable; the delegates had no way to test their speculations about the likely behavior of European powers; and their estimates of the aid America would need fluctuated with their analyses of British intentions and capabilities. In a hastily written letter to James Warren discussing problems of attracting foreign assistance and trade, John Adams managed to raise thirty separate questions deserving serious consideration. If Congress opened American ports to world commerce, would European nations allow their merchants to undertake voyages at the risk of war with Britain? Would even smugglers attempt to evade the British blockade? If Congress were to send ambassadors to Europe—and if so, to which courts?—would they be "received," Adams wondered, "or so much as heard by any Man or Woman in power at any of these Courts." Perhaps an envoy might, "if well skill'd in intrigue, his Pockets well filled with Money and his Person Robust and elegant enough, get introduced to some of the Misses and Courtezans in keeping of the statesmen in France"— Adams allowed his puritanical imagination a brief lurid romp— "but would not that be all?" Even if American requests were seriously entertained, what could Congress offer France or Spain in exchange for their support?[11]

Yet unanswerable as these and other questions inevitably were, the more basic considerations underlying them were hardly obscure. "Our dispute with Britain grows serious indeed," John Penn wrote in mid-February.

Matters are drawing to a crisis. They seem determined to persevere and are forming alliances against us. Must we not do something of the like nature? Can we hope to carry on a war without having trade or commerce some where? Can we ever pay any taxes without it? Will not our paper money depreciate if we go on emitting? . . . The consequence of making alliances is perhaps a total separation with Britain and without something of that sort we may not be able to procure what is necessary for our defence.

The special demands of war could only exaggerate the American economy's normal reliance on foreign imports. Some supplies could be obtained through the enterprising voyages of colonial merchants and clandestine foreign traders. But because Congress needed to be confident that its army would receive substantial, regular shipments of vital supplies, because it was anxious to secure American entrance to foreign ports and, if possible, naval protection for American shipping, most delegates recognized that the negotiation of formal agreements with European powers was a likely prerequisite for American success.[12]

The catch was that diplomatic convention and the hard interests of European nations required the colonies to prove that reconciliation with Britain was impossible before they could expect to receive substantial support from France and possibly Spain, or even to open channels of commerce with neutral nations. No useful agreements could be reached while the colonies remained in their present nebulous state, openly rebellious but still formally connected to Britain. France would have little incentive to support America unless it was convinced that the colonies were absolutely committed to independence. Neutrals would be unwilling to risk provoking Great Britain by conducting commerce with its colonies. The obvious need to form a clearer picture of European attitudes toward the American revolt justified the early March appointment of Silas Deane as the first American agent to France, which Congress "looked upon as the power whose friendship it would be fittest for us to obtain and cultivate." Deane's instructions— framed, it is worth noting, by a committee dominated by four moderates—directed him to ascertain how France would respond to a declaration of independence. But none of the delegates expected that Deane would procure any firm promise of support before independence was actually declared.[13]

Deane was unable to sail for Europe until early April. By then the obstacles that had previously inhibited Congress from actively debating independence were crumbling. Militant delegates who had been privately urging their provincial correspondents to muster support for separation were receiving the signals they knew would allow them to press their case more forcefully. Reports from the individual colonies revealed that the arguments of *Common Sense* and other advocates of independence were gaining the upper hand in the continuing public debate.[14] More important were the revisions of the formal instructions that had previously committed many delegates to reconciliation. South Carolina assumed government under a new constitution and altered its delegates' instructions in late March. The Georgia instructions were revised on April 5, North Carolina's on April 12. By late April it was generally believed that the Virginia Convention would take up the questions of government and independence when it convened May 3. Only the middle colonies remained to be converted to independence, and here too delegates like Samuel Adams anticipated decisive changes within a matter of weeks.[15]

In the meantime skepticism about the rumored arrival of the peace commissioners mounted weekly. Militant delegates had always dismissed this as another ministerial ruse contrived to divide the Americans—an "ideal Phantom," as Oliver Wolcott put it. Moderates were reluctantly coming to share their opinion. Surely a government sincerely interested in peace would have immediately dispatched its commission and publicized the terms of their appointment. "Where the plague are these Commissioners," an exasperated Robert Morris complained in early April; "if they are to come what is it that detains them; It is time we should be on a certainty and know positively whether the libertys of America can be established and secured by reconciliation, or whether we must totally renounce connection with Great Britain and fight our way to a total independence."[16]

New pieces of foreign intelligence reinforced these doubts about the arrival of peace commissioners. Britain may have been rebuffed in its efforts to recruit Russian mercenaries, but by mid-May Congress knew that the government's negotiations with various German principalities were proving more successful. These reports undermined earlier speculations about a multi-power European partition of America. They indicated that the government would be able to mount a vigorous campaign by late summer, and that it would first seek to crush the American rebellion before contemplating any diplomatic resolution of its difficulties. The government was clearly committed to war, and Congress could no longer afford to equivocate about pursuing the additional measures necessary to sustain a long and difficult struggle.[17]

Having consistently recognized how difficult securing independence would be, moderates now ceased to oppose adoption of those measures that their radical colleagues had insisted should be implemented prior to a final declaration. On March 19, Congress authorized privateering voyages against British shipping, an example of "offensive" rather than "defensive" resistance. On April 6, it proclaimed American ports open to foreign vessels.[18] Although moderates did not share the republican enthusiasm that led Jefferson to assert that the creation of new, reformed governments had become "the whole object of the present controversy," they agreed that, in most colonies, the improvisational rule of committees and conventions should be brought to an end. "From the present Appearance of Things it is natural to suppose that the Sword must decide the Controversy," John Jay confessed in mid-April. "And with a View to that Object our Measures should in a great Degree be taken. The first Thing therefore in my Opinion to be done is to erect good and well ordered Governments in all the Colonies, and thereby exclude that Anarchy which already too much prevails."[19]

On May 10, Congress approved its famous resolution authorizing "the respective assemblies and conventions of the united colonies where no government adequate to the exigencies of their affairs have been hitherto established" to set about creating new governments. This resolution passed without major dissent. "The assumption of Governt. was necessary," Carter Braxton, a Virginia moderate, observed, "and to that resolution little objection was made." Moderates could support this resolution because it allowed the existing provincial bodies to decide whether to proceed with the actual creation of new governments. Where, as in the middle colonies, this task might prove more divisive and less efficient than a continuation of the existing arrangements, constitution-writing could still be postponed.[20]

The preamble that Congress added to this resolution only five days later, however, transformed its meaning. Drafted by John Adams and designed to encourage the overthrow of proprietary government in Pennsylvania and Maryland—the two colonies whose restrictive instructions now stood among the last major obstacles to independence—the preamble demanded "that the exercise of every kind of authority under the said Crown shall be

totally suppressed and all the powers of government exerted
under the authority of the people of the colonies." For the first
time, a majority of Congress felt prepared to renounce the king
and to admit that a radical reformation of government had become an American goal. Over the strenuous objections of James
Duane and other delegates from the middle colonies, a divided
Congress narrowly approved the preamble.[21]

One measure of the confidence radical delegates now had was
that they continued to support the preamble even when members of the four delegations opposing it warned that its adoption
might lead their constituents to reject not only the resolution but
the authority of Congress as well. In fact, the Maryland delegation promptly withdrew from Congress, to return some days
later with new instructions reaffirming their colony's opposition
to separation. But in the more important province of Pennsylvania, the preamble achieved its desired effect. After several
weeks of intricate maneuvers, the provincial assembly simply
dissolved, supplanted by a convention dominated by radicals
who had formerly been excluded from the governing élite.[22]
Within Congress, too, most moderates reconciled themselves to
the new measures, although Duane and Thomas Stone, among
others, vented deep misgivings. "Never was a fairer Cause, with
more promising Appearances of final Success ruined by the rash
and precipitate Councils of a few Men," Stone wrote after the
vote of the 15th. But even John Dickinson could be found, a
rueful John Adams noted on the 20th, "confessing himself, now
for instituting Governments, forming a Continental Constitution, making Alliances, with foreigners, opening Ports and all
that—confessing that the defence of the Colonies, and Preparations for defence have been neglected, in Consequence of fond
delusive hopes and deceitfull Expectations."[23]

Through the last fortnight of May, some delegates still imagined that a formal declaration could be postponed while Congress implemented the orderly timetable of preparations that
radicals had originally envisioned.[24] Several new developments
conspired to bring matters to a head, however. Beginning on
May 16, Congress received a series of reports indicating that the
situation of the American army in Canada had deteriorated substantially. Within days it had also received copies of the government's treaties arranging the hire of German mercenaries. By
the end of May, the Rhode Island and Virginia delegations had

instructions authorizing them to support independence, county resolutions favoring separation were arriving regularly in the delegates' correspondence, and signs of decisive shifts in public opinion could be detected in the middle colonies. The final signal needed to initiate direct debate on independence came when Congress learned that the king had curtly rejected a City of London petition that had condemned the government's use of mercenaries, recalled the colonists' long attachment to the mother country, and pointedly suggested that "the most solemn, clear, distinct and unambiguous specification of those just and honourable terms," which the government intended to offer America, "may precede the dreadful operations of your armament."[25]

The inferences to be drawn from these developments were equally obvious to militant and moderate delegates alike. "I fear we cannot proceed systematically," John Adams wrote on June 3, "and that we shall be obliged to declare ourselves independent States, before we confederate, and indeed before all the colonies have established their governments. It is now pretty clear that all these measures will follow one another in a rapid succession, and it may not perhaps be of much importance which is done first." The German treaties and the government's refusal to propose a suspension of fighting, R. H. Lee noted,

leave not a doubt but that our enemies are determined upon the absolute conquest and subduction of N. America. *It is not choice then but necessity that calls for Independence, as the only means by which foreign Alliances can be obtained;* and a proper Confederation by which internal peace and union can be secured. Contrary to our earnest, early, and repeated petitions for peace, liberty, and safety, our enemies press us with war, threaten us with danger and Slavery. And this, not with her single force, but with the aid of Foreigners. Now, altho' we might safely venture our strength, circumstanced as it is, against that of Great Britain only, yet we are certainly unequal to a Contest with her and her Allies without any Assistance from without, and this more especially, as we are incapable of profiting by our exports for want of Naval force.

Moderates predicted that the king's answer to the London petition would be, as Robert Livingston wrote on the 4th, "productive of very good effects since it takes away all hopes of accommodation and shows that nothing less . . . than absolute submission" would satisfy the ministry. Robert Morris concurred. The king's reply to London, Morris informed Silas Deane, had totally destroyed all hopes of reconciliation. . . . [It] breathes nothing but death and destruction, everybody sees it in the same light and it will bring us all to one way of thinking, so that you may soon expect to hear of new governments in every colony, and in conclusion a declaration of Independancy by Congress. I see this step is inevitable and you may depend it will soon take place.[26]

On June 7, R. H. Lee introduced resolutions calling for independence, the formation of foreign alliances, and the preparation of a confederation. When Congress debated them on June 8 and 10, both factions conceded that reconciliation was impossible and independence inevitable. Only the problem of timing remained. The advocates of independence were quick to note "That no gentleman had argued against the policy or right of separation from Britain, nor had supposed it possible we should ever renew our connection: that they had only opposed its being now declared." Moderates now adopted the arguments their opponents had been making for nine months, asserting that independence should follow the other two measures. Their position was tenuous. Drawing on the events of the past month, the proponents of an immediate declaration argued that European nations could only view any further delay as evidence of a deep American reluctance ever to separate from Britain. If the colonies were to receive the assistance they now required, France had to be convinced that reconciliation was impossible, and neutrals had to be able to argue that the colonies were no longer legally subject to British commercial regulation. Reasons of state and diplomatic protocol required a declaration, which "alone could render it consistent with European delicacy for European powers to treat with us, or even to receive an ambassador."[27]

On these points of substantive policy, advocates of independence held a decisive advantage; but on the question of public opinion, they had to yield to the moderates' claim that the people of the middle colonies "were not yet ripe for bidding adieu to British connection," though admittedly "they were fast ripening." Against the argument that the time had finally come for Congress to take the lead in influencing public opinion, moderates insisted "That the conduct we had formerly observed was wise & proper now, of deferring to take any capital step till the voice of the people drove us into it." Their view prevailed. On June 10 Congress agreed to postpone a decision until July 1.

The intervening three weeks brought the developments that

all the delegates, whatever their private feelings, had anticipated. Within a week Delaware, Connecticut, and New Hampshire had authorized their delegations to approve independence; by June 28, Pennsylvania, New Jersey, and Maryland had fallen into line, and only New York remained formally opposed to independence. The debate of July 1 was long but desultory. On the first ballot, nine colonies voted for independence, Pennsylvania and South Carolina voted against, Delaware divided, and New York abstained. When Congress voted again on July 2, New York, lacking positive instructions, still abstained, but the South Carolina delegates reversed their position, and by prior arrangement majorities were mustered in the Pennsylvania and Delaware delegations. Although John Dickinson and a handful of other delegates restated the case against independence, the final decision was almost anticlimactic.[28]

Until the very end, moderates inside and outside Congress had continued to argue that popular support for independence would be more durable if Congress could only wait until the commissioners had arrived, for, as Thomas Stone had noted in May, "upon their deceitful show of reconciliation being detected and open & exposed, the general and unanimous voice of America would have been for separation." But most delegates agreed that Congress had waited long enough, and that an early July separation would alienate few wavering souls. Even the Adamses now recognized that this delay had "many great Advantages attending it," as John Adams wrote his wife on the 3rd. "The Hopes of Reconciliation, which were fondly entertained by Multitudes of honest and well meaning tho weak and mistaken People, have been gradually and totally extinguished." The people had been given ample time "to ripen their Judgments, dissipate their Fears, and allure their Hopes," so that in the end "the whole People in every Colony of the 13, have now adopted it, as their own Act. This will cement the Union," Adams concluded, "and avoid those Heats and Convulsions" that an earlier decision would have produced.[29] This was sound history, but coming months would reveal that the exuberance of July was to be short-lived.

Lessons

EARLY in 1778, as rumors of partisan bickering within Congress were circulating among American politicians, William Livingston recalled how quickly factions had emerged at the First Continental Congress. He had not been there "a fortnight," the New Jersey governor informed Henry Laurens,

> before I discovered that parties were forming, and that some members had come to that Assembly with views altogether different from what America professed to have; and what, baring a designing Junto, I believe she really had. Of these men, her Independence on Great Britain *at all Events* was the most favourite Project. By these, the pulse of the rest was felt on every favourable occasion, and often upon no apparent occasion at all: And by these men, measures were concerted to produce what we all professed to deprecate. Nay at the very time we universally invoked the Majesty of heaven to witness the purity of our Intentions, I had reason to believe the hearts of many of us gave our Invocation the lie!

Livingston agreed that Congress had been perfectly justified in declaring independence "in a moral Consideration of the matter." But like other moderates, he continued to wonder whether the decision had been taken prematurely or even whether it could have been avoided had not the faction led by the Adamses and Lee persistently pressured Congress into adopting measures that made reconciliation ever less likely.[30] These doubts, which arose initially from the frustrations moderates experienced in the months preceding independence, were reinforced by the difficulties the Americans encountered in the months that followed, when the continental army suffered a series of military reverses and the predicted disputes about government erupted in the middle colonies.

Nor were disappointed moderates the only members of Congress who perceived its early politics in factional terms. John Adams's autobiographical account of the deliberations preceding independence projects a similar view, although there it is the overcautious delegates from the middle colonies who come in for criticism. Not surprisingly, then, modern writings on the decision for independence have emphasized the distinctive goals, talents, and shortcomings of the two major factions. The decisions of

Congress accordingly become so many victories and defeats, and because independence rather than reconciliation was the eventual result, such historians as Merrill Jensen and H. James Henderson have in effect argued that a radical caucus dominated the early proceedings of Congress. By maneuvering more cautious members into endorsing belligerent positions that Britain could never accept, by manipulating events outside Congress and debates within, the so-called Adams-Lee junto made independence inevitable.[31]

The preceding chapters have sought to suggest that such an interpretation fails to explain how the decision for independence gradually unfolded. It is deficient in two critical respects. It exaggerates the degree to which militant delegates were actually able to define the agenda confronting Congress, force adoption of the measures they favored, and regulate their colleagues' progress toward independence. And it ignores the determinative contribution that the government's unswerving commitment to a policy of repression made toward narrowing the factional divisions that did exist among the delegates. In the end, independence emerged as a logical conclusion flowing from principles and opinions that most delegates commonly shared and as a response to events they could neither control nor evade.

That does not mean, of course, that congressional politics were always conducted in an atmosphere of forbearance and congeniality. As Livingston's letter suggests, moderates resented their opponents' obvious efforts to control the proceedings. Nor is it surprising, given the intimate character of the delegates' working environment and the natural strain the weight of their responsibilities induced, that some private enmities quickly began to smolder. For months John Dickinson refused to converse with John Adams, and when Edward Rutledge voiced his distaste for the "overruling Influence" and "low cunning" of the New England delegates, he was merely venting an opinion shared by several other delegates from the middle and southern colonies. "It would be better for us," James Duane remarked in early 1777, upon hearing a report that Benjamin Franklin would sail to Europe in a French ship, "if the Devil had him and the Adams's too."[32] And indeed, the three principal members of the Adams-Lee cohort do seem to have assigned themselves distinctive roles: R. H. Lee introducing proposals for military preparations in 1774 and 1775, thereby defusing the charge that Massachusetts was seeking to force its sister colonies into civil war; John Adams, the attorney for independence, tirelessly delivering briefs on the need to initiate measures anticipating a total separation; and Samuel Adams, less debater than parliamentary whip, adept at drafting agendas, monitoring the flow of business, and discreetly lobbying wavering delegates—the natural talents of a man who had used his position as clerk of the Massachusetts House to advance his own political career.

Despite their efforts, however, the militant leaders repeatedly failed to secure the adoption of key elements of their program according to the schedule they urged their colleagues to follow. Time and again they had to accept less than they not only desired but believed vital to the success of the common cause. For they were not the only members of Congress who appeared in debate with an agenda and priorities of their own. Although in 1774 moderates had suffered from Galloway's erratic leadership and Dickinson's absence, they had still managed to block several proposals they deemed dangerously provocative; regrouping in May 1775, they successfully braked the escalation of American resistance for almost a full year. Despite being less politically experienced than their counterparts, moderate leaders such as Duane, Jay, Thomas Johnson, James Wilson, and Robert Morris proved to be remarkably tenacious in debate, a mark of their personal commitment to reconciliation.

As in any deliberative body, then, those who came prepared to make motions, offer amendments, and raise objections could substantially influence the conduct of business by defining the actual alternatives under consideration. But could they also determine the outcome of debate? The record of proceedings suggests that neither of the polar factions was capable of directing or dictating the decisions of Congress. A more accurate model of early congressional politics would recognize that, collectively, the two clusters of militant and conciliatory leaders, with their closest collaborators, always numbered less than a majority of the membership. Each had to solicit the support of less committed delegates, who generally proved susceptible to the claims both groups advanced, and who were thus in a position to encourage the formulation of compromises that enabled Congress to proceed with its principal business, the conduct of resistance. Edmund Pendleton alluded to this process in a letter written from Philadelphia in mid-June 1775:

The Sanguine are for rash Measures without consideration, the Fleg-
matic to avoid that extreme are afraid to move at all, while a third Class
take the middle way and endeavor by tempering the first sort and
bringing the latter into action to draw all together to a Steddy, tho'
Active Point of defense; but till this is done, it is natural to suppose the
extremes will be blaming each other, and perhaps in terms not the most
decent, and each at times will include the third class in that which is
opposite to themselves, this I have frequently experienced: and must
blame, since mutual Charity should lead us, not to censure, but to endeavor to convince the Judgment of each other. . . .

Pendleton may have been referring to his own attempt to draft
a compromise set of resolutions bridging the differences between
the militant and conciliatory proposals that Lee and Dickinson
introduced at the opening of the Second Congress in May 1775.[33]

Nor would it be correct to describe the two opposing clusters
of advocates as tightly disciplined factions. In practice they were
not legislative parties but aggregates of individuals who generally thought alike and sometimes acted together, but who also
felt free to "defect" from their ostensible allies on particular (and
often critical) issues. John Rutledge supported Galloway and
Duane at the First Congress but denounced Dickinson's scheme
of accommodation at the opening of the Second. Samuel Chase
supported Dickinson in May 1775, roundly criticized the Pennsylvania instructions that "the Farmer" drafted six months later,
and cooperated with the Adamses in the months before independence, but then actively solicited Dickinson's advice and
even personal involvement when Maryland began writing a new
constitution.[34] When James Duane was still dreading the creation of new governments, his correspondent John Jay was arguing that the New York Provincial Congress had outlived its use-
fulness, and his colleague Robert Livingston was expressing his
hope that the king's reply to the London petition would end the
conflict between supporters of the old and new regimes in Pennsylvania.[35]

An interpretation emphasizing factionalism would be better
warranted if Congress had fallen victim to internal paralysis, or
found itself unable to frame policy and reach decisions, or if a
substantial fraction of its membership had been dragged unwill-
ingly or unwittingly into measures they thoroughly reprobated.
But that was not the case. Moderates had always known that
resistance could lead to civil war and civil war to independence,

and in practice they had found ways to coexist with their radical counterparts. What requires explanation, therefore, is the process that repeatedly led the delegates to reach compromises and what might even be called a working consensus.

Next to the fundamental gap separating the dominant British view of the sources of the Anglo-American crisis from the comparable colonial orthodoxy, such divisions as did exist within Congress were relatively narrow. Both factions followed the same trajectory of thought: if any one thing distinguished them, it was that militant delegates acted on the basis of their expectations while moderates clung to their hopes. Yet that distinction was real, and it could have been exploited by a British government willing to adopt even a moderately conciliatory approach toward the demands of the First Congress. But the government never gave congressional moderates the one firm signal they needed if they were to be able to argue that candid negotiations could occur or to block successive escalations of American resistance. No delegate so much as suggested that Lord North's "Olive Branch" of 1775 represented a sincere proposal for negotiations, much less an acceptable basis for reconciliation. It was "insidiously devised," Thomas Johnson observed, "to wear the face of peace, and embarrass us in the choice of evils—either to accept and be slaves, or reject and increase the number and power of our enemies."[36] But that and the chimerical peace commission of 1776, which finally arrived only after independence had been declared and with powers that Congress quickly discovered were manifestly inadequate, were the only frail props Britain offered to moderates who would have gratefully seized and exploited any tenuous gesture merely implying that Britain would give American grievances a fair hearing.

Yet even had it possessed accurate intelligence about congressional deliberations, the government at Whitehall would probably have attached little significance to these differences among the delegates. From its perspective, it did not matter whether or not Congress thought Parliament possessed an inherent right to regulate trade. That was a secondary issue, little more than a quibble when laid against the fundamental problem of the indivisibility of parliamentary sovereignty. No conceivable American plan of reconciliation could have overcome the British consensus on this subject. Possibly the government would have been less intransigent had the First and Second Congresses not committed themselves to programs of resistance. Yet here, too, the distinctions that Congress persistently sought to make between "offensive" and "defensive" resistance would have seemed meaningless to the government, even had it grasped the fine logic of the American position. The ministry was convinced instead that the delegates were promoting not only constitutional heresy but a rebellion against all legal authority, and that Britain faced a movement not of protest but sedition.[37]

Perhaps more important, the apparent ease with which Congress moved to adopt and escalate resistance suggested to British observers that the delegates *were* largely united on goals and tactics alike. And in a certain sense this conclusion was accurate: for in fact Congress had not found it very difficult to frame a program of resistance either in 1774 or 1775. By adopting a strategy even of "defensive" resistance—which moderates supported in the hope of preventing worse calamities—Congress took the one step that persuaded the British government of the futility of pursuing negotiations. The government naturally concluded that there were no divisions among the delegates to exploit. British political efforts were accordingly directed instead toward detaching potential loyalist colonies, notably New York, from congressional control—a policy that only reinforced American axioms about the need for union and the inherent duplicity of the ministry, and thus drove the two extremes of Congress closer together.

Like colonial leaders, British policymakers found themselves drawn to conspiratorial explanations for their antagonists' behavior.[38] By 1775 they were acting on a belief that the secret springs of revolution lay in the machinations and ambitions of the delegates themselves. Here their analysis rested on a plausible, if rather superficial, reading of events that was supported by the reports of loyal observers in America who were struck by the sheer intensity and busyness of the delegates' activities. For once Congress had realized that it could not adjourn periodically but would have to meet continuously—a disappointing discovery, given the general aversion to long absences from home—most members began shuttling back and forth between Philadelphia and their provinces, where they were necessarily plunged into advising and directing local measures of resistance. Although royal officials and well-placed loyalists occasionally heard rumors of the moderates' discontent with the course of events, on balance they detected little significant difference in the behavior of militant and moderate delegates. Committed to military resistance in the hope that early American success might bring down the government of Lord North, moderate delegates made no effort to obstruct preparations for war in their individual colonies.

Members of Congress recognized that it was their peculiar duty to preside over the separation from Britain. Immersed in the daily labor of engineering a revolution, sensitive to the nuances of public opinion and the need to preserve a working consensus within Congress, they knew that the success of the common cause depended on their ability to coordinate policy and strategy among the various levels of resistance. Yet despite the intensity of their activity, they never came to believe themselves ultimately responsible for bringing the Revolution about. What alone explained to their satisfaction the coming of independence was the uncannily misguided and yet somehow predictable course British policy had followed over the past decade. In the end, moderate and militant members agreed that British obstinacy constituted the true dynamic of revolution. "Great Britain may thank herself for this event," Robert Morris wrote in early June 1776, when he believed independence inevitable,

for whatever may have been the original design of some men in promoting the present contest, I am sure that America in general never set out with any view or desire of establishing an independent Empire. They have been driven into it step by step with a reluctance that has been manifested in all their proceedings, yet I dare say our enemies will assert that it was planned from the first movements.

However much the colonies might have extended their claims as the quarrel progressed, William Smith, the wavering "loyal whig," wrote, "the present animosities are imputable to the Pride & Avarice of Great Britain."[39]

"All experience hath shown," Jefferson observed in the Declaration, "that mankind are more disposed to suffer, while evils are sufferable, than to right themselves by abolishing the forms to which they are accustomed." That was conventional wisdom, culled from the dismal but familiar history of the decline of liberty in its long struggle against power. Thus when Jefferson detailed the "long train of abuses and usurpation" that justified independence, he was not merely conducting an exercise in revolutionary apologetics. The Declaration also provided an empirical explanation of how the revolution it proclaimed had actually come about. As the colonies could only justify independence by proving the existence of "a design to reduce them under absolute Despotism," so too the coming of revolution itself would have been impossible, and historically inexplicable, had not all the "repeated injuries and usurpations" Jefferson enumerated actually taken place. The people, all whigs knew from their reading of history and their own experience, could not have been otherwise roused from their natural "lethargy" or shaken from their traditional reverence for crown and empire. The Connecticut delegate Oliver Wolcott put the case even more plainly. "A strange Infatuation has possessed the british Councills to drive Matters to the length they have gone," he wrote in mid-May; "every Thing convinces me that the Abilities of a Child might have governed this Country, so strong has been their Attachment to Britain."[40]

This perception of British culpability shaped the basic strategy that Congress would scrupulously follow during the early years of its existence. From their earliest meetings the delegates had been intent on husbanding their political capital, the extensive yet precarious hegemony the First Congress had so quickly acquired. During the first major debate of 1774, one of the Rutledges had declared that "Obedience to our Determinations will only follow the reasonableness, the apparent Utility and Necessity of the Measures We adopt." In 1774, this observation seemed self-evident. But even after Congress had recruited local committees and organized an army to carry out its decisions, the delegates remained strikingly sensitive to what they perceived as the vagaries of public opinion. When in April 1776 Samuel Adams observed that "We cannot make Events[;] Our Business is wisely to improve them," he merely reduced to a proverb the practical lesson most delegates had drawn from the upheaval of the preceding months and, indeed, from the longer history of the Anglo-American controversy.

The delegates believed, as experience showed, that continued demonstrations of British malevolence would provide the strongest and safest arguments for resistance and, eventually, independence as well. Rather than adopt measures that might expose Congress to charges of unilaterally enlarging the grounds of conflict, they timed their decisions to appear as responses to particular British provocations. Usually Congress acted only after receiving evidence that public opinion was prepared for further escalation. Thus while patriot publicists regularly enjoined their readers "to pay great deference to the *learned* and *worthy* gentlemen" of the Congress, the delegates themselves were content to let public opinion coalesce in its own way, occasionally nudged but rarely prodded by congressional pronouncements. Maintaining an aura of secrecy about their deliberations, reminding restless provincial correspondents that "something more than a majority, an unanimity" was, as the Connecticut delegation once remarked, "of the last importance," the delegates moved cautiously toward independence.[41]

The lesson of independence was, quite simply, that this strategy had worked, both within Congress and without. Congress had shepherded thirteen disparate colonies along a common path to independence; and if the decision for separation did not escape the criticism of delegates who had favored conciliation, their allegiance to Congress and the Revolution remained intact. No wonder the normally laconic Samuel Adams allowed himself a brief moment of exultation when he exclaimed: "Was there ever a Revolution brot about, especially as important as this, without great internal Tumults & violent Convulsions!" He had been wrong, Adams now admitted in late July 1776, to believe that independence should have been declared six or nine months earlier.[42]

Of course, one does not explain a revolution simply by recording its leaders' understanding of how it unfolded. Contemporary explanations of the process whereby "thirteen clocks struck as one" may well have been inadequate; certainly they seem surprisingly simple, even naïve, when laid against some of the more sophisticated (if rather speculative) interpretations that modern scholars have offered. Nor did all the delegates believe that patriotic motives alone attracted many apparent supporters of the common cause, or that all the people would act as virtuously and disinterestedly as emerging republican theory demanded they should. The fears that James Duane voiced in the summer of 1775 foreshadowed a darker mood that would grow more pervasive as the war dragged on. "We must think in Time of the means of asserting the Reins of Government when those Commotions shall subside," he had reminded Robert Livingston. "Licenciousness is the natural Effect of a civil discord and it can only be guarded against by placing the Command of the Troops in the hands of Men of property and Rank who, by that means, will preserve the same Authority over the Minds of the people which they enjoyed in the Hour of Tranquility."[43]

Yet before 1776 such fears were initially confined to Duane and his circle, men whose propertied interests and avowedly élitist attitudes made them naturally skeptical of the prospects for the new republic. Others viewed the situation differently. "In the eyes of the Whigs," Gordon Wood has aptly written, these years before independence

always appeared to be the great period of the Revolution, the time of greatest denial and cohesion, when men ceased to extort and abuse one another, when families and communities seemed particularly united, when the courts (many of which were closed) were wonderfully free of that constant bickering over land and credit that had dominated their colonial life.

This period, Wood adds, "marked the time and spirit which best defined the Americans' Revolutionary objectives and to which they clung throughout the war with increasing nostalgia." No group of leaders were to feel this nostalgia more acutely than the members of the Continental Congress. For them, the sunshine patriotism of 1774–76 and the initial ascendancy of Congress would provide an increasingly painful contrast to the political problems and frustrations the war and its aftermath engendered.[44]

CHAPTER VI

A Lengthening War

———— ⌒⋎⌒ ————

E IGHT days after Congress approved the Declaration of Independence, Admiral Lord Richard Howe, head of the peace
commission finally appointed under the provision of the Prohibitory Act, landed at Staten Island. Six weeks later, after Howe's
initial conciliatory gestures had predictably proved futile, the
British landed twenty thousand troops on Long Island and
routed the continental army, which was fortunate to escape to
Manhattan. In mid-September the Americans were again defeated at Manhattan, and in the fall the British gained further
victories by capturing Fort Washington and then Fort Lee. General Washington was forced to withdraw across New Jersey.
Early in December the British occupied Rhode Island, and when
elements of General William Howe's army came dangerously
close to Philadelphia, a nervous Congress decided to retreat to
Baltimore.[1]

These military reverses were the most alarming events Congress had yet confronted. But the months following independence brought other discouraging developments to deflate earlier optimistic forecasts about the prospects for American
success: problems of logistics and recruitment within the army,
political conflicts in the states, rising prices, and an accompanying depreciation in the value of continental currency, which was
by now rolling off the presses to pay the mounting expenses of
war. Reports of popular indifference and disaffection toward the

cause, grew more common, punctuated by occasional outbursts of loyalist activity in the middle states.

The summer of 1776 thus marked a watershed in congressional politics, not only because it resolved the central question of independence, but because the conditions under which Congress held and exercised power began to change. The threatening developments of 1776 and 1777 defined the essential problems Congress would face until the war ended in 1783. Yet only gradually did the consequences of this transition become apparent, and political assumptions formed during the previous phases of resistance continued to exert a powerful influence on congressional thinking. Rather than attempt to devise new avenues of political control, the delegates clung to the methods that had worked so successfully before independence.

Diplomacy on Two Fronts

FOR perhaps a week after Lord Howe's landing on July 12, a few delegates speculated that genuine negotiations might be in the offing. If the Howe Commission could "offer Peace on admissible terms," Robert Morris ventured, "I believe the great Majority of America wou'd still be for accepting it." If they could not, he added, it would become universally obvious that a vigorous war for independence was absolutely necessary. The prospect of peace receded, however, when Howe published a proclamation offering little more than royal pardons for the repentant. Howe's declaration "has now convinced everybody that no offers are to be made us but absolute submission," Josiah Bartlett noted on July 22, which he thought "very happy for America." For had Britain "offered some concessions, there would have been danger of divisions, or at least of our not acting with unanimity and spirit, as I think will now be the case." A grateful Congress voted to reprint Howe's proclamation as graphic proof that hopes for reconciliation were still chimerical.[2]

The British victory at Long Island in late August forced a reassessment of this strategy. On September 2, the captured and paroled American general John Sullivan delivered Howe's obscurely worded request for a conference with several members of Congress, who could appear, Howe had stipulated, only as private individuals. Fearing that "Tories, and *moderate men,* so called, will try to represent the Congress as obstinate, and so desirous of war and bloodshed that we would not so much as hear the proposals," the delegates spent several days debating their response. As John Witherspoon summarized the discussion, all the speakers agreed that Congress had no intention of receding from independence, while "the greatest part, if not the whole, [admitted] that there is not the least reason to expect that any correspondence we can have with him will tend to peace." Most delegates believed that Howe's invitation was, as Samuel Huntington put it, "a finness [*sic*] to Create a belief in the people that he is desirous for peace and we desire to protract the war." The central question was whether Congress would abet the subversive activities of loyalists by spurning a conference or, as Bartlett noted, "intimidate people when they see us catching hold of so slender a thread to bring about a settlement."[3]

"Opposing manoeuvre to manoeuvre," Congress dispatched Benjamin Franklin, John Adams, and Edward Rutledge to hear what propositions Howe might make, but "with a view to satisfy some disturbed minds out of doors," Caesar Rodney reported, "rather than expectation of its bringing about peace." The results of the Staten Island conference of September 11 were precisely what Congress expected. Howe could do nothing more than grant pardons or enter into private conversations with individuals. He had no substantive or discretionary powers of negotiation, and could only give vague personal assurances that the government might be more forthcoming than before. The committee hastily returned to Philadelphia, and on September 17 submitted a brief written account of the conference, which Congress immediately had published. "Thus, it is conceived one great point is gained," William Williams believed: "to strike the Torys dumb, or rather to defeat and kill the impressions they were makeing and would have made on many Friendly but credulous Minds."[4]

Although during these same weeks the plan for a commercial treaty with France was also under review, the delegates apparently failed to consider what repercussions the Staten Island conference might have on Silas Deane's negotiations at the court of France. Not until mid-December did the Committee of Secret Correspondence think to send Deane a copy of the committee's report.[5] Congress was concerned instead with the domestic uses of foreign policy, anxious to exploit this episode because Howe's superficial gestures so conveniently conformed to earlier pat-

terns of British behavior. Like the king's speech to Parliament in
October 1775 or his subsequent dismissal of the London petition,
it demonstrated that the government would offer America no
choice between submission or independence. Publication of all
the relevant documents, which American newspapers dutifully
reprinted, further enabled Congress to reinforce its reputation
for virtue and unanimity. Explicitly in their private letters, implicitly through the published proceedings, the delegates were
careful to stress that the decision to confer with Howe had not
created serious divisions within Congress. The "pleasure" that
John Adams took in assuring a worried Samuel Adams "that there
was no disagreement in opinion among the members of the committee upon any one point" (a reference to Rutledge, who had
resisted a decision for independence until the very end) was
sincere.[6]

Had Howe possessed adequate authority to negotiate, however, it seems likely that the reverses of late 1776 could well have
reopened serious divisions within Congress and exacerbated the
existing signs of popular disillusionment. By the early winter of
1776–77, moderates such as Philip Schuyler and Charles Carroll
privately evinced a pessimism bordering on desperation, and
even Robert Morris, though not inclined toward panic, warned
that if France did not come to its support immediately, "America
must sue for peace from her oppressors." At last the gloomy
predictions moderates had invoked when opposing a final separation seemed to be coming true. "Our people knew not the
hardships and calamities of war when they so boldly dared Britain to arms," Morris wrote the American commissioners at Paris;

every man was then a bold patriot, felt himself equal to the contest, and
seemed to wish for an opportunity of evincing his prowess; but now,
when we are fairly engaged, when death and ruin stare us in the face,
and when nothing but the most intrepid courage can rescue us from
contempt and disgrace, sorry am I to say it, many of those who were
foremost in noise shrink coward like from the danger and are begging
pardon without striking a blow. This, however, is not general; but dejection of spirits is an epidemical disease, and unless some fortunate event
or other gives a turn to the disorder, in time it may prevail throughout
the community.[7]

Yet even among the moderate whig leaders of the middle states,
these discouragements appear to have sparked no more than a

passing interest in suing for peace. After American victories at Trenton and Princeton ushered in the New Year, talk of reconciliation evaporated. When Duane, Robert Livingston, and Gouverneur Morris paid a visit to William Smith in mid-February, the still neutral Smith was stunned to observe that "The Enthusiasm of those who lead the People at this Day if not counterfeited is astonishing. . . . These young heroes seem not apprized of any Danger" from discords in the states, evidence of public support in Great Britain for continuing the war, and the improbability of French assistance.[8] And less than a week later, when another captured American general, Charles Lee, brought a second request from Howe for a conference, Congress quickly rejected the invitation. "It was the General Sense of Congress," Thomas Burke, a newly arrived delegate from North Carolina, observed, "that no Conference ought to be held with any but Embassadors properly authorised by the Court of Britain to treat of Peace."[9]

By then Deane had informed Congress that the Staten Island conference, "however politic the step may have been in America, was made use of to our prejudice in Europe," and few delegates any longer questioned the importance of securing early French intervention in the war. In the summer of 1776, when John Adams had drafted a visionary plan for a model treaty, many delegates had hoped that French assistance could remain largely commercial in nature, thereby enabling the United States to sacrifice as little of its new political independence as possible.[10] But by the end of the year, Congress was prepared to authorize its newly expanded commission at Paris—Deane, Franklin, and Arthur Lee—to offer whatever concessions the French demanded in return for their assistance. Robert Morris, who had previously voiced his horror at the thought "that our own Safety should call on us to involve other Nations in the Calamities of Warr," now marshaled arguments for immediate French intervention.[11] Early reports from the commissioners at Paris had been favorable but inconclusive. Congress had only the scantiest information about the progress of their negotiations with the Comte de Vergennes, the French foreign minister; after the spring of 1777, the British secret service and blockade intercepted every dispatch the commissioners sent. As the weeks passed without further word, the delegates realized that the results of the campaign of 1777 would determine the policies France and other European nations would follow.

But the campaign of 1777 was remarkably slow to unfold. The strategic initiative lay clearly with the Howes. While an army commanded by General John Burgoyne began slogging its way south from Quebec, the two brothers remained largely inactive around New York until late July. Then, instead of marching directly across New Jersey, General William Howe's army made a laborious voyage around the eastern shore of the Chesapeake before landing southwest of Philadelphia. After repulsing the Americans at Brandywine, Howe occupied the American capital, forcing Congress to flee again, this time to York, Pennsylvania. By then, however, the other central element in the British strategy—a junction between Burgoyne and forces under General Henry Clinton, marching north from New York, which was designed to isolate New England from the other states—was doomed to failure when Burgoyne's march bogged down in the face of stiff American resistance. Rather than retreat to Quebec, Burgoyne pressed on, and in October his army was forced to surrender to continental troops and militia commanded by Horatio Gates.[12]

The victory at Saratoga provided dramatic relief from months of uncertainty over the outcome of the campaign and the prospects for a French alliance. Eager to capitalize on the impact Burgoyne's surrender would have throughout Europe, Congress almost immediately acted to provide the French court with additional evidence of its commitment to independence. After months of indecisive debate, it now found the will and energy to finish drafting Articles of Confederation and to approve a set of recommendations proposing remedies for its most puzzling domestic problem, a dangerous inflation caused by a general rise in prices and an accompanying depreciation in the value of continental currency. After both of these actions were completed in mid-November, Congress quickly turned its attention to the situation of the American commissioners in Paris—from whom, in fact, it had heard nothing for months.

Ignorance did not deter the delegates from adopting several resolutions designed to improve the American negotiating position at Paris. The first resolution, approved on November 21, requested Silas Deane to return from Paris. Although this decision would subsequently engender disastrous political conflicts within Congress, it was initially taken for comparatively innocuous reasons, largely because Deane had exceeded his authority by granting scores of commissions in the continental army to French adventurers.* On the next day, November 22, Congress passed additional resolutions authorizing its commissioners to counter predictable British propaganda by declaring that no negotiations had taken place between Britain and America, and that should any ever occur, recognition of American independence would be their point of departure. Within a week Congress also appointed John Adams to replace Deane, even though many members were uncertain whether Adams, away in Massachusetts, would accept the appointment.[13] As was so often the case when Congress sought to supervise transatlantic diplomacy, none of these actions influenced the negotiations that culminated, on February 6, 1778, in the signing of two Franco-American treaties: one regulating commerce, the other creating a defensive alliance that must eventually make France a belligerent. The French decision was a direct outgrowth of Saratoga, which had given Vergennes, the leading advocate of alliance, a decisive advantage within the cabinet.[14]

What the various resolutions of November 1777 do reveal, however, is the extent to which diplomatic considerations continued both to define the central policy objectives of Congress and to establish an outlying perimeter of agreement within which disputes over other issues could still be contained. At the most general level of policy, little had changed since 1776. Convinced of both the necessity of a French alliance and the futility of negotiating with the Howes, delegates who differed over other issues—finance, military appointments, confederation, price controls—were constrained to accept the same imperatives that had governed congressional behavior since 1774. To say that Congress remained committed to independence and alliance may seem merely to restate the obvious; yet ultimately no other issue was more important. Had Lord Howe been able to offer significant concessions, or had any bloc of delegates come to believe that an alliance with France was undesirable or unattainable, the existing tensions within Congress, which would reach an explosive level in 1779, would have been much more difficult to contain at an earlier point. Instead, despite their continued ignorance of the progress of negotiations, the delegates fastened on the benefits of the anticipated alliance and managed to recover

*The recall of Deane is discussed at greater length in Chapter XI.

some of the naïve optimism of 1774 and 1775. Would not French military aid and financial largesse bring the war to a speedy end and alleviate the economic woes that increasingly threatened to split the American polity into rancorous, competing interests?

Thus when in late April 1778 copies of the two conciliatory bills that Lord North had introduced in Parliament in February began circulating in America, Congress showed little interest in reopening negotiations with either the Howes or the new peace commission, headed by the Earl of Carlisle, which arrived in June.[15] Reaction within Congress was again cynical. Some delegates initially challenged the authenticity of the bills; others inferred, correctly, that the bills had been rushed to America to forestall ratification of whatever alliance Franklin, Deane, and Lee had been able to conclude with France. All agreed that even though the terms offered complied essentially with the American demands of 1774, they were no longer satisfactory. Independence, which Britain could still not concede, was now a *sine qua non* of peace. As in 1776 and 1777, the delegates considered this new gesture as merely another attempt at subversion, designed "with a view no doubt of diverting the People of America from their grand object of Preparation and defence." On April 22 Congress published a sarcastic proclamation ridiculing the two bills.[16] Ten days later, Silas Deane's brother Simeon delivered copies of the long-awaited treaties, which Congress ratified after only a weekend's delay. Having been previously prepared, out of desperation, to grant substantial concessions to France, the delegates were taken aback by the generous terms that Louis XVI had extended to the struggling American states.

By the time the Carlisle Commission reached Philadelphia—which the British were embarrassingly about to abandon—Congress was ready to use its presence to bolster American morale and, not incidentally, to reassure the French that there were no prospects for an Anglo-American rapprochement. Through the summer and early fall of 1778, the delegates sought to exploit each of the progressively less temperate pronouncements that the increasingly frustrated Carlisle Commission issued. Drawing on the precedents of 1776, Congress arranged to have all the relevant documents reprinted in patriot journals, sometimes adding suitable commentaries, sometimes allowing the commissioners' miscues to speak for themselves.[17] Leading whig publicists—Thomas Paine, William Livingston, and the New York delegate Gouverneur Morris—denounced them in polished essays. Other writers resorted to different techniques, as, for example, the New England poet who penned these lines:

> *But see a cloud burst, and a seraph appears,*
> *Loud trumpeting peace, while in blood to their ears,*
> *With bulls and with pardons, for us on submission;*
> *To lull us, and gull us, by their sham commission.*
>
> *The haughty great George, then to peace is now prone,*
> *A bully when match'd soon can alter his tone;*
> *'Tis the act of a Briton to bluster and threaten,*
> *Hang his tail like a spaniel, when handsomely beaten.*
>
> *Charge your glasses lip high, to brave Washington sing,*
> *To the union so glorious the whole world shall ring;*
> *May their councils in wisdom and valour unite,*
> *And that men ne'er be wrong, who yet so far are right.*[18]

Within less than a year, this brash note of optimism would become hopelessly dated.

Changing Concerns

THE summer of 1778 marked the end of what might be called the first phase of national politics, a period in which several overriding imperatives of resistance had encouraged virtually all of the members of Congress to develop and accept similar perceptions of their responsibilities. Within this numerically small, admittedly élitist group of politicians, a common attitude toward the manifest implications of British policy and a common sensitivity toward the precarious basis of their own authority proved more influential than the very real tensions and differences that many had expected would convert Congress into the proverbial "rope of sand." Although well into 1777 and even 1778 moderate delegates continued to question the timing of the Declaration of Independence and to resent what they saw as the manipulative propensities of Samuel Adams and R. H. Lee, their criticism of Great Britain remained far more biting than their complaints against congressional protagonists. And the persistently inept maneuvers of the Howe and Carlisle commissions provided a continuing reminder of the importance of preserving a rough measure of harmony within Congress. So long as Britain offered no opening for serious negotiations and the war seemed to be going as well as could reasonably be expected, the delegates were able to suppress their growing personal animosities, or at least confine them within the chambers of Congress or the circles of their closest correspondents.

Yet in other ways the similarities linking the two-year periods preceding and following the Declaration of July 1776 were only superficial. Various developments after the summer of 1776 sharply altered the conditions under which Congress held and exercised power. Although the conclusions to be drawn from the *origins* of the Revolution still constituted the dominant paradigm of the delegates' political thinking, concerns over the *consequences* of independence—all the problems arising from the war itself, the economic dislocations it produced, the political struggles attending the creation of new governments, and the slackening of popular patriotism—increasingly commanded their attention. Their reluctance to abandon the original paradigm, with its emphasis on a virtuous people responding to British oppression, reflected not only nostalgia for the remembered, gradually mythologized fervor of 1774–75, but also the difficulty of devising solutions adequate to the problems that now beset Congress. Indeed, concern about the possible unraveling of congressional authority enhanced the delegates' eagerness to exploit the clumsy mistakes of the two peace commissions.

The most urgent problems confronting Congress after July 1776 involved the administration of the army. By late 1776 the continental army was seriously under strength. Thousands of its troops had been captured, and its size was further reduced by short-term enlistments, desertion, and inadequate recruiting. The establishment of military discipline, a recurrent complaint of officers from the middle and southern states in particular, still seemed as difficult as it had first appeared in 1775. "Where the Principles of Democracy so universally prevail," Joseph Reed observed while serving as Washington's aide, "when so great an Equality & levelling Spirit predominates either no Discipline can be established or he who attempts it must become odious and detestable." And when the officers were not complaining about their men, they indulged in jealous and seemingly incessant bickering over rank and promotion, frequently threatening to resign their commissions if their protests were unappeased. "What shall we say of this phantom *honour:* The soldier's deity & object of worship," asked Charles Thomson. "I would not have a soldier devoid of it: But I think it a plant better suited for the gardens of Monarchy, than those of a republic."[19]

The problem seemed only to worsen the higher one moved along the chain of command: generals proved no more immune to ambition, envy, and thin-skinned pride than their subordinates. The running squabble between Horatio Gates and Philip Schuyler over command of the northern army was particularly disturbing, not merely because the defense of New York was critical to American security, but also because both men had vocal partisans within Congress: Schuyler in the New York delegation, Gates among the New England delegates. An overlapping conflict between Walter Livingston and Connecticut's Joseph Trumbull over control of the northern commissary further agitated these tensions. And Washington's uneven performance in 1776 and 1777 sparked critical murmurings within both the army and Congress—though these had to be vented in rather more subdued tones.[20]

Political divisions within the states provided another source of alarm. From the fall of 1776 until the spring of 1777, the framing of new constitutions in Pennsylvania, Maryland, and New York proved particularly disturbing to many of the moderate whig leaders of these states, themselves wealthy merchants and landowners who feared the creation of excessively democratic governments and harbored little respect for the political abilities of the "lower orders." As early as February 1775 Samuel Chase of Maryland had spoken in favor of creating new governments; but by October 1776 he could inform John Dickinson that the Maryland leaders would "endeavor to postpone the Consideration of our form of Government but I doubt if We shall succeed. A distemper of Governing has seized all Ranks of Men." A dispirited Charles Carroll voiced an even gloomier opinion. If the Americans would not negotiate with Britain, he wrote in October 1776, "they will be ruined, not so much by the calamities of war, as by the intestine divisions and the bad govern[men]ts wh[ich] I foresee will take place in most of the United States: they will be simple Democracies, of all govern[men]ts the worst, and will end as all other Democracies have, in despotism." And from New York, Robert Livingston voiced similar fears. "We see daily more and more strongly the necessity of forming a new government," he wrote in mid-September 1776, "and yet dare not begin it, because of the absurd ideas that some have on that subject. A weak executive, considering the disposition of the people and claims of our neighbors, must end in our ruin; and officers chosen either by the people or the Assembly involve us in perpetual faction, or bring the magistracy into contempt."[21]

Nevertheless, established whig leaders managed to retain an uneasy control over the new regimes of Maryland and New York. The Maryland constitution of 1776 imposed substantial restrictions on officeholding and suffrage, thereby erecting formal barriers against popular political participation; and when problems of popular "disaffection" threatened to become wildly disruptive of internal order, the conservative leadership enacted a program of fiscal legislation and debtor relief that defused popular resentment of their power.[22] In New York, too, the various leaders associated with the Livingston clan exerted a substantial influence over the constitution approved in the spring of 1777—though only by employing a strategy, Robert Livingston noted, of "well timed delays, indefatigable industry, & a minute attention to every favourable circumstance."[23]

Only in Pennsylvania did the framing of a constitution fulfill the worst forecasts moderates had previously ventured. There constitution-writing was dominated by a group of obscure radicals and political newcomers who produced the most democratic of the new governments. Rather than accept the new constitution, which had not been submitted to the people for ratification, moderates led by Robert Morris, James Wilson, and their associates attempted to force its revision and frustrate its operation. The ensuing conflict temporarily paralyzed the state's government and raged unabated for years. And it was the example of Pennsylvania, the state where Congress resided throughout almost the entire war, that continually demonstrated (at least to American moderates) the apparent futility of undertaking dangerous innovations in government when the whole cause was tottering on the brink of collapse.[24]

Yet in the virulence of its constitutional disputes, Pennsylvania was more the exception than the rule. What gradually came to seem more disturbing than the initial divisions of 1776 was the general tenor of the "restructuring of power" achieved in the new constitutions, which took place not in response to the anticipated exigencies of war but in reaction against the old colonial regimes. If these reforms thus expressed some of the deepest impulses of the Revolution, as Gordon Wood has argued, they did not for that reason necessarily serve the immediate demands of resistance. Provincial politicians were no better prepared than members of Congress to foresee the strenuous demands a protracted war would place on their administrative talents. It was one thing to entrust sweeping power to the state legislatures—the distinctive feature of the new constitutions—another to compel the diligent attendance of their members for lengthy and inconvenient sessions; one thing to strip the governors of formal authority, another to leave them burdened with excessive responsibilities during the assemblies' frequent recesses.[25]

When, in early 1776, the Adamses and others had urged the prompt erection of new governments, they believed such a step would greatly reinforce popular commitment to independence —as it may well have done at the time.[26] But that measure alone could scarcely maintain a high level of popular fervor once the other dislocations the war inevitably created came to be felt. "There are two Things, that afford Affliction to all of us, who have the American Cause and Interest at Heart," Samuel Mather, the last of the eminent family of Boston divines, informed Samuel Adams. "These are the secret Cabals, Intreagues and Machinations of those, whom we call *Tories;* and the Selfish and avaritious Spirit, which is so shamefully discovered and manifested among us." Mather talked naturally of the sins of treason and avarice; but beneath his charged language he identified two tasks that would engage Congress in the years to come: maintaining popular support for the war; and countering the diverse unsettling effects, political as well as economic, that flowed inevitably from wartime scarcities of goods and labor and from the depreciation of paper currency. Mather's pained observations, echoed innumerable times by others, merely marked the first phase of the readjustment of American society to the reality of a long, indecisive war, and to the economic hardships and opportunities, social strains, and political conflicts it necessarily produced.[27]

Disloyalty and disaffection, variously defined, were recurrent causes of complaint after the summer of 1776. The British military successes of 1776 and the locus of their campaigns of 1776–77 fostered a resurgence of loyalist military activity in the area stretching from New York City and New Jersey through the eastern shore of the Chesapeake into Delaware and Maryland. Where the British army acted in force, or where it could at least provide regular aid to local sympathizers, patriot authority was gravely weakened, most dramatically in New Jersey in 1776. But conversely, as John Shy has argued, whenever shifting lines of battle or, more simply, General Howe's erratic strategy led the British to abandon such areas, local loyalists were left unprotected and exposed, and patriot militia were generally able to regain effective control, often having become, in the process, more deeply politicized than they had formerly been. Only occasionally did the mobilization of armed loyalist bands become a subject of congressional concern, though in the context of local and state politics—particularly in New York, Delaware, and the Carolinas—such groups continued to pose serious challenges to the whig leadership.[28]

Moreover, by late 1776 whig perceptions of unpatriotic behavior were coming to acquire a more elastic definition; toryism no longer meant merely principled loyalty to Great Britain or to the constitutional supremacy of Parliament. When in October 1776 Franklin and Robert Morris informed Silas Deane that "The only Source of uneasiness amongst us arises from the Number of Tories we find in every State," their classification of tories suggested something of this new meaning of disloyalty.

But Tories are now of various kinds and various principles; some are so from real attachment to Britain; some from interested Views, many, very many from fear of the British Force; some because they are dissatisfied with the General Measures of Congress, more because they disapprove of the Men in power & the measures in their respective States; but these different passions views and expectations are so combined in their Consequences that the parties affected by them, either withhold their assistance or oppose our operations, and if America falls it will be owing to such divisions more than the force of our Enemies.[29]

Though in the eyes of whig leaders toryism retained a strong connotation of subversion, it now also carried an implication of popular indifference toward necessary Revolutionary activities, a mood perhaps better described by a term acquiring more common usage: "disaffection." The patriotic fervor of 1774–75 was impossible to sustain indefinitely, and under the pressure of military setbacks and adjustments to a wartime economy, the bubble burst.

What did the subsequent experience of revolution mean to the vast majority of Americans whose direct participation in politics and the war was largely confined to occasional elections and militia alerts? More than anything else, it meant exploiting or coping with the new economic conditions that the war created. For some, the Revolution offered possibilities for profit: merchants, artisans, and commercial farmers whose products and services were in increasing demand; New England seamen whose zeal for privateering was held responsible for local difficulties in recruiting. For others, the Revolution created genuine hardships: refugees from British-occupied areas, deprived of property and livelihood; wives and widows struggling to maintain family farms. And everyone was affected by inflation: merchants constantly juggling the various currencies in circulation; landlords forced to accept their tenants' rents in depreciated currency; small farmers, whose produce was expropriated by military units, receiving in exchange questionable continental certificates promising future payment; and soldiers' orphans and widows, whose sufferings figured so prominently in public discussions of fiscal policy. Year in, year out, as interest in politics waxed and waned, as news of one indecisive skirmish followed another, the task of coping with these economic dislocations was probably the major preoccupation of most Americans.[30]

The delegates enjoyed no immunity from these changes. Each had an estate or profession to protect—like John Adams, concerned with Abigail's management of their farm and envious of his advancing colleagues in the Massachusetts bar—or ambitions to pursue, like Robert Morris, the great merchant and military contractor. By late 1776, too, Congress was well aware that it was being locked into an inflationary spiral, having to print additional money to meet rising prices and the growing demands of the war, thereby further fueling the depreciation of its currency and credit. The objective causes of inflation were scarcely obscure. Nevertheless, many delegates found it difficult to resist the temptation to blame much of the evil on the excessive self-interest with which their countrymen were reacting to problems that threatened to cripple the entire war effort. Caught between an intellectual understanding and personal frustration, American leaders repeatedly contrasted the economic realism of the late 1770's with the atmosphere of sacrifice and self-reliance that had been evoked by the Association. "Such Avarice! Such Pecula-

tion! such detestable Mismanagement in almost every department," William Livingston exclaimed in early 1778. "Good God!
how different from the glorious spirit with which we embarked
in the Cause of Liberty."[31]

Considered individually, each of these broad problems could,
like inflation, be rationally attributed to discrete, specific causes.
Although effective solutions were difficult to discover, the task of
diagnosis was comparatively simple. Some problems were clearly
traceable to mistaken congressional decisions—poor military appointments in the early days of the war, a naïve confidence that
the war would prove short and the militia reliable. Others, notably the difficulty of levying or collecting taxes in amounts adequate to prevent depreciation, could be ascribed to the ineffectiveness of the state governments. Viewed dispassionately,
without an eye to partisan recriminations, most of these troubles
could be seen to be rooted in the nature of the war itself.

Yet whatever their individual causes, from the perspective of
the Continental Congress all these problems could ultimately be
subsumed under one rubric, their separate features merging into
one image of a society experiencing an abrupt declension from
the vaunted patriotism and public virtue of 1774 and 1775. Different groups of delegates described this transformation in different
ways. To those with a more ideological bent—men with the part-
Calvinist, part-classical republican temperament of a Samuel
Adams—these evils clearly signaled a corruption, or at least a
dilution, of republican virtue, and thus demonstrated the need
for a more thorough reformation of the American character.
Their more cynical or worldly colleagues found these developments equally disturbing but less surprising. To someone like
Morris or Duane, these new patterns of behavior seemed merely
to confirm their earlier warnings against trusting the virtue of
the people too far or too long, and thus pointed toward the need
to adopt policies that would improve the efficiency of the Revolutionary apparatus while leaving the reclamation of public spirit
to a later if not indefinite date. Yet delegates who held contrast-
ing views about the virtue of the American people were reacting
to the same phenomena.

Whether the mood of 1775 could ever be restored was, of
course, quite problematic. There was a school of thought that
held, as Benjamin Rush would argue in 1780, that "Our republics
cannot exist long in prosperity. We require adversity and appear

to possess most of the republican spirit when most depressed."
By then, America had experienced more distressing reverses,
and a notion of redemption through suffering may have come to
appear not only more feasible but possibly unavoidable. But in
1777 and 1778, at least, the delegates continued to hope that
public opinion could be influenced in less drastic ways: by exploiting the errors of the peace commissions, reports of British
and loyalist depredations, and the favorable impact of Saratoga
and the French alliance; and by acting to preserve, as well as
possible, the inherited reputation of Congress itself. For, as
Henry Laurens wrote in September 1777, "If people in America
are once impressed with an opinion that Congress is inadequate
to the business of Government, this Assembly will be presently
blown up & our circumstances will become deplorable."[32] Laurens had no high opinion of the talents of many of his colleagues.
He was one of a growing number of American leaders who
believed, by 1777–78, that the membership of Congress was far
less distinguished than it had been before independence, and
like others he hoped that the states would improve their delegations by selecting better qualified individuals.[33] But in the meantime, he also understood the importance of maintaining popular
confidence in Congress—or at least of preventing its further
diminution.

A growing sense of isolation contributed to the delegates'
uneasiness about the security of their power. Before the summer
of 1776, the overlapping issues of independence and new governments and the early stages of military preparation had kept congressional, provincial, and local politics closely linked. But once
independence was declared, the delegates' channels of communication with their constituents seemed to wither, and their complaints about the unreliability of their private and official correspondents, which had been voiced as early as 1775, grew more
frequent and intense. Far from being able somehow to reach out
to influence politics in the states, either through personal visits
or correspondence, the delegates found themselves struggling to
maintain a barely adequate flow of information between Congress and their constituents.

Ignorance of developments in their own states provided one
mark of the delegates' isolation. "I am really at a loss to account
for my not receiving any intelligence from N. Hampshire," William Whipple wrote to Josiah Bartlett in January 1777. "I am as

great a stranger to what is doing in that state as to what's doing
in the moon." Requests for desired information went unanswered. "It is long since I received a letter from the Assembly,
notwithstanding my repeated requests," William Ellery of Rhode
Island observed. "I know nothing about the affairs of our State
except what I collect from the private letters and newspapers,
which I now and then receive." Philip Livingston reminded
Abraham Yates that the New York delegation "could wish to hear
from you as often as possible. Many particulars that deeply concern us as members of the State and are more interesting now
than ever we are not informed of." Samuel Adams, whose once
numerous correspondents had dwindled to a handful, registered
a more unusual grievance. In February 1777 Adams recounted to
James Warren how he had asked John Hancock (from whom
Adams was already estranged) whether it was true that Hancock
had received a letter asserting there was widespread opposition
within Massachusetts to the regulation of prices, a topic then
under consideration at Congress.

He confirmed it. . . . I beg'd him to let me see his Letter but he refused
in a kind of Pet, telling me it was a private letter, & leaving me to
conjecture whether I had really been impertinent in asking a Sight of
his Letter or whether the Contents of it were such as it was not proper
for me to see. You will easily conceive what a Scituation a Man must be
in here, who having received no Intelligence of the Sentiments of his
Constituents himself is obligd in vain to ask of another upon what Principles they have disapprovd of a Measure if in truth they did disapprove
of it, of which he is calld to give his own opinion. You may see, my
Friend, from this Instance, the Necessity of your writing me oftener.
When I was told upon the forementioned occasion, that I should be
intitled to see the Letters of another whenever I should be disposed to
show those which I receive myself, I could have truly said that I had
scarcely received any.

Benjamin Rush blamed the dearth of reliable news on the removal of Congress to Baltimore. "We live here in a Convent," he
wrote Robert Morris, ". . . precluded from all opportunities of
feeling the pulse of the public upon our measures." But in truth
the brief exiles to Baltimore and later York only aggravated an
existing problem.[34]

The simple mechanical problems of coordinating political activity between two levels of government, each pressed with business and prone to inefficiency, were virtually insurmountable.

Correspondence between the delegates and their official constituents, the state assemblies, was hampered by several obstacles. Although members of Congress were responsible to the legislatures, who elected and occasionally instructed them, most of their official letters were directed to the governors or executive councils, largely because the assemblies met irregularly and were chronically disposed to convene late and adjourn early, often without completing all the business awaiting their decision. The governors would lay the delegates' pending letters and requests before the legislators whenever they convened. Yet while the governors thus became the central link between Congress and the assemblies, they could do little more than transmit requests and replies from one to the other. For the new republican constitutions had sharply circumscribed not only the formal powers of the state executives but much of their political influence as well, leaving them unable to play any significant role in legislative deliberations. This was particularly true during the earlier years of the Revolution, before new political alignments and habits of conducting public business had had time to take hold. Sometimes the governors were informed of the actions a given session had taken only after the members had adjourned and rapidly dispersed to their homes. Writing to Thomas Burke early in the spring of 1777, North Carolina's Richard Caswell ventured a hope that he would soon "have an opportunity of looking over the Journals of the Assembly, not knowing what they have done. At present I am almost a stranger to it, not having received more than two or three messages from that Body, during the whole course of the session; tho' I had sent them many more." Nor did the governors have any authority to instruct the delegates on matters of policy.[35]

At times, too, the provincial executives were hard pressed to keep up their own correspondence. The plight of Meshech Weare, the president of New Hampshire, may have been an extreme case, but it suggests something of the vagaries with which Congress had to cope. When Josiah Bartlett returned to Congress in May 1778, Henry Laurens, then its president, asked if he knew whether Weare had received any letters from Congress during the past eight months, "and seemed very uneasy," Bartlett noted, "that he had received no answers to his letters." Bartlett was distressed but hardly surprised by Laurens's question. "But really Sir," he asked John Langdon in July, "is it to be expected that our very worthy President . . . should be at the trouble to receive, file, copy and answer from time to time all such public Letters without any compensation. To do it properly he ought to be allowed a Clerk for the purpose and receive something handsome for his own time." Writing in his own defense several weeks later, Weare complained that when

letters are laid before the General Court & read, somethings [sic] are taken up & acted on and others forgot and no persons appointed to return any Answers About them; I have never suppos'd that it belong'd to me without perticular direction to do any of these things but that I should be tho't assuming if I did but surely there ought to be some one whose proper business it should be But there seems to be a strange fear that such a one would soon grow up to be a Governor.[36]

The delegates also suffered from overwork, and often complained they had little time free even to write their families. This system of indirect correspondence was thus always prone to inefficiency and delay at both ends, the natural result of the irregularity of assembly sessions, the harassed condition of delegates and governors alike, and the unpredictability of the post. Information and advice the delegates had repeatedly requested never arrived or was received too late to be useful; often Congress as a whole was left uncertain about the status of the various recommendations and injunctions it referred to the states. "I think it not amiss to say," James Lovell wrote Samuel Adams in 1778, "that whenever Congress sends a recommendation to the States it [is] but right & fit that regular public Returns should be made whether the Recommendations are fully or partially complied with or rejected. How, otherwise can future plans be properly laid, or the general continental works carried on?" But state officials complained in turn, as George Walton of Georgia remarked, that "We are shockingly in the dark as to the proceedings of Congress, no resolves, or information of any kind." Even members of the various staff departments of the army often failed to receive copies of the congressional resolutions that were to govern their conduct. "What advantage is it for Congress from time to time to pass resolves respecting the regulation of the army when the army never get them?" Jesse Root asked the Connecticut delegates in 1777. Alexander McDougall voiced the same criticism in 1779, and the New York printer John Holt repeated it again in April 1780, when he admitted that "there has been a very great Defect in communicating Intelligence of the Proceedings of Congress to the Public, tho' highly concerned in it [myself]. They seemed to conclude, that if published in their Journals, or a Philadelphia newspaper, their proceedings would naturally be known all over the United States."[37] Writing as late as 1782, Samuel Osgood noted that the laggardly publication of the journals often left the delegates "at a loss to know what we have done tho we may possibly by the assistance of Charles [Thomson] get a Knowledge of it yet the States are totally in the Dark; where perhaps," Osgood added, "some of our Resolves ever ought to remain."[38]

Comments such as these evoke a political world whose dominant characteristics may well have been confusion and inefficiency. A Congress that encountered such difficulties merely in conducting its essential correspondence could not begin to devise innovative techniques for influencing public opinion. The American Revolutionaries' greatest achievements in political organization had come at the outset, with their creation of the ubiquitous committee system of 1774–76. But although committees or the militia companies that replaced them continued to function in many places after independence, they could command only a grudging loyalty, not enthusiasm, and it was a restoration of some measure of enthusiasm that Congress sought. Rather than attempt to overcome the political obstacles their isolation imposed, the delegates implicitly chose to make a virtue of necessity by striving to perpetuate the reputation that Congress had acquired during earlier phases of resistance. Such a strategy seemed practicable so long as Congress could replay old themes by exploiting the British peace commissions or promising tokens of American success. But as other sources of domestic discontent grew more powerful, this policy became increasingly unrewarding. After 1778, as inflation and depreciation continued unabated and the war dragged on inconclusively, popular criticism of Congress mounted, and its reputation, which could only be maintained by the success of its policies, suffered accordingly. Lacking other channels of political influence, the delegates could do little to recoup the support they had lost.

And yet this growing isolation from state politics did not result solely from mechanical problems of correspondence and coordination. In other ways it was self-imposed and consciously considered, and thus reflected the delegates' views of both the nature of the American union and the prerogatives of Congress. We must turn, therefore, to an examination of the Articles of Confederation, the first federal constitution, and of the patterns of congressional administration that developed while the Articles remained uncompleted.

Part Two

———————◦~◦———————

CONFEDERATION

———————◦~◦———————

CHAPTER VII

Confederation Considered

———————⟨∾⟩———————

O F all the problems in constitutional theory that engaged the
American Revolutionaries, none ultimately proved more
challenging or critical than the framing of a federal union. To
reduce the evolution of their ideas on this subject to manageable
proportions is not an easy task. Much of the difficulty is justly
owing, of course, to our natural absorption with the Constitution
of 1787. The informative records of debate that were kept in both
the Philadelphia and state ratifying conventions, and the polemical literature that appeared during the ratification struggle, are so
rich and complex as to seem capable of supporting an endless
flood of analyses of the founding fathers' theories of federalism,
democracy, representation, human nature, and other topics too
numerous to mention. Although the comparable sources for understanding the Articles of Confederation are far less explicit or
impressive, historians have sometimes felt impelled to treat the
earlier document in much the same way as they do the Constitution, presuming, that is, that it embodied an equally distinctive set
of convictions, consciously held and thoughtfully developed,
about the problem of federal government. Certainly this is the
interpretation developed by Merrill Jensen, the most influential
of modern historians of the confederation. Jensen portrays the
Articles as one of the major achievements of the same radical
groups who drafted the democratic state constitutions of 1776—as
the Constitution was the great work of the conservatives who had
resisted the political reforms of earlier years.[1]

The chapters that follow offer a different view, one that emphasizes the extent to which the halting and at times haphazard progress of confederation allowed new problems to be raised, old ones once thought solved to be reopened, and others to go unexplored. At the outset of the Revolution, the problem of confederation received little sustained attention. When it was first considered in 1774 and 1775, the task of dividing the powers of government between Congress and the colonies proved far less troubling than might have been expected. Instead, the earliest congressional discussions of confederation tended, like other issues, to be more deeply influenced by the demands of resistance. In the political vocabulary of 1774–75, union still meant agreement on the principles and tactics of opposition to Britain and avoidance of the types of jealousy that had troubled American resistance in the early 1770's. The initial efforts to draft plans of confederation concentrated, therefore, on minimizing possible sources of intercolonial conflict, particularly those arising from the apportionment of continental representation and the common expenses of war among the colonies, and from specific disputes involving individual provinces. More thorough discussion of a wider range of issues was inhibited by the intimate link between ideas of confederation and independence. Because the establishment of a formal American union would imply that the colonies were demanding something more than a restoration of the imperial situation of 1763, moderate delegates were able to defer direct consideration of confederation until their hopes for reconciliation had finally disappeared—that is, until well into 1776. Yet critical questions involving the character of the American union had already been raised well before Congress began debating the seminal Articles that John Dickinson and twelve other members prepared in June 1776.

Confederation: An Early Chronology

SIX drafts of a confederation were prepared in 1775 and 1776. Three of these are generally unknown to scholars; indeed, the existence of two of these texts has been discovered only recently.

At least two and probably three drafts were composed during the summer and fall of 1775. One by Benjamin Franklin was presented to Congress on July 21 but never formally considered

—Congress recessed twelve days later—although it was subsequently referred to the North Carolina Provincial Congress.[2] Silas Deane, one of the first delegates to have recorded an interest in confederation, prepared a second plan, possibly with the assistance of his Connecticut colleagues Roger Sherman and Eliphalet Dyer.[3] Though different in several critical provisions, the Franklin and Deane texts are distinguished by the apparent haste with which they were drawn, a common absorption with problems affecting the immediate unity of the colonies, and a striking lack of concern with the task of dividing power between Congress and the colonies.

Because the Deane draft was manifestly inadequate to the expanding responsibilities of Congress, its revision would have been necessary before it could be seriously considered. It appears to have been substantially revised between the late summer of 1775 and early March 1776, when a third text, here labeled the Connecticut plan, was published in the *Pennsylvania Evening Post.* * This plan may have been completed by early December

---

*The editors of the new edition of *Letters of Delegates to Congress* have suggested a November 1775 date for the composition of Deane's proposals for a confederation. Several considerations lead me to believe that the proposals were prepared somewhat earlier, probably in late July or early August 1775: (1) Deane had expressed an interest in confederation as early as January 2, 1775, when he briefly discussed the subject in a letter to Patrick Henry. Shortly after returning to Philadelphia in May 1775, he wrote home to ask his wife to send him a copy of the New England Confederation of 1643 (Paul H. Smith, *et al.*, eds., *Letters of Delegates to Congress, 1774–1789* [Washington, 1976–], I, 291, 347). (2) In their substantive content, the Deane proposals simply seem too terse to have been framed any later than the summer of 1775. (3) Between mid-August and late November 1775, Governor Jonathan Trumbull sent the Connecticut delegates several letters referring (though in disappointingly brief terms) to a draft set of articles they had apparently left with him. His first letter (August 19) simply mentions that he has "not had time yet to consider them." The second letter (September 23) notes that Trumbull has "many things to object to . . . and not time to point them out." But in the third letter (November 17), Trumbull evidently enclosed revisions of his own: "you'l easily discern the Alterations I have made from that I received." There is no reason to believe that the Connecticut delegates had sought or needed Trumbull's comments on the Franklin plan. It is more plausible to infer that the governor was commenting on a draft that he knew the Connecticut delegates were working on themselves and intended to submit to Congress. The laconic tone of the delegates' reply (December 5, quoted in the text just below) strongly suggests that the draft Trumbull had been referring to since August was not Franklin's. (The governor's letters are in the Jonathan Trumbull, Sr., Collection, Connecticut Historical Society, Hartford. I am

1775, when the Connecticut delegates informed Trumbull that "The draught of Articles of Confederation we have not as yet been able to lay before the Congress; business of every kind, and from every quarter, thickening fast at this session." Seven weeks later, moderate delegates successfully opposed a motion introduced by Franklin and Samuel Adams to fix a date for considering the Franklin plan, thereby also precluding the introduction of the Connecticut draft. Instead, at least one of its authors, possibly with the advice of more militant members of Congress, arranged for its publication in a popular whig newspaper; its appearance, following hard on the arrival of texts of the Prohibitory Act, was probably a discreet effort to prod public opinion along the road toward independence.[4] Substantively, the Connecticut plan can be linked to the earlier Deane draft by their common approach to the problem of representation. But in other respects it marked an important step forward, particularly in attempting to sharpen the line separating the spheres of authority allotted to Congress and the individual colonies.

None of these initial three drafts had any major impact on the seminal text that John Dickinson prepared in June 1776; their importance rests instead on what they reveal of the delegates' earliest conceptions of confederation. Each reflects the constraints of the months between the outbreak of war and the growing recognition of the inevitability of independence—the period when Congress was caught, John Adams complained, "between hawk and buzzard." A concern with preserving intercolonial unity, still defined in the rhetoric of harmony, outweighed any perceived need to draft a comprehensive constitution for what was implicitly becoming a federal system

grateful to Professor Christopher Collier for calling my attention to them.)

I would argue, therefore, that the Deane sketch was prepared during the August 1775 recess, but that it served essentially as a working paper from which the Connecticut delegates, perhaps with assistance from Trumbull, went on to prepare a second draft. I would also suggest, though it is impossible to prove, that the *Pennsylvania Evening Post* "Proposals" may have been the draft alluded to in the delegates' letter of December 5. Although different in many key respects, the two texts are strikingly similar in their approach to the critical question of representation. It is also possible that Roger Sherman played the major role in preparing the Connecticut plan, for in June 1779 John Adams recalled that Sherman had "made an Essay towards a Confederation about the same time" as Franklin (L. H. Butterfield, *et al.*, eds., *Diary and Autobiography of John Adams* [Cambridge, 1961], II, 391).

of government. At the same time, moderate delegates refused to allow Congress to exceed the American constitutional claims of 1774 and 1775, thereby requiring each draft somehow to remain consistent with their lingering hope of securing a reconciliation that would leave the colonies within the British empire—something that the unilateral creation of a confederation could only make more difficult.[5]

These considerations no longer applied in June, when, in the wake of the final two-day debate over independence, Dickinson and a committee of twelve other members set to work on a new plan of confederation. Historians have previously labeled the text that the committee presented to Congress on July 12 as the Dickinson plan; but it can now be identified as the committee's revision of an earlier draft that Dickinson submitted to his colleagues and which has been preserved among his own private papers rather than the official papers of the Continental Congress.[6] This first draft apparently served as a working copy for the committee, for on it Dickinson made additions and corrections incorporated in the second draft, and deleted whatever the committee objected to—sometimes lightly, so we know what was proposed, sometimes with tightly curled lines of ink, so that the objectionable phrases are now indecipherable. Debate on this second draft was intermittently conducted in a committee of the whole Congress between July 22 and August 20, when Congress voted to print eighty copies of the Articles as they had been further revised.[7] The existence of these three drafts thus allows us to reconstruct the second major phase of congressional consideration, when, due to Dickinson's innovative proposals, the delegates first began to think systematically about the structure of a confederation.

Initial Conceptions

ON September 12, 1787, as the delegates to the Philadelphia Convention were preparing to sign the new Constitution, Nathaniel Gorham meekly rose to ask—"if it was not too late"—whether the population ratio that was to govern the size of the House of Representatives might not be altered. Many delegates must have groaned inwardly at Gorham's proposal, since this question had been strenuously debated during the preceding weeks; but with an unprecedented endorsement from George Washington, his motion carried.[8] This little episode provided a fitting conclusion to the Convention's labors. For of all the issues that had troubled the Revolutionary generation's attempt to create a federal government, none ultimately proved more difficult than the problem of apportioning representation among the states—not because the theoretical questions involved were especially complex but, perhaps rather ironically, because the conflicting interests they evoked were dismayingly obvious.

Thirteen years earlier, James Duane had launched the opening debate of the First Continental Congress by asking whether voting in Congress would be "by Colonies, or by the Poll, or by Interests." That is, should each colony or, alternatively, each delegate have one vote, or, as Patrick Henry quickly proposed, should each colony possess "a just Weight in our deliberations in proportion to its opulence and number of inhabitants, its Exports and Imports"? The basic conflict that would divide the small and large colonies (states) until 1787 was thus immediately exposed. Spokesmen for the larger colonies, notably Henry, insisted that representation should be apportioned on what was called, in eighteenth-century usage, an "equal" basis, taking into account disparities in population and, if feasible, wealth as well. Delegates from the smaller colonies, already evincing what J. R. Pole has aptly described as their "corporate self-consciousness," argued "that a little Colony had its All at Stake as well as a great one," and therefore deserved an equal vote in Congress.[9]

In fact, as virtually all the delegates admitted, the First Congress had no practical alternative to giving each colony one vote; nor did its agenda demand a different solution. Simply allowing all the delegates to vote as individuals would not have answered the claims of delegates from the larger colonies: Massachusetts, the second most populous colony, had sent only four delegates, while Delaware, the smallest, had sent three. The two central objections against attempting to apportion votes were summarized by Richard Bland, who agreed, with several other speakers, "that we are not at present provided with materials to ascertain the importance of each Colony." The absence of reliable data made it impossible to fix any formula for allocating votes within Congress according to the population—much less the trade, produce, and property—of the colonies. But Bland adduced a second reason that was peculiarly appropriate to the political context of

1774 when he observed: "The Question is whether the Rights and Liberties of America shall be contended for, or given up to arbitrary Power." Bland was reminding his colleagues that their essential task was to frame measures and policies acceptable to all of the colonies. What had justified holding a Congress in the first place was the common conviction that the legislation against Massachusetts endangered the rights of all the colonies. If that were the case, and if, as the Connecticut delegates later noted, Congress hoped to reach decisions through consensus rather than simple pluralities, the apportionment of representation was irrelevant. On September 6, then, Congress resolved to give each colony one vote; but this resolution stipulated that future sessions need not be bound by this precedent.[10]

Once this issue was resolved, even if only temporarily, the First Congress ignored other opportunities to give further consideration to the formal structure of American union. Its emerging positions on American rights emphasized a restoration of the *status quo ante*, and thereby precluded serious discussion of the possibility, explicitly advanced in the Galloway plan, that the creation of some sort of American confederation could be proposed as a step toward reconciliation. Nor did the framing of the Association evoke thoughts of confederation, since the delegates were confident that local committees and conventions would be able to enforce its provisions.

By early 1775, however, a few delegates were beginning to consider the subject of confederation more seriously. To some extent, their initial concern was simply to guarantee that Congress would continue to meet annually—a reflection, perhaps, of a latent belief that developments in 1775 would replicate the experience of 1766 and 1770, when Parliament had repealed offensive legislation without proposing an acceptable solution to the basic issue of its claim to supremacy. Silas Deane went a step further when, in a letter to Patrick Henry, he suggested that the colonies should create a union akin to the New England Confederation of 1643, which had been essentially a defensive alliance against Indian attack.

Something of this kind appears most absolutely necessary, let Us turn which way We will. If a reconciliation with G Britain takes place, it will be obtained on the best terms, by the Colonies being united, and be the more like to be preserved, on just and equal Terms; if no reconciliation is to be had without a Confederation we are ruined to all intents and purposes. United We stand, divided We fall, is our motto and must be. One general Congress has brought the Colonies to be acquainted with each other, and I am in hopes another may effect a lasting Confederation which will need nothing, perhaps, but time, to mature it into a complete & perfect American Constitution, the only proper one for Us, whether connected with Great Britain or not.[11]

This idea grew more compelling with the outbreak of war. Instead of framing policies to be implemented by local committees and conventions, Congress now had to supervise an army and its administrative machinery. Although Congress was removed from the immediate, regular exercise of those coercive powers that most urgently demanded the sanction of constitutional legitimacy—unlike local officials, the delegates did not personally have to collect taxes, raise troops, or stifle dissent—it seemed reasonable to conclude that its own expanding authority required definition. The argument Massachusetts had advanced in requesting permission to resume civil government, that "the sword should in all free states be subservient to the civil powers," could be applied at the continental level as well.[12]

Moreover, the expenses attendant on the organization of an army allowed the problem of representation to be reexamined from a new perspective. Advocates of reapportionment could now argue that it was unreasonable to continue the voting procedures of 1774, since Congress would be taking actions requiring the expenditure of large sums of money and the allocation of other resources necessary to the conduct of war. Massachusetts, Pennsylvania, and Virginia would obviously have to contribute far more than Rhode Island, New Jersey, or Delaware: yet were each of these colonies to have an equal voice in congressional decisions?

Two further developments of 1775 reinforced earlier concerns about the risks of conflict—or "intestine broils," as they were sometimes referred to—among the colonies. One was the deteriorating situation in the Wyoming Valley of northeastern Pennsylvania, where rival settlers from the Quaker colony and Connecticut seemed on the verge of bloodshed over their contested land claims: a graphic reminder of the divergent interests that could pit individual colonies in confrontation with one another.[13] And from Boston came reports of outbursts of provincial and regional animosities among officers and troops drawn from different colonies, a natural result, perhaps, of this encounter of parochial cultures, but nevertheless a painful contrast to the rhetoric of uniting for the common cause. Southern officers, including Washington himself, described the New England regiments in contemptuous terms—"they are an exceeding dirty and nasty people," the commander-in-chief complained—and their arrogance was deeply resented by New Englanders.[14] Congress could do little to alleviate the underlying sources of these petty rumblings, but their simple expression was a reminder of the potential for intercolonial conflict.

Not surprisingly, therefore, both the Franklin and Deane plans of union were primarily concerned with removing possible sources of discord among the colonies, and particularly with providing a solution to the problem of representation. Franklin clearly intended to exploit the circumstances of war to reverse the 1774 resolution favoring the smaller colonies. Articles VI and VII of his draft proposed that representation and the common expenses should both be apportioned according to the same rule: the "Number of Male Polls between 16 and 60 Years of Age" residing in each colony; while Article VIII, though loosely drawn, provided that each delegate would have one vote, with all questions presumably to be decided by a majority of the members present. The equation between expenses and representation was unquestionably designed to dramatize the justice of the larger colonies' claims for reapportionment. But at the same time Franklin may have hoped to allay the smaller colonies' fear of subjugation by incorporating a simple formula for allocating the costs of war within the confederation itself, thereby removing it as a source for later political dispute. Too, by allowing the delegates to vote individually, rather than weighting each delegation's vote, Franklin may have meant to suggest that interests which transcended provincial boundaries would be effectively represented in Congress, and that many questions would arise which would bear no relation to the size or corporate integrity of the colonies.

By contrast, the Deane "Proposals" sought to strike a compromise between the resolution of 1774 and the logic of reapportionment. Deane proposed that each colony be given one delegate for every twenty-five thousand "Souls" of its population, and that "In determining on Supplies of Men, or Money, and in passing Accts. Laid before them & other Concerns of a Lesser Nature," a simple majority of the delegates would be decisive. But, "In determining on Warr, or peace, on the privileges of the Colonies in General, or of any one in particular"—that is, on all those issues of general policy that had been so critical in 1774 and in which all the colonies were presumed to have an equal interest—"a majority both of Colonies, and Numbers [i.e., delegations and delegates]" would be required. In embryonic form, this was the genesis of the Connecticut Compromise of 1787, which would solve the problem of continental representation by allowing the states to be represented both as aggregates of population and corporate units.

The Deane and Franklin drafts shared a second major similarity: both defined the respective powers of Congress and the colonies in terms that seem remarkably brief and imprecise, coming after a decade of sensitive debate over the proper relation between the colonies and Parliament. Only four of Franklin's thirteen Articles and seven of Deane's sixteen dealt with this problem directly; neither draft provided the colonies with explicit safeguards against the abuse of congressional authority. Both implied, in effect, that the duties appropriate to these two levels of Revolutionary government could be readily agreed on. Franklin suggested that "Each Colony shall enjoy and retain as much as it may think fit of its own present Laws, Customs, Rights, Privileges, and peculiar jurisdictions within its own Limits," including a right to "amend" its existing charter. Congress in turn would be entrusted with powers of deciding on war and peace, foreign alliances, and reconciliation; resolving disputes between colonies; planting new colonies; and making "such General ordinances"—commercial, financial, postal, and military—as "particular assemblies cannot be competent to." Deane scarcely bothered to enumerate the powers of Congress, contenting himself instead with allowing each colony, "in every respect, [to] retain its present mode of internal police & legislation," while prohibiting the colonies from entering into separate negotiations "with those with whom they are, or may be, Contending," or from levying duties "on any Wares, or Merchandize," without the permission of Congress. The proceeds of such duties would go to the continental treasury. Congress was empowered to resolve disputes between colonies, but only after their own efforts at mediation had failed. Concerned with the restoration of a semblance of legal government throughout America, Deane also suggested that Congress should appoint the governors and lieutenant governors of the royal, but not the proprietary, governments; councillors, judges, and other royal officials in those colonies were to be elected by the lower houses of assembly, to serve during good behavior, and to have a right of appeal to Congress if they were "displaced" and felt themselves "injured."

If the intended scope of congressional power could be measured by the absence of clear limits and precise restraints, both plans would have given Congress substantial authority indeed. Yet there is little evidence to suggest that Franklin and Deane were consciously thinking of using confederation to enhance the authority of Congress at the expense of the colonies. What seemed to be at stake in 1775 was not the creation of an enduring nation state but the continued legitimation of a resistance movement whose responsibilities were rapidly growing more extensive and complex. Both drafts therefore gave as much if not more attention to confirming the status of Congress—fixing its size and composition, basic rules of procedure, time and place of meeting —as to defining its powers. Such an offhand treatment of what would otherwise be regarded as the central problem of constitution-writing remained possible because the apparent ease with which Congress had acquired and exercised power suggested that the extent of its authority was *not* a subject of major political concern. Congress already possessed unquestioned control over the conduct of war and diplomacy; it was issuing bills of credit to serve as a circulating currency; and through the Association it had enacted regulations affecting the daily activities of thousands of Americans. If in the name of preserving the unity and security of resistance it now seemed sensible to allow Congress to settle disputes between colonies or, as Franklin proposed, supervise Indian relations, did this mark any great departure from prevailing notions of its responsibilities?

Nevertheless, had these plans been exposed to serious discussion, their elastic definition of the authority of Congress would almost certainly have been challenged. The Connecticut plan that was published in early March 1776 seems to have been framed with this consideration in mind. Its clarity and precision contrasted sharply with the verbal looseness of its predecessors —in part a mark of the evident haste with which the two earlier drafts had been written. More revealing were the limits the Connecticut plan would have imposed on the powers of Congress. Unlike the Franklin plan, it did not empower Congress to create new colonies, regulate commercial and financial affairs, or act in those matters affecting the general welfare that "particular assemblies cannot be competent to." Other clauses strengthened the residual rights of the colonies by explicitly reserving to each colony "the sole government and direction of its internal police," while forbidding Congress "to impose or leavy taxes, or interfere with the internal policy of any of the Colonies." In several places it replaced the vague wording of the earlier drafts with explicit clauses that would be easier to interpret. Thus where Franklin had granted Congress a blanket power to resolve disputes between colonies, the Connecticut plan stipulated that Congress could "hear and determine controversies between Colony and Colony according to the right of the parties by the rules of law or equity." And where Franklin barely mentioned the continental army, the Connecticut plan devoted an entire Article to the appointment of officers and the regulation of the militia.

Yet these revisions notwithstanding, most of the provisions of the Connecticut plan remained essentially similar to the two earlier drafts. As before, Congress retained exclusive authority over all major aspects of resistance, including the conduct of foreign policy, decisions of war and peace, and the regulation of the army; as before, all matters of "internal police" were reserved to the colonies, though now somewhat more explicitly. The Connecticut plan preserved Franklin's formula equating the apportionment of representation and common expenses; and it amended the Deane scheme of voting, by proposing that "the concurrence of a majority of the Colonies represented, and also a majority of the Delegates present, shall be necessary to make a vote of the Congress" on all issues—not merely, as Deane had suggested, those involving major policy decisions.

What, then, was the significance of the revisions the Connecticut plan did propose? Again, the absence of any contemporary discussion of its features forces us to rely on inference rather than concrete evidence. The Connecticut plan *was* more sensitive to the preservation of the autonomy of the colonies than the earlier drafts. Yet on balance the restraints it would have imposed were probably intended not so much to redress an emerging constitutional imbalance between Congress and the colonies as to erect a rigorous boundary separating their respective spheres of authority. For the Connecticut plan retreated from Franklin's expansive notions precisely in those areas—the regulation of commerce and settlement of western lands—where the exercise of congressional power might bring the union into conflict with the specific interests of particular colonies. A confederation that confined the authority of Congress to the business of resistance might not prove adequate at some later date—a moot point in 1776—but it would have the advantage of encouraging its prompt and uncontroversial approval. For confederation was, as the debate over representation had already revealed, perhaps the first major issue that stood to compromise the rhetoric of Revolutionary unity by forcing each colony to weigh its interests against those of its "sisters." Its association with the specter of independence made confederation an inherently sensitive issue as it was, as North Carolina's refusal even to discuss the Franklin plan had shown.[15] Enough political contention would be generated by the creation of new colonial governments without the further complication of a controversial confederation. By carefully distinguishing and even isolating the spheres of congressional and provincial authority, the Connecticut plan was implicitly intended to minimize potential sources of conflict between them —a goal entirely consistent with the larger political considerations governing other congressional actions.

Outside of Congress, however, there were several whig leaders who did criticize the notion of strictly separating the provincial and federal levels of government or who believed that the colonies should not be left to their own devices in framing new constitutions. As early as December 1775, Joseph Hawley advised John Adams that "An American Parliament with legislative authority over all the colonies" should be promptly established. To Elbridge Gerry, then preparing to leave Massachusetts for the beginning of a long congressional career, Hawley was even more explicit. A confederation, he argued, should consist of "a Supreme Legislative and Executive instituted in a just proportion from all the colonies . . . with subordinate legislatures for each Colony"; and the decisions of the supreme legislature should be considered as "the most solemn acts instead of Recommendations" and "shall bind the whole and every part."[16] Other writers suggested that Congress should play a direct role in the reconstruction of provincial government. Thomas Ludwell Lee questioned whether the Virginia Convention should have included a "proviso which reserves to this Colony the power of forming its own government" in its resolutions calling for a declaration of independence. "Would not a uniform plan of government prepared for America by the Congress, & approved by the Colonies, be a surer foundation of unceasing harmony to the whole?" he asked his brother Richard Henry Lee. New Hampshire's John Wendell doubted that Congress could "interfere with the Civil Policy of any Colony," but thought it could recommend specific reforms for the new constitutions; while John Langdon believed that after independence Congress could go even further and "interfere in any Government that seems to go wrong."[17]

Nevertheless, these were minority views, possibly more attractive to local observers upset by trends in provincial politics than to members of Congress concerned with husbanding their own authority. While America had remained poised between independence and reconciliation, it had been necessary for Congress to retain the prerogative of sanctioning changes in the colonial governments on an individual basis—the precedent established in the case of Massachusetts. But the pressures of 1776 made this model of reform obsolete. Once independence became imminent, growing popular enthusiasm for a republican reformation and the natural temptation to imagine America as a society reduced to an actual state of nature led most whig thinkers to agree that the authority to reconstitute legal government now rested in the people at large. "Every Province should be viewed as having a right, either with or without an application to the Continental Congress, to alter their form of Government in some particulars," ran the argument of "Spartanus," one of the more radical writers of 1776. When Congress issued its May 15 resolution demanding the creation of new governments "under the authority of the people," it formally recognized the emergence of a new constituent power.[18]

The role of Congress or a confederation received little attention when Americans began debating the reconstruction of their governments, however. Public discussion centered instead on devising suitably republican constitutions for the individual states. Tracts on government seldom gave more than a paragraph to describing the general powers of Congress. Moreover, a broad consensus about its role prevailed among writers with such markedly divergent opinions as John Adams, his Virginian protagonist Carter Braxton, and the anonymous authors of two ardently republican essays, "The Interest of America" and *Four*

Letters on Interesting Subjects. Each could have endorsed Braxton's encapsulated view that Congress should "have power to adjust disputes between Colonies, regulate the affairs of trade, war, peace, alliances, &c. but they should by no means have authority to interfere with the internal police or domestic concerns of any Colony." Adams was similarly succinct. A confederation, he wrote at the conclusion of his *Thoughts on Government,* should consist of a Congress whose "authority should sacredly be confined to these cases, namely, war, trade, disputes between colony and colony, the post-office, and the unappropriated lands of the crown." Braxton, a delegate from land-rich Virginia, would have contested only the last point.[19]

The writers of 1776 found no contradiction between advocating an avowedly republican reform of the provincial governments and recommending that Congress be endowed with substantial authority over matters of general concern. Joseph Hawley could argue that the decisions of Congress should be literally binding on the colonies but still express a hope that "all the colonies . . . will as soon as possible assume Popular forms of Government and indeed become several little republicks—I freely own myself a republican and I wish to see all Government on this Earth republican, no other form is a Security for right and virtue." A writer like "Spartanus" could assert that Congress "should not interfere or meddle with Provincial affairs, more than needs must," and add that not only every colony but "each county, yea, and each town, [should be left] to do as much within themselves as possible." Yet in the end, he admitted, "some things must be left to the General Congress," and his list of its responsibilities was no less generous than others:

1. Making, and managing war, and making peace. 2. Settling differences between provinces. 3. Making some maritime laws, or general regulations respecting trade; otherwise one Province might unjustly interfere with another. 4. Ordering a currency for the whole Continent, for it would be best, that as soon as may be, there should be one currency for the whole. The General Congress might order the quota for each Province. 5. The forming of new Provinces. 6. The sale of new lands. 7. Treaties with other nations, consequently some general direction of our Indian affairs.

Moreover, the powers that such writers agreed Congress should possess were to be exercised freely. The author of *Four Letters*

on Interesting Subjects, one of the most innovative and democratic pamphlets of 1776, argued that "in matters for the general
good," Congress "ought to be as free as assemblies" and unfet-
tered by "[p]ositive provincial instructions [which] have a tendency to disunion."[20]

Perhaps because tory polemicists engrossed the market for
criticism of Congress, none of the whig writers of 1776 subjected
the extensive powers it was exercising to serious constitutional
scrutiny. Thus while the creation of new provincial governments
generated intense and complex debate, the problem of confederation was treated with a remarkable casualness. In part, of
course, this disparity reflected the essentially provincial character of American society, where local arrangements of power
deeply affected areas of vital interest to large numbers of citizens. Yet in 1776 and the years to come, the real power Congress
exercised was also substantial. Its decisions about war and peace,
currency and supply, may often have been difficult to implement, but they were scarcely trivial in their consequences. And
Congress was itself a novel political entity whose anomalous
character defied conventional description and therefore deserved consideration. Nevertheless, the popular impulse to reexamine the basic principles of government exhausted itself at the
provincial level of politics.[21] Only in Connecticut—whose existing charter, widely regarded as a model for republican government, required no revision—was a serious question raised about
the status of Congress when a Litchfield County convention proposed that members of Congress be elected by the people.[22]

For the most part, it was left to the delegates themselves to
raise occasional objections about the authority of Congress. Oliver Wolcott, a new member from Connecticut, wondered
whether the Litchfield proposals would not remove delegates
from the effective supervision of their assemblies and leave the
colony "absolutely bound ... by every Act their Delegates should
do, as they would have all the Authority absolutely and indepen-
dently which the People could give them." Abraham Clark of
New Jersey worried that Congress might gain absolute control
over the colonial militia. Thomas Jefferson thought the new constitutions should restrict the delegates' tenure and eligibility for
reelection. And after Congress partially sanctioned an abortive
scheme to remove the proprietary governor of Maryland, that

colony's delegation expressed reservations about the potential abuse of congressional power.[23]

Such objections were consistent with the Connecticut plan's emphasis on maintaining a clear separation between Congress and the colonies; they did not, however, change the general atmosphere in which the problem of confederation was initially considered. The deference that Congress commanded in the early years of the Revolution left it immune from close theoretical scrutiny. Removed from the daily exercise of coercive power, charged with framing general policies that all patriots felt obliged to support, venerated as "the collective wisdom" of the continent, Congress seemingly did not need to be subjected to the same constitutional restraints that other levels of government required.

The Dickinson Plan

THROUGH the early months of 1776, John Dickinson had resisted allowing Congress to discuss confederation; only in late May did he acknowledge that its preparation could no longer be delayed.[24] Given his reluctance, it might seem surprising that Dickinson rather than Franklin was named as Pennsylvania's representative to the thirteen-man committee appointed on June 12 to draft articles of confederation.[25] But, once appointed, it is less surprising that he played a dominant role in the committee's labors. His colleagues had always valued his literary talents, and framing a confederation was the sort of political activity that Dickinson would have relished, even as he was privately preparing to resign from Congress.

With Dickinson's first draft, far more lengthy and complex than any of its three predecessors, discussion of confederation shifted to new and more expansive ground. Recognizing that only Congress as a whole could resolve the politically sensitive problems of apportioning representation and expenses, he skipped over the issues that had seemed most troublesome in 1774 and 1775, leaving a blank space in his manuscript for the later insertion of the approved solutions. For Dickinson, the problem of confederation involved more than alleviating the most obvious potential sources of jealousy among the states. His ideas reflected instead the fears of division and disunion that moderate delegates, particularly those from the middle colonies, had voiced during the previous months, as America drifted gradually but inexorably toward independence. What concerned Dickinson was not only the allocation of votes and expenses but a wider range of issues that stood to precipitate conflicts both within and between individual states as well as between the states and Congress. Implicit in his conception of confederation, then, was the premise that the states were incapable of entirely regulating their activities in the best interest of union, and that any plan of confederation would therefore have to impose restraints on their sphere of action—and not merely in areas that obviously required the general direction of Congress. Dickinson rejected the underlying thrust of the Connecticut plan, which had sought to block out exclusive spheres of authority for Congress and the states. He envisioned a confederation whose own needs would enjoy clear precedence over the rights of the states; that would be empowered to interfere in some aspects of their internal police; and that would limit their ability to exercise powers inimical to the union.

Dickinson revealed something of his concern by devoting the early portion of his draft to Articles restraining the authority of the states. He accepted the common formula used by the Franklin and Connecticut plans to reserve to each colony "as much as it may think fit of its own present Laws, Customs, Rights, Privileges, and peculiar Jurisdictions," but to it he added the proviso, "in all Matters that shall not interfere with the Articles of this Confederation." Moreover, in Dickinson's view this confirmation of "present" laws and practices did not confer upon the states an absolute control over the future regulation of their internal police. For in the very next Article—the most innovative of the entire draft—Dickinson plunged into a topic that was intimately connected with government and politics in virtually all of the states: the rights of religious dissenters. Here Dickinson sought to freeze the pattern of church-state relations existing in each of the states by prohibiting the new governments from enacting any additional laws requiring dissenters to support established churches, imposing religious tests as a qualification for holding office or exercising any other civil liberty, and compelling "persons conscientiously scrupulous of taking an oath" to swear the same, "it being the full Intent of these united Colonies," the Article concluded,

that all the Inhabitants thereof respectively of every Sect Society or religious Denomination shall enjoy under this Confederation, all those Liberties and Priviledges which they have heretofore enjoyed, without the least abridgement of their civil Rights for or on Account of their religious Persuasion, profession or practise.

Although such language implicitly endorsed liberal notions of religious toleration, Dickinson was not calling for an immediate, total disestablishment of religion. Each of these clauses contained a stipulation sanctioning the validity of "the usual Laws & Customs subsisting at the Commencement of this war." His immediate concerns were more narrowly political, and thus provide a key for understanding his distinctive approach toward confederation. Recognizing the extent to which sectarian rivalries lay at the very center of domestic political strife—most dramatically in the middle colonies, where a Presbyterian "interest" stood opposed to Quakers in Pennsylvania and Anglicans in New York, but to lesser degrees elsewhere as well—Dickinson hoped to use the confederation to prevent religious hostilities from being injected into the foreseeable struggles for power that would accompany the formation of new state governments. By allaying fears that dominant sects might use their political power to harry their opponents, adoption of this Article might dampen, and possibly even eliminate, a dangerous source of internal conflict.

Succeeding Articles sought to assert the superiority of the confederation in other ways. There was nothing novel in forbidding the states to conduct negotiations with foreign nations, but Dickinson went further by proposing that the states not be allowed to "enter into any Treaty, Confederation, or Alliance whatever" with each other, "without the previous and free Consent & Allowance of the Union." The next two Articles would have prohibited the states from enacting measures discriminating against the inhabitants of other colonies, most importantly in matters of trade, where it was provided that "The Inhabitants of all the united Colonies shall enjoy all the Rights Priviledges Exemptions & Immunities in Trade Navigation & Commerce in every Colony, and in going to & from the same, which the Natives of each Colony enjoy." The states were individually authorized to lay duties on imports and exports, but not in violation of foreign treaties concluded by Congress. Where the Connecticut plan had prohibited Congress from maintaining a standing army in time of peace, Dickinson reversed the prohibition and applied it to the states. He also proposed that, under certain circumstances, Congress could raise troops within a state without the approval or participation of local authorities. And in case a state felt that it had been unfairly treated by Congress in matters regarding the amount of its "Losses or Expenses," it could not "endeavour by Force to procure Redress of any Injury or Injustice supposed to be done . . . by not granting to such Colony or Colonies such Indemnification, Compensation, Retribution, Exemption or Benefits of any kind, as such Colony or Colonies may think just and reasonable." Nor could individual states make war against Indian tribes without the permission of Congress. A further Article barred the purchase of any Indian lands until the territorial limits of the colonies had been ascertained; after which time all future purchases were to be made through the authority of Congress and for the benefit of the union.

The committee on confederation, which met "at all opportunities" during the second fortnight of June 1776, did make several changes in Dickinson's prohibitory Articles.[26] It rejected outright the Article on religious toleration and the provision authorizing Congress to raise troops without the intercession of state officials.[27] A clause prohibiting the states from laying duties or regulatory fees on imports from other states was also deleted. But the drafting committee let stand the other restrictions Dickinson had proposed to circumscribe the residual authority of the states. Changes in wording clarified their meaning or made them seem slightly more innocuous but did not defuse their essential implications. Although we know virtually nothing about the internal workings of the committee, it seems likely that Dickinson was able to persuade his colleagues that most of these restrictions should be retained.

The committee may have been more actively involved in the task of detailing the positive powers and functions of Congress, which were extensively described in Article XVIII of the revised draft that was presented to Congress on July 12. The manner in which this Article appears in the first draft—with numerous interlineations, marginal notes and queries, deletions, and a separate sheet of revisions and additions—strongly suggests that it was subjected to considerable debate and emerged as the work of the whole committee.

The committee rejected several of Dickinson's most innovative proposals. It deleted a clause assigning Congress sole power for "establishing & regulating Fees" arising from interstate commerce, and it was unresponsive to Dickinson's suggestions that Congress be empowered to lay embargoes or call out the militia without the approval of the state governments. A provision for the appointment of "a Chamber of Accounts, an Office of Treasury, a Board of War, & a Board of Admiralty" was likewise omitted, thereby precluding discussion of the utility of formally dividing the confederation into legislative and executive branches. Dickinson himself questioned whether the status of these administrative agencies had to "be defined, as they are to act under the Congress." The committee decided instead that it would be sufficient to empower Congress to appoint a "Council of State" —whose authority, because it would operate only during the recess of Congress, was detailed at length in the following Article —"and such committees and civil Officers as may be necessary for managing the general Affairs of the United States."

Despite these revisions, however, the powers that Article XVIII would have given Congress were extensive. The most important, granting exclusive control over peace and war and the conduct of foreign relations, were probably also the least controversial. Other clauses relating to the administration of the army and navy and the general conduct of the war were unlikely to have produced serious differences of opinion. To give Congress exclusive control over war and diplomacy, to allow it to emit bills of credit, borrow money, and apportion the common expenses among the states, merely ratified the pragmatic and virtually instinctive decisions and precedents that had been adopted since 1774, and that only tories had opposed.

Where the Dickinson plan went further was in conferring on the union the exclusive power of "Settling all Disputes and Differences now subsisting, or that hereafter may arise between two or more Colonies concerning Boundaries, Jurisdictions, or any other Cause whatever," and in giving Congress virtually absolute control over the disposition of western lands, including the powers of "Limiting the Bounds" of colonies whose charters, like Virginia's, purportedly ran to the South Seas, and creating new states in territories "to be thus separated" from the older states or purchased from Indians. Just as sectarian differences loomed as one of the most ominous sources of political dispute within the states, so the control of unsettled or disputed lands seemed to constitute the greatest obstacle to harmony among them. The Susquehannah controversy remained a source of conflict between Pennsylvania and Connecticut. Within Congress, much of the animosity that regularly separated the New York and New England delegations could be traced to the problem of Vermont, whose residents had taken advantage of the Revolution to secede from New York.

Even more important were the resentments that states lacking western lands harbored against those whose colonial charters gave them possession of enormous tracts across the mountains. Although the politics of western lands were often manipulated by small groups of speculators who were intent on invalidating the claims of Virginia, the landless states' persistent efforts to create a national domain also had a more substantive foundation. States such as Virginia and Connecticut could expect to defray much of their share of the war's cost by selling their western lands to the settlers who were likely to emigrate there in the near future. But the landless states would be obliged to raise their portion by taxation, a problem that would be exacerbated in the case of Maryland, Delaware, and New Jersey—the three states most strongly committed to the idea of a national domain—by their commercial dependence on either Philadelphia or New York.[28]

Against the potential abuse of all these powers, Article XVIII offered four securities. Congress could not "impose or levy any Taxes or Duties . . . nor interfere in the internal police of any Colony, any further than such Police may be affected by the Articles of this Confederation." None of its major powers could be exercised without the approval of delegations from nine states, or any other question decided without the votes of seven. Finally, certain restrictions would be placed on the delegates themselves: they could serve only three years out of every six in Congress; must not simultaneously hold any other salaried office under the United States; and would be subject to recall at any time. Congress would be required to publish its journals monthly, and to record and enter roll calls whenever any delegate requested. But nothing in the Dickinson plan suggested that the states enjoyed a discretionary right to judge or refuse to obey decisions of Congress.

In drafting and revising these Articles, Dickinson and the committee seem to have intended to present as comprehensive a plan as possible, recognizing that many of their proposals were inherently controversial and would have to be, as Dickinson periodically noted on his copy of the second draft, "submitted to Congress" for thorough reconsideration. This would clearly be the case with all provisions relating to the disposition of western lands, as well as the solutions the committee proposed for the familiar problems of voting and expenses: retaining the formula of one vote for each colony, but apportioning the quota of expenses according "to the Number of Inhabitants of every Age, Sex and Quality, except Indians not paying Taxes." Whether the committee in general supported Dickinson's conception of confederation or merely believed that it provided a usefully broad basis for further debate is uncertain; none of its members figured prominently in the fragmentary notes of later debates recorded by Jefferson and John Adams.

But for Dickinson, at least, these Articles were consistent with the concerns he and other moderates had previously voiced while warning Congress of the dangers of disunion. When to both drafts Dickinson added a marginal query suggesting "The Propriety of the Union's garranteeing to every colony their respective Constitution and form of Government," he certainly conveyed his fear that the creation of new constitutions would produce political turmoil within the states. When he proposed creating a national domain or prohibiting the states from discriminating against each other's citizens, he recognized how easily questions of interest could evoke interstate conflicts. Dickinson clearly intended to use confederation as a vehicle not only for defining the powers of Congress but also for limiting the authority of the states. Yet in its essential provisions, the Dickinson plan was neither a blueprint for consolidating thirteen provinces into one unitary polity, nor an attempt by alarmed "conservatives" to counter excessively democratic or "leveling" tendencies in the states by transferring power to a strong national government. The right of the states to maintain their own systems of taxation, economic regulation, currency finance, and jurisprudence—all those aspects of "internal police" that most substantially affected actual competition among rival classes and

CONFEDERATION

interests—remained unimpaired. Expansive as the Dickinson plan was, its dominant concerns were still centered on resistance. The restraints to be imposed on the states were largely designed to preserve existing congressional prerogatives and autonomy in all matters affecting the conduct of war and diplomacy, or to minimize the most obvious sources of internal conflict capable of disrupting the unity that all whig leaders continued to agree was necessary to American success.

Congress Debates

THE committee submitted its report to Congress on July 12. By then, John Dickinson had left Congress, apparently with a sense of relief, for in early August he informed Charles Thomson that "no youthful Lover ever stript off his Cloathes to step into Bed to his blooming beautiful bride with more delight than I have cast off my Popularity." In his absence, there seems to have been no one left to defend his conception of confederation, and in the debates that took place between mid-July and August 20, important revisions were made by the committee of the whole.[29]

Yet on two critical questions the committee's recommendations survived the general debate intact. Despite strenuous objections from members representing more populous states, Congress agreed to continue to vote by states. The opposing arguments had changed little since 1774, but now they were expressed with a new vehemence and impatience, perhaps in part because two Scots, James Wilson of Pennsylvania and John Witherspoon of New Jersey, played a leading role in the debate. The apparent absurdity of according Rhode Island equal weight with Massachusetts—"by the effect of magic," Wilson scoffed, "not of reason"—again encountered the insistent fear that, as Witherspoon asserted, "if an equal vote be refused, the smaller states will become vassals to the larger." How their enfeoffment would come about remained obscure; Jefferson and Adams recorded no answer to Wilson's retort that "I defy the wit of man to invent a possible case or to suggest any one thing on earth which shall be for the interests of Virginia, Pennsylvania & Massachusetts, and which will not also be for the interest of the other states." But there was little room for compromise. Roger Sherman repeated the cumbersome suggestion advanced in the Connecticut plan, that a majority both of delegations and delegates should be required for any decision; while Samuel Chase proposed that all money matters should be approved with "the voice of each colony . . . proportioned to the number of it's [*sic*] inhabitants," an ingenious suggestion that would have applied the logic of reapportionment to the one area of public policy where it seemed particularly appropriate. Neither of these hybrid schemes was considered practicable. John Adams attempted to break this impasse by reminding Congress that "the question is not what we are now, but what we ought to be when our bargain shall be made . . . we shall no longer retain our separate individuality, but become a single individual as to all questions submitted to the confederacy." Therefore, he concluded, "all those reasons which prove the justice & expediency of equal representation in other assemblies, hold good here." Logic alone, however, could not overcome the instinctive objections of the smaller states. They were more stubborn, while the larger states at least knew they could never be "swallowed" by the smaller. The practice of voting by states therefore remained unchanged.[30]

The committee of the whole also approved the proposed formula for apportioning expenses to the total population of each state. When Samuel Chase moved that only "white inhabitants" should be counted, an ugly debate ensued, centering on the question whether slaves should be regarded as property akin to farm animals, or as productive workers who contributed as much to the wealth of a state as the free farmers and artisans of the north. Here, too, the opposing interests were too sharply drawn for compromise, and Chase's amendment was defeated in a strictly sectional vote.[31]

On these two questions, then, the suggestions of the drafting committee were adopted. But when Congress began debating the substantive powers to be lodged in the confederation, it made several major changes in the Dickinson plan. Every provision giving Congress exclusive authority over the American interior was struck out: Article XIV, governing the purchase of Indian lands; Article XV, on determining state boundaries; and those clauses of Article XVIII empowering Congress to create a national domain from the excessive western claims of the landed states and other territory wrested from British control during the war. The claims of Virginia had, for the moment, prevailed against the ambitions of Maryland, some of whose leading politicians were personally interested in overturning Virginia's title. In addition to these revisions, Congress rejected the sixth and seventh Articles, which contained the prohibitions against state measures that would discriminate against citizens of other states.

These deletions suggest that most delegates had consciously repudiated Dickinson's essential notion of confederation. For while Congress did retain the clause giving the confederation sole authority to resolve disputes between states, it eliminated a potentially broad area in which its powers and the vested interests of individual states could easily overlap and come into conflict. The result was a plan whose remaining provisions were still largely the work of John Dickinson but whose conception lay closer to the notion of confederation advanced several months earlier in the Connecticut plan. The effective powers of government were to be divided into two general spheres of authority, with the respective functions of Congress and the states clearly and exclusively distinguished. The delegates thereby stripped the Dickinson plan of its original thrust. The "intestine divisions" that were now to be avoided no longer involved political conflict within or between states but centered instead on the possibility of competition between the states and Congress. Here as on other occasions Dickinson had devised a complex scheme designed to allay fears and answer objections that he found peculiarly alarming. Some of his colleagues certainly shared his fears, but Dickinson's remedies, which would have required Congress to impose its authority upon the states, threatened to raise as many problems as they would solve. This was what Edward Rutledge meant when he complained that the Dickinson draft shared "the Vice of all his Productions . . . I mean the vice of refining too much."[32] The American union would enjoy greater stability if the powers that seemed most appropriate to Congress and the states were rigorously defined and separated.

Underlying these revisions of July–August 1776 were growing doubts as to whether any draft of confederation that Congress could approve would be promptly ratified by the states. When debate had begun in July, several delegates predicted that the whole business could be quickly completed; but their optimism was soon dispelled. By late August, when Edward Rutledge complained that "we have made such a Devil of it already that the Colonies can never agree to it," the future progress of confederation seemed highly uncertain.[33] The decisions regarding representation, expenses, and western lands embodied in the text that Congress ordered printed on August 20 reflected no compromise or consensus but loomed instead as formidable obstacles to final agreement within Congress or ratification by the states. Each delegation had been forced to calculate how the interests of its constituents would be served as each of these issues was resolved, and each delegation had to ask whether any formal confederation should be concluded at all if satisfactory compromises were not reached. During the debate of 1776 threats of disunion flowed freely. James Wilson warned that Pennsylvania would never confederate if Virginia clung to its western claims. The Virginia delegates replied that those claims were inviolable, and that their constituents would never accept a confederation that required their sacrifice. Thomas Lynch, Jr., spoke for many southern delegates when he warned: "If it is debated, whether their slaves are their property, there is an end of the confederation." John Witherspoon was similarly adamant in opposing the arguments for proportional representation.[34]

The revisions made by the committee of the whole removed several of the provisions that the states in general might have found most objectionable, but they could not assuage all the reservations particular states would inevitably feel. After August 20 other concerns intervened to prevent the further consideration of confederation. But delay was, in any event, unavoidable: these three issues had evoked such conflicting interests that they were, for the time being, insurmountable. In the late summer of 1776, when Congress was still reasonably confident of its authority, it seemed more prudent to defer public discussion of confederation than to raise potentially controversial issues touching, in different ways, on the interests of all the states.

This caution and the character of the amendments made to the Dickinson plan suggest, therefore, that Congress was sensitive to the likely reception confederation would encounter in the states. Yet nothing in any of the three versions of the Dickinson plan indicates that the delegates believed that Congress was to be subject to the supervision or control of the states. As Congress would not be allowed to tamper with their internal police, the states were expected to obey and implement its decisions unequivocally. Indeed Article XII, which had enjoined the states from forcibly resisting congressional decisions "concerning the Services performed and Losses or Expenses incurred by every

Colony," was amended to read simply: "Every State shall abide by the Determinations of the United States in Congress Assembled, on all questions which by this Confederation are submitted to them."

In practice, then, this division of power meant that, in their separate spheres, both Congress and the states were to exercise certain functions of sovereign government, and that a division of sovereignty was implicit in the structure of American federalism from its very inception. The theoretical difficulties raised by such a division of power were formidable. Few political adages were more familiar than that which stated that *imperium in imperio* —a state within a state, or two sovereign authorities in one society—was "a solecism in politics." Although in their opposition to Parliament the colonists had in fact been groping toward modern theories of federalism, the notion that sovereignty ultimately had to reside in some one discernible place was still orthodox. Yet the most surprising feature of the drafts and deliberations of 1775–76 was, finally, that the question of sovereignty was never directly raised. No one had yet asked where sovereignty would be located when the principal functions of government were parceled out between Congress and the states.

CHAPTER VIII

Confederation Drafted

F OR eight months after the summer of 1776, discussion of
confederation ceased, a victim of more pressing concerns and
the delegates' inability to envision satisfactory solutions to the
problems of representation, expenses, and western lands. When
debate resumed in May 1777, the delegates quickly realized that
these issues remained intractable. Once again discussion lagged,
not to be resumed until early fall, when the British occupation
of Philadelphia forced Congress to flee to York. There confederation finally acquired an urgency it had previously lacked. Congress was anxious to capitalize on the victory at Saratoga to secure a French alliance at long last, and it was preparing to issue
its first set of comprehensive recommendations designed to cope
with the alarming specter of inflation. Because completion of the
Articles of Confederation would provide a vital boost for both
policies, Congress resolved to issue a recognizably imperfect
confederation. Some confederation, any confederation, was necessary, whatever defects it contained, and where satisfactory
compromises could not be arranged, solutions had to be imposed.[1]

Although the substantive differences between the final version of the Dickinson plan and the text Congress ultimately approved in mid-November 1777 scarcely warranted fifteen
months of delay, one critical change had been adopted during
the opening debates of May. With the arrival of Thomas Burke
from North Carolina, the membership of Congress included at

least one delegate who was prepared to articulate a theory of confederation founded on a belief in the primacy of state sovereignty. His arguments seemed compelling, and Congress quickly adopted a new Article affirming that the states were sovereign and that the confederation could exercise only those powers that were expressly delegated to it.

Yet it is questionable whether this redefinition of the theoretical nature of the union actually altered most delegates' perceptions of the extent and character of congressional authority. Few of Burke's colleagues shared his intense interest in the constitutional principles that the Articles of Confederation were to embody. They simply hoped that the Articles would be immediately ratified by the states. The opposition of Maryland destroyed that hope. Still insisting that the union should acquire control over western lands, Maryland refused to ratify until early in 1781. Unratified, the Articles could give Congress none of the additional support it desired; once ratified, they scarcely seemed adequate to the worsening problems Congress faced.

Thomas Burke
and the Problem of Sovereignty

IN the absence of a confederation, it was inevitable that awkward questions would occasionally arise about the proper relations between Congress and the states, many of which were themselves now operating under new constitutions of government. Although the reverses America experienced during the months after independence gave Congress little time to reconsider confederation, several discrete developments revealed how uncertain many delegates were about the precise extent of their authority. What, for example, was the legal status of a congressional recommendation? When Congress advised each state to offer grants of land to soldiers enlisting in the army, the Maryland Convention fired one of the first rounds of its campaign for a national domain by voting to substitute a cash bounty instead. Congress responded by passing a resolution that not only reaffirmed its initial proposal but declared that "the faith, which this house, (by virtue of the power with which they were vested,) has plighted, must be obligatory upon their constituents; [and] that no one state can, by its own act, be released therefrom. . . ." After Maryland issued another protest, however, Congress adopted a more conciliatory resolution, which temporarily prevented further controversy but left the basic constitutional issue unresolved.[2] A different problem was raised in November 1776 when Congress briefly considered sending continental troops to Delaware to suppress a resurgence of loyalist activity, even though Delaware officials had not requested assistance. Some members thought such an intervention would have exceeded the proper bounds of congressional authority.[3]

Two overlapping debates that took place in February 1777 evoked a more thoughtful examination of the respective rights of Congress and the states. One involved deciding whether Congress should approve the proceedings of a convention of the four New England states that had been held at Providence in December to discuss two pressing problems: the British occupation of Rhode Island and the general rise in prices.[4] Much of this debate centered on the wisdom of endorsing a plan of price regulation adopted by the meeting, an intricate and controversial subject in its own right. From the outset, however, the delegates were also concerned with another question: whether the meeting itself "was a proper one and whether it did not stand in need of the Approbation of Congress to make it *valid.*" Samuel Adams and R. H. Lee argued that the states had an inherent right to consult one another whenever they wished, and that because "we were not yet confederated . . . no law of the Union infringed." James Wilson and John Adams replied that congressional approval was necessary because the convention had "touched upon continental Subjects." It was left to Benjamin Rush to restate the issue in more general terms. The real question, Rush asserted, was not whether the Providence proceedings required approval, but whether any meeting should have been held at all. "Their business was chiefly continental," he declared, "and therefore they usurped the powers of congress as much as four counties would usurp the powers of legislation in a state should they attempt to tax themselves." Partly because it would have been impolitic to offend New England by repudiating the convention, "All the Members agreed that the Meeting was right considering the circumstances"; but, William Ellery added, "after a long metaphysical debate which took up Part of three Days Congress were equally divided" as to whether the states had an inherent right "to meet without the prior or subsequent Approbation of Congress." This question, too, was thus left unresolved.[5]

The results of the other debate of February 1777 were less equivocal. At issue was a report recommending that the states should authorize "any constable, freeholder, or Keeper of any public ferry" to apprehend suspected deserters. The report had been amended to allow local committees of inspection to exercise the same power during the interval that would elapse before the states framed suitable enabling legislation. Protesting vehemently against the adoption of this amendment, Thomas Burke was able to procure its reconsideration, and in the ensuing debate he and James Wilson presented radically different views of the nature of the union.[6]

The central question in dispute was whether Congress, acting solely on its own authority, could continue to direct local agencies to execute its policies without the intermediate approval of the states. As Burke summarized the debate, "Mr. Wilson argued that every object of Continental Concern was the subject of Continental Councils, that all Provisions made by the Continental Councils must be carried into execution by Continental authority." Congress could therefore directly empower local officials to apprehend deserters. Wilson's position was predicated on the absence of any formal confederation defining or limiting the powers of Congress and, perhaps more forcefully, on precedents set during earlier phases of resistance, when "Congress had always directed their resolves to be put in Execution by Committees of Inspection and it was never denied that they had Power" to do so. Like other moderates from the middle states, Wilson believed that the creation of new constitutions had weakened rather than strengthened the hand of government by generating divisive political conflicts within the states, and thus that Congress might see its decisions implemented more efficiently if it continued to work directly through local committees and militia companies.[7]

In reply, Burke argued, repetitively but convincingly, that it was inherently dangerous to allow Congress to exercise coercive powers within the states,

That it would be giving Congress a Power to prostrate all the Laws and Constitutions of the states because they might create a Power within each that must act entirely Independent of them, and might act directly contrary to them, that they might by virtue of this Power render ineffectual all the Barriers provided in the states for the Security of the Rights of the Citizens . . . [that] the subject of every state was entitled to the Protection of that particular state, and subject to the Laws of that alone, because to them alone did he give his consent. . . . That the states alone had Power to act coercively against their Citizens, and therefore were the only Power competent to carry into execution any Provisions whether Continental or Municipal.

In this debate the advantage lay decisively with Burke because, unlike Wilson, he could support his position by pointing to the actual provisions of the new state constitutions and their attendant bills of rights. While Congress had postponed confederation, most of the states had acted to define the powers of their governments and the rights of their citizens. They had thereby ended the general state of constitutional uncertainty that had previously enabled Congress to operate much in the way Wilson described and hoped to perpetuate. The good of the "common cause" no longer provided a sufficient justification for the exercise of congressional power. Burke's argument was powerful, and when he was through, Wilson was forced to back down. R. H. Lee scoffed that "it was a Misfortune to be too learned," but John Adams admitted that the "articles of War must be enacted into Laws in the several States," if they were to have their desired effect.

What was striking about Burke's role in this debate was not only his success but his presumption. He had first appeared in Congress only three weeks earlier, as the Providence convention was coming under consideration. Unlike other new members who typically entered Congress somewhat unprepared for the duties and burdens awaiting them, Burke arrived with an acutely defined sense of his responsibilities. No other delegate was more determined to act strictly as an ambassador from a sovereign state or found that role, which was not easily maintained in the close quarters of Congress, more comfortable. On his first day in Congress he informed Governor Richard Caswell of his intention "hereafter to trouble you with a letter every post," and to "give my sentiments of the different political principles which I shall perceive to actuate the several States, the measures intended to be pursued, the intelligence we receive, and the important decisions in Congress." He was a scrupulous correspondent, and if Caswell actually had little use for the stream of letters and abstracts of debates he received from Burke, the historian is more fortunate, for they provide not only a valuable record of the doings of Congress and Burke's opinions but also, in their ingeniously, almost pompously self-serving style, a revealing insight into his character and temperament as well. In Burke, personality and politics fused: assertive and unyielding in debate, acutely sensitive to private honor and personal privilege, this youthful and ambitious Irish immigrant felt few compunctions about calling Congress back to what he perceived to be the first principles of republican government.[8]

The debates he witnessed during February and March 1777 only confirmed his intuitive reservations against concentrating power in Congress. Precisely because he was so intent on representing the interests of North Carolina, he detected numerous occasions when the rights and interests of other states seemed threatened. On his first day in Congress he noticed that "a considerable jealousy is entertained of the northern states." Three days later a debate about the declining level of attendance in Congress produced an attempt to "Embarrass several states." The next day a motion to raise the interest on loan office certificates seemed contrived to benefit some states at the expense of others. Another week passed, and Burke thought North Carolina slighted when arrangements were made for the middle and southern states to hold conferences similar to the Providence convention.[9]

At first Burke concluded that the threat to liberty lay in the ambitions of the landless states, which would "endeavour by degrees to make the authority of Congress very extensive" in order eventually to "pass resolves injurious to the rights of those states who claim to the South Seas." But when, in early March, he composed a lengthy letter summarizing his first five weeks of attendance at Congress, he found it less easy either to pinpoint the source of danger or to provide a coherent explanation for the conduct of his colleagues. Two seemingly contradictory observations troubled him. He was convinced that his fellow delegates were sincere patriots who were neglecting domestic pleasures and interests "to attend public business under many insurmountable difficulties and inconveniences," and who had no discernible "motives for increasing the Power of their body Politic." Yet his brief experience at Congress had already taught him "that *unlimited Power can not be safely Trusted* to any man or set of men on Earth." Why, then, was a Congress composed of "generous and disinterested" men so often preoccupied with debates about increasing its own power?[10]

Had Burke been able to identify factions that consistently favored or opposed the growth of congressional power, this question could have been quickly answered. But so convenient an alignment did not in fact exist. "The advocates do not always keep the same side of the Contest," he informed Caswell.

> The same persons who on one day endeavour to carry through some Resolutions, whose Tendency is to increase the Power of Congress, are often on an other day very strenuous advocates to restrain it. From this I infer that no one has entertained a concerted design to increase the Power; and the attempts to do it proceed from Ignorance of what such a Being ought to be, and from the Delusive Intoxication which power naturally imposes on the human Mind.

It was this "Delusive Intoxication" that would prove destructive of liberty, he believed, rather than any overt clash of parties committed to rival ideologies of nationalism or state sovereignty —parties whose existence this intensely suspicious man was unable to detect. Indeed, Burke's attempts to identify more immediate dangers and sinister motives were inconclusive. Although his most vivid fear was that Pennsylvania, Massachusetts, and Virginia would combine to subvert the liberties of the smaller states, he offered no example of the common interests they shared to make such a project reasonable. "Patriotism in America must always be partial to the particular States," he argued, for no man could gain political preferment except by satisfying his constituents; but he then illogically concluded that it was this provincial chauvinism that would make the confederacy dangerous to the states.

Burke was, in short, an unreconstructed whig whose image of power reflected the traditional axioms of eighteenth-century opposition thought, with its obsession with the insatiable and corrupting nature of power itself. His initial reaction against the dangers of an overmighty Congress was in part derived, it is true, from a genuine attachment to the importance of preserving the independence of the states—an attachment that many other delegates shared, but in a more abstract, less compelling way. It may also have reflected a sensible reaction to the history of his native Ireland, whose patronage-ridden subordination to a central government provided almost a perfect example of the dangers of corruption. Still, the remarkable rapidity with which Burke found his doubts confirmed suggests that his convictions were sparked by an academic understanding of power rather than the experience of its exercise, and this set him apart from most of his colleagues. Their approach to the problem of confederation was increasingly governed by immediate pressures of finance, diplomacy, and the need to enhance the authority of Congress. But Burke, the newcomer, viewed this issue in terms of framing an enduring federal constitution, and was more concerned about indefinite future threats to liberty than current dangers. Indeed, as confederation was being completed in the fall, Burke confessed to Caswell: "I fear I differ very widely on this subject with a majority of Congress. I deem a time of peace and tranquility the proper time for agitating so important a concern"—a luxury other members felt Congress could not afford.[11]

Nevertheless, when Congress resumed its consideration of confederation in late April, the novelty of Burke's perspective enabled him to secure what would become the most important addition to the Articles finally completed in November: a thorough revision of the Article reserving to each state "the sole and exclusive Regulation and Government of its internal police, in all matters that shall not interfere with the Articles of this Confederation." Burke thought this provision "resigned every other power" to the confederacy, and would allow later Congresses "to explain away every right belonging to the States and to make their own power as unlimited as they pleased." He therefore moved an amendment designed to affirm that "all sovereign power was in the states separately, and that particular acts of it, which should be expressly enumerated, would be exercised in conjunction, and not otherwise; but that in all things else each State would exercise all the rights and power of sovereignty, uncontrolled." The actual wording of his amendment was somewhat more ambiguous. It declared that each state would retain "its sovereignty, freedom, and independence, and every power, jurisdiction, and right, which is not by this confederation expressly delegated" to Congress.[12]

Everything we know about this revision comes from a letter Burke wrote a few days later, in which he recorded four intriguing aspects of its passage: that it was "at first so little understood that it was some time before it was seconded"; that R. H. Lee and James Wilson voiced the principal opposition; that eleven states voted in its favor, Virginia against, and New Hampshire divided; and finally, his own surprised pleasure in discovering "the opinion of accumulating powers to Congress so little supported." What inferences can be drawn from these statements?

One is that most delegates apparently found this amendment not merely less controversial than Burke anticipated they would, but also, as their initial lack of interest in it perhaps suggests, less significant than he believed it to be. Burke's conviction that his amendment was necessary rested, after all, on an opinion that his colleagues were insensitive to the growth of congressional power. Yet however dangerous he found the wording of the earlier draft of this Article to be, none of the delegates who had participated in the debates of 1776 would have imagined that it opened a path for the sort of tyranny Burke envisioned. They may have thought that Burke's amendment provided a modest shift in emphasis or a useful clarification of meaning, but not the critical transformation its author assumed it portended. The expansive language of the amendment would have the advantage of reassuring the states about the security of their rights—an important consideration, given existing doubts about the prospect for ratification—but until the powers that were to be "expressly delegated" to the union were enumerated, its actual impact on the authority of Congress remained speculative. Indeed, the excessive character of Burke's fears probably prevented him from realizing that his amendment was less innovative than he thought. Certainly Congress could scarcely have disposed of this issue so easily had it believed the basic structure of the confederation hinged on its outcome.

Although Burke did not summarize the arguments that were made against his amendment, the very fact that Lee and Wilson joined together in opposition is significant, for the two could not normally be called political bedfellows. Lee, the old radical, had been an early proponent of armed resistance, independence, and republican government; Wilson, an active member of the moderate caucus, had supported independence reluctantly and remained a severe critic of the new constitutions. Lee represented Virginia, with its vast western claims; while Wilson, a delegate from landless Pennsylvania, was himself one of the speculators interested in overturning Virginia's title. In 1787, of course, the two men also divided over the federal Constitution. At the very least, then, their joint opposition to Burke suggests the difficulty (if not futility) of attempting to transpose what little we know about alignments on other issues to the question of confederation, or of assuming that simplistic labels—"radical" and "conservative"—can be applied to the participants in this debate. If this vote did reflect some overt clash of nationalist and states'-rights ideologies, it is also difficult to explain why the New York members, who composed as "conservative" a delegation as any, would have supported Burke.

With these qualifications, it is nevertheless unquestionable that Burke made a critical contribution to the evolution of American notions of confederation. He was the first to ask how conventional ideas of sovereignty were to be reconciled with the establishment of a confederation. And once this question, hitherto surprisingly ignored, was posed, there could be little doubt that the states were a more appropriate repository for sovereignty than was the union. The states were the constituent parties of the union: they elected and instructed the members of Congress, and their consent was indisputably necessary for the ratification of confederation. The states possessed governments constructed in the normal meaning of the term, exercising legislative, executive, and judicial functions, while Congress remained, so to speak, structurally anomalous.

Yet Burke's solution was satisfactory only in the theoretical sense of defining the one locus where sovereignty ultimately had to reside. For a pragmatic division of the functions of sovereignty was, as has already been suggested, inherent in the nature of American union from the very start. The same confederation that would acknowledge the sovereignty of the states would also simultaneously detach substantial areas of authority from their control and expressly delegate these powers to Congress. And in the exercise of its exclusive responsibilities, Congress was not to be subject to the veto or even the supervision of the states. The framers of the Articles did not presume that the states were free to accept or reject congressional decisions as they pleased. Where the authority of Congress was clearly defined, implicit obedience was due to its decisions. The final draft of 1777 thus preserved the language of 1776: "Every State shall abide by the determinations of the United States, in Congress assembled, on all questions which, by this confederation, are submitted to them." The Articles contained no provision empowering Congress to use coercive authority against the states because, quite simply, it was difficult to believe they would willfully defy its decisions. By the early 1780's that presumption would seem naïve —though even then the inability of the states to comply with congressional policies was often more important than their refusal to do so; but in the context of 1777, it was consistent with the early experience of Congress.*

From this first success Burke evidently concluded that his colleagues would prove receptive to further changes, and in early May he introduced a second amendment, which sought both to provide additional safeguards against congressional power and to solve the persistent problem of apportioning representation. Burke proposed converting Congress into a bicameral legislature, composed of a General Council, where members

---

*Richard B. Morris has recently suggested that "The adoption of Burke's amendment does not necessarily mean that the Articles endorsed a 'compact' view of the formation of the Union, in which the states agreed to confederate and delegate limited aspects of their sovereignty to a central government. Rather, since the Articles recognized in Congress exclusive authority over peace and war . . . [it] may be read as simply retaining in the states all aspects of internal sovereignty not expressly delegated to the United States" (Morris, "The Forging of the Union Reconsidered: A Historical Refutation of State Sovereignty over Seabeds," *Columbia Law Review*, 74 [1974], 1057). Although Burke was critical of the range of powers the Articles assigned to Congress, he himself also admitted that "The United States ought to be as one Sovereign with respect to foreign Powers, in all things that relate to War or where the States have one Common Interest" (Burke, Notes on the Articles of Confederation [November 1777], in Edmund Burnett, ed., *Letters of Members of the Continental Congress* [Washington, D.C., 1921–36], II, 554). The question of where sovereignty initially resided is, of course, one of the oldest topics in American constitutional history, the source of what Gordon Wood has aptly characterized as "a continuing if fruitless debate . . . over the priority of the union or the states" (Wood, *The Creation of the American Republic, 1776–1787* [Chapel Hill, 1969], 355). Morris's essay provides, in my opinion, the most important and sensible analysis of this issue. His principal conclusion is that "The central government [i.e., Congress] alone possessed those attributes of external sovereignty which entitled it to be called a state in the international sense, while the separate States, possessing a limited or internal sovereignty, may rightly be considered a creation of the Continental Congress, which preceded them in time and brought them into being."

This conclusion is essentially consistent with the interpretation I have sought to develop in this book. A reconstruction of the precedents, events, and atmosphere of 1774–76 does not validate a states'-rightist interpretation of the origins of the union. In addition to congressional prerogatives over war and diplomacy, the procedures used to authorize the creation of new governments in 1775–76 clearly demonstrate that sovereign powers were vested in Congress from the

would vote as individuals and the states be represented according to some unstated rule of apportionment, and a Council of State, where each state would have one member. Every proposed act of Congress would be introduced in the General Council, "read three times and three times assented to," and would then require the approval of the Council of State. Once properly passed, "every act, Edict and ordinance" was to be considered "binding on all and Every of the United States."[13]

On this proposal, however, Burke met defeat: "the Qu: Shall the Congress consist of two houses passed in the Negative," Charles Thomson noted, "So whole dropt." According to the terse notes recorded on Burke's own copy of these resolutions, several objections were raised against his proposal. One was that it would produce "Delays in Execution." Procedural safeguards were laudable in theory but could well prove unwisely obstructive in time of war, when Congress had to act expeditiously. Indeed, some delegates questioned whether Congress was really

---

start and that the emerging provincial regimes were regarded as subordinate bodies. This view has recently been endorsed by Samuel H. Beer in his 1977 presidential address to the American Political Science Association, "Federalism, Nationalism, and Democracy in America," *American Political Science Review*, 72 (1978), 9–21.

In the search for constitutional precedents, then, "the national theory . . . is a superior version of what actually happened," as Beer has observed. Yet it is equally important to recognize the extent to which the location of sovereignty remained a potential source not only of conflict but—what was perhaps more revealing—of confusion as well. The precedents of 1774–76, the location of sovereign powers in Congress, many delegates' intuitive sense of responsibility to the union, and the detailed provisions of the Articles, all militated against what might be called an implicitly states'-rightist conception of the union. But other considerations worked against a protonationalist view: the framing of many state constitutions by specially elected conventions, the apparent thrust of Burke's Article, the inability of Congress to enforce its decisions, and a sense that the notions of popular sovereignty enshrined in emerging republican theory were workable at the state level but difficult to apply on any larger scale (a point Edmund Morgan has recently advanced in his review of the new edition of the delegates' correspondence, *New York Review of Books*, March 9, 1978, 17). The reconciliation of the conception of unitary sovereignty with the realities of an implicitly federal polity was thus a source of controversy and uncertainty even before 1787, not because the Articles endorsed state sovereignty, but because the issues were imperfectly understood. It was hardly surprising, therefore, that the post-Revolutionary decades produced a growing dispute over the priority of the union or the states. The emerging debate has been reexamined in Kenneth Stampp, "The Concept of a Perpetual Union," *Journal of American History*, 65 (1978), 5–33.

a legislative body at all, arguing instead that it was an "Executive Body resembling [the] King." According to this view, Congress had simply supplanted the crown in the exercise of two functions traditionally at the heart of royal power, war and diplomacy, functions that were executive in nature. Its apparent resemblance to a legislative body was thus both superficial and illusory, and Burke's proposal would merely compound the illusion. Finally, even admitting that Congress was a representative body, some delegates argued that Congress should represent either the states as corporate units or as aggregates of population, but not both. There should be "No Combination Except one or the other," because the "Idea of Distinctions resembl[ed the] British Constitution."

By rejecting this amendment, Congress lost a useful opportunity to consider two issues of more general importance. First, the very idea of bicameralism carried with it an implicit suggestion that the formal structure of the confederation should somehow conform to the divisions of authority customarily expected of other governments. Despite the substantial scope of its authority, Congress thus remained something of a theoretical anomaly, apparently not subject to the same laws and precautions that were meant to check the abuse of power in other governments. It was difficult even to find a term that would accurately describe the nature of Congress. Was it "a deliberating Executive assembly," as Burke would observe in 1779; "not a legislative but a diplomatic assembly," as John Adams asserted in 1787; or "both legislative and executive," as Thomas Jefferson noted in challenging Adams's definitions?[14] Second, though Burke favored bicameralism primarily as a check against the abuse of power, his amendment did offer a promising solution to the familiar problem of representation, one that in fact directly anticipated the eventual solution of 1787. That problem was in effect left unsolved, for any scheme of apportionment worked out within the confines of a single-chamber Congress would antagonize either the small or large states or require some hybrid scheme of voting that might well prove as cumbersome, and thus objectionable, as bicameralism.[15]

The defeat of this amendment marked the beginning of a growing separation between Burke and the rest of Congress over the importance of confederation. Even before these opening debates Burke had questioned whether a formal confederation was necessary or need comprise anything more than a "defensive alliance." During the months that followed, he continued his attacks against entrusting too much power to Congress, carrying them at year's end to the North Carolina assembly, which at first, under his prodding, gave the completed Articles only a partial ratification.[16] Other delegates who shared his belief in the importance of preserving the autonomy of the states came to detest him. James Lovell criticized his "obstinate Vanity"; William Whipple, who had once thought Burke "the best man I have seen from that Country," spoke derisively of his "Oratory and impudence"; and when Burke returned from North Carolina in March 1778, Eliphalet Dyer observed that "The Disturber—I mean B—ke has just come after Inducing N[or]th C[aroli]na to dissent from Confederation in a great part of it. [I]s now in Congress to the universal sorrow &c of every Member." Ironically, the man who had succeeded in incorporating the principle of state sovereignty in the Articles of Confederation emerged as that document's first major critic.[17]

Confederation Completed

ONCE the two Burke amendments were disposed of, discussion of confederation quickly foundered. The familiar problem of representation created the first snag, but the two other critical issues of 1776—western lands and common expenses—also reappeared in an obstructive role. Having discovered that these problems had survived the winter intact, Congress soon lost momentum. "We every now and then take it into Consideration," Samuel Adams noted at the end of June, but during the rest of the summer formal debate about confederation apparently ceased. Little that was new could be said about the old issues: the basic arguments and positions were too well defined. "I believe most if not all the Members have already made up their Minds," Adams informed James Warren, adding, "The Sentiments in Congress [on these issues] are not various, but as you will easily conceive, opposite." Turnover in the membership of Congress may have been a further source of delay; late in July, James Lovell observed that confederation had fallen a "martyr to the change in Delegation which takes place between the periods of second and third distant discussions upon the same point."[18]

With no workable compromises in sight, Congress turned to more pressing business. Privately, however, many delegates were chafing at this further delay. "I grant it should be well considered, and digested with judgement," R. H. Lee noted in mid-July during a brief stay at his Virginia plantation; "but such excessive refinement, and pedantic affectation of discerning future ills in necessary, innocent, and indeed proper establishments, I cannot bear with patience."[19] By early summer there was a growing feeling that Congress might soon be forced to decide whether a flawed confederation was not better than none at all. Even Charles Carroll, whose Maryland constituents had instructed him to oppose any plan that failed to give Congress control over western lands or that included slave labor in the assessable wealth of a state, thought that the impasse could not be allowed to continue indefinitely. "The absurd claim to the back lands will not be given up," he informed his father on June 23; "however I think it better to confederate even on these terms than not to confederate at all." Three days later he wrote:

I am pleased to find a very considerable, nay a very great majority of Congress as anxious for a confederacy as I am or you can be: the necessity of this measure is now obvious to every man, yet I fear the confederacy will not be formed on principles so mutually advantageous as it ought & might be, but in my opinion an imperfect & somewhat unequal Confederacy is better than none.[20]

Another three months would elapse, however, before Congress, fleeing Philadelphia and Howe's army for the isolated security of York, finally forced itself to resume discussion of confederation in early October.

No sudden compromise or conceptual breakthrough preceded this decision. The major outstanding issues remained immune to satisfactory compromises because each was too intimately involved with the calculated interests of the states to be neatly resolved. Yet after months of delay and equivocation, a point had been reached where virtually all of the delegates agreed that the necessity of completing confederation at last outweighed the inevitable danger that some states would be antagonized by whatever solutions were eventually imposed. Like other issues, confederation ultimately proved susceptible to the larger demands of resistance; and in the fall of 1777, two considerations—one financial, the other diplomatic—warranted its prompt completion and ratification.

After months of growing apprehension over the steady depreciation of continental currency, Congress was finally preparing its first comprehensive program to cope with inflation. Framed during the same period when it was debating confederation, this program called upon the states to initiate several drastic measures. They were to collect $5 million in taxes to be remitted to the continental treasury, cease their own emissions of paper currency, and impose both regional price restraints on "labour, manufactures, internal produce, and commodities imported from foreign parts" and temporary price controls on military supplies. Because these recommendations were more controversial and potentially more explosive than any of the requisitions for men and supplies that Congress had previously made upon the states, and because inflation was increasingly coming to be seen as the most dangerous source of popular "disaffection," the delegates realized they could no longer afford to ignore the nebulous character of their own authority. By itself confederation could not make tolerable measures that were inherently unpalatable. But it could help induce the state legislatures to enact the necessary taxes and regulations and, in more elusive ways, work to enhance popular confidence in Congress itself—a vital if unmeasurable component of the value of any paper currency. Simply demonstrating that a permanent federal union did exist might go a long way toward reassuring the public that its various financial instruments would ultimately be redeemed. The final approval and publication of this financial program was therefore to be delayed, William Williams noted in late October, because the delegates "conceive it will go out with much more weight with or after the Confederation."[21]

Diplomatic considerations were the second source of this new sense of urgency about confederation. Although the delegates lacked any reliable intelligence about the progress of their commissioners' negotiations with France, the course of the 1777 campaign fostered a new confidence that an alliance would soon be concluded, particularly after Congress received word of Burgoyne's surrender in mid-October. In 1777, as in 1776, the delegates believed that the existence of a formal confederation would strengthen their commissioners' bargaining position, partly as a matter of protocol, but also by providing the French court and other European powers with reassuring evidence of the new nation's political stability and its determination to secure independence. Like the Declaration of Independence before it, confederation was a diplomatic signal to potential allies; and in the fall of 1777, when Congress was eager to capitalize on Saratoga, it was a signal that could no longer be withheld.

Once the decision to resume debate was taken, Congress needed only ten days to resolve the issues that had impeded confederation so long. The questions of representation and western lands each required only a day of debate. On October 7, Congress rejected three motions for apportioning representation by population or the size of state contributions to the continental treasury, and reaffirmed that each state would have one vote. Only Virginia and a handful of other delegates, including John Adams, favored reapportionment; against the interests of their own states, Massachusetts and Pennsylvania voted with the majority.[22] The question of western lands was similarly resolved on October 15, when Congress rejected three proposals to allow the union to ascertain western boundaries and dispose of the lands lying beyond them. On the final vote on this issue, only Maryland and a lone New Jersey delegate were recorded in favor of national control of the American interior, though here too other states were interested in contesting the sweeping claims of the landed states.[23]

The problem of apportioning expenses among the states was more troublesome, and ultimately consumed five days of debate before Congress narrowly approved an amendment making the value of all granted lands, "and the buildings and improvements thereon," the standard to be employed. Here no compromise at all was possible. The four New England states voted solidly against this provision, believing that it was highly discriminatory against their region, whose lands were more densely settled and better improved than most of the other states. The four southern states present voted solidly in its favor, largely because slaves had been exempted from the formula. Pennsylvania and New York divided. New Jersey cast the deciding vote and may even have dictated this solution, since John Witherspoon had introduced an identical amendment during the debates of 1776.[24]

The remaining Articles of the August 1776 draft were reconsidered between October 21 and November 7. Six were approved as written. The states were still prohibited from negotiating with foreign powers; nor could they make formal agreements with one another or maintain naval or permanent military forces without the consent of Congress. Canada was again invited to join the union, but no other new state could be admitted without the approval of nine states. Perhaps most important, Congress again confirmed that "Every State shall abide by the determinations" of Congress "on all questions which by this Confederation are submitted to them." Two other Articles were marginally amended.

Two significant changes were made, however, in Article XIV, which detailed the powers and authority of Congress. After considerable debate, the delegates approved a proviso stipulating that "the legislative rights of any State, within its own limits [shall not be] infringed or violated" by any treaty Congress might make. Congress imposed a second limitation on its authority when it established a carefully detailed procedure for mediating disputes between states, an area where John Dickinson had originally hoped to see the union vested with broad powers. Although many of the clauses Dickinson had inserted toward that end had been trimmed during the revisions of 1776, the committee of the whole had retained a clause allowing Congress to decide "all disputes and differences" between states. This was now struck out. The quasi-judicial procedure erected in its place made Congress "the last resort on appeal" for resolving such disputes, but only after an aggrieved state had lawfully requested a hearing and other intermediate processes in which Congress would play a merely supervisory role had been exhausted. Article XV, which had initially enumerated the powers of the Council of State that was to meet when Congress recessed, was also thoroughly revised. The Committee of the States, as it was now called, was to perform whatever functions "the consent of nine states, shall, from time to time, think expedient," but not to reach decisions on matters normally requiring the assent of nine states.[25]

While each of these changes suggests that Congress was sensitive to the need for safeguards against its own power, the final phase of discussion witnessed the adoption of several additional provisions that marked a significant reversion toward John Dickinson's original conception of confederation. On November 10,

Congress appointed a committee to consider "sundry propositions" submitted as additional Articles. The committee acted
quickly, reporting seven Articles the next day. Of these, four
were adopted essentially as reported, two were approved with
significant amendments, and one authorizing Congress to discipline its own members was rejected. One clause pledged the
states and the public faith to the "Payment and Satisfaction" of
all charges and debts Congress had previously contracted, and
thus confirmed the states' obligation to implement the fiscal decisions of Congress while incidentally reinforcing the plan of financial reform Congress was about to recommend to the states. The
states would also be required to give "full Faith and Credit" to
each other's legal acts and to extradite persons accused or con-
victed of "treason, felony, or other high misdemeanor in any
State"—though Congress balked at extending the former provision to include the recovery of private debts or the latter to apply
to persons "charged or Suspected of any Crime." The new procedures for adjudicating disputes between states were extended to
cover "all controversies concerning the private right of soil,
claimed under different grants of two or more states." Finally,
Congress carefully considered and approved a set of four restrictions on the residual powers of the states. First, citizens of each
state "shall be entitled to all privileges and immunities of free
citizens in the several states"; second, they could travel freely
between states, "and shall enjoy therein all the privileges of trade
and commerce, subject to the same duties, impositions, and restrictions, as the inhabitants"; third, such restrictions could not
prevent them from removing personal property to their state of
residence; and fourth, no state could lay duties "on the property
of the United States, or either of them."[26]

Although these changes added nothing to the powers already
"expressly delegated" to Congress, the new restrictions they imposed on the states were similar to those originally proposed by
John Dickinson in 1776, and in apparent contradiction with the
theory of state sovereignty Thomas Burke had advanced in April
1777. Each of these prohibitions involved some function of government related to the internal police of the states but whose
exercise could prove inimical to the tranquility of the union.
The exercise of these prerogatives of sovereignty was not, however, to be transferred to the union, but simply denied to the
states. There were, in other words, some rights of sovereignty

that would neither be reserved for the states nor delegated to Congress. Without materially impairing the states' ability to regulate their own affairs, the confederation would nevertheless establish certain limits on their sovereignty other than those required by the exigencies of war and diplomacy.

With these additions approved, Congress immediately appointed a committee "to revise and arrange the articles." Their work, too, was quickly completed and laid before Congress two days later (on November 15). Their editorial labors made the final text agreed to that day more elegant and compact than its predecessor. Previously dispersed but related clauses were now united to produce a text numbering three fewer Articles than before, although little had been expunged while several new provisions had been added. Congress immediately ordered the Articles to be printed, but met with a few delays from its Lancaster printer, who would do only a page a day. "I had rather be a Hogg-driver," Jonathan Dickinson Sergeant complained, "than attend his press."[27]

In the meantime it approved a circular letter to the states that recalled "the difficulty of combining in one general system the various sentiments and interests of a continent divided into so many sovereign and independent communities," and urged that the Articles be given prompt consideration. Against the wishes of several New England delegates, who possibly hoped to organize opposition against the formula for apportioning expenses, Congress fixed March 10, 1778, as the date for proceeding with final ratification. If this note of haste contrasted all too visibly with their own dilatory proceedings, the delegates could nevertheless adduce numerous reasons for prompt ratification. "More than any other consideration," the circular letter observed, "it will confound our foreign enemies, defeat the flagitious practices of the disaffected, strengthen and confirm our friends, support our public credit, restore the value of our money, enable us to maintain our fleets and armies, and add weight to our councils at home, and to our treaties abroad."[28]

The Limits of Constitutional Thought

As it is difficult to avoid approaching the Articles of Confederation from the perspective of the Constitution, so, too, it is customary to portray these documents as the embodiments of two antithetical theories of federalism, one emphasizing the sovereignty of the states, the other the supremacy of the nation, and to conclude that the Revolutionary generation had to choose between their alternative conceptions of the nature of the union. In the context of 1787–88, that choice could clearly be made, since the perceived failings of the Articles inspired the framing of the Constitution. It does not therefore follow, however, that the Articles represented an explicit, conscious, prescient disavowal of the Federalist principles of 1787–88. The basic issues that were posed during the framing of the Articles differed sharply from many of those that arose a decade later; the Continental Congress and the Constitutional Convention did not confront the same alternatives. Although there were several important similarities between the two sets of debates—the problems of apportioning representation and expenses were as much at issue in 1787 as they had been before—the political conditions governing the framing of these two documents were radically different, and they deeply affected the way in which the critical issues were defined. The 1787 Convention drew upon years of congressional experience and of constitutional experiments in the states, and was able to conduct its deliberations at a leisurely pace, free from interruption and troubled only by the discomfort of a Philadelphia summer. The framers of the Articles enjoyed no similar advantages. The membership of Congress changed between different periods of debate, and even when the delegates mustered the will to resume discussion, they found, as Eliphalet Dyer complained in September 1777, that "ten thousand necessaries are dayly Crouding in" to hinder sustained progress.[29]

Conducted under these and other constraints, the debates of 1776–77 did not encourage the development of coherent, systematic, and rival ideologies of nationalism or state sovereignty. Thomas Burke and James Wilson were, in this respect, exceptional; they spoke, as Burke recognized, for no discernible factions in Congress but from their own unusually refined grasp of the central importance of the location of sovereignty. Most delegates probably accepted Burke's definition of state sovereignty without sharing his exaggerated fear of congressional power; most probably rejected Wilson's view of the inherent sweep of congressional authority without giving up an intuitive belief that in certain critical cases Congress must reign supreme.

Nor would it be accurate to describe the Articles as a victory of radical democrats over conservative nationalists. There is little evidence to suggest that those who were most critical of the prevailing character of state politics looked to the creation of a strong confederation for relief. It was James Duane who described the Articles as "a liberal Plan, calculated to establish general Security, and Social Intercourse, among the States; and to extinguish All territorial Disputes," and who thought that "There are only two points that can admit of much Debate: The *Equality* of each State in Congress; and the Ratio, for assessing their respective Quotas of the publick charges." It was Benjamin Harrison, commercial and political ally of Robert Morris, who worried that Congress had been endowed, through its treaty power, with the "power of regulating the Trades, and of course granting a monopoly of the whole, or any part of it to any Nation it pleases," and who was relieved when Morris relayed his personal opinion that Congress had no such authority.[30] And if, on the other hand, the Articles fulfilled the intentions of American radicals seeking to secure maximum autonomy for the states, it is difficult to understand why Burke so vigorously condemned the excessive powers they gave to Congress or why R. H. Lee should have criticized the "pedantic affectation of discerning future ills in necessary, innocent, and indeed proper establishments" that the North Carolinian, more than anyone else, evinced.[31]

The intellectual and imaginative boundaries that surrounded these first attempts at framing a national government are thus as revealing as the initial solutions mapped within them. At a time when constitution-writers in the states were displaying an acute sensitivity to redesigning the architecture of government, transferring power from executive to legislature, the framers of the Articles never thought of confederation as an exercise in creating a conventional structure of government. For the idea that the confederation was essentially only a league of sovereign states was ultimately a fiction. Congress was in fact a national government, burdened with legislative and administrative responsibilities unprecedented in the colonial past, and the most debilitating weakness it suffered ultimately lay in its own inefficiency. Aware that its reluctance to delegate power squandered time and energy, Congress nonetheless continued to concentrate its constitutional labors on distinguishing the powers of the union and the states, never considering whether its own internal workings did not pose more serious questions.

By the same token, the Articles did not establish regular procedures for coordinating the administration of the critical financial and logistical policies that were to be framed by Congress but largely implemented by the states. Most of the difficulties Congress later experienced in seeing its recommendations put into practice reflected the delegates' inability to imagine or devise effective means of coordinating state and national politics. Abstract designs of sovereignty could barely be tested in a system so prone to mechanical inefficiency, where the clash of sovereign wills mattered far less than irregular correspondence, dilatory proceedings in the assemblies and Congress alike, and the staggering array of problems that the war itself created. The delegates' failure to give serious attention to these aspects of confederation, understandable as it may have been, marked the limits of their earliest conceptions of the problem of union.

Nothing in the general reception the Articles received suggests that Americans were deeply interested in discussing the nature of the union they were forming. No pamphlets were written about them, and when the Articles were printed in American newspapers they appeared only as another scrap of news, probably less important than reports of victory at Saratoga and almost certainly less controversial than a growing number of essays proposing remedies for inflation. Only in New England were the people at large asked to comment on the Articles,[32] and the town meeting replies that the assemblies received were predictably concerned with the valuation of lands proposed in Article 8.*

The occasional references to confederation that appear in surviving private correspondence are either cursory or concerned with the necessity of its prompt completion. It was "of such infinite importance," General Henry Knox fulminated, "that my heart turns with horror from the man or men who

---

*The final draft of the Articles used arabic rather than roman numerals.

would in any wise impair it—it is so essential to our existence that
. . . I damn him who has any local attachments whatever" that
might impede its ratification, although that, he admitted, "perhaps is carrying the matter too far." The Articles must be
"Ratified by all the States," Josiah Bartlett was told by a New
Hampshire constituent, "for this Simple Reson that when any
Sociaty Gets Divided in Sentiment it is verry hard to unite
them." The New Hampshire assembly apparently agreed. Its
members had agreed to ratify the confederation, Bartlett informed the state's delegates, not from "an Opinion of the per-
fectness of the Articles," but rather because they believed it was
"a Matter of so much Importance" and because they appreciated
"the Difficulties naturally attending such an Union by so many
States differing in so many Circumstances."[33] It was thus the act
of confederating that mattered, not the substance of confederation. "An indifferent one is better than none," John Jay reminded
James Duane; "upon this Principle I mean for my own Part to
act." If the Articles and the exhortatory address accompanying
them have their "Weight," Duane replied, "the States will come
to a Conclusion to endeavour to obtain Improvements which
they conceive important, but to consent to the present Plan
rather than delay a Measure essential to their Safety."[34] Only
rarely did someone like Elisha Boudinot, a minor New Jersey
official, wonder whether a confederation based only on mutual
fear of a common enemy could last, or venture a "weak Opinion"
that "Congress have not reserved enough Power for themselves." Criticism of the Articles from the opposite perspective
was similarly rare. Thomas Burke did prepare a lengthy memorandum attacking their aggrandizing tendencies, while an anonymous newspaper essayist declared it would be dangerous to
allow Congress to appoint postal officials, "for it invests them
with too great a Power of Multiplying their Dependents, and
thereby endangering the States in Future."[35] But not until the
early 1780's did allegiance or antipathy to the Articles come to
represent reasonably coherent views about the nature of federal
government.

   Congressional reaction to the various amendments to the Articles that were proposed by the states demonstrated the delegates' continuing commitment to ratification for its own sake.
Not surprisingly, the initial March date for proceeding with ratification proved impractical. Another three months elapsed before,

on June 20, 1778, Congress began considering the state amendments, and even then several states had yet to be heard from.[36] Anxious to complete confederation before the anticipated arrival of the first French minister to the United States, Congress made up for this delay with a vengeance. It raced through the thirty-six proposed amendments in a week, seriously debating few, rejecting all, recording only one roll call of individual delegates, before finishing with a rush on June 25. Only one amendment received the support of as many as five states, while fully twenty-five found one or two delegations alone voting in their favor.[37] Even before debate began, most members had agreed that the Articles should be ratified exactly as drafted, and that it was best to avoid the new round of delays that the resubmission of a revised text to the states would inevitably evoke. "There were many Amendments proposed from the States, but none were adopted," the Connecticut delegates reported in early July; "it seemed to be the Opinion of Congress that an immediate Confederation was of greater moment to the Interest of the States, than any present Alteration of the Articles to accomodate the Opinion of particular States on the Amendments proposed."[38]

The one serious threat to ratification came from the instructions that the Maryland assembly had issued to its delegates. Arriving just as debate was to begin, these instructions seemed so critical that Congress departed from its prescribed order of business to consider them first. In December 1777, Maryland had adopted resolutions reiterating its firm conviction that Congress should be vested with both the control of the unsettled American interior and the power to ascertain the western boundaries of the states. In June 1778, noting that "they have hitherto received no answer" to these resolutions, the assembly ordered its delegates not to ratify the Articles until its amendments had been considered and appropriate answers conveyed to the state, and until the delegates in turn received express authorization to sign.[39]

Probably hoping to issue its response before the assembly adjourned, Congress took up the Maryland amendments first, not, however, with the intention of bowing to their demands, but in the belief that a prompt reply reaffirming the priority of completing confederation would induce Maryland to yield. Even before they presented their case, the Maryland delegates themselves conceded the futility of their assignment.[40] Congress quickly and overwhelmingly rejected the two lesser Maryland proposals. But the third, pertaining to western boundaries, required more debate before it too was defeated, although narrowly, six states to five, with New York divided and North Carolina, which would have voted with the majority, absent. The five landless states—Maryland, Delaware, New Jersey, Rhode Island, and Pennsylvania—comprised the minority. The margin of defeat might possibly have been greater had not the Maryland delegates requested a roll call, since that forced other delegates to vote as the particular interests of their states demanded. Significantly, this was the only amendment on which a roll-call vote was taken; on all the others, Congress took the unusual step of noting only the number (not the names) of states voting on either side of the question.

The rejection of the Maryland amendments sealed the fate of all the others, which in fact received only perfunctory attention. Many of these were trivial or could properly be called perfecting amendments; but several raised more serious objections. Massachusetts and Connecticut predictably challenged apportioning common expenses according to the value of improved lands, while several other states recommended that the property of each state should be reassessed at fixed intervals. Three northern states favored apportioning troop requisitions according to the total population of each state rather than "the number of white inhabitants," a provision that obviously favored the southern states. South Carolina in turn sought to restrict the guarantees of reciprocal rights to whites alone. New Jersey was the only state to propose giving Congress a significant new power, suggesting, as it would continue to do into the 1780's, that Congress be authorized to regulate interstate commerce. Finally, only two substantial limitations on the authority of Congress were proposed by the states. Connecticut and New Jersey moved that Congress not be allowed to maintain a peacetime army, while South Carolina proposed that the consent of eleven states be necessary for major decisions within Congress.

Rather than wait for Maryland and New Jersey to authorize their delegates to sign, Congress proceeded with the formalities of ratification. Eight delegations were already empowered to sign the Articles; North Carolina was known to have repealed its partial ratification and agreed to confederate in full; Georgia, though not yet heard from, was expected to sign; while Delaware, it was learned in mid-June, had not issued express instructions because it had never received an official copy of the Articles.[41] On July 9, the authorized delegations signed the confederation, and on the 10th Congress approved an imploring letter that appealed to the "patriotism and good sense" of the dissenting states to trust "to future deliberations to make such alterations and amendments as experience may shew to be expedient and just."[42]

Many members clearly expected that Maryland, New Jersey, and Delaware would now abandon their obstructive campaign, and in pursuing this strategy of *fait accompli*, the majority may well have been joined, perhaps even encouraged, by delegates from the dissenting states themselves. Thomas McKean, Delaware's lone representative, favored immediate ratification, and on July 13 Nathaniel Scudder wrote a lengthy letter to John Hart, the speaker of the New Jersey assembly, lamenting that Hart had not "taken more Pains to convince the members of the Necessity of granting the Powers of Ratification." For, Scudder argued, "every State must be expected to be subjected to considerable local Disadvantages in a general Confederation. Indeed upon the whole I am fully [of the] Opinion that no Plan can or will ever be adopted more equal or less generally injurious to the confederated States than the present." Samuel Chase had informed him, Scudder added, that Maryland might well follow New Jersey if the latter yielded; and the two men had agreed to use their influence among their constituents to further the cause of ratification.[43]

The congressional appeal apparently did work in New Jersey and Delaware, which voted final approval of the Articles in November 1778 and January 1779 respectively. Both states were still committed to the creation of a national domain; when the Delaware act of ratification was laid before Congress, it was accompanied with a memorial justifying the claims of the landless states. Nevertheless, contemporary accounts suggest that the congressional letter of July 10 had influenced the decisions of both assemblies. New Jersey "had acceded to the Confederacy," Elisha Boudinot reported, "not from a Conviction of the Equality & Justness of it, but merely from an absolute Necessity there was of complying to save the Continent," even though in so doing it had "sacrificed its particular Rights on the publick Alter."[44]

Samuel Chase's prediction that Maryland, too, would capitulate proved characteristically rash, however. In mid-December 1778 its assembly again refused to ratify the Articles until Congress was empowered to ascertain the western bounds of the states and until all of the states enjoyed common rights to the lands that would then lie beyond.[45] Maryland clung to this position for another two years, and the Articles remained an empty letter. Leading Maryland politicians were directly interested in preventing the confederation from sanctioning the rights of the landed states, for they were shareholders in the speculating companies whose prewar Indian purchases could be redeemed only by the annihilation of Virginia's title. During the next two years, Maryland, Virginia, the land companies, and Congress itself engaged in a tangled series of maneuvers, issuing remonstrances, protests, and resolutions whose immediate effect was to leave the Articles of Confederation unratified until 1781.[46]

In the end, the simple passage of time perhaps mattered more than the maneuvers that first prevented and then eventually produced ratification. By 1781 many delegates were convinced that the Articles were obsolete, irrelevant to changing political circumstances. As finally drafted, they had given Congress no authority to formulate a national land policy; but by 1781 the cessions of individual states were pointing toward the creation of a national domain. The Articles said little about the exercise of executive power; Congress was about to launch a major administrative reorganization. In 1777 the delegates had generally presumed that the states would pay implicit obedience to their recommendations; four years later Congress was desperately wondering how to command and compel that obedience. In 1777 and 1778 Congress had rushed to complete confederation to bolster its sagging currency; but depreciation continued unabated, so in February 1781 Congress asked the states for authority to collect an impost. Each of these developments revealed new gaps between the naïve expectations of 1776–78 and the uncomfortable reality of the early 1780's.

An examination of the conditions and circumstances governing the framing of the Articles of Confederation thus suggests, more than anything else, the extent to which political exigencies imposed powerful limits on the sweep of formal constitutional thought. It was not only in the Articles, however, that members of the Continental Congress defined and expressed their earliest conceptions of the nature of the federal union. Informally and implicitly, the procedures and working habits of the delegates tell us as much about these ideas as the occasional notes of debate, letters, and memoranda that remain our principal sources for the framing of the Articles.

CHAPTER IX

The Beginnings
of National Government

W HILE the Articles of Confederation remained in abey-
ance, the delegates' working assumptions about the nature
of the American union were most clearly revealed in their conduct of the daily business of Congress. Well after heady debates
about independence, new governments, and confederation had
run their course, the delegates were left to discharge their more
prosaic responsibilities, meeting early mornings and late eve-
nings in committee, attending tedious debates of the whole
house, reviewing endless requests from the army and the states
for money and supplies, maintaining their own official and private correspondence, and continuously struggling with financial
and logistical problems that often seemed incapable of solution.
It was in their responses to these burdens and problems that the
delegates expressed their intuitive understanding of the nature
of the American confederation.

Much like the framing of the Articles of Confederation, the
evolution of a congressional system of administration was sharply
influenced by the exigencies of war, finance, and politics. Many
of the precedents and habits that governed congressional operations throughout the war first took hold in 1775, at a time when
Congress could scarcely anticipate the full range of difficulties
that lay ahead. After independence, growing complaints about
the inefficiency of Congress, widespread abuses in the logistical

branches of the army, and the ineffectiveness of the state governments made many delegates painfully sensitive to their administrative shortcomings. Yet through the 1770's Congress continued
to scrape along, moving piecemeal from one partial expedient to
another until, by late 1779, the war effort seemed on the verge
of collapse.

Despite this endemic dissatisfaction with their own failings,
most delegates consistently recognized the importance of preserving the prerogatives of Congress itself. They were reluctant
to transfer discretionary authority to other officials, either in the
army or the states; and, the acknowledgment of state sovereignty
in the Articles notwithstanding, Congress often acted as if the
states were merely its administrative auxiliaries. Moreover, the
state assemblies were given little opportunity to influence congressional deliberations, in part because the problems of coordinating policymaking between two levels of government were
almost insuperable, but also because the delegates consciously
avoided involving their constituents in many issues under debate.

This chapter examines how the congressional system of administration operated until 1781, when Congress finally created
permanent executive departments. The next chapter will ask
how the ambitions, motives, and experiences of the delegates
shaped their own conception of their political responsibilities as
well as their attitudes toward the exercise of power itself.

Precedents

PROBLEMS of administration had not seemed important in 1774.
The members of the First Congress had concentrated their
efforts on resolving major questions of principle and policy, confident that the decisions they eventually reached would be effectively implemented by the apparatus of committees and conventions that had coalesced during the summer of 1774. When they
adjourned in October, they left behind no standing committee
to preside over the conduct of resistance during the half year that
would intervene before the opening of the Second Congress. The
delegates who returned to Philadelphia in May 1775 found, of
course, that the outbreak of war had substantially enlarged their
concerns and responsibilities. No longer merely a deliberative

assembly composed of spokesmen from individual colonies, Congress now began to function much like a national government. While the delegates still had to review major questions of policy, their energies were increasingly devoted to the problems involved in recruiting, staffing, and supplying the continental army, approving expenditures and issuing bills of credit, and advising provincial conventions and local committees to undertake specific measures deemed necessary for the general defense.

At the outset, the administrative procedures Congress adopted seemed reasonably efficient. To deal with the wide variety of problems that arose as the war effort gathered momentum, it created a series of committees, composed exclusively of its own members, to frame either general recommendations of policy or expedient solutions for particular problems. Their recommendations and reports were generally returned to the whole Congress for discussion and decision. Once approved, they were transmitted to the relevant military or provincial authorities for execution or, in other instances, entrusted to particular delegates or delegations for further action. As had been the case with the Association, Congress continued to treat resistance leaders in the colonies as its administrative subordinates, and much of the actual labor of organizing for war naturally devolved upon them. Under supervisory regulations devised by Congress, provincial conventions and local committees were expected to enforce commercial restrictions, raise and arm troops, fortify harbors, requisition supplies and send them wherever they were needed, and undertake a hundred other miscellaneous tasks necessary to place America in a state of military preparedness.

In the context of 1775, this reliance on the apparatus of resistance was not only the most sensible but the only feasible solution to the problem of organizing men and resources as rapidly as possible. Local leaders presumably enjoyed the active support of the politically mobilized inhabitants of their communities; moreover, they would understand best how to translate general directives into the desired results. Thus the Massachusetts General Court was instructed "to use all the means in their power, that the army before Boston be supplied with wood and hay, on the most reasonable terms"; while the Pennsylvania Committee of Safety was asked "to supply the armed vessels, nearly ready for sailing, with four tons of gun powder, at the continental expense."[1] Although such resolutions were nominally phrased as recommendations, in delegating these responsibilities Congress did not assume that local officials were free to obey or ignore them as they saw fit. Local discretion was meant to apply only to those problematic circumstances Congress could not be expected to foresee; it was not intended to allow challenges to the general strategy of resistance.

Under the hectic conditions prevailing early in the war, Congress was unable to devise, much less impose, any clear or systematic division of labor among the provincial conventions, the newly created staff departments of the army, and itself. The delegates frequently found themselves charged with carrying out a wide variety of administrative tasks, many involving seemingly minor problems. The New Jersey delegates, for example, were instructed to "take care" that "a quantity of Gunpowder belonging to the Continent . . . be safely conveyed to Dobbs Ferry"; while James Wilson was ordered to ask the Philadelphia Committee of Inspection to ascertain how much "Duck, Russia sheeting, tow cloth, Oznaburgs and ticklenburgs can be procured in this City."[2] In the meantime, the delegates were expected to fulfill their other committee assignments and attend the daily sessions of the whole Congress. These demands placed a severe strain on members who enjoyed their colleagues' confidence and found themselves elected to numerous committees. Men like Silas Deane, John Adams, and Robert Morris would attend committee meetings in the early morning, sit in Congress much of the day, and return to committee sessions in the evening, sometimes working there until midnight.[3]

Although most delegates found these novel demands on their time and energy tiresome, they did not at first seem overwhelming. Before independence, Congress was well attended and its membership included a number of unusually capable and conscientious men. Moreover, during the fall of 1775 and the winter of 1776 Congress moved to simplify some of its burdens through the creation of several standing committees responsible for areas of major concern. In September 1775 a Secret Committee was appointed to arrange for the importation of munitions and other supplies necessary for the continental army. A Committee of Secret Correspondence was named in November to maintain communications with American agents and informants overseas. A thirteen-member Marine Committee was formed in January

1776 to supervise naval operations, and during the same month another committee began drafting a plan for the establishment of a Board of War, though final action on their proposal was not taken until June. Finally, in February five delegates were named to a standing committee charged with overseeing the operations of the Treasury, complementing the work of the Committee on Accounts, appointed earlier to handle requests for reimbursement from continental funds.[4]

While these changes helped to correct an early propensity to appoint a new committee for every problem, they did little to improve the efficiency of Congress or reduce the flow of business demanding its attention. The standing committees did take over some routine matters but, with the exception of the Secret Committee, they were hardly autonomous bodies; anything of significance and much that was trivial had to be referred to the whole Congress for decision. Nor did the new committees reduce the workload of the delegates themselves: conscientious members were still obliged to spend most of their waking hours attending committee and general meetings and maintaining their official and personal correspondence. Yet while the delegates grumbled freely about these burdens, before independence only a few reservations were voiced about the wisdom of concentrating so much responsibility in Congress itself. In May 1776, Samuel Chase did complain that "Congress are not a fit Body to act as a Council of War; they are too large, too slow and their Resolutions can never be kept secret."[5] But for the most part the delegates were content to see how well the new standing committees operated before concerning themselves with questions of administrative reform.

This early lack of sustained interest in their own procedures reflected the delegates' natural absorption in the organization and direction of the army, the most pressing of their concerns. The subordination of the military to civilian control was a central axiom of the whig ideology that had led the colonists into rebellion. But broad agreement on this principle hardly provided Congress with useful guidelines for determining how direct and close its supervision of the army should be. In 1775 Congress was necessarily involved in every aspect of military activity, from recruitment and logistics to troop movements and strategy, which still had to be subordinated to the increasingly tenuous policy of escalating resistance only in response to British provocation. Active congressional supervision of strategy declined some-what after independence, though even then the famous rivalries involving Washington, Schuyler, Gates, Mifflin, Lee, Conway, and lesser officers generated major controversies not only within Congress but between it and the army as well. These subsided only after 1778, when Washington's preeminence was irrevoca-bly established. Other problems involving the army proved less sensational but consistently more burdensome. From 1775 to 1781, Congress was intimately concerned with the organization and administration of the army. It established rules of war and discipline, pay scales, terms of enlistment, and detailed regula-tions governing the procurement of supplies and provisions by the quartermaster and commissary departments; it also seemed to be regularly beset with the incessant complaints—sometimes petty, sometimes substantive, but never forgotten—of its officer corps.[6]

As they evolved in 1775 and 1776, then, congressional notions of administration had three major characteristics. One was that provincial authorities were, in many ways, subordinate officials of Congress who were expected to implement many of its direc-tives and policies. A second was that Congress was not merely a deliberative body responsible for framing broad policies but, in the phrase Thomas Burke later used, a "deliberating executive assembly," whose concerns were as much administrative as polit-ical. Indeed, shortly after independence John Adams proposed that many of the current members should be replaced by men skilled in "either military or Commercial Branches of Knowl-edge or Business, for which hundred of others in our Province," he hastily added, "are much better qualified than I am."[7] Finally, among the executive duties of Congress, none was more impor-tant than a close supervision of the army, particularly in those areas that most affected the costs of war—supply and salaries—and thus aggravated the inherently inflationary tendencies of congressional reliance on currency finance.

None of these notions was systematically examined in 1775 or 1776: there was time only for action, not reflection, and the politi-cal restraints that inhibited the early discussion of confederation also discouraged serious consideration of problems of administra-tion. And while in his first draft of confederation John Dickinson had recommended the permanent establishment of "a Chamber of Accounts, an Office of Treasury, a Board of War, & a Board of

Admiralty,"[8] the drafting committee eliminated this provision from the text it submitted to Congress. The ensuing debates apparently witnessed no further attempts to incorporate an internal division of responsibilities within the Articles themselves. In many ways this was a sensible omission. Congress left itself free to revise its administrative arrangements as experience and expediency subsequently demanded; and, in any event, most of the actual labor of implementing its decisions naturally devolved on the army and the states, whose efforts the Articles could scarcely regulate in any practical sense. Yet this reluctance to explore problems of administration foreshadowed and perhaps helped to create the increasingly inefficient conditions that would hamper the operations of Congress throughout the war.

Problems

THE military reverses that followed the Declaration of Independence deflated much of the naïve optimism that had characterized the early months of war and thus made the delegates more sensitive to their potential failings. Early doubts about Washington's generalship were one consequence of these setbacks, but the delegates seem to have been more troubled by signs of their own growing inefficiency. With the completion of the Declaration and the August debates over confederation, an emerging pattern of irregular attendance began to impair the effectiveness of Congress in several ways. A decline in the number of members in attendance, changes in the composition of various delegations, and the frequent arrivals and departures of individual delegates placed heavier responsibilities on those who remained, complicated the task of reaching decisions, and retarded much of the work that had to be done in committee.

Members left Congress or postponed returning for a variety of reasons. Some departed to assume different offices in the states or, like the anxious members of the New York and Maryland delegations, to participate in the framing of the new constitutions. "You little know my dear Edward the State of this Colony when you press Jay and me so warmly to quit it and take our seats in Congress," Robert Livingston wrote the younger Rutledge; "that much depends upon a good representation there is undeniable but every thing is at stake here." A few, like Carter Braxton of Virginia, failed to be reelected. His long campaign to forestall independence defeated, John Dickinson withdrew from active politics; while Benjamin Franklin was named a commissioner to the court of France. Private considerations were often more important than political excuses, however. Many delegates simply needed or wanted a rest. Samuel Adams was so "completely worn out," John Adams noted in July 1776, ". . . his strength, Spirit and Abilities so exhausted, that an hundred such delegates, here would not be worth a Shilling. My case is worse," he added, begging that he, too, might be relieved.[9]

Complaints such as this reflected most delegates' natural reluctance to spend more than a few months at a time away from home, and were a response to one simple but important development in congressional proceedings: the realization that Congress could not afford to recess, but would have to sit in continuous session indefinitely. Prior to the fall of 1775, Congress had been able to recess twice, and even as late as December 1775 some delegates were anticipating another adjournment.[10] But in fact not until 1784 would Congress again be able to recess for more than a few days at a time, and the delegates were thus regularly forced to weigh official responsibilities against private interest and convenience or, occasionally, against competing public obligations in the states. The result was a body whose constantly fluctuating membership made the achievement of any sort of continuity precarious at best. To operate efficiently, Congress required the attendance of men who could remain for several months at a stretch, if not longer. It generally took some weeks to master the details of pending business, and delegates who felt compelled to leave Congress just as they were catching up with its affairs could hardly serve usefully. Yet during the years to come, weather, family, private business, and simple relief at being away from Congress produced a regular turnover in its composition; and despite frequent pleas from attending members and Congress itself, the states did little to compel the attendance of absent delegates.[11]

It was the decline in attendance that accompanied the congressional withdrawal to Baltimore that first forced the delegates to confront the issue of their own inefficiency. At the prodding of Robert Morris, who was managing the interim Executive Committee left behind in Philadelphia, Congress appointed a committee "to prepare a plan for the better conducting the executive business of Congress, by boards composed of persons, not members of Congress."[12] The central problem, Morris and others argued, was that executive committees composed exclusively of members of Congress could not function efficiently under the burdensome conditions prevailing after independence. Congress lacked the manpower and the expertise to act as both a deliberative and an executive body. Dividing their limited time and energies between two such disparate tasks merely guaranteed that neither would receive the attention it deserved, a condition that was further aggravated by the turnover in the membership of Congress. Who could ever expect continental finances to be capably managed, William Duer fumed, when one

considers how few Members of Congress could ever attend to the Character of Financiers, the Evils which flow from a constant Fluctuation of Members of the Treasury, the Partiality in public Advances too often shewn, to particular States, and individuals, from a political Complaisance which Members are inclined to shew each other, and the Impracticality there is of Members of Congress giving up sufficient Time to the Boards, to make themselves Masters of the Business. . . .

The solution Morris and others envisioned, however, was not to replace the existing membership of Congress with more suitably talented men, as John Adams had proposed, but to "pay good executive men to do their business as it ought to be, and not lavish millions away by their own mismanagement. I say mismanagement," Morris added, "because no man living can attend the daily deliberations of Congress and do executive parts of business at the same time." His own experience on the Executive Committee at Philadelphia convinced Morris that this division of labor was practicable. For although he complained to John Jay that the committee's business had made him "the veriest Slave you ever saw," he was eventually able to boast that "we dispatch about 7/8ths of that damned trash that used to take up 3/4ths of the debates in Congress; and give them no trouble about the matter."[13]

Although the proposal to create executive boards of nonmembers apparently met with general approval—it was endorsed by Samuel Adams and R. H. Lee as well as men like Morris and Benjamin Harrison—good intentions yielded few results.[14] The committee's first report, which dealt only with the office of the secretary of Congress, was not delivered until late March 1777. Its second, which proposed reconstituting the Board of War, was read a fortnight later, but further delays and revisions occurred before an amended plan was approved in October. Even then the new board included members of Congress, though the bulk of its work was done by the appointed commissioners and their staff. The Board of Treasury, initially composed of five delegates, was not reorganized until 1778, and then underwent further reform a year later; while the Marine Committee was not superseded by a Board of Admiralty until 1779.[15] Ironically, the halting progress of administrative reform was in part a result of the very pressures it was intended to reduce. "A flood of small Business from every Quarter continues to crowd out the great important Matters," the Connecticut delegate Andrew Adams observed in 1778; delay was unavoidable, Josiah Bartlett noted, because Congress simply did not have enough "time to make the proper arrangements and form proper systems for conducting the business."[16]

Complementing their doubts about the committee system, many of the delegates were equally concerned with the amount of time that was tediously squandered, often on trivial points, during the daily sessions of the whole Congress. A succinct if acerbic description of these proceedings was recorded by Titus Hosmer, a Connecticut delegate, in 1778. After morning committee meetings that ran from as early as 6:00 A.M. until 10 or 11 o'clock, Congress attempted to muster a quorum, sometimes with difficulty. "Some states have delegates so very negligent, so much immersed in the pursuit of pleasure or business," Hosmer complained, "that it is very rare we can make a Congress before near eleven o'clock, and this evil seems incapable of a remedy as Congress has no means to compel gentlemen's attendance, and those who occasion the delay are callous to admonition and reproof, which have been often tried in vain." Once a quorum of nine states had assembled and prayers were read, Congress proceeded with the order of the day, which first required "the public letters [to be] read & disposed off, next reports from the Treasury & then reports from the Board of War." Thereafter the delegates were free to raise whatever points they wished. Nothing prevented Congress from taking immediate action on these matters or the various letters and reports it received daily, but anything requiring research or further reflection was referred either to one of the standing committees or to a committee specially appointed for the purpose. What most troubled Hosmer and other delegates, however, was the erratic character of the parliamentary procedure that Congress barely followed. Although a certain informality might have been expected to prevail in a body that generally numbered between two and three dozen members, Congress often bogged down in procedural wrangling. "When we are assembled," Hosmer complained,

several gentlemen have such a knack at starting questions of order, raising debates upon critical, captious, and trifling amendments, protracting them by long speeches, by postponing, calling for the previous question, and other arts, that it is almost impossible to get an important question decided at one sitting; and if it is put over to another day, the field is open to be gone over again, precious time is lost, and the public business left undone.

Moreover, many procedural questions were resolved by appeals to the house itself, which gave the disputants "much the same, indeed a greater Latitude than in debating points of Common Law in our Courts."[17]

Members of Congress offered various explanations for the unusual and unwieldy character of its proceedings. If many of its parliamentary rulings would "readily appear extraordinary to legislative assemblies," Thomas Burke argued, their peculiarity was

Occasioned by the Nature of Congress, which is a deliberating Executive assembly, to whose proceedings the rules of order Established for deliberating Legislative assemblies will not always apply without manifest Inconvenience and as Utility is the principle which gives rise to all rules of order, so whatever rule appears to a Majority to be contrary to utility must necessarily be rejected as not order.

And if the congressional calendar always seemed overcrowded, Burke continued, it was because Congress "cannot reject any Business, addressed to them by way of despatch through the President, before it has undergone some Consideration." Other delegates cited different reasons for the slow pace of debate. Oliver Ellsworth sensibly attributed it to the variety of interests and opinions that had to be reconciled before any major decision could be reached. Writing in 1781, Samuel Johnston blamed it on the turnover in membership and the fact that "there is no man of sufficient credit or influence to take the lead, or give a tone to the business"—a useful reminder that however partisan congressional politics periodically became, such factions as did exist were too small in size and ephemeral in duration to exercise effective control over the course of business. Josiah Bartlett blamed the delay in transacting business on the amount of "time it takes to transact matters in so large an Assembly filled with lawyers and other gentlemen who love to talk as much as they."[18]

Congress, in short, was too inefficient to correct its own inefficiency. But there were other reasons why it took so long to implement even the comparatively modest plan to create standing committees composed of bureaucrats rather than delegates. Beneath the general agreement about the utility of executive boards lay the inherent difficulties of deciding exactly what powers they were to be given and who would compose them. This was particularly true of the reconstituted Board of War after Generals Horatio Gates and Thomas Mifflin were appointed to it. Since both men were suspected of hostility toward Washington, any substantial delegation of power to the new board risked increasing internal dissension within both Congress and the American officer corps.[19] Nor did the new boards themselves prove to be models of administrative efficiency. After the treasury was reorganized in 1779, a series of petty clerical disputes among the staff of its various offices eventually required a congressional investigation.[20]

Early efforts at improving the efficiency of Congress were necessarily tentative for another reason. The line between broad considerations of policy and details of administration proved less easy to draw than Robert Morris and others had initally assumed. As financial and logistical problems became their obsessive concerns, the delegates' reluctance to waive the supervision of even routine expenditures grew less difficult to understand. Widespread reports of corruption, profiteering, and inefficiency in the purchase and distribution of military supplies, and recurrent feuding among the principal officers of the staff departments, suggested, after all, that executive agencies were not to be trusted implicitly. Periodic reports from correspondents in the states or the army probably led some delegates to conclude that Congress should continue to play an active supervisory role. Writing from New Jersey in early 1778, William C. Houston provided John Witherspoon with a graphic account of the "Corruptions abuses and Enormities" that continental officers were daily perpetrating. What was particularly "alarming," Houston wrote, was

to see People of the firmest principles so struck with the publick mismanagements as to be pondering and balancing can there be any thing better than for a man of spirit who has an Estate to spend it out of the way, rather than suffer it to come into the Hands of a sett of contemptible wretches, the very Fag-end of the Species who are rolling and wantoning in the hard-earned substance of their neighbours, for doing no earthly thing to deserve it.

Two years later, the New Hampshire delegate Nathaniel Peabody described these staff officers as "Legions of Continental Sinecures who appear in Swarms like Locusts . . . and not only draw Numberless rations; but are in every other respect rioting upon the blood and Treasures of the virtuous Citizens (if any Such there be) in these united States." As observations such as these suggest, the underlying problems of military procurement and finance posed questions that were as much political as administrative in nature, and that went to the heart of the task of preserving public morale during an indecisive war. Any temptation to simplify the congressional calendar had to be weighed against the fear that executive officials, free from supervision, might prove so untrustworthy that popular support for the war would be jeopardized even further. The most important problems of finance and supply could not be relegated to functionaries, therefore, but had to be resolved by the delegates themselves.[21]

In the meantime, candid complaints about congressional inefficiency continued to be voiced by delegates, state officials, and military officers alike. The committee system remained an object of strong criticism. "Our commercial, marine and treasury affairs are in a very bad situation," Josiah Bartlett wrote in September 1778,

and will never be otherwise while they are managed by Committees of Congress who are many of them unacquainted with the business and are continually changing and by the time they begin to be acquainted with the business they quit, others come in who know nothing that has been done: thus we go on from time to time to the great loss of the public.[22]

Quartermaster General Nathanael Greene's regular dealings with Congress left him dispirited and cynical. "They are always beginning but never finishing business. They act from the spur of the ocassion [*sic*]," he informed Alexander McDougall in early 1779, after spending a month at Philadelphia. "[I] went upon the special application of a Committee of Congress; and all the business they did with me might have been done in a few hours." Another year's experience only soured Greene further. "I have been among the great at Philadelphia, and have a worse opinion of our cause than ever," he wrote McDougall in April 1780. "Never was there a people that employed themselves so much about trifles. Their whole policy is a chapter of new expedients, and long debates upon little matters of form." No one judged Congress more harshly than the officers of the continental army, of course, and Greene's assessment of its failings has to be evaluated with that in mind. Yet his comments had been echoed innumerable times by the delegates themselves, many of whom recognized, as Henry Laurens once grumbled, that if the American cause ultimately prevailed, it would do so only because "Our Antagonist is as Idle, as profligate as ourselves & keeps pace with us in profusion, mismanagement & family discord."[23]

Representation Without Taxation

MONEY was not the root of all the evils afflicting Congress, but after 1776 it became the most persistent and oppressive problem on its agenda. Nothing proved more frustrating to the delegates than their inability to frame and implement measures that would keep the depreciation of the continental dollar within tolerable bounds.

In 1775, with some trepidation but little dissent, both Congress and the states had chosen to defray the costs of war through a system of currency finance. Rather than levy taxes, which for obvious reasons seemed politically inadvisable, Congress issued bills of credit whose value was secured not by any specific fund or revenues but only by the pledged faith of the united colonies. Depreciation was slow to begin, because the American economy, then being redirected toward the higher demands of wartime production, needed an expanding money supply. By late 1776, however, continental and state emissions were beginning to exceed what the economy could usefully absorb, and popular confidence in their value suffered with the military setbacks that followed independence. General economic conditions exacerbated the inherently inflationary pressure of a constantly expanding money supply. Wartime shortages of goods and labor and the purported activities of "forestallers" and "engrossers" who held commodities off the market or monopolized their sale also contributed to the general price rise. To meet the ever-growing demands of the war, Congress opened a domestic loan office and sponsored a lottery, but it necessarily continued to rely on its printing presses for the bulk of its expenses. The gradual but ominous depreciation of continental currency continued in 1777 and 1778, possibly retarded by Saratoga and the French alliance, before worsening drastically in 1779.[24]

Taxation was the remedy the colonies had traditionally used to maintain the value of public bills of credit issued during previous wars; and in theory, it remained the most obvious method of limiting the total money supply and thus preserving the value of the currency remaining in circulation. But in 1775 and 1776, when Congress and the new provincial regimes were anxious to attain maximum popular support, the political liabilities of taxation outweighed its financial benefits. By November 1777 when, in conjunction with the completion of the Articles of Confederation, Congress issued its first comprehensive response to the looming fiscal crisis, taxation was still politically unattractive but seemingly no longer avoidable. In the first of a series of requisitions designed to limit the volume of currency in circulation, Congress asked the states to levy $5 million in taxes, to be remitted to the continental treasury. Congress also advised the states to refrain from issuing further emissions of their own and, where adequate quantities of continental paper were available, "to call in by loans or taxes" the currency they had previously issued. In the future the states were asked to meet their current expenses through annual taxes. Finally, Congress advised the states to implement a wide-ranging program of price regulation—a measure it had earlier considered but only tepidly endorsed, since many delegates rightly doubted whether any durable system of price controls could be enforced.[25]

Congress retracted its endorsement of price regulation in

1778,[26] but the other provisions of the November 1777 resolutions defined the essential financial program it followed, unsuccessfully, during the next two years. Why did this program fail? In any discussion of the financial debility of Congress, it is obligatory to point out that Congress lacked the effective power or, once the Articles were ratified, the constitutional right either to levy taxes on its own authority or to compel the states to obey its recommendations. It is certainly true that the states would never have ratified the Articles had they contained such provisions, and that during the 1780's the absence of these powers contributed substantially to the growing weakness of the confederation. Yet it is highly questionable whether Congress initially attributed its wartime financial problems to its want of powers of direct taxation or coercion. From the outset, most delegates probably recognized that the task of devising a workable, equitable scheme of taxation for thirteen states was, quite simply, something Congress could accomplish only with great difficulty. As the continual haggling merely over the *apportionment* of expenses had already revealed, any attempt to determine rates and objects of taxation would likely prove highly controversial and disruptive within Congress. But more important, few delegates could be confident that they knew which types of taxes would in fact prove most productive and least objectionable in each of the states. Here as on other occasions pragmatic obstacles mattered far more than constitutional scruples. Given the uneven, fluctuating economic dislocations the war had produced, and the diverse political conditions prevailing in different states, it was certainly more sensible to allow the individual assemblies to determine how taxes could best be raised among their constituents.

But would the states levy the taxes Congress requested? The delegates were certainly aware of the political resistance any program even of moderate taxation would inevitably evoke—a consideration that may have encouraged them to require the assemblies rather than Congress to decide which taxes actually to impose. But in the context of the 1770's, before there had been any major clashes between the sovereign wills of the states and Congress, the delegates fully expected the states to make a conscientious, sustained effort to comply with their recommendations. This was not only the inference to be drawn from the first three years of congressional experience, but the implicit logic underlying the Articles of Confederation. And since Congress deliberately completed and issued the Articles and the November 1777 resolutions simultaneously, in the hope that they would reinforce each other, it seems reasonable to conclude that a presumption of the states' responsibility to implement the proposed financial program did reflect the delegates' genuine understanding of the nature of the confederation.

In fact, most of the states did attempt to levy taxes and fulfill the other elements of the congressional program, with the exception of price regulations, which were too controversial and too difficult to enforce to be effectively set in motion. Nor did the states challenge the propriety or rationale of the November recommendations. Where they did fall short was, first, in the size of the levies they nominally adopted; but second—and what was probably more important—in their simple inability to collect taxes or, once collected, to remit the currency to the treasury when their own pressing demands required its immediate return to circulation. Again we are thrown back to the political world of the eighteenth century, where government officials were habitually inefficient and where, given the political character of the Revolution itself, there were important considerations inhibiting local tax collectors from discharging their duties at the risk of increasing popular "disaffection" toward the war in general. Hesitant to tax as heavily as the financial situation seemingly required, incapable of efficient tax collection, the states' efforts were an inadequate response to the rapid depreciation of continental currency that took place in 1779; yet it seems unlikely that any different result would have occurred had Congress rather than the states been vested with the power of taxation. The lag between the initial congressional requisition, state legislative action, and actual tax collection was itself enough to guarantee that the eventual sums withdrawn from circulation would be inconsequential in relation to further emissions.[27]

It is difficult to assess the extent to which delegates actually believed that their recommendations would, if adopted, reduce inflation to acceptable proportions. Some doubtless viewed depreciation with a cynical equanimity, recognizing that it gave Congress a tacit power of taxation by progressively reducing the real value of its emissions. For, as Benjamin Franklin observed, depreciation itself was "a kind of imperceptible Tax, every one having paid a Part of it in the Fall of Value that took place between his receiving and Paying such Sums as pass'd thro' his hands." On balance, however, the persistent if futile efforts that Congress made to "appreciate" the value of its currency suggest that it hoped to stave off repudiation as long as possible, for political if not for financial reasons. Most delegates were reluctant to confess that a bankrupt Congress might be forced to repudiate its own financial instruments, since such an admission naturally implied that Congress deserved neither the confidence nor conceivably the loyalty of its constituents.[28]

Similar political concerns sharpened the delegates' criticisms of the logistical departments of the army, whose shortcomings were frequently held responsible for much of the rising cost of essential goods and commodities. Allegations of corruption and inefficiency in these departments dated from the very beginning of the war and, much like the dire predictions about the destiny of the currency, began to be taken seriously by Congress by early 1777. The system of military procurement that operated through 1779 was believed to embody two major flaws. First, its purchasing agents were paid not by salary but through a fixed commission on the amount of money they disbursed. With their personal incomes thus increasing with their expenditures, military purchasers had no incentive to economize or drive hard bargains for supplies. Second, the lines of administration within the commissary, quartermaster, and other supportive departments were too loosely drawn and distended to allow active supervision of the scattered officials who actually spent the continental funds. Congress attempted to impose stricter controls on the commissary when it passed a revised and comprehensive series of regulations for that department in 1777, but ironically these proved too detailed and complex to be followed closely, and there were even complaints that many officers never received copies of the regulations that were supposed to govern their conduct.[29]

The reputed vices of these officials offered a much easier target for attack than the complexities of public finance. Next to the sums of money these useless appendages consumed, William C. Houston complained, the actual expenses of the army were "a Cypher, a Feather in the Balance." As Congress grew progressively more concerned about restoring the value of its currency, such allegations could scarcely be ignored. "A general opinion prevails," the Committee on the Treasury reported in April 1779, "that one cause of the alarming expenses in these Departments,

arises from allowing commissions to the numerous persons employed in purchasing for the Army; and that a very general dissatisfaction has taken place on that account, among the citizens
of these United States."[30] Serious students of public finance probably recognized that these practices merely aggravated conditions whose deeper roots lay elsewhere. When John Dickinson
asked Joseph Reed to collect recommendations for reforming the
national finances from the Philadelphia mercantile community,
Reed reported that his consultants "did [not] reckon upon any
great Savings by a Change in the System of procuring for the
Army . . . for tho we suppose [that system] has contributed its
Share to the Depreciation, we think the true & great Cause has
been the Surplus [of money] beyond the necessary Medium of
Trade, or the ordinary Occasions of the People." Many delegates
nevertheless agreed that, as Charles Carroll put it, "next to high
taxation," a careful and strict management of military procurement would "be found the most effectual measure to appreciate
your Bills of Credit."[31]

Although discussions of finance and procurement were virtually standing items on the congressional agenda, all the conditions that customarily retarded its deliberations obstructed the
serious reformation of policy until well into 1779, when the precipitate decline of the continental dollar indicated that a crisis
was imminent. By late spring the exchange ratio of paper to
specie at Philadelphia was roughly twenty to one, and the currency requirements of the commissary and quartermaster departments were reaching truly astronomical proportions.[32] By
early summer few if any members of Congress would have disputed the conclusions Joseph Reed reported in response to Dickinson's request for advice. The central question, Reed observed,
was "By what Means can the Presses be soonest & most effectually stopp'd? Or in other Words how can future Supplies be raised
so as to prevent any farther Emissions?" The answer lay, he
argued, in "fixing the farther Sum beyond which the Emissions
shall not go," and in the meantime, before this final round of
currency was exhausted, in inaugurating some new mode of
securing supplies and provisions for the army.[33]

The continued decline of continental currency during the
summer of 1779 made the decision to halt the presses comparatively easy to reach. On September 3, Congress resolved to cease

further emissions as soon as the total paper value of its circulating currency reached $200 million, which would be in a matter of weeks. A new plan of supply took longer to develop, but as 1779 drew to a close Congress approved several resolutions indicating the course it intended to take. Individual states would be asked to raise designated quantities of specific supplies needed by the army. Initially this was done on a piecemeal basis, but on February 25, 1780, Congress passed a comprehensive resolution requiring each state to collect exact amounts of the foodstuffs necessary to provision the army during the ensuing campaign. With currency emissions halted, the commissary would no longer be able to expend huge sums of money in the purchase of supplies.[34]

On the question of reorganizing the staff departments, Congress acted reluctantly and, in the end, inconclusively. Although several committees appointed to propose reforms did submit detailed reports during the summer of 1779, their suggestions were generally deferred for later consideration or left unapproved. During the winter of 1780 a special commission was appointed to review the whole problem of logistics. But although this commission produced the most comprehensive scheme of reform yet proposed, their efforts also proved fruitless. In April 1780 Congress merely referred their report to a new committee of three members dispatched to army headquarters, where they were instructed to confer extensively with Washington on the general situation of the army. In this pathetic sequence of committees and reports, Congress revealed its perennial inability to act decisively when confronted by problems of administration. Only one significant innovation was made in the supervision of the staff departments: on July 9, 1779, Congress requested the state executives "instantly to make the strictest enquiry into the conduct" of every commissary and quartermaster agent operating within their states, simultaneously authorizing them to remove and replace those who were strongly suspected "of any kind of misbehaviour." This resolution amounted, in effect, to an admission that Congress itself was incapable of supervising its own administrative subordinates.[35]

Between the fall of 1779 and the spring of 1780, congressional fiscal policy underwent a similar reorientation toward reliance on state authority. In deciding to halt further emissions of bills of credit, Congress did not abandon a hope of "appreciating" the value of its previous emissions. It again urged the states to lay taxes payable in continental money and to remit the proceeds to Congress, and it also launched a new attempt to attract substantial loans. When these efforts proved ineffective, it devised one last plan to salvage something from its voluminous past emissions. On March 18, 1780, it officially revalued its old currency at a rate of forty to one of specie. The states were again asked to tax the old money out of existence and to remit their collections to Congress. As these receipts came in, Congress would in turn release new bills of credit whose total value was "not to exceed, on any account, one-twentieth part of the nominal sum of the bills brought in to be destroyed." The new bills, which would collect interest at an annual rate of 5 percent, were to be distributed between Congress and the states. Perhaps more important, the states were asked to provide specific funds for the payment of interest and the redemption of the new bills. Although the states again made serious efforts to comply with this plan, their collections fell far short of what was intended or necessary. The practical consequence of the various steps Congress had taken to restore some value to its emissions was the repudiation of $200 million of paper currency. Little over a year later it was worthless.[36]

Each of these decisions of 1779–80 was designed to transfer power and responsibility to the states. Congress not only renounced its own principal source of funds but attempted to force the states to impose heavier taxes of their own. By asking the states to assume much of the responsibility for collecting supplies and even urging them to prosecute continental officials suspected of dereliction, Congress confessed its own administrative failings. And in a further effort to curtail demands on the depleted continental treasury, Congress also shifted to the states the critical responsibility of paying military salaries. Moreover, in adopting policies that theoretically enlarged the responsibilities of the states, the delegates barely contemplated alternatives that might have tended to increase rather than reduce their own power. Immediately before approving the devaluation of March 18, 1780, for example, Congress tabled a motion, ironically offered by Thomas Burke, requesting the states to authorize it to lay a duty of 1 percent on all imports and exports. Only four members voted even to take Burke's proposal under consideration.[37]

Congress might have acted otherwise had it believed that ratification of the Articles of Confederation might soon take place. But in 1779, when the conflict between Virginia and Maryland was, if anything, intensifying, the prospects for ratification seemed to be receding. Popular confidence in Congress was also at the lowest point of the Revolution, depressed not only by the collapse of the currency but by the outbreak of rancorous factional disputes within Congress, which quickly became public knowledge. Because from 1777 on the problem of bolstering the credit of the currency had always been linked to the completion of confederation and to a restoration of confidence in Congress itself, these developments doubtless made many delegates wonder whether any program of reform operating strictly under congressional auspices could succeed. The delegates harbored few illusions about the efficiency of the states, known to be laboring under heavy liabilities of their own. But in operating under the sanction of written constitutions, the states enjoyed one major advantage over Congress, and an advantage that seemed all the more significant when Congress was exposed to harsher criticism than it had ever known.

The considerations that led Congress to rely on the states had thus become obvious by the summer of 1779, when the North Carolina delegation offered this explanation for the imminent change of policy:

The Continental Currency is so much depreciated, that every one sees the necessity of putting an entire stop to emissions; and relying on the Exertions of the States for Supplying the public necessaries. The power of the States, internally is much better understood, much better Established, much more simple and vigorous in its Operation relative to public Credit, and, let us add, much more relied on, than that of Congress. It is therefore more competent to give Securities, which will give value to paper Currency, than Congress, in their unconfederated State, can give. The Congress, sensible of this, also Sensible, that increasing the Continental Emissions must be attended with very injurious Consequences, have taken up Ideas very different from such as heretofore prevailed. Should the War continue longer than the present Campaign, the States must furnish the supplies, either by Contributions in kind or by Taxes in money; and these are the chief Resources which the Congress have at present in view.

In his Philadelphia consultations, too, Joseph Reed found it "a prevailing Sentiment that any Measure for the Restoration of

publick Credit will be more effectual if executed by the States
individually after a Recommendation of Congress than if attempted by Congress itself."[38]

In consciously choosing to rely more heavily on the states,
members of Congress evinced little if any concern with the constitutional implications of this shift in policy. Their doubts centered not on the effect these reforms would have on the power
of Congress but, more pointedly, on the question of their likely
success. As the tone of resignation that pervaded the delegates'
correspondence suggests, necessity rather than ideology governed their decisions. "Congress are at their wit's end," William
Ellery observed starkly as 1779 drew to a close, and his comment
would be echoed by others during the months ahead. However
problematic these expedients might prove, their adoption was
depicted as unavoidable. The devaluation of continental currency, James Lovell confessed, was "one of those Decisions about
which very much may and will be said on both Sides"; yet he
believed that "most of those who said nay here on the Determination were glad it was carried against them." Once Congress
had committed itself to these policies, the delegates closed ranks
to exhort their constituents to do what was expected, presenting
them, in effect, with a *fait accompli*. "Unless the states exert
themselves" in collecting their designated supplies, the North
Carolina delegates informed Governor Caswell, "the Cause is
utterly lost"; if they did not "vigorously proceed in collecting the
old money and establishing funds for the credit of the new,"
James Madison wrote Thomas Jefferson, ". . . we are undone."[39]

Newly arrived from Virginia, where he had observed something of the shortcomings of state government, Madison privately confessed that he had "the most pungent apprehensions"
about the wisdom of relying on the states. In the months to come,
when the inadequacies of the system of specific supplies and the
revaluation of the currency left most members receptive to more
decisive measures, Madison would emerge as a leading exponent
of consolidating authority in Congress rather than dispersing it
to the states. In the meantime, however, Congress could only
hope that the states, once confronted with a crisis, would recognize their obligations to sustain the war effort. Had Congress
believed that the states would balk at these new burdens, it
scarcely seems likely that so much dependence would have been
placed on their efforts. What was new in 1779 and 1780 was the

delegates' acceptance of their own limitations and failures and their inability to supervise the procurement of supplies. But the decision to turn to the states remained consistent with earlier assumptions about the character of the American confederation.

CHAPTER X

Ambition and Responsibility: An Essay on Revolutionary Politics

———————— ⚬⚭⚬ ————————

M ANY of the problems that incessantly oppressed Congress were rooted in the circumstances of the war itself, and are best explained in terms of the inherent difficulty of collecting taxes, regulating prices, enlisting troops, and obtaining supplies. But if inattendance and a continuing turnover of delegates provided important additional sources of inefficiency, one must also ask why Congress found it so difficult to recruit a diligent and stable membership. The malaise that usually afflicted the delegates might be attributed to the limited authority Congress enjoyed under the Articles of Confederation. A government that met frustration at every turn could hardly prove attractive to ambitious politicians or even to those who accepted election from motives of civic responsibility. Such an explanation may perhaps be applied to the mid-1780's, when the embarrassment Congress suffered simply in maintaining a quorum was one obvious mark of its "imbecility." But this argument is less persuasive for the period before 1783, when Congress still actively supervised the conduct of war and foreign policy. Its wartime duties remained formidable, and if Revolutionary leaders were desirous of power, responsibility, or administrative experience, few more promising opportunities existed than those it provided.

Yet to judge from their own personal writings, few of these men enjoyed politics or government. Their continuing complaints about the burdens of office cannot be regarded simply as the sort of ritual griping any group of workers ordinarily makes, nor was it merely a natural response to the recurring frustrations Congress encountered. The delegates' grumblings deserve serious examination for other reasons. They make it possible to reconstruct the attitudes and expectations that these men brought to their involvement in politics, and to appreciate as well the novelty of the demands the Revolution made on American leaders.

To ask why the delegates found service at Congress so unsatisfactory calls into question familiar assumptions about the behavior of politicians. James S. Young faced a similar problem when he sought to analyze the attitudes and careers of those who served in the federal government during the early nineteenth century. "Ambivalence about power among men in power jars one's expectations," Young writes:

a Machiavellian image of those who rule is, after all, much more congenial to the democratic mind. And an uneasy conscience among powerful men is an idea so very alien to the modern understanding of why politicians in government behave the way they do that to suggest it at all is to appear naïve or at best Shakespearean in one's approach toward men in power.

And yet, Young continues, modern scholars have rarely sought "to view politics and power through the eyes of the rulers themselves," or "to grasp what it meant to hold power, to comprehend the human experience involved."[1]

Although there were important differences between the Revolutionary and Jeffersonian phases of early national politics, the similarities between the attitudes of the members of the Continental Congress and Young's "Washington community" are equally striking. In the late eighteenth even more than the early nineteenth century, politics was still far more of an avocation than a career. Because the delegates were forced to assume burdens more staggering than any that government had previously required, the adjustment they had to make proved uncomfortable, inconvenient, and a source of frequent resentment. Any explanation of the inefficiency that regularly beset Congress must, therefore, examine the interplay between the frustrations inherent in the office and the character of the delegates' political ambitions and private aspirations.

. . .

ARTICLE 5 of the confederation stipulated that "no person shall be capable of being a delegate for more than three years in any term of six years." This prohibition clearly reflected the Americans' early commitment to the republican principle of rotation in office, and in that sense may also have been a mark of the naïveté with which they initially weighed the merits of experience in government against the dangers of entrenched power. Because the Articles went unratified until 1781, this provision did not actually take effect until 1784, when a handful of members became ineligible for reelection. But in practical terms Article 5 would have been largely irrelevant to the actual composition of Congress even had the Articles been promptly completed. Of the 235 delegates who attended Congress for a minimal period of four weeks during any one calendar year between 1774 and 1783, 56 appeared in Congress during one year only, another 65 were present during each of two years, while 53 attended during each of three. Thus fully three-quarters of the active wartime membership of Congress were present during each of three years or less. On the other hand, only 31 delegates, or one-eighth of our total, served in Congress during each of five calendar years or more. By the end of 1776, more than half of those who had attended Congress prior to the Declaration of Independence had left its chambers for good.[2] "The members of Congress are so perpetually changing," R. H. Lee wrote his brother Arthur in May 1778, "that it is of little use to give you their Names."[3]

The continuing turnover in Congress can be attributed to several causes. Some are immediately obvious. Those who resisted the movement toward independence left Congress as quickly as possible. The creation of new governments in the states, the organization of the army, and a handful of diplomatic appointments diverted others away from Congress during the early years of the war. Washington, Schuyler, George Clinton, and Thomas Mifflin left Congress to assume major military commands. Patrick Henry, Thomas Johnson, Caesar Rodney, and William Livingston quickly became the chief executive officials in their states. Franklin, Jay, John Adams, Henry Laurens, and William Carmichael entered the much-troubled diplomatic corps. But if it can be assumed that only military commands, major state offices, and ambassadorial posts were as important

positions as membership in Congress itself, the number of delegates who left Congress to assume *higher* responsibilities was
hardly significant. It was not the appeal of more powerful positions that lured men away.

Nor is there much evidence to suggest that legislative dis-
pleasure or competition to gain election to Congress were major
causes of rotation, though here, too, there are some prominent
examples that may be cited. Elbridge Gerry displaced Thomas
Cushing when the former Massachusetts speaker lost the confidence of the Adamses.[4] Silas Deane lost his seat when political
rivals in Connecticut capitalized on his absence.[5] Benjamin Rush
was turned out because of his opposition to the new Pennsylvania
constitution (though Robert Morris was not). Other legislatures
occasionally punished delegates whom they felt had not represented their interests correctly. The Massachusetts assembly
refused to reelect several members who reluctantly voted for the
commutation of military pensions in 1783. On the other hand,
several delegates who unexpectedly lost their seats treated their
involuntary retirement as affairs of honor and successfully
secured reappointment as an act of vindication, among them
Benjamin Harrison, R. H. Lee, and Francis Lee in Virginia,[6] and
Joseph Hewes and Thomas Burke in North Carolina.[7]

Still, there is little reason to believe that constituent jealousy
or electoral competition had a major impact on overall patterns
of attendance. Within the constraints that eighteenth-century
political etiquette imposed, most delegates who were willing to
retain their places in Congress were not likely to be turned out
of office. The number of members who refused reelection or
simply declined to attend during a given term outnumbered
those who lost their seats involuntarily. Given the recurring difficulties most states experienced in maintaining adequate representation at Congress, the assemblies were probably grateful to
find individuals who were willing to serve there repeatedly.
There is no evidence that those delegates who served the longest
terms—a group including Samuel Adams, Elbridge Gerry, James
Lovell, Samuel Holten, Roger Sherman, William Ellery, James
Duane, William Floyd, Abraham Clark, and Thomas McKean—
were ever seriously criticized by their constituents for lusting
after power or turning themselves into federal placemen. When
John F. Mercer asked James Monroe if his political interest would
be better served by attending a session of the Virginia assembly

or remaining at Congress, Monroe justified doing the latter by reminding Mercer of the reputation James Madison had obtained by dint of constant attendance at Congress.[8]

The most plausible explanation for the persistent turnover in Congress is, quite simply, that most members chose not to remain there longer than propriety dictated. Their letters reveal that they left Congress neither because they had been defeated for reelection nor appointed to higher office, but rather because they disliked the burdens Congress imposed and preferred to be at home. Retirement from Congress did not mean withdrawal from politics. Most remained active in state affairs. Conceivably, their departure from Congress represented less an aversion to national politics than a greater absorption in state issues. There is some merit to this hypothesis. Constitution-writing in the states certainly did prove more exciting than the framing of the confederation. Decisions about finance, taxation, and economic regulation may have been guided by congressional recommendations, but the hard questions of how general policies were to be implemented—and at whose expense—could be hammered out only in the assemblies. These considerations clearly influenced some delegates, particularly those representing states where the establishment of new governments and the dislocations generated by the war combined to produce bitter disputes over control of the new regimes.

Yet there was another major difference between congressional and state politics that probably had a greater effect on the delegates' decisions. The personal costs of attendance at Congress were not comparable to the burdens borne by most state officials. Measured in terms either of the amount of time spent away from family, community, and occupation, or the sheer length of each working day, Congress was far more demanding than the state assemblies. Whereas Congress sat in continuous session, the assemblies met irregularly, and they were often slow to assemble and quick to disperse. Rural legislators were generally inclined to tailor their fulfillment of public commitments to the seasonal demands of agriculture: legislation could be enacted any time, but plowing, planting, and harvesting had to follow a more rigorous schedule. Apologizing to the Virginia governor, Patrick Henry, for the North Carolina assembly's failure to consider a common problem involving the Cherokees, Richard Caswell could only observe that the legislators had been intent on "getting home to their plantations at a season in which Planters in general have so very much to attend to." Lawyers and merchants who served in the assemblies were less severely constrained, but they too were self-employed and had to weigh private obligations and interests against the requirements of office. State politics attracted them because it was less disruptive of personal life and private interests than attendance at Congress. By contrast, effective service at Congress required a willingness to absent oneself from home for some months rather than mere weeks. For, as the North Carolina delegate Cornelius Harnett observed, "it will take a *young man* of Genius, ability and *application,* three months at least to make himself well acquainted with the business of Congress," by which point he was either anxious to return home or likely to be relieved, usually before either Congress or his state could fully capitalize on his acclimation.[9]

So, too, the arduous and tedious character of the congressional working day contrasted sharply with the lesser burdens of the assemblies. Committee appointments, general debates, and the conduct of personal and political correspondence left the delegates some time for food, sleep, and perhaps a little recreation, but until executive departments were organized in 1781, the claims on their energy and time seemed limitless. Much of this was due, to be sure, to the procedural inefficiency of Congress. "I have frequently heard heavy complaints in our Assembly, of the tedious progress of business," the South Carolina delegate John Mathews noted, "but I will venture to say, you do more business in one day, than we do, in three."[10] In some ways, as Mathews implied, Congress and the assemblies were exposed to similar criticism. The legislatures were rarely praised for their efficiency. Like Congress, they naturally preferred to avoid choosing among unpalatable alternatives and often failed to act on business requiring timely decision. State governors frequently had to inform Congress that the assemblies had abruptly adjourned without resolving federal matters referred for their action. The legislatures, too, experienced high rates of turnover in membership, which did little to foster improved efficiency.[11]

Although much has been written about the changing social composition of the assemblies, it is not at all clear how seriously the new men who entered state politics with the Revolution took their responsibilities. The extensive criticism directed against legislators drawn from the "middling" classes has to be discounted in part—for much of it did emanate from undisguisedly élitist sources—but it can hardly be ignored.[12] Yet however one assesses the "democratization" of the assemblies, there is little in surviving correspondence to suggest that legislative service was particularly strenuous. We know far less about the wartime routines of the assemblies than Congress, but one suspects that much of the actual labor was probably still done, as in the colonial period, by comparatively few members.[13] In any event, even if a particular session did prove demanding, legislators had the consolation of knowing that it would not last long, that their homes were reasonably close, and that if it did grow too tiresome, a critical mass of restless backbenchers would simply move to adjourn. What distinguished attendance at Congress from legislative service, then, were the special inconveniences the former imposed on its members. Congress had larger responsibilities to be divided among fewer men. The delegates had to work more arduous days, travel further, and stay away from home longer. Nor, once arrived, could they be certain how long they would have to stay. Though some members came and went as convenience dictated, others felt obliged to guarantee that their state would be represented in their absence or to remain until some issue of importance to their constituents had been resolved— which might mean indefinitely.[14]

The delegates' grievances thus sprang both from their personal dissatisfaction with the pace of congressional business and from a genuine resentment of the personal inconvenience that attendance at Congress required. The complaints that recur so often in their private correspondence represented something more than the mere release of daily frustrations. To sample this litany is to realize not only that few of these men enjoyed politics for its own sake, but also that their discomfort was in large measure a response to the simple novelty and extent of their responsibilities. For virtually nothing in the history of American politics could have prepared them for the range of problems Congress confronted during the war. A political education relevant to these concerns became possible only after 1774, and even these early lessons grew obsolete as the conflict dragged on.

On the eve of the Revolution, it is true, the Americans could draw upon an impressive tradition of self-government. Yet it is naïve to think that men who spent a few days a month mixing business and pleasure at the county court or occasional intervals of some weeks attending a provincial assembly were actually learning how to run a war, or coax supplies from farmers angry over inflation and expropriation, or maintain the morale of a war-weary populace.[15] Nor were they acquiring the stamina to stay at these tasks for months at a time. Before the Revolution, politics was still essentially an avocation, a secondary activity that local dignitaries pursued as a function of social status, some sense of civic responsibility, and certain types of ambition. It was something one did either in addition to a private calling or after achieving a measure of financial security. The attainment of public office did, of course, bestow practical advantages, and some of these were substantial: the fees of administrative office, enhanced standing at the bar, influence in the disposition of lands, simple prestige, and the power to transmit higher status to one's children—all important commodities in a society where the competition for visible marks of social superiority was intense. Yet *as an activity*, officeholding was rarely demanding of time and energy. Particularly at the colony-wide level of politics, its attractions were as much social as political. A session of a colonial assembly created its own social season. Legislators could expect to attend balls, dinners, and horse races; to renew old acquaintances and make new connections; to sample whatever cosmopolitan diversions the provincial capital offered.[16]

The wartime experience of the Continental Congress did not conform to the leisurely ambience of colonial politics. It marked instead a first, though still tentative, step toward an era when the pursuit of office and the exercise of power would become far more demanding, and when politics would ultimately become both an occupation and a career. The delegates' experience was transitional to the extent that their wartime responsibilities imposed changes in their working habits. Their reluctance to remain at Congress any longer than necessary thus embodied the tension between the novel conditions the Revolution created—and which perhaps affected Congress more acutely than any other body—and traditional patterns of political activity. Sharing the attitudes characteristic of American officials during the late colonial period, the delegates were ill-prepared, either by experience or inclination, for their new tasks. Their griping over the daily tedium of Congress did not anticipate the acceptance of unending obligations and unrewarding chores that we associate with the professional politicians of the nineteenth and twentieth centuries. Their attitudes toward work were still attuned to the daily and seasonal patterns of eighteenth-century agriculture, law, and commerce, when planters could spend at least an hour or two a day on horseback and when lawyers and merchants frequented coffeehouses, clubs, and taverns as a regular part of their business.

In a very simple sense, these men were not used to the indoor confinement Congress required. At the opening of the First Congress, Samuel Ward noted that "The southern Gentlemen have been used to do no Business in the afternoon so that We rise about 2 or 3 o'clock & set no more that Day." When the Second Congress had been in session less than two weeks and was still meeting only seven hours a day, William Hooper complained that "the little leisure we have is not sufficient for the common functions of life & exercise to keep us in health." And after William H. Drayton died at Congress in 1779, when he was only thirty-eight, a newspaper obituary merely converted these private complaints into a clinical autopsy. "His health had been almost insensibly impaired by a sedentary life, and incessant attention to business for near two years attendance on Congress, which his constitution, though naturally strong, was unable longer to sustain." (No wonder John Adams thought he had performed a great patriotic service when he coaxed his namesake Samuel into taking up horseback riding.)[17] The restlessness that infected the first two meetings of Congress after only a few weeks of deliberation was thus a harbinger of greater difficulties to come, once the major questions of policy that were so critical before independence gave way to the tiresome, unheroic, yet vital problems of sustaining the war.

The difficulty with which the delegates adjusted to these conditions resulted not from a lack of political experience per se but rather from the limited character of their previous involvement in affairs of state. In fact, few of the 235 members who served between 1774 and 1783 entered Congress as political novices. Four out of every five had held office at the colony- or statewide level of government prior to their election, mostly in the assemblies or provincial conventions. At least twenty-four had been speakers of assembly, and roughly another forty had been members of the provincial committees of safety that exercised such sweeping powers in the early years of the war. The primary political experience of another score of delegates had been within the confederation itself, principally in the army. For only a residual group of perhaps two dozen delegates did election to Congress mark the very beginning of their public careers. Almost a hundred had held office at the provincial level of government before the crisis of 1774; the remainder could fairly be called "new men," whose active political participation began only with the creation of the resistance apparatus of 1774–75.[18]

If the argument is correct that there was a significant disparity between Congress and other offices, such evidence has little explanatory power when it comes to assaying the delegates' attitudes toward politics. Far more important, but also far more difficult to recapture, were the particular motives and ambitions that induced men to enter Congress. As might be expected, these varied widely and cannot be subsumed under any one simple formula; yet in many ways a discussion of divergent careers conveys the real nature of Revolutionary leadership far more accurately than aggregate data about wealth, occupation, status, education, previous experience, and the other indices of collective biography.

We can speak with some confidence of the motives that led certain delegates to attend Congress, particularly those who served lengthy terms. Samuel Adams's regular attendance at Congress (1774–81) was a logical extension of his longstanding commitment to a united resistance, which he maintained even at the cost of a reduction of influence in his native Massachusetts. Although in his adherence to old whig principles and the faith of his Puritan forebears Adams was avowedly traditional, he was perhaps the most "modern" of Revolutionary leaders in the sense that he lived, quite simply, for politics alone.[19] In this respect the delegate who bears closest comparison to Adams may well have been James Madison (1780–83, 1787–88). For while the two men held few positions in common on questions of policy, they shared an untiring absorption in political activity—an absorption that deeply impressed, indeed sometimes astonished their closest colleagues. There were other veteran delegates who served lengthy terms because, like Adams, they had been among the earliest leaders of resistance: Roger Sherman (1774–81, 1784), Eliphalet Dyer (1774–79, 1782–83), Elbridge Gerry (1776–80, 1783–85), William Ellery (1776–85), Thomas McKean (1774–76, 1778–81), and R. H. Lee (1774–79, 1784–87). Politics became a career for these men in large part because they thought of themselves as the original Revolutionaries.[20]

Of more interest, perhaps, are those delegates who became politically active not in anticipation of, but rather in response to, the crises immediately preceding independence. Some were moderates who hoped to promote a negotiated reconciliation, like James Duane and his New York colleagues John Jay, Robert Livingston, and Gouverneur Morris. Duane's career was particularly revealing. Although he had been involved in the non-importation campaign of 1768–70, he was hardly a political enthusiast. In 1767 he had passed up an opportunity to become recorder for the city of New York, arguing that "the most I cou'd have derived from it wou'd have been £100 a year; and for this I must have been led into party and dirty politicks which I despise as beneath a man who would wish to be honest & wise." In 1770, when his marital relation Peter R. Livingston publicly supported Alexander McDougall, the notorious Son of Liberty, Duane questioned "the Policy of a great and respected Family becoming Obnoxious to Government." Were "popular Honours" worth seeking, he asked, "at the Expense of Quiet and a Certainty almost of an ungrateful Return for the most faithful Services?" After the First Congress adjourned in 1774, Duane found himself moving reluctantly toward active involvement. "Addicted like you to a close Attention to the Duties of my profession," he wrote Maryland's Thomas Johnson, "I have ever avoided both from the want of Inclination & Leisure an active part in politics. Unhappily for my Repose the alarming state of our publick affairs & the Acts of my Countrymen oblige me at once to plunge into the midst of a Tempest which I find myself unable to direct." There was much about Congress that he never learned to like; yet Duane appeared there every year from 1774 until 1783. Some of his interest may be attributed to his land speculations, particularly his lost investments in Vermont, but in the end his conversion to public life remains impressive. After the war he sought and secured election as mayor of New York, and he was later appointed a federal judge under the new Constitution.[21]

Had he so desired, Duane could have held office long before 1774; but for others, such as James Lovell, the Revolution provided opportunities that otherwise would not have existed. Lovell, a former Boston schoolteacher, entered Congress in 1777. Though moderately active in resistance in Boston before 1774, he had not previously held public office. Lovell may well have been the only delegate who was financially dependent on his salary. He remained at Congress for five uninterrupted years without once returning home, in the meantime frequently complaining about the impoverishment of his family and his own difficulty in meeting expenses. In 1781, after the tory printer James Rivington reported that Lovell was so diligent because he was keeping a mistress at Philadelphia, Gerry advised him to return to Boston if only for the sake of propriety. "You speak of my seeing Boston," Lovell replied;

I own no Horse or I might run away from my Debts and ask Charity on the Road for a Delegate of Mass[achusetts] to enable him to reach Home. But really my Friend are you not in Opinion that it is a ridiculous Way of proving that I did not keep Madam Clymar, to go and spend a Number of Months with my Family without one Shilling of Income *the Day after my arrival in Boston,* or without the least Hint from any Man that he will employ me in any Way within the Compass of my Abilities . . . ? Is it a Crime to serve here as a Delegate for a Living more than to do it in the Church or in an Academy? I thought not when I undertook it.

Lovell finally left Congress in 1782. Once a vitriolic critic of Silas Deane and his supporters in Congress, Lovell soon accepted an appointment from Robert Morris as receiver of continental taxes in Massachusetts, even though Morris, by then superintendent of finance, had been one of Deane's intimates. In 1785 Lovell became naval officer for the port of Boston, but was removed from office by the General Court two years later. In February 1789, with the new federal government about to begin operation, he could be found soliciting the patronage of R. H. Lee, just elected to the Senate. What he now desired, Lovell informed his "much esteemed Friend," was an opportunity to pursue "an honest Livelyhood on the Tenure of *good Behavior* instead of one upon the tottering Foundations of an *annual choice* liable to every petty & unfair Art of Electioneering."* Lovell received the ap-

---

*Disillusionment with the fickle loyalties of legislators and voters was a recurring theme in the writings of Revolutionary politicians. Near the end of his short life, Thomas Burke dismissed the "enthusiastic public Spirit" which he had once possessed as "a species of madness with which I was long infected, [and] which was too powerful for my reason . . . but to which the ingratitude of republican society [has] applied, I hope, a radical Remedy." (Burke to an unidentified recipient, draft, n.d., Thomas Burke Papers, microfilm reel 5, Southern Historical Collection, University of North Carolina Library.)

pointment he sought, and died a customs officer—hardly an appropriate ending for an old radical.[22]

The career of Abraham Clark provides a third variation on this theme of transition. Clark had had some involvement in government before 1774, as a sheriff and as clerk of the New Jersey assembly, but he was probably better known as a surveyor and something of an amateur lawyer. He was already fifty when he was sent to Congress only days before it declared independence. At first the prospect of being a delegate staggered Clark. "I regret my being moved to this Congress," he wrote after a month's attendance;

> I think I could have been of more service in our own Province than here. I remember what Cesar said in passing the Alps, "That he had rather be the first in a small village in the Alps, than the Second in Rome." This will not exactly apply to myself, as I did not esteem myself, the first in the Jersey Convention, and I am sure I am far below the second here.

But Clark's diffidence soon disappeared—a function not only of the experience he accumulated but perhaps also of the declining abilities of his colleagues, a phenomenon much commented on after 1777. Clark attended Congress fairly regularly into the spring of 1778, returned as a reliable member from 1780 to 1783, and again in 1787–88—even though, as he reminded a friend in 1781, "it is well known Attendance in Congress hath long been a painful service to me, and I feel a strong desire to be free from it." Rather than seek a seat in the assembly, however, Clark chose to remain in Congress, arguing that "The present situation of our publick affairs requires the Assistance of such as have a thorough knowledge in the business before Congress." Though Clark, an anti-Federalist in 1788, is usually described as a "radical republican," he believed that continuity of personnel was vital to the stability of Congress, justifying his own career accordingly. He was elected to the House of Representatives in 1790, when he was already sixty-four, and served there until shortly before his death in 1794.[23]

Some delegates, then, were prepared to accept either the obligations Congress imposed or the opportunities it offered. Though they grumbled like other members, their experience testified to an adjustment to politics as a career or occupation. Almost by definition, those who remained active through the war and into the 1780's and beyond were to become the most famous of Revolutionary leaders, recognizable either among the select circle of founding fathers or at least—as in the case of Duane, Lovell, and Clark—familiar to historians. Yet most members of the Continental Congress were historically obscure. Who remembers Titus Hosmer, Nathaniel Peabody, James McLene, Jonathan Elmer, John Harvie, Whitmill Hill, and scores of other delegates who scattered some months of attendance across one, two, or three years of membership and then left? Yet they were not cyphers. Individually and collectively, their presence exerted a substantial influence on the character of congressional proceedings and thus on the conduct of the war and national politics. Their ambivalence toward office illustrates both the diverse ambitions that shaped participation in the Revolution and the survival of the more traditional attitudes of the amateur, attitudes embodying cultural norms often shared by such prominent American leaders as John Adams, Robert and Gouverneur Morris, Robert Livingston, and Thomas Jefferson.

What considerations governed the behavior of those who sought to retire from Congress as soon as they gracefully could? Sustained attendance at Congress generally proved most troubling to those who had the greatest family responsibilities. In practical terms, these obligations fell most heavily on married men in middle age—that is, in their late thirties and forties—whose children were approaching maturity and thus needed to be settled in an occupation or a marriage. Comparative youth or maturity could therefore enhance (or at least remove obstacles against) a member's willingness to absent himself from home, as several prominent examples suggest. Among the youthful bachelors who served long terms were Madison (twenty-nine when he entered Congress), Gerry (thirty-two and wealthy), and Samuel Osgood (thirty-three). John Jay was a newlywed of twenty-eight when he was elected to the First Congress, and his friends Robert Livingston and Gouverneur Morris (another bachelor) were respectively twenty-eight and twenty-five when they subsequently joined him in the New York delegation. Thomas Burke (1777–81) was only thirty when he came to Congress, and when he died in 1783, he was survived only by his wife, toward whom he was reputedly indifferent, and a daughter.[24]

At the other end of this scale were those older delegates who felt less constrained by the need to provide for their children. Joseph Jones (1777, 1780–83), Clark, Samuel Adams, Henry Laurens (1777–79), Dyer, Sherman, and John Witherspoon (1776–82) were all in their early fifties when they entered Congress; Francis Lewis (1775–79) was sixty-two. Family affairs apparently mattered little to Adams. "Occasional letters to his daughter," Pauline Maier has observed, "resemble nothing so much as replies from the Boston Committee of Correspondence."[25] The children of Roger Sherman's first marriage had already reached maturity when he was elected to the First Congress; his second wife, herself descended from a prosperous mercantile family, produced five daughters who helpfully married well and two sons as yet too young to require active concern.[26] Laurens and Lewis were both semiretired merchants who had already made their fortunes well before the Revolution.

But for a larger number of delegates, career and family concerns did indeed seem too pressing to ignore. Prolonged service at Congress created real difficulties for younger men anxious to establish a legal practice or commercial connections or for those in middle age with large families to support. A few members, such as Rhode Island's William Ellery and David Howell, found the office a satisfactory alternative to careers disrupted by the Revolution, but the more common and sensible reaction was to regard it as a precarious foundation for a family's security. "How much I wish to be at Congress!" George Walton wrote Robert Morris in 1778. "Yet I dare not give up to the public yet. I am determined to pursue your advice"—presumably to establish his private fortune—"because it leads to permanent ease and happiness." Election to Congress might greatly enhance a lawyer's prestige and reputation, but this advantage could be capitalized on only by developing and maintaining one's practice at home. "This Trade of Patriotism but ill agrees with the profession of a practising Lawyer," Duane wrote after six weeks attendance at the First Congress. "I have lost my Clients the Benefit of a Circuit and now despair of doing any thing the ensuing Term." The same nagging concern regularly agitated John Adams as he enviously followed the rise of former colleagues in the Massachusetts bar.[27] Merchants and planters who could rely on some trusted family member to manage their interests and estates might find one or two terms in Congress acceptable but anything longer worrisome. Even Robert Morris found his attendance at Congress an increasingly irritating drain on his time, though its location in or near Philadelphia enabled him to keep a constant watch on his commercial ventures.

Yet in the end the delegates' willingness to attend Congress was fully as important as their eagerness to retire. There were no trimmers in Congress after 1776; no one who was not deeply committed to independence was likely to be elected, much less to attend. Almost by definition, the delegates were men whose personal sense of commitment to the Revolution made them susceptible to patriotic appeals to step into the breach. Such appeals worked in different ways: by acting upon the élitist sensibilities of men already distinguished in public life; or by asserting the superior claims that society enjoyed in times of crisis over the private inclinations of individuals, an argument that the new republicanism greatly enhanced. If it is impossible to measure which of these appeals carried greater weight—and apparent that at times neither worked very well—it is certain that both coexisted throughout the war. Although occasional contemporary comments suggest that the élitist strain grew feeble during the late 1770's, it later proved effective in mobilizing the Federalists of 1787–88.[28]

Cornelius Harnett, the old North Carolina Son of Liberty, was one delegate whose congressional tenure illustrated the convergence of these appeals. When first elected to Congress in 1777, he had already served as president of the provincial congress and the state council. Although still in his mid-fifties, he thought himself "*too* old to be sent here," and in fact suffered from a case of gout that impaired his ability to attend Congress. There is no question that he detested being away from his plantation. "I heartily desire to be at home," he wrote after four months of attendance, "& whenever I get there I shall with pleasure give up this very disagreeable & troublesome office." It was not only that he was "heartily tired of eating the flesh of four footed animals," a mainstay of the congressional diet when it was mired at York, and longed for his favorite delicacy of pickled oysters or even "a few dryed fish of any kind," which "if they even stank, they would be pleasing." Harnett was simply homesick.

If I once more return to my family all the Devils in Hell shall not separate us. The honor of being once a member of Congress is sufficient for me, I acknowledge it is the highest honor a free state can bestow on one of its members. I shall be careful to ask for nothing more, but will sit down under my own vine & my own Fig tree (for I have them both) at Poplar Grove where none shall make me afraid except the boats of the British Cruisers.

A year later, when he was about to leave Congress after serving four months of a second term, Harnett declared his intention "never more to return in the character my Country has been pleased to honor me with, unless I am forced in to it." But the North Carolina assembly reelected him once more, and so Harnett returned to Congress late in 1779. He departed for home before winter set in, but the retirement he desired was tragically brief. Captured by loyalist troops in 1781, he died from their mistreatment.[29]

As an early leader of resistance, Harnett may have found it peculiarly difficult to refuse election. Yet there is substantial evidence to suggest that similar considerations governed the conduct of many others who had been less intimately involved in opposition to Britain before 1774. The republican values of the Revolution did not permit conscientious leaders casually to reject an appointment to office merely because it was inconvenient. Republicanism not only glorified the individual who risked private interest for the public weal, it also bestowed on the act of election the sovereign imprint of the popular will. Even if conferred unexpectedly, the act of election was not easily renounced. "I am ordered to the Congress," Henry Laurens wrote shortly after his election; ". . . many reasons were & more might have been urged in excuse for me but . . . the Vote was confirmed, I call it therefore as I feel it, a Command—I go." Thomas Adams was apparently exposed to similar pressures. In the summer of 1777 his brother informed him that many members of the Virginia assembly had asked if Adams would be willing to go to Congress. "I told them you was fond of retirement & that I thought it would be most agreeable to you to stay at home," his brother wrote, "but if your Country called for your assistance I thought it the Duty of every man at this time to accept any appointment his Country should call him to, unsolicited." Whether Thomas Adams thanked his brother for the encouragement he had given the legislators is not known, but later in the year he was elected to Congress. He attended Congress for four months in 1778 and, after reelection, another four months in 1779; then he resigned. "Contrary to my expectation I am appointed a Deputy to Congress," Charles Carroll wrote his fa-

ther the day after independence, "and much against my inclination I find myself obliged to set off for Ph[iladelphia] in a week
at farthest." Robert Livingston complained bitterly when he was
reelected to Congress in 1779, after an absence of three years.
"The Legislature have again drawn me from domestick peace, to
bustle in the great world," he wrote. "I am to have the supreme
felicity of making them a second sacrifice of my health, fortune
& enjoyments at Congress: to this I submit, but with the reluctance of the shipwrecked wretch who embarks again after having once safely landed."[30]

Attendance at Congress was thus an obligation to be discharged, not an ambition to be fulfilled. "Ambition had no share
in bringing me forward into Public life," Robert Morris wrote in
September 1778, shortly before he left Congress,

nor has it any charms to keep me there, the time I have spent in it has
been the severest Tax of my life and really I think those who have had
so much, shou'd now be relieved and let some fresh hands take the
Helm, these notions prompt me to get out of Congress at the next
appointment of Delegates, but my namesake [Gouveneur Morris]
swears I shall not depart.[31]

The urgings of the younger Morris were probably a case of mis-
ery seeking company. He had allowed eight months to elapse
between the time of his election and his first visit to Congress
early in 1778. It took him only another fortnight to conclude: "I
would that I were quit of my congressional Capacity which is in
every Respect irksome. . . . There are no fine Women at York
Town," he informed Livingston. "Judge then of my situation."
Writing to his mother two months later, Morris admitted that
"The natural Indolence of my Disposition hath unfitted me for
the Paths of Ambition and the early Possession of Power taught
me how little it deserves to be prized." Morris was nevertheless
an active member of Congress, and he criticized Livingston,
among others, for sulking at home. Yet after leaving Congress in
1779, he was anxious to avoid being forced to return. In 1781 he
begged Livingston to "keep me out of Congress if it should ever
be ment[ione]d," reminding him that "from the Beginning I
never asked nor sought the public Confidence. Many are wit-
nesses that when I came to Congress it was by Virtue of a *positive
Order.*"[32] These protests notwithstanding, neither of the Morrises can be described as lukewarm patriots. Robert Morris was

deeply critical of the trimmers who had abandoned politics during the discouraging months after independence, even though
he longed to tend strictly to his commercial affairs. When he
returned to office in 1781 as superintendent of finance, he did so
despite a sincere belief that it was "contrary to my private Interest." That he was able to enlist Gouverneur Morris as his assistant
may well have been a tribute to the force of his example rather
than the latter's eagerness to reenter public life.[33]

If these two men remained as ambivalent about political activity as their personal correspondence indicates, less prominent
or influential delegates must have been even more disposed to
limit the time and resources they were required to invest in
Congress. Having accepted election because refusal would have
been impolitic, embarrassing, and unpatriotic, they nevertheless
sought to leave office once they thought their obligation had
been adequately discharged. Claims of conflicting private interest or simple lack of ability did not always provide a potent
justification for declining an initial election, but after a year or
two of sacrifice they offered a plausible objection against reappointment.

The North Carolina delegate John Williams provided a model
statement of the formula many delegates used to request permission to resign. He had not felt himself qualified to be a delegate
when he was elected, Williams wrote, but despite his private
doubts, he did not believe he had a right to decline.

To have refused might have been imputed to a Reluctance to have
Stepped forth into a Distinguished point of View, least distinction should
mark me for the Resentment of our Enemies, or that I wished to reap
the fruits of the Active Counsels and Endeavors of Others in peace and
Retirement without making any Sacrifice of my own personal Ease or
Interest to obtain them.

After less than a year's attendance at Congress, however, the
state of his private affairs and family concerns led him "with
Reluctance" to "ask leave to Retire." The New Jersey delegate
Jonathan Elmer had phrased a similar request several months
earlier. "A willingness to comply with your requisition, and an
earnest desire to serve my country, as far as my slender abilities
would enable me, were the sole motives that induced me to
accept of the appointment," he reminded the state assembly.
Now the circumstances of his family and private affairs rendered

his continued attendance impracticable. Explaining his decision to decline reelection to Congress, William Hooper informed Robert Morris that "the situation of my own private affairs, the importunity of my wife and little ones, that delicacy which I felt as a friend"—a reference to the North Carolina assembly's failure to reelect Joseph Hewes—"did not leave me a moment in suspense whether I should decline the honor intended me." Thomas Stone justified his resignation rather more curtly. "Being convinced that I cannot attend Congress so constantly, as every Delegate ought to do, without giving up the Practice of the Law: I beg Leave to resign the appointment with which I have been honoured."[34]

Some delegates were convinced that the interests of their constituents would indeed be better served if they were replaced by "men of extensive political Knowledge," as John Harvie informed Jefferson late in 1777. If his resignation would "not be Imputed to Unworthy Motives," he would gladly "make room for one of this Character," Harvie wrote, "for to you who know me so well it is Needless to say I do not possess talents for State Affairs and yet truly I am one of the Board of War without having the Skill in Military affairs of an Orderly Sergeant." (Yet George Mason, one of the potential replacements Harvie doubtless had in mind, occasionally justified his refusal to accept election to Congress by arguing, as he wrote R. H. Lee in 1779, that "you will hardly blame me for taking care, in time, to keep out of such Company.")[35]

It was not only good manners but sound tactics for a delegate seeking retirement to recall his own meager talents, since that widened the pool of eligible replacements. The more significant feature of these letters, however, is their candid acknowledgment of the urgency of private concerns and family affairs. That these constituted a legitimate plea for retirement is itself revealing, for such interests are expected to suffer during patriotic wars and republican revolutions. Had it not been for inflation and its attendant consequences, such excuses might have proved less permissible. But inflation was an issue that concerned the delegates in their private as well as public capacities; and because all segments of society had to adjust to its implications, it provided a rationale for rotating delegates that the state assemblies ultimately had to respect. More than simple homesickness or boredom with the male ambience of Congress, anxiety over their absence from family, property, occupation, and other personal interests was the obsessive concern that ran through their private correspondence. Each had an estate to maintain, and as the inflationary spiral began to accelerate after 1776, any prolonged absence from home increased their disquiet. Not even genuinely wealthy delegates were free from these concerns. "It is extremely unreasonable in my Countrymen to compel me to this useless Service," Henry Laurens complained in September 1777, when he had been in Congress less than seven weeks, "if they had only considered how much of my time had been devoted to theirs & how little to my own affairs, I think common gratitude would have induced them to give me a moment's respite."[36] The tendency to attribute inflation not merely to an expanding money supply but, more crudely, to the common avarice of the citizenry only aggravated their discomfort. If the rest of American society was indeed intently pursuing private interest to the exclusion of public good, some members must have begun to wonder why they had been singled out for obligations their countrymen disdained.

Living mostly as travelers, the delegates experienced daily reminders of the difficulty of meeting expenses in times of inflation. They were exposed, like all travelers, to extraordinary expenses. In fashionable Philadelphia they felt obliged to maintain a decent appearance; in their more primitive accommodations at Baltimore and York, they were subjected to the boomtown prices of local innkeepers and laundresses. Inflation steadily reduced the purchasing power of their salaries and expenses, which the state legislatures were often slow to adjust, and the press of other demands on state treasuries often prevented the timely forwarding of necessary funds. Those delegates who had substantial independent incomes probably expected only to see their salaries cover their expenses, but those whose attendance impaired their ability to practice their occupations naturally desired an adequate income.

"I am by no means desirous of raising my fortune at the expense of the public," William Whipple wrote his colleague Josiah Bartlett in 1778, "but justice to my family requires that I should afford them some support," which the New Hampshire assembly's allowance of twenty-five shillings a day did not provide. The collapse of the continental dollar in 1779 exacerbated their situation. It was bad enough, the New Jersey delegate John

Fell complained, that his colleagues Witherspoon and Frederick Frelinghuysen treated him "with the greatest impoliteness," leaving Congress "when they please" and "without ever saying one word to me on the occasion"; but "not to be able to live in the manner I have ever been used to, without spending my own money as well as time, is rather too unreasonable for the public to desire of any individual." When William Fleming wrote Jefferson to ask that he not be renominated, he noted that

> besides my own loss of time; and the long separation from my family, my expenses are so enormous that I find my fortune quite insufficient to support them. I am in private lodgings, with only a servant and two horses, which are in the continental stable, and I live as frugal as possible, notwithstanding which it costs me, at least, 25£ a week, over and above my wages. If our assembly do not determine to support their delegates in congress, they will shortly find that none of those of small fortunes will be able to continue here long enough to make themselves acquainted with the business. . . .[37]

The only alternative to providing "a more respectable Footing" for the New York delegation, Gouverneur Morris argued in 1778, was to elect men "who possess such Property that they can afford to sacrifice a few Thousand to the general Cause." Four years later, however, the New York delegation reminded Governor Clinton that "tho' they cheerfully submit to the Loss and Inconvenience necessarily arising from their Absence from home and Neglect of their domestic Concerns, [they] cannot possibly maintain themselves in the public Service at their own private Expense." By then, with the presses long since stopped, needy delegates could no longer draw on the continental treasury in a pinch. While waiting to receive an overdue remittance from Virginia in June 1781, Theodorick Bland found himself unable to purchase dinner for himself and oats for his horses. "The anxiety I feel in this situation (new, to me) is insupportable," Bland wrote to Jefferson, "especially as it in some degree incapacitates me from turning my thoughts with that application I would wish to do to those important concerns which I would wish to engross my attention."[38]

Samuel Adams might have been oblivious to so trivial an inconvenience as starvation. But Bland's distress, temporary as it was, symbolizes the link between the delegates' complaints and the substantive history of the Congress. Petty and idiosyncratic as these complaints often were, the diverse anxieties and frustrations they reflected contributed to the troubled mood that usually pervaded Congress. Not only did they act to confirm the delegates' initial misgivings about jeopardizing private interests for public good; they also worked, ironically, to inhibit sustained efforts to reform congressional procedures. Men who rarely associated their own ambitions with the future of Congress could not seriously commit themselves to remedying its dilatory and inefficient habits. It was far easier to put in one's required time at Congress and then leave, having learned that the office was a mark of distinction but not a political objective worth pursuing in a serious way or for any length of time. Their reactions probably had little to do with the ideological aversion to the corruptive tendencies of power that was so much a part of Revolutionary political thinking, for the war provided a sufficient justification for the assumption of office. The delegates' manifest edginess had a more immediate, practical source. The exercise of power was tedious, fatiguing, and damaging to their private interests. So long as most delegates thought their attendance a concession to patriotism rather than the fulfillment of their ambitions, Congress would be condemned to muddling through to independence. Internal reform became possible only after the military and logistical crises of 1780–81 proved it could no longer be avoided. Even then, attendance proved little more attractive than it had been before, and instability of membership continued to trouble Congress through the 1780's.

And yet those who left Congress gladly sometimes found themselves growing unexpectedly nostalgic for news of its affairs. "I find in spight of all my Philosophy that I have a strange Hankering to know what is going forward in the great Houses in Chestnut Street," Nathaniel Scudder wrote to Nathaniel Peabody from his home in New Jersey after leaving Congress in 1779. "I pray you therefore to be speedy in administering to me a cardiac Dose." Some years later, when the former Massachusetts delegate Stephen Higginson renewed his correspondence with Theodorick Bland, he reported that "I have done attending to the motions of the great political wheel," adding that "my taste for public life was always very inadequate." But two former colleagues in the delegation, Elbridge Gerry and John Lowell, "are this day to eat with me part of a leg of mutton," he noted:

when the table shall be cleared, I expect from Gerry the history of the last session, or rather the present session thus far of congress; to hear of all their manoeuvres and little paltry acts to carry points. I wish you could be one of our party; we would scrutinize and characterize every action and all their conduct.[39]

Perhaps there was something to be said for politics after all. Higginson may have found it less convenient and certainly less profitable than attendance at his countinghouse, but at times it had also been more exciting.

What Higginson seemed to miss, though, was not so much the actual business of government as such social pleasures as Congress had afforded: the congeniality of the boardinghouse and the diversion of political gossip. From a distance, Higginson could permit himself a moment of nostalgia, but nothing more. Yet he had been politicized: in the aftermath of Shays's Rebellion he would emerge as an active Federalist, plunging into politics in the same way that the earlier crisis of independence had mobilized others who had previously had little interest in public life. The Revolution had not converted all of these men into professional politicians or officeseekers, but it had freed many of them from the prudently bourgeois ambitions that had once limited their horizons to the quiet, respectable routines of late colonial society.

Part Three

CRISES

CHAPTER XI

Factional Conflict and Foreign Policy

———————— ⚬⚬ ————————

DURING the four years that separated the imposition of the Coercive Acts and the completion of the French alliance, the framing of the central decisions of the Continental Congress had been greatly facilitated by the pressure of external events, a seemingly limited range of acceptable alternatives, and the delegates' common recognition of the importance of preserving the authority of Congress itself. None of these considerations obscured the existence of personal animosities and substantive differences of opinion within Congress, but they did act to constrain their effects and, more often than not, to impose compromises most members could accept. It seems all the more surprising, therefore, that these restraints rapidly began to dissolve shortly after Congress had achieved its long-sought goal of a French alliance and at a time when American leaders believed victory would soon be within their grasp. For 1779 was to prove the most disillusioning year yet of the Revolution, not only because the war and inflation both took ominous turns, but also because Congress was wracked with an internal partisan conflict too severe to remain hidden from public knowledge.

The convergence of older enmities and new issues of policy paralyzed Congress at a time when it needed to take decisive initiatives in the administration and financing of the war as well as the conduct of foreign policy. For the first time, supporters of the Revolution felt free to criticize its proceedings openly. Yet although the aftershocks of this eruption would continue to affect national politics well into the 1780's, the experience of 1779 also confirmed earlier political lessons. A careful examination of these developments therefore reveals not only the character but also the limits of congressional partisanship.

Sources of Partisanship

To argue that partisan activities were generally *not* a critical determinant of major congressional decisions does not require us to ignore either the reality or the persistence of factional conflict. From the opening weeks of the First Congress, through the debates leading to independence, and well into the disillusioning aftermath of the Declaration, identifiable clusters of delegates had differed in their assessments of the priorities, requirements, tactics, and prospects of resistance. And in the hothouse atmosphere of a Congress where vital decisions were indeed being made, disputes over policy inevitably impaired the preservation of harmonious relations among the delegates. The considerations that persuaded moderate leaders such as James Duane, John Jay, and Robert Morris to accept the agenda of their more militant colleagues enabled Congress to implement essential policies; but they did little to assuage the mutual suspicions and antipathy of the rival spokesmen.

Congressional factions were initially linked to the debate over resistance and independence. Although any attempt to correlate geography and ideology too closely predictably falters, at the heart of congressional partisanship was a conflict between a nucleus of militant delegates centered on New England, and their moderate protagonists, who were concentrated in the delegations from New York, Pennsylvania, and Maryland. What bound this latter coalition together was less a sense of common regional interest than a mutual recognition and fear of the political upheaval that could occur in each of their provinces once reconciliation was abandoned and Congress authorized the creation of new governments. It was this issue that most directly sustained the initial pattern of factional conflict during the months after independence, when the actual business of constitution-writing was taking place. Residual doubts about the wisdom of creating republican governments in the midst of a difficult war were reinforced by the reverses of late 1776. Living and working in close proximity to the Pennsylvania government—the most controversial and, it sometimes seemed, the least effective of the new regimes—moderate delegates were neither able nor willing to remain neutral on this question. Duane, Jay, Robert and Gouverneur Morris, James Wilson, and Robert Livingston were all vocal critics of the radical Pennsylvania constitution, and in 1776 and 1777 they entertained hopes that the new government would quickly collapse. Their congressional opponents, on the other hand, tended to be more sympathetic toward the Pennsylvania experiment, or at least felt that further controversy should be deferred for the sake of the common cause.

A second issue that encouraged earlier animosities to survive past 1776 involved the controversy over the command and administration of the northern army. Here delegates from the middle states were particularly intent on preserving the authority and reputation of Philip Schuyler against the rival claims of Horatio Gates, the favorite general of the New England delegates. Skirmishing between the respective partisans of the two generals provoked congressional strife throughout 1777, and even Gates's victory at Saratoga did not end the wrangling. Moreover, the disruptive impact of this rivalry was compounded when Walter Livingston, deputy commissary for the northern army and a Schuyler intimate, repeatedly clashed with his superior, Joseph Trumbull, son of the Connecticut governor, Harvard graduate, and a confidant of several New England delegates.

Some of the vindictiveness that colored relations between delegates from New York and New England stemmed from pre-Revolutionary sources. A long dispute over the location of the eastern boundary of New York, though peacefully settled in 1773, had helped to inspire mutual suspicions; conflicts between New York landlords anxious for docile tenants and New England emigrants seeking to acquire land on freehold tenure had generated other ill feelings. "I fear these people will spread over the whole Continent," James Duane had written in May 1773; and when the outbreak of the Revolution enabled the secessionist Yankees of Vermont to renounce their allegiance to New York, his prejudices were confirmed. By 1777 both the New York and New Hampshire delegations were preparing to assert their respective claims over Vermont, an issue that further widened the basis for regional conflict.[1]

Personal antagonisms, doubtless magnified by the intimacy of a body that usually numbered fewer than three dozen members, also contributed to congressional factionalism. The celebrated incident of 1775 that saw John Dickinson refusing to speak to John Adams provided the most pungent example of how irritable some delegates could become, but the snide references that periodically occurred in many members' private correspondence testified to the existence of a larger reservoir of animosity. Some of this can clearly be attributed to the provincial sensibilities most delegates shared. Various parochial and personal biases played into disputes over policies and appointments: regional mannerisms of speech; the familiar denominational prejudices of Anglicans, Congregationalists, and Presbyterians; differences in status, wealth, and occupation. There was never any love to be lost between someone like James Duane, an Anglican lawyer and land speculator who was openly contemptuous of New Englanders, and the arch republican Samuel Adams, loyal son of Puritan Boston and an unreconstructed Calvinist who was inconspicuous in dress and so indifferent to his own family's security that he was reluctant to help his physician son obtain a military commission. Nor could James Lovell, the impecunious Boston schoolteacher, ever feel comfortable in the company of Robert Morris, the merchant prince of Philadelphia, or such cronies of Morris as George Plater, a wealthy Maryland planter, or Gouverneur Morris, the urbane New Yorker.

Some delegates, like Thomas Burke and R. H. Lee, simply took an instant dislike to each other, while the self-righteous posturing of such egotists as Burke or Henry Laurens could unilaterally raise the temperature of any debate. By 1777 and 1778 the cumulative grievances, real or fancied, that some delegates harbored toward others could no longer be concealed, and when they coincided with differences over important issues of policy, their repercussions were doubly disturbing. Newcomers to Congress occasionally recorded disillusionment at finding how sharply their previous images of Congress clashed with the petty enmities that marked many of its deliberations.[2]

A basis for sustained factional conflict did exist, then, before Silas Deane's return from France precipitated the major political controversies of 1778 and 1779. Some issues had already encouraged clusters of delegates to collaborate over a period of time and form effective factions within Congress, and personal animosities had sometimes reinforced differences over policy. It would nevertheless be wrong to argue that partisanship had consistently provided the dominant motif of congressional politics. Until late 1778, the barriers against overt factional behavior remained more powerful than the conditions that might have encouraged its open expression. What requires explanation, in short, is why the circumstances of 1778–79 released the delegates from restraints that had previously kept congressional factionalism within tolerable limits.[3]

How had the potential for factional conflict been checked before 1778? Many of the restraints on partisan behavior were, as we have already seen, inherent in the situation of Congress itself. The delegates' common recognition of the importance of preserving the extensive yet fragile authority of Congress worked to confine factional activities within its chambers rather than permit internal divisions to become public knowledge. Candid criticisms of Congress could be broached among confidential correspondents, but were rarely intended for a larger audience. Few delegates attempted to organize external sources of pressure to influence congressional debates, in part because the simple difficulty of coordinating state and national politics always posed major obstacles, but also because most members were sensitive to the preservation of their own prerogatives.

Other circumstances restricted the scope of factionalism. The progressive turnover in membership meant that new delegates were regularly arriving who were unacquainted with divisive issues and personalities, and who might therefore be reluctant to commit themselves too hastily to one group or another. The seasonal rotation of experienced delegates and the comparatively brief terms served by many others who attended Congress only begrudgingly would have impaired any efforts to maintain a cohesive faction over any significant period. The entire membership of Congress was rarely if ever divided into neat factional groupings; at almost any point, a substantial or even decisive portion of the membership was free from partisan allegiance and thus receptive to appeals from opposing clusters of more committed delegates.

Several aspects of the working procedures of Congress also suggest that factionalism had relatively little impact on the ordinary conduct of business. There is no evidence, for example, that any group of delegates was ever able to use its voting strength to manipulate the proceedings by stacking committees, managing debates, or using other parliamentary devices to outmaneuver its opponents. No faction ever acquired the strength or cohesion to form a legislative majority capable of controlling the flow of congressional business. And if, as in any deliberative body, some delegates exercised superior powers of persuasion over their colleagues, none ever occupied a position equivalent to the role played by a modern legislative whip; nor did the president of Congress exercise powers comparable to those of a speaker of the house. Before 1779, in other words, congressional factions were too fluid in composition, small in size, and primitive in function to act as modern legislative parties do. They were essentially clusters of delegates who thought alike on certain issues and sometimes managed to cooperate toward common ends.[4]

Much of what we do know about the shifting lines of congressional partisanship comes from analyzing the more than a thousand roll calls that Congress recorded, beginning in the summer of 1777. These certainly suggest, as H. James Henderson has argued, that important cleavages persisted in Congress and that regional loyalties constituted the most critical determinant of factional alignments. Yet there is another aspect of congressional voting that also deserves attention: for the frequency with which roll calls were recorded itself provides a rough index of the changing levels of partisanship. It is striking that it took Congress three years to begin recording selected roll calls in its journals, and that even then that decision was the result not of the delegates' intrinsic desire to have their positions publicized, but of pressure from the Maryland assembly, which was anxious to know how its own and other delegations were voting on questions involving the disposition of western lands.[5]

Nor were roll calls ever taken systematically; sometimes months passed while only a handful were recorded. Roll-call votes were taken only when individual delegates requested them, and this frequently occurred when a member wanted either to publicize his own actions for his constituents or to embarrass the supporters of a measure he opposed. In many ways a request for a roll call was an exercise of personal privilege, and it is not a coincidence that Elbridge Gerry and Thomas Burke, who were particularly sensitive to such matters, were more likely to demand recorded votes than most of their colleagues. Despite their frequent requests, however, it is still impossible to reconstruct how or why Congress divided on a number of major issues, which suggests that many delegates retained a belief in the importance of preserving the traditional façade of congressional unanimity. Conditions of severe partisan stress, of course, undermined this resolve, and the number of recorded votes proliferated—as was the case in 1779. But if frequent roll calls suggest periods of intense partisan feelings, intervals when comparatively few were taken imply that factionalism had subsided, or at least that most delegates were prepared to restrain the expression of partisan loyalties in deference to the greater importance of preserving the authority of Congress.

On balance, then, what is remarkable about the early years of congressional politics is not that some factional strife occurred—it would have been surprising only if it had not—but that it was so well contained. Nevertheless, the events that produced the divisive conflicts of 1778–79 had their origins in 1777, when Congress recalled Silas Deane from his diplomatic position in France; and an explanation of the later controversies must begin by untangling the circumstances of this earlier resolution.

The Affairs of Silas Deane

FOR its mysterious and bizarre turnings, the career of Silas Deane bears fair comparison, perhaps, only to the later enterprises of Aaron Burr. Deane had been one of the hardest-working members of Congress in 1774 and 1775, and when the Connecticut assembly unexpectedly dropped him from its delegation, his colleagues' esteem and his background as a Yankee trader helped procure his appointment as the first American agent to France. In the fall of 1776 he was named one of the three American commissioners to the court of France, along with Benjamin Franklin and Arthur Lee. Once in France, Deane entered into a bewildering maze of commercial activities that brought substantial benefits to the American cause and lucrative profits for his partners (who included, most notably, Robert Morris) and himself. Through his ill-conceived employment of the spy Edward Bancroft, Deane also inadvertently provided the British

government with an almost embarrassing largesse of secret intelligence about Franco-American relations.[6]

But no allegations of financial improprieties had been leveled
against Deane before August 5, 1777, when his recall was first
moved, or even late November, when it was finally approved.
The issue that led to his return involved a comparatively minor
aspect of his activities. Deane had granted scores of commissions
in the continental army to adventurous French gentlemen, and
these unauthorized recruiting efforts threatened to embarrass
Congress in two ways. The continental army, as Washington repeatedly made clear, had little use for the stream of French
officers Deane was sending across the Atlantic, and the cantan-
kerous American officer corps resented the liberal terms Deane
had been offering. Particularly controversial was the extravagant
contract he had signed with Major Philippe Du Coudray, an
unimpressive artillerist whose career abruptly ended when his
horse plunged off a ferry, drowning its rider in the Schuylkill
River. Perhaps more important, many members thought that
Deane's conduct, as well as impugning his judgment, could also
make him a liability at the court of Versailles, which might resent
congressional reluctance to honor his contracts.[7]

To some extent, the debates about the recall of Deane did
reflect the major factional division within Congress. His principal
critics included the Connecticut delegates;[8] James Lovell, who
had had to deal directly with many of the French officers; Samuel
Adams, whose suspicions of Deane dated to 1774; and R. H. Lee.
Deane's defenders were led by James Duane and possibly Robert
Morris. By November the arguments against his continuance in
office had evidently become conclusive. "He died at last very
easie," William Williams noted, "tho there had been at sund[ry]
Times before, the most violent and convulsive throes and Exertions on the same Question." His supporters did not request a roll
call, and Lee reported that the final recall motion passed "without dissent." When Duane sought to have the recall annulled,
Congress approved an additional resolution asking Deane "to
embrace the first opportunity of returning to America."[9]

The decision to recall Deane was nevertheless not an act of
partisan spite. Although several delegates from his own state of
Connecticut were bitterly critical of Deane, R. H. Lee felt that
he had "pursued his best judgment for the good of his Country
when he made those distressing contracts," and as late as May

1778 James Lovell proposed giving Deane a new position as American agent in Holland, where his mercantile talents could presumably be put to good use.[10] Nor in November 1777 did Congress as yet know anything of the personal quarrels that were splitting its diplomatic corps in two, setting Franklin and Deane against Arthur Lee, his brother William (commissioner to Vienna and Berlin), and Ralph Izard (commissioner at the court of Tuscany). The fear that Deane's continued presence in France might jeopardize negotiations for an alliance was legitimate, for his recall came at a time when Congress, hoping to capitalize on Saratoga, was anxious to see an alliance with France finally concluded.

Despite his recall, Deane did not choose to return to America until early summer, when he astutely sailed as an honored passenger on board the ship carrying the first French minister to the United States, Conrad Alexandre Gérard. By then, Congress was beginning to learn something of the disputes that had wracked the American commission at Paris. Deane's brother Simeon had returned to America in May 1778 as the official bearer of the French treaties, and he had doubtless briefed his brother's confidants about the troublesome meddling of Arthur Lee. During the early spring, too, R. H. Lee began receiving informative and accusatory letters from *his* brothers, which included serious allegations about a commercial contract Deane had concluded with Pierre Beaumarchais. In early June, Henry Laurens could note that "Frequent Items have been given in public of the disagreements of our Commissioners."[11]

Even so, Deane returned to a Congress that had merely sought to remove him from Paris, not to examine his affairs, and that now had little use for his presence in America. Nor were his detractors yet prepared to press an investigation. Their information was still shadowy and incomplete, and they quickly learned that Deane had judiciously left his accounts in France. It was not, therefore, an inquisitive Congress that sought to interview Deane, but an impatient Deane who demanded an audience with Congress.[12] Deane's desire for public vindication was no doubt sincere: once before, in 1775, his reputation had been gratuitously impugned by his constituents. Private interest complemented public honor. His commercial enterprises had been interrupted, and Deane was anxious, as he informed John Hancock, to "return to France, and attend to my private affairs."

Congress did not share his sense of urgency, however. During the third week of August Deane did make three appearances before Congress, where he gave a "general account of his transactions" in France and "his commercial transactions in Europe, especially with Mr. Beaumarchais."[13] But Congress took no action on his report.

One month later, however, substantive accusations were finally brought against Deane. R. H. Lee charged that William Carmichael, recently returned from France, could provide evidence that Deane had "misapplied the public money" and treated Arthur Lee unfairly; and Henry Laurens presented letters from Ralph Izard which, though not uncritical of Arthur Lee, placed greater blame for the discord at Paris on Deane and Franklin. On October 4 a lengthy letter from Arthur Lee, containing new allegations about Deane's handling of public money, was also read. But while Congress did examine Carmichael twice, it again took no decisive action, and on October 7 it tabled Deane's latest request for another hearing.[14]

Deane was convinced that this indecision, as well as his recall, was the work of a small knot of personal enemies, principally Arthur Lee and "a certain Triumvirate, who have been from the first members of Congress"—Roger Sherman ("my old Colleague Roger the Jesuit"), Samuel Adams, and "their Southern associate," R. H. Lee.[15] Almost immediately upon his return, Deane began to disseminate reports and rumors designed to undermine Arthur Lee's own position. His principal charge, which was essentially correct, was that some members of the French court harbored such serious suspicions about Lee's true loyalties—not to mention his diplomatic ineptitude—that his continued presence at Paris was not only useless but potentially harmful to American interests.

In early October, when the campaign against him was escalating, Deane counterattacked more vigorously. On October 10 the *Pennsylvania Packet* printed six queries strongly implying that Arthur and R. H. Lee had had traitorous communications with Dr. John Berkenhout, a mysterious figure whose activities following his recent appearance in America had led some to believe (correctly) that he was a British agent. The anonymous "Querist" was Deane himself. By mid-autumn, "tir'd with a four Months Attendance" that he believed served only the vindictive "purpose of the Junto" opposing him, Deane had resolved to go fur-

ther. "I design before I leave America if nothing is done, to lay
my Case at large before the public," he wrote to another brother,
Barnabas. "I have hitherto delayed it, hoping I should not be put
to the disagreeable Necessity, & knowing the Effects it must have
on public affairs, but the Law of Self defence being the first of all
I shall not longer be silent." On December 5, Deane's address
"To the Free and Virtuous Citizens of America" appeared in the
Pennsylvania Packet. Essentially an extended assault on the
Lees, its publication broke the veil of obscurity that still limited
public understanding of his recall, and (what was more important) provided a critical precedent for other politicians to appeal
for popular support against their opponents in Congress. It also
constituted the most widely publicized breach in the ranks of the
original patriot leadership that had taken place since independence.[16]

Deane's broadside took his antagonists by surprise. R. H. Lee
had returned to Virginia—though another brother, Francis
Lightfoot Lee, was still in Congress—and Samuel Adams had just
abandoned the idea of launching a newspaper campaign against
Deane, something he had been considering since October.[17] Although Thomas Paine was quickly recruited to counteract
Deane, the Lee supporters were initially outmatched.[18] On balance, however, most delegates apparently considered the skirmishing of December 1778 as more a literary curiosity than a
looming political crisis. "You will see by our papers a ridiculous
squabble between Deane and the Lees," James Duane, an early
Deane supporter, wrote George Clinton. "It may amuse a leisure
hour." James Lovell adopted a similarly casual tone: "I do not
think that the Public will be any Losers by the Time they spend
in view'g [Deane and Paine] tie and untie a few Knots, since the
former has been pleased to call up that Species of Diversion." For
his part, Edward Langworthy of Georgia noted, "I shall rejoice
to see more publications on the proceedings of Congress. A little
gentle Satyr will be useful on many occasions and will restrain
the Spirit of Intrigue and Cabal."[19]

Langworthy was wrong. The delegates' growing willingness
to tolerate appeals to the public at large gave that "Spirit" free
rein. Far from requiring the respective factions to reach some
tacit compromise at least preserving the traditional privacy of
Congress, this perceptible shift in attitudes encouraged them to
marshal popular support that they hoped to use for further parti-

san purposes within Congress. By the New Year of 1779 the repercussions of this change were becoming more apparent, as other members took to the newspapers or found themselves publicly impeached. Samuel Adams was rebuked for having met with John Temple, who had come to America in the company of Berkenhout. Responding to the insinuations of Thomas Paine, Robert Morris published a signed defense of his conduct as a member of the Secret Committee of Commerce, only to discover that Henry Laurens was on the verge of publishing additional charges against him. Laurens, who had resigned as president of Congress when his colleagues refused to condemn Deane's address, found himself forced to print an explanation of his resignation. Paine and Deane continued their exchanges, periodically joined by the two Lee delegates.[20] An unrelated series of disputes between Congress and the government of Pennsylvania generated another newspaper controversy.

Deane's publication of December 5 was the catalyst for all this. Yet it would be a mistake to conclude that the Deane-Lee quarrel was by itself capable of disrupting the course of congressional politics or obstructing the formulation of policies on other issues. Despite mounting levels of partisan animosity, Congress as a whole remained reluctant to distract itself from more pressing concerns in order to sort out the mushrooming accusations and countercharges. Deane appeared before Congress again in late December, but not until January 20, 1779, was a committee finally appointed to consider "the foreign affairs of these United States, and also the conduct of the late and present commissioners." And as late as the last week of February, Meriwether Smith voiced his hope that people "will not think that the Disputes of Messrs. Lee and Deane can be attended with any Serious Consequences to these united States. Believe me they would not deserve the serious Attention of a Moment if they did not interrupt the Business which is of more Importance."[21]

None of these allegations of corruption and treason had as yet posed questions of policy demanding immediate attention. But in mid-February 1779, Conrad Gérard informed Congress that Spain might attempt to mediate an end to the war, and the Deane-Lee quarrel became inextricably linked with new and more important questions of peace terms and diplomacy. Once that fusion took place, problems of foreign policy, formerly a source of congressional unity, acquired a divisive potential, and congressional partisanship reached the highest level it would attain during the war.

The Year of Division, 1779

As with the recall of Silas Deane, the domestic repercussions of the protracted foreign policy debate of 1779 proved far more important than its diplomatic consequences. The negotiations that Gérard asked Congress to anticipate did not materialize; under the careful prodding of his successor, the Chevalier de la Luzerne, the instructions Congress so laboriously composed for its peace commission would be thoroughly revised by 1781. The composition of the American diplomatic corps, another critical issue of 1779, also underwent later alterations. Nevertheless, despite the apparent futility of these debates, the substantive questions they raised clearly affected the tensions that were unleashed, and to understand how the political controversies of 1779 became so severe, it is first necessary to outline the essential issues involved.[22]

Early in February 1779, Gérard informed Congress that Spain had decided to present an ultimatum to Great Britain, offering its services as a mediator of peace but also declaring its intention of entering the war on the side of its Bourbon ally, France, should its offer be rejected. In an initial memorandum and then in a personal audience, Gérard made two requests of Congress. He asked it to appoint a minister plenipotentiary capable of joining the peace negotiations whenever they might occur; and also to determine its conditions of peace, which should specify not only what the United States would demand of Britain but its policy toward Spain as well. Gérard knew that the Spanish ultimatum would be tendered in clear expectation of its rejection, and that some Spanish participation in the war was therefore likely. He nevertheless urged Congress to adopt positions that would reassure Spain about the security of its possessions in North America once the United States achieved its independence. Gérard hoped, too, that Congress would not endorse stringent demands that might complicate the task of reaching an eventual peace with Britain. Accordingly, his primary goal was to induce Congress to limit its territorial ambitions, thereby protecting Spanish interests in the southwest while preventing extravagant claims against other British mainland possessions. To this end, Gérard hoped Congress would appoint a minister sympathetic to the objectives of French policy and subservient to French direction —preferably John Jay, who had replaced Laurens as president of Congress. He was irreconcilably opposed to the appointment of Arthur Lee, whom he, like his superiors in Paris, held in particularly low esteem.[23]

Although Gérard asked Congress to act quickly—even pressing it, rather tactlessly, "to overcome [its] usual inertia"[24]—his requests launched a series of debates and maneuvers whose four major phases took almost eight months to run their course. The first of these phases began in late February, when Congress took under consideration a draft text of peace terms that had been promptly prepared by a five-member committee. Congress agreed, with its committee, that Britain must recognize American independence preliminary to any negotiations. It also approved, without major modification, the committee's first two ultimatums, which defined the boundaries of the United States and demanded the evacuation of all British troops. The delegates rejected the committee's fourth and fifth ultimatums, which demanded free navigation of the Mississippi and access to "some port or ports" on that river beneath the southern boundary of the United States. But the most controversial problem arose with the committee's third ultimatum, which sought to guarantee American access to the Newfoundland fisheries—a matter of particular importance to New England. In committee of the whole, Congress initially diluted this provision, but in late March a completely rewritten article, favorable to the New England claims, was narrowly approved. It was this issue that was destined to provide the greatest source of controversy.[25]

The acceptance of an ultimatum on the fisheries closed the first phase of debate. The second began on March 24, when Congress received a report from another committee, composed of thirteen members, that had been examining the various allegations compiled against the American commissioners in Europe. This committee proposed that the appointments of Franklin, Deane, Izard, Arthur and William Lee should all "be vacated, and new appointments made." During the ensuing six weeks of debate, the status of Arthur Lee was the major focus of concern. But Franklin's position was also uncertain, for unlike Deane and Lee, he had no group of supporters—no "interest"—

personally committed to his defense. Several of Deane's supporters, in fact, apparently hoped to see Franklin recalled, possibly
because they had their own diplomatic ambitions to pursue.
When the vote came on Franklin's recall (on April 22), however,
only eight members voted against him.[26] Arthur Lee's position
was far more precarious, largely because Gérard, anxious to have
Lee recalled, provided his congressional detractors with information severely damaging to the expatriated Virginian's reputation. Even so, when on May 3 Congress voted on the question of
recalling Lee, the result was a stalemate: four states each voted
for or against him, while four other delegations divided evenly.
Lee's position had been gravely weakened, but for the time
being he retained his commission.[27]

This effectively completed the second phase of debate,
though another five weeks passed before Congress vacated the
appointments of William Lee and Izard.[28] From May until mid-
August, Congress resumed consideration of its peace terms, concentrating almost exclusively on the question of the fisheries—or,
as James Lovell put it, "Cod and Haddoc." After further revisions
of the article approved in late March, Elbridge Gerry (a resident
of the Massachusetts fishing port of Marblehead) introduced a set
of five complementary resolutions that provided a new framework for discussion. Gerry sought to convince Congress not only
to acknowledge the essential importance of the fisheries to the
postwar prosperity of the United States, but also to have provisions confirming American fishing rights incorporated in the
treaty of alliance with France (as an additional "explanatory article"), in the peace treaty itself, and in any postwar commercial
treaty with Britain. On four of the Gerry proposals, the pro-
fishery forces were able to command a solid plurality of the
states. They enjoyed a solid core of five votes, consisting of the
four New England states and Pennsylvania, whose current delegation was more representative of the radical Constitutionalist
faction than the moderates grouped around Robert Morris and
James Wilson. They could also count on the support of three
delegates—Nathaniel Scudder of New Jersey, Thomas McKean
of Delaware, and Henry Laurens of South Carolina—who almost
invariably prevented their states' votes from going to the other
side. By contrast, their opponents could rely on only three states:
Maryland, Virginia, and North Carolina; even New York, rarely
known to be sympathetic to New England, wavered. But on the

critical third article, which would have reinstated the demand for access to the fisheries as an ultimatum of any peace treaty, the pro-fishery coalition broke down. On this question Connecticut defected, and their obstructive support in the New Jersey and Delaware delegations disappeared. By July 31, when discussion of the Gerry proposals was completed, it was clear that access to the fisheries would not be made a necessary condition of peace.[29]

Although in early August Congress learned that Britain had rejected the Spanish offer of mediation, it was still deemed necessary to appoint a peace commissioner and a representative to the court of Spain. The maneuvers surrounding both of these appointments were an extension of the controversies of the preceding months. Recognizing that securing American access to the fisheries now depended on the diplomatic skill and perseverance of the American peace commissioner, the surviving nucleus of the pro-fishery coalition favored the election of someone who could be relied upon to pursue that goal vigorously. Their candidate was John Adams, recently returned to Massachusetts after his year in France, where he had become critical of the conduct of each of the American commissioners at Paris. His opponent was John Jay, still the candidate preferred by Conrad Gérard, who believed that Jay would accept French guidance and not allow the question of fishing rights to become a major barrier to the timely conclusion of the war. Similarly, the need to open diplomatic relations with Spain forced Congress to reexamine the status of Arthur Lee, who was still designated the American commissioner to Madrid. Several of his closest supporters, notably Lovell, hoped that a reaffirmation of his appointment would redeem his much-abused reputation, and they accordingly withheld from Congress a letter of resignation that Lee had already transmitted to them.[30]

They soon discovered, however, that Gérard's account of the suspicions surrounding Lee's activities in Europe constituted an insuperable obstacle to his appointment. The real contest lay, therefore, between Adams and Jay. After two indecisive ballots for the peace commission, an explicit compromise was reached that saw Jay deputed to Spain while Adams was designated to represent the United States in any peace negotiations that might occur.[31] With their appointments, the protracted debates over foreign policy were at last completed, and a relieved Congress turned its attention to more urgent business.

In greatly simplified form, then, these were the major issues of 1779. Merely identifying what issues were in dispute, however, does not explain why they evoked such severe strains within Congress or why Congress found itself subjected to an unprecedented level of popular disenchantment with its policies. Although inherently disruptive elements were certainly present in this matrix of issues and personalities, it is by no means obvious why these should have generated political tensions that transcended earlier controversies. For ultimately what is striking about the crisis of 1779 is not that it simply exemplified or magnified divisions normally present in Congress, but that its explosiveness disarmed the mechanisms Congress usually employed to restrain the potential for such outbreaks. The force and bitterness this struggle acquired reflected a peculiar configuration of personalities, issues, and attitudes that had not existed before and would never be fully reproduced once the crisis subsided.

Four factors explain how and why these issues had such an abrupt and drastic impact on the character of national politics. First, once Silas Deane and the supporters of Arthur Lee appealed for popular support, the personal and invidious nature of their multiplying allegations induced the major combatants to demand vindication outside Congress and revenge within. Second, easy as it sometimes must have seemed to lampoon the importance of the fisheries, the issues raised during the debate over peace terms did have genuine importance, and they forced individual delegations to calculate the nature of American war aims more precisely than had yet been necessary. Third, the role played by Conrad Gérard, who had his own objectives to pursue, was critical, for the French minister greatly encouraged those delegates who were sympathetic to his goals to persist in their opposition to Arthur Lee and the fisheries. Finally, the disputes of 1779 took place against a background of sagging public morale, when the glaring defects of congressional adherence to currency finance made Congress more vulnerable to criticism than it had ever been before and thus magnified the impact of the public reports of its internal strife and paralysis.

Much of the rancor released during these debates and their attendant polemics reflected the peculiar temperaments of the disputants. It would have been difficult to assemble a more contentious group of politicians than Thomas Paine, Lovell, Laurens, and the various Lee brothers—the major spokesmen for one faction—and Deane, Burke, William Henry Drayton, Gouverneur Morris, and William Paca of Maryland, their antagonists. Volatile, self-righteous, and intensely suspicious, they were not men who could suppress their mutual animosities once hostilities had begun. Deane was determined to procure vindication less by justifying his own conduct than by destroying his detractors; R. H. Lee called him "the Innuendo-Man." Of Arthur Lee, Deane's principal accuser, John Adams has left this portrait: "His Countenance is disgusting, his Air is not pleasing, his Manners are not engaging, his Temper is harsh, sour and fierce, and his Judgment of Men and Things is often wrong."[32] Burke and Laurens were perhaps the two most abrasive delegates who ever attended Congress; both invoked parliamentary privilege so often that they regularly antagonized many of their colleagues. Burke had tangled with R. H. Lee within a fortnight of the North Carolinian's arrival at Congress. Laurens and his fellow South Carolinian, Drayton, constituted the least harmonious delegation in Congress and were personally reconciled only when Drayton was on his deathbed in late August.[33] Burke, Deane, and R. H. Lee had all been denied reelection to Congress at one time or another, an experience that left them especially sensitive to the questions of personal honor that the Deane-Lee quarrel raised. Lovell's acerbic disposition was well recorded in the unflattering nicknames he and William Whipple bestowed on several of Deane's supporters. "The reading of Doctor Lee's vindication," Whipple wrote in late August, discussing a statement Lee had submitted to Congress in refutation of Deane's charges,

afforded me high entertainment; envy, malice, and every vindictive passion that disappointed malevolence could inspire, appeared on various countenances around the room. Fiddle head [Meriwether Smith of Virginia] shook, swivel eye [James Duane] nestled and turned pale, the chair [Jay] changed colour at every sentence, some others forced a sneer, endeavouring to conceal their chagrin and confusion; this, you may well suppose, afforded me no small degree of enjoyment. The Base-Viol [Smith again] has tarried a fortnight beyond the time he some time ago set for his departure. . . .[34]

We can guess that Gouverneur Morris, who had a satirical bent of his own, must have accorded similar honors to the Lee supporters.

Yet personal resentments and idiosyncrasies affect the workings of every legislative body to some degree, and their presence in 1779 does not by itself explain why members of Congress began ignoring previously accepted conventions of behavior. What was critical was that the specific allegations at the heart of the Deane-Lee imbroglio involved the reputations of politicians who were, one feels, understandably yet acutely sensitive to questions of honor. Deane, Robert Morris, and, by extension, their supporters stood accused of blending public business and private commerce to an exceptionable degree, improper even by the relatively tolerant standards of the eighteenth century. Members of the pro-Lee faction were similarly suspected of pursuing their own political ambitions with a zeal that mocked their ostensible attachment to the principles of virtuous republicanism.[35] Yet the particular substance of these charges and countercharges mattered less than the essentially similar responses they triggered among both sets of antagonists. For one thing, despite some differences in the rhetoric of their respective arguments, the contrasts between the two factions can be overdrawn. Samuel Adams may indeed have perfected the style of the virtuous republican, the visionary who looked to the creation of "a Christian Sparta"; but many of his collaborators knew how to reconcile patriotism with private interest. Whipple and Gerry were war profiteers, Lovell was financially dependent on his salary as a delegate, and the Lee brothers were more assiduous than most in their efforts to further their political careers.[36]

More important, both groups shared a common exasperation with the burdens and tedium of attendance at Congress—a malaise that the inconclusive debates of 1779 only aggravated. Convinced that attendance at Congress meant the subordination of personal interest and convenience, inhibited by conventional standards of political propriety from portraying their accession to office as a fulfillment of personal ambition, the delegates gave questions of honor and reputation an exaggerated importance because such motives alone seemed to justify their acceptance of office. For the friends of Arthur Lee, distressed by the obloquy heaped on a seemingly vigilant patriot, the true moral of this whole episode lay in a familiar couplet from Addison's *Cato:*

> *When vice prevails, and impious men bear sway,*
> *The post of honour is a private station.*

262

But when in the spring of 1780 Robert Morris reviewed for Benjamin Franklin the sufferings of Silas Deane, he noted that "My own fate has been in some degree similar, after four years Indefatigueable Service, I have been reviled and traduced for a long time by Whispers and insinuations. . . ." Now, believing the charges against him at last disproved, Morris hoped he could finally enjoy "the peaceable possession of the most Honourable Station my Ambition aspires to, that of a private Citizen of a Free State."[37]

Despite these considerations, the animosities of the Deane-Lee quarrel might have been confined to the increasingly tiresome potshots of the principals, had not Gérard's mid-February audience forced Congress to formulate its peace terms and frame a policy toward Spain. The foreign policy issues that confronted Congress prior to 1779 had been comparatively easy to resolve. Reconciliation with Britain had seemed inconceivable, while assistance from France appeared absolutely necessary. The nature of both of these issues thus enabled Congress to think in terms of a broad national interest that concerned all the states equally. But the debate over peace terms raised questions that affected the immediate interests of particular states more acutely than almost any other issue Congress had previously encountered. New England's vital interest in the fisheries was pitted against southern delegates' fears that a continuation of the war would prove disastrous to their region, whose military position was growing increasingly precarious as the new British strategy unfolded. Much of Georgia had already been occupied by the enemy, neighboring South Carolina was endangered, and in May 1779 a brief amphibious assault was launched against Virginia. The southern delegates who dominated the anti-Lee, antifishery coalition were so concerned about this situation that they did not insist upon Congress adopting a strong position on securing American navigation rights along the Mississippi, even though this question was generally deemed critical to the postwar economic development of their region. Prepared to yield so much in the interest of peace, concerned about the possibility of a peace settlement that would leave occupied territory in British possession, they naturally resented their opponents' stubborn insistence on the importance of fishing rights.

The fact that the pro-fishery coalition was only marginally stronger than its opponents tempted the latter to solicit support outside Congress. Some basis for public concern had existed since Gérard's initial audience with Congress, for rumors about the changing diplomatic situation and prospects for peace began to circulate almost immediately, though usually in garbled and erroneous form.[38] In early April the North Carolina delegation made a clumsy attempt to force Henry Laurens to alter his position, preparing letters to be sent to the South Carolina delegation and to their own constituents arguing that North Carolina should not provide military aid to its neighbor so long as Laurens defied the regional interests of the south.[39] A similar "very artful Attempt" to alter the vote of the Pennsylvania delegation was made in the very early spring, when the supporters of French objectives—or "Deane's Friends," as Joseph Reed identified them—sought to induce the assembly to issue explicit instructions concerning peace terms to its delegates.

But they could not be perswaded to interfere [Reed informed Alexander McDougall], alledging that it was properly the Business of Congress, & that Interposition might give Offence to some of their Sister States—a Sentiment which had all my Weight & Influence—indeed it appeared to me to be a strange Policy, to tell our Enemies so plainly, that we are sick of the War, & sought Peace on any Terms & I believe it was the first Instance or would have been, for a Power about to treat, to tell its Ultimatum to the World. Finding it would not take, the Measure was wholly withdrawn, but I have no doubt but it was framed by some Member of Congress, as it opened up plainly what had been in Agitation there, & our honest Country Members were told, there were some Men who did not desire Peace on any Terms.

Six weeks later, Thomas McKean complained to Congress that "our Ultimatum was subject of common conversation in every Country town [in Pennsylvania], the secret disclosed by Members of Congress at Reading in Berks."[40] By late April, discussions of the importance of the fisheries were beginning to appear in several New England newspapers, suggesting that the pro-fishery delegates were also preparing to organize popular support.[41]

The normal congressional reticence about disclosing details of secret business crumbled further after the May 3 deadlock over the recall of Arthur Lee. Two items printed in the *Pennsylvania Packet* in the days that followed—both obviously submitted by delegates—finally revealed how bitterly the Deane-Lee quarrel had divided Congress. The first disclosed not merely that a motion to recall Lee had been entertained but also how each member had voted. Since this vote was recorded only on the secret journals, its publication marked as flagrant a violation of congressional secrecy as had ever taken place. According to Charles Carroll, who had met with Thomas Adams, a Virginia delegate and Lee opponent, in early May, the decision "to publish the proceedings on this affair" had been taken by "the minority in Congress" who sought Lee's recall. The supporters of Lee responded quickly. In its next edition, the *Packet* printed a less explicit but more tantalizing countercharge. In whatever light Lee might be considered, "T." argued (but only after alluding to "his long and faithful services"),

nobody, that I have heard of, can guess at any honest motive for recalling Dr. Franklin, whose abilities, integrity and patriotism is [*sic*] acknowledged by all. . . . And yet it is certain that his recall has actually been moved for in Congress, and put to the vote. This may throw a light on the former question [of Lee's recall]. You will add to the obligation already conferred by procuring and publishing the Yeas and Nays, on the question relating to this venerable patriot.

This was, of course, a clear allusion to the fact that seven of Deane's supporters had voted to recall Franklin. "Will it be possible to ascertain who were intended for our new foreign Ministers if the recall had taken place?" asked "T." in conclusion. "If it could, it would throw a further light on this dark business."[42]

Just as Silas Deane's address had earlier precipitated open conflict with the Lees, so too the appearance of these pieces cleared the way for a public discussion of foreign policy. By late May, supporters of Lee and the fisheries were publishing additional articles on these subjects, and their antagonists, actively coached and supported by Gérard, replied immediately. As a result, the whole subject of peace terms was laid before the public in June and July, accompanied by further, more vicious recriminations between the two factions.[43]

Gérard's active involvement in congressional factionalism had begun much earlier, however. From the time of his arrival in America, his sympathies had clearly resided with his fellow passenger Silas Deane, from whom he absorbed a deep distrust of R. H. Lee and Samuel Adams. At first, Gérard acted with some discretion. He replied evasively when Lee and Adams asked him to comment on the rumors of Arthur Lee's unpopularity in

Europe. As early as December 1778, however, he had informed
Vergennes, the French foreign minister, that he hoped "to free
you and the Minister of Spain of a man who is very troublesome
if not dangerous." By year's end, if not earlier, several of Deane's
ʾupporters knew that Gérard hoped to see Lee recalled, and that
he might be prepared, under suitable conditions, to make his
sentiments known in Congress.[44] This issue came to a head in
mid-April, when Adams distorted Gérard's earlier noncommittal
statement by declaring that "he had the highest authority for
believing that Mr. Arthur Lee was in the full confidence of the
Court of France." Gérard immediately informed Henry Laurens,
a Lee sympathizer, that this statement was incorrect and that if
Adams went uncontradicted, Gérard would be forced to clarify
his position to Congress. Two weeks later, shortly before the vote
to recall Lee was taken, William Paca and William H. Drayton
gave Congress a written account of an interview they had had
with Gérard, during which he had shown them a letter from
Vergennes containing the pregnant statement, *"je crains M. Lee
et ses entours."* Thomas Burke and Thomas Nelson also personally confirmed Gérard's distrust of Lee.[45] Despite this indirect
intervention, however, Lee was not recalled, and a disappointed
Gérard now had to organize his congressional supporters to
make a successful stand on the question of the fisheries, knowing
that the pro-fishery, pro-Lee forces were growing openly critical
of his own conduct.

Gérard was aware of both the dangers and opportunities that
a public debate over foreign policy posed. He had previously
hired Samuel Cooper, the patriotic Boston minister, to publish
essays defending the French alliance; now he secured the services of Hugh Henry Brackenridge and of an unnamed former
delegate, probably Edward Langworthy of Georgia, who as
"Americanus" had already written several pieces and who now
offered "to write under my direction." Gérard hoped that moderate public pressure, judiciously applied, would finally force
Congress to reach a decision favorable to French purposes. At
the same time, he feared that newspaper polemics might not
only lead to the disclosure of information better kept secret but
also exacerbate partisan tensions within Congress. He had not
welcomed the published revelations of the motions for recalling
Franklin and Lee; and in mid-July, after matters had passed
beyond his control, he wrote Vergennes that he was "trying to

inspire some restraint in the principal writers on both sides. It is infinitely unfortunate that these discussions break out at such a critical moment." But Gérard's editorial efforts were ineffective and inconsistent; he did not object, for example, to the circulation and eventual publication of the Paca-Drayton deposition revealing his and Vergennes's suspicions of Arthur Lee.[46]

In his dealings with "Americanus" and his other writers, Gérard attempted to "moderate [their] zeal as much as it is in my power. My method is not to provide them with any information relative to current affairs, but to suggest some remarks on the facts that they know."[47] Despite their relatively evenhanded tone, however, the early pieces of "Americanus," the most important of the essayists, raised potentially damning allegations about the motives of the opponents of French policy. The first essay, which appeared in the *Pennsylvania Gazette* of June 2, not only argued that Spain would enter the war only after it knew "what terms are insisted on by each contending party," but also revealed that Congress had inexplicably failed to define its terms of peace even though it had been "applied to early in February" for that purpose. Without precisely explaining the source of this delay, "Americanus" posed two dangling questions for his readers. "Are we disposed to continue the war at all events?" he wondered. "Have we men in our public councils who object to the making any overtures in return, but such as shall put us in the possession of what the treaties of Paris never stipulated for or guaranteed to us?" A subsequent essay published three weeks later went even further, providing new details about the delays afflicting Congress, analyzing the attitudes and objectives of France, and specifically identifying the fisheries as the critical obstacle to a decision. Securing that right, "Americanus" conceded, though clearly in the national interest, was too extravagant a demand to be made a condition of peace. When Thomas Paine promptly began a series of three letters justifying the importance of the fisheries, "Americanus" devoted additional essays to that question.[48]

Gérard's naïve hope that a restrained public debate might prove useful was exploded at the end of June with the appearance of an essay entitled "O Tempora! O Mores!" Although its author was almost certainly a member of Congress, Gérard professed not to know his identity and apparently had no control over his activities. Dropping all pretense of restraint, this writer argued that Congress was being governed by "a Junto" consisting of the delegates from New England, their Pennsylvania and New Jersey supporters, and a few scattered allies. The foundation of this "Junto" dated to 1774, and now, through their secret meetings and machinations, its members controlled all the proceedings of Congress. The author revealed that it was their insistence on a fisheries ultimatum that had frustrated Gérard's repeated requests for prompt action, and also reported that Congress had failed to recall Arthur Lee despite its knowledge of his dubious stature in France. "By this one instance," he concluded, "you will be able to judge of the strength of this minority, and to what lengths they will go in promoting private views, and supporting of their party, family connections, and interest."[49]

Within a fortnight copies of the Paca-Drayton affidavit were circulating in Boston, where, as Thomas Cushing wrote Samuel Holten, the general opinion was "that let Mr. Lee's attachment to the United States be ever so strong . . . yet if he was disgustfull to the Courts of Versailles & Madrid it is to the highest Degree absurd to continue him a Commissioner at either." In August, with the fisheries question resolved, copies of the affidavit began appearing in American newspapers, perhaps with the tacit approval of Gérard, still intent on recalling Lee. In August, too, Paca and Burke laid detailed accounts of the problems and maneuvers troubling Congress before their assemblies.[50] All of this did not go unanswered by the other side. In addition to Paine's essays on the fisheries, R. H. Lee, who had left Congress in late May, composed new letters defending his family, which James Lovell arranged to have printed in Philadelphia. Early in September a reply to "O Tempora! O Mores!" was written by Oliver Ellsworth, a Connecticut delegate who had left Congress immediately after Gérard's February audience. Other squibs continued to appear.[51]

Gérard's willingness to tolerate these appeals reflected his own jaundiced attitude toward the group of delegates he erroneously described as *"la faction angloise"*—the label which, he informed Vergennes, "one must bestow . . . on those individuals who have the effrontery to treat as a French faction [other] Americans who work only for the fulfillment of their agreements and the general good of America." His earlier involvement with Deane left Gérard intuitively suspicious of Samuel Adams and R. H. Lee. Perhaps more important, it also enabled Deane's friends in Congress to form a cordial working relationship with the French minister, and not surprisingly Gérard's analyses of congressional politics mirrored their own vitriolic feelings, hardened during earlier years of partisan skirmishing.

But if the opponents of Arthur Lee and the fisheries were thus able to prejudice Gérard's understanding of American politics, he himself also played a critically active role in fomenting the partisanship of 1779. Convinced that his own diplomatic aims were being frustrated by the machinations of an entrenched clique, he consciously acted to expand the small nucleus of delegates with whom he worked closely into a broader and more cohesive coalition. "Until now," he wrote Vergennes in June, "they have presented so little of the character of a faction that although they have been united on principles, it has not been possible to bring them together in one plan or on a uniform way of proceeding. Each acts only on his own interior motives and feelings rather than in concert [with others]."[52]

One month later, when the fisheries issue still seemed unresolvable, John Jay and two other delegates visited Gérard one evening to propose yielding to their opponents in Congress. They argued that "sooner or later the fisheries would create serious difficulties in which France would be obliged to take part, if she wished to save America, and that it would be better to resolve this great quarrel now than to see the flame of war rekindled after two or three years of peace." Finding "our friends dejected, discouraged, and resolved to abandon a struggle that has become absolutely unequal," Gérard took forceful steps to revive their spirits and recommit them to further debates over the fisheries. After five hours of discussion, one of his visitors—a delegate "of an ardent temper and character," which calls to mind Thomas Burke—dramatically "became pale, as if awakening from a long dream," and, turning to his colleagues, "told them in a penetrating tone [of voice] that I was right, and that it was absolutely necessary to make the last efforts . . . to disrupt the measures of the anti-Gallican leaders." With their cooperation, Gérard proposed a new strategy, which involved another personal appearance before Congress on his own part. And his gambit ultimately succeeded: Congress did not make access to the fisheries a condition of peace.[53]

Gérard's account of his role has its self-serving aspects, of course, and it is also possible that he was not fully enlightened about the extent of his own supporters' political activities. His remarks nevertheless provide a useful reminder of how, even in 1779, conventional limits on the expression and character of factional activities retained something of their force. It is in the first place striking that Jay was prepared to acknowledge the validity of the New England delegates' insistence on the importance of the fisheries. At a critical point when compromise might have begun to seem possible, it was Gérard who coaxed the opponents of fishing rights into further activities that kept Congress involved in partisan maneuvers for another two months. And Gérard's skeptical analysis of the cohesiveness of his own congressional supporters suggests the need to distinguish between partisan alignments and partisan actions. The repetitive quality of the wrangling over the fisheries, the intimate connection between that issue and the status of Arthur Lee, and the frequency of roll-call votes forced most delegates to take one side or the other. But that in itself does not prove that all the delegates consciously thought of themselves or acted as members of a legislative faction. Some clearly did, of course— Adams, the Lees, Lovell, Jay, Paca, Burke, Drayton—but others continued to feel that circumstance rather than inclination had forced them, somewhat begrudgingly, to join one group or the other.

One suspects that William Churchill Houston spoke for many delegates when, in the course of a candid review of the whole proceedings against Arthur Lee, he provided William Livingston with a personal assessment of the mood prevailing in Congress in early October:

At all events I am happy this troublesome affair is ended, and I hope it will never rise up to disturb the counsels of America more. Subjects of contention and animosity are retiring one after another, and unanimity reviving in Congress where it is so essentially necessary. Trifles have had their day, and too long a one it has been; matters of moment have a claim to this, and that it may not only be longer but perpetual, I am persuaded is the ardent wish of every honest man.

By then other delegates were also attempting to convince their correspondents that Congress was again operating in a reasonably harmonious atmosphere. "The Inconveniences resulting from the Derangement of our Foreign Affairs are at length removed," Jay informed Governor Clinton in late September, announcing the recent diplomatic appointments. "All this was done with most uncommon unanimity and Concord." Gouverneur Morris offered a more realistic appraisal a month later when, he told Washington "that we are united as much as is safe for the public."[54]

The desire to restore a façade of unity was a natural response to the final determinant of the political controversies of 1779: the steadily mounting level of public criticism that had been directed against Congress since spring. For the foreign policy disputes of 1778–79 took place against a background of domestic unrest which was generated by the collapse of continental currency and the steady progress of inflation and which was accompanied by the formation of numerous extra-legal popular committees intent on regulating prices. Mired in inconclusive debates over foreign affairs, its members leaking innuendoes and scandalous revelations, Congress seemed incapable of dealing with the pressing financial and logistical problems that threatened to cripple the American war effort, instead "wasting Days & even weeks," as Joseph Reed complained, "in unprofitable Debates upon Subjects beneath the Robin Hood Society." Publicly and privately, Americans began criticizing Congress as they had never done before, comparing it unfavorably with its vaunted predecessors and concluding, with Charles Carroll, that "they have not abilities equal to the conducting of matters intrusted to them."[55]

The highly publicized Deane-Lee dispute provided not only evidence of congressional inefficiency but a precedent for candid public critiques of its proceedings, something that would have been inconceivable before 1779. Thus, after pointing out that the Deane-Lee accusations inevitably left many people wondering about the integrity of Congress, "A True Patriot" posed harder questions about the abuses attributed to continental commissaries and quartermasters:

Are these not the servants of Congress? Is Congress only ignorant of these abuses, which the whole public beholds with grief and concern? Does Congress know what becomes of the public money? Can it be possible that even the greatest part of our national debt has been accounted for? . . . The *strict secrecy* which Congress seems to enjoin on its Members with respect to almost all its business is by no means calculated to remove the conceived suspicions.

Congress responded to these criticisms by deciding to publish its journals weekly, but that decision only produced new complaints. "Let the journals of the first and second Congress be inspected," wrote "Phocion":

we find no such crooked lines drawn there; the path of public business was made plain: Whereas the journals of Congress as now published are unintelligible to half the world, for whose information they were designed. These are the devices of some modern Machiavel, who not being able to rise to that simplicity and grandeur which ought to distinguish a Republican Government, seek to effect by artifice and strategem what cannot be accomplished by fair and open methods.

Similar criticisms were voiced by "Gustavus Vasa," who after complaining that Congress gave greater attention to "the interests of a *Deane* or *Lee*" than the more pressing demands "of a *pining* army," went on to raise more general questions about its status:

Every true whig must, from principle, venerate *a Congress;* but *the Congress* may meet (when merited) with the disapprobation of the most public spirited whig in America—every loyal whig should always hold out, and at heart [feel] the most profound respect for the institution, even in the very moment the principles of the institution suffer abuse from that body, either *collectively or individually*—But to assert that Congress is paramount to the *just* censure of its *constituents,* would be to assert the institution of Congress unconstitutional—it would exclude the idea of their being the servants of these States, and of course of the people who compose them. . . .

In one sense, these were commonplace notions, already being applied with increasing frequency to the functioning of the state governments. Not since 1775, however, had Congress been exposed to similar criticism, and even then, as "Gustavus Vasa" implicitly recalled, such remarks had emanated from loyalists, not from "true whigs."[56]

For a time, some delegates seemed to welcome this scrutiny. Members of both factions hoped it might work to expose or at least restrain the vicious behavior of their antagonists. A few, like Henry Laurens, even proposed that Congress should open its doors to the public, a suggestion that was endorsed by R. H. Lee, recuperating at his Virginia plantation, Chantilly. "I believe our affairs will not go on well," Lee told Laurens, "until the plotting secret Divan is converted into an open Assembly of the people's

representatives." Other delegates tolerated public criticism because they thought it justified. Thus when Benjamin Rush, a
former delegate, published a searching indictment of congressional finance, Gérard was able to report that a few delegates
"wished to deal severely with the author, but a large majority
thought it more valuable to profit from the justice of his reflections and advice."[57]

Yet older reservations about the wisdom of encouraging open
discussion and criticism of congressional deliberations had only
been temporarily undermined, not destroyed. The notion of appealing to popular opinion was still regarded as something of an
aberration, an experiment sparked by the distinctive circumstances of 1779. When the newspaper campaign over the fisheries
was reaching its height, even Gouverneur Morris confessed that

It is peculiarly unfortunate for the People and for Congress that Subjects
of this Sort should be thus publickly agitated. Without divulging the
Secrets of Congress it is impossible to place the Subject in its proper
Light and yet unless that is done the People will probably be deluded
and if it is done Congress must become contemptible abroad and consequently insignificant at home.

Once the debates over foreign affairs finally ran their course in
the early fall, most delegates, anxious to turn their full attention
to the long-delayed reformation of financial policy, quickly lost
their enthusiasm for pursuing these animosities further. "There
seems to be an Infinity of Good Humour in Consequence of the
late Elections," Lovell observed the day after Jay and Adams
received their new appointments.[58] The continuing turnover of
delegates also helped tensions to subside. The two Lee brothers
had left Congress by late May; Samuel Adams went home in
mid-June, Thomas Burke in mid-July. Drayton took fatally ill in
August, Gouverneur Morris lost his seat, and Jay, Laurens, and
William Carmichael all accepted diplomatic positions. And, with
the arrival of the Chevalier de la Luzerne, an ailing Conrad
Gérard was finally able to depart for France.

For a time, this tacit resolution to minimize the appearance
of internal conflict proved effective. It passed an early test in
1780, when Arthur Lee returned to America and promptly jour-
neyed to Congress to demand the recall of Franklin and an opportunity to refute Deane's allegations. These were not requests
that Congress wanted to answer. "I have had great anxiety lest

the flame of faction which on a former occasion proved so injurious be kindled anew," James Madison wrote, "but as far as I can judge the temper of Congress is in general by no means prone to it, although there may be individuals on both sides who would both wish and endeavour it." The experience of 1779 had seemingly confirmed the older tradition of congressional behavior and responsibility. Although 1780 and 1781 were years of major decisions and changes in policy, Congress recorded fewer roll calls, delegates stopped submitting candid accounts of their deliberations to the press, and in their correspondence some members again sought to project an image of relative harmony prevailing at Philadelphia.[59]

These changes were not lost on some observers. In July 1780, for example, the Virginia assembly approved a resolution criticizing Congress for "the omission of the Yeas and Nays" in its published journals and instructing its delegates "to use their best endeavors to have the Yeays [*sic*] and Nays on every important question printed . . . as formerly."[60] Although Madison and his colleagues did not consider this instruction binding, its implications were nevertheless apparent. The deference that Congress had enjoyed before the disputes of 1778–79 could not be restored. For the remaining decade of its existence, Congress was increasingly exposed to expressions of pity, derision, suspicion, and contempt. Even without these controversies, a substantial loss of prestige was inevitable, for the difficult financial and logistical decisions that now had to be made were bound to prove unpopular. But the loss of confidence Congress had already suffered guaranteed that its subsequent decisions could be criticized with a candor and cynicism not possible before. Thus while the lessons of 1779 encouraged the delegates to close ranks enough to deal with the pressing questions that arose as the war entered its bleakest phase, their efforts to project a façade of unanimity were at best a means of preventing further damage. The political capital squandered over the fates of Silas Deane, Arthur Lee, and the Newfoundland fisheries could not be recouped.

Nor could the personal conflicts and sectional tensions evoked during these disputes be confined to 1779. In 1781 Gérard's successor waged a successful campaign to revise American peace terms and circumscribe John Adams's diplomatic independence.[61] In 1779 New England delegates had been more critical of Gérard as a diplomat than France as an ally; after 1781 a genuine Francophobia infected their positions not only on foreign policy but also on critical issues of domestic politics, largely because supporters of French objectives played major roles in national politics during the early 1780's. Robert Morris was superintendent of finance, Gouverneur Morris his assistant, and Robert Livingston the new secretary for foreign affairs. When Arthur Lee entered Congress in early 1782, the fusion between foreign and domestic policy thus became inevitable. From the perspective of Lee and some of his closest supporters, the issues of the 1780's were merely an extension of the earlier struggle. In their origins and extent, the disputes of 1778–79 had their accidental components; but their legacy would have a lasting effect on the politics of the confederation.

CHAPTER XII

A Government
Without Money

————————⟳————————

TO many Revolutionary leaders the foreign policy disputes
of 1778–79 seemed particularly harmful because they hindered congressional attempts to devise effective measures for
halting the depreciation of the currency and properly supplying
the army and also because they raised false hopes of peace. "It
has been the Misfortune of this Country, that every Year, has
afforded some amusement to retard its Exertions against the
common Enemy," Alexander McDougall complained in the
spring of 1779. "At one time Reconciliation, another our Assistance from France is to effect our Deliverance—this failing, our
Alliance with that People, was to accomplish our Redemption—
now Spain's acceding to our Independency" provided the latest
delusion.[1] By early fall, however, Congress knew that the war
would continue indefinitely, and once the diplomatic debates
had run their course, the delegates rapidly acted to fashion a new
system of finance and logistics. As we have already seen, this
reformation embodied three principal measures: a halt to the
further printing of continental currency; a plan to transfer responsibility for provisioning the army to the states, which were
asked to furnish specific supplies of food, clothing, and other
essentials; and an attempt to create a stable circulating currency
through a program of devaluating the old currency, taxing it out
of existence, and issuing a new emission whose total value would

be carefully restricted. One effect of these measures was to make Congress and the army more dependent on the efforts of the states.

How the states responded to this challenge constituted an implicit test of one of the central assumptions underlying the early American theory of federalism, namely, that in certain areas the states were the administrative agencies of Congress, obliged to implement its decisions when they lay within its legitimate sphere of responsibility. Thus when the states proved unable—though not necessarily unwilling—to carry out these new policies successfully, a number of American leaders, both in Congress and out, began to consider other alternatives. Some, like McDougall, had always questioned the wisdom of relying on the states and saw the looming crisis as evidence of defects in American institutions and manners alike. "While we are pleasing and amusing ourselves with Spartan Constitutions on paper, a very contrary Spirit reigns triumphant, in all Ranks," he told Joseph Reed in the letter quoted earlier. "Our political Constitutions and Manners, do not agree, one or the other must fall—give way —otherwise America is a Phenomenon in Civil Society—Spartan Constitutions, and Roman Manners, peculiar to her declining State, never will accord." By the summer of 1780, the disappointing results of the new programs were leading some delegates to propose other measures pointing toward an increase in the authority of Congress and to wonder whether the Articles of Confederation, once ratified, would constitute an adequate frame of national government. The conditions of 1780 thus introduced a new phase of thinking about the problems of federalism, but a phase in which the exigencies of war rather than any grandly nationalistic visions continued to determine the scope of thought.

The Problem of Supplies

CONGRESS had not adopted the system of specific supplies without foreboding. "For my part I dislike the plan altogether," Abraham Clark wrote, "as purchases ought to be made where most Convenient having regard to the places where they are to be consumed and the prices in the several states which must depend upon the seasons." Ezra L'Hommedieu hoped the new plan would be seriously pursued, but "at the same time I fear more difficulties will be experienced in carrying it into execution than is at present imagined." Such reservations initially mattered less than the absence of viable alternatives. The new system of procurement, the North Carolina delegates observed, was "such as the Necessity of our affairs, rather than choice, has determin[ed] us to adopt."[2] State officials who knew the limits of their own resources and perhaps had a better opportunity to witness the system in operation entertained similar doubts. Writing on behalf of the Massachusetts Council in late September, James Bowdoin felt obliged to give Congress what was virtually an elementary lesson in civics:

With respect to supplies for the Army, Experience has taught us that by calling on the several States (whose Assemblies are composed of a great number of Persons who must deliberate upon every Measure & consequently must be very slow in their final Determinations) for the specific Articles that are wanted, the Army has been fed only from day to day & at some times almost intirely destitute of any provision at all. . . .

Officials in other states echoed Bowdoin's complaints, while even more scathing criticism arose from the army.[3]

The inherent inefficiency of the system of supplies also helped to cripple the financial plan of March 18, 1780—the last attempt to salvage something from the voluminous emissions of past years. To keep the army fed and clothed while requisitions were being collected and transported, commissaries and quartermasters were increasingly obliged to impress whatever commodities and goods they needed. Instead of cash, the disgruntled owners received certificates, which were "drafts which federal officers drew upon their respective departments," and which had no more value than the continental currency they first supplemented and then replaced. "Wherever the armies went they littered the country with certificates," E. James Ferguson, the historian of Revolutionary finance, has written, and this "massive certificate debt foredoomed Congress' efforts to restore its currency." Popular pressure forced the state governments to accept certificates in lieu of currency for the payment of taxes, thereby undercutting the intended plan of removing the old money from circulation and issuing a new emission in its place. As the months passed, the continental treasury remained empty, while Congress was daily exposed to continued demands for cash.[4]

Until alternative policies could be developed, Congress had no choice but to pursue these expedients as best it could. But from the spring of 1780 through the following winter it appointed a series of committees whose cumulative recommendations constituted a thorough repudiation of the reforms just set in motion. The first of these committees was elected in mid-April, when Philip Schuyler, John Mathews, and Nathaniel Peabody were dispatched to army headquarters. The "Committee at Camp," as it was called, was given broad responsibilities: to confer with Washington and other key officers on the condition of the army; to act to implement the plan of specific supplies; and to undertake a thorough examination of the whole logistical apparatus with an eye to recommending further reforms. One of the committee's major functions was exhortatory: it issued a steady stream of circular letters urging the states to forward the supplies that had been demanded of them.[5]

From the start of their mission, the committee seems to have been convinced that the system of specific supplies was poorly calculated to sustain an active campaign. The news that France had finally decided to send a large force to America confirmed Schuyler's opinion that "to Depend entirely on the States for *effectual* Supplies . . . would be hazarding too much."[6] It was Schuyler, the controversial former general from New York, who emerged as the leading critic of the new system. Schuyler had little inclination to defer to the judgment of Congress. Although he had been reelected to Congress in October 1778, immediately after his acquittal by a court-martial convened to determine his responsibility for the loss of Ticonderoga in 1777, Schuyler resisted the pleas of his friends in the New York delegation and allowed another year to elapse before he consented to take his seat. Still bitter over the treatment he had received from Congress in 1776 and 1777, he refused to accept a place on a commission Congress appointed in January 1780 to reform the staff departments, citing his reluctance to "accept of any employment under Congress in a Station either less honorable or less Important than that which I once had the honor to hold." In April, however, he agreed to serve on the new committee Washington asked Congress to send to his headquarters. John Mathews had a similarly low opinion of Congress, which as early as 1778 he had concluded was no longer "competent to do the great public business intrusted to them." Given other delegates' awareness of Mathews's and Schuyler's feelings toward Congress, it scarcely proved surprising when the committee's activities came to be viewed suspiciously from the perspective of Philadelphia.[7]

The issue that worked to alienate Congress from the Committee at Camp stemmed from a proposal the committee made shortly after its arrival at the Middletown headquarters, where it was able to observe the miserable condition of the troops under Washington's immediate command—an embarrassing sight also witnessed only days earlier by the Chevalier de la Luzerne. With Washington's active encouragement and support, the committee asked Congress to give it or another small committee "ample Powers for Drawing forth the Resources of the Country," and permission to request the states "to invest for a limited time in Congress or such persons as Congress may appoint Dictatorial Powers" sufficient to keep the army well supplied.[8]

Like most of the officers with whom it consulted, the committee believed that Congress was too habitually inefficient to act with the "dispatch" that the military situation of 1780 required. "A degree of inertia pervades all popular bodies, they are unequal to that celerity so requisite to the effectual prosecution of Military operations," Schuyler observed in a private letter to James Duane; "perhaps Congress labours in a greater degree under this misfortune than any popular body that ever existed at the head of an Empire." Although Congress did issue supplemental instructions to the committee, it persistently balked at granting the additional extensive authority that had been requested. Some delegates apparently bridled at the peremptory language the committee had used in addressing Congress, and relations deteriorated further when the committee sided with General Nathanael Greene in a nasty dispute over the reorganization of the quartermaster department. The committee remained at camp, doing its utmost to implement the requisitions Congress had levied on the states, before being finally discharged on August 11.[9]

Although the central recommendations of the committee went unadopted, its communications, reinforced by additional pleas from Washington, did succeed in conveying to Congress a disturbing picture of the precarious and impotent condition of the army. Neither Schuyler nor Mathews bothered to mince words. Both had concluded that Congress needed to reclaim rather than disperse its powers. "By invariably holding up to the States that it had only a Recommendatory power, they have been taught to pay little attention to any decision of Congress," Schuyler wrote Duane in mid-May, "but it is for the weal of the Empire that [Congress] should assume, or even take new powers." Two months later Schuyler endorsed Jeremiah Wadsworth's belief that "Congress must have new and extensive Powers. . . . It involves an Absurdity that the propriety of the recommendations of the directing power of the Empire should be complied with or not as It may be thought expedient by the States." And there were delegates at Philadelphia who shared his fears, including Duane and Robert Livingston, Schuyler's Albany intimates, and two new members from Virginia, James Madison and Joseph Jones. Madison had been at Congress less than a week when, in a letter to Jefferson, he outlined the predicament of a body that was "from a defect of adequate Statesmen more likely to fall into wrong measures and of less weight to enforce right ones, recommending plans to the several states for execution and the states separately rejudging the expediency of such plans." Yet, as Jones realized, its recent decisions had only made the recovery of congressional powers all the more difficult, for

by these and several other proceedings Congress have been gradually surrendering or throwing upon the States the exercise of powers they should have retained and to their utmost have exercised themselves, until at length they have scarce a power left but such as concerns foreign transactions, for as to the Army the Congress is at present little more than the medium through which the wants of the Army are conveyed to the States. This Body never had or at least in few instances have exercised powers adequate to the purposes of War and such as they had, have been from embarrassment and difficulties frittered away and it will be found I fear very difficult to recover them.[10]

Jones may well have been unfairly pessimistic. From the vantage point of Congress, the states' inefficiency in collecting supplies and raising taxes seemed tantamount to a willful defiance of its authority; but there were other signs that officials in the states were prepared to concentrate additional powers in Congress. Schuyler again played a critical role in launching a new series of maneuvers designed to encourage Congress to take stronger action. Frustrated in his dealings with Congress, Schuyler had returned to New York rather than resume his seat after the dissolution of the Committee at Camp. It was almost certainly at his prodding that the New York legislature approved a resolution urging Congress to "exercise every Power which they may deem necessary for an effectual Prosecution of the War," including vesting Washington with the authority to use the army to compel "any State [which] is deficient in furnishing the Quota of Men, Money, Provisions or other Supplies . . . to furnish its deficiency." The New York delegates remaining at Congress thought this latter clause "not perhaps proper for publick Inspection" and chose to withhold it.[11]

In November 1780, however, a convention of deputies from the four New England states and New York met at Hartford and approved similar resolutions, which were subsequently submitted to Congress. British activity on Lake Champlain prevented Schuyler from making the journey to Hartford, but he made sure that Egbert Benson, a fellow commissioner, was "strongly Impressed" with his views. In February 1781 Governor Clinton of New York also dispatched a strongly worded letter to Congress, reminding it that it had always exercised "extensive Powers" over war, finance, and diplomacy. "No Objection has, that we know of, been made by any State to any of these Measures," wrote Clinton, who later became a major opponent of a strong national government. "Hence we venture to conclude that other States are in Sentiment with us, that these were Powers that necessarily existed in Congress, and we cannot suppose that they should want the Power of compelling the several States to their Duty and thereby enabling the Confederacy to expel the common Enemy."[12] If the governments of the northern states, which were no longer the scene of major fighting, were prepared to advance such sentiments, it is at least plausible to suggest that consent for drastic measures could have been procured from the imperiled southern states.

Despite these suggestions, Congress was not prepared to assert or solicit coercive powers over the states; even James Duane, a man of few illusions, seemed to feel that such proposals went too far. Congressional reluctance to pursue the measures Schuyler had propagated may have reflected a belief that the Articles of Confederation, then finally nearing ratification, should go into effect first. In the meantime, acting in its characteristically cumbersome fashion, Congress began reconsidering its standing problems of money, supplies, and administration. On the same day that the Committee at Camp was discharged, a new committee was appointed to prepare an estimate of expenses for the next two years and "to provide ways and means for [procuring] such further supplies as may be necessary." This committee produced several reports designed both to carry the earlier reforms into effect and to propose ways for Congress to resume direct control over finance and logistics. Some of its duties were apparently assumed by another committee, appointed in November to prepare "a plan for arranging the finances, paying the debts and economising the revenue of the United States." Finally, several overlapping committees were asked to draft plans for organizing "civil executive departments." Their reports at last allowed Congress to divest itself of numerous administrative burdens that had clogged its proceedings for years.[13]

These committees did not directly address the troubling questions Schuyler and Mathews had raised about the relations binding Congress and the states. They were appointed instead to cope with the pressing needs of the army and treasury; their immediate concerns were with beef and flour, old money and new, outstanding debts and ongoing expenses. Nevertheless, the reports they prepared during the autumn of 1780 and the early winter of 1781 inaugurated a new phase in both the theory and politics of American union. Two of their recommendations—both initially moved by Robert Livingston—proved particularly influential in shaping the politics of the early 1780's. The first, which was approved on February 3, 1781, asked the states to empower Congress to collect an impost duty on foreign goods, thereby suggesting that the national government should at last acquire independent sources of revenue.[14] The second, adopted four days later, saw the creation of three executive departments —Finance, War, and Marine—to supplement the Department of Foreign Affairs established a month earlier.[15] Robert Morris quickly returned to national politics as the superintendent of finance—the preeminent position—and his proposals and policies effectively came to define the major domestic issues confronting Congress until 1783.

Although historians have sometimes regarded the passage of the impost as the opening wedge in a campaign to give Congress broad powers of taxation—adopting, in effect, the argument of its opponents—it was initially designed with more modest, though still important, purposes in mind. Livingston's original proposal was to have the states, not Congress, levy two sets of duties for specific uses: one on exports to provide a security that would enable America to attract foreign loans, the other on captured prizes to be applied to the expenses of the continental navy. The impost was only one of several financial proposals that Congress considered during the waning months of 1780, and probably not the most important. Proposals for taxing specie and establishing a national bank evidently attracted greater attention, while current negotiations with New York and Virginia over the cession of their western lands raised the possibility that Congress would soon acquire control over that vast and, it was believed, immensely profitable resource.[16]

But as the plan for an impost took shape, the constitutional precedent it would set gave it a significance greater than the admittedly limited financial relief it would immediately produce. Much of the discussion over its adoption centered not on its utility, which seemed self-evident, but on the mode of its collection. Instead of asking the states to "pass laws, granting [an impost] to Congress," as had been initially proposed, the final text requested that "they vest a power in Congress to levy" a duty of 5 percent—a revision apparently designed to obviate the possibility that the states could repeal their acts of authorization as they might any piece of legislation. As finally passed, the restrictions that Livingston had proposed on the use of the impost were relaxed: revenues were to be applied against the principal and interest of the national debt.[17] The impost was thus designed not to raise operating expenses but to enable Congress to attract other sources of revenue—most notably foreign loans—by providing security for the extension of additional credit.

The decision to create executive departments directed by individuals was meant to answer two longstanding complaints made inescapably urgent by recent events. One was the familiar belief that the delegates wasted too much time, both in committees and sessions of the whole house, on minor matters of administration. With its calendar incessantly cluttered with all the lesser questions that were raised and debated almost daily, Congress had repeatedly found it difficult to set ample time aside for the systematic consideration of major issues of policy. In the second place, Congress was also dissatisfied with its earlier administrative reforms, which had created various multimember boards whose own deliberations and mutual relations were fre-

quently marked by petty bickering and inefficiency. As recently
as January 12, for example, Congress had had to review charges
leveled by two members of the Board of Treasury against the
Chamber of Accounts, alleging: "1, neglect of duty; 2, indolence;
3, inattention to the public interest; 4, incapacity; and 5, partiality."[18] By consolidating these boards and placing them under the
supervision of responsible heads of departments, Congress
hoped to end both these disputes and the confusion created by
the continuous process of appointing and replacing commissioners. But much like the limited role prescribed for the executive
branch under the first state constitutions, the responsibilities of
the new department heads were meant to be largely administrative in nature. Congress did not intend to surrender its own
policymaking prerogatives or even its right to interfere in the
basic operations of the departments—although during the next
two years it would discover that Robert Morris had a more expansive notion of his own responsibilities.

With these actions of early February, Congress completed a
first phase of reconsidering its earlier decisions to transfer major
responsibilities to the states. It did so, however, without explicitly
repudiating either the system of specific supplies or the finance
plan of March 1780. Although several of the expedients discussed
did foreshadow more radical proposals that would be advanced
in the months to come, on balance there is little evidence to
suggest that Congress was seriously contemplating a reapportionment of the balance of authority between the union and the
states. The discussions of 1780 and early 1781 arose in direct response to the crisis in supply, recruitment, and finance, each an
area of responsibility where it had generally been assumed that
Congress would establish basic policy, even if details of execution
were to be left to the states. If in reaction to the apparent failings
of the states, Congress now sought additional authority to implement as well as frame policy, its intentions reflected not a grasping after power but an attempt to fulfill the purposes for which
the union had been created. It was nevertheless inevitable that
the mood of 1780–81 would produce a more thoughtful and critical attitude toward the Articles of Confederation than had previously existed. And when Maryland finally ratified the Articles in
early February, some members began to propose amendments
that were consistent with the questions Philip Schuyler had
raised several months earlier.

Confederation Reconsidered

CONGRESSIONAL hopes for the prompt ratification of the Articles of Confederation had withered during the early months of 1779. When the Virginia legislature declared void all the controversial land purchases that the speculators of the Illinois-Wabash and Indiana companies had made before the Revolution, Maryland responded by reasserting its unwillingness to ratify the Articles until all the states were given common rights to the western lands. In 1779 Virginia concluded a detailed investigation of the speculators' claims by rejecting the purchases made by the non-Virginian companies; the assembly then enacted legislation opening a land office for the orderly sale of its western lands. The speculating companies were thus forced to appeal to Congress. There they met with some success, for on October 30, 1779, over the strenuous objections of the Virginia and North Carolina delegations, Congress asked the landed states "to suspend the sale, grant, or settlement of any land unappropriated at the time of the declaration of independence, until the conclusion of the war."[19] This was at best a limited victory, however. Even if land sales were postponed, the revisions Maryland sought in the structure of the confederation still seemed unattainable, for the simple reason that Virginia appeared likely to prove as obstinate as its northern neighbor should its charter rights be endangered without its acquiescence.

But the landless states did have two increasingly useful advantages working in their favor. One was that a number of Virginia leaders were prepared to cede much of the state's western claims if the right conditions could be obtained. Perhaps more important, as the financial crisis deepened in 1779, many delegates began to hope, more longingly than ever, that congressional acquisition of a national domain would provide a secure and lasting foundation for the reestablishment of public credit. The lure of land, always one of the central themes in American history, acquired in this context the special attraction of a panacea. When the speculating companies appealed to Congress, therefore, delegates from the landless states were preparing to launch a new campaign to encourage the major landed states to cede their claims to the union. The overwhelming support they mustered for the resolution of October 30 provided an early demonstration of the growing appeal of their position.

Although this action predictably elicited a further protest from Virginia, its immediate target was New York, which also had significant western claims but now seemed susceptible to judicious pressure from Congress. The validity of the New York claim was problematic because it conflicted with Virginia's. But the status of Vermont offered another, more pressing consideration. New York leaders still hoped to procure congressional support for the return of the "revolted" territory to their state's possession. A sacrifice of New York's questionable western claims might produce dividends along its eastern borders. By late November 1779, Robert Livingston and Philip Schuyler were convinced that national and state interest both required New York to cede its claims to land north of the Ohio River.

I find a violent inclination in most of the states to appropriate all the western Lands to the use of the United States [Livingston wrote], and in proportion as they feel the weight of taxes, that inclination will increase, till I fear it will at last overpower us, unless we contrive to make a sacrifice of part to secure the remainder. This I think we may do to advantage now, while they treat our title with some respect. . . . It will put our claim out of dispute, [and] enable Congress and us to apply our Lands to counter secure our money.

Two months later, Schuyler gave the New York assembly a detailed account of the threats and inducements to which their delegates had been exposed. In the letter that effectively set the New York cession in motion, he reported that within Congress "an idea prevailed that this and some other States ought to be divested of part of their Territory for the Benefit of the United States." Support for this proposal no longer came, he warned, from the landless states alone, but "was strenuously insisted upon, in private Conversation, and even supported by Gentlemen who represented States in Circumstances seemingly similar to our's." If the states with extravagant claims "would consent to a reasonable Western Limitation," he continued, it would "prevent Controversy and remove the Obstacle which prevented the completion of the Confederation." Schuyler then went on to outline the general details of a territorial settlement, a subject that had also been privately discussed at Philadelphia. The assembly responded with alacrity. Within three weeks it had approved a suitable act of cession.[20]

Schuyler carried a copy of this act with him upon returning to Congress in March 1780. Despite the subsequent reading of the new Virginia remonstrance, by early May James Duane was able to inform Washington that he was "much engaged in another attempt to get the Confederation accomplished," and perhaps more important, "that the Delegates from Virginia are warmly disposed to give it all the Aid in their Power."[21] For the recent arrival of James Madison and Joseph Jones meant that the delegation now included two influential politicians who agreed, with Governor Thomas Jefferson, that Virginia should yield its claims on principles acceptable to the state and, moreover, that ratification of the Articles was absolutely necessary. In late June Congress appointed a five-member committee, drawn from the four states possessing major western claims plus Maryland, to consider the various state actions that had been taken during the past year. Their report, delivered four days later, called upon "those states which can remove the embarrassment respecting the western country" to make "a liberal surrender of a portion of their territorial claims," which, it noted, "cannot be preserved entire without endangering the stability of the general confederacy." The report then reminded the landed states of the importance of completing the confederation "on a fixed and permanent basis, and on principles acceptable to all its respective members." Although the report was not finally approved until early September, its eventual adoption demonstrated, after the contention of previous years, the extent to which the delegates continually had to balance their responsibility to their states against considerations of national interest. No roll call was taken on this resolution.[22]

Once the report was adopted, Joseph Jones immediately returned to Virginia to lobby for the passage of an act of cession similar to New York's. By the winter of 1781 its approval seemed imminent (though subsequent negotiations and controversy over the terms of the cession would delay its acceptance by Congress until 1784).[23] In the meantime, after British naval activity in the Chesapeake Bay had led Maryland to ask the Chevalier de la Luzerne for naval assistance, the French minister diplomatically reminded state officials of the importance of completing the confederation. Maryland voted to ratify the Articles on February

2, 1781; ten days later, Congress fixed March 1 as the day the confederation would finally take effect.[24]

Serious doubts about the adequacy of the Articles were beginning to grow even while these final maneuvers unfolded. As drafted, the Articles granted Congress no powers it had not previously exercised, nor did they confer the additional authority some members thought the situation of 1780–81 demanded: the right to raise an independent revenue and to compel state compliance with its requisitions. Indeed, by substituting a written charter for the less precise mandate of the public good, the Articles threatened to impose rather than remove obstacles to the assertion of any inherent power to act as the national interest demanded. Dissatisfaction with the substantive content of the Articles, a topic few members had previously pondered, thus increased as ratification became imminent. By early 1781 some delegates were arguing that the Articles were "defective" or "inadequate," and confidently predicting that Congress would immediately ask the states to approve "such additional Articles as will give vigour and authority to Government."[25]

Those who held this opinion nevertheless thought ratification imperative. In 1780 a few American leaders had flirted with the idea of calling a national convention to revise the pending confederation before it took effect. Thomas Paine briefly mentioned such a proposal in his pamphlet *Public Good,* a commissioned tract calling for the creation of a national domain; Schuyler discussed it in a private letter to Jeremiah Wadsworth and doubtless in conversation with Alexander Hamilton, soon to become his son-in-law; and Hamilton considered the idea more thoughtfully when he prepared a lengthy and devastating critique of the Articles at the request of James Duane.[26] But unless, as Hamilton suggested, a convention "vested with plenipotentiary authority" could be assembled—which was not likely—such a tactic could scarcely have seemed practical in 1780 or 1781. For several reasons it probably appeared more advisable to amend rather than supplant the draft of 1777. Time was certainly one critical factor. The crisis of the American war effort was immediate and urgent, but, assuming that the states would insist on their right to ratify a new draft, months or even years might elapse before another document could be approved. Moreover, the success of any scheme for the restoration of public credit virtually presupposed the prompt completion of the Articles; without it, pledges of public faith would remain meaningless. Finally, many delegates recognized that recent events, beginning with the acrimonious disputes of 1779, had so damaged the reputation of Congress that it could no longer rely solely on the implicit goodwill of the people and the states. These considerations outweighed the anticipated flaws in the Articles. "Tho' the powers of the confederation are very inadequate to a vigorous prosecution of the present war," John Mathews observed, "yet we must endeavour to make the most of them we can, and it is better to have some authority to regulate us, than, (as for some time past has been the case,) to have none."[27]

Some delegates, then, saw ratification of the Articles as drafted as a prerequisite to the approval of additional amendments whose significance, though not anticipated in 1777, had been confirmed by recent developments. Certainly the completion of confederation would facilitate both the creation of a national domain and state approval of the continental impost, two measures that commanded the support of virtually the entire membership. But no similar consensus emerged when other measures for strengthening the authority of Congress were discussed during the months surrounding the inauguration of the confederation. Congress "have been disputing for a long time past, what powers were necessary to enable them to prosecute the business intrusted to them," Mathews noted in late January, "and were at this moment, as far from agreeing about it, as when we began." During the spring and summer of 1781, three separate committees prepared reports suggesting various amendments to the Articles. Although none of their proposals was adopted by the whole Congress, these documents nevertheless deserve examination because they expressed the first substantive criticisms leveled against the perceived shortcomings of the confederation.

The first of these reports was drafted in early March by a committee composed of Madison, Duane, and James Varnum, a former continental general from Rhode Island who shared his collaborators' doubts about the adequacy of the Articles. Their report began with a lengthy preamble asserting that Congress possessed "a general and implied power . . . to carry into effect all the Articles of the said Confederation against any of the States which shall refuse or neglect to abide by such their determinations," but which also admitted that "no determinate and particular provision" had been drawn to show how that power could be implemented. To remedy this oversight, the committee proposed an additional Article authorizing Congress to use military or naval force "to compel . . . [delinquent] States to fulfill their federal engagements." This report was not taken into consideration until early May, when it was referred to a grand committee of thirteen members, which in turn did not report until late July. By then the idea of coercing the states had been rejected. The grand committee merely proposed that Congress ask the states, first, to allow it to impose temporary embargoes in time of war; and second, to appropriate for the specific use of Congress whatever funds they collected in compliance with its requisitions. This report was in turn referred to a third committee, "appointed to prepare an Exposition of the Confederation, a plan for its complete execution and supplemental articles." Varnum was the leading member of this committee.[28]

Their report, which was read on August 22 but never acted upon, constituted the most detailed commentary on the Articles that 1781 produced. Even so, the committee declined to give an "exposition of the Confederation"—a complex and presumptuous task—revealingly arguing that any current "omission to enumerate any Congressional powers [would later] become an argument against their existence, and it will be early enough to insist upon them, when they shall be exercised and disputed." The report then went on to detail fully twenty-one areas in which Congress needed to devise plans for carrying specific provisions of the confederation into execution, including, last but not least, "providing means of animadverting on delinquent States." Finally, the committee proposed seven additional Articles. These would enable Congress to impose embargoes in wartime, establish rules governing the impressment of private property for military use during the current war, appoint collectors of taxes "imposed according to the requisitions of Congress," and seize property belonging to states that had proved delinquent in furnishing their quotas of men and money. Other provisions related to the admission of new states into the union, the negotiation of consular agreements with foreign nations, and the clarification of the number of states needed to compose a quorum and a majority in Congress (a subject on which the Articles were found to be ambiguous).[29]

The temptation to think of enabling Congress either to coerce the states or to circumvent their authority was a natural response to the sense of despair that afflicted American leaders in 1780 and 1781. They knew that their own repeated efforts to mobilize men and supplies had proved inadequate, and they were well aware that masses of the people were simply exhausted with the war and its demands. The officer corps of the army and former soldiers now holding political office were increasingly attracted to radical measures, and by the early summer of 1781 even R. H. Lee was arguing that Congress should follow the precedent of 1776–77 and vest some form of dictatorial powers in Washington.[30]

Nevertheless, the indifferent reception that Congress gave to these proposed amendments suggests that they constituted less an agenda for reform than a basis for private discussion and speculation. Few references to them are to be found in the delegates' correspondence, nor did they elicit any roll calls in Congress. It is therefore difficult to determine why they were never acted upon or even whether delegates who were sympathetic or opposed to such amendments constituted a majority of Congress. The support Robert Morris enjoyed in 1781 suggests that whatever factional alignments did exist did not by themselves preclude their approval. Yet the presence of even a small nucleus of hostile delegates would have raised serious problems. State ratification of these amendments would depend on the existence within Congress of a solid consensus of opinion, capable of binding all the delegates to their support. But in fact, as Varnum complained, many members, "especially those of a long standing," displayed "an extreme, tho perhaps well-meant Jealousy" of these measures.[31]

Other pragmatic considerations probably militated against their adoption. By late August 1781, when the third committee's report lay before Congress, two developments were working to defuse the pressure for constitutional change. Washington had begun moving a major part of the northern army, long investing the British forces at New York, south toward Virginia, where the position of the enemy army commanded by Cornwallis and the anticipated arrival of a French fleet had suddenly raised the possibility of a decisive allied victory. At the same time, the early efforts of Robert Morris, the new superintendent of finance, had helped to alleviate the distressed condition of the continental army, which, though still undermanned and precariously sup-

plied, at least seemed capable of waging an active fall campaign.
Political experience suggested other doubts about the prospects
for the ratification of additional amendments. Congress was already encountering minor problems in securing approval for the
impost, which led some delegates to conclude that further requests should be postponed until this first trial proved successful.
Even those who favored vesting coercive powers in Congress
believed that the impetus for change had to come from the
states. Varnum thought that the dissenting delegates would
never alter their position without pressure from their constituents, while Joseph Jones argued that it would be better for the
states to make "a voluntary declaration . . . of their Sentiment
upon the Right of Congress to exercise such a power . . . for I
suspect such a Recommendation coming from Congress wo'd
excite fears in the States, that there was a disposition in Congress
to grasp dangerous Powers."[32]

Whenever frustration gave way to reflection, it was difficult
to avoid concluding that no expedient, however drastic, could
achieve a miraculous reformation. By the early 1780's, political
leaders had come to understand that the problems besetting the
war effort were inherent in the character of American society
and its new governments. "General Washington complains of us
all," Joseph Reed, his former aide, noted in June 1781. "Engrossed
with military affairs, he has not the time or opportunity to know
the real state of the country, or the difficulties which environ
men in civil life." Five months later Robert Morris offered a more
reflective view of the American situation. It was true, he reminded Franklin, that American finances were in a very unpromising state.

But what else could be expected from us? A Revolution, a War, the
Dissolution of Government, the creating of it anew, Cruelty, Rapine and
Devastation in the midst of our very Bowels, these Sir are Circumstances
by no means favorable to Finance. The wonder then is that we have
done so much, that we have borne so much, and the candid World will
add that we have dared so much.

In fact, Morris concluded, "the Exertions of our Country have
really been very great," and "as soon as more Consistency shall
have been put in the Administration" they would be so again;
"but this is the Period of weakness between the convulsive La-

bors of Enthusiasm, and the sound and regular Operations of Order and Government."[33]

Constitutional scruples and thoughtful assessments of American failings did not always satisfy those who were attracted to the idea of coercive powers. Varnum still wondered how "political and civil liberty can be enjoyed amidst the Din of Arms, in their utmost platonic Extent." If reforms were to be adopted, they would have to be devised by "a Convention, not composed of Members of Congress, especially those whose political Sentiments have become interwoven with their Habits, from a long Train of thinking in the same way." Yet Varnum was not proposing a permanent alteration of the confederation: whatever measures this convention enacted "should expire at a given or limited Time." Proponents of coercive powers thus recognized the legitimacy of the objections they encountered. The right to use coercive force against a state, Jones admitted, "is certainly a transcendant power, never to be used but in cases of absolute necessity and extremity"; he hoped that the simple vesting "of such a power in Congress might possibly supercede [*sic*] the use of it." For his part, Madison naïvely believed that the imposition of simple naval blockades against recalcitrant states would render any actual exertion of force relatively painless.[34]

Such qualifications could not obscure the impact that the addition of coercive powers would have had on the structure of the confederation. To the extent that such a shift would have enhanced the authority of Congress at the expense of the states, it may fairly be seen as a harbinger of the deeper feelings of nationalism that ultimately led to the Philadelphia Convention. And there were, in fact, a few American leaders whose thinking was not inhibited by the political obstacles constraining Congress. Of these the most important was clearly Alexander Hamilton. In the critique of the Articles that he submitted to Duane in September 1780, and again in the "Continentalist" essays he published a year later, Hamilton expressed ideas that directly anticipated the overt Federalism of 1787–88 and the distinctive policies he would pursue as secretary of the treasury under Washington. Even in 1780 Hamilton was prepared to advance a broad interpretation of the inherent powers Congress enjoyed in the absence of a formal confederation. "Undefined powers are discretionary powers," he reminded Duane, "limited only by the object for which they are given—in the present case, the independence and freedom of America." If each state retained "an uncontrolable sovereignty . . . over its internal police," the American union would remain "feeble and precarious." Congress needed to recognize "the advantages of securing the attachment of the army," if it were to acquire "a solid basis [for its] authority and consequence," he wrote; "for to me it is an axiom that in our constitution an army is essential to the American union." Hamilton proposed that Congress should assume control of the public debt rather than allow it to devolve on the states; it should also acquire independent sources of revenue and support the establishment of a national bank. The creation of executive departments administered by single individuals "would give new life and energy to the operations of government." Drawing (as would Madison several years later) on the experience of the ancient Greek and modern Swiss and Dutch confederacies, Hamilton concluded that the greatest danger confronting the American polity was not that "the [common] sove[re]ign will have too much power to oppress the parts of which it is composed," but rather that it "will not have power sufficient to unite the different members together, and direct the common forces to the interest and happiness of the whole."[35]

These were powerful ideas, more strikingly innovative in 1780 than they would be seven years later, and they testify to the brash iconoclasm that always characterized Hamilton's thought. No comparable commentary on the confederation was composed until Madison prepared his memorandum on the "Vices of the Political System of the United States" in April 1787. Yet in the context of 1780—and his intimate connections with key members of the New York delegation notwithstanding—Hamilton's analysis must be seen as the work of a political outsider. It was academic in the sense that his perspective, so reflective of the frustrations endured by the continental army, did not correspond with the views that members of Congress, increasingly sensitive to the range of political difficulties confronting them, necessarily had to adopt.

Equally important, Hamilton's animus against the Articles greatly exceeded the reservations its congressional critics shared. For while Madison, Duane, and Varnum clearly understood the novelty of their own proposals for vesting coercive powers in Congress, they viewed them as a vehicle for fulfilling rather than subverting the Articles. Their criticisms were not conceived, in other words, as a blueprint for what later came to be known as consolidation: the concentration of the responsibilities of government at the national level and a corresponding reduction in the sphere of authority reserved to the states. The proposed amendments were essentially a response to the problems of a nation at war, a drastic but hopefully expedient solution to the immediate crisis that had left the continental army at the brink of ineffectiveness. Several of the amendments designed to compel state compliance with federal requisitions were meant to operate during the present conflict only. None of the amendments envisioned transferring any of the substantial responsibilities of government from the states to Congress; in that sense, the underlying division of authority outlined in the Articles would remain intact. And while Washington, Schuyler, Madison, and others were beginning to wonder whether a confederation that could barely function in war would survive in peace, the future problems the union might face were at most of peripheral concern.

The 1781 proposals for amending the Articles were consistent with what their advocates believed to be the legitimate ends of the confederation. It was neither disingenuous nor accidental that Madison, Duane, and Varnum prefaced their report with a reminder that Article 13 "stipulated and declared . . . 'that every State shall abide by the determination of the United States in Congress assembled on all questions which by this Confederation are submitted to them.' " They believed that the confederation had been framed to give Congress virtually exclusive responsibility for the conduct of war and foreign policy. Where discretionary functions had been left to the states, the framers had sensibly recognized that administrative efficiency required deferring to the local circumstances that distinguished the individual regions and states.

But this deference was not an acknowledgment of a state's right to obey or disregard the legitimate requisitions and recommendations of Congress as it saw fit. For the Articles had also expressly stipulated that the determinations of Congress on such questions as the payment of funds to the continental treasury or the recruitment and provisioning of troops—the critical problems of 1780–81—were binding on the states, and not conditionally but "inviolably." Indeed, the proponents of coercive powers were prepared to argue that, in a strict sense, amendments should have been unnecessary. "I hope our new constitution will prove the means of introducing a more clear and perfect understanding between Congress and the states," John Mathews wrote immediately after final ratification, "and while the first continues to confine themselves within the strict limits of their authority, the latter will conceive themselves bound by the most sacred ties, implicitly to support them."[36]

CHAPTER XIII

The Administration of Robert Morris

————————————⟨∽⟩————————————

SHORTLY before Congress appointed the heads of its new executive departments, Gouverneur Morris composed a short essay detailing the qualifications that each of the ministers should possess. Some of the traits he deemed desirable in a minister of finance were predictable: he should be "persevering, industrious, & severe in exacting from all a rigid compliance with their Duty," and knowledgeable about the circumstances of the different states. Other requirements of the office seemed more prescriptive, however:

He should be habituated to Business, on the most extensive Scale, particularly that which is usually denominated *Money Matters.* He should, therefore, be not only a regular bred Merchant, but also one who hath been long and deeply engaged in that Profession. At the same time, he should be practically acquainted with our political Affairs, and the Management of public Business. He should be warmly and thoroughly attached to America, not bigotted to any particular State; and his Attachment should be founded not on Whim, Caprice, Resentment, or a weak Compliance with the Current of Opinion, but on a manly and rational Conviction of the Benefits of Independence. His Manners should be plain and simple, sincere and honest; his Morals pure, his Integrity unblemished; and he should enjoy general Credit & Reputation, both at Home and abroad.[1]

Whether Robert Morris was the conscious model for this portrait cannot be determined. Nevertheless, his political experience and extensive mercantile connections on both sides of the ocean made Morris the preeminent candidate for superintendent of finance. He brought to his new position the same energy that had distinguished his commercial enterprises, and his ability, influence, and reputation enabled him to emerge as the leading national policymaker of the early 1780's. Morris scrupulously portrayed himself as a dutiful public servant called to office against his private wishes, yet he was also a calculating, determined minister who launched an ambitious campaign to convince a reluctant Congress to adopt his comprehensive financial program.

Although Congress ultimately rejected his leadership and severely diluted his program, historians have often described Morris as a virtual prime minister and the dominant leader of a "nationalist" or "centralist" faction that had finally gained ascendancy in Congress.[2] Such a view must be seriously questioned, for it misrepresents the actual relationship between Morris and Congress while oversimplifying the substantive thrust of his program. As with the other measures for revising the Articles that were also under discussion in the early 1780's, any interpretation of the Morris program must begin by examining the actual alternatives and issues as they were perceived at the time, rather than by assuming that they merely embodied goals essentially identical with the explicitly nationalist movement that emerged in 1787.

The Morris Program

IN their politics and personalities, few leading Revolutionaries were less alike than Robert Morris and Samuel Adams. From the historian's perspective, however, they seem to share one common trait: an elusiveness or opaqueness that leaves any reconstruction of their deepest political motives and ambitions always vaguely unsatisfying. At least with Adams—a man whose public mask and private personality became so tightly fused that even he no longer knew where one ended and the other began—one can recover the orthodoxy that consistently defined his political creed. But for Morris, a statesman by circumstance rather than inclination, our sources are less informative. Many of his underlying political ideas can only be inferred from his actions, and few of his surviving letters offer the revealing insights that regularly recur in the private writings of such contemporaries as John Adams, Henry Laurens, James Madison, or even James Duane. He evinced little interest in the problems of political theory that agitated many of his colleagues: despite his leading role in the early 1780's, the unassuming posture he adopted at the Constitutional Convention was entirely characteristic of his attitude toward politics. He was always more comfortable in committee than debate and, like so many public men of his generation, more anxious to return to the management of his private interests than to continue to accept the responsibilities of office. At the start of the Revolution, Morris certainly took advantage of his official position to further his commercial ventures; but once they were established, he apparently concluded that his time would be most profitably spent if he were out of office entirely. When he left Congress in 1778, it was with a genuine sense of relief.[3]

The positions he espoused in congressional and state politics reflected both the temperament of a man of business and the doubts that he and other moderates had expressed about the difficulty of securing American independence. By late 1776 he had emerged as the leading advocate of administrative reform within Congress and a public opponent of the new Pennsylvania constitution, which seemed designed to promote not only divisive controversy but also inefficiency in a state whose size and location made its contributions to the war effort critically important. Neither of these positions, however, required Morris to challenge the way in which the Articles had divided the sovereign powers of government between Congress and the states. The belief that Congress should devote its limited energies to policymaking rather than administration involved no change in existing federal relations. Nor were the defects of the state constitution to be cured by transferring additional functions to Congress. Despite periodic friction between Congress and the Pennsylvania government, constitutional reform remained an internal affair, to be achieved through electoral politics or the gradual adoption of amendments. Given the political context of the late 1770's, when the Articles as drafted received little critical scrutiny, there is no reason to believe that Morris and those who shared his general views were hoping to enhance the powers of the confederation at the expense of the states.

Morris, like others, became convinced that Congress needed additional authority only after the financial and logistical crisis of 1779–80 had demonstrated that its resources were inadequate to its responsibilities. His recognition of the magnitude of this crisis was probably the critical consideration that convinced him to return to office as superintendent of finance.

The unmeritted abuse I had formerly received as the reward of Exertions as disinterested and pure as ever were made by Mortal Man had determined me against every public Station [Morris wrote Washington in May 1781], and God knows my Sentiments are not changed; Contrary to my Inclination, to my Judgement and to my Experience have I consented to make an other Attempt in favour of this poor distressed Country at a time when only one consideration could have influenced me thereto . . . the absolute Necessity of a reformation being attempted and the difficulty of getting any other person on whom Congress could agree.[4]

Self-serving as this statement may have been, it was consistent with his other recorded comments on public life.

Given this attitude, it is scarcely surprising that Morris asked Congress to approve several conditions before he formally accepted his appointment. Over the objections of Samuel Adams, then in his final weeks of attendance, Congress quickly agreed to permit Morris to fulfill his current commercial engagements and to appoint his immediate subordinates. But it balked at his request for broad powers of dismissal over any official whose duties involved handling public funds. Morris was insistent, however. If "the most Essential part" of his duty would be to disburse public funds "in the most frugal Fair and honest manner," he had to be empowered to discharge those he found "unnecessary, unequal to their Stations, inattentive to their duty or dishonest in the exercise of it." For otherwise, he informed Congress, "a Minister who would *Venture* to execute the Duties of his office with Vigour . . . would in a few Months put it out of his own Power to proceed in his Business," while Congress would predictably find itself inundated with the aggrieved complaints of the accused.[5] Morris understood as well as anyone the possibilities for wartime profit and knew how important the possession of disciplinary powers would be in executing any scheme of retrenchment. In early May Congress approved this request with some modifications, and Morris promptly accepted his appointment, though another six weeks elapsed before he formally took office.[6]

This first mild clash between Morris and Congress was resolved in his favor because every passing week added new urgency to his assumption of office. It nevertheless provided an early hint of problems that were to grow more serious later. In the ordinance creating the Office of Finance, Congress had already given the superintendent substantial authority not only in matters of administration but also in assisting and advising Congress in the formulation of policy. But the precise working relationship that would exist between them was as yet untested and perhaps inherently ambiguous. When it came to procuring supplies and managing the paltry resources of the continental treasury, the delegates willingly deferred to Morris's expertise, even promptly endorsing, without alteration, the "Plan for Establishing a National Bank" that he submitted only three days after accepting office.[7] He had been appointed with just such purposes in mind. But there were other areas in which many delegates were reluctant to relinquish congressional prerogatives. Vesting the power of dismissal in an executive official, for example, was conceivably antirepublican, for it implied that his subordinates owed their primary loyalty not to the body that was ultimately representative of the people—the Congress—but merely to its servant. This was an ephemeral concern. What proved more important was the clash of wills that gradually developed after Yorktown, when the superintendent's aggressive efforts to frame a comprehensive, enduring fiscal program for the confederation collided with the delegates' strong residual sense of responsibility for framing basic national policies. Many members who shared the Revolutionary generation's characteristic suspicion of executive power thought it appropriate for Morris to act as their adviser, but not as an advocate.

In requesting broad powers over his subordinates, Morris had indeed argued that his duties would be primarily administrative in nature. It was for Congress and the state legislatures to devise ways "to raise the Publick Revenues by Such Modes as may be most easy and most equal to the People," he reminded a congressional committee in late March, "because the Powers of Taxation Can not be delegated."[8] Despite this perfunctory bow to constitutional propriety, Morris's subsequent activities indicated that he did not take this division of powers seriously. Congress and the states would have to approve changes in policy, of course, but Morris clearly hoped to be their author. His early submission of a plan for a national bank, boldly titled the Bank of North America, provided the first evidence of his intentions. During the summer of 1781, when he was largely preoccupied with procuring supplies for the army, Morris nevertheless found time to draft a lengthy message outlining several of his essential proposals for reforming continental finances. The greater urgency of the 1781 campaign delayed its transmission to Congress until November.[9] But its very preparation suggests that, from the outset, Morris intended to fashion a program that would not be confined to imposing sound procedures on an unwieldy bureaucracy, but would also provide for the settlement of accounts between the union and the states and the creation of secure sources of revenue for Congress. This program did not emerge full-blown in mid-1781, but the financier's conception of his role apparently developed very quickly.

As it gradually took shape between the spring of 1781 and the summer of 1782, the Morris program comprised a number of innovations.[10] His earliest proposals were naturally a response to the prevailing crisis of supply and finance. One was the establishment of the Bank of North America, to be funded by private subscriptions but incorporated by Congress. The Bank's notes were to be receivable as payment for both state taxes and congressional requisitions, and were thus designed to provide a stable circulating currency to replace the by now worthless bills of credit issued during earlier emissions. To supplement these notes, Morris also began issuing a second currency, the so-called Morris notes, backed by his own private credit. And to introduce economies in the procurement of supplies, Morris instituted a policy of obtaining provisions by granting specific contracts to the lowest bidder.

These three measures, buttressed by other efforts to impose administrative efficiency, were important reforms; but by themselves they could not reestablish continental credit on a secure foundation. The heart of the Morris program thus came to embody four broader goals. First, the state of national accounts— that is, the balance of debts and credits between Congress, on the one hand, and the states and general public on the other—would have to be determined and settled. Second, once that enormous task was completed, the expenses of the war would be apportioned among the states, which would be responsible for allocating funds to satisfy the claims of private creditors. But, in the third place, certain critical obligations—notably the interest on loan office certificates and the redemptive value of commissary and quartermaster certificates—would not be included among the quota of debts assigned to the states, but would remain the responsibility of the confederation itself. Finally, it was the preservation of this national "public debt" that would provide the strongest arguments for granting Congress independent sources of revenue capable of covering the continuing expenses of the national government. These revenues would be derived not only from the impost of February 1781 but also from additional land, poll, and excise taxes, which the states were to be asked to grant to Congress.

Such a program differed sharply from the other reform proposals discussed in Congress in 1781. Although Morris privately criticized the dilatory efforts of the states and frequently issued blunt letters urging governors and assemblies to approve congressional requisitions and recommendations, his program did not include vesting Congress with coercive powers over the states. Indeed, what distinguished his approach to the problem of confederation from the thinking of Madison or Hamilton, for example, was that, except in matters of finance, Morris did not envision any major redistribution of authority between Congress and the states. He did not suggest allowing Congress to regulate interstate or foreign commerce or to divert its anticipated income toward undertaking internal improvements. Nor did he propose impinging on the internal police of the states or even depriving them of authority to lay concurrent taxes on the same objects that were to provide revenue for the union. Innovative and imaginative as Morris's financial program was, it was not designed to further the political consolidation of the union or to place the states in a new and more rigorous subordination to Congress—two of the cardinal themes that would later dominate Madison's approach to the problem of federalism. When, in July 1782, Hamilton and Philip Schuyler induced the New York assembly to approve a resolution calling for a national constitutional convention—already a pet idea of Hamilton's—the superintendent's response was vaguely sympathetic but lukewarm; that was not a scenario he was interested in pursuing.[11]

The Morris program was instead preeminently directed to-

ward one immediate end: the restoration of public credit on a
permanent foundation, predicated on the establishment of a
recognized national debt, to be serviced by Congress through
the allocation of specific revenues to its treasury. The beneficial
consequences that would flow from the achievement of this goal
were twofold. First, in conjunction with the operations of the
new national bank, funding the debt with permanent revenues
would provide the nation with a stable currency of obvious value
to a domestic economy visibly poised for peacetime growth. The
confederation would thereby play an influential supportive role
in fostering economic development, not by pursuing overtly
mercantilist or protectionist policies, but by creating essential
conditions of monetary stability and introducing modern institutions of finance. Such a policy would be particularly appealing,
Morris believed, not merely to the existing creditors of the union
but also to those propertied elements of American society most
eager to invest in the anticipated postwar expansion of the national economy. It would also create an important popular con-
stituency attached to the confederation itself and thus willing to
exert political pressure on the state governments. Hamilton, of
course, pursued a similar strategy in 1789–90.

But the funding of a national debt had another, more important political purpose. If adequate independent revenues were
granted to Congress, it would be able not only to service the debt
but to defray the operating expenses of the union without having
to rely on the precarious payment of requisitions levied on the
states. Without independent funds, Congress seemed destined to
languish in the condition of lassitude into which it was beginning
to sink even before the level of fighting subsided in 1782. Yet the
purposes for which Morris intended to use these revenues did
not involve the expansion of congressional authority, but simply
the fulfillment of those responsibilities delegated to Congress by
the Articles of Confederation. In a very real sense, the "conservatism" of the Morris program lay not in any reaction against the
Articles as a naïve federal system excessively balanced in favor
of the states, but instead in its attempt to make the existing
division of authority envisioned in the confederation a workable
one. His proposals marked a reversion not to John Dickinson's
original conception of a confederation capable of imposing specific restraints on the autonomy of the states, but rather to other
efforts of 1775–77 to erect clear and rigid distinctions between

the separate spheres of authority allotted to Congress and the states.[12]

It can of course be objected that the framers of the Articles had consciously intended to enhance the residual authority of the states by denying to Congress any intrinsic power of taxation. To "eighteenth-century Americans," E. James Ferguson has written,

[t]he power of the purse was . . . the determinant of sovereignty, and upon its location and extent depended the power of government, the existence of civil rights, and the integrity of representative institutions. . . . After independence, they tried to safeguard the sovereignty of their new states under the Articles of Confederation by denying Congress the right to tax.[13]

The issue was never perceived that simply. For one thing (as has been argued earlier), regardless of the constitutional scruples involved, a number of pragmatic political considerations militated against any program of substantial taxation. At the outset of the Revolution, as Gouverneur Morris wrote in an essay on finance he drafted in 1779, the colonies "had no Funds to support the War notwithstanding [their] Riches and Fertility. America having never been much taxed [and] for a continued Length of Time Being without fixed Government . . . and the Contest being on the very Question of Taxation," Morris concluded, "the laying of Imposts unless from the last Necessity would have been Madness." Even when the depreciation of the currency seemingly left no alternative to taxation, "the Weakness of Governments yet in their Infancy and not arrived to that Power Method and Firmness which are the Portion of elder States" still rendered it impractical.[14]

American reliance on a scheme of currency finance requiring the continual printing of bills of credit was thus a risk that the duration of the war made increasingly costly. But it was nevertheless a policy that the Articles had specifically endorsed and that the states, through their acts of ratification, had explicitly pledged to support by levying the taxes necessary to redeem the emissions. Although by 1780–81 many Revolutionary leaders clearly recognized that the Articles had placed excessive confidence in the good faith or ability of the states, the initial assumption had been that the states would comply with the appropriate requisitions of Congress. If they did not, the depreciation of the currency would itself implicitly constitute an involuntary tax, which would ultimately act on most of the citizenry. From the start, then, Congress had enjoyed a substantial degree of financial autonomy that the states, with pressing monetary needs of their own, had sanctioned and even enlarged by repeatedly soliciting advances of continental emissions. Moreover, once the presses were finally shut down in 1779, the accelerating movement to create a national domain revealed that local officials *were* willing to give Congress control of a resource many thought capable of underwriting national credit for decades to come—probably because they hoped the tax burdens of their own constituents would thereby be reduced.

Thus while it was certainly true that granting Congress unrestricted powers of taxation would have been considered ideologically questionable, taxation was merely one aspect of a larger financial matrix. Neither in 1777 nor in 1781 did congressional leaders presume that the Articles were meant to reduce Congress to a choice between insolvency and a precarious reliance on the voluntary gifts of the states. The novelty of the impost of February 1781 and the additional taxes Morris requested lay less in the ends than in the ways and means of raising revenue. In seeking independent sources of revenue, the delegates were asking the states to enable Congress to discharge its acknowledged responsibilities. Moreover, far from maintaining that Congress had implied or inherent powers to procure the revenue it required, Morris explicitly sought to conform to principles of constitutional legitimacy. To blunt predictable objections that Congress was insufficiently representative of the people to levy taxes, he conceded that the specific objects and rates of taxation had to be approved by the state legislatures. Each tax would then acquire the juridical status of an amendment to the confederation. Once approved, these taxes could presumably not be revoked without the unanimous consent of the states—admittedly a major advantage for Congress. Yet Morris and his supporters probably believed that the actual collection of the impost and land, poll, and excise taxes would not prove controversial in practice. It took no profound knowledge of social statistics to predict that America would soon witness prodigious increases in imports, population, land under cultivation, and (not least of all) liquor consumption. Low rates of taxation would still produce sizable revenues, while the sale of western lands would provide another relatively painless source of income.

All of these considerations suggest, in short, that the Morris program was not a model for leviathan. Although its financial provisions directly foreshadowed the policies Hamilton later pursued, its constitutional ambitions were far more modest than the goals of the Federalist movement of 1787–88. Morris was willing to accept the essential constitutional framework outlined in the Articles of Confederation, and sought only to detach Congress from its debilitating dependence on the states—a dependence he and other national politicians believed had never been intended to arise. Whether he privately shared the more advanced visions of continental empire already held by his assistant Gouverneur Morris or by Alexander Hamilton cannot be ascertained. But there is no evidence that he thought in such grandiose terms or that his political strategy transcended the restoration of national credit. In any event, the obstacles Morris quickly encountered demonstrated that even his limited professed objectives were more expansive than the political conditions prevailing at war's end could support.

Morris and Congress: A Reassessment

ONCE Congress accepted his conditions for employment, Robert Morris initially commanded the willing support of most delegates. During the campaign of 1781, when his energies were largely absorbed in the urgent task of supplying the army, Congress granted virtually all of his requests. A few members with long memories still distrusted Morris, but they were a small minority, and circumstances left little choice but to comply with his recommendations. For the first time in years the congressional calendar was no longer littered with details of petty expenses. On logistical questions Morris was clearly the master of Congress, and it was this situation Joseph Reed had in mind when, in November 1781, he sketched a sarcastic portrait of a body "relieved from all business of deliberation or executive difficulty with which money is in any respect connected . . . very much at leisure to read dispatches, return thanks, pay and receive compliments, &c."[15]

Reed and Morris had shared similar political views during the early stages of the Revolution. But they grew estranged after differing sharply over what position moderate whigs should adopt toward the new Pennsylvania constitution, and thus, as with other hostile assessments of the superintendent's influence, Reed's opinion cannot be taken uncritically. In fact, it would be wrong to conclude that Morris continued to enjoy the same automatic deference that Reed attributed to him at the outset of his administration. Different conditions prevailed when Congress debated major questions of financial policy, and indeed at almost the same time that Reed was writing, Morris was beginning to realize how difficult a road lay ahead if his program were to be adopted. Although a majority of delegates apparently concurred with his basic objectives, on critical questions of ways and means this consensus broke down and was never satisfactorily repaired. Morris was accordingly forced to divert increasing attention to attempting to exert pressure on Congress and the states—a campaign that was bound to agitate ingrained sensibilities about the dangers of entrusting too much power to executive officials.

Morris's difficulties with Congress were foreshadowed as early as the autumn of 1781, when Congress approved a set of resolutions apportioning a requisition for $8 million among the states. Although Morris had not been consulted while these resolutions were under preparation, they contained provisions that would have affected any settlement of accounts between the union and the states, and that clashed with the comprehensive financial plan Morris had drafted in August but never submitted to Congress. The superintendent immediately dispatched a letter detailing his objections and enclosing the plan of August 28. Congress gave him only partial satisfaction. One objectionable provision was repealed, but two others were not, including a statement implying that the settlement of accounts would not take place until some indefinite future date. This action constituted something of a rebuff to Morris.[16] But in late November he was given a new opening when Congress asked him to report on a New Jersey memorial calling for the prompt adjustment of accounts. On December 10, Morris submitted a new plan for their settlement; and though this proposal was recommitted several times, Congress eventually adopted an ordinance giving the superintendent the essential authority he desired.[17]

Morris immediately tried to capitalize on this success by requesting Congress to ask the states to allow it to collect additional revenues in the form of land, poll, and excise taxes. This suggestion, too, had been broached in his report of August 28 but ignored by Congress. But if Morris now thought the rest of his program would be approved, he was quickly disillusioned. His new letter was referred to a committee of three members, including his old and inveterate enemy Arthur Lee, who had entered Congress a fortnight earlier as a delegate from Virginia. Convinced that the collapse of his own diplomatic career had been due to the efforts of Morris, Silas Deane, and their allies, Lee arrived at Congress determined to subject the superintendent's policies to the closest scrutiny. Whether the committee's discouraging report of March 25, 1782, was the result of Lee's vengeful influence cannot be determined, but in any event the committee found the means proposed "for raising a revenue . . . too exceptionable to meet with the approbation of Congress; as it would operate very unequally, as well with respect to the different States, as to the inhabitants of each State." No provision for granting Congress new revenues should be approved, they suggested, until the national accounts were finally settled, a process that conceivably could take years to complete. In the meantime, the proposals for new taxes lay effectively tabled.[18]

By the early spring of 1782, then, Morris understood that his plans faced major obstacles. He could not assume that Congress would automatically endorse his proposals. The presence of Arthur Lee was an unexpected nuisance, but more important was the delegates' habitual inclination to assert their prerogatives over deliberation and policymaking. Even less faith could be placed on the states, which so far had done little to comply with the requisitions of 1781. Nor had the impost of February 1781 yet been approved. Several states had attached awkward conditions to their acts of ratification; neither Rhode Island nor Massachusetts had yet acted. In the spring, too, news arrived that the twelve-year ministry of Lord North had finally collapsed, and with that report the prospects for peace suddenly grew more realistic.

The end of active combat on the American mainland deprived Morris of the one argument that Congress had always invoked to call for new patriotic sacrifices. The superintendent was by no means as cynical as his assistant, Gouverneur Morris, who almost seemed to wish that the war would continue so that

Congress would have legitimate and decisive grounds for augmenting its power. "It is not much for the Interest of America
that [peace] should be made at present," Gouverneur Morris
wrote in early August. Since the writing of the original state
constitutions, which had secured "Freedom in the extreme," the
new nation had been making "a silent but rapid and constant
Progress toward Strength and Greatness. . . . Nothing remained
but Vigor, Organization & Promptitude to render this a considerable Empire," he concluded, but "These can only be acquired
by a Continuance of the War, which will convince People of the
necessity of Obedience to common Counsels for general Purposes." For Robert Morris, the benefits of peace probably outweighed the political regrets his assistant had expressed. But he
too agreed that war provided the most telling arguments for
strengthening the confederation, and he recognized—what
was obvious—that the onset of peace would severely hamper his
own efforts to secure an ample and reliable revenue for Congress.[19]

These perceptions led Morris to launch a complex series of
political maneuvers that gathered momentum during the second
half of 1782 and eventually fomented an atmosphere of near-
crisis in early 1783. His campaign was necessarily ambitious, for
it had to be aimed simultaneously at manipulating not only Congress but the state assemblies and the public creditors, who now
included the officer corps of the continental army as well as
holders of various securities. To induce Congress to adopt his
proposals, Morris offered ever gloomier accounts of the depleted
continental treasury and the mood of the public creditors. He
sent frequent letters to the states soliciting, cajoling, and even
demanding their compliance with the recommendations and
requisitions of Congress. When Congress balked at the text of
one letter, a compromise was reached whereby four delegates
were dispatched to visit those states that seemed most disposed
to furnish their quota of current expenses.[20]

In an effort to neutralize the opposition of Arthur Lee, Morris
appointed two of the Virginian's former defenders, James Lovell
and William Whipple, to be receivers of continental taxes in
Massachusetts and New Hampshire. (In New York, however, his
refusal to name Abraham Yates, Jr., to this position may have
helped to convert Yates into a militant opponent of further congressional powers.)[21] Morris hoped the receivers would function

as his local political agents. They were instructed to "use the most strenuous and unremitting Efforts" to impress the local legislatures with the importance of levying the required taxes, avoiding additional emissions, and complying with the finance plan of March 1780, nominally still in effect. Morris also asked the receivers to keep him closely informed of local developments, "among which the Characters and Dispositions of public Men are to be numbered."[22] Morris was even more direct in his dealings with the public creditors. To mobilize them to exert pressure on Congress, he halted interest payments on loan office certificates, the most important of continental securities. When the aggrieved creditors then met in protest, Morris urged them to carry their complaints to Congress and to lobby their state assemblies for the establishment of continental funds.[23]

It was this maneuver that led Congress in mid-July 1782 to appoint a grand committee of thirteen members, "to take into consideration and report the most effectual means for supporting the credit of the United States." Morris immediately completed and submitted to Congress his most important message on public finance. This letter, dated July 29, offered a sharply critical assessment of the proceeds to be derived from foreign loans and the sale of western lands—two remedies always appealing in their simplicity—and argued that the financial security of the confederation required the funding of the national debt through permanent revenues. The stage was thus set for the difficult deliberations that would preoccupy Congress from the summer of 1782 into the spring of 1783.[24] Two considerations would prove particularly troublesome. One was the predictable difficulty of reconciling any specific scheme of taxation with the delegates' perception of the interests of their individual states. The other involved new doubts about the likelihood of any revenue plan receiving the unanimous approval of the states required by Article 13 of the confederation.

In proposing a comprehensive plan of land, poll, and excise taxes, Morris had explicitly repudiated Article 8 of the confederation, which provided that the common expenses were to "be defrayed out of a common treasury, which shall be supplied by the several states, in proportion to the value of all land within each State, granted to or surveyed for any person, as such land and the buildings and improvements thereon shall be estimated according to such mode" as Congress devised. The states would then levy the taxes necessary to fulfill their quotas. To Morris and others, this scheme seemed suspect not only because the states had hitherto failed to raise the sums required, but also because it established a cumbersome and inherently controversial formula for apportioning expenses. In his message of July 29, Morris argued that such a procedure would be "improper, because . . . attended with great delay expence and inconvenience," and also because its "uncertain" results would make it unreliable "as a fund for public Debts." It seemed unlikely that "any estimate would be just, and even if it were it must be annually varied," in which case it "would cost more than the Tax" would raise. A uniform land tax based simply on acreage would be far easier to administer and, if set at the proposed rate of $1 per 100 acres, well within the abilities of American farmers to pay. It would also have "the salutary operation of an agrarian law without the iniquity," Morris wrote in terms that sound almost Jeffersonian in thrust, for it would encourage those "great landholders" claiming large tracts of unimproved land to sell their estates rather than hold them for monopolistic speculations that would "impede the settlement and culture of the Country."[25]

Such a change in the basis on which the appropriated lands of America were to be assessed or taxed was certainly acceptable to the New England states, whose densely settled farmlands would be rated disproportionately high under Article 8, but which would benefit from a uniform land tax because of their comparatively small size.[26] Conversely, many southern delegates, particularly those from the Carolinas, thought any fixed land tax would be "insufferably unequal" to their constituents. "The vast tracts of sandy barren land in North Carolina," wrote that state's delegation, "can never be measured with the same scale as the uniformly fertile Lands in some of the Northern States." Led by John Rutledge of South Carolina, these members argued that Article 8 should be given a fair trial.[27]

The ever-tempting alternative of funding the debt largely through the sale of western lands posed a similar threat to congressional acceptance of the proposed taxes. Even before Morris submitted his message on public credit, the grand committee on finance had recommended that Congress decide whether to accept the Connecticut, New York, and Virginia cessions on the terms offered. Although this resolution was tabled, interest in exploiting western lands continued to run high among the delegates. Morris attempted to deflate their enthusiasm by arguing that the current difficulties of acquiring clear congressional title portended further delays and that the backlands would be far less remunerative than was commonly believed. Nevertheless, when the grand committee delivered its report, its opening statement noted: "That it is their opinion that the western lands if ceded to the U.S. might contribute towards a fund for paying the debts of these States." The committee then proceeded to endorse the program of taxes the superintendent had requested. When Congress debated this report, however, each of the taxes was rejected. The one measure that came close to adoption was a set of resolutions designed to facilitate the cessions; but the absence of a single New Hampshire delegate prevented these resolutions from obtaining the seven votes necessary for passage.[28]

Thus for the second time in eight months Morris found himself unable to secure congressional approval for his plan of taxation. The next phase of his campaign did not begin until January 1783, when the arrival in Philadelphia of a three-man delegation carrying the financial complaints of the army encouraged him to launch one final effort to overcome the impasse in Congress. In the meantime, however, a further complication had arisen. By the fall of 1782 it was apparent that Rhode Island's delay in ratifying the impost was not due to the vagaries of legislative politics but reflected deep and principled opposition to the measure itself. If Rhode Island refused to accept the impost, there seemed little reason to hope that other taxes could ever be unanimously approved by the states.

Opposition to the impost had originally seemed strongest in Massachusetts, which had not ratified until early June, even then attaching several conditions to its assent.[29] Morris probably hoped that the accession of Massachusetts would carry its small southern neighbor in its wake. James M. Varnum, who had returned to Rhode Island in November 1781, was directing a public campaign for ratification, and as late as July 1, Varnum predicted that the impost would soon be approved.[30] But the arrival of David Howell, a new Rhode Island delegate elected on the basis of his opposition to the impost, destroyed that illusion. At first Howell revealed little about his constituents' true attitude toward the impost. But when in July he was called before a congressional committee appointed to review its progress, Howell spoke freely, and after this interview it was clear that prospects for passage in his state were hardly encouraging.[31]

David Howell did not indulge in the self-righteous posturing that had characterized Thomas Burke's behavior in Congress, but in other ways these two delegates were remarkably similar. Both shared a militantly states'-rightist view of the nature of the confederation and a firm conviction that their primary obligation as delegates was to protect the specific interests of their constituents. Neither man allowed his inexperience at the national level of politics to inhibit an early and vigorous participation in debate or to foster a receptivity to arguments and positions developed prior to his entrance into Congress. Both incurred the enmity of many of their colleagues, and together they enjoyed the distinction of being the only two delegates ever to be reprimanded by vote of Congress.

For Howell, a political novice and former professor of mathematics, the campaign against the impost was at once an exhilarating and emotionally draining experience. "I find a field sufficiently extensive for the exertion of every faculty I possess, nay more if I had them," he wrote to one Rhode Island correspondent in early August;

Business to me entirely new daily arises, and such a variety of objects are presented that I am ready to admire what I have been doing all my days not to have turned my attention to them heretofore. But the truth is, the course of my Studies & thoughts has heretofore been confined to books, Systems, & Speculations; I am now concerned with life itself. . . . I have much to learn. I am about it; I lose no time.

A mere three days later his enthusiasm seemed to be verging toward depression, in part because so few people in Congress or Philadelphia in general shared his feelings about the impost. "My mind is at times deeply oppressed with the weight of public affairs," he wrote to Moses Brown.

You know I always was subject to be low spirited. I feel so much of it at times now as utterly disqualifies me for all business. The vanity to which I am subject when in full spirits, adds poignancy to my reflections at such times, and having no particular friend here to whom my difficulties are known to converse freely with, I am the more overcome. Never did tears flow more freely from my eyes than since I have been in this City.

The fact that Ezekiel Cornell, his initial colleague in the state delegation, disagreed with everything he said further upset Howell. Only after Jonathan Arnold had replaced Cornell in October did Howell admit that he was now "cheerful as usual."[32]

What really braced Howell's spirits, however, was his sense of being on a sacred mission to preserve the interests of Rhode Island and the constitutional framework of the Articles of Confederation. Like his patrons at home in Providence, Howell believed the impost would be harmful to Rhode Island's highly commercialized economy. Part of the state's opposition may have reflected the peculiar character of its commerce, which depended on reexporting foreign imports for sale through the coasting trade. Because the impost contained no provision granting drawbacks on such reexports, Rhode Island merchants feared its adoption would place them at a competitive disadvantage.[33] There were other arguments from interest. As a representative of the smallest of the landless states, Howell repeatedly declared that the sale of western lands offered the most attractive means of servicing the national debt. But the political implications of the impost were equally important in his thinking. Indeed, Howell's views provide almost a stereotype of the attitudes one would attribute to a localist politician from a small New England state. The more one traveled south from New England—he noted to Theodore Foster—the more "Government verges toward Aristocracy. In New-England alone have we pure & unmixed Democracy & in Rhode Island & P[rovidence] P[lantations] is it in its Perfection." And, he added, "Should our little State have the credit of preventing the 5 p Cent from taking effect it would be to us an additional gem." The impost was "but an entring wedge, others will follow—a land tax, a poll tax & an Excise. Is it not best to oppose the first in such a manner as to discourage application for the others?" Moreover, "it derogated from the Sovereignty and Independance of the State for the Ud. Ss. to draw a Revenue for their benefit out of our State and to collect it by their officers," particularly when these revenues would injure "the morals of the community at large . . . by nourishing in idleness and Luxury a numerous train of Collectors, Comptrollers, Searchers, tide-waiters, Clerks, etc. etc."[34]

Such fears were directly evocative of the convictions that had led the Americans into revolution, and they heralded the arguments that, though rarely expressed previously, would be heard with increasing frequency during the next five years. They did not represent the ideas now shared by most members of Congress, whose own views were largely shaped by the frustrations of their experience rather than the sort of academic whiggism Howell embodied. The uncanny obstinacy with which Howell dismissed what had become something of a consensus among his colleagues was peculiarly maddening. Whatever its defects, by late 1782 the impost had become a *sine qua non* for any further reformation of congressional finance, and to have it challenged by a new delegate from one of the two smallest states in the union seemed intolerable. Moreover, many members began to suspect that Howell was actively coordinating the Rhode Island struggle against the impost from his seat in Congress. In fact, their suspicions barely touched the real skill with which Howell was using accounts of his experiences at Congress to influence his connections at home.

Alarmed by the forthright position Howell asserted, Robert Morris hired Thomas Paine to write a series of essays defending the impost, and Congress issued an explicit plea urging its ratification. The Rhode Island assembly nevertheless unanimously rejected the impost in early November. Congress then dispatched a three-man committee to Rhode Island to lobby for a reconsideration.[35] But the committee's journey was abruptly suspended when Congress learned that Virginia had unexpectedly repealed its ratification. Explanations for this distressing development were hard to come by. Benjamin Harrison and Edmund Randolph eventually informed Madison that the Virginia legislators had expressed a variety of objections, both constitutional and economic. But the two men also suggested that Arthur and Richard H. Lee—both in attendance at the October session of the assembly—had somehow connived to extract a measure of revenge against Robert Morris, a suspicion that was also commonly voiced at Philadelphia.[36]

Even before the news from Virginia arrived, Congress had vented its frustration on Howell, who was suspected of having leaked for publication selected and misrepresentative extracts from diplomatic dispatches in which John Adams had assessed the prospects for foreign loans. After some sheepish behavior, Howell admitted his responsibility. Howell's conduct, James Madison noted, had "exited great & (excepting his Colleagues or rather Mr. Arnold) universal indignation and astonishment in Congress." A full account of these proceedings was ordered to be transmitted to Rhode Island, accompanied with a more complete statement of the disappointing results of efforts to attract foreign loans.[37]

The extensive abuse that was heaped on Howell measured not only most delegates' irritation but also, it may be suggested, their rejection of the arguments and principles he had advanced. It was nevertheless apparent that Congress would again have to reconsider the still deteriorating state of continental finance. The delegates did not require the prodding of Robert Morris to resume their deliberations. But the superintendent's own activities were clearly contrived to influence their debates. By late December 1782, Morris had realized that he was unable either to command a reliable working majority in Congress or to bring effective political pressure to bear against recalcitrant states. Thus when the delegation from the army arrived in Philadelphia on the 29th, little more than a week after the censure of Howell and the news of the Virginia repeal, he was probably already disposed to pursue more drastic measures. The organization of the public creditors into a coherent interest group, capable of exerting pressure on Congress and the assemblies alike, now became a paramount goal. He had already enjoyed some success in manipulating the holders of continental securities; now he sought to create a broader coalition that would unite the interests of the army with those of other public creditors. Rather than scale down his program to the emerging though inauspicious realities of 1783, Morris committed himself to manufacturing a crisis that he hoped would alarm Congress into adopting his scheme of public finance. The tactics he pursued were ingenious, risky, and fairly short-sighted, focused as they were on Congress far more than the states.[38]

Led by Alexander McDougall, the army delegation sought prompt congressional action on long-overdue arrears of pay and assurances that the half-pay pension which Congress had begrudgingly granted continental officers in 1780 would actually be funded. It was not difficult for Morris to convince them to demand that the confederation, rather than the states, assume the responsibility for satisfying their requests.[39] By adding these military obligations to other debts already charged to Congress, Morris obviously hoped to strengthen the arguments for his compre-

hensive revenue program. In a sense this was a cynical maneuver
—Morris understood the importance of exploiting the opportunity that the soldiers' unrest presented—but one that was consistent with his central policies. Although McDougall was primarily
concerned with the interests of the army, he sympathized with
the superintendent's goals and cooperated with his plans. When
on January 13 the delegation met with a grand committee specially appointed by Congress, McDougall and his two colleagues
therefore were careful to describe not only the bitter feelings
prevalent within the army but also the growing difficulty of preserving normal discipline and restraint. When asked what might
happen should back pay not be immediately advanced, the officers responded that

> it was impossible to say precisely, that altho' the Sergeants & some of
> the most intelligent privates had been often observed in sequestered
> consultations, yet it was not known that any premeditated plan had been
> formed; that there was sufficient reason to dread that at least a mutiny
> would ensue, and the rather as the temper of the officers, at least those
> of inferior grades, would with less vigor than heretofore, struggle agst.
> it.[40]

During the weeks to come, rumors of mutiny, violent protests,
a refusal of the army to disband, or even a military coup, were
commonly bruited about.

How seriously such rumors were taken is difficult to resolve.
It is clear that Alexander Hamilton (who had entered Congress
in November 1782) and Gouverneur Morris actively attempted to
manipulate the activities of their military connections at the
main encampment at Newburgh in order to influence the course
of congressional debate; it also seems highly probable that Robert
Morris must have endorsed their efforts.[41] But while the developments at Newburgh, culminating in Washington's dramatic intervention at the abortive camp meeting of March 15, added
urgency to the already oppressive atmosphere under which Congress labored, they did not play a decisive role in its debates.
Military disorders may or may not have posed a credible threat,
but they offered no useful solution to the political impasse any
revenue program would face whenever it was submitted to the
states. This was a point that Henry Knox, Washington's general
of artillery, emphasized in resisting McDougall's efforts to en-

hance the political impact of the army. "Much has been said," Knox wrote on February 21,

about the influence of the Army being united with the influence of the other public creditors to procure a General System of Finance or permanent continental funds—I wish it was more apparent how such a measure is to be effected—and how & in what manner the influence of the Army is to be exerted. . . . Rhode Island and Virginia are refractory and will not grant the impost of 5 per cent. I do not see how the influence of the Army can work any conversion of those states.[42]

It was on this objection that the attempt to exploit the army foundered. The legitimate grievances of the soldiers dramatized the urgency of the revenue question—though that was hardly necessary—but they provided no answers to the practical problems that had troubled Congress all along.

Robert Morris tried to pressure Congress in other ways. In late January he announced his intention to resign from office if adequate provisions for securing continental funds were not made by May.[43] Morris also conferred regularly with committees and individual delegates, and in Hamilton and James Wilson, who had returned to Congress after an absence of five years, he had two allies who were prepared to act as his spokesmen. At first the superintendent's efforts seemed to have some effect. Although Congress refused to publish his letter of resignation—a request Morris clearly made with the intention of agitating the public creditors—it did resume debate over funding immediately. Aware of its need to appease the army, and perhaps Morris as well, Congress approved a proposition affirming that "the establishment of permanent and adequate funds on taxes and duties, which shall operate generally and on the whole in just proportion throughout the United States, are indispensably necessary towards doing complete justice to the public creditors, for restoring public credit, and for providing for the future exigencies of the war." After much debate, this proposition passed "without opposition" in committee of the whole, though when it was later entered on the journals, five of twenty-nine members present recorded their votes against it.[44]

From the beginning of debate, however, it was apparent that this general commitment embodied no new consensus but simply cloaked persistent differences of opinion on several key issues. During the first fortnight of February, for example, Congress tediously rehashed the old problem of implementing the land censuses mandated under Article 8, largely because John Rutledge and several other members insisted on resolving this question before other "measures for restoring public credit" were pursued. By February 11, an exasperated Madison was complaining that "after all the projects & discussions which have taken place, we seem only to have gone round in circle."[45] Six days later a plan was finally accepted, though "with great reluctance by almost all, by many from a spirit of accomodation only, & [from] the necessity of doing something on the subject." Even this compromise, manifestly an outgrowth of futility, was ephemeral. Congress subsequently approved a recommendation asking the states to revoke the relevant section of Article 8 and substitute a new rule dividing expenses among the states in proportion to population, with slaves being enumerated according to the fateful three-fifths ratio, here sanctioned for the first time.[46]

In the meantime, the discussion of revenue measures was also encountering major difficulties. Although David Howell did not attend Congress in early 1783, the ideological attack against any program of general taxation was sustained by Arthur Lee, just returned from Virginia. The whole subject, Lee declared, "was a waste of time," since "the states would never agree to those plans which tended to aggrandize Congress." Their "jealousy [of its power was] not an unreasonable one," he added, for "no one who had ever opened a page or read a line on the subject of liberty, could be insensible to the danger of surrendering the purse into the same hand which held the sword"—a point he illustrated, sound whig that he was, by recalling the history of Stuart England. A new impost might be ratified, Lee suggested, if its duration and means of collection were carefully limited, but other taxes would never be granted. Against this position, however, Hamilton and Wilson continued to argue for a general revenue program. Where Lee and several others suggested distinguishing between the just claims of the army and those of other public creditors—many of whom, they alleged, were speculators rather than the original holders—Hamilton and Wilson pressed for the consolidation of the public debt.[47]

Although through early March Hamilton continued to invoke the specter of military unrest, the basis for the compromise that ultimately emerged was apparently determined at a February 20 meeting, held at the home of Thomas FitzSimons, a Pennsylvania delegate, and attended by Madison, Hamilton, Nathaniel Gorham, Richard Peters, and Daniel Carroll—all supporters of general revenues. Much of the evening's conversation was given over to Peters and Hamilton's reports on the turbulent situation at Newburgh. But the six men also discussed the revenue question and, over the dissent of Hamilton, jointly admitted "the impossibility of adding to the impost on trade any taxes that wd. operate equally throughout the States, or be adopted by them." In a lengthy speech the next day, Madison introduced the proposals that eventually formed the heart of the revenue system of 1783. After first arguing that permanent congressional revenues would be entirely consistent with both the meaning and intent of the Articles—a position Lee immediately condemned —Madison declared that

the discussions which had taken place had finally satisfied him that it would be necessary to limit the call for a general revenue to duties on commerce & to call for the deficiency in the most permanent way that could be reconciled with a revenue established within each State separately & appropriated to the common Treasury.

After further debate, the committee of the whole ended its deliberations, and responsibility for fashioning a comprehensive funding plan was transferred to a new committee of five: Madison, Hamilton, Gorham, FitzSimons, and (the one member not present at the previous night's meeting) John Rutledge.[48]

The committee reported quickly, submitting a comprehensive proposal on March 6; but not until mid-April did Congress complete action on its new financial program. One stumbling block was the question of pensions for army officers. Approval of a "commutation" of half-pay for life to full pay for five years was delayed until Eliphalet Dyer, under the intense pressure of his colleagues, reluctantly disregarded the known objections of his Connecticut constituents to cast the vote that enabled the compromise to pass.[49] The arrival of texts of the provisional peace treaty with Great Britain led to a second delay, which had more controversial overtones. Disregarding their formal instructions to defer to French guidance, the three American peace commissioners—John Adams, Franklin, and Jay—had instead chosen to negotiate a treaty on their own. No one could criticize the favorable terms they had secured, but their independent action and the revelation of a secret article pertaining to a possible British seizure of Florida from Spain raised embarrassing implications for the Franco-American alliance.[50]

Notwithstanding these interruptions and the agitation at Newburgh, the compromise Madison had outlined on February 21 survived to form the central provisions of the recommendations Congress approved on April 18. The new impost would last no longer than twenty-five years, and it would be collected by officials appointed by the states, though subject to removal by Congress. Hamilton and Wilson reiterated the case for vesting other taxes in the union, but their pleas were unavailing. The states were instead asked to supplement the impost by appropriating "substantial and effectual revenues of such nature as they may judge most convenient," which were to be applied toward servicing the national debt. The final vote of April 18 saw four New England delegates (including Howell) recorded in the negative, accompanied in their dissent by a fifth member, Alexander Hamilton.[51] For the remaining two dozen members who supported these resolutions, this decision represented something of a compromise; however, it was a compromise that evoked neither enthusiasm nor any deep sense of accomplishment, but reflected instead their recognition of the political obstacles prevailing both within Congress and without.

Nor did Robert Morris find satisfaction in the passage of these resolutions. Two parts of his program, it was true, had been approved. Military pensions and other obligations to the army had been incorporated in the national debt, not assigned to the states; and Congress had approved an alteration in Article 8. Morris had also helped shape the final version of the impost: at his suggestion, it included differential tariffs on specific goods as well as a flat duty of 5 percent on other imports not enumerated. But the new revenue scheme fell so far short of his proposals that Morris, in a sulk, initially declined to endorse it. He had been consulted while the resolutions were taking shape, yet his influence and advice were scarcely determinative. When asked for his comments on the plan drafted by the committee appointed on February 21, Morris had advised Congress to present the states with an ultimatum: "either to establish these permanent revenues"—that is, land, house, and excise taxes, as well as an impost —"for the interest [on the debt], or to comply with a constitutional demand of the principal within a very short time." Congress dismissed this proposal without bothering to take a vote, "its impropriety," Madison noted, "being generally proclaimed."[52] By deciding instead to ask the states to set aside revenues collected entirely under their own authority for the payment of national expenses, Congress repudiated the essential principle Morris had sought to establish all along.

After some reflection, Morris apparently resolved to give the new system his support. His personal intervention helped to salvage the impost from defeat in Massachusetts, and notwithstanding his earlier threat of resignation, he remained in office until 1784. His attention, however, was increasingly devoted to his private affairs, which had suffered considerably during his first two years in office. In Congress, too, his administration came under severe criticism. The implacable Arthur Lee pursued every hint of impropriety, and other members who had bridled at his heavy-handed tactics also questioned his conduct. Lee found allies in Elbridge Gerry, Stephen Higginson, and Samuel Osgood, who were critical of the superintendent's high-handed dealings with Congress, suspicious of his commercial ambitions, and who resented Morris for convincing the Massachusetts assembly to ratify the impost over their objections. In their minds, the superintendent's long and close association with French interests and objectives was also suspicious; they had not forgotten how Gérard and Luzerne had sought to subordinate the interests of New England and the independence of John Adams to French aims and control. They found a new pretext for attacking Morris when Massachusetts instructed its delegates to seek a reorganization of the Department of Finance.[53] In May 1784, when Morris again announced his resignation, Congress passed an ordinance vesting the supervision of financial affairs in a three-member commission, thereby retreating from the principle of individual responsibility it had endorsed in the executive reforms of 1781. The new Board of Treasury, as eventually constituted, included Lee and Osgood.[54]

Unpleasant as his final months in office may have been, it would be wrong to conclude that Morris's political influence went into eclipse only after the winter of 1783. As his repeated inability to secure the adoption of a general revenue program demonstrates, there was never a time when Morris was able to dictate to Congress. To describe this phase of national politics as either the "Reign of the Financier" or a "Nationalist Ascendancy" thus misrepresents the actual tenor of his relationship with Congress.[55] Despite the forceful and direct arguments Morris advanced, Congress continued to move at its customary cautious pace; and in the end, when an impatient Morris fabricated a crisis, it fashioned a policy he could support halfheartedly at best. Morris clearly grasped just how precarious his position actually was. If anything, his gambling tactics reflected a calculated assessment of the mounting obstacles his program would face as the war wound down and other states began emulating the self-interested example of Rhode Island. From the perspective of Congress, however, this strategy seemed unattractive and inherently unrealistic. The unfortunate fate of the first impost confirmed the lessons learned during the struggle to ratify the Articles: any decision affecting the structure of the confederation required a broad consensus within Congress if it were to have a chance for unanimous ratification by the states; and even with such a consensus, ratification remained problematic. However maddening the objections of Lee or Howell must have appeared to someone like Madison, their influence in their states clearly had to be reckoned with, as did the doubts of John Rutledge, whose opposition seemed more sincere. Lee and Howell could be expected to denounce any measure even vaguely tainted with the superintendent's imprint; but if a substantial majority of delegates could be mustered around a carefully balanced compromise, their objections might be undercut once the program was submitted to the states.

The real architects of the financial program of 1783 were thus the five delegates who left Thomas FitzSimons's house on February 20 understanding that compromise, however unsatisfying, was unavoidable. Their independence further suggests the difficulty of arguing that Morris was at the head of a "nationalist party" in Congress. Each of these men had actively supported his recommendations, but none of them can be considered his obedient partisan. There was no nationalist party, in any meaningful sense of the term, in Congress in the early 1780's. Robert Morris had a devoted assistant in Gouverneur Morris and two articulate supporters in Hamilton and Wilson; but while their concerted activities were clearly partisan in character, four men do not a party make.

Omens

THE considerations that produced the compromise financial plan of April 1783 continued to shape subsequent efforts to reform the Articles. An awareness of the difficulty of securing the unanimous consent of the states, and the familiar problem of creating a consensus within Congress, conspired to commit critics of the Articles to a strategy of gradual, piecemeal reform. Until the failure of the Annapolis Convention of 1786 proved the bankruptcy of this strategy, such an approach worked to discourage American politicians from attempting to rethink the basic problems of federal government in radical or incisive terms. In both the early and the mid-1780's, most discussions of the weaknesses of the confederation took place within fairly narrow and familiar parameters.

And yet by 1782 and 1783 there were some politicians who were beginning to raise questions and develop arguments that explicitly anticipated the Federalism of 1787–88. Occasional references to the idea of calling a constitutional convention—a tactic Morris had briefly considered but declined to endorse—suggest that, at least in private conversations, the conservatism of the reforms that dominated congressional debate was being questioned. No one played a more vigorous role in this respect than Alexander Hamilton, who had broached the idea of a convention in 1780 and who tried to advance it again in 1782 after the New York assembly approved resolutions recommending such a meeting to Congress. It is clear that Hamilton was already developing positions that ran far in advance of prevailing assumptions about the problems of union. Because he saw little wisdom in pursuing partial solutions, Hamilton refused to support the revenue plan of 1783. "This plan was framed to accommodate it to the objections of some of the states," he wrote Governor Clinton; "but this spirit of accommodation will only serve to render it less efficient, without making it more palatable." In early April he informed Congress that, in accordance with the New York resolutions, he would soon introduce a plan for "a General Convention," whose "object would be to strengthen the federal constitution." Hamilton proceeded to draft a characteristically bold and imaginative set of resolutions outlining the central defects of the confederation. He criticized the Articles for "confounding legislative and executive powers in a single body," for failing to establish "a Federal Judicature" capable of upholding the authority of the union, and for giving Congress substantial autonomy over the expenditure of public funds without providing corresponding powers of taxation. Hamilton similarly complained that the Articles unduly compromised the union's ability to discharge its military and diplomatic responsibilities. And he argued that Congress should exercise "a general superintendence of trade." At the end of this lengthy document he attached a resolution calling for a constitutional convention. But the entire proposal was never introduced; it was "abandoned," Hamilton noted, "for want of support."[56]

Our interest in this manuscript is a natural outgrowth of our fascination with its author. Like Hamilton's earlier memorandum of 1780, these resolutions enable us to trace the precocious development of his constitutional thought. But Hamilton was not alone in expressing ideas destined to become more compelling later. In April 1783, for example, Jonathan Jackson, recently returned to his Newburyport commercial ventures after a brief stint at Congress, wrote a remarkable letter which, despite its syntax, deserves to be quoted at length. "Is it possible," he asked Benjamin Lincoln, the secretary of war,

to throw the States into one large Family & the separate Sovereignties into one united (Forgetting Distinctions & swallowing up Names in one only that of Columbians if you please) laying out the whole into convenient districts, & as equal as possible for Territory & Inhabitants, distinguishing the Boundaries by large Rivers, giving each district separate Legislatures for internal Police & for Reference & Deliberation in all great Matters where the supreme ought to go to the People for their Opinions—making the Representation always according to Numbers & equal in all deliberative Bodies throut the Nation? Perhaps two Councils, with a veto in each, but with some Insignia & prerogatives distinguishing the upper from the lower the first of which may consist of a less number would be as useful in the great affairs of the Nation as they are found to be in our smaller Assemblies and if so more necessary, their concerns being of more Magnitude—I have always looked with Concern upon the Inequality of Representation established by our Confederation [i.e., not apportioning voting in Congress to the population of the states] —it has worked evils—it may work many—I have supposed more Sifting or Sublimation would be usefull in the Elections throut the States for members of that Body—in such case puny Fellows like myself would never be sent—could we add to these two Councils a Stadtholder [the title of the chief executive of the Dutch republic]? so limited as to do us no essential Harm were he inclined—& so endowed as to preserve the Balance of Power & do us all possible Good? and as we can't make such an one immortal, can we hit upon a mode of Election, that without Turbulence or Cabal shall supply his place when needed with the best or nearly so?

In this rambling outline, Jackson managed to articulate four of the critical questions that would preoccupy the Philadelphia Convention: the apportionment of representation, bicameralism, the difficulty of selecting suitable representatives, and the need for an independent executive. It was an amazing performance, but one that found no echo in the years that followed. As Jackson himself admitted, such ideas were "Utopian Animadversions"; and indeed in a curious sense this letter corroborates the opinion that, even in 1783, few national politicians were thinking in such expansive terms. For while Jackson had just come from Philadelphia, Lincoln, the recipient, was still there, and as the tone of this letter itself suggests, Jackson presumably intended to raise ideas the secretary had not considered.[57]

While these two documents demonstrate that Hamilton and Jackson were able to break through the ordinary boundaries of debate, their political irrelevance also confirms how powerful a restraint was imposed by the pragmatic considerations governing congressional action. Moreover, it could well be argued that such protonationalist notions did not mark the most innovative development in the constitutional thinking of the early 1780's. That distinction belonged instead to Arthur Lee, David Howell, William Gordon (the Roxbury minister and budding historian), and others who elaborated an explicitly states'-rightist interpretation of the Articles of Confederation, and whose writings against both impost measures and commutation had deep public impact, particularly in New England.[58] Their view of the confederation expressed a degree of ideological attachment to its ostensible principles that had not been present in the more expedient arguments Congress had previously employed in urging the states to abide by its provisions.

Even more important, with the approach of peace their conception of the Articles as a constitution framed with the primary purpose of securing the liberties of the states acquired a new and compelling force. That view had not been commonly advanced during the war. When James Madison asserted that "the federal constitution was as sacred & obligatory as the internal constitutions of the several States; and that nothing could justify the States in disobeying acts warranted by it, but some previous abuse or infraction on the part of Congs.," he was not expressing an opinion that would have been considered controversial before 1782. The greater novelty lay in the rejoinders his remarks elicited from his Virginia colleagues, Arthur Lee, who declared "he had rather see Congress a rope of sand than a rod of Iron," and John F. Mercer, who argued that "if Congs. had a right to borrow money as they pleased and to make [binding] requisitions on the States"—which was what the Articles in fact stipulated—"the liberties of the States were ideal."[59] For Howell and his colleague Jonathan Arnold, the struggle against the impost similarly involved nothing more or less than an application of the same principles that had led the colonies into revolution: Congress now seemed no less dangerous than Parliament had been in 1774. If Congress "obtained a Perpetual permanent revenue at their disposal," they asked, "will it not be a Temptation to that August body . . . either to vote themselves Perpetual, or to apply to the states for such a grant[?]" A year later Howell reminded a correspondent that "however good & virtuous the present members of Congress may be supposed, that body might degenerate into lordly aristocrats." It was hardly surprising, then, that Howell proudly declared he had opposed the New York resolutions for a convention "*tooth* & *nail,*" believing as he did that "No future confederation will ever give equal Liberty to the people, or equal power to the Small States."[60]

Where earlier disputes about the Articles had been confined to such specific issues as western lands or representation, rival interpretations of the substantive purposes of the confederation now constituted a foundation for ideological divisions within Congress. Although both the opponents and most advocates of amendments to the Articles asserted their allegiance to the essential structure of the confederation, the debates of 1782–83 had thus allowed two alternative positions to crystallize, one stressing strict adherence to the Articles as written, the other calling for revisions consistent with the broad purposes of the union. In embryonic form, the debate over the revenue measures of 1783 had raised and clarified the basic arguments that would be applied to the further discussions of the mid-1780's. Moreover, it was already apparent that the opponents of reform enjoyed certain advantages. Their criticism of any extension of federal authority consciously invoked familiar and orthodox fears of power long ingrained in American political rhetoric. In their attacks on Rober⁺ Morris and his complicated financial schemes they could conjure up an image of a latter-day Robert Walpole, intent on corrupting a liberty-preserving constitution; in their opposition to commutation they could exploit traditional prejudices against military pensions and the danger of standing armies. And in Article 13, which required unanimous state approval for any amendment to the confederation, they possessed a tactical advantage that proponents of change were to find impossible to overcome.

"As our present Constitution is so defective," Henry Knox asked Gouverneur Morris in February 1783, "why do not you great men call the people together and tell them so; that is, to have a convention of the States to form a better Constitution[?]" Those who seriously considered that alternative found it impractical. "A new Convention to settle a Constitution is a measure proposed," John Lowell, a Massachusetts delegate, had written Benjamin Lincoln the previous fall.

I have with you great doubts of its Efficacy. The business of Government making however easy it may be esteem'd, or however plausible it may appear, I have long been of opinion is rarely if ever accomplish'd by consultation. Governments make themselves or grow up out of the ground, that is, out of the Habits, the wants, the wishes of the People, & if all the wise men of the East & of the South were to meet in the Center & form a system that other people would admire & lavishly extol, I suspect it would turn out like Shakespears "baseless fabrick of a vision."

"What then is to be done?" Lowell asked; "blunder on—mend where we can, bear where we cannot—lose on this side gain on that & leave to time, accident, or artifice the formation of a better plan." He had accurately forecast the future course of the confederation.[61]

Part Four

REFORM

CHAPTER XIV

Union Without Power:
The Confederation in Peacetime

———————⟡———————

I T has always been difficult to avoid viewing the political developments of the mid-1780's from any perspective other than
the Constitutional Convention of 1787. However one assesses the
true character of the four years separating the coming of peace
from the assembling of the Convention, the framing and ratification of the Constitution indisputably marked the culminating
event in the history of Revolutionary politics and political thinking. In one sense, then, it is of only secondary importance to
determine whether the new republic actually lay at the brink of
chaos—the admittedly exaggerated image we have inherited
from John Fiske—or was a basically prosperous society recover-
ing as rapidly as could be expected from the dislocations of the
war, as Merrill Jensen persuasively argued some years ago. As
Bernard Bailyn has recently written,

Despite depressions, doubts, and fears for the future, and despite the
universal easing of ideological fervor, the general mood remained high
through all of these years. There was a freshness and boldness in the tone
of the eighties, a continuing belief that the world was still open, that
young, energetic, daring, hopeful, imaginative men had taken charge
and were drawing their power directly from the soil of the society they
ruled and not from a distant, capricious, unmanageable sovereign.

At last "free from the corruption and inflexibility of the tangled
old-regime whose toils had so encumbered Americans in the late

colonial period," the citizens of the newly independent United States discovered a "sense of enterprise and experimentation" whose impulses were expressed "in every sphere of life."[1]

Such a portrait reminds us, of course, not merely that healthy societies experience political malaise, but also that politics may well have mattered little to an overwhelming majority of the population intent, as anyone would sensibly be, on returning to the private joys and ambitions of ordinary life. If Alexander Hamilton could retire from Congress to practice law and, it seems, ignore politics almost completely until 1786, one can only conclude that masses of his fellow citizens shared his relative unconcern.

Even so, some American leaders were consistently troubled by the visible debilities in the governments of the new republic, and in the end their concerns grew sufficiently strong to enable the Convention to assemble, rethink the basic premises of republicanism, and draft a radically innovative Constitution, which eleven states had ratified by the summer of 1788. Explaining how the Constitution was framed thus remains, as it always has been, one of the most challenging problems in American history. A reconstruction of the various problems that vexed Congress once the war ended provides the logical starting point for such an inquiry. This chapter will briefly survey the major problems of policy and politics that troubled Congress during the mid-1780's. The next will trace the evolving strategy of reform that led to the Convention of 1787 and attempt to explain the conditions that governed the outcome of its deliberations.

Capital

DURING the final years of the war, Congress had groped for ways to enhance its authority; in the first months of peace, it found itself struggling simply to maintain its dignity. The first insult came in late June 1783, when a small contingent of Pennsylvania soldiers mutinied, marched on Philadelphia, and surrounded the building where both Congress and the state council regularly met. After the council refused its request to call out the militia, Congress resolved to quit Philadelphia. The delegates adjourned to nearby Princeton, a college town that they soon discovered was no better prepared to accommodate Congress in a sudden flight than Baltimore and York had been in 1776 and 1777. The removal to Princeton added a new element of bathos to the political plight of Congress. "The high and mighty and most *gracious* Sovereigns the C[ongres]s," a Boston newspaper scoffed, "not being stars of the *first* magnitude, but rather partaking of the nature of *inferior* luminaries, or *wandering* comets, again appear in their eccentric orb, assuming various directions and courses, sometimes regular and uniform, at other times, vain and retrograde." A postwar fascination with air balloons suggested another sardonic metaphor for the rootless Congress. This device, one wag wrote, would "exactly accommodate the *itinerant Genius of Congress,* who being raised in a little Balloon, can float along from one end of the continent to the other, observe that the systems of government are properly supported, and when occasion requires can suddenly pop down into any of the states they please." Congress had been publicly criticized before, most notably in 1779, but never so mockingly.[2]

Although some Philadelphians—including Charles Thomson, still secretary of Congress—hoped that conciliatory gestures could induce the delegates to return, public opinion in the nation's leading city turned against its former guests when resolutions to that effect narrowly failed to pass Congress. By late October, Benjamin Rush observed, Congress was being "abused, laughed at, pitied & cursed in every Company." Thomas Willing, a former delegate and merchant partner of Robert Morris, took the whole episode lightheartedly. "I have never said any thing to you about the removal of the Congress from this City," he wrote William Bingham; "it was not worth while. [W]e shall laugh at it hereafter over a glass of Wine." In the end, Willing believed, Congress "must finally sitt down *here,* & *here* only. The Bank itself, together with the enterprizing spirit of the people of Pennsylvania, will ever support their measures, better than they can be supported elsewhere."[3]

That, however, was precisely the reason why some delegates hoped Congress would never return to Philadelphia. For those members who were still bitterly opposed to Robert Morris, Princeton was a welcome refuge from a city where the superintendent's measures had always commanded visible popular support. In the view of Arthur Lee, David Howell, the Massachusetts delegation, and several other members, Congress had made a providential escape from what Howell called "the unhealthful &

dangerous atmosphere of Philadelphia." "It is observed by some Gentlemen," the Rhode Islander reported in late July, "that an obvious alteration has taken place in the House on some debates . . . wherein the office of Finance is concerned." Samuel Osgood put the case more bluntly in December, when he wrote John Adams that Congress could never "have been a free and independent Body," had it returned to Philadelphia. "Plans for absolute Government, for deceiving the lower Classes of People, for introducing undue Influence, for any Kind of Government, in which Democracy has the least possible share, originate, are cherished and disseminated from thence." In the minds of the New England delegates in particular, Philadelphia had become a symbol of economic corruption and political reaction.[4]

Princeton was not itself a promising site for a permanent capital. James Madison and Joseph Jones were forced to share a bed in a tiny room, while Howell and William Ellery were housed in a former store. Even before Congress fled Philadelphia, it had begun discussing proposals for creating a permanent national capital; the move to Princeton gave this matter a new urgency. Since Congress could conceivably relocate almost anywhere between the lower Hudson and the Potomac, and because no fewer than five states were actively competing to have it settle within their borders, this question was not easily resolved. After some tangled maneuvers, in late October 1783 a majority was mustered in support of a plan to construct two capitals along the Delaware and Potomac rivers, with Congress alternately meeting, in the meantime, at Annapolis and Trenton. Late in the fall Congress removed to Annapolis, where it adjourned in the spring of 1784, leaving a Committee of the States to sit, first restlessly and then abortively, in its recess. By prior arrangement, Congress reassembled at Trenton in the fall. There it scrapped the dual capital plan in favor of the erection of a single residence along the Delaware. Two days before Christmas, Congress adjourned to New York, where it sat for the duration of the confederation.[5]

The ultimate location of the national capital was destined to remain unresolved until the famous Compromise of 1790 led to the planning and construction of Washington. Although hardly the most critical issue confronting the Continental Congress in the mid-1780's, this problem did symbolize several major aspects of the transition to peacetime politics. Its residence in five sepa-

rate cities and towns during a period of little more than a year
and a half did nothing to enhance the wounded dignity of Congress. The adamant opposition against returning to Philadelphia
demonstrated the persistence of the partisan rancor nurtured
during the final years of the war, when a small cluster of delegates centered on New England but abetted by Arthur Lee had
been aroused against Robert Morris and the two principal interests he seemed to represent—the commercial ambitions of Philadelphia and the diplomatic designs of France. Parochial in their
loyalties and almost paranoid in their suspicions, these men saw
Morris resurgent in every proposal for augmenting the power of
Congress. Finally, the capital issue foreshadowed the role sectionalism would play in the politics of the mid-1780's. It was
hardly surprising that sectional feelings influenced the outcome
of this question. But other substantive issues soon arose that exposed the potential conflict among major regional interests in
equally obvious but also more dangerous ways, ultimately raising
the question of whether or not there was one common national
interest the states could mutually support. The establishment of
a national capital at least presupposed the survival of the confederation; other issues pertaining to commercial policy toward foreign powers and the settlement of the west seemed to point
toward its dissolution.

Revenue

FINANCE, the great dilemma of the early 1780's, remained the
central test of the authority Congress would be able to exercise
after the peace. The revenue plan of April 1783 had embodied
three major proposals: a revised impost, a request for supplemental funds to be appropriated by the states for the use of Congress,
and a recommendation that population replace land values as the
basis for apportioning the common expenses. Having framed a
compromise that most members felt answered the reasonable
objections of the states, Congress had agreed that none of these
resolutions would take effect until all had been unanimously approved. This stringent condition apparently reflected an opinion
that further modifications of this program would effectively reduce Congress to precisely the situation it sought to escape: a
precarious dependence on the goodwill and efficiency of the

states. Congress was anxious to deter individual states from attaching the sorts of restrictive conditions that had been incorporated in several of the acts ratifying the impost of 1781.[6] As a result, the new revenue program remained a dead letter.

The impost nevertheless came close to adoption. It survived critical tests in Virginia, where Washington intervened in its behalf, and Massachusetts, where Robert Morris overcame forceful opposition by transmitting extracts from diplomatic dispatches in which John Adams had emphasized the importance of securing national credit. But Rhode Island remained obstinate and refused to ratify until 1785. In Connecticut feelings against the commutation of military pensions ran particularly high, and the impost was rejected twice before being approved in the spring of 1784. Georgia had never ratified the first impost—an omission largely overlooked during the furor over Rhode Island—and delayed ratifying the amended version until 1786.[7]

By then New York was the only state that had yet to grant the impost in some form. In the early 1780's its acquiescence could have been taken for granted. But resentment over congressional failure to aid its efforts to reclaim Vermont and a conviction that New York had always contributed more than other states to the common cause had soured the feelings of many state officials, most notably Governor George Clinton, toward the union. Abraham Yates, Jr., still bitter that Robert Morris had refused to appoint him receiver of continental taxes, emerged as an effective public critic of the impost, publishing a number of essays attacking the proposal.[8] In 1785 the New York Senate rejected the impost, and when in 1786 the assembly did pass an act of ratification, it contained provisions that Congress deemed unacceptable. During the five years that an impost had been under consideration, all the states had accepted it at one time or another; but although Congress made a last futile effort to set it in operation, the New York rejection constituted the final verdict.

Other provisions of the program of 1783 also came to nothing. Congress did not receive unanimous approval for its amendment proposing the apportionment of expenses according to population. Foreseeing that this recommendation might go unratified, Congress had also asked the states to complete the censuses of land and buildings required under Article 8, but the states never made a serious effort to carry out what would have been, in any case, an extremely difficult task. And although many of the states did agree to levy the supplemental taxes Congress had requested, unanimous ratification was again unattainable, while many of the state acts contained provisions Congress deemed unacceptable. To meet its current operating expenses, Congress continued to rely on requisitions on the states. The results were hardly satisfying. Remittances proved inadequate to the servicing of the foreign debt, which had remained the indisputable obligation of the confederation, and Congress was forced to postpone payments to major foreign creditors. The one sign of hope in this otherwise gloomy picture was the completion in 1784 of the major western land cessions, which finally enabled Congress to begin to plan for the disposition of the new national domain. Disagreements over the plans for settling and governing these territories prevented the immediate exploitation of this resource, however.

The desultory progress of these measures effectively defeated Robert Morris's plan to use the creation of a consolidated national debt to justify endowing Congress with independent revenues. Rather than provide the funds Congress wanted or wait until they were unanimously ratified, the states began to make separate provisions for satisfying the public creditors whom Morris had hoped to make dependent on Congress. State notes were issued in exchange for federal securities, making the states, in effect, the creditors of Congress. As the states responded to the demands of their own citizens by absorbing a substantial proportion of the domestic debt, the rationale for granting Congress independent revenues was progressively weakened.[9]

Those delegates who had most deeply resented Morris were not overly alarmed about these difficulties, at least before 1786. The task of first weakening and then eliminating the vestiges of his power seemed more urgent than mere problems of finance, and their already intense suspicions were further inflamed when his artful intervention secured Massachusetts's approval of the impost. In a lengthy letter to John Adams, which was intended, in part, to question the opinions Morris had quoted, Samuel Osgood pointedly noted that "if you were here, you would find it very difficult to establish Funds, that would not have a Tendency to destroy the Liberties of this Country." The great danger, Osgood and his collaborators believed, was "That if permanent Funds are given to Congress, the aristocratical Influence, which predominates in more than a major part of the United States, will fully establish an arbitrary Government." Far from being troubled by the slow progress of the impost, they candidly rooted for its rejection, hoping, as Samuel Holten put it, that "the states will be daily more & more convinced of the propriety & necessity of . . . establishing revenues within themselves & retaining the absolute controul over their own purse strings." If the claims of legitimate public creditors remained unsatisfied, Arthur Lee wrote John Adams in August 1784, it was not the fault of the Articles of Confederation. The problem was instead "owing to the heavy weight the war had laid upon us," and, Lee added in his characteristic vein, to "the placing two men in the first offices of trust and power, who have constantly aimed at exalting themselves by depreciating [sic] the public"—namely, Morris and Franklin, his two nemeses. Popular opposition to the impost and commutation thus seemed a healthy sign because it could be equated with opposition to Morris himself. When Congress reorganized the Office of Finance in May 1784, David Howell attributed this decision to a growing realization that a repudiation of Morris had become "the only remaining expedient of regaining the confidence of the states, and obtaining the long expected funds."[10]

When Morris finally left office in the fall of 1784, his opponents were still cautiously optimistic about the financial prospects of Congress. Lee and Osgood soon comprised a majority of the new Board of Treasury, and while it was true, as Holten complained, that "there is not much pleasure in being a member of Congress, unless a man can bear duning very well," it now seemed possible that the states would grow less suspicious of Congress and more willing to support it. Osgood had his doubts on this score, but Lee was more optimistic. The prospective opening of the west, Lee believed, could yet do wonders. "With this fund well managed," he informed John Adams, "the public debt may soon be annihilated." Howell agreed. "The western world opens an amazing prospect as a national fund," he wrote in February 1784; ". . . it is equal to our debt."[11]

By early 1786, however, the experience of administering the treasury was providing Lee and Osgood with evidence not of the inherent dangers of power but rather of the frustration of exercising it under the circumstances prevailing in the mid-1780's. As E. James Ferguson has observed, they eventually found themselves writing "diatribes against the states almost in the style of the Financier whom they had displaced." The conclusion seemed unavoidable that a financial system based on requisitions and the levying of state taxes would never work, as Osgood admitted in January 1786 in a revealing letter to William Gordon, a long-time critic of Morris and the impost. "I am clear in one point," Osgood observed,

that the united states must be entrusted with Monies other than the scanty Pittance that they obtain from the annual Requisitions—Ten Months will more explicitly show all that we cannot exist as a Nation without more prompt & effectual Supplies—Congress must either be vested with coercive Powers as to the Collection of Money or with the Impost which last for many Years to come will not be equal to the Necessities of the Nation; they must therefore if vested with the last be vested with the former also—or cease to be a Congress of any Consequence to the Union.

For Osgood, once so fearful of the dangers of federal power, Congress was now a "Sovereign Body [which] ought always to have a Power to do Justice" to its creditors. If that meant it might also "do Injustice," it had to be remembered that "Without the Power Injustice must certainly ensue." He had formerly shared the reservations Gordon still held, Osgood recalled, "but four or five Years close Attention to the Subject, confronted with Facts as stubborn as ungrateful obliged me to yield." Now he was convinced that "Americans have no more Virtue than other People," and that "We must be governed by Laws, or we shall be no Nation at all." Although Osgood, like Lee, subsequently opposed the Constitution, his disillusionment in 1786 was profound; Gouverneur Morris could hardly have spoken more cynically.[12]

One month after Osgood wrote this letter, the New Jersey assembly approved a resolution declaring it would refuse to honor the requisitions of Congress until New York ratified the impost. New York had previously enacted a state impost to which the citizens of New Jersey, lacking any significant port of their own, necessarily contributed, and the assembly argued that these revenues should be appropriated to the use of Congress rather than the state. Most delegates understandably regarded the New Jersey announcement as a well-meant but short-sighted show of zeal more likely to weaken further the authority of Congress than to strengthen it; "however New Jersey may suffer by her paying taxes to N. York," Nathaniel Gorham commented, "her refusal to comply with the requisition is unjustifiable, and unless she recinds, her resolution must work the end of all federal Government." Gorham was one of three delegates dispatched to ask the assembly to reconsider its position. The legislators apparently accepted the committee's argument that their action had been impolitic, and subsequently retracted their resolution. But the assembly took no further steps to comply with the pending requisition of 1785. Several months later, the New York assembly approved its defective ratification of the impost.[13]

Congress had lived from hand to mouth for six years, and there was nothing new to be said about its financial plight. The delegates had continually appealed to their private political connections, and Congress had repeatedly beseeched the states. The results were the same, and equally disappointing.

Dilemmas of Foreign Policy

MORE complex and, if possible, even more alarming than these financial problems were the major questions of foreign policy that beset Congress after 1783. Within a year of the conclusion of peace three external threats to the security and welfare of the United States had become evident; yet Congress lacked not only the resources but the authority and political support necessary to counteract them. It could not compel Great Britain to relinquish the military posts it continued to occupy within the new nation's northern boundaries. It could not induce Britain and France to remove the discriminatory restrictions they quickly imposed on American commerce. And it could not force Spain to reopen the Mississippi to American navigation. Because the conduct of foreign affairs had always been considered the prerogative and the preeminent responsibility of Congress, its inability to respond to these challenges raised further questions about the adequacy of the Articles of Confederation. Perhaps even more ominously, these problems affected the interests of different states and regions disproportionately, so both within Congress and without it became increasingly difficult to define a common national interest deserving the unanimous support of the states. Where financial issues encouraged criticism of the Articles, by 1786 problems of foreign policy were evoking fears for the survival of the union.[14]

The Treaty of Paris ending the war contained two provisions that brought Congress into conflict with the states. Article IV stipulated that "creditors on either side shall meet with no lawful impediment to the recovery of the full value in sterling money, of all bona fide debts heretofore contracted." Article V required Congress to recommend that the states provide for the restitution of property confiscated from British subjects or American loyalists, and that they also allow the claimants of this property to return to America to institute the appropriate legal proceedings.[15] Both articles were predictably unpopular in the states, where animosities against British creditors and the loyalists showed few signs of evaporating. Acting on the recommendation of Congress, the states had earlier enacted a considerable body of confiscatory legislation; and in the wake of a long war and a late upsurge in British naval activity against American commerce, there was little enthusiam for the payment of prewar debts, particularly when it was rumored that creditors would demand cumulative interest.[16]

These were sensitive issues, and most state legislatures found it politically inexpedient to defend these provisions against the wishes of their constituents. Some question existed as to whether Britain actually expected the restitution of confiscated property. Congress had only been asked to recommend appropriate measures to the states, and it was commonly suspected that Britain had insisted upon this provision only to appease loyalist refugees in England.[17] The sincerity of British interest in the repayment of debts was not in doubt, however. In either event, the states' failure to honor these articles gave the British government a convenient pretext for refusing to abandon its strategically situated posts according to the terms set by the treaty.[18] In the immediate aftermath of finishing one war, and with its treasury impoverished, Congress was in no position to attempt to seize the forts by force; nor could it persuade the states that the national interest took precedence over local political considerations.

That legislation hostile to the claims of loyalists and British creditors was proving popular was hardly difficult to understand: it was no more surprising than the legislatures' reluctance to fulfill congressional requisitions by levying additional taxes on their constituents. Yet whatever the circumstances, in both cases many delegates believed the states were willfully defying the

explicit provisions of the Articles of Confederation and the legitimate authority of Congress. Even George Mason, on other issues
an increasingly bitter critic of Congress, thought state legislation
restricting debt collections by British creditors indefensible. For,
as he reminded Patrick Henry, "the power of War & Peace, and
of making Treatys, being in Congress, and not in the separate
States, any such act wou'd be considered as an unwarrantable
Assumption of Power in the State adopting it."[19] With foreign
treaties as with requisitions, however, the central problem was
to bridge the gap between the responsibilities formally delegated to Congress and the failure of the Articles to anticipate,
much less devise remedies for situations where the states might
obstruct or contravene its actions.

Charles Thomson attempted to grapple with the awkward
questions this issue raised in a private memorandum he prepared
sometime in 1784 or 1785, which was specifically addressed to the
problem of enforcing treaties. Thomson began by examining the
second and ninth Articles of Confederation, which stated that
Congress would exercise delegated powers, but also that some of
these powers, including that of making treaties, were to be under
its "sole and exclusive" control. Once a treaty had been properly
concluded, Thomson argued,

> every state in the confederacy & every individual in every state is bound
> to observe it. It is a law paramount in the state so long as the state
> continues a member of the confederacy. The legislature have no right
> to interfere with it. . . . On the contrary it is their duty to remove every
> obstacle (if any there be) within their state to the faithful performance
> & observance of the treaty.

The secretary admitted that the precise legal status of foreign
treaties was still uncertain. Nevertheless, Thomson was clear in
his opinion that in these matters the determinations of Congress
must ultimately prevail. Even where preexisting state legislation
militated against the terms of a treaty, local judges were obliged
to recognize "that the promulgation of the treaty is a virtual
repeal of the law. To decide otherwise would be to declare their
state in rebellion against the Confederacy, which is not to be
presumed." Thomson's argument followed the logic Madison
had earlier adduced to demonstrate that congressional requisitions were binding on the states, and, it may be argued, his
interpretation was consistent with the intended meaning of the

Articles themselves. That did not, however, give his position the political impact necessary to overcome the practical difficulty of securing its acceptance in the states.[20]

Although British retention of the frontier posts had little effect on the lives of most Americans, British restrictions on American commerce posed a more palpable threat to the general welfare. As early as the summer of 1783 Britain began to pursue a series of measures limiting the access of American products to imperial markets, notably in the West Indies, and preventing the American merchant marine from regaining its previously substantial share of Atlantic commerce. French commercial policy was somewhat less discriminatory, but the concessions offered by the nation's sole ally disappointed American expectations. By the fall of 1783 it was apparent that Britain was committed to following an illiberal and, it was thought, vindictive commercial policy toward the United States—one that could be most effectively countered if Congress could impose retaliatory restrictions on the glut of British imports that began flooding American markets immediately after the peace. Strongly influenced by a series of blunt dispatches from John Adams, whose diplomatic frustrations in Europe were already turning him into an advocate of greater powers for Congress, the delegates began considering asking the states to allow Congress to regulate foreign trade. Committee reports and appropriate recommendations were under preparation by late September 1783, but action was delayed until the following spring, in large measure because of the low level of attendance that barely carried Congress through the winter of 1784 at its new residence in Annapolis.[21]

Discussions of commercial retaliation seem to have escaped the controversial aura surrounding other issues that concerned Congress in the final months before its adjournment in early June 1784. There were different opinions as to how stringent and comprehensive such measures should be, but the animosities and ideological sparks that matters of finance still evoked did not affect this issue—at least as it was discussed in 1784. On the last day of April, Congress approved two recommendations which, the New Hampshire delegates noted, "we think to be so guarded that no ill consequences are to be apprehended from adopting that measure." The first would empower Congress to prohibit the importation or exportation of goods shipped in vessels owned or navigated by citizens of nations that had not concluded com-

mercial treaties with the United States. The second would authorize Congress to bar foreign subjects trading in America from
importing goods produced in any country but their own. Both
recommendations were intended to bolster the American bargaining positions in the anticipated negotiation of commercial
treaties with European states.[22]

The two recommendations of April 1784 said nothing about
imposing restraints on American commerce, though some delegates already believed that the country had to be protected from
its own lust for British goods. "If we have been prevented from
making any Commercial stipulations with Great Britain," the
North Carolina delegates observed as early as September 1783,
"it is because the Merchants without System or caution rushed
into the British Ports and courted an intercourse with that Country."[23] When Congress slowly reassembled at Trenton late in
1784, a widening trade depression affecting American merchants
and tradesmen suggested that further commercial reforms
might be pursued, particularly since this depression was commonly attributed to the competitive advantages British manufac-
turers and merchants were believed to enjoy over their American counterparts. The absence of an effective quorum provided
those delegates who were in attendance with ample leisure to
discuss the general problems of the union. After the idea of a
constitutional convention had been briefly considered and dismissed,[24] a committee was appointed to consider whether Congress should solicit a general power to regulate commerce. Its
report, delivered at New York in mid-February 1785, proposed
that Congress seek an amendment to the Articles authorizing it
to regulate both foreign and interstate commerce and to levy
duties on imports and exports. To divorce this amendment from
the revenue plan of April 1783, the report stipulated that these
duties were to be collected by and appropriated to the states
where they were payable.[25]

This report was intermittently though thoroughly debated
well into the summer of 1785, but never approved. Its principal
supporters, led by the young Virginian James Monroe, quickly
realized that its prospects for adoption, either by Congress or the
states, were few. Two objections were critical. First, a number of
southern delegates thought this measure was designed to further
the interests of northern merchants at the expense of southern
planters. As James McHenry of Maryland summarized their ar-

guments, they feared it would lead to a northern monopoly of the carrying trade, which would in turn produce lower prices for their commodities and higher charges for their voluminous imports. Not all southern delegates shared this fear that the eight states from Delaware to the north would exploit their five sisters to the south, but these objections could be expected to be duplicated by their constituents.[26] Second, the committee's report revived the same fears of unchecked power that had informed the earlier opposition to Robert Morris and proposals for an independent congressional revenue. Richard Henry Lee (now president of Congress), Elbridge Gerry, Rufus King, David Jackson, and others criticized these proposals on traditional whiggish grounds, arguing (as Monroe summarized their position) that "it was dangerous to concentrate power, since it might be turned to mischievous purposes," and that "all attacks upon the confederation were dangerous and calculated even if they did not succeed to weaken it."[27] Writing from Albany, Abraham Yates, Jr., informed David Howell that he was "rather Suspitious that the advocates for augmenting the powers of Congress will try to Effect their Scheme under the Cloak of investing Congress with power to make Commercial Regulations."[28]

The claim that Congress needed stronger authority over foreign affairs also aggravated those New England delegates who still resented the success Gérard and Luzerne had achieved in inducing Congress to defer to French interests when peace instructions had been drafted in 1779 and 1781. In their minds it was still an open question whether the United States should be much concerned with foreign affairs at all. Even Francis Dana, the first American minister to Russia, could argue in January 1785 that

there is nothing clearer in my opinion than that our Interests will be more injured by the residence of foreign Ministers among us, than they can be promoted by our Ministers abroad. The best way to get rid of the former, is not to send out the latter. And therefore let those already appointed die off, or resign as fast as they may, I never wish to hear of another being sent to any Country or Court in Europe, after we shall have settled our commercial Treaties with them. . . . We have a World to ourselves; and if we do not know how at present, we shall learn to govern it as well at least as any other part of the Globe is governed, and sooner and better without foreign interference than with it.[29]

John Adams, the recipient of this outburst, thought otherwise, but his personal experience in Europe provided him with a perspective radically different from that of many of his New England correspondents.

The extent to which these lingering fears clashed with and overrode the sectional interests of the New England delegates was demonstrated in a revealing episode that occurred during the summer of 1785. Few states were more seriously affected by the depression than Massachusetts. Yet when the General Court instructed its delegates to propose the calling of a constitutional convention, the state's delegation (Gerry, King, and Holten) decided not to present their constituents' resolutions for the consideration of Congress. Their private tabling of these instructions provided a remarkable example not only of the independence that delegates sometimes exercised but also of the residual force the conflict of the early 1780's still exerted.

They had suppressed their instructions, the delegates informed Governor James Bowdoin, in part because they saw little prospect for any substantial revision of the Articles actually taking place—an opinion most members of Congress shared. But the Massachusetts delegates also believed that it was too soon to be certain what amendments were necessary or whether they should be adopted on a permanent or merely temporary basis. Underlying these expedient reservations was a more disturbing concern: any movement to amend the Articles would provide a tempting and dangerous opportunity for those who wished to convert "our republican Governments, into baleful Aristocracies." As Congress needed time to determine whether American commerce might not revive naturally, so too the state legislatures and the people were obliged to reflect on the risks of precipitate action, and to recall that

the powers, once delegated to the Confederation, cannot be revoked without the *unanimous Consent* of the States—that *this* may be earnestly sought for, but never obtained—that the federal and State Constitutions, are the great Bulwarks of Liberty—that if they are subject, on trivial and even important Occasions, to be revised, and re-revised, altered and re-altered, they must cease to be considered as effectual and sacred Barriers; and like land Marks frequently changed, will afford no certain Rule for ascertaining the Boundaries, no criterion for distinguishing between the Rights of Government and those of the people, and therefore, that every Alteration of the Articles, should be so thoroughly understood and digested, as scarcely to admit the *possibility* of a Disposition for a Reconsideration.

Although somewhat less shrill than the prophecies and warnings of 1783, this letter revealed that the principles that had fueled the campaign against the impost were hardly forgotten.[30]

For different reasons, the advocates of these amendments were also prepared to confess that further delays in strengthening Congress were not only unavoidable but necessary. Monroe, the leading proponent of commercial reform, had realized this by April 1785, when he informed Jefferson that it would probably be best for Congress not to approve the report but simply refer it to the states for their consideration. Fearing that its further agitation in Congress would create "prejudices" among dissenting delegates, who would then organize opposition in their states, Monroe concluded that "If it is [to be] carried it can only be by thorough investigation and a conviction carried to the minds of every citizen that it is right; the slower it moves on therefore in my opinion the better." Four months later he reaffirmed his opinion. Conceding the sincerity of the objections raised by the report's critics—"for I have the most confidential communications with them and am satisfied they act ingenuously"—Monroe remained confident that "the longer it is delay'd the more certain is its passage thro the several states ultimately. Their minds will be better informed by evidence within their views of the necessity of committing the power to Congress, for the commerce of the union is daily declining."[31]

Monroe's assessment reflected both a candid concession to political reality and the curious optimism that, prior to 1786, colored many private discussions of the weaknesses of Congress. It was naïve in minimizing the potentially disruptive pressures Congress faced as issues that had strong sectional overtones acquired increasing importance. Each passing year saw this problem raised in more ominous terms. The debate over commercial powers for Congress had exposed the divergent interests of the major regions in a way that earlier maneuvers over the location of a capital had not anticipated. The third major issue of postwar diplomacy—American policy toward Spain—not only carried this process one step further but encouraged speculation about the dissolution of the union.

In 1784 Spain had closed the Mississippi River to American

navigation. When negotiations for a Spanish-American treaty of
commerce began at New York in the summer of 1785, John Jay,
now secretary for foreign affairs, was instructed to procure the
repeal of this prohibition. The Spanish negotiator, Don Diego de
Gardoqui, was under equally firm instructions not to open the
Mississippi. Jay, who had spent two frustrating years as the
American minister in Madrid, initially agreed with his instructions. But by late May 1786, months of laborious negotiations had
convinced him to ask Congress to agree to a revision under
which the United States would abjure the navigation of the Mississippi for a limited term of years. In exchange for this concession, it seemed possible that a liberal commercial agreement
could be reached with Spain. Jay's request was widely interpre-
ted by southern delegates to require their region to sacrifice its
expansionist interests for the benefit of northern commerce. The
bitter debates that ensued during the summer of 1786 were further complicated by the parliamentary tactics of the northern
delegates. The seven states from Pennsylvania to New Hampshire approved the revised instructions Jay wanted, even though
they knew that the five southern states would be able to block
the ratification of any treaty Jay negotiated, since nine votes
were necessary for that purpose. This issue produced the starkest
sectional division Congress had ever known, and southern members began to suspect what some northern delegates were in fact
considering: that the impasse over this question portended the
creation of two or three separate confederacies.[32]

The foreign policy problems of the mid-1780's thus raised two
major questions about the future of the confederation. First,
would Congress enjoy sufficient authority and support to enable
it to protect American interests in the world of nations? Second,
and perhaps more disturbing, was there a general, coherent national interest that Congress could defend, or had the very success of the struggle for independence undermined the strongest
foundation of American unity? Because the conduct of foreign
policy was clearly the principal responsibility that Congress
would exercise in time of peace, these posed the most alarming
questions the delegates encountered between the Treaty of Paris
and the calling of the Philadelphia Convention. Even the states'
failure to supply the continental treasury could be subsumed
under their larger inability to recognize the existence of a legitimate sphere of national interest. An impoverished Congress

could neither satisfy foreign creditors nor keep up military forces capable of defending American claims and interests along its extensive frontiers, nor even maintain a diplomatic corps that European nations could take seriously. When the Committee of the States abruptly adjourned in August 1784, Charles Thomson was forced to reflect on how much Americans had yet to learn about the character of their mutual interests. "Whatever little politicians may think," he wrote Jacob Read,

time will evince that it is of no small consequence to save appearances with foreign nations, and not to suffer the federal government to become invisible. A government without a visible head must appear a strange phenomenon to European politicians and will I fear lead them to form no very favourable opinion of our stability, wisdom or Union.

When critics of the Articles talked of amendments and reforms, what they had in mind were primarily these responsibilities of foreign relations, the great affairs of state as they were traditionally conceived.[33]

These were concerns, however, that for the most part only experienced politicians could find deeply troubling, and that the majority of Americans deemed largely irrelevant to their own immediate interests. Even those issues that did impinge upon particular communities or classes of individuals lacked the potential to create a national consensus in support of specific reforms. The depression of 1784–85 had a disproportionate impact on urban merchants and tradesmen. British retention of frontier posts affected speculators and migrants looking toward the settlement of the northwestern territories, but not southern planters and small farmers vehemently opposed to the payment of prewar debts or the return of loyalist refugees to areas where British troops and their American sympathizers had committed acts of personal violence and property damage. The occlusion of the Mississippi troubled southern leaders anticipating regional expansion into the southwest, but not New Englanders fearful that their own sectional influence and interests would suffer as western migrations gathered momentum. The conversion from the wartime politics of patriotism to the candid pursuit of local and private interests foredoomed any attempt to secure the unanimous approval that amendments to the Articles required. The comparatively modest amendments Congress had proposed in April 1784 were never adopted, and there was little reason to

believe that the broader commercial powers under consideration in 1785 and 1786 would soon enjoy a different reception.

Land

WHEN, in 1785, James Monroe argued that a strategy of delaying
agitation for major amendments was the wisest course Congress
could take, he may well have been drawing lessons from the
history of another issue that interested him intensely: the organization and development of the new national domain. The disposition of western lands had been among the most difficult questions Congress had confronted during the war, precisely because,
like the issues of the mid-1780's, it had forced the states to balance
considerations of self-interest against the pressing demands of
national welfare. This was the issue that had led Maryland to
obstruct the ratification of the Articles and inspired Connecticut
and Virginia to propose that the remaining states confederate
without Maryland. Even after Virginia had agreed to yield its
extensive claims, continuing disputes over the terms of its cession
delayed its final acceptance until March 1, 1784.[34] By then, however, Congress had already been considering for some months
further plans for governing, surveying, and settling these new
territories. On April 23, it adopted its first ordinance on the
subject of territorial government—the forerunner of the celebrated Northwest Ordinance of 1787. Plans for settling the land
proved more controversial, and another year elapsed before further provisions were adopted. Nevertheless, after years of
acrimony and calculated maneuvers, the gradual emergence of
a generally acceptable policy must have been tremendously
heartening to many members of Congress. If this issue, seemingly so intractable in 1776 and so intimately connected with the
particular interests of the states, had finally been resolved in
favor of the confederation, might it not provide a model for
compromise and common sense on other matters as well?

So Monroe might have reasoned. The framing of a policy for
the opening of the west *was* the one undisputed postwar
achievement of Congress and, as several historians have recently
argued, an achievement that represented not merely the visionary imprint of Thomas Jefferson (who played a leading role in the
deliberations of 1784) but also the shared concerns of most dele-

gates. Indeed, one of the most recent students of the evolution of the 1787 Ordinance has concluded that "its history is apparently nothing more or less than that of a rather ordinary piece of noncontroversial legislation," and that throughout the mid-1780's the "continuity and consensus of thought" about key provisions of territorial government "are obvious."[35] Had other problems not intervened, the creation of the national domain might conceivably have fulfilled some of the expectations it had evoked within Congress all along, enhancing its influence, replenishing its treasury, and demonstrating that substantial power could be safely entrusted to the federal government, thereby weakening objections against the further revision of the Articles.

Yet the success of any western policy was itself contingent on the extent to which Congress could exercise authority in other matters, and by 1786 its debilities were threatening to undermine the anticipated results of the long struggle to acquire a national domain. The mere enactment of provisions for territorial government and settlement could not guarantee that Congress would be able to discharge its mandate effectively or retain the loyalty of western settlers. Would migrants to the west maintain their allegiance to the confederation if it proved incapable of defending the frontiers or forcing Spain to open the Mississippi? If the process of settlement proceeded as slowly as many members now believed it would, and if it were as carefully regulated as Congress intended, difficulties could presumably be avoided. Still, it was hard enough to imagine how the geographical barriers inhibiting the integration of the seaboard and the interior would be overcome even if political disputes between these disparate regions did not arise.

By the summer of 1786, the collapse of the revenue plan of 1783 and the bitter rift within Congress over the Mississippi converged to point toward more ominous conclusions. Even Rufus King, who was hardly an enthusiast for rapid western development, was alarmed when the Board of Treasury was forced to "explicitly declare their utter inability to make [a] pitiful advance" of $1,000 to transport ammunition to American posts along the Ohio River. Monroe and other southern delegates believed that the northern willingness to acquiesce in the occlusion of the Mississippi was designed "to break up . . . the settlements on the western waters, prevent any in future, and thereby keep the States southward as they now are"—that is, a numerical minority of the existing union—"or if settlements will take place, that they shall be on such principles as to make it the interest of the people to separate from the Confederacy, so as effectually to exclude any new State from it." And in fact King, his Massachusetts colleague Theodore Sedgwick, and other New England leaders were toying with the idea of a separate confederation and wondering whether any "paper engagements, or stipulations, can be formed which will insure a desirable connection between the Atlantic States" and those on the other side of the mountains should the Mississippi be opened. "[T]he pursuits and interests of the people on the two sides, will be so different," King argued, "and probably so opposite, that an entire separation must eventually ensue."[36]

As the furor over the Mississippi subsided somewhat in early 1787, such fears receded as well, and Congress went ahead to complete the Northwest Ordinance. Nevertheless, far from being the notable exception to the otherwise pathetic history of Congress in the 1780's, the still problematic fate of its western policy indicated just how dangerous the unresolved difficulties of the confederation could become.[37] If the confederation could not surmount its postwar lassitude and internal divisions, it was entirely conceivable that Britain and Spain would emerge as the dominant political forces in the interior of the continent, leaving the thirteen original states clinging to the ocean, deprived of the resources of the west, and still bickering over explosive issues of foreign affairs.

Reputation

UNTIL the final months before the Philadelphia Convention, serious concern about the future of the confederation was in all probability confined to a small and élite circle of American politicians and their connections. Discussions of the peacetime plight of Congress appeared only infrequently in American newspapers and never developed into a full-fledged, much less incisive debate over the state of the union. Popular interest in the affairs of Congress occasionally mounted, as in the widespread protest against commutation that roiled Connecticut politics in 1783–84, or the calls for vesting commercial powers in Congress that were frequently printed in leading urban newspapers in 1785. But in general the proceedings of Congress commanded little attention. Americans probably knew as much if not more about Parliament, whose debates were often reprinted in their newspapers, as they did about Congress, which still sat behind closed doors even after the coming of peace effectively undercut the claim that its deliberations were best conducted in secret. "We know little more of Congress here than you do in France," Francis Hopkinson informed Jefferson in the spring of 1785, "perhaps not so much. They are seldom or ever mentioned in the Papers and are less talked of than if they were in the West Indies Islands."[38]

One reason why Congress received so little attention was that it was often incapable of reaching decisions. Caught between various sources of sectional rivalry and the conflicting interests that periodically set Congress at loggerheads with the states, the delegates were hard pressed to frame policies they could realistically expect to be endorsed or executed by the states. But its constitutional handicaps hampered congressional efficiency in another way. Its lack of power could not make service at Congress attractive to veteran politicians whose own prestige might serve to enhance its precarious influence. When Jefferson expressed a belief that "the best effects [would be] produced by sending our young statesmen" to Congress, he hoped their exposure to national issues would eventually lead them to "befriend federal measures" whenever they returned to their states.[39] But his statement also implied a certain doubt as to whether Congress would be able to do anything of real importance in the near future. In its weakened state, Congress could command neither the regular attendance nor the personal loyalties of many of its members, and both its reputation and the progress of business suffered accordingly.

From the time of its retreat to Princeton until the very demise of the confederation, Congress struggled almost constantly to maintain the quorum of seven states required by the Articles. The transaction of even minor business required the approval of all seven, and major decisions could be taken only with the affirmative vote of nine states. A state that was represented by two members—the minimum fixed by the Articles—always risked losing its vote if both disagreed, or whenever one member was ill, or decided he had more pressing business of his own to attend to, or left unexpectedly for home when his overdue relief failed to appear. Congress suffered as well, since the indisposition of a

single delegate could prevent a quorum, while a divided delegation lessened any possibility of creating a majority. To have anything passed in Congress in the mid-1780's required a fair amount
of luck and a substantial level of consensus. Neither came readily
to hand.

In 1783 and 1784, the problem of locating a comfortable residence did little to encourage attendance. Princeton was charm-
ing in its tranquility but hardly comfortable. Annapolis offered
much more in the way of diversions. Elbridge Gerry, for one, was
struck by the variety of entertainments available. "The object of
the Inhabitants here is altogether pleasure," he wrote Stephen
Higginson; "Business is no part of their System, and of Consequence, Congress are altogether free from external Influence"—
a pointed comparison with the pressure the public creditors of
Philadelphia had exerted in behalf of Robert Morris. This
glimpse of the leisurely pursuits of the southern gentry seems to
have offended the sensibilities of several New England members,
although Jonathan Blanchard of New Hampshire relished the
opportunity to dine "in the Company of a number of very fine
Ladies, who seemed not averse, to a small Squeze from a Member of Congress." Such diversions did not compensate, however,
for the prospect of spending an entire summer in the heat of
Annapolis, and in August Blanchard joined Francis Dana and
Samuel Dick in taking an abrupt departure, leaving the Committee of the States to dissolve in a fit of recriminations. Nor, to judge
by the slowness with which Congress reassembled in November,
did the pleasures of wintering at Trenton prove any more entic-
ing.[40]

The decision to relocate temporarily in New York while a
permanent residence was constructed along the Delaware
helped make attendance at Congress somewhat more comfortable. New York had two advantages: it was not Philadelphia, still
an object of resentment in some members' eyes; and with its
mercantile fortunes and wealthy heiresses it offered a promising
field for the bachelors who comprised a significant portion of the
membership. Whether the delegates were equally eligible is
open to question. Catherine Livingston has left this portrait of
William Hindman of Maryland:

he looks more shocking than I can describe, I congratulated myself that
he was destined for the Kitty he was instead of another [i.e., herself]; her

coming to Town had a wonderful effect on his spirits, which animated his poor emaciated frame so that he rolled out of bed, quit his chamber and in a few minutes with the assistance of a hack, was conveyed to his beloved, but good Heavens what a subject for a matrimony! she told me she was waiting for me, alluding to a promise we mutually made last spring, I looked very arch at her; at the same time giving a glance to the *spectre* between us, I thought she had a better reason for suspending the nuptials.

A flurry of congressional marriages in 1786 provided the only occasions for celebration in an otherwise discouraging year. Since the delegates had little to do while they were waiting for the states to comply with their requisitions, Abigail Adams was informed by a correspondent, "the interim of business they improve in getting married." "Every now and then we hear of an Honble. Gentleman getting a wife," Eliza House Trist wrote Jefferson, "or else we shou'd not know there existed such a Body as Congress."[41]

To suggest that marital ambitions encouraged some men to go to Congress does not mean that they took politics any less seriously for that reason: King, Monroe, Gerry, and Osgood were among the newlyweds, and their private correspondence evinces a deep concern about the issues confronting the confederation. Nevertheless, comments like those just quoted suggest how peripheral such concerns had become to the daily interests of most Americans. Charles Thomson had recognized this when he contrasted the "unfavourable impressions" the dissolution of the Committee of the States would make in Europe with the "little effect [it would have] on our affairs here, or on the minds of the citizens," who would simply "view it in no other light than the rising or dissolution of their several legislatures." After Congress reconvened, however, other members began to share the secretary's alarm about the embarrassing inferences that "this invisibility of a federal head" would produce.[42] Despite the difficulty of maintaining a congressional quorum, the Committee of the States never met again, perhaps because the status of the union seemed so precarious that some members feared it actually might dissolve if Congress adjourned. Yet ironically one of the most obvious ways to improve the image of a body that met continually but accomplished little would have been to have Congress assemble for a limited period each year.

George Washington made a compelling argument for this

reform in a letter he wrote to Jefferson in March 1784. Complaining that "the inertitude [sic] which prevails in Congress, and the non-attendance of its Members" were both "discouraging" to the supporters of the union and "disgraceful" to the nation, Washington predicted "the case will never be otherwise" until Congress substituted "annual" for "constant" sessions. In peacetime there was no legitimate reason for Congress to meet in continual session, but the advantages of an annual meeting were numerous.

Annual sessions would always produce a full representation and alertness in business. The Delegats [sic] after a recess of 8 or 10 months would meet each other with glad Countenances. They would be complaisant. They would yield to each other as much as the duty they owed their constituents would permit, and they would have opportunities of becoming better acquainted with the Sentiments of them, and removing their prejudices, during the recess.

Drawing on his own experience in the army, Washington recalled that "Men who are always thrown together get tired of each others Company," losing the "proper restraint," doing things that are "personally disgusting," and thus fostering antagonisms that eventually left public business "at a stand." If, on the other hand, Congress appointed executive boards or committees to prepare their business, "an Annual Session of two Months would dispatch more business than is now done in twelve; and this by a full representation of the Union." Pragmatic and sensible, this proposal was revealing in another way: it suggests that even as ardent a "nationalist" as Washington foresaw little need in peacetime for a vigorous, powerful federal government.[43]

But in the end, these injuries to the dignity and efficiency of Congress only reflected the adjustment of national politics to the reality of peace. The transition was pervasive. It affected the political indifference of much of the public, the clashing interests of different states and regions, and the ambitions of the delegates themselves. In its internal proceedings and its relations with the states, Congress was a victim of the clash of interests that shaped the course of politics in the mid-1780's. The major issues of these years—revenue, commerce, expansion—forced each state to calculate the benefits and costs that would flow from particular decisions. Freed from the patriotic constraints that had always operated, although unevenly, during the war, the states were no longer obliged to defer to the wisdom of Congress and the overriding demands of the common cause. The delegates, too, enjoyed greater liberty and, in a sense, a greater obligation to serve as the actual representatives of their constituents. They felt less impelled to subordinate the particular desires of their states to the larger good of the union. Most members agreed that Congress deserved greater support from the states than it was receiving—particularly after the influence of Robert Morris was, for better or worse, curtailed—but they themselves were often uncertain how far their personal loyalties to its interest extended. Few shared the sort of disinterested commitment that can be attributed to Madison. Until they grew more convinced that the problems of the union demanded a clear priority over the demands of the states, the task of strengthening Congress could only proceed on a piecemeal, gradual basis.

CHAPTER XV

Toward
the Philadelphia Convention

———————⟨∿⟩———————

THE Constitutional Convention of 1787 was the climactic
and transforming event in the history of the Revolutionary
experiment in creating republican governments. After two centuries of interpretation, the task of explaining and analyzing the
Convention's achievement still retains its inherent fascination.
Two central concerns have dominated modern approaches to
the framing of the Constitution. One, stemming from the much
disputed writings of Charles Beard, has sought to reconstruct
how specific interests and individuals aligned over the issue of
creating a stronger national government. The second approach,
which took its initial inspiration from the essays of Douglass
Adair,[1] has concentrated instead on tracing the origins and evolution of the ideas that found their fullest expression in the debates conducted first at Philadelphia and then in the state ratifying conventions of 1787–88.

Any convincing explanation of the triumph of the Constitution requires understanding what made the arguments of the
Federalists so compelling and their innovative blend of élitist
and popular politics so effective. But there is an anterior problem
that also deserves consideration. What conditions and circumstances enabled the Convention to transcend the trite and un-
imaginative terms in which the difficulties of the confederation
had been discussed during the mid-1780's? For on the eve of the

Convention even well-placed observers could not have anticipated the actual course its deliberations were to take. In the early months of 1787 there was little reason to believe that the delegates could even agree on a plan, much less produce comprehensive reforms acceptable to the states. The most sensible predictions about the Convention's outcome were thus healthily skeptical if not pessimistic. An understanding of the Convention has to begin by explaining how it was able to break through and radically recast the existing terms of debate, and that in turn entails asking how the cautious tactics that the putative reformers of the Articles of Confederation had originally pursued ultimately produced results they had barely hoped to achieve.

Full Circle:
The Tactics of Reform

IN several respects, the predicament that advocates of a stronger confederation confronted in the mid-1780's was remarkably similar to the conditions the leaders of American resistance had struggled against in the early 1770's. The problems of organizing a cohesive movement in thirteen separate states seemed as overwhelming in 1785 as they had in 1772. Proponents of reform recognized that the approval of congressional requisitions and recommendations required the creation of an effective supporting consensus in each of the states. Yet they also believed that their own efforts to foster an enlightened sense of national interest were, by themselves, likely to prove unavailing. However carefully they were worded, the requests and pleas Congress emitted were inherently tainted: if Congress sought powers adequate to its responsibilities, in the eyes of its critics that merely confirmed its aggrandizing designs. Congress thus stood discredited in much the same way that American radicals had found their warnings impeached after the collapse of non-importation in 1770.

Those who thought the union could not survive unless the Articles were revised found themselves relying, as had Samuel Adams before, on a belief that Americans would recognize their true national interest only after they had fully understood and experienced the character of postwar British policy. Robert Morris gave early expression to this theory in the fall of 1783, when he argued that if Britain actually persisted in closing the West Indies to American commerce, "it will operate in favour of Amendment to our Articles of Confederation," because "the effects of that Proclamation will very soon apply to our Feelings & like the rest of Mankind we are sooner stimulated to action by our passions than by our reason." The British had apparently not absorbed the most obvious lesson of the Revolution: that it was only their myopic and vengeful policies that had enabled the colonists to discover their national identity. "Great Britain seems determined to pursue the same ruinous line of conduct, that guided her thro' the late War," John Langdon reminded Jefferson late in 1785; "she values not the ruin of her own Commerce, if she can thereby injure us." Like other American leaders, Langdon believed that "every step Britain takes to prevent our increase of Commerce . . . will be eventually for our advantage, by driving us into manufactures," and by demonstrating "the absolute necessity of vesting Congress with full power to regulate our Commerce, both external, and internal."[2]

This argument, which was made repeatedly during the mid-1780's, presupposed that the specific injuries Britain imposed would gradually bring the people and legislatures of the thirteen states to recognize the existence of a larger national interest. But advocates of reform also encountered resistance based on less tangible yet pervasive fears of the inherent dangers of power itself. Here, too, the rhetoric of the mid-1780's resembled earlier opposition to the claims of Parliament. If the address and documents Congress had issued in support of its revenue plan were "carefully and impartially examined," wrote George Mason, "they will be found to exhibit strong proofs of lust of power. They contain the same kinds of arguments which were formerly used in the business of ship money and to justify the arbitrary measures of the race of Stuarts in England."[3]

Mason's views were stridently echoed in New England during the polemical campaign that was waged against the impost and commutation in 1783–84. Opposition to commutation, which evoked the traditional resentment of military pensions and standing armies, was particularly strong in Connecticut, where several towns approved resolutions condemning Congress and calling for popular conventions to assemble in protest. "Is it not highly probable that Congress, at present, are feasting their imaginations on the prospect of future pensions?" asked the citizens of Torrington. "For the attainment of which, do they not rejoice at the present opportunity of introducing a custom, into which, they artfully habituate the country under cover of the officers?" Espousing a radical theory of popular government, Torrington declared that because "Congress are delegated by the people, therefore Congress must be responsible to the people, in all cases whatever. And the disputes, which have arisen, respecting the power, assumed by Congress, must be determined by the unanimous voice of the people." Other towns, such as Farmington, were more cautious about challenging the authority of Congress. Yet while the citizens of Farmington were "not disposed to charge Congress with criminal views," and were even willing to concede that it may have acted legitimately in approving half-pay, they too argued that the delegates were ultimately "accountable for their high trust, as servants, to their constituents, the great body of the people, to whose decision they must finally submit."[4]

Although the clamor over commutation and (to a lesser extent) the impost subsided after 1784, other issues evoked similar objections rooted in traditionally whiggish suspicions of government. When the Massachusetts General Court was actively supporting proposals to vest commercial powers in Congress, "Jonathan of the Valley" argued that such an amendment to the Articles would work to "pull down the goodly fabric of freedom in this western world." The legislators should consider "whether a grant of this nature, without restrictions and limitations, will not lay a foundation for one consolidated government over the whole union, annihilate all your legislatures, and swallow up the separate sovereignty of the States so carefully preserved in the Confederation."[5] Abraham Yates, Jr., developed similar themes in his writings against the impost. For Yates, even annual elections offered little security against congressional schemes of profit, as an animal fable he was fond of quoting suggested. " 'Friend!' says the fox, 'I desire you by no means to disturb those honest bloodsuckers, that are now quartered upon me, and whose bellies are, I fancy, pretty well filled, for if they should leave me, a fresh swarm would take their place, and I should not have a drop of blood left in my body.' "[6]

There were reasonable responses to be made against these and other objections, of course. The satirical resolutions attributed to the town of Geeseburrow—signed by Quack Gander, town clerk—were meant to show the citizens of Connecticut how little danger they actually faced from Congress.

2. That there is the utmost danger of ruin to these states from the present exorbitant power and wealth of Congress; because Congress have neither wealth, power, nor influence, and were lately unable either for love or money to support their authority against the insults of eighty mutineers. . . .

10. That since we had the utmost difficulty in prevailing on the Delegates from this state to attend on Congress, we have no doubt that Congress intend very soon to retire on pensions and half-pay.[7]

Supporters of Congress argued that its powers would still be carefully defined by the Articles and whatever additional amendments the states ultimately approved; that its members were subject to "that fundamental part of our constitution—that great palladium of civil liberty, *Annual Elections*"; that its wartime services demanded postwar confidence. Popular jealousy and the countervailing authority of the states would still provide ample security against any conceivable congressional encroachments on liberty. "This bug bear of the power of Congress . . . is the most flimsy tale of a falsehood ever invented," wrote "C.S.," the author of a lengthy essay contesting the anticongressional claims George Mason had advanced in a new set of Fairfax County instructions.

There is some consistency in being jealous of power in the hands of those who assume it by birth, or without our consent and over whom we have no controul, as was the case with the crown of England over America. But to be jealous of those whom we chuse the instant we have chosen them, shews either the folly of our choice, or the absurdity of our politics; and that in the transition from monarchy to a republic, we have unfortunately bastardized our ideas, by placing jealousy where we ought to erect confidence.[8]

When John Treadwell, Farmington's representative in the Connecticut assembly, sought to dissuade his constituents from condemning Congress, he reminded them that the doctrine "that no confidence can be placed in any public body" was itself evidence that the people were "incapable of supporting any longer a democratical government, and that nothing can restrain their licentiousness, but the iron rod of monarchy." What interest did Congress have different from that of the nation as a whole, other than the responsibility for resolving its problems? For, as "Pro Bono-

Republicae" argued, "If they behave remiss, we can remove them: They are chosen annually from the body of the people; they are accountable to us for their conduct; they feel our wrongs the same with ourselves but cannot redress them."[9]

Congress was not alone in being subjected to what one writer called "that paltry unnatural jealousy of power."[10] As Gordon Wood has shown, emerging American notions of popular government implied that all branches of government, even those most directly representative of the people, required continuous and close supervision from a vigilant citizenry.[11] The implications of this attitude were, however, perhaps more ominous for Congress than they were for the state governments. Not only was it the most distant element of American government; it was also the least influential and effective, and thus the one most seriously in need of additional powers. Locally based politicians had ways of mitigating these populistic suspicions that were not available to members of Congress, whose carefully articulated defenses of its requests could do little to allay visceral fears of power by now long imbedded in American political consciousness.

All of this helps to explain why the proponents of amendments were content to allow Great Britain to make the most persuasive case for strengthening the confederation. The tone of passivity that runs through the political correspondence of these years—and that also recalls the mood of the early 1770's—reflects an inability to imagine how more aggressive agitation could materially alter the pace of events. The prevailing ideological aversion against power itself was not something that could be relieved simply through disinterested appeals to the national welfare. Thus beyond the barrier of securing unanimous ratification for any amendment, Congress also had to be mindful of the danger of demanding too much. These considerations were clearly what convinced James Monroe, the leading advocate of the committee report recommending broad commercial powers for Congress, to admit that it would be better not to push this question too strenuously either within Congress or without. Postwar congressional requests for additional powers were therefore confined to the revenue plan of April 1783 and the limited authority over foreign trade solicited a year later.

Moreover, despite occasionally gloomy outbursts, few American leaders believed that the new nation was actually poised on the brink of crisis. After eight years of war and the turbulence of the pre-Revolutionary years, it was scarcely surprising that most Americans showed little interest in public affairs. "I think great Allowances are to be made for a people just shaking Themselves from the Horrors & Calamities of a War; unused to the great and arduous Task of making and giving Laws to Millions; and of entering into the deep Policy of the great and [illegible] Nations of the World with whom we are now to walk," Henry Marchant reminded Richard Price, the prominent English radical whose *Observations on the Importance of the American Revolution* had candidly criticized the weakness of the confederation. And Charles Thomson wrote to Franklin: "Those who know the difficulty which old established nations experience in their attempts to introduce new arrangements either in government, police or finance, will readily conceive what we have had to encounter." At the start of the Revolution, Thomson recalled, the Americans had long been "kept apart by local interests and prejudices," and British mediation had left them "secluded . . . almost from all intercourse with foreign nations." The people had been "thrown into a state of nature," and with "property being equally divided and the feudal system unknown in this country," there were few individuals "who could influence their conduct or opinions." Nor had the new constitutions, with their prevailing "ideas of liberty," provided the "opportunity of acquiring national sentiments. Notwithstanding all this," the secretary of Congress concluded, "we have made remarkable progress in the short period of eight years."[12] That the Articles required amendment seemed obvious to many American leaders, but in 1784 and 1785 the consequences of failing to enact reforms still seemed to exist only in some indefinite future. "We are neither so wise nor so weake as our Friends & Enemies represent us," John Jay wrote in 1785, "and the fact is, that tho' much remains to be done, yet we are gradually advancing towards system & order."[13]

A lengthy and characteristically thoughtful letter that Charles Thomson wrote to John Dickinson in July 1785 conveyed this mood remarkably well. Dickinson had initiated the correspondence by proposing several additional measures to aid Congress that went beyond the amendments usually discussed. Confessing that he was "greatly at a loss how to answer" Dickinson's letter, Thomson first suggested that it was difficult to identify the precise causes of the weakness and inefficiency of the federal gov-

ernment. Were they due "[t]o an imperfection in the confederation or to a defect in the constitutions of the several states?"
Thomson asked; "to a want of energy in the executives or a
disinclination in the people to submit to such regulations restrictions & government" as the general welfare demanded? In either case, the secretary continued,

Will the vesting greater power in the federal council conquer the aversion which the people too generally seem to have to a strict government? Will it reconcile them to a more punctual payment of taxes? Or
rather, taught as too many have been of late to think & speak disrespect-
fully of Congress, will not an attempt to exercise power, should it be
granted, render the federal council odious, & in case of a failure, contemptible?

It was clear, he admitted, that amendments were necessary; but
they had to be solicited cautiously. "I am not unnecessarily for
overturning foundations already laid," he continued, "nor for
attempting to give at once all that is necessary." Considering the
present temper of the people, Thomson believed it would be
useless to propose giving Congress larger powers than those that
had already been requested.

It would only tend to awaken jealousy & might enable designing men
to divert the people from what a concurrence of circumstances seems
to be preparing them to grant; and which if granted would in my opinion answer our present purpose, give weight to the federal council and
dignity to the nation, and would relieve us from the embarrassed &
humiliating state under which we now labour: I mean the power of
regulating commerce and of imposing duties at least on importations for
the purpose of raising a revenue. The conduct of our late enemy since
the peace has done a great deal towards preparing the minds of the
people to grant this.

If these specific and limited powers could be granted, Thomson
concluded, the people would become "better disposed for granting other necessary powers and the federal government will
without any convulsion be gradually improved as circumstances
require, until it attains some degree of perfection."[14]

One year later this prudent analysis would have seemed
naïve. Even in 1785 Thomson's views were perhaps more sanguine than circumstances warranted. James Madison, for one,
already feared that southern obstruction of commercial powers
could endanger the survival of the union. "Should G. B. persist

in the machinations which distress us," he warned Monroe in August, "and seven or eight of the States be hindered by the others from obtaining relief by federal means, I own, I tremble at the anti-federal expedients into which the former may be drawn."[15] Where Thomson still believed that foreseeable events would progressively enlighten the people and their representatives, Madison recognized that a strategy of reform based on trusting to external events could just as easily play into the hands of the opponents of American nationalism, both at home and overseas. In one sense, the difference between these perspectives can be overstated. Both men agreed as to what powers Congress should have—revenue and trade remained the two preeminent objects—and both were convinced that the process of reform could go forward only gradually. The principal question, however, involved deciding how that process was to be initiated, and here it was Madison who was soon to emerge as both the leading tactician and theoretician of reform.

The Emergence of Madison

MADISON had left Congress in the fall of 1783, an early victim of Article 5 of the confederation, which prohibited an individual from serving in Congress more than three years out of every six. But retirement from Congress did little to slacken his interest in national affairs. Throughout this period he kept in close contact with the Virginia delegates James Monroe and William Grayson, and in the early fall of 1785 he visited Philadelphia and New York, where he had "several conversations" with Grayson and Samuel Hardy, another Virginia member, "on the affairs of the Confederacy." (Monroe was away on a tour of the west, a journey that was to have important consequences for the development of congressional territorial policy.) From these conversations, Madison apparently concluded that he should attempt to convince the coming session of the Virginia assembly to grant Congress the power to regulate trade. Positive instructions from the largest southern state might help to break the impasse within Congress, defuse the sectional tensions that had already alarmed Madison, and facilitate later ratification by the states. Madison returned to Virginia, and during the ensuing session he vigorously argued the case for vesting permanent regulatory powers in Congress. The assembly diluted the proposals he favored, however, and Madison concluded that nothing would be gained by granting Congress the restricted and temporary powers his fellow legislators were willing to surrender. "I think it better to trust to further experience and even distress, for an adequate remedy," he informed Washington in early December, "than to try a temporary measure which may stand in the way of a permanent one, and must confirm that transatlantic [i.e., British] policy which is founded on our supposed distrust of Congress and of one another."[16]

At the very close of the session, however, the assembly approved a substitute resolution calling for an interstate conference that would consider the utility of uniform commercial regulations and also frame an act vesting appropriate powers in Congress, which could actually be ratified by the states. Madison supported this resolution because it was "better than nothing," but he initially thought that it was "liable to objections and will probably miscarry," if only because the Virginia commissioners themselves seemed unlikely to agree on proper reforms.[17] He remained uncertain through the early months of 1786. Given all the obstacles that had to be overcome, the chances for the conference's success scarcely seemed promising, while the risks of failure were increasingly ominous, for it was in March that New Jersey balked at complying with further congressional requisitions and in April that New York effectively rejected the impost. Should the Convention now set for Annapolis in September prove abortive, further efforts to augment the powers of Congress could not be regarded optimistically.

For Madison, however, the decisive consideration was that there no longer seemed to be any practicable alternative to calling some sort of convention. "Something it is agreed is necessary to be done, towards the commerce at least of the U.S.," he wrote Monroe in March, "and if anything can be done, it seems as likely to result from the proposed Convention, and more likely to result f[rom] the present crisis, than from any other mode or time." Monroe evidently disagreed, arguing that if the defects of the confederation were to be remedied by a convention rather than through the piecemeal recommendations of Congress, the proposed conference was too narrowly conceived to do much good. Madison's reply revealed how closely the idea of a convention and the cautious tenor of other proposals for reform could still be intertwined. "If all on whom the correction of these vices depends were well informed and well disposed, the mode would be of little moment," he replied.

But as we have both ignorance and iniquity to control, we must defeat the designs of the latter by humouring the prejudices of the former. The efforts of bringing about a correction thro' the medium of Congress have miscarried. Let a Convention then be tried. If it succeeds in the first instance, it can be repeated as other defects force themselves on the public attention, and as the public mind becomes prepared for further remedies.

The key to Madison's position was his opinion that the Virginia assembly would neither approve amendments emanating from Congress nor give its commissioners broad "plenipotentiary" powers to revise the Articles. Those objections would not threaten a convention appointed for limited and carefully defined purposes and meeting under the auspices of the states rather than Congress. Despite his continued aversion to "temporizing or partial remedies," Madison had now decided that excessive "rigor in this respect . . . may hazard every thing. If the present paroxism of our affairs be totally neglected," he concluded, "our case may become desperate."[18]

In Congress, too, the early months of 1786 saw some delegates entertaining "serious thoughts . . . to recommend to the States the meeting of a general Convention" to revise the Articles, an idea that had been periodically bruited about since 1780 but never taken seriously. Late in March William Grayson informed Madison that a motion to that effect had already been introduced. Its probable author was Charles Pinckney of South Carolina, who had been one of the committee sent to convince the New Jersey legislature to rescind its resolution rejecting further compliance with the requisitions of Congress. In his speech, Pinckney had urged the legislators to issue a call for a national convention, promising that he would support such a proposal whenever it reached the floor of Congress.[19] On May 3 Pinckney again urged his colleagues to consider calling a general convention and moved that Congress appoint a grand committee to review national affairs. Two months elapsed before this motion was finally approved, the delay resulting, perhaps, from a desire to determine first whether New York's unsatisfactory action on the impost might not be rectified. The committee's report, comprising seven additional Articles of Confederation, was delivered in early August but never accepted, although Congress took the unusual step of allowing texts to be published in newspapers and apparently transmitted to the states.[20]

Substantively, the committee's report marked a last attempt to propose constitutional reforms consistent with the essential purposes of the Articles. Six of the seven amendments were concerned with the regulation of trade and the collection of federal revenues and requisitions. Following the abandoned recommendations of 1785, Congress would receive "sole and exclusive power" over foreign and interstate commerce, though whatever duties were collected as a result of trade regulations would accrue to the states. Congress would be given limited remedies against states delinquent in paying their share of requisitions. Subsequent revenue amendments would require the assent of eleven states only. The most striking innovation the report proposed involved the creation of a seven-member court to try cases brought against federal officials, and to receive appeals from state judicial proceedings pertaining to questions of foreign relations, international law, or whatever regulations Congress later made in matters of commerce and revenue. A final Article concerned the increasingly annoying problem of maintaining a quorum of delegates.

In scope and detail, these amendments went beyond anything Congress had ever seriously considered. Yet they did not envision a confederation whose responsibilities would be significantly larger than those projected in earlier discussions of the need to amend the Articles. Instead, the report of August 7 represented a final attempt to enable Congress to discharge its duties as traditionally conceived, and to acquire the single additional power that had recently become the focus for so much debate: the regulation of trade. The report did recognize the critical importance of clarifying the constitutional relationship between the union and the states. Yet enforcement of the legitimate actions of Congress would entail not the blunt use of coercive power Madison and others had contemplated in the early 1780's, but rather the establishment of specific judicial remedies that would give those actions the effective sanction of law. In this respect, perhaps, the report did anticipate the deliberations of

1787; but on balance its proposals stopped well short of scrapping the Articles or reconstituting the union on radically different principles.

There is little in the surviving correspondence of the delegates to reveal what Congress actually thought about the objective merits of these amendments. Issued at the very height of debate over the Spanish negotiations and the navigation of the Mississippi, the report was in part a victim of the sectional tensions that question aroused, possibly shunted aside because many delegates were already assessing the likelihood that the confederation might dissolve before any realistic scheme of amendments could be pursued.[21]

But it was objectionable for another reason. In May, Pinckney had argued that Congress had to choose between soliciting additional powers directly or issuing a call for a national convention. He was opposed by Monroe, and it is Monroe's position, soon endorsed by Madison, that helps to explain why neither alternative was acceptable. Their evolving strategy of reform was now committed to the success of the forthcoming meeting at Annapolis. They assumed that further congressional requests would be fruitless, for, as Monroe noted, "recommendations from that body are received with such suspicion by the States that their success however proper they may be is always to be doubted." That could not be said, however, of "a body assembled under the particular direction of the States for a temporary purpose in whom the lust for power cannot be supposed to exist." Equally important, they were still convinced that popular opinion was not yet prepared for sweeping constitutional reforms. "Will it not be best on the whole to suspend measures for a more thorough cure of our federal system, till the partial experiment shall have been made[?]" Madison wrote in mid-May, after Monroe had informed him of the renewed discussions of a convention. If the Annapolis meeting went well, its results and the return of its members to "their respective states will greatly facilitate any subsequent measures which may be set on foot by Congress, or by any of the states."[22]

But the Annapolis Convention itself faced numerous pitfalls. When the Virginia commissioners had set early September as the date for assembling, they had doubtless hoped an interval of six months would encourage appointments by all the states. By mid-August only eight states had complied, and some began to wonder whether a poorly attended conference might not do more harm than good. For as Jacob Broom, a Delaware commissioner, fretted, "if one half the states should not then have made similar appointments, how ridiculous will all this parade appear?" It was critical that the meeting "run no risque of being rendered contemptible." At least two states refused to appoint commissioners because they were reluctant to condone a meeting that would have, as the Maryland Senate feared, "a tendency to weaken the authority of Congress" by implying that it was no longer competent to handle matters of national concern.[23]

Beyond these questions of propriety, the expectations of commissioners and members of Congress alike were inevitably affected by the foreign policy disputes of the summer and the predictions of disunion they evoked. Several New England delegates, already contemplating the idea of separate confederacies, noted that the Virginia commissioners were not commercial experts and began to suspect that the ostensible occasion for the meeting might mask more sinister political ambitions.[24] On the other hand, William Grayson feared that if the declared purposes of the conference were actually met, the task of vesting Congress with other necessary powers might grow more, not less difficult. Turning Madison's logic on its head, he argued that

affairs are not arrived at such a crisis as to ensure success to a reformation on proper principles; a partial reformation will be fatal; things had better remain as they are than not to probe them to the bottom. If particular States gain their own particular objects, it will place other grievances perhaps of equal importance at a greater distance: if all are brought forward at the same time one object will facilitate the passage of another, & by a general compromise perhaps a good government may be procured.

On balance, Grayson thought it best that the Annapolis meeting not "produce any thing decisive." If it did prove successful, the more commercial states might lose interest in pursuing further reforms.[25]

Others were less skeptical, however. Writing from Philadelphia in mid-August, Madison was able to inform Jefferson that "Many Gentlemen both within & without Congs. wish to make this Meeting subservient to a Plenipotentiary Convention for amending the Confederation." For his own part, Madison was nonetheless still committed to proceeding cautiously. "Tho' my wishes are in favor of such an event," he added, "yet I despair so much of its accomplishment at the present crisis that I do not extend my views beyond a Commercial Reform. To speak the truth *I almost despair even of this.*" Madison's pessimism reflected his concern over the Mississippi question, a subject on which Monroe kept him closely informed.[26] The prevailing aura of suspicion that issue had generated, the diverse assessments of the motives underlying the original Virginia invitation for the Annapolis meeting, doubts about how well it would be attended, and the inherent difficulty of framing acceptable resolutions, all conspired to create an atmosphere of confusion and uncertainty. This was a far cry from the initial hope that the commissioners would be able to assemble under conditions favorable to a calm and rational examination of the immediate subject of commerce.

Had the Annapolis Convention actually been well attended, Madison would probably have attempted to carry out the strategy he had come to favor, which was to frame a specific amendment, limited to the regulation of trade, whose adoption would benefit Congress over the short run while creating an attractive precedent for further reforms. But when commissioners from only five states appeared, confirming the possibility of embarrassment Madison and others had dreaded all along, the logic underlying this strategy was effectively destroyed. Any substantive recommendation issued by a meeting so poorly attended would carry little weight with either Congress or the states. Yet if the Convention adjourned without accomplishing anything, the movement to strengthen the confederation would receive a critical, perhaps decisive setback.

It was precisely this predicament that enabled the commissioners to recommend the calling of a second convention, set for Philadelphia nine months later, "to devise such further provisions as shall appear to them necessary to render the constitution of the federal government adequate to the exigencies of the Union." The celerity with which the Annapolis Convention endorsed this measure has sometimes justified the suspicion that a more radical expedient had been in contemplation from the start. In view of the customary tardiness of eighteenth-century politicians, the Convention does seem to have acted with undue haste. It is possible, too, that Alexander Hamilton, now returning to national politics, had come to Annapolis predisposed to argue for more drastic measures. Nevertheless, the call for a second convention was more likely the result of desperation than calculated forethought. Given the political situation prevailing in the late summer of 1786, the dozen commissioners who actually assembled had little reason to believe that the appearance of a handful of additional members would materially enhance the authority of the Convention. Nor had they suddenly discovered any evidence to support the idea that a general convention would now prove more compelling than it had been previously. They merely hoped that a further delay of nine months might bring the emergence of a climate more favorable to reform. The decision to call a second convention was recognizably a gamble, justified not by any change in the odds against such a measure actually succeeding but rather by the need to salvage something from the potentially harmful consequences of adjourning without reaching any decision at all.[27]

In taking this step, the commissioners had consciously concluded that further constitutional reform could not emanate from Congress. "Propriety" dictated that their recommendations be formally submitted only to their own states. When they sent a copy of their report to Congress, it was only done, they noted, "from motives of respect." Those members of Congress who supported the Annapolis recommendation concluded that a congressional endorsement would nevertheless be useful. But this measure "was objected to by the Eastern States," Monroe noted, and while on October 11 the Annapolis report was assigned to a grand committee, Congress took no action on it for another four months. The initial opposition against congressional endorsement was based on two objections: first, that Congress could not approve a blatantly unconstitutional procedure for amending the Articles; second, that the duties of the proposed Convention were too vaguely defined. Several New England delegates, notably Nathan Dane, still harbored the suspicions of constitutional change that David Howell and others had enunciated in the early 1780's.[28] Their opinions began to change only after they could assess the defects of the Articles in the light of the political unrest that broke out in western Massachusetts late in 1786.

By February 1787, when Congress finally endorsed the forthcoming Convention, Madison was able to observe that the essential issue that "divided and embarrassed" Congress was "whether their taking an interest in the measure would impede or promote it." Even then, William Irvine noted, "the Eastern

men were all much against the measure," acceding only when
"they saw it would be carried without them." In exchange for
their acquiescence, the Massachusetts delegates extracted a significant concession, for the resolution stipulated that the Convention was to meet "for the sole and express purpose of revising
the Articles of Confederation"—a phrase that could be interpre-
ted as imposing carefully limited responsibilities on the delegates
who assembled at Philadelphia three months later.[29]

By the time Congress acted, seven states had already voted
to appoint delegates, and New York, whose participation might
have been doubted, seemed inclined to do so as well. Those who
openly supported the Convention considered a congressional
sanction useful but not essential. In the view of Madison and
others, establishing the strict legitimacy of the Convention was
less important than creating other conditions favorable to the
success of its deliberations. As Madison approached this problem
during the waning months of 1786, three considerations were
paramount. First, the Philadelphia Convention would have to be
respectably attended, which meant not only that most states
would have to be represented, but also that their delegates
should be men of reputation and influence. Second, some restraints had to be placed on growing sectional animosities and
loose talk of disunion, notably arising from the continuing debate
over American policy toward Spain. Finally, some thought had
to be given to devising a suitable agenda for the Convention
itself.

By early 1787, the first two of these conditions seemed well on
the way to being satisfied. Despite intense resentment against
congressional action on the Mississippi question, the Virginia assembly had unanimously approved the Annapolis recommendation for a second convention, issued a circular letter of invitation
to the other states, and appointed a delegation made eminently
respectable by the inclusion of George Washington and Edmund
Randolph, the state governor. Madison was already at work
courting Washington's participation, which could not be taken
for granted.[30] By early January five other states had agreed to
appoint delegates, and their decisions helped to exert pressure
on others, notably Massachusetts, that were at first reluctant to
act. Ultimately every state was represented but Rhode Island,
whose internal controversies over paper money had made it
something of an object of continental derision.[31]

Not all the delegates were the luminaries Federalist propaganda and historical mythology later made them out to be. One does not have to accept Forrest McDonald's sardonic claim that well over half the members "were voices that few would have listened to anytime, anywhere" to recognize that the Convention, like any public body, contained mediocrity as well as talent.[32] But the presence of Madison, Hamilton, James Wilson, Gouverneur Morris, John Dickinson, George Mason, Elbridge Gerry, and others did guarantee that the Convention would include a critical nucleus of members capable of addressing fundamental issues and articulating innovative positions. In any event, attaining broad representation from the states *was* a prerequisite to accomplishing anything, and that was achieved with surprisingly little difficulty. Although very little is known about how this participation was produced, such evidence as there is suggests that the separate state decisions were neither the result of an intensive coordinated effort by committed "nationalists" nor a source of significant partisan divisions within the legislatures. It is difficult to avoid concluding that most legislators simply agreed that something had to be done about the "imbecility" of Congress and found the idea of a special convention relatively acceptable. Had they anticipated the results of its deliberations, they would have been less compliant; but even in early 1787 few discussions of the defects of the Articles foreshadowed the sweeping changes proposed in the Constitution.[33]

Neutralizing the dangers of sectional tensions that could impede either initial agreement on reforms or their subsequent ratification proved more difficult. In late February Madison observed that, "after long confinement to individual speculations & private circles," the idea of separate confederacies "is beginning to shew itself in the Newspapers." Debate over the Mississippi question still continued in Congress, and Madison knew that Patrick Henry was already likely to throw his enormous influence in Virginia against whatever measures the Convention adopted solely out of resentment over this issue alone.[34] On the other hand, there was reason to believe that this most urgent sectional issue had been somewhat defused. The stark north-south division that had emerged within Congress at the height of the Mississippi debate in 1786 had dissolved as Madison, Monroe, and others managed to recruit support for their position against occlusion among delegates from the middle states. Even should John

Jay succeed in negotiating a Spanish treaty inimical to the southern states, which still seemed improbable, it could never be ratified by Congress. At the very least, then, the prospect for a major crisis over the Mississippi had been greatly reduced. Moreover, the aftershocks of Shays's Rebellion in Massachusetts had made various New England politicians more receptive to the idea of a stronger federal union.[35] Stephen Higginson, once one of the most vitriolic critics of Robert Morris, now found himself "ready for any measures that will promise an efficient government." "Let it be fair & energetic," he wrote Samuel Osgood, "& you may christen it by what name you will." For, Higginson argued, even if Massachusetts succeeded in "brac[ing] up Our Government; what can it avail, or how can it last, while the Union & Our Sister States remain feeble as at present?"[36]

Neither of these developments—the gradual appointment of twelve delegations and the temporary weakening of sectional obstacles—guaranteed that the Convention would meet with success; they merely removed or reduced potential sources of failure. Once the delegates actually assembled, American newspapers began printing optimistic rumors about the course of its deliberations. But in the early months of 1787, leading American politicians were quite skeptical about its prospects. James Varnum had been one of the earliest advocates of a constitutional convention, but his prediction of April scarcely breathed a spirit of optimism. "It cannot be expected," he wrote from Congress,

that the Convention at Philadelphia will frame and recommend a system that will ever be federally adopted. They will probably investigate the defects of our present national government, and point out the means of removing them. The respective states will greatly differ in their ideas upon the subject, and their increasing animosities will precipitate the period of anarchy and confusion. From these exuberant sources will arise a government that may be assisted in its formation and principles by the wisdom of the convention.

William Grayson, who in 1786 had doubted whether "a reformation on proper principles" could yet be secured, still believed "the whole will terminate in nothing"; either the Convention "will not agree, or if they do agree, the States will not ratify; our distresses are not sufficiently great to produce decisive alterations." Writing to John Adams in late February, John Jay noted that "I do not promise myself much further immediate Good from the Measure than that it will tend to approximate the public Mind to the Changes which ought to take place." Rufus King was "rather inclined to the measure from an idea of prudence, or for the purpose of watching, than from an expectation that much Good will flow from it." In early April he still thought its outcome "doubtful," for while the southern states were sending "many well disposed men . . . the projects are so various, and so short of the best, that my fears are by no means inferior to my Hopes on this subject." Even Madison verged toward pessimism. "What the issue of it will be is among the other arcana of futurity and nearly as inscrutable as any of them," he informed Edmund Pendleton in late February. "In general I find men of reflection much less sanguine as to a new than despondent as to the present System." As late as April 15 Madison was still wondering whether Washington should "postpone his actual attendance, until some judgment can be formed of the result of the meeting?" His immense prestige would be squandered, Madison feared, if he were to "participate in any abortive undertaking."[37]

To a large extent, these doubts about the outcome of the Convention reflected the difficulty of imagining the agenda it would actually pursue once it met. Given the constricted boundaries of earlier discussions of reform, the indefinite character of the Convention's mandate, and the potentially broad field for its deliberations, such diffidence was understandable. More than his colleagues, it was Madison who grasped the advantage this prevailing mood of uncertainty would bestow on anyone who came to Philadelphia prepared to seize the initiative in defining the issues confronting the Convention. Madison had thus reserved for himself the responsibility for fulfilling the third of his preconditions for the Convention's success. His affinity for such a role was, by now, almost intuitive, for Madison's own political career and influence rested, quite simply, on the recognition that a man who did his homework and thought through issues and alternatives before debate began could often lead his lazier colleagues —of whom there would always be many—along the avenues he had selected. In a state legislature, of course, where specific interests were represented, such a posture had its limitations. But a national convention offered as promising a field for Madison's distinctively intellectual approach to politics as he could reasonably desire, and when in 1786 and 1787 Madison committed himself to a study of the history and theory of federal government, his motives were intensely and consciously pragmatic.[38] That he succeeded in launching the Convention in the direction he desired was thus a tribute to his preeminence at a certain style of élitist politics; but it was also a measure of how little systematic thought the problems of the confederation had previously engendered. When the Convention adjourned in September, the sheer audacity of the proposed Constitution proved no less astonishing to its instinctive supporters than its early detractors. How the Convention was able to transcend and thus transform earlier perimeters of debate remains an immensely intriguing question, to be explained only in part by the catalytic role of Madison.

The Deadlock of Thought

IN both its origin and its result, the Philadelphia Convention marked a decisive repudiation of all earlier efforts to create a national government adequate to the needs of the new republic. It was thus the beneficiary of previous failures to strengthen the confederation: the Morris program of 1782–83, the revenue plan of 1783, the limited commercial amendments of 1784, the tabled committee reports of 1785–86, and the Annapolis Convention. The adoption of one or more of these proposals would actually have undermined the logic that ultimately justified sweeping reform, either by remedying the outstanding problems confronting the union or by demonstrating that the Articles could be amended when necessary.[39] The idea of a constitutional convention became compelling only after other avenues of reform proved uniformly futile. Even more important, substantive changes of the dimensions proposed in 1787 could not have been formulated without the additional lessons of the mid-1780's. Although at any time after 1780 Madison, Wilson, Hamilton, Washington, the Morrises, and others would certainly have favored a stronger confederation, it is unlikely that the full range of nationalist principles embodied in the Constitution would have been either the object or result of their labors before 1787. To argue otherwise would be anachronistic.

Viewed from this perspective, the disappointments of the mid-1780's were significant not only because they created the occasion for the Convention but also because they affected its deliberations in at least two critical ways. In the first place, the constraints that had inhibited earlier proposals for reform were what ultimately enabled the Convention to attain its distinctive position in the history of Revolutionary political thought—to become, that is, the definitive reassessment of the republican experiment that had been launched with independence. And, in the second place, the cumulative frustrations Congress had experienced in its relations with the states encouraged the delegates at Philadelphia to link two concerns that had hitherto been considered separately: the strengthening of the union and the political reformation of the states.

Far from liberating constitutional thought from the defining assumptions set by the Articles, the difficulties Congress encountered after 1780 ironically hindered efforts to rethink the complex problems inherent in the creation of any federal system. In an almost perverse sense, those difficulties seemed either too obvious or too oppressive to provoke searching thought. The same pragmatic considerations that committed Madison and Monroe to their cautious strategy provided little incentive for devising additional measures to strengthen the confederation. The requirement of unanimous ratification posed one barrier; but equally discouraging was the knowledge that the presentation of comprehensive schemes of reform would merely confirm the suspicion that Congress was grasping for power. Earlier discussions of the character of the confederation had also left an unpromising legacy. No major alteration of the Articles could take place without appropriate adjustments in prevailing conceptions of the location of sovereignty, the nature of Congress itself, and the apportionment of continental representation. Yet it was difficult to imagine how well-hardened opinions on these subjects could be opened for reconsideration or conflicting interests and interpretations reconciled.

Almost all discussions of the additional authority that Congress needed were confined to the familiar subjects of revenue and trade. These were admittedly substantial powers. But the purposes for which they were solicited did not presuppose a radical alteration in the nature of the confederation. Permanent revenues were necessary for Congress to discharge its existing responsibilities and to service the national debt; the authority to regulate trade was justified largely as a means of counteracting European restrictions on American commerce. Both measures were consistent with the existing conception of a confederation

whose principal concerns centered on external affairs rather
than "internal police."

Only occasionally did commentators of the mid-1780's envis-
age more radical adjustments of the spheres of authority allotted
to Congress and the states. The most drastic suggestion was advanced in a remarkable pamphlet published in 1784, *The Political Establishments of the United States of America*. Its unknown
author argued, quite simply, that "no reformation, or amendment can effectually answer any good purpose, short of the abol-
ishment of our state governments and the forming a constitution,
whereby the whole nation can be united in one government."[40]
This was a nationalism that went beyond even Hamilton's sweeping condemnations of the Articles. A similar solution appealed,
if only in theory, to "Observator," who in 1785 argued that a
"political system" based on the existence of "so many separate
and independent interests" could never "maintain a unanimity
in views and measures; nor render any act of government effica-
cious." Even if the states did authorize Congress to regulate
trade—"the furthest any proposal has extended"—little good
would be accomplished, "for every political interest of a nation
is so blended together, and dependent on one another, that,
unless there be a sovereign power sufficient to govern them all,
the end of public measures will be lost."[41]

Such statements, though evocative, hardly justified optimism, for as "Observator" himself noted, "a sacrifice of this
favourite Hobby-Horse" of state sovereignty was "an event
scarcely to be hoped for at this time." Only a few writers attempted to sketch intermediate positions that went beyond
the existing agenda of reform while stopping prudently short
of demands for national consolidation. Reviving a proposal he
had advanced in his initial draft of the Articles, John Dickinson suggested empowering Congress to quell dissensions endangering the constitution of any of the states. This idea was
also advanced by a New York writer who in 1786 presented a
brief "Plan for a New Federal Government." But most commentators contented themselves with reiterating the call for
state compliance with congressional requisitions and ratification of the amendments of 1783–84. By 1786, if not earlier,
there was little new to be said about these questions. "The
necessity of some federal adequate regulation of the commerce of the united states has been so often enforced and

descanted on," one writer observed, "that the subject appears to be worn thread-bare."[42]

Other restraints on debate could be traced to seemingly unresolvable problems in constitutional theory. The anomalous character of Congress posed strong objections against any increase of its authority. American writers were still groping for a satisfactory description of Congress. To John Adams, writing his *Defence of the Constitutions of Government of the United States* while American minister to London, it seemed clear that Congress was "not a legislative assembly, not a representative assembly, but only a diplomatic assembly." To Thomas Burke it had been "a deliberating Executive assembly"; others described it as the "Supreme Executive" or "Supreme Executive Council."[43] The idea that Congress was essentially an executive body persisted because its principal functions, war and diplomacy, were traditionally associated with the crown, "whose executive, political prerogatives, bear a very striking resemblance to the powers of Congress." The powers enumerated in the Articles were almost "as extensive as the *prerogatives* of the crown of Great-Britain, about which they make so much noise and bustle."[44] Opponents of the impost therefore argued that Congress should never be allowed to levy taxes because, as Arthur Lee had reminded Congress, "the purse ought not to be put into the same hands with the Sword."[45]

This equation between crown and Congress naturally reinforced the position of those who held that sovereignty could reside only in the states. An executive body could not be deemed sovereign, nor could it be entrusted with powers of legislation and taxation. "A supreme executive Council, which Congress represent, can never consonant to republican principles be vested with a full and exclusive right of taxation," the New Hampshire essayist "Solicitor" wrote; "for the union of these two different rights and powers . . . constitutes one very essential aspect of despotic government." Far from fulfilling the underlying purposes of the confederation, the proposed amendments would subvert and ultimately destroy the proper relation between Congress and the sovereign legislatures that were intended to control it. For when the analogy to the British constitution was completed, the assemblies were logically seen to "stand in the same situation, and have the same restraint on Congress that the parliament or rather the commons once had on the crown; that authority which *grants money,* most certainly have a right to *refuse granting,* when they can neither see the *necessity or righteousness* of the measure for which it is to be granted."[46]

More radical theorists carried this assault on Congress even further. Those who were now asserting that sovereignty resided continually in the people argued that even the assemblies lacked the authority to ratify amendments to the Articles. It would be "no less than treason in those to whom the people have delegated the exercise of the sovereign power, to attempt, without their constituents' express consent, fairly and fully given, to assign it over to others."[47] Whether the state legislatures could be the actual repositories of sovereignty in a republican polity was itself very much at issue in the mid-1780's; ultimately, as Wood has argued, such populist criticisms of the assemblies' authority did more to weaken the claim that the state legislatures were sovereign than demands for obedience to Congress.[48] But before 1787, proponents of the conflicting doctrines of popular and legislative sovereignty could agree on at least one point: sovereignty was clearly not an attribute of Congress.

Yet while the political climate of the 1780's seemed to demonstrate just how subordinate a status Congress actually possessed, the arguments for unrestricted state sovereignty were far from conclusive. The language of the Articles was, in fact, ambiguous. Article 2 explicitly recognized the sovereignty of the states; but other provisions delegated certain powers expressly and exclusively to Congress and declared its decisions in these matters "binding" on the states. The political history of the Revolution similarly lent support to both interpretations. The notion that Congress was executive militated against the adoption of additional amendments, but it was less effective when applied to the powers it already possessed. It was thus entirely possible for a writer such as "Solicitor" to warn against uniting "legislative, judicial, and executive authority" in Congress, yet simultaneously to assert that Congress was not "amenable to any body of men in the states, for the lawful exercise" of its authority. Other writers put the case for divided sovereignty more plainly. "In all matters that respect the United States in general, the powers of Congress are ascertained by the confederation and they authorise Congress to make laws and regulations that shall be binding upon every State," one Connecticut writer observed. "But in all internal matters, each state is still sovereign and independent; nor can Congress by virtue of any prerogative, encroach upon the rights or abridge the privileges of a single State."[49]

The ambiguity that Thomas Burke had helped to incorporate in the Articles in 1777 was thus perpetuated into the 1780's. Its legacy was aptly illustrated in 1787 when John Adams sent Jefferson one of the first copies of his *Defence.* Of the many points that he could have found controversial, Jefferson singled out only one for criticism. "I doubt whether [Congress] are at all a diplomatic assembly," he wrote from Paris. "Separating into parts the whole sovereignty of our states," he noted, "some of these parts are yielded to Congress. Upon these I should think them both legislative and executive, and that they would have been judiciary also, had not the Confederation required them for certain purposes to appoint a judiciary." Adams politely replied that he hoped his statement would be regarded "as a Problem, rather for Consideration, than as an opinion." Whether Adams or Jefferson was more nearly right matters less than the simple fact that these two statesmen, themselves participants in the framing of the Articles, could still disagree over a point seemingly so rudimentary.[50]

This exchange symbolizes how little progress had been made in rethinking the problems of federal government. Theoretical discussions of the nature of Congress and the location of sovereignty had reached an impasse, and most writings of the mid-1780's were confined within the limits it imposed. Only a few essays ventured proposals that anticipated the solutions the Convention would devise to recast the terms of debate.

One obvious response to the anomalous character of Congress was to reconstitute the confederation as a normal government whose structure would conform to the familiar examples of the states. In a pamphlet written in 1783, the political economist Pelatiah Webster proposed dividing Congress into a "senate" and "commons," whose mutual concurrence would be required for the passage of every act. Webster also suggested appointing two additional bodies to assist Congress: a council of state composed of the heads of the executive departments, and a chamber of commerce, consisting of merchants, who could *"relieve Congress from the pain and trouble of deciding many intricate questions of trade which they do not understand."* With the addition of three members of Congress, chosen from each of the major regions, the Council of State would also serve as a national execu-

tive. Three years later, Benjamin Rush advanced a similar proposal, suggesting that Congress be divided "into two distinct,
independent branches," which would in turn annually elect a
president who would "possess certain powers in conjunction
with a privy council, especially the power of appointing most of
the officers of the United States." By the summer of 1786, John
Jay confessed that he had "long thought and become daily more
convinced that the Construction of our federal Government is
fundamentally wrong. To vest legislative, judicial and executive
Powers in one and the same Body of Men, and that too in a Body
daily changing its Members, can never be wise."[51]

A second solution to the theoretical deadlock of the mid-
1780's could have developed had American writers reconsidered
the nature of continental representation. Here, too, occasional
essays asked why Congress should be considered less representative of the popular will than the assemblies. Its members were
subject to annual elections, legislative instructions, and, as citizens, to the consequences of their decisions. "Why in the name
of reason should we trust men in Connecticut and yet distrust
them in Maryland or New Jersey?" a Connecticut writer asked
in 1784 (when Congress was to meet at Annapolis and Trenton).
"Does a change of climate corrupt the heart and pervert the
understanding?" "Power is as safe in the hands of Congress, as in
the hands of the General Assembly," another writer argued
three years later, "for the members of both are equally the representatives of the people."[52]

Such appeals had their force, and they, too, foreshadowed the
eventual results of the Convention. Yet none of the commentators of the 1780's actually advocated the popular election of members of Congress, the one step that could have unilaterally placed
it on the same footing as the assemblies. As Edmund Morgan has
noted, "the idea of popular sovereignty on a national scale began
to appear more and more implausible," particularly at a time
when many groups were challenging the representative adequacy of the state legislatures.[53] Opponents of a stronger confederation never asked for popular election of delegates—though a
modified form of it was already in practice in Rhode Island and
Connecticut—precisely because the idea would have conceded
too much. But the notion probably seemed no more attractive,
or feasible, to those who already, in Hamilton's phrase, thought
continentally. They, too, were puzzled to understand how direct

representation could work on such a scale, and they must also have doubted whether a people whose current legislators were of questionable ability would act more wisely in choosing members for Congress. The idea of popular election was never given serious attention. Indeed, as late as April 1787 Madison was still uncertain whether the new national legislature he was envisioning should be elected by the assemblies or the people.[54]

The striking feature of the discussions of these years, then, is that they do *not* foreshadow the intensity, scope, and sophistication of the debates of 1787–88. The few proposals that did anticipate the deliberations of the Convention can be said to have marked only the outer limits of speculation, not the familiar, dominant terms of debate. Through the waning months of 1786 public essays and private letters differed little, not only from each other but from arguments worked out by the end of the first year of peace. Most writers reiterated old arguments and familiar themes: the just claims of public creditors, the sufferings of widows and orphans, the need to establish public faith and national honor, and the futility of pursuing national interests through the partial and conflicting measures of individual states.

Were more sophisticated and innovative proposals, too controversial for publication, being discussed in cloistered chambers? In some private letters, it is true, one glimpses allusions to conversations not confined to the usual narrow agenda for reform. In the late fall of 1786, Samuel Osgood was able to inform John Adams that "a few Men in every State" were contemplating truly radical alterations in the balance of power between the states and the union. "It is therefore not uncommon to hear the principles of Government stated in common Conversation," Osgood wrote; "Emperors, Kings, Stadtholders, Governors General, with a Senate, or House of Lords, & House of Commons, are frequently the Topics of Conversation." Still, such allusions to the need for a "more energetic" government were so vague that it is difficult to avoid concluding that whatever discussions did take place were academic rather than conspiratorial. "Many are for abolishing all the State Governments, & for establishing some Kind of general Government," Osgood observed, "but I believe very few agree in the general Principles; much less in the Details of such a Government." "Various are the conjectures as to the issue" of the Convention, Edward Carrington informed Jefferson

five months later, "and still more various are the suggested remedies to the defects of our system."[55]

The search for specific antecedents of the Convention thus
proves disappointing—but perhaps it is misguided as well. What
may have contributed more to the Convention's success was a
continuing belief that a rational reassessment of the republican
experiment was still possible. In the face of all the obstacles the
putative reformers of the Articles encountered, this was in itself
striking. Politicians in the 1780's no longer felt the exultation that
John Adams had discovered in 1776 at being "sent into life at a
time when the greatest lawgivers of antiquity would have wished
to live." That mood had since given way to more sober if not
pessimistic views. Yet in 1784 the author of *The Political Establishments of the United States* could still argue that "America
enjoys a privilege, no other nations now existing ever did." For
while other governments had been "established, either by force,
or an undue influence" that had paid little interest to "the general good of the people," the Americans still possessed "the peculiar advantage of establishing a government on the best principles." Indeed, now that the war was over, they had a better
opportunity "of considering and debating the subject, and of
making a deliberate choice," than had existed in 1776, when "the
confusion of the times put it out of the power of the people, to
pay that attention to the subject, its nature and importance required." The conclusion to be drawn was accordingly simple: "If
therefore our government is defective, (which every candid observer must acknowledge,) why not reform it?"[56]

Benjamin Rush expressed the same sentiments more forcibly
in 1786, when he published his famous essay decrying the common tendency "to confound the terms of the American revolution with those of the late American war." Although the war was
over, "nothing but the first act of the great drama is closed. It
remains yet to establish and perfect our new forms of government, and to prepare the principles, morals, and manners of our
citizens, for these forms of government, after they are established and brought to perfection." In Rush's view, the reform of
the confederation was the most urgent of the tasks still confronting the Americans, and it was a task he professed to face optimistically.[57] It was this sense of possibility, rather than the skeptical
predictions that were still being voiced well into 1787, that ultimately set the tone for the Convention's deliberations.

The Idea
of a National Government

AN awareness of the scope of the discussions that were likely to occur at Philadelphia began to dawn early in 1787. Even then few politicians were eager to draft their own sketches of a reconstituted confederation. George Read and John Dickinson discussed the threat that a reapportionment of representation would pose to the small states.[58] Stephen Higginson prepared a carefully reasoned argument recommending that the results of the Convention be submitted not to the assemblies but to popularly elected ratifying conventions. A writer signing himself "Harrington" published an essay that resembled Madison's emerging theory of the extended republic. At least in élite circles, the gathering of the Convention produced a sudden heightening of hopes and predictions. "I find the Expectations of Politicians from the wisdom & Magnanimity of the Convention are much raised," Stephen Mix Mitchell reported from Connecticut; "all our Difficulties are to be removed, and we are to have almost a new Earth."[59]

Nevertheless, the months preceding the Convention did not produce the same sharp clarification of issues and alternatives that had occured, for example, prior to the meeting of the First Continental Congress. One senses in the early debates of the Convention that most members were individually prepared to draw lessons from their own observations and experiences, but that few arrived inclined to direct the course of debate. Of these Madison was the most important. Yet even Madison apparently began to draft the outlines of what would become the Virginia Plan only in late March. With the unimportant exception of Charles Pinckney, other members were content to postpone formulating their own responses until the initial debate on the Virginia resolutions was completed.

The limited and indefinite character of the earlier discussions of the 1780's had a liberating effect on the Convention's actual work. The delegates who assembled at Philadelphia in late May had to explore basic issues not only because events demanded innovation, but more important, because many of the relevant questions had not been systematically canvassed before. A few problems, notably the apportionment of representation and taxation, were of course too familiar. But a wider range of questions had never been seriously considered in the context of previous discussions of confederation: the proper distribution of power among three branches of government or between two houses of Congress; the extension and variation of terms of office; the proper relationship between the people at large and their elected representatives; a radical transfer of authority from the states to the union; the propriety of a national bill of rights; and so on. The delegates' ability to debate these issues candidly and thoroughly depended in large measure on the absence both of prior discussions and of instructions their constituents could never have issued because such extensive changes were not foreseen. They were thus free to assess these questions afresh and on their merits, and to initiate a wide-ranging and open inquiry into the fundamentals of republican government, precisely because such speculations had previously been pointless. In its very scope, then, the Convention became both the antithesis and the result of earlier failures to probe deeper questions of constitutional theory from the perspective of the problems of the confederation.

These considerations alone do not explain, however, why the Convention was able to accept an agenda whose radical implications would have been inconceivable less than a year earlier. For what enabled the Convention to transcend the old boundaries of debate was the realization that it had to analyze not merely the specific problems of Congress but, in effect, the whole history of the American republican experiment, thereby subsuming the debility of Congress and the political troubles of the states under one common rubric.[60] Before 1786 there had been little if any discussion of the idea of actively using the confederation to correct the internal political vices of the states. Many members of Congress and their correspondents were, of course, freely critical of the shortcomings of the state governments. But their plans for strengthening the Articles were designed to free Congress from its precarious and frustrating dependence on the states, not to remedy the situations of the individual states by creating an overawing national government. The Articles of Confederation had to be reformed for its own sake, not to correct errors incorporated in the state constitutions during the early flushes of republican enthusiasm. Some hoped that a reinvigorated confederation would provide a useful example for the states to emulate; but even if it did, that process would clearly unfold only gradually and indirectly. Insofar as the weaknesses of both Congress and the states were commonly attributed to a loss of virtue in the people at large, it was difficult to see how constitutional revisions alone could work the necessary reformation in the habits of the people. In the meantime, the immediate object remained simply to strengthen the ability of Congress to meet its existing obligations and new challenges to the national interest.

There was thus no necessary connection between the revision of the Articles and the reformation of state politics. The states could conceivably have granted Congress the powers it sought, thereby allowing it to function more effectively, while continuing to pursue their own uneven courses toward greater stability. Had the states been less indifferent to the plight of Congress, the fusion between these two issues might not have been made even in 1787. But in the end nothing so vividly demonstrated the shortcomings of the state governments as their reluctance to grant Congress a handful of additional powers necessary for the general welfare and their failure to comply with its legitimate requisitions. By late 1786 these failings could no longer be plausibly attributed to the temporary dislocations of the war, but now seemed symptomatic of deeper defects in the state constitutions and the political manners of the people and their representatives. Even Samuel Osgood was complaining that the states were so "weak & selfish" that they would eventually "annihilate" Congress. "Their stubborn Dignity," he wrote Adams, "will never permit a federal Government to exist."[61]

Reinforcing this general perception were the specific lessons to be drawn from the current controversy over paper money in Rhode Island and from Shays's Rebellion in Massachusetts. Not all national leaders saw in these developments the specter of anarchy that key New England politicians imagined had been unleashed, but there was common agreement that the recovery of domestic order seemed as distant as ever. Nothing that happened in Rhode Island was ever surprising, of course, but if (as appeared likely) other states resorted to similarly ill-secured schemes of currency finance, the resulting monetary instability would doom any plan for supplying the continental treasury. The situation in Massachusetts was different—the disorders in the western part of the state were a reaction against the sort of program of heavy taxation that orthodox fiscal theorists had demanded all along—but its political implications were no less disturbing. If a state with a history of relative stability and a constitution less radical than many others was prone to insurrection, could other states expect to avoid similar troubles? Few national politicians would have been comforted by Jefferson's famous calculation of the infrequency of rebellion in America.[62]

Again it was Madison who most clearly understood how the connection between the defects of the Articles and the internal difficulties of the states could substantially broaden the perspective of the Convention. The association was explicitly forged in his famous memorandum detailing the "Vices of the Political System of the United States," which Madison drafted only weeks before the Convention opened. The initial items in this catalogue were familiar enough, though compiled with his customary thoroughness. Madison indicted the states for ignoring congressional requisitions, encroaching on federal authority, violating foreign treaties, trespassing on each other's rights of commerce and property, and refusing to recognize their common interests. He also criticized the Articles for failing to give acts of Congress the sanction of law; for not initially requiring ratification by the people rather than the legislatures, an omission that further compromised the status of the confederation; and for not authorizing Congress to assist the states in protecting themselves against "internal violence." This last point clearly drew upon the experience of Massachusetts, but not until the ninth item did Madison make the transition in his concerns explicit. "In developing the evils which viciate the political system of the U.S.," he wrote, in language that conveys his own sense of discovery, "it is proper to include those which are found within the States individually, as well as those which directly affect the States collectively, since the former class have an indirect influence on the general malady and must not be overlooked in forming a compleat remedy." The immediate objects of his concern were the "multiplicity" and "mutability" of state legislation, which respectively constituted "a nuisance of the most pestilent kind" and proof that laws were being carelessly framed and rashly revised. But it was in explaining why these "evils" existed that Madison demonstrated how state and federal issues could now be made to converge.[63]

There were two complementary explanations for the "vicious" character of state legislation, Madison argued. One was that the assemblies were too commonly filled by men who sought office from motives of "ambition" and "personal interest," and who had proved adept at pursuing "base and selfish measures, masked by pretexts of public good and apparent expediency." More serious were the conditions that enabled a majority of interested citizens to coalesce within their states in support of measures injurious either to the national welfare or to the private rights of other citizens. Taken separately or together, these two phenomena of American politics challenged "the fundamental principle of republican Government, that the majority who rule in such Governments, are the safest Guardians both of public Good and of private rights." The antidote to both maladies, Madison concluded, was to construct a national polity whose simple extent would simultaneously inhibit the formation of "the requisite combinations" of self-interested groups of citizens while facilitating the election of those individuals best qualified to act responsibly for the common good. Turning on its head the orthodox notion that only small, homogeneous societies could sustain republican governments, Madison now followed David Hume in concluding that a geographically extensive and socially diverse polity would be more likely to provide the stability and security that republics were known to put at risk. In concurrent letters to Randolph and Washington, Madison suggested that the new federal government could best exercise this function if it were given a veto over state legislation. This would allow it not only to protect itself from obstructive acts by the states but also to prevent factious majorities in individual states from violating the rights of their fellow citizens.[64]

Because Madison's position was incorporated in the Virginia Plan, which in turn defined the initial framework of debate, the Convention was induced to approach the task of reform from the elevated perspective he had fashioned. In this respect, several features of the Virginia Plan were critical. One was that it took almost for granted that the powers to be transferred from the states to the union would be substantial indeed. Rather than enumerating the specific objects of federal concern, the Virginia Plan simply asserted that the new national legislature

ought to be impowered to enjoy the Legislative Rights vested in Congress by the Confederation & moreover to legislate in all cases to which

the separate States are incompetent, or in which the harmony of the
United States may be interrupted by the exercise of individual Legislation; [and] to negative all laws passed by the several States, contravening
. . . the articles of Union. . . .[65]

The revision of the Articles was now understood to require more
than the reinvigoration of Congress. It had become instead a
struggle to preserve the republican experiment, not only by sav-
ing Congress from the states but the states from themselves. Such
a perspective demanded, in effect, that the debates of the Convention involve more than an expedient reapportionment of the
powers of government. And how extensive a revision would
occur now depended not on the visible weaknesses of Congress
but on a reassessment of the character and temperament of the
American people. In the end, the delegates' rejection of Madison's pet scheme of a federal veto mattered less than their agreement that what was at stake was the relationship between the
institutions of government and the nature of American society,
broadly conceived.

A second critical aspect of the Virginia Plan was its application of the still fluid doctrine of separation of powers to the
reconstruction of the federal government—a subject that engaged fully six of its fifteen articles. The Virginia Plan called for
the establishment of a bicameral legislature, a national executive,
and a national judiciary. By outlining the architecture of the new
government at the very outset, Madison and his colleagues
cleared the way for an open-ended discussion of its powers. As
a South Carolina delegate, Pierce Butler, observed on May 30,
"he had opposed the grant of powers to Congs. heretofore, because the whole power was vested in one body. The proposed
distribution of the powers into different bodies changed the case,
and would induce him to go great lengths."[66] But the converse
proposition was equally true. Once it was realized that the
union's new powers would greatly exceed anything seriously
considered before, it became obvious that such powers could
never be exercised by the Continental Congress as currently
organized. In part this was because Congress had to be protected
from its own inefficiency. But more important, neither the people nor the states could be expected to ratify any plan of major
reform that did not embody the essential internal safeguards
constitutional orthodoxy demanded of all governments. The

confederation had to be reconstituted as a government in the full and normal meaning of the term.

This was a simple, virtually intuitive discovery; but once it was made, the Convention's perspectives were substantially widened. For prior to 1787 the doctrine of separation of powers had not been consciously applied to the case of confederation. The framers of the Articles had been content instead to divide the major functions of government between Congress and the states. When members of Congress had talked of delegating power to subordinate executive agencies, they had been primarily concerned with improving the efficiency of Congress, nothing more. But now it was realized that those notions of separation of powers that were designed to prevent governments from becoming too efficient, and thus dangerous to liberty, had to be applied to the internal organization of the federal government. Moreover, by proposing that the members of the lower house be elected by the people, the Virginia Plan at last established a direct link between the federal government and the people, thus giving its enactments the status of legislation and removing the major obstacle to bestowing powers of taxation.[67]

These proposals cut through the theoretical anomalies that had complicated previous discussions of the nature of the federal government, and enabled the delegates to draw upon a far more provocative body of critical thought than any that the affairs of Congress had ever generated. For it was in the creation of the state constitutions and ensuing appraisals of their success that American thinkers had most carefully developed their new conceptions of separation of powers and representation. It was the experience of the states that had called into question the Americans' initial commitment to the supremacy of the legislature and the evisceration of the executive. It was in the states that the problem of protecting constitutional charters and rights from legislative encroachment had become apparent and that the doctrine of judicial review had begun to take shape. And it was there, too, that the difficulty of reconciling the traditional forms of mixed government with a republican conception of popular sovereignty had led toward a new understanding of the meaning of representation.[68]

Only in 1787, then, were the richly detailed and innovative arguments that had accompanied the creation of republican polities in the states brought to bear on the problem of national government. As a result, the Convention was able to consider the issues inherent in establishing a national government with a sophistication that had been absent from all previous discussions. At the same time, its debates necessarily amounted to a mature reassessment of the merits and defects of the original state constitutions. The new Constitution was thus framed less in reaction to the Articles of Confederation than in response to a seasoned critique of politics and government at the level of the states. More than anything else, it was this shift of perspective that allowed the Convention to acquire its preeminent place in the history of American political thought.

The Virtue of Isolation

THERE was, as well, one final condition that worked to release the deliberations of 1787 from earlier constraints, and that also represented the peculiar legacy of the Continental Congress.

Despite the aftershocks of Shays's Rebellion and the Mississippi controversy, it would be incorrect to assert that the Convention assembled in an atmosphere of true crisis. The popular mood of America in 1787 cannot be compared to the fearful anxieties of 1774–75 or the deepening disillusionment of 1779–80. The First Continental Congress had had "materials to work with & the strong Impression of Fear to support their Influence," Stephen Mix Mitchell reminded William Samuel Johnson, a member of the Convention from Connecticut. "The Convention is in a very different predicament, no fears of the people to co-operate with them," and assembled in "a time of profound peace within & without."[69] Although shrill warnings of social upheaval were occasionally heard from New England, few American leaders believed that the nation was literally ripe for anarchy. On the eve of the Convention, a number of well-placed national leaders, including Washington, still doubted whether affairs had yet plunged to the nadir necessary to ensure the success of a reformation.[70]

Yet the fact that there was to be a convention itself constituted a new variable in political calculations. "Should this plan fall thro, or meeting, should their System be rejected . . . what is to become of the confederacy?" asked Tench Coxe, the Philadelphia merchant and political economist. "I confess it appears to me but short-lived." Once it was known that the meeting would be well and capably attended, speculation about the consequences of failure proved unavoidable. Would it then be possible to return to the strategy of patient and partial reform that had been pursued since 1781? Would Congress and the Articles then be seen in a newly favorable light? Neither question could be answered confidently. "I cannot sit still & see a Dissolution of the Confederacy without making an effort to save it from Anarchy & Ruin," wrote the New Jersey congressional delegate, Lambert Cadwalader. "How far the Measure in Question may prevent it I am not Prophet enough to say—in it however we have some chance—but if we leave our Affairs to go to Pieces, silently acquiescing in the Consequences which must ensue, it will in my Idea be criminal in the highest Degree."[71]

These considerations were of course apparent to the members of the Convention and help to explain their perseverance through months of deliberation. But the imminence of the Convention had a similarly galvanizing effect on a widening circle of articulate, respectable, but politically inactive citizens—in Coxe's view, "Men of real Virtue, knowledge, and clear property," but who had to be "forced into public life." By the time the Convention assembled, there were clear signs that the political torpor of the preceding years was giving way to a new sense of engagement. "Men are brought into action who had consigned themselves to an eve of rest," Edward Carrington informed Jefferson, "and the Convention, as a Beacon, is rousing the attention of the Empire." But more was to be required of these men than attention. If the Convention produced a satisfactory plan, Benjamin Lincoln wrote in early May, "men of property and principle and all who wish for *government* must combine and carry it down." Anticipating the reliance on the socially respectable classes that would soon typify the Federalist campaign for ratification, Lincoln argued that "the whole artillery of the wealth & address of the good men of the community must be levelled against" those who would pass judgment on the Convention. "The weakness of some must be managed—the vices of others turned to account—their virtues (and here & there a virtue is yet to be found among them) must be cherished and improved."[72]

Brief items inserted in the more cosmopolitan newspapers implied that the people themselves might need little convincing, since there was a "general determination among all classes of people to receive the government they [the members of the Convention] are now framing." Such comments were themselves harbingers of the imminent Federalist campaign for ratification, "artfully calculated," a few skeptics already suspected, "to prepare the minds of the people, implicitly to receive any form of government that may be offered to them."[73] Whether any meaningful currents of public opinion had as yet taken shape is doubtful, however. Among active politicians and within certain élite circles there was considerable anticipation of the Convention's outcome. But other writings from the summer of 1787 do not depict a society already chafing to begin the frenetic political activity that did follow the publication of the Constitution. Writing to Coxe in mid-June, Edward Goold of New York could only describe his astonishment at seeing "with what indifference people in general speak of [the Convention] and how little anxiety they betray for an event that in *all* probability must produce some very important Changes in the Government of this Country." Yet if the Americans displayed "more Coolness in affairs when they are nearly Concerned than any other People I know," that in itself was comforting. For, "whatever Revolutions we may undergo," Goold concluded, "no great violence or enormities will ensue & the property of individuals [will] remain unmolested."[74]

Deference on the part of those who were predisposed to favor a stronger federal government, indifference or simple ignorance among those who might later see the Constitution as a reaction against local autonomy: this is perhaps the most that can be said about the state of public opinion during the summer of 1787. There are important differences between periods of genuine crisis and the political atmosphere that existed in 1787. It was very much to the Convention's advantage that it met *after* the worst fears arising from the developments of 1786 had managed to subside. Had the Convention assembled at a time when public interest in politics had been running high, its deliberations would almost certainly have proved futile. But, as Goold's comments suggest, that was not the case in 1787. The dominant motif that runs through the public and private writings from these summer months evokes a curious mixture of expectancy and passivity toward the results of the Convention. It is the pervasive expression of this attitude, which was essentially deferential, that suggests a final link between the Convention and the Continental Congress.

For the most remarkable aspect of the Convention's four-month inquiry was that it was conducted in virtually absolute secrecy, uninfluenced by external pressures of any kind. No detailed instructions bound the delegates to specific goals, nor did the Convention even feel constrained to confine itself to proposing mere revisions of the Articles, as some of the members' credentials stipulated. No crowds assembled in the streets outside to shout for the redress of grievances or to protest its decision to meet behind closed doors. Except for the occasional rumors—many of them inaccurate—that American newspapers published, the general public knew nothing of the Convention's deliberations. It was a curious counterpoint to the tumult of state politics in the 1780's and indeed to a whole generation of political ferment, suggesting that the turbulence of the preceding years had crested somewhere below the national level, held within the limits of local conflicts over debts and taxes, roads and banks, and the rights of religious dissenters and loyalist refugees.

And yet the freedom that the Convention enjoyed, and that was indispensable to its success, was hardly accidental. That the Convention wished to deliberate in private could not have been surprising, but its ability to shield itself from public scrutiny was the legacy of the isolation that had traditionally separated the Continental Congress from the other spheres of American politics. The independence and originality the Convention demonstrated could not have been achieved had Congress ever succeeded in establishing efficient channels of influence and habits of communication with the states. The Convention realized that the new government must not remain similarly aloof; but in the meantime it was prepared to extract one last advantage from the tradition that had served Congress so well at the height of its power, and so poorly in its decline.

NOTES,
A NOTE ON
PRIMARY SOURCES,
INDEX

Abbreviations

BCC   Boston Committee of Correspondence

CHS   Connecticut Historical Society, Hartford

Colls.   Published *Collections* of the Connecticut, Massachusetts, and New-York Historical societies

HSP   Historical Society of Pennsylvania, Philadelphia

HUL   Houghton Library, Harvard University, Cambridge, Massachusetts

JCC   Worthington C. Ford, *et al.*, eds., *Journals of the Continental Congress, 1774–1789* (Washington, D.C., 1904–37)

LC   Library of Congress, Washington, D.C.

LDC   Paul H. Smith, *et al.*, eds., *Letters of Delegates to Congress, 1774–1789* (Washington, D.C., 1976–)

LMCC   Edmund C. Burnett, ed., *Letters of Members of the Continental Congress* (Washington, D.C., 1921–36)

MHS   Massachusetts Historical Society, Boston

MdHS   Maryland Historical Society, Baltimore

NYHS   New-York Historical Society, New York City

NYPL   New York Public Library, New York City

NYSL   New York State Library, Albany

PCC   Papers of the Continental Congress, 1774–1789, Record Group 360, National Archives, Washington, D.C.

RIHS   Rhode Island Historical Society, Providence

SCHS   South Carolina Historical Society, Charleston

UVa   Alderman Library, University of Virginia, Charlottesville

WMQ   *William and Mary Quarterly,* 3d series (1944–)

Complete bibliographic information for printed sources and secondary works is provided only for the first reference. Similarly, when a particular document is cited more than once within the same chapter, the full description of its location is not repeated. I have chosen to preserve the original spelling, punctuation, and capitalization of eighteenth-century documents, except in a few instances where changes strongly enhanced the clarity of the passage.

Notes

___

Chapter I: Resistance Without Union, 1770–1774

1. For a more detailed account of the events of the early 1770's, see Merrill Jensen, *The Founding of a Nation: A History of the American Revolution, 1763–1776* (New York, 1968), 354–433.

2. Francis Dana to Henry Marchant, Cambridge, 18 Oct. 1771, Henry Marchant Papers, Correspondence 1769–1771, RIHS. For general discussions of the beliefs and perceptions of colonial leaders, see Bernard Bailyn, *The Ideological Origins of the American Revolution* (Cambridge, 1967), 55–159, and Pauline Maier, *From Resistance to Revolution: Colonial Radicals and the Development of American Opposition to Britain, 1765–1776* (New York, 1972), *passim*. By the leaders of opposition I mean to refer to those politically active individuals whom Maier has identified as "colonial radicals."

3. A. Lee to R. H. Lee, London, 14 Feb. 1773, in Paul P. Hoffman, ed., *Lee Family Papers, 1742–1795* (microfilm, Charlottesville, Va., 1966), reel 2 (original in HUL; subsequent references to the microfilm will also cite repository for manuscript); and see Andrew Eliot to Thomas Hollis, Boston, 26 Jan. 1771, and Thomas Cushing to Roger Sherman, 21 Jan. 1772, *Colls.* MHS, 4th ser., 4 (1858), 458, 358.

4. A. Lee to S. Adams, London, 10 Jan. 1771, in Richard Henry Lee, *Life of Arthur Lee, LL.D.* (Boston, 1829), I, 250; Adams to Lee, 27 Sept. 1771, in Harry Alonzo Cushing, ed., *The Writings of Samuel Adams* (New York, 1904–08), II, 234. On the creation of the Boston Committee of Correspondence (hereafter cited as BCC), see Richard D. Brown, *Revolutionary Politics in Massachusetts: The Boston Committee of Correspondence and the Towns, 1772–1774* (Cambridge, 1970), 38–57.

5. Charles Thomson to the BCC, Phila., 19 Dec. 1773, in Letters of

the BCC, Bancroft Collection, NYPL. On the general inactivity of the provincial committees, see Edward D. Collins, "Committees of Correspondence of the American Revolution," American Historical Association, *Annual Report for 1901*, I, 250–4.

6. Shippen to R. H. Lee, Phila., 25 Aug. 1770, Lee Family Papers, reel 2 (UVa); Dickinson to S. Adams, 10 April 1773, S. Adams Papers, box 2, NYPL.

7. Hannah Arendt, *On Revolution* (New York, 1963), 26.

8. Dickinson to A. Lee, Phila., 31 Oct. 1770, in R. H. Lee, *Life of Arthur Lee*, II, 302; Thomson to BCC, 19 Dec. 1773; and see Maier, *From Resistance to Revolution*, 220–8.

9. Dickinson to S. Adams, 10 April 1773.

10. Cushing to A. Lee, Boston, September 1773, *Colls.* MHS, 4th ser., 4 (1858), 360; and see Franklin to Cushing, London, 5 Jan. 1773, in William B. Willcox, *et al.*, eds., *The Papers of Benjamin Franklin* (New Haven and London, 1959–), XX, 10, and the general discussion in James H. Cassedy, *Demography in Early America: Beginnings of the Statistical Mind, 1600–1800* (Cambridge, 1969), 180–205.

11. Thomson to BCC, 19 Dec. 1773; Franklin to Cushing, London, 7 July 1773, Willcox, ed., *Papers of Franklin*, XX, 280–2; A. Lee to S. Adams, London, 11 June 1773, in R. H. Lee, *Life of Arthur Lee*, I, 230.

12. On Hutchinson's debate with the General Court, see Bernard Bailyn, *The Ordeal of Thomas Hutchinson* (Cambridge, 1974), 196–220; the entire debate is reprinted in Alden Bradford, ed., *Speeches of the Governors of Massachusetts, from 1765 to 1775* . . . (Boston, 1818), 336–400.

13. S. Adams to Darius Sessions, *et al.*, Boston, 28 Dec. 1772 and 2 Jan. 1773, S. Adams Papers, boxes 1 and 2 (respectively), NYPL.

14. S. Adams to Dickinson, Boston, 27 March 1773, S. Adams Papers, box 2, NYPL; Cushing to Franklin, Boston, 20 April 1773, in Willcox, ed., *Papers of Franklin*, XX, 172.

15. The house reply is reprinted in Cushing, ed., *Writings of Adams*, II, 401–26; the reference to a congress is at 424.

16. S. Adams to A. Lee, 9 April 1773, *ibid.*, III, 21; Cushing to Franklin, 20 April 1773. For other early references to a congress, see Samuel H. Parsons to S. Adams, Providence, 3 March 1773, S. Adams Papers, box 2, NYPL; "Proposals for the good of the Colonies . . . ," *Boston Gazette*, 15 March 1773.

17. A. Lee to R. H. Lee, 14 Feb. 1773; A. Lee to S. Adams, 11 June 1773 and 23 June 1773, S. Adams Papers, box 2, NYPL; Franklin to Cushing, 7 July 1773.

18. Hutchinson to an unknown correspondent, 21 Aug. 1773, Massachusetts Archives, XXVII, 534–5.

19. "Observation," *Boston Gazette*, 27 Sept. 1773; reprinted in at

least three colonial newspapers: *Newport Mercury*, 4 Oct., *Connecticut Courant*, 12 Oct., and *Virginia Gazette* (Purdie and Dixon), 11 Nov. For Hutchinson's comments, see his undated letter to Lord Dartmouth, an unsent letter to John Pownall, 18 Oct. 1773, and another letter to Dartmouth, 19 Oct. 1773; all in Massachusetts Archives, XXVII, 542–4, 557–8.

20. On resistance to the Tea Act, see Benjamin W. Labaree, *The Boston Tea Party* (New York, 1964), 80–169.

21. S. Adams to James Warren, Boston, 28 Dec. 1773, in Worthington C. Ford, ed., *Warren-Adams Letters* (*Colls.* MHS, 1917–25), I, 20–1; Cushing to A. Lee, Boston, 23 Jan. 1774, Boston Public Library. In early December, Henry Marchant informed a London correspondent that "a General Congress of Deputies from all the Colonies is much talked of," but that is virtually the only reference to a congress that I have been able to discover during the period of the Tea Act resistance; Marchant to Joseph Jennings, Newport, 4 Dec. 1773, Marchant Papers, Letter Book 1773–1785, RIHS.

22. Labaree, *Boston Tea Party*, 218–19.

23. Thomson to BCC, 19 Dec. 1773.

24. On the scheme for a post office, see Thomas Young to John Lamb, Boston, 18–19 March 1774; Goddard to Lamb, Boston, 23 March and May 1774; Paul Revere to Lamb, Boston, 28 March 1774; and Whitehead Humphreys to Lamb, Phila., 1 April 1774; all in the John Lamb Papers, reel 1, NYHS.

25. Richard D. Brown, *Revolutionary Politics in Massachusetts*, 152–5; the Massachusetts provincial committee's circular is reprinted in *Proceedings* of the MHS, 13 (1873–75), 161–3; Young to Lamb, 18–19 March 1774; Gerry to S. Adams, Marblehead, April 1774, Gerry-Knight Collection, MHS.

26. J. Adams to James Warren, Boston, 9 April 1774, in Robert J. Taylor, *et al.,* eds., *Papers of John Adams* (Cambridge, 1977–), II, 83.

27. John Hancock, *An Oration; Delivered March 5, 1774 . . .* (Boston, 1774), 17–18; S. Adams to Dickinson, Boston, 19 April 1774, R. R. Logan Collection, box 2, HSP. For another proposal for a congress, see "Americanus," *Virginia Gazette* (Rind), 10 March 1774.

28. *Boston Gazette*, 23 Dec. 1771 and 27 Jan. 1772.

29. See the suggestive essay by Patricia Bonomi, "The Middle Colonies: Embryo of the New Political Order," in Alden T. Vaughan and George A. Billias, eds., *Perspectives on Early American History: Essays in Honor of Richard B. Morris* (New York, 1973), 63–92.

30. George A. Billias, *Elbridge Gerry: Founding Father and Republican Statesman* (New York, 1976), 12.

31. See Richard L. Merritt, *Symbols of American Community, 1773–1775* (New Haven, 1966).

Chapter II: The Creation of a Mandate

1. On the passage of the Coercive Acts, see Bernard Donoughue, *British Politics and the American Revolution: The Path to War, 1773–1775* (London, 1964), 36–126, and Labaree, *Boston Tea Party*, 170–216.

2. More detailed accounts of the maneuvers of the summer of 1774 can be found in Arthur M. Schlesinger, *The Colonial Merchants and the American Revolution, 1763–1776* (New York, 1917), 305–405, and in David Ammerman, *In the Common Cause: American Response to the Coercive Acts of 1774* (Charlottesville, Va., 1974), 19–51.

3. Alexander McDougall, "Political memorandums relative to the Conduct of the Citizens on the Boston Port Bill," n.d., Alexander McDougall Papers, reel 1, NYHS; Sears and McDougall to the BCC, 15 May 1774, Letters of the BCC, NYPL; New York Comm. to BCC, 23 May 1774, in Peter Force, ed., *American Archives . . .* (Washington, D.C., 1837–46), 4th ser., I, 297–8. A succinct account of the tangled situation in New York can be found in Roger Champagne, *Alexander McDougall and the American Revolution in New York* (Schenectady, N.Y., 1975), 52–66.

4. Phila. Comm. to BCC, 21 May 1774, Force, ed., *American Archives*, I, 341–2; Mifflin to S. Adams, 21 and 26 May 1774 (quotation is from the latter), and Thomson to Adams, 3 June 1774; all in S. Adams Papers, box 2, NYPL.

5. An initial letter from Deane, written in the name of the Connecticut Committee of Correspondence, is not extant, but its criticisms can be inferred from the contents of Samuel Adams's reply, Boston, 18 May 1774, Cushing, ed., *Writings of Adams*, III, 114–16; Deane to S. Adams, Hartford, 26 May 1774, Letters of BCC, NYPL.

6. BCC to Providence, 21 May 1774, to New York Comm., 30 May 1774, and to Phila. Comm., n.d., all in BCC Minutebook, 796–8, 807–8, 817, NYPL; and see S. Adams to Thomson, 30 May 1774, and to Deane, 31 May 1774, Cushing, ed., *Writings of Adams*, III, 122–7; and Josiah Quincy to John Dickinson, Boston, 27 May 1774, R. R. Logan Collection, box 2, HSP.

7. On the Solemn League, see Brown, *Revolutionary Politics in Massachusetts*, 188–209, and Stephen Patterson, *Political Parties in Revolutionary Massachusetts* (Madison, 1973), 75–90. In an intriguing letter to an unidentified Boston leader, Joseph Reed had argued that the New England colonies would have to demonstrate their willingness to support Boston through a boycott before other colonies could be expected to endorse commercial resistance; Reed to [John Hancock?], 22 May 1774, Fogg Collection, vol. 54, Maine Historical Society, Portland.

8. Deane to BCC, Wethersfield, Conn., 13 June 1774, Letters of

BCC, NYPL; Thomson to S. Adams, 3 June 1774; and see McDougall to Adams, New York, 26 June 1774, S. Adams Papers, box 2, NYPL; and McDougall and Sears to Adams, New York, 20 June 1774, McDougall Papers, reel 1, NYHS.

9. R. H. Lee to S. Adams, Chantilly, Va., 23 June 1774, in James C. Ballagh, ed., *The Letters of Richard Henry Lee* (New York, 1911–14), I, 111–13; the various proceedings of the official and rump sessions of the Virginia Burgesses are reprinted in Julian P. Boyd, ed., *The Papers of Thomas Jefferson* (Princeton, 1950–), I, 105–12. On Maryland, see David Ammerman, "Annapolis and the First Continental Congress: A Note on the Committee System in Revolutionary America," *Maryland Historical Magazine*, 66 (1971), 169–80; and Baltimore Comm. to BCC, in J. Thomas Scharf, *History of Maryland from the Earliest Period to the Present Day* (Hatboro, Pa., 1967 [originally published 1879]), II, 146–7.

10. Robert Treat Paine, "Account of Stratagem used to keep Daniel Leonard from Voting on the Cont Congress," Robert Treat Paine Papers, MHS; Force, ed., *American Archives*, I, 421–3.

11. Palmer Comm. to BCC, 8 Aug. 1774, enclosing town resolutions of 29 June, Letters of BCC, NYPL; see Brown, *Revolutionary Politics in Massachusetts*, 199–209.

12. Dickinson to Quincy, 20 June 1774, in Josiah Quincy, *Memoir of the Life of Josiah Quincy, Jun. of Massachusetts* (Boston, 1825), 169; Deane to Samuel H. Parsons, Wethersfield, Conn., 13 April [i.e., June] 1774, in "Correspondence of Silas Deane, 1774–1776," *Colls.* CHS, 2 (1870), 130; and see Sears and McDougall to S. Adams, New York, 25 July 1774, S. Adams Papers, box 2, NYPL.

13. Clymer to Quincy, Phila., 13 June 1774, Quincy, *Memoir of Josiah Quincy*, 164–8; Mifflin to S. Adams, 30 July 1774, S. Adams Papers, box 2, NYPL. Early in June it was rumored in New York that Dickinson had "declared the Boston Port Act was a Constitutional Law"; McDougall to C. Thomson, New York, 1 June 1774, McDougall Papers, reel 1, NYHS. On Dickinson, see David L. Jacobson, *John Dickinson and the Revolution in Pennsylvania, 1764–1776* (Berkeley and Los Angeles, 1965).

14. In this and the following paragraphs discussing the resolutions of the summer of 1774, I have relied on Force, ed., *American Archives*, I, 331–741, for proceedings in New York, New Jersey, Pennsylvania, Delaware, and Maryland; on the records of the BCC, NYPL, for Massachusetts and Connecticut; on W. J. van Schreeven, comp., and Robert L. Scribner, ed., *Revolutionary Virginia: The Road to Independence* (Charlottesville, Va., 1973–), I, *Forming Thunderclouds and the First Convention: A Documentary Record*, 111–68, for Virginia; and on William L. Saunders, ed., *The Colonial Records of North Carolina* (Raleigh, N.C., 1886–1905), IX, 1030–41.

15. Jere R. Daniell, *Experiment in Republicanism: New Hampshire*

Politics and the American Revolution, 1741–1794 (Cambridge, 1970), 74–91; Robert J. Taylor, *Western Massachusetts in the Revolution* (Providence, 1954), 64–9. On the overall continuity of local leadership in New England towns, see Edward M. Cook, Jr., *The Fathers of the Towns: Leadership and Community Structure in Eighteenth-Century New England* (Baltimore and London, 1976), 186–9.

16. L. H. Butterfield, *et al.*, eds., *Diary and Autobiography of John Adams* (Cambridge, 1961), II, 96–7.

17. Saunders, ed., *Col. Recs. of N.C.*, IX, 1035.

18. [Isaac Wilkins?], *Short Advice to the Counties of New York* (New York, 1774), 8.

19. The provincial resolves are reprinted in Force, ed., *American Archives*, I, 355–6, 421–2, 439–40, 525–6, 606–7, 624–5, 667–8, 686–90, 734–7.

20. Boyd, ed., *Papers of Jefferson*, I, 143.

21. [John Randolph], *Considerations on the Present State of Virginia* ([Williamsburg], 1774), 15; Saunders, ed., *Col. Recs. of N.C.*, IX, 1034.

22. Jefferson, *A Summary View of the Rights of British America* ([Williamsburg], 1774), reprinted in Boyd, ed., *Papers of Jefferson*, I, 121–35 (quotation from opening paragraph); Force, ed., *American Archives*, I, 647, 756.

23. Force, ed., *American Archives*, I, 757; [Randolph], *Considerations*, 8.

24. Boyd, ed., *Papers of Jefferson*, I, 135; [James Wilson], *Considerations on the Nature and Extent of the Legislative Authority of the British Parliament* (Philadelphia, 1774), reprinted in Robert G. McCloskey, ed., *The Works of James Wilson* (Cambridge, 1967), II, 744; Iredell, "To the Inhabitants of Great Britain," in Don Higginbotham, ed., *The Papers of James Iredell* (Raleigh, N.C., 1976–), I, 251–67. See, in general, the discussion of the constitutional issues in Bailyn, *Ideological Origins*, 160–229, esp. 219 ff.

25. McCloskey, ed., *Works of Wilson*, II, 746.

26. The Fairfax Resolves are reprinted in Robert Rutland, ed., *The Papers of George Mason, 1725–1792* (Chapel Hill, 1970), II, 201–9.

27. *Virginia Gazette* (Rind), 21 and 28 July 1774. For expression of similar sentiments, see Henry Marchant to Harford and Powell, Newport, 13 March 1773, Marchant Papers, Letter Book 1772–1791, RIHS; Edward Burd to Edward Shippen, Reading, Pa., 4 July 1774, in Lewis Burd Walker, ed., *Selections from Letters Written by Edward Burd, 1763–1828* (Pottsville, Pa., 1899), 66–70; Boyd, ed., *Papers of Jefferson*, I, 135.

28. [John Dickinson], *An Essay on the Constitutional Power of Great-Britain over the Colonies in America* (Philadelphia, 1774), reprinted in Samuel Hazard, *et al.*, eds., *Pennsylvania Archives* (Philadel-

phia and Harrisburg, 1880–1949), 2d ser., III, 565–622 (quotations from 612, 616); Bailyn, *Ideological Origins*, 23; and see "Z.," *New York Gazette*, 15 Aug. 1774.

29. [Jonathan Boucher?], *A Letter from a Virginian, to the Members of the Congress* . . . ([New York], 1774), 26–7; [William Henry Drayton], *A Letter from Freeman, to the Deputies of North America* . . . (Charleston, S.C., 1774), 15–16.

30. *Letter from Freeman*, 24.

31. *Letter from a Virginian*, 4; [Thomas Bradbury Chandler], *The American Querist* . . . ([New York], 1774), 28–9; cf. [Richard Wells], *A Few Political Reflections* . . . (Philadelphia, 1774), 57–61.

32. Samuel Patterson to Levi Hollingsworth, 6 July 1774, quoted in Arthur Jensen, *The Maritime Commerce of Colonial Philadelphia* (Madison, 1963), 214; William Smith to Philip Schuyler, in W.H.W. Sabine, ed., *Historical Memoirs from 16 March 1763 to 25 July 1778 of William Smith* (New York, 1969), I, 190; Christopher Leffingwell to Silas Deane, Norwich, 22 Aug. 1774, in "Correspondence of Deane," 140; and see "B.N.," *New York Journal*, 4 Aug. 1774.

33. Thomas Willing to the Mechanics, 11 July 1774, quoted in Charles S. Olton, *Artisans for Independence: Philadelphia Mechanics and the American Revolution* (Syracuse, N.Y., 1975), 67.

34. S. Adams to Samuel Cooper, Phila., 30 April 1776, Cushing, ed., *Writings of Adams*, III, 282.

35. See, by way of example, the following: Jack P. Greene, "An Uneasy Connection: An Analysis of the Preconditions of the American Revolution," in Stephen Kurtz and James H. Hutson, eds., *Essays on the American Revolution* (Chapel Hill, 1973), 32–80; Greene, "Search for Identity: An Interpretation of the Meaning of Selected Patterns of Social Response in Eighteenth-Century America," *Journal of Social History*, 3 (1970), 189–220; Gordon S. Wood, "Rhetoric and Reality in the American Revolution," *WMQ*, 23 (1966), 3–32; Gary B. Nash, "Urban Wealth and Poverty in Pre-Revolutionary America," *Journal of Interdisciplinary History*, 6 (1976), 545–84; Robert M. Weir, "Who Shall Rule at Home: The American Revolution as a Crisis of Legitimacy for the Colonial Elite," *ibid.*, 679–700; and Edwin G. Burrows and Michael Wallace, "The American Revolution: The Ideology and Psychology of National Liberation," *Perspectives in American History*, 6 (1972), 167–306.

Chapter III: The First Continental Congress

1. Butterfield, ed., *Diary of Adams*, II, 97–114; Deane to Elizabeth Deane, New York, 29 Aug. 1774, in "Correspondence of Deane," *Colls. CHS*, 2 (1870), 144.

2. *LDC*, I, 6–9. For convenience, citations from Adams's diary will be made from this source rather than the Butterfield edition.

3. For events in Massachusetts, see Patterson, *Political Parties in Massachusetts*, 91–108; on the scope of the Powder Alarm, see the entry for 17 Nov. 1774 in Franklin B. Dexter, ed., *The Literary Diary of Ezra Stiles* (New York, 1901), I, 476–85.

4. Carroll to Charles Carroll of Annapolis (hereafter cited as Carroll, Sr.), 12 Sept. 1774, in Thomas O'Brien Hanley, ed., The Charles Carroll Papers (microfilm, Wilmington, 1972), reel 1, f. 422; and see Carroll's other letters to Carroll, Sr., 7 and 9 Sept., *ibid.*, f. 420, 421. Though not himself a delegate, Carroll was in Philadelphia at the time and enjoyed close connections with the Maryland delegation.

5. Hawley to J. Adams, Northampton, 25 July 1774, Taylor, ed., *Papers of Adams*, II, 117–21; Carroll to Carroll, Sr., 9 Sept. 1774; Reed to [Charles Pettit?], 4 Sept. 1774, Joseph Reed Papers, reel 1, NYHS; J. Adams to William Tudor, 29 Sept. 1774, *LDC*, I, 130–1.

6. Joseph Warren to S. Adams, 15 and 21 Aug. 1774, in Richard Frothingham, *Life and Times of Joseph Warren* (Boston, 1865), 339–40. Adams's reply, written from Hartford, is not extant, but its contents can be inferred from Warren's second letter.

7. The first draft of the Suffolk Resolves is in the Joseph Palmer Papers, MHS; the text received and approved by Congress is in *JCC*, I, 32–7; on the framing of the Resolves, see John Cary, *Joseph Warren: Physician, Politician, Patriot* (Urbana, Ill., 1961), 151–60.

8. *JCC*, I, 35.

9. Joseph Galloway, *Historical and Political Reflections on the Rise and Progress of the American Revolution* (London, 1780), 67.

10. On the impact the Resolves had in England, see Bailyn, *Hutchinson*, 303–5.

11. S. Adams to Joseph Warren, 25 Sept. 1774; J. Adams to William Tudor, 29 Sept. 1774, and to Joseph Palmer, 26 Sept. 1774; all in *LDC*, I, 100, 129–31, 106. For examples of the proposals for more forceful measures that the Massachusetts delegates were receiving from their correspondents, see Tudor to J. Adams, 17 Sept. 1774, Taylor, ed. *Papers of Adams*, II, 167; Thomas Young to S. Adams, Boston, 4 Sept. 1774, S. Adams Papers, box 2, NYPL; Joseph Warren to S. Adams, Boston, 12 Sept. 1774, in Frothingham, *Warren*, 376; and Benjamin Kent to Robert Treat Paine, Boston, 15 Sept. 1774, and Joseph Greenleaf to Paine, Boston, 16 Oct. 1774, R. T. Paine Papers, MHS.

12. *JCC*, I, 55–62; for Samuel Adams's draft of the Gage letter, see *LDC*, I, 158–60; and see the draft resolutions that John Adams prepared *circa* Sept. 30., *ibid.*, 131–2. For later explications of Congress's intentions toward Massachusetts, see Joseph Hawley to Thomas Cushing, Northampton, 22 Feb. 1775, in *Colls.* MHS, 4th ser., 4 (1858), 393–7;

James Duane to Thomas Johnson, New York, 29 Dec. 1774; John Dickinson to Cushing, 26 Jan. 1775; and Cushing to Dickinson, Boston, 13 Feb. 1775; all in *LDC*, I, 276–8, 301–2, 310–11.

13. This motion was made by George Ross and seconded by Galloway, probably during the October debate on Massachusetts; J. Adams to [Edward Biddle?], 12 Dec. 1774, *LDC*, I, 265–6.

14. *JCC*, I, 41, 43, 51–2; John Adams, Notes of Debates for 26 and 27 Sept., *LDC*, I, 103–5.

15. P. Livingston to Duane, New York, 27 Sept. 1774, "The Duane Letters," *Publications* of the Southern History Association, 8 (1904), 53.

16. *JCC*, I, 53, 62–3, 74–81; J. Adams, Notes of Debates, 6 Oct. 1774, and Deane, Diary, 6 Oct. 1774, *LDC*, I, 151–4; cf. Ammerman, *In the Common Cause*, 73–87.

17. *LDC*, I, 103. On the assumptions underlying American faith in commercial resistance, see Maier, *From Resistance to Revolution*, 251–5, and Paul L. Ford, "The Association of the First Congress," *Political Science Quarterly*, 6 (1891), 613–24.

18. Maier, *From Resistance to Revolution*, 235–7.

19. *JCC*, I, 79.

20. Randolph to Henry Tazewell, 3 Feb. 1775, Frederick Dearborn Collection, pt. I, box 4, HUL.

21. For more comprehensive discussions of the American acceptance of republicanism, see Willi Paul Adams, "Republicanism in Political Rhetoric Before 1776," *Political Science Quarterly*, 85 (1970), 397–421; Pauline Maier, "The Beginnings of American Republicanism, 1765–1776," in *The Development of a Revolutionary Mentality* (Washington, D.C., 1974), 99–117; and Gordon S. Wood, *The Creation of the American Republic, 1776–1787* (Chapel Hill, 1969), 46–124.

22. *JCC*, I, 27–9; and see Edmund Burnett's notes on the proceedings of the two committees, *LMCC*, I, 45–7 n.

23. On Galloway, see Robert M. Calhoon, " 'I Have Deduced Your Rights': Joseph Galloway's Concept of His Role, 1774–1775," *Pennsylvania History*, 35 (1968), 356–78, and Julian P. Boyd, *Anglo-American Union: Joseph Galloway's Plans to Preserve the British Empire, 1774–1788* (Philadelphia, 1941).

24. Other identifiable moderates included Isaac Low and John Alsop (N.Y.) George Ross (Pa.), Thomas Johnson (Md.), William Hooper (N.C.), and John Rutledge (S.C.).

25. J. Adams, Notes of Debates, 8 Sept. 1774; James Duane, Speech, 8 Sept. 1774; and Samuel Ward, Diary, 9 Sept. 1774; *LDC*, I, 46–8, 51–4, 59.

26. J. Adams, Notes of Debates, 28 Sept. 1774, and Galloway's Plan of Union, *LDC*, I, 109–12, 117–18.

27. Galloway, *Historical and Political Reflections*, 66.

28. Similar conclusions have been reached by Ammerman, *In the Common Cause*, 57–60, and by the editors of *LDC*, I, 112–17 n.

29. *LDC*, I, 133.

30. *LDC*, I, 133–4. It is possible that Duane's resolution also included provisions promising that the assemblies would "provide a Competent and honourable Support" for royal officials, including judges, in the colonies. In an earlier set of resolutions presented to the committee on rights, he had linked expenditures for defense and civil government; and in describing the delegates' decision to postpone debate on Duane's motion until October 3, Silas Deane referred to it as "respecting Administration of Justice." Cf. Duane, Propositions, *LDC*, I, 42.

31. *LDC*, I, 138–40.

32. *JCC*, I, 53–4. Because Congress voted by delegations rather than individually, the meaning of a "unanimous" decision is ambiguous.

33. *LDC*, I, 143–5; *JCC*, I, 42, 54–5; cf. Ammerman, *In the Common Cause*, 63–6, for a somewhat different interpretation.

34. J. Adams, Diary, 14 Oct. 1774; and see the other notes of debates kept by Duane, R. T. Paine, and Samuel Ward, 12–13 Oct. 1774, *LDC*, I, 180–92.

35. *JCC*, I, 63–71; Duane, Propositions, and Galloway to Samuel Verplanck, 30 Dec. 1774, *LDC*, I, 40–2, 284. It now seems possible that John Dickinson participated in the drafting of the statement on grievances and rights *prior* to his late election to Congress; *LDC*, I, 193–4 n.

36. *JCC*, I, 71; cf. Ammerman, *In the Common Cause*, 63–71, for a fuller treatment.

37. *JCC*, I, 115–21; drafts by Patrick Henry, R. H. Lee, and Dickinson are in *LDC*, I, 222–33; Edwin Wolf, 2d, "The Authorship of the 1774 Address to the King Restudied," *WMQ*, 22 (1965), 189–224. The editors of *LDC* have suggested that "Dickinson played a more prominent role at the First Continental Congress than has been previously appreciated," as his participation in the drafting of the statement on grievances and rights, the memorial to the colonists, and the address to the king all attest. It is also apparent that he was in regular contact with members of Congress prior to his election. Still, his absence from the floor of debate would almost certainly have circumscribed his influence as positions were being hammered out in late September and early October.

38. *JCC*, I, 119.

39. Conn. Delegates to Gov. Trumbull, 10 Oct. 1774; Samuel Ward to Gov. Wanton, 3 Oct. 1774; *LDC*, I, 141, 169.

40. Cf. Ammerman, "A Note on Consensus," *In the Common Cause*, 89–101.

Chapter IV: War and Politics, 1775–1776

1. *JCC*, I, 102; Ward to R. H. Lee, Westerly, R.I., 14 Dec. 1774, *LDC*, I, 271–3.

2. William Williams to Thomas Williams, Hartford, 27 April 1775, Gratz Collection, case 12, box 1, HSP.

3. On the emergence of loyalism, see, in general, William Nelson, *The American Tory* (Oxford, 1961); Robert M. Calhoon, *The Loyalists in Revolutionary America* (New York, 1973); and Mary Beth Norton, *The British-Americans: The Loyalist Exiles in England, 1774–1789* (Boston, 1972), 10–41.

4. [Isaac Wilkins?], *Short Advice to the Counties of New-York*, 8; *Pills for the Delegates: Or the Chairman Chastised* . . . (New York, 1775), 24.

5. [Samuel Seabury], *The Congress Canvassed* . . . ([New York], 1774), 10; [Crean Brush], *Speech of a Member of the General Assembly of New-York* . . . (New York, 1775), 8–9; [Thomas Bradbury Chandler], *What Think Ye of the Congress Now?* . . . (New York, 1775), 6–7, 15.

6. On the implementation of the Association, see Ammerman, *In the Common Cause*, 103–24. "In effect the state was being created anew," Pauline Maier has written, "and those who chose to abstain from the new arrangements were free to remain, suffering all the perils of a state of nature, or to leave"; *From Resistance to Revolution,* 279. For justifications of the popular basis of Congress's authority, see "Philadelphus," *Pa. Gazette,* 11 Jan. 1775; "Political Observations, without Order," *Pa. Packet,* 14 Nov. 1774; Robert Ross, *A Sermon, in which the Union of the Colonies Is Considered and Recommended* . . . (New York, 1776), 7–8.

7. Wentworth to Lord Dartmouth, 2 Dec. 1774, Force, ed., *American Archives,* I, 1013; Dunmore to Dartmouth, 24 Dec. 1774, in K. G. Davies, ed., *Documents of the American Revolution, 1770–1783* (Dublin, 1972–), VIII, 265–6; and see Gov. Josiah Martin to Dartmouth, New Bern, N.C., 10 March 1775, *ibid.,* IX, 71–2.

8. Cf. Calhoon, *Loyalists in Revolutionary America,* chaps. 32, 34, 37, and 39.

9. Duane to Samuel Chase, New York, 29 Dec. 1774, *LDC,* I, 277–80; and see Bernard Mason, *The Road to Independence: The Revolutionary Movement in New York, 1773–1777* (Lexington, Ky., 1966), 42–54.

10. Wentworth to Dartmouth, 2 Dec. 1774; Galloway to W. Franklin, 28 Feb. and 26 March 1775, and W. Franklin to Galloway, 12 March 1775, Davies, ed., *Documents,* IX, 57–9, 84–8, 76–8.

11. On the origins and result of Lord North's "Olive Branch" of 1775, see Weldon A. Brown, *Empire or Independence: A Study in the Failure*

of Reconciliation, 1774–1783 (Baton Rouge, La., 1941), 35–74; Boyd, ed., *Papers of Jefferson*, I, 170–4; Dunmore to Dartmouth, 25 June 1775; and see other letters to Dartmouth from W. Franklin, 6 May and 5 June 1775; Gov. Martin (N.C.), 18 May 1775; and Lt. Gov. William Bull (S.C.), 1 May 1775; all in Davies, ed., *Documents*, IX, 202, 125–8, 152–3, 139–40, 111–12.

12. Arthur and William Lee were the principal sources for the rumors of New York's bribery; see A. Lee to S. Adams, 21 Feb. 1775, S. Adams Papers, box 2, NYPL; and to John Dickinson, London, 8 April 1775, R. R. Logan Collection, box 2, HSP; Thomas Johnson to Horatio Gates, Annapolis, 18 Aug. 1775, *LDC*, I, 703.

13. Reed to Pettit, 31 Jan. 1775, in William B. Reed, *Life and Correspondence of Joseph Reed* (Philadelphia, 1847), I, 92.

14. "Marcus Brutus" [i.e., Alexander McDougall] to S. Adams, New York, 29 Jan. 1775, McDougall Papers, reel 1, NYHS; Johnson to Duane, Annapolis, 16 Dec. 1774, *LDC*, I, 273–4.

15. Dickinson to Samuel Ward, 29 Jan. 1775, *LDC*, I, 303.

16. A. Lee to Cushing, 6 Dec. 1774, C.O. 5/118, Public Record Office, London (I owe this reference to Pauline Maier); for another comment on a reported rift between Adams and Cushing, cf. Robert T. Paine to Stephen Collins, Taunton, 25 Feb. 1775, *LDC*, I, 317–18.

17. Deane to Patrick Henry, Wethersfield, Conn., 2 Jan. 1775; Samuel Ward to Dickinson, and to R. H. Lee, Westerly, R.I., 14 Dec. 1774; Chase to Duane, 5 Feb. 1775, and to Dickinson, 6 Feb. 1775; all in *LDC*, I, 291, 269–73, 304–8.

18. Randolph to Landon Carter, 6 Jan. 1775, Fogg Collection, vol. 21, Maine Historical Society.

19. Events in Britain are briefly surveyed in Jensen, *Founding of a Nation*, 569–83, and Ammerman, *In the Common Cause*, 125–38.

20. Hancock to Dorothy Quincy, New York, 7 May 1775, in Edward E. Salisbury, *Family-Memorials: A Series of Genealogical and Biographical Monographs . . .* ([New Haven], 1885), I, 329.

21. Ward to R. H. Lee, 14 Dec. 1774; *JCC*, II, 13–22.

22. *JCC*, II, 53; Deane, Diary, 16 May 1775, *LDC*, I, 351–2.

23. Deane, Diary, 23 May 1775; Dickinson, Notes for a Speech and Proposed Resolutions [23–25? May 1775]; *LDC*, I, 371–86 (quotations at 371, 375, 384).

24. Deane, Diary, 23 and 24 May 1775; and see a second set of notes that Dickinson prepared as a rejoinder to his critics; *LDC*, I, 371, 386–91, 401–2. Dickinson's intentions are analyzed in Jacobson, *John Dickinson*, 86–91. For an attempt to strike a compromise position, see Edmund Pendleton's Proposed Resolutions [24–26? May 1775], *LDC*, I, 402–6.

25. *JCC*, II, 64–6.

26. *JCC*, II, 80; Benjamin H. Newcomb, *Franklin and Galloway: A Political Partnership* (New Haven and London, 1972), 259–70.

27. J. Adams to James Warren, 6 July 1775, *LDC*, I, 589.
28. J. Adams to James Warren, 24 July 1775, 6 July 1775, *LDC*, I, 658, 589.
29. Massachusetts Prov. Congress to Cont. Congress, Watertown, 16 May 1775, *JCC*, II, 76–8, 83–4; S. Adams to Joseph Warren, 24 Sept. 1774, *LDC*, I, 94–5.
30. N.Y. Prov. Congress to N.Y. Delegates, New York, 29 June 1775, and Gouverneur Morris to John Jay, New York, 30 June 1775, both in Richard B. Morris, ed., *John Jay: The Making of a Revolutionary* (New York, 1975–), I, *Unpublished Papers, 1745–1780*, 155–8; N.Y. Delegates to N.Y. Prov. Congress, 6 July 1775, *LDC*, I, 596–7.
31. *JCC*, II, 75.
32. *JCC*, II, 109–10. The immediate cause of the revocation of the earlier resolution was a report of British incitement of an Indian invasion of northern New York, but that information scarcely overshadowed the general policy considerations implicit in an invasion of Canada.
33. On the evolution of the "Declaration of the Causes and Necessity for Taking Up Arms," see the introductory notes to the four drafts of that document published in Boyd, ed., *Papers of Jefferson*, I, 187–219, esp. 190–2.
34. *JCC*, II, 157–62; cf. John Jay's draft of the royal petition, *LDC*, I, 440–1; on Congress's response to Parliament's conciliatory proposal, see *JCC*, II, 62–3, 202, 224–34.
35. *JCC*, II, 85–6, 89–94, 103, 111–22.
36. S. Adams to Elizabeth Adams, 30 July 1775, *LDC*, I, 683.
37. Johnson to Horatio Gates, Annapolis, 18 Aug. 1775, *LDC*, I, 703.
38. Texts of the royal proclamation and speech are reprinted in Merrill Jensen, ed., *American Colonial Documents to 1776* [*English Historical Documents*, IX (New York and London, 1955)], 850–2; Duane to Robert Livingston, 5 Jan. 1776, Duane Papers, reel 1, NYHS.
39. Pauline Maier has argued that American disillusionment with the king can be traced to the early 1770's; *From Resistance to Revolution*, 198–219, 236–41.
40. *JCC*, III, 319, 326–7; N.H. Delegates to Matthew Thornton, 3 Nov. 1775, *LDC*, II, 292–3.
41. Wood, *Creation of the American Republic*, 127–32.
42. On New York, see Edward Countryman, "Consolidating Power in Revolutionary America: The Case of New York, 1775–1783," *Journal of Interdisciplinary History*, 6 (1975–76), 645–77; on Maryland, Ronald Hoffman, *A Spirit of Dissension: Economics, Politics, and the Revolution in Maryland* (Baltimore, 1973), 152–95; and on Pennsylvania, Wood, *Creation of the American Republic*, 226–37.
43. J. Adams, Notes of Debates, 4, 5, 6, 12, 20, 21, and 27 Oct. 1775,

LDC, II, 106–12, 126–7, 165–9, 211–15, 220–4, 261–2; and see J. Adams to James Warren, 7 Oct. 1775; Robert Livingston, Notes for a Speech, 27 Oct. 1775; and Franklin to C. W.F. Dumas, 9 Dec. 1775; all in *LDC*, II, 135–8, 263–71, 466–7.

44. J. Adams, Notes of Debates, 7 Oct. 1775, *LDC*, II, 132–3.

45. Richard Smith, Diary, 13 March 1776, *LMCC*, I, 386.

46. Dickinson, Proposed Instructions, November 1775, *LDC*, II, 319–20; Chase to J. Adams, 8 Dec. 1775, Adams Family Papers, reel 345, MHS.

47. Johnson to Gates, 18 Aug. 1775; J. Adams, Notes of Debates, 6 Oct. 1775.

48. Morris to Inglis, 30 Jan. 1776, Dearborn Collection, pt. I, box 3, HUL.

49. Livingston to Duane, 16 Feb. 1776, R. R. Livingston Papers, Bancroft Transcripts, NYPL; to Robert T. Paine, 26 Feb. 1776, R. T. Paine Papers, MHS.

50. *JCC*, IV, 146; for other uses of this motto, see William Hooper to Samuel Johnston, 6 Feb. 1776, and John Penn to Thomas Person, 14 Feb. 1776, *LMCC*, I, 348 n. 4, 349.

51. *JCC*, II, 253–5, III, 392; Notes of Delegates' Remarks to N.J. Assembly [5 Dec. 1775], *LDC*, II, 443–5.

Chapter V: Independence

1. Bernard Bailyn, "The Central Themes of the American Revolution," in Kurtz and Hutson, *Essays*, 16; Pettit to Reed, 25 March 1776, Joseph Reed Papers, reel 1, NYHS; see Reed to Pettit, Cambridge, 29 Aug. 1775, and Phila., 13 Jan. 1775 [i.e., 1776], *ibid.*

2. From the postscript to the second edition of *Common Sense*, reprinted in Philip Foner, ed., *The Complete Writings of Thomas Paine* (New York, 1945), I, 40.

3. On this celebrated pamphlet, see Bernard Bailyn, "Common Sense," in *Fundamental Testaments of the American Revolution* (Washington, D.C., 1973), 7–22, and Eric Foner, *Tom Paine and Revolutionary America* (New York, 1976), 71–106.

4. Richard Smith, Diary, 9 Jan. 1776, *LMCC*, I, 304; Morris, ed., *John Jay*, I, 198–200.

5. *JCC*, IV, 87, 134–46; R. Smith, Diary, 13 Feb. 1776, and S. Adams to J. Adams, 15 Jan. 1776, *LMCC*, I, 348, 311. The curious tone of Wilson's address is discussed from a slightly different perspective in Bailyn, *Ideological Origins*, 281–3.

6. S. Adams to J. Adams, 15 Jan. 1776; Richard Smith, Diary, 16 Jan. 1776, 22 March 1776, *LMCC*, I, 313, 404.

7. Tudor to J. Adams, Cambridge, 29 Feb. 1776, Adams Family Papers, reel 345, MHS.

8. S. Adams to Samuel Cooper, 30 April 1776, Cushing, ed., *Writings of Adams*, III, 281–3; and see J. Adams to Henry Knox, 2 June 1776, Letter Book, May 1776–February 1778, Adams Family Papers, reel 89, MHS.

9. Jensen, ed., *American Colonial Documents*, 853.

10. R. Smith, Diary, 15 March 1776, and Smith to Pres. of N.J. Convention, 16 March 1776, *LMCC*, I, 393, 396; James H. Hutson, "The Partition Treaty and the Declaration of American Independence," *Journal of American History*, 58 (1971–72), 875–96.

11. J. Adams to James Warren, 7 Oct. 1775, *LDC*, II, 135–8.

12. Penn to Thomas Person, 14 Feb. 1776; R. Smith, Diary, 16 and 29 Feb., 11 March 1776; Carter Braxton to Landon Carter, 14 April 1776; all in *LMCC*, I, 349, 350–2, 369, 385, 420.

13. Comm. of Secret Correspondence to Deane, 3 March 1776, *LMCC*, I, 375–7.

14. A number of letters tracing the progress of popular support for independence can be found in the Adams Family Papers, reels 345–6, MHS, and the S. Adams Papers, box 2, NYPL.

15. For the removal of instructions against independence, see Jensen, *Founding of a Nation*, 677–81; Archibald Bulloch to S. Adams, Savannah, 1 May 1776, S. Adams Papers, box 3, NYPL; Bulloch to J. Adams, 1 May 1776, Adams Family Papers, reel 346, MHS; J. Penn to J. Adams, Halifax, N.C., 17 April 1776, *ibid.*, reel 345; James McClurg to Jefferson, Williamsburg, 6 April 1776, Boyd, ed., *Papers of Jefferson*, I, 287; and John Page to R. H. Lee, Williamsburg, 12 April 1776, Lee Family Papers, reel 2 (UVa).

16. Wolcott to Laura Wolcott, 17 April 1776, and R. Morris to Horatio Gates, 6 April 1776, *LMCC*, I, 427, 416; and see Pettit to Reed, 25 March 1776; John Jay to Alexander McDougall, 11 April 1776, Morris, ed., *John Jay*, I, 253–4; C. Carroll to Carroll, Sr., 18–19 March 1776, Charles Carroll Papers, reel 1, f. 497, MdHS; Joseph Reed to Washington, 15 March 1776, in W. B. Reed, *Life of Reed*, I, 173; Joseph Hawley to S. Adams, Northampton, 17 May 1776, S. Adams Papers, box 3, NYPL.

17. John Hancock to Mass. Assembly, 16 May 1776, and Josiah Bartlett to John Langdon, 19 May 1776, *LMCC*, I, 450, 458; and see Burnett's note, 458 n. 5. James H. Hutson argues that "the fear of a partition treaty, fantastic though its origin may have been, commanded the minds of American leaders in the spring and summer of 1776 and appears to have been the most important factor which produced the July 2, 1776, resolution of Congress, declaring America independent"; Hutson, "Partition Treaty," 896. There are, it seems to me, two critical flaws in this argument. One is that during the final debates over independence the

specter of a partition treaty was invoked as a reason for *not* declaring independence. See Jefferson's Notes of Proceedings in the Continental Congress [7 June–4 July 1776], Boyd, ed., *Papers of Jefferson*, I, 310–11; and J. H. Powell, "Speech of John Dickinson Opposing the Declaration of Independence, 1 July 1776," *Pennsylvania Magazine of History and Biography*, 65 (1941), 458–81. The second and more important weakness is that the advocates of independence no longer believed partition was likely. Although it is true that, early in the spring, R. H. Lee and Patrick Henry had seriously discussed the possibility of partition, by June American radicals were convinced that the government was committed to war. It therefore became necessary to solicit French assistance not to preclude a partition treaty but to acquire much-needed support against the British and their new mercenary recruits. Compare Lee's candid acknowledgment of his fear of partition in his April 20 letter to Henry in Ballagh, ed., *Letters of Lee*, I, 177–9, with his June 2 letter to Landon Carter in *LMCC*, I, 468–9.

18. *JCC*, IV, 213, 229–33, 257–9.

19. Jefferson to Thomas Nelson, 16 May 1776, Boyd, ed., *Papers of Jefferson*, I, 292; Jay to McDougall, 11 April 1776.

20. *JCC*, IV, 342; Braxton to Landon Carter, 17 May 1776, Fogg Collection, Maine Historical Society.

21. *JCC*, IV, 357–8; J. Adams, Notes of Debates [13–15 May 1776], Butterfield, ed., *Diary of Adams*, II, 238–40.

22. Hoffman, *A Spirit of Dissension*, 163–8; David Hawke, *In the Midst of a Revolution* (Philadelphia, 1961).

23. Duane to Jay, 18 and 25 May 1776, Morris, ed., *John Jay*, I, 266–9; Stone to an unknown recipient, 20 May 1776, Stone Family Papers, LC; J. Adams to James Warren, 20 May 1776, *LMCC*, I, 461.

24. Braxton to Carter, 17 May 1776; William Whipple to John Langdon, 18 May 1776, *LMCC*, I, 456.

25. *JCC*, IV, 358–63; Hancock to John Thomas, 24 May 1776; Elbridge Gerry to James Warren, 20 May 1776; both in *LMCC*, I, 463, 457–8. The petition and the king's reply are reprinted in Force, ed., *American Archives*, 4th ser., V, 462–3.

26. J. Adams to Patrick Henry, 3 June 1776, and R. H. Lee to Landon Carter, 2 June 1776, both in *LMCC*, I, 471, 468–9; Livingston to Jay, 4 June 1776, Morris, ed., *John Jay*, I, 273; Morris to Silas Deane, 5 June 1776, in Charles Isham, ed., *The Deane Papers* (*Colls.* NYHS, 1886–90), I, 137–9.

27. Jefferson, Notes of Proceedings, Boyd, ed., *Papers of Jefferson*, I, 309–15.

28. Jensen, *Founding of a Nation*, 691–701; Eliphalet Dyer to Gerry, Hartford, 18 June 1776, Gerry Papers II, MHS; on Maryland, see Md. Delegates to Md. Council of Safety, 11 and 15 June 1776, *LMCC*, I, 485,

492; and Benjamin Rumsey to William Rumsey [mid-June 1776], Rumsey Family Papers, box 2, LC; Powell, "Speech of John Dickinson"; *JCC*, V, 507.

29. Stone to unknown recipient, 20 May 1776; J. Adams to Abigail Adams, 3 July 1776, in L. H. Butterfield and Marc Friedlaender, eds., *Adams Family Correspondence* (Cambridge, 1963–), II, 30.

30. Livingston to Laurens, 5 Feb. 1778, in Philip Hamer, ed., *The Papers of Henry Laurens in the South Carolina Historical Society* (microfilm, Charleston, 1966), Livingston-Laurens Letters, reel 15.

31. Merrill Jensen, *The Articles of Confederation: An Interpretation of the Social-Constitutional History of the American Revolution, 1774–1781* (Madison, 1940), 54–103; H. James Henderson, *Party Politics in the Continental Congress* (New York, 1974), 32–69; Joseph L. Davis, *Sectionalism in American Politics, 1774–1787* (Madison, 1977), 7–22.

32. E. Rutledge to Jay, 29 June 1776, Morris, ed., *John Jay*, I, 281; W. Sabine, ed., *Historical Memoirs of William Smith*, II, 64.

33. Pendleton to Joseph Chew, 15 June 1775, *LDC*, I, 488.

34. Deane, Diary, 24 May 1775, *LDC*, I, 402; Chase to J. Adams, 8 Dec. 1775, 21 and 28 June 1776, Adams Family Papers, reels 345 and 346, MHS; Chase to Dickinson, Annapolis, 29 Sept. 1776, 19 Oct. 1776, and undated [October 1776], R. R. Logan Collection, box 2, HSP.

35. Jay to McDougall, 11 April 1776; Livingston to Jay, 4 June 1776.

36. Johnson to Horatio Gates, 18 Aug. 1775, *LDC*, I, 704.

37. On the rigidity of British belief and policymaking, see Jack P. Greene, "The Plunge of Lemmings: A Consideration of Recent Writings on British Politics and the American Revolution," *South Atlantic Quarterly*, 67 (1968), 141–75; for other discussions of the government's inability to compromise, see Greene, "An Uneasy Connection," in Kurtz and Hutson, *Essays*, 32–80; and John Shy, "The Spectrum of Imperial Possibilities: Henry Ellis and Thomas Pownall, 1763–1775," in Shy, *A People Numerous and Armed: Reflections on the Military Struggle for American Independence* (New York, 1976), 35–72.

38. Ira Gruber, "The American Revolution as a Conspiracy," *WMQ*, 26 (1969), 360–72.

39. Morris to Deane, 5 June 1776; W. Sabine, ed., *Historical Memoirs of William Smith*, I, 273.

40. Wolcott to Laura Wolcott, 16 May 1776, *LMCC*, I, 449; and see Wolcott to Samuel Lyman, 27 March 1776, Dreer Collection, HSP.

41. J. Adams, Notes of Debates, 6 Sept. 1774, *LDC*, I, 28; S. Adams to Cooper, 30 April 1776; Robert Ross, *A Sermon . . .*, 13–14; Conn. Delegates to Gov. Trumbull, 10 Oct. 1774, *LDC*, I, 169.

42. S. Adams to Benjamin Kent, 27 July 1776, Cushing, ed., *Writings of Adams*, III, 304–5.

43. Duane to Robert Livingston, 7 June 1775, *LDC*, I, 454; Arthur

Middleton to William H. Drayton, 14 Sept. 1776, *South Carolina Histori-cal Magazine*, 27 (1926), 144.

44. Wood, *Creation of the American Republic*, 102.

Chapter VI: A Lengthening War

1. On the campaign of late 1776, see Piers Mackesy, *The War for America, 1775–1783* (Cambridge, 1965), 82–120; Ira Gruber, *The Howe Brothers and the American Revolution* (Chapel Hill, 1972), 89–157; the creation of the Howe Commission is analyzed in Brown, *Empire or Independence*, 75–107.

2. Morris to Joseph Reed, 21 July 1776, and Bartlett to John Langdon, 22 July 1776, *LMCC*, II, 19–21; Charles Carroll to Carroll, Sr., 29 July 1776, Carroll Papers, reel 1, f. 451, MdHS; *JCC*, V, 592–3.

3. Bartlett to William Whipple, 3 Sept. 1776; Witherspoon, Speech [5? Sept. 1776]; Huntington to M. Griswold, E. Dyer, and W. Pitkin, 7 Sept. 1776; all in *LMCC*, II, 66–7, 70–4, 76–7.

4. Rodney to George Read, 7 Sept. 1776, and Williams to Joseph Trumbull, 13 Sept. 1776, *LMCC*, II, 77, 85–7. The committee's report is in *JCC*, V, 765–6. For other comments see J. Adams to Abigail Adams, 6 Sept. 1776, and Bartlett to Whipple, 14 Sept. 1776, *LMCC*, II, 74–5, 88–9.

5. Comm. of Secret Correspondence to Commissioners at Paris, 21 Dec. 1776, *LMCC*, II, 181–3.

6. J. Adams to S. Adams, 17 Sept. 1776, *LMCC*, II, 91–3. Samuel Adams and William Whipple had both left Congress shortly before Sullivan's arrival and were surprised and concerned to learn that Congress had reversed its earlier decision against meeting with Howe; S. Adams to J. Adams, Boston, 16 and 30 Sept. 1776, Cushing, ed., *Writings of Adams*, III, 312–15; Whipple to Bartlett, Portsmouth, 23 Sept. 1776, Declaration of Independence Collection, HUL.

7. W. Sabine, ed., *Historical Memoirs of William Smith*, II, 62–4; Carroll to Carroll, Sr., 10 and 18 Oct. 1776, 15 March 1777, Carroll Papers, reel 1, f. 550, 551, 566, MdHS; Morris to American Commissioners, Phila., 21 Dec. 1776, in Francis Wharton, ed., *Revolutionary Diplomatic Correspondence of the United States* (Washington, D.C., 1889), II, 235–6.

8. W. Sabine, ed., *Historical Memoirs of William Smith*, II, 81.

9. Burke, Abstract of Debates, 21 Feb. 1777; Benjamin Rush to R. Morris, 22 Feb. 1777; *LMCC*, II, 268–71.

10. Deane to Comm. of Secret Correspondence, Paris, 28 Nov. 1776, Wharton, ed., *Rev. Dipl. Corr.*, II, 197–8; E. Gerry to John Wendell, 11 June 1776, Gratz Collection, case 1, box 19, HSP; J. Adams to John Winthrop, 23 June 1776, *LMCC*, I, 502. On the framing of the model treaty

of 1776, see Felix Gilbert, *To the Farewell Address: Ideas of Early American Foreign Policy* (Princeton, 1961), 44–75, and the more recent argument, critical of Gilbert, developed by William Stinchcombe, "John Adams and the Model Treaty," in Lawrence S. Kaplan, ed., *The American Revolution and "A Candid World"* (Kent, Ohio, 1977), 69–84.

11. Morris to Jay, 23 Sept. 1776, Morris, ed., *John Jay*, I, 317; and to American Commissioners, 21 Dec. 1776.

12. On the campaign of 1777, see Mackesy, *War for America*, 103–44; Gruber, *Howe Brothers*, 158–267.

13. *JCC*, IX, 946, 951–2, 975. Adams was appointed not only to replace Deane, but also because some delegates apparently believed Franklin might be too old and infirm to carry on strenuous negotiations —see James Lovell to J. Adams [28 Nov. 1777], Adams Family Papers, reel 348, MHS; Henry Laurens to John Rutledge, 12 Aug. 1777, and Gerry to J. Adams, 29 Sept. 1779, *LMCC*, II, 448, IV, 454–5.

14. On the French decision, see Edward S. Corwin, *French Policy and the American Alliance of 1778* (Princeton, 1916); Samuel Flagg Bemis, *The Diplomacy of the American Revolution* (New York, 1935), 41–69; and Jonathan Dull, *The French Navy and American Independence: A Study of Arms and Diplomacy, 1774–1787* (Princeton, 1976), 68–101.

15. On the appointment and frustrating career of the Carlisle Commission, see Brown, *Empire or Independence*, 205–93.

16. Virginia Delegates to Gov. Henry, 21 April 1778, *LMCC*, III, 180–1; *JCC*, X, 374–80; and see Laurens to Duane, 17–20 April 1778; Samuel Chase to Gov. Johnson, 20 April 1778; and John Henry, Jr., to Johnson, 20 April 1778; all in *LMCC*, III, 170–1, 179–80.

17. *JCC*, XI, 572–5, 605–6, 614–15. For comments on the motives of the commissioners and how Congress should respond, see Charles Thomson, Memorandum, and drafts of replies to their proclamations by R. H. Lee and John Witherspoon, all prepared *circa* 16 June 1778, *LMCC*, III, 295–7; S. Adams to R. H. Lee, Boston, 20 April 1778, Cushing, ed., *Writings of Adams*, IV, 22–4; Lovell to J. Adams, 15 May 1778, Adams Family Papers, reel 349, MHS; Schuyler to McDougall, Saratoga, 1 May 1778, McDougall Papers, reel 2, NYHS; Schuyler to Gouverneur Morris, Albany, 17 May 1778, Gouverneur Morris Papers, folder 1212, Columbia University Library, N.Y.; Robert R. Livingston to William Duer, Clare Mount, N.Y., 3 July 1778, R. R. Livingston Papers, box 4, NYHS; William Livingston to Laurens, Morristown, N.J., 22 July 1778, Livingston-Laurens Letters, Laurens Papers, reel 15, SCHS.

18. "The Gamester: A New Song," *Boston Gazette*, 24 Aug. 1778; for the publication of other articles, see *LMCC*, III, 359 n. 2, 360 n. 2, 421 n. 2, 514 n. 2.

19. Reed to Elizabeth Reed, Headquarters, 11 Oct. 1776, Reed Pa-

pers, reel 1, NYHS; Thomson to Dickinson, 29 July 1776, John Dickinson Papers, box 2, item 26, HSP.

20. Jonathan G. Rossie, *The Politics of Command in the American Revolution* (Syracuse, N.Y., 1975), 107–53; Henderson, *Party Politics*, 112–20.

21. Chase to Dickinson [Annapolis, October 1776], R. R. Logan Collection, box 2, HSP; Carroll to Carroll, Sr. [Annapolis], 18 Oct. 1776, and see his other letters of 4, 10, and 20 Oct. 1776, Carroll Papers, reel 1, MdHS; Livingston to George Clinton, 15 Sept. 1776, Sparks Papers, XII, p. 7, HUL.

22. Hoffman, *A Spirit of Dissension*, 169–241.

23. Mason, *Road to Independence*, 213–49, discusses the framing of the New York constitution; Livingston to William Duer, 12 June 1777, R. R. Livingston Papers, box 3, NYHS.

24. Robert Brunhouse, *The Counter-Revolution in Pennsylvania, 1776–1790* (Harrisburg, Pa., 1942), 18–52. For early comments on constitutional strife in Pennsylvania, see Duane to Jay, *et al.*, 19 April 1777, and William Duer to Jay, 28 May 1777, Morris, ed., *John Jay*, I, 386–7, 406–7; Henry Laurens to John Laurens, 30 Aug. 1777, Laurens Papers, reel 5, SCHS.

25. Wood, *Creation of the American Republic*, 127–96; still useful as a survey of constitution-writing is Allan Nevins, *The American States During and After the Revolution* (New York, 1924), 117–70.

26. J. Adams to Horatio Gates, 23 March 1776, and to Abigail Adams, 17 May 1776, *LMCC*, I, 406, 453. Adams also recognized, however, that this process could hurt the war effort if it distracted attention from other urgent matters; see his letter to Benjamin Hichborn, 29 May 1776, Adams Family Papers, reel 89, MHS.

27. Mather to S. Adams, Boston, 22 April 1777, S. Adams Papers, box 4, NYPL. These themes are so pervasive in the political correspondence of the late 1770's that further citation seems unnecessary; but the correspondence of Henry Laurens for 1777 and 1778 contains a number of detailed and pungent discussions of the deterioration of public "virtue"; Laurens Papers, reels 5 and 6, SCHS.

28. John Shy, "The Military Conflict Considered as a Revolutionary War," in *A People Numerous and Armed*, 193–224; Ronald Hoffman, "The 'Disaffected' in the Revolutionary South," in Alfred Young, ed., *The American Revolution: Explorations in the History of American Radicalism* (DeKalb, Ill., 1976), 275–316.

29. Franklin and Morris to Deane, 1 Oct. 1776, Isham, ed., *Deane Papers*, I, 298. For a small sample of similar comments, see James Warren to S. Adams, Watertown, 24 Oct. 1776, Ford, ed., *Warren-Adams Letters*, II, 440; S. Adams to John Pitts, 15 Feb. 1777, Cushing, ed., *Writings of Adams*, III, 359–60; Laurens to John L. Gervais, 5–9 Aug.

1777, and to John Wereat, 30 Aug. 1777, Laurens Papers, reel 6, SCHS; and John Harvie to Jefferson, 29 Dec. 1777, Boyd, ed., *Papers of Jefferson*, II, 125-7.

30. For a succinct account of economic change after 1775, see Jackson T. Main, *The Sovereign States, 1775-1783* (New York, 1973), 222-68. A satisfactory social history of the Revolution—one exploring the intersection of public events and private experience—remains to be written, although recently some scholars have begun to move in this direction, most notably John Shy's work on the militia, the essays collected in Young, ed., *The American Revolution*, and Robert A. Gross, *The Minutemen and Their World* (New York, 1976). Still, one longs for the sort of insight found, for example, in Richard Cobb's recent books on the French Revolutionary era, *Reactions to the French Revolution* (Oxford, 1972), and *Paris and Its Provinces* (Oxford, 1976).

31. Livingston to Henry Laurens, Springfield, N.J., 8 Jan. 1778, Laurens Papers, reel 15, SCHS.

32. Rush to J. Adams, 13 July 1780, in L. H. Butterfield, ed., *Letters of Benjamin Rush* (Princeton, 1951), I, 253; Laurens to John L. Gervais, 5-9 Sept. 1777, Laurens Papers, reel 6, SCHS.

33. For other examples, see John Harvie to Jefferson, 18 Oct. 1777, Boyd, ed., *Papers of Jefferson*, II, 35; Alexander Hamilton to George Clinton [Valley Forge], 13 Feb. 1778, in Harold C. Syrett and Jacob E. Cooke, eds., *The Papers of Alexander Hamilton* (New York, 1960-78), I, 425-8; and John Mathews to Thomas Bee, 17 Oct. 1778, *LMCC*, III, 453.

34. Whipple to Bartlett, 13 Jan. 1777, Josiah Bartlett Papers, Dartmouth College Library; Ellery to Gov. Cooke, 4 Dec. 1776, in William Staples, ed., *Rhode Island in the Continental Congress* (Providence, 1870), 104; Livingston to Yates, 30 Aug. 1776, Signers Collection, NYSL; Adams to Warren, 1 Feb. 1777, Cushing, ed., *Writings of Adams*, III, 350-1; and Rush to Morris, 8 Feb. 1777, *LMCC*, II, 240.

35. See Margaret Burnham Macmillan, *The War Governors in the American Revolution* (New York, 1943), 112-33; Caswell to Burke, New Bern, N.C., 13 May 1777, in Walter Clark, ed., *The State Records of North Carolina* (Winston and Goldsboro, N.C., 1895-1906), XI, 471; and see Caswell's apologies for not having the constitutional authority to call a special session of the legislature to transact necessary business, Caswell to the N.C. Delegates, New Bern, 7 Feb. 1778, *ibid.*, XIII, 31-2. For another example of a governor ignorant of legislative actions important to his state's delegates, see Virginia Delegates to Benjamin Harrison, 6 Aug. 1782; Harrison's reply of 16 Aug. 1782; and another letter from Harrison to the Delegates, 3 May 1783; all in William T. Hutchinson and William M. E. Rachal, eds., *The Papers of James Madison* (Chicago, 1962-), V, 25, 57-8, VII, 5 n.

36. Bartlett to Langdon, 13 July 1778, Sparks Papers, LII, vol. 2, p.

211, HUL; Weare to Bartlett, Hampton Falls, N.H., 8 Aug. 1778, Meshech Weare Papers, MHS.

37. Lovell to S. Adams, 10 March 1778, S. Adams Papers, box 4, NYPL; Walton to Laurens, Savannah, 26 April 1778, Laurens Papers, reel 9, SCHS; Root to E. Dyer and W. Williams, Peekskill, 31 Aug. 1777, Fogg Collection, vol. 21, Maine Historical Society; McDougall to Joseph Reed, Peekskill, 25 March 1779, Reed Papers, reel 2, NYHS; and Holt to Gov. Clinton, 15 April 1780, in Hugh Hastings, *et al.*, eds., *Public Papers of George Clinton* . . . (Albany and New York, 1899–1914), V, 622.

38. Osgood to Lovell, 2 March 1782, S. Adams Papers, box 6, NYPL.

Chapter VII: Confederation Considered

1. Jensen's views have been restated most recently in his essay "The Articles of Confederation," in Boyd, ed., *Fundamental Testaments of the American Revolution.*

2. *JCC*, II, 195–9; Saunders, ed., *State Recs. of N.C.*, X, 175–9, 191–2.

3. Deane's Proposals are printed in *LDC*, II, 418–19, from the original manuscript in the Silas Deane Papers, CHS. I am grateful to Professor Christopher Collier of the University of Bridgeport for calling the existence of this document to my attention.

4. *Pennsylvania Evening Post*, 5 March 1776; subsequently reprinted in at least four New England newspapers: *Essex Journal*, 29 March; *Connecticut Courant*, 15 April; *Boston Gazette*, 22 April; and *Newport Mercury*, 29 April; Conn. Delegates to Gov. Trumbull, 5 Dec. 1775, *LDC*, II, 440; Richard Smith, Diary, 16 Jan. 1776; and see S. Adams to James Warren, 7 Jan. 1776, and to J. Adams, 15 Jan. 1776; all in *LMCC*, I, 313, 302, 311–12.

5. John Dickinson had discussed a more limited conception of confederation during his May 1775 campaign to induce Congress to initiate negotiations. The fourth resolution that Dickinson introduced on May 23 stipulated that *after* Congress had decided what "Demands & Concessions" his proposed embassy to Britain could make, the delegates would then "associate and confederate" to continue their opposition until these objectives were achieved. Here Dickinson apparently envisioned confederation not as a scheme of government but as an agreement on the terms and duration of American opposition. In notes for a later speech, Dickinson seemed to imply that he would refuse to countenance the framing of a confederation unless Congress adopted the conciliatory measures he was advocating; *LDC*, I, 384–5, 390.

6. The first draft of the Dickinson plan is in the John Dickinson Papers, box 2, R. R. Logan Collection, HSP; I am grateful to Peter Parker of the HSP for calling it to my attention. It will be reprinted in *LDC*,

IV, under the date of 17 June 1776. Josiah Bartlett of New Hampshire prepared what is apparently a copy of Dickinson's first draft, which will be printed in a parallel format in *LDC*. Paul H. Smith has informed me that the differences between these two texts are minor, except that Bartlett omits the article on religious toleration discussed below in the text (pp. 152–3). The second draft of the Dickinson plan—that is, the draft submitted to Congress on July 12—is printed in *JCC*, V, 674–89.

7. *JCC*, V, 674–89.

8. Max Farrand, ed., *The Records of the Federal Convention of 1787* (New Haven, 1911), II, 643–4.

9. Notes of this debate (6 Sept. 1774) were kept by J. Adams and James Duane, *LDC*, I, 27–31; Jack R. Pole, *Political Representation in England and the Origins of the American Republic* (London, 1966), 344–8; and for other discussions of this issue, see Ezra Stiles's notes of a November 1774 conversation with Samuel Ward and R. T. Paine, in F. B. Dexter, ed., *Diary of Stiles*, I, 487, and S. Ward to Henry Ward, 31 Dec. 1775, *LDC*, II, 539–40.

10. Conn. Delegates to Gov. Trumbull, 10 Oct. 1774, *LDC*, I, 169; *JCC*, I, 25.

11. Deane to Henry, Wethersfield, Conn., 2 Jan. 1775, Isham, ed., *Deane Papers*, I, 38–9; and see Deane's draft of resolutions calling for an annual Congress [October 1774], Silas Deane Papers, CHS; S. Ward to R. H. Lee, 14 Dec. 1774, *LDC*, I, 271–3.

12. *JCC*, II, 77.

13. See the discussion in Julian P. Boyd and Robert J. Taylor, eds., *The Susquehannah Company Papers* (Ithaca, N.Y., 1962–71), V, xliv–lii. The Connecticut delegates' concern with this issue would have provided them with a strong incentive to advocate the necessity of a confederation; see Deane to Thomas Mumford, 16 Oct. 1775, *LDC*, II, 188–90.

14. Washington to Lund Washington, Cambridge, 20 Aug. 1775, and to R. H. Lee, 29 Aug. 1775, in John C. Fitzpatrick, ed., *The Writings of George Washington* (Washington, D.C., 1931–44), III, 433, 450–1; a number of letters complaining about southern attitudes toward New England soldiers can be found in the Adams Family Papers, reel 345, MHS; and see William Palfrey to S. Adams, 3 Oct. 1775, S. Adams Papers, box 3, NYPL.

15. See Samuel Johnston to James Iredell, Hillsborough, N.C., 5 Sept. 1775, and Iredell to Henry McCulloh, Edenton, N.C., 1 Nov. 1775, in Higginbotham, ed., *Papers of Iredell*, I, 317, 324.

16. Hawley to J. Adams, Watertown, 18 Dec. 1775, Adams Family Papers, reel 345, MHS; Hawley, "Hints for the consideration of Mr. Gerry," Gerry Papers, MHS; and see Hawley to S. Adams, 1 April 1776, and to Gerry, 13 Oct. 1776, S. Adams Papers, boxes 2 and 3, NYPL.

17. T. L. Lee to R. H. Lee, 18 May 1776, Lee Family Papers, reel 2 (UVa); Wendell to Gerry, Portsmouth, 25 June 1776, Gerry Papers II, MHS; Langdon to Bartlett, Portsmouth, 28 July 1776, Bartlett Papers, Dartmouth College Library.

18. "Spartanus," *New Hampshire Gazette,* 29 June 1776; *Pa. Packet,* 1 July 1776; and see James Sullivan to J. Adams, Watertown, 9 May 1776, Adams Family Papers, reel 346, MHS.

19. [Carter Braxton], *An Address to the Convention of . . . Virginia; on the Subject of Government* (Philadelphia, 1776), 25; [John Adams], *Thoughts on Government* (Philadelphia, 1776), 25.

20. Hawley to J. Adams, 18 Dec. 1775; *N.H. Gazette,* 29 June 1776; *Four Letters on Interesting Subjects* (Philadelphia, 1776), 23, and see 7–9.

21. Wood, *Creation of the American Republic,* 354.

22. The Litchfield resolutions were printed in the *Connecticut Courant* of 27 May 1776 and subsequently discussed by other writers in the issues of 3, 10, and 17 June 1776 and 15 and 29 Sept. 1777; and see the Norwich, Conn., resolves printed in the *Norwich Packet,* 5 Jan. 1778.

23. Wolcott to Samuel Lyman, 17 April 1776, Gratz Collection, case 1, box 20, HSP; Clark to Samuel Tucker, Elizabethtown, N.J., 29 March 1776, Roberts Collection, No. 722, Haverford College Library, Haverford, Pa. Jefferson's reservations were expressed in his second and third drafts of the Virginia constitution of 1776, Boyd, ed., *Papers of Jefferson,* I, 351, 360. On the reaction to the abortive kidnapping of Robert Eden, the last proprietary governor of Maryland, see Maryland Delegates to Council of Safety, 18 April 1776, and Thomas Johnson to Daniel of St. Thomas Jenifer, 23 April 1776, both in *LMCC,* I, 427–9; Benjamin Rumsey to William Rumsey, Westminster, Md., 3 June 1776, Rumsey Family Papers, box 2, LC; and Hoffman, *A Spirit of Dissension,* 157–63.

24. J. Adams to James Warren, 20 May 1776, *LMCC,* I, 461.

25. *JCC,* V, 431, 433.

26. Bartlett to Nathaniel Folsom, 1 July 1776, Gratz Collection, case 1, box 19, HSP.

27. Although there is no evidence that John Adams knew of Dickinson's proposed article on toleration, in a letter of 22 June 1776 to Benjamin Kent he wrote: "I am for the most liberal toleration of all denominations of religionists, but I hope that Congress will never meddle with religion further than to say their own prayers, and to fast and give thanks once a year. Let every colony have its own religion without molestation"; C. F. Adams, ed., *The Works of John Adams* (Boston, 1850–6), IX, 401–2.

28. See Jensen, *Articles of Confederation,* 150–60, for a succinct account.

29. Dickinson to Thomson, Elizabethtown, N.J., 7 Aug. [1776], *Colls.,* NYHS, 11 (1878), 29. Notes of the July and August debates on

confederation were kept by Jefferson and John Adams, and are re-printed in Boyd, ed., *Papers of Jefferson*, I, 320–7, and Butterfield, ed., *Diary of Adams*, II, 238–50.

30. Jefferson, Notes, 323–7; Adams, Notes, 247–8.

31. Jefferson, Notes, 320–3; Adams, Notes, 245–7.

32. E. Rutledge to Jay, 29 June 1776, Morris, ed., *John Jay*, I, 280–1.

33. E. Rutledge to R. R. Livingston [19? Aug. 1776], *LMCC*, II, 56.

34. Adams, Notes, 242, 246, 249; for Witherspoon, see Jefferson, Notes, 324–5; and see William Williams to Oliver Wolcott, 12 Aug. 1776, *LMCC*, II, 48.

Chapter VIII: Confederation Drafted

1. For other accounts of the deliberations of 1777, see Jensen, *Articles of Confederation*, 140–84, and Henderson, *Party Politics*, 130–56.

2. Charles Carroll to Carroll, Sr., 10 Oct. 1776 and 8 Nov. 1776, Carroll Papers, reel 1, f. 550, 556, MdHS; *JCC*, VI, 912–13; Hancock to Washington, 5 Nov. 1776, and B. Rumsey to Daniel Jenifer, 24 Nov. 1776, *LMCC*, II, 140, 162–3, and see Burnett's editorial comment, 140 n. 3.

3. George Read to R. Morris, Newcastle, Del., 4 Nov. 1776, Gratz Collection, case 1, box 10, HSP; Morris to Read, 6 Nov. 1776; B. Rush to Thomas Wharton, Jr. [1 Nov. 1776]; both in *LMCC*, II, 141, 138.

4. The proceedings are printed in C. J. Hoadly and L. W. Labaree, eds., *The Public Records of the State of Connecticut* (Hartford, 1894–1951), I, 585–99.

5. B. Rush, Diary, 4 and 14 Feb. 1777; Thomas Burke, Abstract of Debates, 12 and 15 Feb. 1777; Ellery to Gov. Cooke, 15 Feb. 1777; all in *LMCC*, II, 234–5, 249–55; *JCC*, VII, 124–5.

6. *JCC*, VII, 115–18, 154–5; Burke, Abstract of Debates, 25 Feb. 1777, *LMCC*, II, 275–81; the quotations in the following two paragraphs are taken from this source.

7. On the advantages of the committee system over the recon-stituted governments, see N.Y. Delegates to Abraham Ten Broeck, 21 and 29 April 1777, *LMCC*, II, 337, 344, and Philip Schuyler to William Duer, 7 July 1777, Sparks Papers, LX, 133–4, HUL.

8. Burke to Caswell, 4 Feb. 1777, *LMCC*, II, 235; Caswell to Burke, New Bern, N.C., 10 June 1777, Clark, ed., *State Recs. of N.C.*, XI, 494. The best discussions of Burke's career are Jennings B. Sanders, "Thomas Burke in the Continental Congress," *North Carolina Historical Review*, 9 (1932), 22–37, and Elisha P. Douglass, "Thomas Burke, Disillu-sioned Democrat," *ibid.*, 26 (1949), 150–86.

9. Burke to Caswell, 4 Feb. 1777, and Abstracts of Debate for 7, 8, and 15 Feb. 1777, *LMCC*, II, 235, 238–42, 253–4.

10. Burke to Caswell, 10 [16?] Feb. 1777, *LMCC*, II, 257, and 11 March 1777, Clark, ed., *State Recs. of N.C.*, XI, 417–23 (partly reprinted in *LMCC*, II, 294–6).

11. Burke to Caswell, Tyaguin, N.C., 4 Nov. 1777, *LMCC*, II, 542; and see Samuel Johnston to Burke, Hayes, N.C., 19 April 1777, Clark, ed., *State Recs. of N.C.*, XI, 453–4.

12. Burke to Caswell, 29 April 1777, *LMCC*, II, 345–6. Burke's revision of Article III of the August 1776 draft became Article 2 of the final draft approved in November 1777; *JCC*, IX, 908. The discussion in the following paragraphs is based on Burke's letter of the 29th.

13. The motion as well as the terse comments recorded on it are reprinted in *JCC*, VII, 328–9.

14. Burke to N.C. Assembly [August 1779], *LMCC*, IV, 367–8; John Adams, *Defence of the Constitutions of Government of the United States* (Boston, 1788), II, 362–4; and see Jefferson to Adams, Paris, 23 Feb. 1787, and Adams's reply, London, 1 March 1787, Boyd, ed., *Papers of Jefferson*, XI, 177, 190.

15. Writing to John Adams from Williamsburg on 16 May 1777, Jefferson proposed reviving the scheme of dual voting that the Connecticut delegates had previously proposed. Adams replied (26 May) that he would be willing to reconsider the merits of that scheme, "if we cannot Succeed in our Wishes for a Representation and a Rule of voting, perfectly equitable [i.e., apportioned to population], which has no equal, in my Mind"; Boyd, ed., *Papers of Jefferson*, II, 18–19, 21–2. For two further brief allusions to the unicameral nature of Congress, see [Benjamin Rush], *Observations upon the Present Government of Pennsylvania* (Philadelphia, 1777), 8, and "Whitlocke," *Pa. Gazette*, 11 July 1777.

16. Johnston to Burke, 19 April 1777; Burke to Caswell, 4 Nov. 1777; and see the two sets of Burke's comments on the confederation reprinted in *LMCC*, II, 552–8; for the action of the North Carolina assembly, see Clark, ed., *State Recs. of N.C.*, XII, 221, 229, 263, 400, 449.

17. Lovell to R. H. Lee, 22 July 1777, Lee Family Papers, reel 3 (UVa); Whipple to Bartlett, 7 Feb. 1777, *LMCC*, II, 238; Whipple to Lovell, Portsmouth, 15 July 1777, Sparks Papers, LII, vol. 2, p. 182, HUL; Dyer to William Williams, 10 March 1778, Boston Public Library.

18. Burke to Caswell, 11 May 1777, and S. Adams to James Warren, 30 June 1777, *LMCC*, II, 360, 391–2; Lovell to R. H. Lee, 22 July 1777.

19. R. H. Lee to S. Adams, Chantilly, Va., 12 July 1777, Ballagh, ed., *Letters of Lee*, I, 308; Lee's reference is almost certainly to Burke.

20. Carroll to Carroll, Sr., 23 and 26 June 1777, Carroll Papers, reel 1, f. 601–2; the Maryland instructions of 19 April 1777 are in *Votes and Proceedings of the House of Delegates of the State of Maryland. February Session, 1777* [Annapolis, 1777], 105.

21. *JCC*, IX, 953–8, 971; Williams to Jabez Huntington, 20 Oct. 1777,

and E. Dyer to Joseph Trumbull, 7 Sept. 1777, *LMCC*, II, 529, 485; and see Roger Sherman to S. Adams, New Haven, 25 Aug. 1777, S. Adams Papers, box 4, NYPL.

22. *JCC*, IX, 779–82.

23. *JCC*, IX, 806–8.

24. *JCC*, IX, 788–9, 793, 797–8, 800–1. For Witherspoon's earlier introduction of this formula, see Jefferson, Notes of Proceedings, Boyd, ed., *Papers of Jefferson*, I, 322.

25. *JCC*, IX, 841–4, 845. Merrill Jensen has argued (*Articles of Confederation*, 178) that the Council of State proposed by Dickinson "was apparently designed as the beginning of an executive organization, a permanent bureaucratic staff of the central government," while the Committee of the States provided for in 1777 was to sit only during the recess of Congress. I believe Jensen has misread Dickinson's language, and that the surviving drafts of the Dickinson plan clearly indicate that the Council was to meet only when Congress adjourned. Each of the drafts of 1776 provided that Congress, not the Council of State (or Safety, as it was called in the earliest text), would supervise the activities of all subordinate committees, boards, and offices; only when Congress recessed would the Council act in that capacity.

26. *JCC*, IX, 879–80, 885–90, 895–6, 899–900. The members of the committee were R. H. Lee, James Duane, and Richard Law.

27. The final text is printed in *JCC*, IX, 907–25; Sergeant to [Lovell], 20 Nov. 1777, S. Adams Papers, box 4, NYPL.

28. *JCC*, IX, 932–5; Folsom to Weare, 21 Nov. 1777, *LMCC*, II, 564.

29. Dyer to Joseph Trumbull, 7 Sept. 1777; and see Carroll to Carroll, Sr., 5 Oct. 1777, Carroll Papers, reel 1, f. 623, MdHS.

30. Duane to Jay, Livingston Manor, N.Y., 23 Dec. 1777, Morris, ed., *John Jay*, I, 458–9; and see Duane to R. R. Livingston, 2 Dec. 1777, R. R. Livingston Papers, box 3, NYHS; Harrison to R. Morris, 18 Dec. 1777 and 19 Feb. 1778, in Stan. V. Henkels, *The Confidential Correspondence of Robert Morris* (Philadelphia, 1917 [Henkels's Catalogue #1183]), 15, 18 (the second letter is now in the Dearborn Collection, HUL).

31. Burke's comments on the Articles, *LMCC*, II, 552–8; R. H. Lee to S. Adams, 12 July 1777.

32. William Williams to S. Adams, Lebanon, N.H., 9 Feb. 1778, S. Adams Papers, box 4, NYPL; Richard F. Upton, *Revolutionary New Hampshire* (Hanover, N.H., 1936), 73–5.

33. Knox to Henry Jackson, Derby, Pa., 25 Aug. 1777, Boston Public Library; Samuel Philbrick to Bartlett, 12 Aug. 1778, Bartlett Papers, Dartmouth College Library; and see Samuel H. Parsons to S. Adams, White Plains, 9 July 1778, S. Adams Papers, box 4, NYPL; Bartlett to N.H. Delegates, Exeter, 14 March 1778, in Frank C. Mevers, ed., The Papers of Josiah Bartlett, 1729–1795 (microfilm, Concord, N.H., 1976), reel 2.

34. Jay to Duane, Fishkill, N.Y., 14 Dec. 1777, and Duane to Jay, 23 Dec. 1777, Morris, ed., *John Jay*, I, 454, 458–9.

35. Boudinot to Alexander McDougall, 22 Jan. 1779, McDougall Papers, reel 2, NYHS; "Independens," *N.H. Gazette*, 13 Jan. 1778, offers the only substantive newspaper comment I have discovered.

36. State response is analyzed in greater detail in Jensen, *Articles of Confederation*, 185–97, and George D. Harmon, "The Proposed Amendments to the Articles of Confederation," *South Atlantic Quarterly*, 24 (1925), 298–315.

37. *JCC*, XI, 628, 631–2, 636–40, 647–56. The largest number of amendments was submitted by South Carolina, which had been spurred on by William Henry Drayton's ambitious but pointless attempt to put forward a completely revised set of articles; see Hezekiah Niles, *Principles and Acts of the Revolution in America* . . . (Baltimore, 1822), 98–115. For a letter strongly critical of Drayton's opposition to the Articles as drafted, see Christopher Gadsden to Drayton, 15 Aug. 1778, in Richard Walsh, ed., *The Writings of Christopher Gadsden, 1746–1805* (Columbia, S.C., 1966), 146.

38. Conn. Delegates to Gov. Trumbull, 9 July 1778, typescript, Oliver Wolcott, Sr., Papers, I, 112, CHS (MS at Beinecke Library, Yale University); Titus Hosmer to Richard Law, 10 July 1778, transcript, Ernest Law Papers, CHS.

39. The Maryland resolutions of December 1777 are in *Votes and Proceedings of the House of Delegates of the State of Maryland. October Session, 1777* [Annapolis, 1777], 55; the instructions of June 1778 are in *Votes and Proceedings . . . Second Session, 1778*, 129.

40. Hosmer to Thomas Mumford, 26 June 1778, MS 76123, CHS; Maryland Delegates to Governor and Assembly of Maryland, 22 June 1778, *LMCC*, III, 314–15.

41. On Delaware's failure to ratify, see Caesar Rodney to Henry Laurens, Dover, 31 July, 22 Aug., and 4 Nov. 1778, and to Thomas McKean, 11 June 1778, in George H. Ryden, ed., *Letters to and from Caesar Rodney, 1756–1784* (Philadelphia, 1933), 278, 280, 285–6, 272.

42. *JCC*, XI, 662–71, 677–8, 681.

43. McKean to George Read, 3 April 1778; Scudder to John Hart, 13 July 1778; both in *LMCC*, III, 149, 326–8.

44. *JCC*, XII, 1162–4, XIII, 187; on ratification in Delaware, see Thomas Rodney to Dickinson, Dover, 17 July 1779, R. R. Logan Collection, box 3, HSP, and Dickinson's reply, Phila., 22 July 1779, Gratz Collection, case 1, box 21, HSP; on New Jersey, Boudinot to McDougall, 22 Jan. 1779.

45. For the public positions assumed by Maryland in defense of its claims, see *JCC*, XIV, 619–22, and PCC, Item 70, ff. 293–9. According to George Plater, a Maryland delegate, reports of New Jersey's and Dela-

ware's willingness to ratify the Articles came as a surprise to Maryland leaders. "This staggers some of our deep Politicians," he wrote Gouverneur Morris, Annapolis, 4 Dec. 1778; and see his letters of 10 Dec. 1778 and 27 Dec. 1778, the latter written from his plantation, Sotterley Hall; Gouverneur Morris Papers, folders 1108, 1109, 1111, Columbia University Library, N.Y. Plater himself believed that Maryland should accede.

46. These maneuvers are judiciously reviewed in Jensen, *Articles of Confederation*, 198–238.

Chapter IX: The Beginnings of National Government

1. *JCC*, III, 399, 436.
2. *JCC*, II, 190, 212. In early November 1775, Francis Lewis, John Alsop, and Roger Sherman were appointed a committee to purchase clothing for Schuyler's army, *JCC*, III, 317–18; see Lewis's Memorandum [November 1775], *LDC*, II, 289.
3. Deane to Elizabeth Deane, 3 Oct. 1775; J. Adams to Abigail Adams, 12 Nov. 1775; both in *LDC*, II, 102, 331–2.
4. The appointment and early evolution of these committees are traced in Jennings B. Sanders, *Evolution of Executive Departments of the Continental Congress, 1774–1789* (Chapel Hill, 1935), 6–92.
5. Chase to R. H. Lee, Montreal, 18 May 1776, Lee Family Papers, reel 2 (UVa).
6. For a general discussion of civilian-military relations, see Don Higginbotham, *The War of American Independence: Military Attitudes, Policies and Practice, 1763–1789* (New York, 1971), 81–97, 204–25; on problems of logistics, Victor L. Johnson, *The Administration of the American Commissariat During the Revolutionary War* (Philadelphia, 1941); and see Henderson, *Party Politics*, 100–29.
7. J. Adams to Abigail Adams, 11 July 1776, Butterfield, ed., *Adams Family Correspondence*, II, 44.
8. Dickinson Papers, R. R. Logan Collection, box 2, HSP.
9. R. R. Livingston to E. Rutledge, Fishkill, N.Y., 10 Oct. 1776, R. R. Livingston Papers, Bancroft Transcripts, NYPL; J. Adams to James Warren, 27 July 1776, Ford, ed., *Warren-Adams Letters*, I, 265.
10. Richard Smith, Diary, 15 Dec. 1775; Deane to Elizabeth Deane, 15 Dec. 1775; both in *LDC*, II, 483, 488.
11. For a small sample of these complaints, see Henry Laurens to William Livingston, 27 Jan. 1778, and to Robert Howe, 30 Jan. 1778, Laurens Papers, reel 6, SCHS; and William Duer to R. R. Livingston, Baskenridge, Pa., 10 March 1778, R. R. Livingston Papers, box 4, NYHS.
12. *JCC*, VI, 1041–2.
13. Duer to F. L. Lee, Reading, Pa., 14 Feb. 1777 [i.e., 1778], Lee

Family Papers, reel 4 (UVa); Morris to Comm. of Secret Correspondence, 16 Dec. 1776, *LMCC*, II, 178; Morris to Jay, 12 Jan. and 4 Feb. 1777,
Morris, ed., *John Jay*, I, 364, 370; and see William Hooper to Morris, 28
Dec. 1776, *LMCC*, II, 195–6.

14. S. Adams to J. Adams, 9 Jan. 1777; R. H. Lee to Washington, 20
Oct. 1777; both in *LMCC*, II, 210, 528. These letters contradict the assertion sometimes made that "radicals" such as Adams and Lee deeply
opposed the creation of executive departments. That was the case, it is
true, in the early 1780's, when the appointment of Robert Morris as
superintendent of finance revived earlier partisan disputes; but in
1776–77 their views apparently differed little from those of other members. What was controversial was not the existence of these boards but
their composition, particularly when the Board of War was rightly suspected of being a center of opposition to Washington; cf. Sanders, *Executive Departments*, 3–5.

15. *JCC*, VI, 1041–2, VII, 193–5, 241–2, and IX, 818–20; *LMCC*, II,
210–11 n.; Sanders, *Executive Departments*, 6–92.

16. A. Adams to Oliver Wolcott, 29 Aug. 1778; Bartlett to John Langdon, 21 Sept. 1778; both in *LMCC*, III, 391, 420.

17. Hosmer to [Oliver Ellsworth?], 16 Aug. 1778, Gratz Collection,
case 1, box 7, HSP; Hosmer to Gov. Trumbull, 31 Aug. 1778; A. Adams
to Samuel Lyman, 17 Aug. 1778; and John Mathews to Thomas Bee, 22
Sept. 1778; all in *LMCC*, III, 394–5, 378, 420–1.

18. Burke to N.C. Assembly [August 1779]; [Ellsworth], "A Friend to
Truth and Fair Play," 7 Sept. 1779; Johnston to James Iredell, 8 April
1781; and Bartlett to Langdon, 18 Aug. 1778; all in *LMCC*, IV, 367–8,
408–11, V, 49, and III, 379.

19. Joseph Jones to Washington, Williamsburg, 22 Jan. 1778,
LMCC, III, 44; Nathanael Greene to Alexander McDougall, Valley
Forge, 25 Jan. 1778, and McDougall's reply, 14 Feb. 1778, McDougall
Papers, reel 2, NYHS; Benjamin Harrison to Joseph Hewes, Berkeley,
Va., 3 March 1778, Clark, ed., *State Recs. of N.C.*, XIII, 61–2; and for the
most recent assessments of the so-called Conway cabal, see Higginbotham, *War of Independence*, 216–22; Rossie, *Politics of Command*, 188–
202; and Paul D. Nelson, *General Horatio Gates: A Biography* (Baton
Rouge, La., 1976), 157–85.

20. Sanders, *Executive Departments*, 73–4.

21. Houston to Witherspoon, Trenton, 2 Feb. 1778, Laurens Papers,
reel 9, SCHS; Peabody to M. Weare, 13 March 1780, *LMCC*, V, 70; for
other comments, see William Livingston to Laurens, Springfield, 8 Jan.
1778, Laurens Papers, reel 15, SCHS; Nathanael Greene to Jay, 18 Jan.
and 1 Feb. 1779, Morris, ed., *John Jay*, I, 533, 542–3; Patrick Henry to
Virginia Delegates, Williamsburg, 20 Jan. 1778, Hutchinson, ed., *Papers
of Madison*, I, 220; and see E. James Ferguson, *The Power of the Purse:*

A History of American Public Finance, 1776–1790 (Chapel Hill, 1961), 94–102.

22. Bartlett to Langdon, 21 Sept. 1778; Jay to Washington, 26 April 1779; both in Morris, ed., *John Jay*, I, 587–8.

23. Greene to McDougall, Camp Middle Brook, N.J., 11 Feb. 1779, and Phila., 15 April 1780, McDougall Papers, reels 2 and 3, NYHS; Laurens to Livingston, 27 Jan. 1778.

24. The early phases of congressional finance are analyzed in Ferguson, *Power of the Purse*, 25–47; on inflation, see Anne Bezanson, *et al.*, *Prices and Inflation During the American Revolution, 1770–1790* (Philadelphia, 1951).

25. *JCC*, IX, 953–8, 971.

26. *JCC*, XI, 569–70.

27. The most useful and accessible survey of state finances is still Nevins, *American States During the Revolution*, 470–543; and see Robert A. Becker, "Revolution and Reform: An Interpretation of Southern Taxation, 1763–1783," *WMQ*, 32 (1975), 432–42; Ralph V. Harlow, "Aspects of Revolutionary Finance, 1775–1783," *American Historical Review*, 35 (1929), 46–68.

28. Franklin quoted in Harlow, "Aspects of Revolutionary Finance," 62–3; and see G. Morris to Washington, 26 Oct. 1778, *LMCC*, III, 462. Robert Morris was so confident the currency would recover some of its lost value once the presses were stopped that he advised one of his business correspondents to purchase continental bills of credit—advice for which he later apologized. Morris to Stacey Hepburn, 23 Sept. and 10 Dec. 1779, 17 March 1780, Small Collections, HSP.

29. *JCC*, VII, 355–9, VIII, 433–8, 469–70, and X, 51, 248–52, 344–8, 356–7.

30. Houston to Witherspoon, 2 Feb. 1778; *JCC*, XIII, 492.

31. Reed to Dickinson, 14 June 1779, R. R. Logan Collection, box 3, HSP (a fair copy is in the Henry Laurens Papers, HSP); Carroll to William Carmichael, 8 Feb. 1779, William Carmichael Collection, MdHS; and see "A True Patriot," *Pa. Gazette*, 31 March 1779. By 1779 Congress had grown more sensitive about the question of profiteering because allegations had been made against the delegates themselves; see Daniel Jenifer to an unknown correspondent, 26 May 1779, *LMCC*, IV, 235–6; Alexander Hamilton's attack on Samuel Chase, in Syrett and Cooke, eds., *Papers of Hamilton*, I, 562–3, 567–70, 580–2; and Ferguson, *Power of the Purse*, 70–105, for the charges directed against Robert Morris and his connections.

32. Ferguson, *Power of the Purse*, 39–43; Bezanson, *Prices and Inflation*, 44–5.

33. Reed to Dickinson, 14 June 1779.

34. *JCC*, XV, 1019, 1311, 1371, 1377, and XVI, 196–201; Ferguson, *Power of the Purse*, 44–56.

35. *LMCC*, IV, 235 n. 3; *JCC*, XVI, 293–311, 332–3, and XIV, 812–13. Only one delegate, Meriwether Smith, dissented from the resolution of July 1780.

36. *JCC*, XVI, 262–7; Ferguson, *Power of the Purse*, 51–2, 64–6. For contemporary comment, see Schuyler to Greene and to Washington, 22 March 1780, *LMCC*, V, 90–2; Ezra L'Hommedieu to R. R. Livingston, Kingston, 29 March 1780, R. R. Livingston Papers, box 5, NYHS; Samuel A. Otis to Elbridge Gerry, Boston, 8 April 1780, Gerry-Knight Collection, MHS; Charles Carroll to John Hanson, 15 Aug. 1780, and Daniel Carroll to Charles Carroll, Annapolis, 10 Sept. 1780, Carroll Papers, reel 2, f. 826, 831, MdHS.

37. *JCC*, XVI, 261.

38. N.C. Delegates to Gov. Caswell, 15 July 1779, *LMCC*, IV, 318; Reed to Dickinson, 14 June 1779.

39. Ellery to Gov. Greene, 21 Dec. 1779, and Lovell to J. Adams, 21 March 1780, *LMCC*, IV, 545, V, 85; N.C. Delegates to Caswell, 15 July 1779; Madison to Jefferson, 27 March 1780, Hutchinson, ed., *Papers of Madison*, II, 6; and see Conn. Delegates to Gov. Trumbull, 20 March 1780, *LMCC*, V, 83.

Chapter X: Ambition and Responsibility: An Essay on Revolutionary Politics

1. James S. Young, *The Washington Community, 1800–1828* (New York, 1966), 61.

2. These calculations are based on the attendance records printed at the beginning of each of the volumes of *LMCC*.

3. R. H. Lee to A. Lee, 19 May 1778, Ballagh, ed., *Letters of Lee*, I, 408.

4. The open split within the Massachusetts delegation, which pitted the Adamses against Cushing, Hancock, and Paine, was precipitated by a dispute between the provincial council and house over the appointment of militia officers. Hancock and Cushing supported the council, the Adamses the house. A succinct account of the dispute can be found in Patterson, *Political Parties in Massachusetts*, 128–32; and there is a substantial amount of correspondence about the political controversy that followed. See Gerry to J. Adams, 11 Nov. 1775, Adams Family Papers, reel 345, MHS; James Warren to J. Adams, 3 Dec. 1775, and to S. Adams, 5 Dec. 1775, Ford, ed., *Warren-Adams Letters*, I, 190, II, 427–8. See also J. Adams to James Otis, 23 Nov. 1775; S. Adams to Otis, 23 Nov. 1775; Hancock and Cushing to Mass. Council, 24 Nov. 1775; and S. Adams to

J. Adams, 22 Dec. 1775, all of which appear in *LDC*, II, 373–5, 383, 506; Cushing to Paine, 13 and 29 Feb. 1776, R. T. Paine Papers, MHS; Cushing to Hancock, 30 Jan. 1776, Gratz Collection, case 1, box 4, HSP; and Hancock to Cushing, 7 Feb. 1776, Misc. Bound MSS, MHS.

5. Deane to Elizabeth Deane, 26 Nov. 1775, and Conn. Delegates to Gov. Trumbull, 5 Dec. 1775, *LDC*, II, 391–2, 442; Christopher Collier, *Roger Sherman's Connecticut: Yankee Politics and the American Revolution* (Middletown, Conn., 1971), 130–4; and see the brilliant letter by John Trumbull to John Adams, New Haven, 14 Nov. 1775, Adams Family Papers, reel 345, MHS.

6. See William Fleming to Jefferson, Mt. Pleasant, Va., 27 July 1776, Boyd, ed., *Papers of Jefferson*, I, 475; R. H. Lee to Patrick Henry [26 May 1777], and to [Landon Carter?], Williamsburg, 25 June 1777, Ballagh, ed., *Letters of Lee*, I, 297–304; F. L. Lee and Mann Page, Jr., to George Wythe, 10 June 1777; Page to R. H. Lee, Mann's Field, Va., 27 Oct. 1777; and Henry to R. H. Lee, Williamsburg, 18 June 1778; all in Lee Family Papers, reels 3 and 4 (the first letter is at UVa, the other two at American Philosophical Society).

7. On Hewes, see James Iredell to Hannah Iredell, New Bern, N.C., 28 April 1777, Higginbotham, ed., *Papers of Iredell*, I, 445–6; William Hooper to R. Morris, Cape Fear, N.C., 27 May 1777, *Colls.* NYHS, XI, 427; Caswell to Burke, New Bern, N.C., 13 May 1777, Clark, ed., *State Recs. of N.C.*, XI, 470–1. Burke was denied reelection in 1778 after refusing to comply with an instruction concerning the promotion of two North Carolina officers. He was reelected only after he had quarreled with the rest of Congress over a matter of personal privilege. His earlier embarrassment was nevertheless an ironic reflection on his diligent efforts to act as the ambassador of a sovereign state. See the legislative records reprinted in *State Recs. of N.C.*, XII, v, 711–18; Burke to Caswell, 25 April 1778, and to Laurens, 28 April 1778; Cornelius Harnett to Burke, 19 Sept. 1778; *LMCC*, III, 187–9, 193–5, 418.

8. Monroe to Mercer, 14 March 1783, in Curtis Garrison, ed., James Monroe Papers in Virginia Repositories (microfilm, Charlottesville, Va., 1969), reel 12 (original in Swem Library, College of William and Mary).

9. Caswell to Henry, Newington, N.C., 3 June 1777; Harnett to Caswell, 28 Nov. 1778; Clark, ed., *State Recs. of N.C.*, XI, 484–5, XIII, 306.

10. Mathews to Thomas Bee, 22 Sept. 1778, *LMCC*, III, 420–1.

11. William Livingston to Henry Laurens, Princeton, 9 Oct. 1778, Laurens Papers, reel 15, SCHS.

12. Jackson T. Main, *The Upper House in Revolutionary America, 1763–1788* (Madison, 1967); Main, "Government by the People: The American Revolution and the Democratization of the Legislatures," *WMQ*, 23 (1966), 391–407. James Kirby Martin, *Men in Rebellion: Higher Governmental Leaders and the Coming of the American Revolution*

(New Brunswick, N.J., 1973), makes an analogous case for executive appointments. Gordon Wood describes the increased emphasis on notions of actual representation that accompanied the framing of the new constitutions, but also examines the strains that thereafter developed between the rulers and the ruled—*Creation of the American Republic*, parts II and III.

13. The most suggestive study of pre-Revolutionary legislative behavior is Robert Zemsky, *Merchants, Farmers, and River Gods: An Essay on Eighteenth-Century American Politics* (Boston, 1971), esp. 1–38. Zemsky characterizes assembly leaders and other provincial notables as "professional politicians," which is fair enough; but it is clear from his discussion of the business of government that this term has to be understood in an eighteenth-century context. The most burdened officeholders in pre-Revolutionary America were royal and proprietary appointees holding executive positions, that is, precisely that class of politicians who were least likely to participate in government after independence.

14. John Fell to W. Livingston, 25 March 1779; E. Dyer to Trumbull, 21 May 1783; *LMCC*, IV, 118, VII, 171.

15. It could be objected that the Seven Years War constituted something of a preparation, but I would argue that comparatively few Revolutionary leaders gained experience then, and that much of the responsibility for conducting the earlier war was borne by imperial officials. I do not mean to question the conclusions about increasing colonial political maturity drawn, for example, in Jack P. Greene, *The Quest for Power: The Lower Houses of Assembly in the Southern Royal Colonies, 1689–1763* (Chapel Hill, 1963), only to point out the disparity between the burdens of late colonial and Revolutionary politics and government.

16. See, for example, Carl Bridenbaugh, *Seat of Empire: The Political Role of Eighteenth-Century Williamsburg* (Williamsburg, 1950), 11–28; Charles Sydnor, *Gentlemen Freeholders: Political Practices in Washington's Virginia* (Chapel Hill, 1952), 85–93, for a discussion of the activities of county courts and parish vestries.

17. Ward to Samuel Ward, Jr., 9 Sept. 1774; Hooper to Samuel Johnston, 23 May 1775; and J. Adams to James Warren, 17 Sept. 1775; all in *LDC*, I, 59, 398, II, 24–5. For Drayton, see *Virginia Gazette* (Dixon and Hunter), 25 Sept. 1779. James Iredell kept a diary that provides a revealing description of the leisurely habits of a young lawyer and customs official in North Carolina in the early 1770's; see Higginbotham, ed., *Papers of Iredell*, I, 171–213.

18. This information is compiled from Allen Johnson, Dumas Malone, *et al.*, eds., *Dictionary of American Biography* (New York, 1928–58), and from the *Biographical Directory of the American Congress, 1774–1961* (Washington, D.C., 1961), a source that cannot be trusted im-

plicitly; and see Richard D. Brown, "The Founding Fathers of 1776 and 1787: A Collective View," *WMQ*, 33 (1976), 465–80.

19. See Pauline Maier, "Coming to Terms with Samuel Adams," *American Historical Review*, 81 (1976), 12–37.

20. See Collier, *Roger Sherman's Connecticut;* George C. Groce, "Eliphalet Dyer, Connecticut Revolutionist," in Richard B. Morris, ed., *The Era of the American Revolution* (New York, 1939); Billias, *Elbridge Gerry;* William Fowler, *William Ellery: A Rhode Island Politico and Lord of Admiralty* (Metuchen, N.J., 1973); G. S. Rowe, "Thomas McKean and the Coming of the Revolution," *Pennsylvania Magazine of History and Biography*, 96 (1972), 3–47; and Rowe, " 'A Valuable Acquisition in Congress': Thomas McKean, Delegate from Delaware to the Continental Congress, 1774–1783," *Pennsylvania History*, 38 (1971), 225–64. I am grateful to Pauline Maier for allowing me to read her as yet unpublished essay on R. H. Lee.

21. Duane to Col. Robert Livingston, New York, 2 Feb. 1767 and 19 Feb. 1770, Livingston-Redmond MSS, Franklin D. Roosevelt Library, Hyde Park, N.Y., Duane to Johnson, 29 Dec. 1774, *LDC*, I, 280; and see Edward P. Alexander, *A Revolutionary Conservative: James Duane* (New York, 1938).

22. Lovell to Gerry, 11 Sept. 1781, Gerry Papers II, MHS; and to R. H. Lee, Boston, 20 Feb. 1789, Lee Family Papers, reel 7 (UVa). For other discussions of his situation, see his letters to S. Adams, 17 Aug. 1779 and 13 Dec. 1781, S. Adams Papers, boxes 5 and 6, NYPL; and to Gerry, 13 July 1781 and 14 Sept. 1781, Gerry-Knight Collection, MHS.

23. Clark to James Caldwell, 7 Aug. 1776, Fogg Collection, vol. 54, Maine Historical Society; Clark to Caldwell, 3 Oct. 1781, Roberts Collection, No. 720, Haverford College; and see Clark to Elias Dayton, Elizabethtown, N.J., 26 Oct. 1776, Fogg Collection, vol. 17.

24. Hooper to Iredell, Hillsborough, N.C., 4 Jan. 1784, in Griffith I. McRee, *Life and Correspondence of James Iredell* (New York, 1857–58), II, 83.

25. Maier, "Samuel Adams," 33–4.

26. Collier, *Roger Sherman's Connecticut*, 317–31.

27. Walton to R. Morris, Savannah, 3 Sept. 1778, Signers Collection, HUL; Duane to John Tabor Kempe, 11 Oct. 1774, *LDC*, I, 173; J. Adams to James Warren, Passi, 26 July 1778, Ford, ed., *Warren-Adams Letters*, II, 36.

28. Wood, *Creation of the American Republic*, 497–8.

29. Harnett to Caswell, 28 Nov. 1778; to William Wilkinson, 20 Nov. 1777, and 28 Dec. 1777; all in Clark, ed., *State Recs. of N.C.*, XIII, 305–6, and XI, 809, 827; and see Robert D. W. Connor, *Cornelius Harnett; An Essay in North Carolina History* (Raleigh, N.C., 1909).

30. Laurens to John Laurens, 3 Feb. 1777, Laurens Papers, reel 6,

SCHS; Richard Adams to Thomas Adams, Richmond Hill, Va., 1 July 1777, *Virginia Magazine of History and Biography*, 22 (1914), 392–3; Carroll to Carroll, Sr., 5 July 1776, Carroll Papers, reel 1, f. 536, MdHS; R. R. Livingston to John Livingston, 5 Nov. 1779, R. R. Livingston Papers, box 5, NYHS; and see Elias Boudinot to Nathaniel Scudder, 18 June 1781, Boudinot Papers, Princeton University Library,

31. R. Morris to Duane, 8 Sept. 1778, Duane Papers, reel 1, NYHS.

32. G. Morris to R. R. Livingston, 5 Feb. 1778, R. R. Livingston Papers, box 4, NYHS; to Sarah G. Morris, 16 April 1778, Gouverneur Morris Papers, folder 702, Columbia University Library, N.Y.; to R. R. Livingston [January 1781] and 21 Feb. 1781, R. R. Livingston Papers, box 6, NYHS.

33. R. Morris, Diary, 21 Feb. 1781, and G. Morris to R. Morris, 7 July 1781, E. James Ferguson, *et al.*, eds., *The Papers of Robert Morris, 1781– 1784* (Pittsburgh, 1973–), I, 8–9, 252; and see Robert Morris's comments on John Dickinson in a letter to John Jay, 12 Jan. 1777, Morris, ed., *John Jay*, I, 364–5.

34. Williams to Thomas Benbury, Halifax, N.C., 1 Feb. 1779, Clark, ed., *State Recs. of N.C.*, XIV, 258–9; Elmer to N.J. Assembly, 17 Sept. 1778, Roberts Collection, No. 722, Haverford College; Hooper to Morris, 27 May 1777, *Colls.* NYHS, 11 (1878), 427–8; Stone to William Fitzhugh, 29 Oct. 1778, Signers Collection, NYSL.

35. Harvie to Jefferson, 18 Oct. 1777 and 29 Dec. 1777, Boyd, ed., *Papers of Jefferson*, II, 35, 126; Mason to R. H. Lee, Williamsburg, 19 June 1779, Rutland, ed., *Papers of Mason*, II, 524; and see James Monroe to [William Woodford?], Williamsburg, September 1779, Monroe Papers in Virginia Repositories, reel 12 (UVa).

36. Laurens to John L. Gervais, 5–9 Sept. 1777, Laurens Papers, reel 6, SCHS.

37. Whipple to Bartlett, Portsmouth, N.H., 11 March 1778, Sparks Papers, LII, vol. 2, p. 207, HUL; Fell to Livingston, 25 March 1779, *LMCC*, IV, 118–19; Fleming to Jefferson, 10 May 1779, Boyd, ed., *Papers of Jefferson*, II, 264.

38. G. Morris to R. R. Livingston, 17 Aug. 1778, R. R. Livingston Papers, box 4, NYHS; N.Y. Delegates to Gov. Clinton, 29 March 1782, Duane Papers, reel 2, NYHS; Bland to Jefferson, 3 June 1781, Boyd, ed., *Papers of Jefferson*, VI, 72–3; and see Va. Delegates to Gov. Nelson, 18 Sept. 1781, Hutchinson, ed., *Papers of Madison*, III, 259.

39. Scudder to Nathaniel Peabody, Freehold, N.J., 6 Dec. 1779, Roberts Collection, No. 732, Haverford College; Higginson to Bland, Boston, 31 March 1785, in Charles Campbell, ed., *The Bland Papers* (Petersburg, Va., 1840–43), II, 117–18.

Chapter XI: Factional Conflict and Foreign Policy

1. Duane to Col. Robert Livingston, New York, 29 May 1773, Livingston-Redmond MSS, Franklin D. Roosevelt Library; Duane to R. R. Livingston, 1 July 1777, and N.Y. Delegates to Council of Safety, 2 July 1777, *LMCC*, II, 395–7.

2. John Harvie to Jefferson, 18 Oct. 1777, Boyd, ed., *Papers of Jefferson*, II, 34–5; John Mathews to Thomas Bee, 22 Sept. 1778, *LMCC*, III, 420–1; Henry Laurens to John L. Gervais, 5–9 Sept. 1777, Laurens Papers, reel 6, SCHS.

3. For a different perspective, see Henderson, *Party Politics*, 192–3.

4. I would argue, in other words, that voting blocs alone do not constitute an adequate criterion for the existence of party, even in the sense of legislative rather than mass parties. See Ronald P. Formisano, "Deferential-Participant Politics: The Early Republic's Political Culture, 1789–1840," *American Political Science Review*, 68 (1974), 473–87, for a systematic exposition of the criteria of party and their application to the immediate post-Revolutionary period. Henderson is himself sensitive to this problem, as his summary of his model of congressional politics suggests: "All things considered, congressional politics are best characterized as a politics of interest that took the form of contention between regionally oriented nascent legislative parties. It will not do to make too much of the organization, or even the self-awareness, of the congressional parties"; *Party Politics*, 159–64.

5. *Votes and Proceedings of the House of Delegates . . . of Maryland. February Session, 1777*, 105; Burke, Abstract of Debates, 27 Feb. 1777, and Laurens to John Rutledge, 1 Dec. 1777, *LMCC*, II, 285, 579.

6. On Deane's career, see Ferguson, *Power of the Purse*, 81–94; Thomas P. Abernethy, "Commercial Activities of Silas Deane in France," *American Historical Review*, 39 (1934), 477–85; and Julian P. Boyd, "Silas Deane: Death by a Kindly Teacher of Treason," *WMQ*, 16 (1959), 165–87, 319–42, 515–50.

7. Hancock to Washington, 17 March 1777; Comm. of Secret Correspondence to Commissioners at Paris, 25 March 1777; R. H. Lee to Washington, 22 May 1777; Lovell to Joseph Trumbull, 6 June 1777; William Williams to Jonathan Trumbull, 5 July 1777; and Lovell to William Whipple, 7 July 1777; all in *LMCC*, II, 302–3, 310–11, 368–9, 379, 400, 403.

8. Williams to S. Adams, Lebanon, Conn., 30 June 1774, S. Adams Papers, box 2, NYPL.

9. Laurens to Gervais, 5–9 Sept. 1777, and to John Rutledge, 12 Aug. 1777; Williams to Jonathan Trumbull, 28 Nov. 1777; R. H. Lee to S. Adams, 23 Nov. 1777; all in *LMCC*, II, 448, 574–5, 569; *JCC*, VIII, 605

n., IX, 946, 1008–9; and see Lovell to R. H. Lee, and to J. Adams, both dated 8 Dec. 1777, *LMCC*, II, 581–2.

10. R. H. Lee to S. Adams, 23 Nov. 1777; Lovell to Franklin, 15 May 1778, *LMCC*, III, 242; Lovell to J. Adams, 15 May 1778, Adams Family Papers, reel 349, MHS.

11. R. H. Lee to A. Lee, 12 and 19 May 1778; Laurens to Washington, 8 June 1778; all in *LMCC*, III, 231, 257, 283; and see S. Adams to J. Adams, 21 June 1778, Adams Family Papers, reel 349, MHS. Arthur Lee's letter of 6 Oct. 1777, which raised pointed questions about the contract Deane had negotiated with Beaumarchais, was not received until 2 May 1778; see Comm. of Foreign Affairs to Lee, 14 May 1778, *LMCC*, III, 238.

12. Deane to Laurens, 28 July 1778, Isham, ed., *The Deane Papers*, II, 474–5.

13. Deane to Hancock, 4 Sept. 1778, Dreer Collection, Members of Old Congress, I, HSP; *JCC*, XI, 726, 787, 799–802, 826.

14. *JCC*, XII, 927–8, 935–6; Izard's letters are reprinted in Wharton, ed., *Rev. Dipl. Corr.*, II, 477–80, 497, 547; on Carmichael's appearance, see Charles Thomson's notes, *LMCC*, III, 428–30, 433–5, 438–40; Deane to Laurens, 8, 11, and 22 Sept. 1778, 7 Oct. 1778, Isham, ed., *The Deane Papers*, II, 480–1, 486–8, III, 1.

15. Deane to Hancock, 4 Sept. 1778; Deane to an unknown recipient, 25 Aug. 1778, Peck Collection, box 4, RIHS.

16. Deane to Barnabas Deane, 30 Nov. 1778, Isham, ed., *The Deane Papers*, III, 61–3; Deane to Hancock, 26 Oct. 1778, Roberts Collection, No. 722, Haverford College; Deane's two publications are reprinted in *The Deane Papers*, III, 2–3, 66–76.

17. Four letters that Samuel Adams wrote to James Warren between July and December 1778 indicate his uncertainty about whether or not Deane should be attacked publicly; see his letters dated 20 July, 11 Oct., 23 Nov., and 9 Dec. 1778, *LMCC*, III, 339, 446–9, 503–6.

18. For evidence that Deane enjoyed a decided advantage in the early rounds of this skirmishing, see Francis Dana to Gerry, Cambridge, 11 Oct. 1778, Gerry-Knight Collection, MHS; F. L. Lee to R. H. Lee, 22 Dec. 1778, Lee Family Papers, reel 5 (American Philosophical Society); Richard Parker to R. H. Lee, Williamsburg, 8 April 1779, *ibid.*, reel 6 (UVa); William Whipple to Joseph Whipple, 2 and 19 Jan. 1779, Sturgis Papers, box 3, HUL; Samuel Cooper to S. Adams, Boston, 19 Jan. 1779, S. Adams Papers, box 5, NYPL.

19. Duane to Clinton, 15 Dec. 1778; Lovell to Horatio Gates, 15 Dec. 1778; and Langworthy to William Duer, 8 [18] Dec. 1778; all in *LMCC*, III, 535–6, 540.

20. Many of these are reprinted in Isham, ed., *The Deane Papers*, III.

21. *JCC*, XII, 1265–6, XIII, 93–4; Smith to John Page, 21 Feb. 1779, *LMCC*, IV, 80.

22. For a general account of the diplomatic situation of 1779 and its ramifications in America, see Bemis, *Diplomacy of the American Revolution*, 81–7. William Stinchcombe, *The American Revolution and the French Alliance* (Syracuse, N.Y., 1969), 32–47, 62–76, offers an account critical of Gérard; more sympathetic to the French minister is John J. Meng, ed., *Despatches and Instructions of Conrad Alexandre Gérard, 1778–1780* (Baltimore, 1939), 91–122.

23. Gérard's memorial is reprinted in Wharton, ed., *Rev. Dipl. Corr.*, III, 39–40; for his conference with Congress, see W. H. Drayton, Memorandum, *LMCC*, IV, 69–71; and see Gérard to Vergennes, 17 and 18 Feb. 1779, Meng, ed., *Despatches*, 525–32.

24. Gérard to Vergennes, 15 Feb. 1779, Meng, ed., *Despatches*, 522.

25. *JCC*, XIII, 194–5, 239–44, 260, 263, 272, 329, 339–41, 348–52, 369–73.

26. *JCC*, XIII, 363–9, 455–7, 479–90, 499–500. John Adams was not named in the committee's report. His closest supporters subsequently disagreed over a motion to add his name to the others, some believing that this would imply misbehavior, others arguing that he deserved a vote of confidence; see Lovell to J. Adams, 13 June 1779, and Gerry to J. Adams, 29 Sept. 1779, *LMCC*, IV, 262–3, 455–7. For an extended discussion of the question of foreign appointments, see Henderson, *Party Politics*, 187–206.

27. *JCC*, XIV, 533–7, 542–3.

28. *JCC*, XIV, 700–6.

29. *JCC*, XIV, 749–52, 765–70, 790–3, 850–1, 863–7, 884–6, 896–7, 909–12, 918–22.

30. R. H. Lee to A. Lee, Virginia, 12 Oct. 1779, *LMCC*, IV, 481.

31. Henry Laurens, Notes of Proceedings, 25 Sept. 1779; Laurens to John Laurens, 27 Sept. 1779; Lovell to R. H. Lee, 27 Sept. 1779; Lovell to J. Adams, 27–28 Sept. 1779; and Gerry to J. Adams, 29 Sept. 1779; all in *LMCC*, IV, 437–8, 441–50, 454–8; *JCC*, XV, 1005–13. See also Henderson, *Party Politics*, 206–10, and John Dickinson's explanation of his vote and the actions of Congress in his letter to A. Lee, 30 March 1780, John Dickinson Papers, box 2, item 19, HSP.

32. Lovell to R. H. Lee, 31 July 1779, and to A. Lee, 6 Aug. 1779, *LMCC*, IV, 350, 355; J. Adams to Lovell [21 Sept. 1779], Butterfield, ed., *Adams Family Correspondence*, III, 231 n.

33. On Burke and Lee, see the former's Abstract of Debates, 15 and 20 Feb. 1777; on Laurens and Drayton, see the former's memorandum on his colleague's conduct [3 June 1779]; for a different view of Laurens, see Charles Thomson's complaints about his imperious behavior, 6 Sept. 1779; all in *LMCC*, II, 253–4, 265–6, IV, 247–9, 401–8.

34. Whipple to R. H. Lee, 23 Aug. 1779, *LMCC*, IV, 385–6.

35. On this point, see William Livingston to Laurens, Lebanon Valley, N.J., 5 Feb. 1778, Laurens Papers, reel 15, SCHS.

36. For Adams's reference to "a Christian Sparta"—a phrase historians have recently been fond of quoting—see his letter to John Scollay, 30 Dec. 1780, Cushing, ed., *Writings of Adams*, IV, 238; Whipple to Joseph Whipple, 9, 19, and 25 March 1777, 1 April 1777, Sturgis Papers, box 3, HUL, demonstrate his commercial interests while a delegate; on Gerry's pursuit of profit, see the fascinating analysis in Billias, *Elbridge Gerry*, 123–37.

37. F. L. Lee to A. Lee, Annapolis, 22 April 1779, Lee Family Papers, reel 6 (HUL); R. Morris to Franklin, 30 March 1780, Burnett Collection, box 7, LC.

38. Francis Lewis to Gov. Clinton, 20 Feb. 1779, *LMCC*, IV, 78–9; Washington to Jay, Camp Middle Brook, N.J., 1 March 1779, Fitzpatrick, ed., *Writings of Washington*, XIV, 165–6; *Boston Gazette*, 22 March 1779.

39. N.C. Delegates to S.C. Delegates [2 April 1779]; N.C. Delegates to Gov. Caswell [2 April 1779]; Laurens to Drayton, 3 April 1779; Drayton to Laurens, 4 April 1779; all in *LMCC*, IV, 129–37. Alexander Hamilton was apparently also recruited to use his friendship with John Laurens as a way of influencing the South Carolina delegate to alter his position; see Hamilton to John Laurens, 22 May 1779, Syrett, ed., *Papers of Hamilton*, II, 53.

40. Reed to Alexander McDougall, 11 April 1779, McDougall Papers, reel 3, NYHS; Laurens, Minutes of Debates, 27 May 1779, *LMCC*, IV, 237.

41. "An Inquirer," Boston *Independent Chronicle*, 22 April 1779; "Confederatio," *ibid.*, 29 April 1779.

42. *Pa. Packet*, 6 and 8 May 1779; Carroll to Carroll, Sr., 8 May 1779, Carroll Papers, reel 2, f. 735, MdHS.

43. *Boston Gazette*, 24 May 1779; *Providence Gazette*, 29 May 1779; "Americanus," *Pa. Gazette*, 2 and 23 June 1779.

44. S. Adams to James Warren, 23 Nov. 1778, *LMCC*, III, 505; Gérard to Vergennes, 12–14 Dec. 1778, Meng, ed., *Despatches*, 421–3.

45. Laurens, Statement [21 April 1779]; Burke, Account of Interview with Gérard [21? April]; R. H. Lee, Statement [21 April]; Laurens, Notes [30 April]; William Carmichael, Statement, 3 May 1779; Burke to N.C. Assembly [August 1779]; all in *LMCC*, IV, 166–71, 186–93, 371–3; the so-called Paca-Drayton Information is in *JCC*, XIV, 533–7; and see Gérard to Vergennes, 20 April 1779, Meng, ed., *Despatches*, 605–6.

46. Gérard to Vergennes, 29 May 1779, 7–8 May 1779, and 9 July 1779, Meng, ed., *Despatches*, 689–91, 630, 762.

47. Gérard to Vergennes, 17–18 June 1779, *ibid.*, 733.

48. Paine's essays on the fisheries are reprinted in Foner, ed., *Writings of Paine*, II, 195–208.

49. "O Tempora! O Mores!" *Maryland Journal*, 29 June 1779, reprinted in Isham, ed., *The Deane Papers*, III, 485; Gérard to Vergennes, 18 July 1779, Meng, ed., *Despatches*, 801.

50. Cushing to Samuel Holten, Boston, 28 July 1779, Boston Public Library; *New York Journal*, 12 Aug. 1779; "A Copy of the Minutes left by Mr Wm Paca at the House of Delegates" [after 24 July 1779], Stone Family Papers, LC; Burke to N.C. Assembly [August 1779].

51. R. H. Lee's "Rowland" letters began appearing in the *Pa. Packet* of 10 Aug. 1779; Ellsworth's essay, "A Friend to Truth and Fair Play," was printed in the *Connecticut Courant*, 7 Sept. 1779, and is reprinted in *LMCC*, IV, 408–41.

52. Gérard to Vergennes, 12 June 1779, Meng, ed., *Despatches*, 719.

53. Gérard to Vergennes, 14 July 1779, *ibid.*, 777–85.

54. Houston to Livingston, 5 Oct. 1779; Jay to Clinton, 29 Sept. 1779; G. Morris to Washington, 21 Oct. 1779; all in *LMCC*, IV, 472–4, 459, 496. Daniel of St. Thomas Jenifer had earlier sought to downplay the significance of factional strife in a letter to Charles Carroll, 21 June 1779, Carroll Papers, reel 2, f. 745, MdHS; and also in a conversation with Gérard, reported in the latter's letter to Vergennes, 9–11 July 1779, Meng, ed., *Despatches*, 763–5.

55. Reed to McDougall, 11 April 1779, McDougall Papers; Carroll to Carroll, Sr., 22 May 1779, Carroll Papers, reel 2, f. 740, MdHS. For other comments emanating from outside Congress, see John Jones to Dickinson, Phila., 15 March 1779, Dickinson Papers, box 3, item 44, HSP; William Livingston to Laurens, Trenton, 23 April 1779, and Jonathan Trumbull to Laurens, 22 June 1779, both in Laurens Papers, reel 9, SCHS; Arthur Middleton to Burke, Charleston, 18 Oct. 1779, Gratz Collection, case 1, box 20, HSP; and Jefferson to William Fleming, Williamsburg, 8 June 1779, Boyd, ed., *Papers of Jefferson*, II, 288.

56. "A True Patriot," *Pa. Gazette*, 31 March 1779, reprinted from *N.J. Gazette*; "Phocion," *Pa. Packet*, 27 May 1779; "Gustavus Vasa," *Pa. Gazette*, 1 Sept. 1779; and see the Pennsylvania assembly's instructions to its delegates, 10 Oct. 1779, *Minutes of the Third General Assembly of the Commonwealth of Pennsylvania* (Philadelphia, 1779), 153.

57. R. H. Lee to Laurens, 15 Oct. 1779, Ballagh, ed., *Letters of Lee*, II, 160–1; Rush's essay, published under the pseudonym "Leonidas," is reprinted in Butterfield, ed., *Letters of Rush*, I, 229–35; Gérard to Vergennes, 6 July 1779, Meng, ed., *Despatches*, 749–50.

58. G. Morris to R. R. Livingston, 22 July 1779, R. R. Livingston Papers, box 5, NYHS; and see the draft of Livingston's reply, 8 Aug. 1779, misfiled *ibid.*, box 3; Lovell to J. Adams, 28 Sept. 1779, and McKean to R. H. Lee, 25 March 1780, *LMCC*, IV, 450, V, 95.

59. Madison to Edmund Pendleton, 7 Nov. 1780, Hutchinson, ed., *Papers of Madison*, II, 165; Joseph Jones to Washington, Virginia, 2 Oct. 1780, Worthington C. Ford, ed., *Letters of Joseph Jones* (Washington, D.C., 1889), 33–4.

60. Hutchinson, ed., *Papers of Madison*, II, 43.

61. Stinchcombe, *American Revolution and the French Alliance*, 153–82; Richard B. Morris, *The Peacemakers: The Great Powers and American Independence* (New York, 1965), 210–17.

Chapter XII: A Government Without Money

1. McDougall to Joseph Reed, Peekskill, 25 March 1779, Reed Papers, reel 2, NYHS; and see Reed's reply, Phila., 11 April 1779, McDougall Papers, reel 3, NYHS. McDougall's letter was reprinted in the *Pa. Gazette*, 28 April 1779.

2. Clark to Caleb Camp, 17 Feb. 1780; L'Hommedieu to Gov. Clinton, 22 Feb. 1780; N.C. Delegates to Gov. Caswell, 29 Feb. 1780; all in *LMCC*, V, 40, 45, 55.

3. Bowdoin to Pres. Samuel Huntington, PCC, Item 65, I, ff. 456–7; N.Y. Assembly to N.Y. Delegates, PCC, Item 67, II, ff. 278–80.

4. Ferguson, *Power of the Purse*, 57–69 (quotations at 60, 64); for an extensive argument that taxation could still prove effective, see the lengthy letter of Charles Thomson to John Dickinson, 25 Dec. 1780, Dickinson Papers, box 1, item 7, HSP.

5. The committee's activities are thoroughly described in Edmund C. Burnett, *The Continental Congress* (New York, 1941), 442–71; many of its communications with the states are reprinted in *LMCC*, V.

6. Comm. at Headquarters, Minute, 15 May 1780, *LMCC*, V, 141–2.

7. Schuyler to Pres. Huntington, 6 March 1780; Mathews to Thomas Bee, 17 Oct. 1778; *LMCC*, V, 61, III, 453.

8. Comm. at Headquarters, Minute, 14 May 1780, *LMCC*, V, 140–1.

9. Schuyler to Duane, Morristown, N.J., 13 May 1780, *Publications* of the Southern History Association, 8 (1904), 380–1; *JCC*, XVII, 438–41, 720; and see Comm. at Headquarters to Pres. Huntington, 28 May 1780; Duane to Schuyler, 6 June 1780; and Committee to Huntington, 18 and 30 July 1780, 19 Aug. 1780; all in *LMCC*, V, 173–5, 198, 271–8, 301–4, 336–8.

10. Schuyler to Duane, 13 May 1780; Schuyler to Wadsworth, 16 July 1780, James Wadsworth Collection, LC; Madison to Jefferson, 27 March 1780, 6 May 1780, Hutchinson, ed., *Papers of Madison*, II, 6, 20; Jones to Washington [19 June 1780], *LMCC*, V, 227.

11. The resolutions are reprinted in *LMCC*, V, 445–6 n. 6; Duane to Clinton, 14 Nov. 1780, *ibid.*

12. The Hartford proceedings are reprinted in Boyd, ed., *Papers of*

Jefferson, IV, 138–41; Schuyler to Hamilton, Poughkeepsie, 10 and 16 Sept. 1780, 12 Nov. 1780, Syrett, ed., *Papers of Hamilton*, II, 425, 433, 499; Clinton to Pres. Huntington, Albany, 5 Feb. 1781, PCC, Item 67, II, ff. 344–59 (quotation at 358).

13. *JCC*, XVII, 723, 791, XVIII, 1028; see *LMCC*, V, 405–6 n. 6, 446 n. 3.

14. *JCC*, XVII, 758–9, XIX, 105–6, 110–13, 124–5.

15. *JCC*, XVII, 791, XIX, 126–8.

16. *JCC*, XVIII, 1157–64; John Sullivan, Proceedings and Observations of the Committee of Finance, November 1780, *LMCC*, V, 464–72.

17. *JCC*, XIX, 112–13.

18. *JCC*, XIX, 53–4.

19. Thomas P. Abernethy, *Western Lands and the American Revolution* (New York, 1937), 217–41; *JCC*, XV, 1226–30.

20. R. R. Livingston to Gov. Clinton, 30 Nov. 1779, and Schuyler to Pierre Van Cortlandt and Evert Bancker, 29 Jan. 1780, *LMCC*, IV, 530, V, 22; *JCC*, XVI, 236.

21. Duane to Washington, 4 May 1780, *LMCC*, V, 125.

22. *JCC*, XVII, 559–60, 580, 806–7.

23. Jones to Washington, 6 Sept. 1780, and Madison to Pendleton, 12 Sept. 1780, *LMCC*, V, 364–5, 369–70; and see Pendleton's reply, still critical of Maryland, Edmundsbury, Va., 25 Sept. 1780, in David J. Mays, ed., *The Letters and Papers of Edmund Pendleton, 1734–1803* (Charlottesville, Va., 1967), I, 309–10; and George Mason to Jones, 27 July 1780, Rutland, ed., *Papers of Mason*, II, 655–62.

24. Jensen, *Articles of Confederation*, 235–8.

25. Duane to Washington, 29 Jan. 1781; Joseph Jones to Washington, 27 Feb. 1781; both in *LMCC*, V, 553, 584.

26. Foner, ed., *Complete Writings of Paine*, II, 332; Schuyler to Wadsworth, 16 July 1780; Hamilton to Duane, Liberty Pole, N.J., 3 Sept. 1780, Syrett, ed., *Papers of Hamilton*, II, 400–18.

27. Mathews to Washington, 30 Jan. 1781, *LMCC*, V, 553–4. The quotation in the next paragraph is from the same letter.

28. *JCC*, XIX, 236, XX, 469–71, 773.

29. *JCC*, XXI, 894–6; on the definition of a quorum and a majority, see Thomas Rodney, Diary, 5–6 March 1781, *LMCC*, VI, 7–9.

30. R. H. Lee to Va. Delegates, Chantilly, Va., 12 June 1781, Boyd, ed., *Papers of Jefferson*, VI, 90–2; and see the recent essays by Richard H. Kohn, "American Generals of the Revolution: Subordination and Restraint," and Richard Buel, Jr., "Time: Friend or Foe of the Revolution?" in Don Higginbotham, ed., *Reconsiderations on the Revolutionary War* (Westport, Conn., 1978), 104–43, for discussions of the political implications of the logistical, financial, and economic problems created by the war.

31. Varnum to Gov. Greene, 2 April 1781, *LMCC*, VI, 41–2.
32. Jones to Jefferson, Spring Hill, Va., 16 April 1781, *LMCC*, VI, 57–9.
33. Reed to Nathanael Greene, Phila., 16 June 1781, in W. B. Reed, *Life of Reed*, II, 358; R. Morris to Franklin, 27 Nov. 1781, Ferguson, ed., *Papers of Morris*, III, 268, 282.
34. Madison to Jefferson, 16 April 1781, Hutchinson, ed., *Papers of Madison*, III, 71–2.
35. Hamilton to Duane, 3 Sept. 1780; and see his "Continentalist" essays, reprinted in Syrett, ed., *Papers of Hamilton*, II, 649–52, 654–7, 660–5, 669–74, III, 75–82, 99–106.
36. Mathews to Gov. Livingston [6 March 1781], *LMCC*, VI, 15.

Chapter XIII: The Administration of Robert Morris

1. Gouverneur Morris Papers, folder 810, Columbia University Library, N.Y.
2. Ferguson, *Power of the Purse*, 109–76; Merrill Jensen, *The New Nation: A History of the United States During the Confederation, 1781–1789* (New York, 1950), 54–84; Henderson, *Party Politics*, 281–321.
3. On Morris's career prior to his appointment as superintendent of finance, see Clarence L. Ver Steeg, *Robert Morris: Revolutionary Financier* (Philadelphia, 1954), 1–42.
4. Morris to Washington, 29 May 1781; and see Morris to William Livingston, 12 April 1781; both in Ferguson, ed., *Papers of Morris*, I, 96, 26–7.
5. Morris to Pres. Samuel Huntington, 13 March 1781; and to a Committee of Congress, 26 March 1781; *ibid.*, 17–25.
6. *JCC*, XIX, 287–91, 337–8, 432–3.
7. Ferguson, ed., *Papers of Morris*, I, 66–74; *JCC*, XX, 546–8.
8. Morris to Committee, 26 March 1781.
9. The financial message dated 28 Aug. 1781 is reprinted in Ferguson, ed., *Papers of Morris*, II, 124–35.
10. The summary of the Morris program in this and the following two paragraphs is based on the masterful analyses in Ver Steeg, *Robert Morris*, 78–110, and Ferguson, *Power of the Purse*, 125–45. The financial objectives of this program are not in dispute, but its political implications remain controversial. The interpretation advanced below is deeply indebted to the position that Ver Steeg first suggested but did not develop extensively. Ver Steeg argued, in effect, that while the financial aspects of the Morris program clearly anticipated later Hamiltonian policies, its political objectives were not equivalent to the Federalism of 1787–88. Ferguson follows Merrill Jensen in arguing that Morris was pursuing financial and economic goals essentially similar to the overtly

nationalist program that emerged triumphant in the late 1780's.

11. New York resolutions, 20 July 1782; Hamilton to Morris, Poughkeepsie, 22 July 1782; Morris to Hamilton, 28 Aug. 1782; all in Syrett, ed., *Papers of Hamilton*, III, 110–15, 152–6. Although these resolutions are traditionally attributed to Hamilton, two contemporary letters make no mention of his authorship; George Clinton to R. R. Livingston, Poughkeepsie, 5 Aug. 1782, and Egbert Benson to Livingston, 22 July 1782, R. R. Livingston Papers, box 9, NYHS. It is possible that these resolutions had actually been drafted by Benson the previous fall. In a letter to Livingston of 24 Nov. 1781 (*ibid.*, box 7), Benson reported that he had moved that the assembly propose that Congress call a convention for amending the Articles, but that in the rush of business his proposal was deferred to the next session.

12. See Ver Steeg, *Robert Morris*, 155–6, 173–4.

13. Ferguson, *Power of the Purse*, xiv–xv.

14. Gouverneur Morris, Observations on the Finances of America, G. Morris Papers, folder 804, Columbia University Library.

15. Reed to Nathanael Greene, 1 Nov. 1781, W. B. Reed, *Life of Reed*, II, 374–5. On Morris's role in the 1781 campaign, see Ver Steeg, *Robert Morris*, 72–7.

16. *JCC*, XXI, 1090–1, 1112; Morris to Pres. McKean, 5 Nov. 1781, Ferguson, ed., *Papers of Morris*, III, 142–6; and see Morris to Franklin, 27 Nov. 1781, *ibid.*, 269.

17. *JCC*, XXI, 1132, XXII, 12–14, 14–16 n.; Morris to Pres. Hanson, 10 Dec. 1781, Ferguson, ed., *Papers of Morris*, III, 357–63.

18. Morris to Pres. Hanson, 27 Feb. 1782, PCC, Item 137, I, f. 347; *JCC*, XXII, 447.

19. G. Morris to Ridley, 6 Aug. 1782, and R. Morris to Ridley, 6 Oct. 1782, Matthew Ridley Papers, MHS. For other comments, see G. Morris to Nathanael Greene, 24 Dec. 1781, and R. Morris to Franklin, 27 Nov. 1781, Ferguson, ed., *Papers of Morris*, III, 439–40, 280–2.

20. Ver Steeg, *Robert Morris*, 132–5; Ferguson, *Power of the Purse*, 146–52; on the congressional committee's reception in New York, see George Clinton to R. R. Livingston, Poughkeepsie, 6 June 1782, R. R. Livingston Papers, box 9, NYHS.

21. Yates to Duane, Albany, 7 Sept. 1782; Yates to Duane and Ezra L'Hommedieu, 19 Oct. 1782; Yates to R. Morris, 4 Nov. 1782; Morris to Yates, 29 Nov. 1782; L'Hommedieu to Yates, 2 Aug. and 18 Oct. 1782; all in Abraham Yates, Jr., Papers, box 2, NYPL.

22. Morris to Whipple, 13 April 1782, Sturgis Papers, box 2, HUL; Morris to Hamilton, 2 July 1782, and Hamilton to Morris, 13 Aug. 1782, Syrett, ed., *Papers of Hamilton*, III, 98, 132–44; Ver Steeg, *Robert Morris*, 100–2.

23. Ferguson, *Power of the Purse*, 149–52.

24. *JCC*, XXII, 407–8, 429–46; Ver Steeg, *Robert Morris*, 124–8.

25. *JCC*, XXII, 440.

26. Morris needed no reminder of New England's opposition to Article 8, but see Gov. Trumbull to Morris, Lebanon, 7 Nov. 1781, Ferguson, ed., *Papers of Morris*, III, 162.

27. N.C. Delegates to Gov. Martin, 22 Oct. 1782, and Hugh Williamson to Martin, 2 Sept. 1782, *LMCC*, VI, 516–19, 462; Madison, Notes on Debates, 20 Nov. 1782, Hutchinson, ed., *Papers of Madison*, V, 294.

28. *JCC*, XXII, 423, XXIII, 545–7, 604–6.

29. Jeremiah Powell to Pres. Huntington, Boston, 10 March 1781, PCC, Item 65, I, f. 521; Nathaniel Appleton to S. Adams, 24 April 1782, S. Adams Papers, box 6, NYPL; and see Jackson T. Main, *The Antifederalists: Critics of the Constitution, 1781–1788* (Chapel Hill, 1961), 85–6; R. Morris to Governors of Mass., R.I., and Md., 3 Jan. 1782, Ferguson, ed., *Papers of Morris*, III, 481–2.

30. Morris to Varnum, 16 July 1782, Robert Morris Papers, Letter Book D, LC. For a general account of Rhode Island's opposition to the impost, see Irwin H. Polishook, *Rhode Island and the Union, 1774–1795* (Evanston, Ill., 1969), 53–80.

31. Howell to Gov. William Greene, 30 July 1782, *LMCC*, VI, 399–403.

32. Howell to Welcome Arnold, 3 Aug. 1782, Gratz Collection, case 1, box 7, HSP; to Moses Brown, 6 Aug. and 6 Nov. 1782, Moses Brown Papers IV, RIHS; and see Howell to Nicholas Brown, 3 Aug. 1782, Nicholas Brown Papers, John Carter Brown Library, Brown University, Providence, R.I.

33. James B. Hedges, *The Browns of Providence Plantations: Colonial Years* (Providence, 1952), 324.

34. Howell to W. Arnold, 3 Aug. 1782; Howell to Theodore Foster, 9 Oct. 1782, Theodore Foster Papers, RIHS; Howell to Greene, 30 July 1782.

35. Harry H. Clark, ed., *Six New Letters of Thomas Paine: Being Pieces on the Five Per Cent Duty Addressed to the Citizens of Rhode Island* (Madison, 1939); *JCC*, XXIII, 770–2, 783–4.

36. Madison, Notes on Debates, 6 and 24 Dec. 1782; Edmund Pendleton to Madison, Virginia, 9 Dec. 1782; Harrison to Va. Delegates, 4 Jan. 1783; Randolph to Madison, Richmond, 7 Feb. 1783; and Madison to Randolph, 22 Jan. 1783; all in Hutchinson, ed., *Papers of Madison*, V, 373–4, 442, 383, VI, 14, 207, 55.

37. Madison, Notes on Debates, 6, 12, 13, and 16–18 Dec. 1782, *ibid.*, V, 372–3, 398–9, 407, 411, 419–20; *JCC*, XXIII, 813–19, 822; Polishook, *Rhode Island*, 81–93.

38. There are numerous accounts of the deliberations of early 1783 and the related developments at the army encampment at Newburgh.

See Ferguson, *Power of the Purse*, 155–71; Ver Steeg, *Robert Morris*, 166–86; Henderson, *Party Politics*, 318–49; and Richard H. Kohn, *Eagle and Sword: The Federalists and the Creation of the Military Establishment in America, 1783–1802* (New York, 1975), 17–39.

39. Champagne, *Alexander McDougall*, 181–200.

40. Madison, Notes on Debates, 13 Jan. 1783, Hutchinson, ed., *Papers of Madison*, VI, 31–4; A. Lee to S. Adams, 29 Jan. 1783, *LMCC*, VII, 28.

41. G. Morris to Henry Knox, 7 Feb. 1783, Knox Papers, XI, MHS; Hamilton to Washington, 13 Feb. 1783, Syrett, ed., *Papers of Hamilton*, III, 253–5.

42. Knox to McDougall, West Point, 21 Feb. 1783, Knox Papers, XI, MHS; and see Washington to Hamilton, Newburgh, 4 March 1783, Syrett, ed., *Papers of Hamilton*, III, 277–9; "Brutus" [McDougall] to Knox, 12 and 27 Feb. 1783, Knox Papers, XI, MHS.

43. R. Morris to Pres. of Congress, 24 Jan. 1783, Wharton, ed., *Rev. Dipl. Corr.*, VI, 228–9.

44. *JCC*, XXIV, 126–7; Madison, Notes on Debates, 27–29 Jan. 1783, Hutchinson, ed., *Papers of Madison*, VI, 134–53, 158–69.

45. Madison, Notes on Debates, 4–7 and 11 Feb. 1783, and Madison to Randolph, 11 Feb. 1783, *ibid.*, 188–9, 195–9, 215–16, 223; Hamilton to Gov. Clinton, 24 Feb. 1783, Syrett, ed., *Papers of Hamilton*, III, 268–74.

46. Madison, Notes on Debates, 17 Feb., 27–28 March, and 1 April 1783, Hutchinson, ed., *Papers of Madison*, VI, 247, 402, 407–8, 425.

47. Madison, Notes on Debates, 28–29 Jan. and 21 Feb. 1783, *ibid.*, 141–9, 158–65, 270–4.

48. Madison, Notes on Debates, 20–21 Feb. 1783, *ibid.*, 265–74.

49. Madison, Notes on Debates, 17, 20, and 22 March 1783, *ibid.*, 348, 370, 375. Dyer's anxiety over his position is reflected in his letters to Gov. Trumbull, 18 March, 3 and 12 April 1783, Jonathan Trumbull, Sr., Papers, CHS; and see Samuel Holten to Aaron Wood, 31 July 1783, Samuel Holten Papers, box 1, LC.

50. Morris, *The Peacemakers*, 438–45.

51. *JCC*, XXIV, 207–9, 256–61. On Hamilton's dissent, see his letter to Clinton, 14 May 1783, Syrett, ed., *Papers of Hamilton*, III, 354–6.

52. Ver Steeg, *Robert Morris*, 176–8; Madison, Notes on Debates, 11 March 1783, Hutchinson, ed., *Papers of Madison*, VI, 322–3.

53. Higginson to S. Adams, 20 May 1783, S. Adams Papers, box 6, NYPL; Higginson to [Samuel Holten?], Boston, 14 Oct. 1783, Etting Collection, Members of the Old Congress, II, HSP; Osgood to J. Adams, 7 Dec. 1783, S. Adams Papers, box 6; Osgood to J. Adams, 14 Dec. 1783, Adams Family Papers, reel 362, MHS; and on the General Court's criticism of various aspects of congressional financial policy, see S. Adams and Tristam Dalton to Pres. Boudinot, Boston, 14 July 1783, and Hancock to Boudinot, Boston, 28 Oct. 1783, PCC, Item 65, II, ff. 185–8, 225–8. For

a general account, see Stephen Patterson, "Aːter Newburgh: The Struggle for the Impost in Massachusetts," in James Kirby Martin, ed., *The Human Dimensions of Nation Making* (Madison, 1976), 218–42.

54. *JCC*, XXVI, 465–71.

55. These are the terms used by Ferguson, *Power of the Purse*, 107, 125.

56. Hamilton to Clinton, 14 May 1783; Madison, Notes on Debates, 1 April 1783; Hamilton, Resolutions; all in Syrett, ed., *Papers of Hamilton*, III, 354, 314, 420–6.

57. Jackson to Lincoln, Boston, 19 April 1783, Fogg Collection, vol. 19, Maine Historical Society.

58. On Gordon, see his letters to Nicholas Brown, Jamaica Plain, Mass., 30 Sept. 1782 and 22 Dec. 1783, Nicholas Brown Papers, John Carter Brown Library, Providence, and to J. Adams, 7 Sept. 1782, Adams Family Papers, reel 361, MHS.

59. Madison, Notes on Debates, 21 Feb. 1783, Hutchinson, ed., *Papers of Madison*, VI, 272–3.

60. R.I. Delegates to Gov. Greene, 15 Oct. 1782, *LMCC*, VI, 504; Howell to Thomas Hazard, 26 Aug. 1783, RIHS; Howell to Nicholas Brown, 19 Sept. and 12 Oct. 1782, N. Brown Papers, John Carter Brown Library.

61. Knox to G. Morris, 21 Feb. 1783, Knox Papers, XI, MHS; Lowell to Lincoln, Boston, 20 Nov. 1782, Miscellaneous Bound MSS, MHS; and see Lincoln to Lowell, 24 Sept. 1782, Sparks Papers, XII, 502–3, HUL; and Higginson to Knox, 8 Feb. 1787, in J. Franklin Jameson, ed., "Letters of Stephen Higginson, 1783–1804," American Historical Association, *Annual Report for the Year 1896*, I, 745.

Chapter XIV: Union Without Power: The Confederation in Peacetime

1. Merrill Jensen, *The New Nation;* Bailyn, "The Central Themes of the Revolution," in Kurtz and Hutson, eds., *Essays*, 19–20; but see also Wood, *Creation of the American Republic*, 393–429.

2. *Boston Evening Post*, 22 Nov. 1783; Boston *American Herald*, 5 April 1784 (reprinted from *Pa. Journal*). On the flight to Princeton, see Burnett, *Continental Congress*, 575–80.

3. Rush to John Montgomery, 30 Oct. 1783, and see his other letters of 7 and 29 July, 9 and 24 Oct. 1783, Benjamin Rush Papers, vol. 41, Library Company of Philadelphia; Willing to Bingham, 12 Sept. 1783, Provincial Delegates Collection, II, HSP; Thomson to John Dickinson, 11 July 1783, and Dickinson's reply of the same date, Dickinson Papers, box 1, item 6, HSP.

4. Howell to Nicholas Brown, 30 July 1783, N. Brown Papers, John Carter Brown Library, Providence; Osgood to J. Adams, 7 Dec. 1783, *LMCC*, VII, 378.

5. The politics of this issue is discussed in Lawrence D. Cress, "Whither Columbia? Congressional Residence and the Politics of the New Nation, 1776–1787," *WMQ*, 32 (1975), 581–600, and in Joseph Davis, *Sectionalism in American Politics, 1774–1787*, 59–75.

6. Neither Madison's notes of debates nor the delegates' extant correspondence contain any detailed discussion on this point, with the exception of a speech by Theodorick Bland on 29 Jan. 1783. See Madison's notes for that date and the draft of the committee report that became the basis for the resolutions of 18 April 1783, Hutchinson, ed., *Papers of Madison*, VI, 164, 312; and Joseph Jones to Washington, 6 May 1783, *LMCC*, VII, 159.

7. On the progress of the impost, see Main, *The Antifederalists*, 72–102, and Jackson T. Main, *Political Parties Before the Constitution* (Chapel Hill, 1973), 77, 89–90, 139, 167, 228, 303, 306. For comments on the reception of the impost in Virginia, see Joseph Jones to Madison, Richmond, 25 and 31 May, 14 and 28 June 1783, Hutchinson, ed., *Papers of Madison*, VII, 76, 99, 143–5, 197; R. H. Lee to R. W. Carter, Richmond, 3 July 1783, and to William Whipple, Chantilly, Va., 1 July 1783, Ballagh, ed., *Letters of Lee*, II, 281–4; and see Whipple's reply, critical of Lee's objections, from Portsmouth, N.H., 15 Sept. 1783, Lee Family Papers, reel 7 (American Philosophical Society); and Washington's circular letter to the states, 12 June 1783, Fitzpatrick, ed., *Writings of Washington*, XXVI, 483–96. On the reception of the impost in Massachusetts, see Patterson, "After Newburgh," in Martin, ed., *Human Dimensions*, 218–42; and see Polishook, *Rhode Island*, 98–9, 110–11.

8. Clinton's growing resentment of congressional handling of the Vermont question is clearly reflected in two letters to the N.Y. Delegates, 25 Aug. and 18 Sept. 1781, Legislative Papers 1780–1803, Nos. 2435, 2442, NYSL. Manuscript drafts of Yates's various essays against the impost and other proposals for increasing the power of Congress can be found in the Abraham Yates, Jr., Papers, box 4, NYPL.

9. On the deteriorating financial situation of Congress and state action to assume the debt, see Ferguson, *Power of the Purse*, 220–50.

10. Osgood to J. Adams, 14 Dec. 1783, Adams Family Papers, reel 362; Holten, quoted in David Howell to Nicholas Brown, 30 July 1783, N. Brown Papers, John Carter Brown Library, Providence; A. Lee to J. Adams, 12 Aug. 1784, Adams Family Papers, reel 363, MHS; Howell to Jabez Bowen, 31 May 1784, Staples, *Rhode Island in the Continental Congress*, 514; but for a more balanced assessment of Morris's administration of his office, see Osgood to Stephen Higginson, 2 Feb. 1784, *LMCC*, VII, 430–6.

11. Holten to S. Adams, 11 April 1785, S. Adams Papers, box 6, NYPL; Osgood to Gerry, Boston, 3 Jan. 1784 [i.e., 1785], 18 Feb. 1785, Gerry Papers II, MHS (discussing Osgood's appointment to the treasury); A. Lee to J. Adams, 6 March 1785, Adams Family Papers, reel 364, MHS; Howell to J. Arnold, 21 Feb. 1784, Staples, *Rhode Island in the Continental Congress*, 479; and see Gerry to J. Adams, 16 June 1784, Adams Family Papers, reel 363; and R. H. Lee to S. Adams, 20 May 1785, *LMCC*, VIII, 122.

12. Ferguson, *Power of the Purse*, 242; Osgood to Gordon, 19 Jan. 1786, Samuel Osgood Papers, NYHS.

13. On New Jersey's action, see Richard P. McCormick, *Experiment in Independence: New Jersey in the Critical Period* (New Brunswick, N.J., 1950), 233–44; Gorham to James Warren, 6 March 1786, and Charles Pinckney, Speech Before N.J. Assembly [13 March 1786], *LMCC*, VIII, 318, 321–30.

14. These problems are reviewed in Frederick W. Marks, III, *Independence on Trial: Foreign Affairs and the Making of the Constitution* (Baton Rouge, La., 1973), 3–95. I agree with the major thesis advanced by Marks, that congressional inability to cope with problems of foreign relations provided the major stimulus for criticism of the Articles in the mid-1780's.

15. The definitive treaty is reprinted in *JCC*, XXVI, 23–31.

16. See Emory G. Evans, "Private Indebtedness and the Revolution in Virginia, 1776–1796," *WMQ*, 28 (1971), 357–67; on commercial losses in 1782, see Ver Steeg, *Robert Morris*, 138.

17. Richard Peters to Horatio Gates, 13 March 1783; William Floyd to Gov. Clinton, 17 March 1783; *LMCC*, VII, 79, 88.

18. On the formulation of postwar British policy, see Charles R. Ritcheson, *Aftermath of Revolution: British Policy Toward the United States, 1783–1795* (Dallas, 1969), 3–87.

19. Mason to Henry, Gunston Hall, Va., 6 May 1783; for expressions of his criticism of Congress on other issues, see his letters to Samuel Purviance, 17 July 1782, and to Edmund Randolph, 19 Oct. 1782; all in Rutland, ed., *Papers of Mason*, II, 771, 738–41, 751–3. It could be argued that Mason was a strict constructionist in the literal sense of the term, defending congressional supremacy in foreign affairs yet criticizing its attempts to create a national domain because the Articles had clearly granted authority over the former while withholding the latter.

20. Thomson, Memorandum [n.d., probably 1784 or 1785], Charles Thomson Papers, vol. II, LC; and see Hamilton to Clinton, 1 June 1783, Syrett, ed., *Papers of Hamilton*, III, 367–72.

21. See the draft report of a committee appointed to consider Adams's letters [25 Sept. 1783], *LMCC*, VII, 304–7.

22. N.H. Delegates to Meshech Weare, 5 May 1784; Hugh William-

Notes 455

son to Gov. Martin, 29 April 1784; both in *LMCC*, VII, 514, 506; see also *JCC*, XXVI, 317–22.

23. N.C. Delegates to Gov. Martin, 26 Sept. 1783, *LMCC*, VII, 311.

24. R. H. Lee to Madison, 26 Nov. and 27 Dec. 1784; and John F. Mercer to Madison, 26 Nov. 1784; all in Hutchinson, ed., *Papers of Madison*, VIII, 151–2, 202.

25. *JCC*, XXVIII, 70, 201–5; and see Monroe to Jefferson, 14 Dec. 1784, Boyd, ed., *Papers of Jefferson*, 573, and to Madison, 18 Dec. 1784, Hutchinson, ed., *Papers of Madison*, VIII, 188–90. Monroe's letters indicate that the need to distinguish between laying duties for purposes of regulation and revenue was apparent from the start.

26. McHenry to Washington, 26 Aug. 1785, *LMCC*, VIII, 182–3.

27. Monroe to Madison, 26 July 1785, Hutchinson, ed., *Papers of Madison*, VIII, 329–30.

28. Yates to Howell, Albany, 29 Aug. 1785, Abraham Yates, Jr., Papers, box 2, NYPL; and see Gerry to S. Adams, 30 Sept. 1785, Rufus King to Nathan Dane, 17 Sept. 1785, *LMCC*, VIII, 224, 218–19; David Jackson to George Bryan, 18 July 1785, and Samuel Bryan to George Bryan [May 1785], George Bryan Papers, box 2, HSP.

29. Dana to J. Adams, Cambridge, 30 Jan. 1785, Adams Family Papers, reel 364, MHS.

30. Mass. Delegates to Gov. Bowdoin, 3 Sept. 1785, and see their earlier letters to Bowdoin, 18 and 25 Aug. 1785, *LMCC*, VIII, 206–10, 188–90, 196–7. The resolves are reprinted in Charles H. King, ed., *The Life and Correspondence of Rufus King* (New York, 1894–1900), I, 58; and for a careful analysis of the General Court's action, see Nathan Dane to King, Boston, 8 Oct. 1785, *ibid.*, 67–70.

31. Monroe to Jefferson, 12 April and 15 Aug. 1785, and another letter of 16 June 1785, Boyd, ed., *Papers of Jefferson*, VIII, 76–80, 382–3, 215–17; and see Joseph Jones to Monroe, Richmond, 21 May 1785, Monroe Papers, reel 9, LC.

32. This issue and the ensuing debates and manuevers it evoked are carefully detailed in Henderson, *Party Politics*, 387–99.

33. Thomson to Read, 27 Sept. 1784, *LMCC*, VII, 593. For a general discussion of the conclusions that were drawn from congressional impotence and indecision in foreign affairs, see Marks, *Independence on Trial*, 96–141.

34. Merrill Jensen, "The Creation of the National Domain, 1781–1784," *Mississippi Valley Historical Review*, 26 (1939), 323–42; and see the recent interpretation advanced in Peter S. Onuf, "Toward Federalism: Virginia, Congress, and the Western Lands," *WMQ*, 34 (1977), 353–74.

35. Jack Eblen, *The First and Second United States Empires: Governors and Territorial Government, 1784–1912* (Pittsburgh, 1968), 17–51

(quotation at 47); and see Robert F. Berkhofer, Jr., "Jefferson, the Ordinance of 1784, and the Origins of the American Territorial System," *WMQ*, 29 (1972), 231–62.

36. King to Gerry, 18 June 1786; Monroe to Gov. Henry, 12 Aug. 1786; King to Gerry, 4 June 1786; all in *LMCC*, VIII, 393, 421–5, 380–2.

37. This was particularly apparent to Madison, as Linda K. Kerber has recently pointed out in a review of *Papers of Madison*, III–X: "Despite Madison's obvious concern for the implications of Shays's Rebellion, the Mississippi question and the status of the region west of Virginia were more influential in leading him to wish for a government strong enough to resolve such issues"; *WMQ*, 35 (1978), 150–1.

38. Hopkinson to Jefferson, 20 April 1785, Boyd, ed., *Papers of Jefferson*, VIII, 99. Distribution of the congressional journals was still a problem; see Hugh Williamson to Charles Thomson, Edenton, N.C., 14 Jan. 1786, Gratz Collection, case 14, box 31, HSP.

39. Jefferson to Madison, 20 Feb. 1784, Boyd, ed., *Papers of Jefferson*, VI, 548–9.

40. Gerry to Higginson, 4 March 1784, and Howell to J. Arnold, 21 Feb. 1784, *LMCC*, VII, 461, 451; Blanchard to Gerry, 18 June 1784, Gerry-Knight Collection, MHS; on the dissolution of the Committee of the States, see Burnett, *The Continental Congress*, 595–612.

41. Catherine Livingston to Matthew Ridley, 10 Dec. 1786, Matthew Ridley Papers, box 3, MHS; Charles Storer to Abigail Adams, Boston, 13 April 1786, Adams Family Papers, reel 367, MHS; Eliza H. Trist to Jefferson, Phila., 24 July 1786, Boyd, ed., *Papers of Jefferson*, X, 169.

42. Thomson to Jefferson, 1 Oct. 1784, Boyd, ed., *Papers of Jefferson*, VII, 432.

43. Washington to Jefferson, Mt. Vernon, 29 March 1784, *ibid.*, 49–52; and see Samuel Holten to William Gordon, 22 Aug. 1785, Holten Papers, box 1, LC.

Chapter XV: Toward the Philadelphia Convention

1. The most important of these are " 'Experience Must Be Our Only Guide': History, Democratic Theory, and the United States Constitution," and " 'That Politics May Be Reduced to a Science': David Hume, James Madison, and the Tenth Federalist," reprinted in Trevor Colbourn, ed., *Fame and the Founding Fathers: Essays by Douglass Adair* (New York, 1974).

2. R. Morris to Matthew Ridley, Phila., 5 Nov. 1783, Ridley Papers, box 2, MHS; Langdon to Jefferson, Portsmouth, N.H., 7 Dec. 1785, Boyd, ed., *Papers of Jefferson*, IX, 84; David Ramsay to J. Adams, 14 May 1786, Adams Family Papers, reel 368, MHS; G. Morris to Jay, Phila., 25 Sept.

1783, 10 Jan. 1784, G. Morris Papers, folders 723, 728, Columbia University Library.

3. [Mason], Fairfax County (Va.) Freeholders' Address, 30 May 1783, Rutland, ed., *Papers of Mason*, II, 781.

4. The Torrington and Farmington resolutions were reprinted in the *Connecticut Courant*, 29 July and 12 Aug. 1783. Numerous articles against commutation appeared in Connecticut newspapers throughout the fall of 1783 and into the following spring.

5. Boston *Independent Chronicle*, 16 June 1785.

6. "A Rough Hewer," *New York Gazetteer*, 4 Aug. 1783, reprinted in *Boston Evening Post*, 30 Aug. 1783.

7. *Connecticut Courant*, 5 Aug. 1783.

8. "Observator," Boston *American Herald*, 12 Sept. 1785; "C.S.," "To the Printers Throughout the United States," *Boston Evening Post*, 26 July 1783, much reprinted in other newspapers; and see "Solicitor," *N.H. Gazette*, 15 Nov. 1783.

9. Treadwell, writing in the *Connecticut Courant*, 23 Sept. 1783; "Pro Bono-Republicae," Boston *American Herald*, 25 April 1785, reprinted in *Pa. Packet*, 11 May 1785; and see Washington to William Gordon, Newburgh, 8 July 1783, Fitzpatrick, ed., *Writings of Washington*, XXVII, 51.

10. *Connecticut Courant*, 25 May 1784.

11. Wood, *Creation of the American Republic*, 319–43, 363–89.

12. Marchant to Price, Newport, 4 Aug. 1785, Adams Family Papers, reel 365, MHS; Thomson to Franklin, Phila., 13 Aug. 1784, Bache Collection, American Philosophical Society; and see Rufus King to J. Adams, 4 Dec. 1785, King, ed., *Life of King*, I, 116–17.

13. Jay to Matthew Ridley, 31 March 1785, Ridley Papers, box 3, MHS; and see Thomas Cushing to J. Adams, Boston, 26 Nov. 1783, Adams Family Papers, reel 361, MHS.

14. Thomson to Dickinson, 19 July 1785, Dickinson Papers, box 1, item 6, HSP; and see Dickinson to Thomson, 12 June 1783, *Colls.* NYHS, 11 (1878), 171–2.

15. Madison to Monroe, Orange, Va., 7 Aug. 1785, and to Jefferson, 20 Aug. 1785, Hutchinson, ed., *Papers of Madison*, VIII, 333–6, 344–5.

16. Madison to Jefferson, Phila., 3 Oct. 1785, and to Washington, Richmond, 9 Dec. 1785; and see Madison's drafts of resolutions and notes on debates, November–December 1785; *ibid.*, 373–5, 438–9, 409–10, 413–14, 431–2.

17. Madison to Monroe, Richmond, 22 Jan. 1786, and to Jefferson, same date, *ibid.*, 483, 476–7.

18. Madison to Monroe, Orange, Va., 14 and 19 March, 1786, *ibid.*, 497–8, 505–6; Monroe's letter of 16 Feb. 1786 is missing, but its contents can be inferred from Madison's reply of 19 March.

19. Grayson to Madison, 22 March 1786, *ibid.*, 509–10; Pinckney, Speech Before N.J. Assembly [13 March 1786], *LMCC*, VIII, 323–4.

20. Thomas Rodney, Diary [3 May 1786], Charles Pettit to James Wilson, 2 July 1786, *LMCC*, VIII, 350–1, 359; *JCC*, XXX, 387, XXXI, 494–8.

21. Timothy Bloodworth to Gov. Caswell, 4 Sept. 1786, *LMCC*, VIII, 462. Abraham Yates, Jr., published a lengthy criticism of the committee's recommendations in the *New York Gazetteer*, 29 Jan. 1787, reprinted in Boston *American Herald*, 19 Feb. 1787.

22. Rodney, Diary [3 May 1786]; Monroe to John Sullivan, 16 Aug. 1786, *LMCC*, VIII, 430; Madison to Monroe, Orange, Va., 13 May 1786, Hutchinson, ed., *Papers of Madison*, IX, 55.

23. Jacob Broom to Tench Coxe, Wilmington, 4 Aug. 1786, Tench Coxe Papers, Incoming Correspondence, box 8, HSP; Daniel Carroll to Madison, Annapolis, 13 March 1786, Hutchinson, ed., *Papers of Madison*, VIII, 496.

24. Rufus King to Jonathan Jackson, 11 June 1786, Theodore Sedgwick to Caleb Strong, 6 Aug. 1786, *LMCC*, VIII, 389–90, 415–16; Stephen Higginson to Samuel Osgood, Boston, 22 July 1786, Osgood Papers, NYHS. On Connecticut's failure to appoint delegates, see Jeremiah Wadsworth to Samuel Ward, Hartford, 13 Aug. 1786, Samuel Ward Papers, 1785–91, RIHS.

25. Grayson to Madison, 28 May 1786, Hutchinson, ed., *Papers of Madison*, IX, 64.

26. Madison to Jefferson, 12 Aug. 1786, and Monroe to Madison, 31 May 1786, *ibid.*, 95–7, 68–70.

27. Madison to Monroe, Annapolis, 11 Sept. 1786, *ibid.*, 121–2.

28. Monroe to Madison, 2 and 7 Oct. 1786, *ibid.*, 139, 143; and see the remarks of Rufus King (11 Oct. 1786) and Nathan Dane (9 Nov. 1786) before the Mass. General Court, *LMCC*, VIII, 479, 504.

29. Madison to Washington, 21 Feb. 1787, and his Notes on Debates in Congress, same date, Hutchinson, ed., *Papers of Madison*, IX, 285–6, 290–2; Irvine to Wilson, 6 March 1787, *LMCC*, VIII, 551. For the proceedings of Congress, see Merrill Jensen, ed., *The Documentary History of the Ratification of the Constitution* (Madison, 1976–), I, 185–7.

30. Madison to Washington, 1 and 8 Nov. 1786, 7 and 24 Dec. 1786; Washington to Madison, 18 Nov. and 18 Dec. 1786; all in Hutchinson, ed., *Papers of Madison*, IX, 155, 166, 199, 224, 170–1, 215–16.

31. State actions on the appointment of delegates are reprinted in Jensen, ed., *Doc. His. of the Constitution*, I, 195–229.

32. Forrest McDonald, *E Pluribus Unum: The Formation of the American Republic, 1776–1790* (Cambridge, 1965), 162.

33. Notes of the Connecticut Assembly's debates over appointing delegates were printed in the *Connecticut Courant*, 21 May 1787; and

see Owen Ireland, "Partisanship and the Constitution: Pennsylvania, 1787," *Pennsylvania History*, 45 (1978), 322.

34. Madison to Edmund Pendleton, 24 Feb. 1787, and Edmund Randolph to Madison, Richmond, 1 March 1787, Hutchinson, ed., *Papers of Madison*, IX, 294–5, 301.

35. These developments are traced in Henderson, *Party Politics*, 399–408.

36. Higginson to Osgood, 21 Feb. 1787, Osgood Papers, NYHS; on the changing perceptions of Massachusetts leaders who had formerly been suspicious of any efforts to amend the Articles, see, in general, Robert East, "The Massachusetts Conservatives in the Critical Period," in Morris, ed., *Era of the American Revolution*, 349–91.

37. Varnum to Samuel Ward, 2 April 1787, Samuel Ward Papers, 1785–91, RIHS; Grayson to William Short, 16 April 1787, *LMCC*, VIII, 581; Jay to J. Adams, 21 Feb. 1787, Adams Family Papers, reel 368, MHS; King to Gerry, 18 Feb. 1787, and to Theophilus Parsons, 8 April 1787, King, ed., *Life of King*, I, 215, 218; Madison to Pendleton, 24 Feb. 1787, and to Randolph, 15 April 1787, Hutchinson, ed., *Papers of Madison*, IX, 294, 378. For similar comments, see Henry Knox to Higginson, New York, 25 Feb. 1787, and Jeremiah Wadsworth to Knox, Hartford, 15 April 1787, Knox Papers, XIX, XX, MHS; and Stephen Mix Mitchell to William Samuel Johnson, Wethersfield, Conn., 26 July 1787, W. S. Johnson Papers, II, CHS.

38. See Madison's Notes on Ancient and Modern Confederacies [April–June? 1786], and his Memorandum, "Vices of the Political System of the United States," April 1787, Hutchinson, ed., *Papers of Madison*, IX, 3–24, 345–57.

39. The same point is made in Ver Steeg, *Robert Morris*, 195.

40. Reprinted in Edmund S. Morgan, ed., "The Political Establishments of the United States, 1784," *WMQ*, 23 (1966), 286–308 (quotation at 305).

41. Boston *American Herald*, 12 Sept. 1785.

42. Dickinson to Charles Thomson, Phila., 12 June 1783, *Colls*. NYHS, 11 (1878), 171–2; and see the two draft memoranda briefly elaborating on these ideas in the John Dickinson Papers, box 5, item 65, and box 15, item 250, HSP; "Plan for a New Federal Government," first printed in *New York Journal*, 19 Oct. 1786, reprinted in Boston *American Herald*, 6 Nov. 1786, and *N.H. Gazette*, 11 Nov. 1786; Boston *American Herald*, 21 Aug. 1786.

43. Adams, *Defence of the Constitutions*, II, 362–4; Burke to N.C. Assembly [August 1779], *LMCC*, IV, 367–8; "Grotius," Boston *American Herald*, 10 Feb. 1783; "Solicitor," *N.H. Gazette*, 15 Nov. 1783; and see "Tullius," *Three Letters Addressed to the Public* (Philadelphia, 1783), 8; and "Sydney" [Abraham Yates, Jr.], "Considerations upon the Seven

Articles reported, and now lying on the Table of Congress," Boston *American Herald*, 19 Feb. 1787 (a draft is in the Yates Papers, box 3, NYPL).

44. *Three Letters*, 6; "A Connecticut Farmer," *Remarks on a Pamphlet, Entitled "A Dissertation on the Political Union and Constitution of the Thirteen United States of North-America"* ([New Haven], 1784), 18. I consider the attribution of the latter pamphlet to Roger Sherman dubious.

45. Lee, quoted in Madison, Notes on Debates, 21 Feb. 1783, Hutchinson, ed., *Papers of Madison*, VI, 272.

46. *N.H. Gazette*, 15 Nov. 1783; *Remarks on a Pamphlet*, 21.

47. "Jonathan of the Valley," Boston *Independent Chronicle*, 20 Oct. 1785; "Grotius," *Boston Gazette*, 3 Feb. 1783.

48. Wood, *Creation of the American Republic*, 362.

49. *N.H. Gazette*, 15 Nov. 1783; "To the Members of the Convention, whether good or bad," *Connecticut Courant*, 6 April 1784; *Three Letters*, 8–10.

50. Jefferson to Adams, Paris, 23 Feb. 1787, and Adams to Jefferson, London, 1 March 1787, Boyd, ed., *Papers of Jefferson*, XI, 177, 189–90; and see John Jay to Adams, 12 May 1787, Adams Family Papers, reel 369, MHS.

51. Pelatiah Webster, *A Dissertation on the Political Union and Constitution of the Thirteen United States* (Philadelphia, 1783), quotation at 33; Rush's widely reprinted essay, published under the pseudonym "Nestor," first appeared in the Philadelphia *Independent Gazetteer*, 3 June 1786; Jay to Jefferson, 18 Aug. 1786, and see Jay to Washington, 7 Jan. 1787, both in Henry P. Johnston, ed., *The Correspondence and Public Papers of John Jay* (New York, 1890–93), III, 210, 226–9.

52. "To the Members of the Convention," and "The Republican," *Connecticut Courant*, 6 April 1784 and 19 March 1787.

53. Morgan, "The Great Political Fiction," *New York Review of Books*, 9 March 1978, 17.

54. Madison to Randolph, 8 April 1787, and to Washington, 16 April 1787, Hutchinson, ed., *Papers of Madison*, IX, 370–84. Madison was convinced, of course, that representation had to be proportioned to population, which itself perhaps implied that representatives should be popularly elected, but he still left this question open.

55. Osgood to J. Adams, 14 Nov. 1786, Adams Family Papers, reel 368, MHS; Carrington to Jefferson, 24 April 1787, Boyd, ed., *Papers of Jefferson*, XI, 311–12; and see Rufus King to Jonathan Jackson, 3 Sept. 1786, *LMCC*, VIII, 458–9.

56. [John Adams], *Thoughts on Government* (Philadelphia, 1776), 27; Morgan, ed., "Political Establishments," 288, 300, 304; see "The North-American," *Pa. Journal*, 17 Sept. 1783.

57. Rush, in Philadelphia *Independent Gazetteer*, 3 June 1786; see Wood, *Creation of the American Republic*, 425–32.

58. Read to Dickinson, 6 Jan. 1787, R. R. Logan Collection, box 4, HSP; Read to Dickinson, Newcastle, Del., 17 Jan. 1787, and Phila., 21 May 1787, in William T. Read, *Life and Correspondence of George Read* (Philadelphia, 1870), 438–9, 443–4. The last of these letters indicates, incidentally, that the Virginians were still undecided about popular elections of members of the lower house.

59. Higginson to Henry Knox, 8 Feb. 1787, Jameson, ed., "Letters of Higginson," 745–9; "Harrington," Boston *American Herald*, 11 June 1787; Mitchell to Charles Thomson, 6 June 1787, Gratz Collection, case 14, box 30, HSP. For a more unusual discussion, see the pamphlet *Fragments on the Confederation of the American States* (Philadelphia, 1787), published just on the eve of the Convention.

60. See Wood, *Creation of the American Republic*, 463–75.

61. Osgood to J. Adams, 14 Nov. 1786.

62. Jefferson to Madison, Paris, 20 Dec. 1787, Boyd, ed., *Papers of Jefferson*, XII, 442.

63. Hutchinson, ed., *Papers of Madison*, IX, 345–58.

64. Adair, " 'That Politics May Be Reduced to a Science,' " in *Fame and the Founding Fathers*; Madison to Randolph, 8 April 1787, and to Washington, 16 April 1787.

65. Farrand, ed., *Records of Federal Convention*, I, 20–2.

66. *Ibid.*, 34.

67. Such a proposal did not, of course, unilaterally erase all the ambiguity inherent in creating a bicameral legislature that ultimately came to represent not only population but the states as corporate units. See the fuller discussion in Pole, *Political Representation*, 353–73, and Wood, *Creation of the American Republic*, 519–64.

68. My general debt to the interpretation advanced by Gordon Wood is obvious. On the evolution of the doctrine of judicial review, see the still valuable essay by Edward S. Corwin, "The Progress of Constitutional Theory Between the Declaration of Independence and the Meeting of the Philadelphia Convention," *American Historical Review*, 30 (1924–5), 511–36.

69. Mitchell to Johnson, Wethersfield, Conn., 26 July 1787, William Samuel Johnson Papers, vol. II, CHS.

70. Cotton Tufts to J. Adams, 15 May and 30 June 1787, Adams Family Papers, reel 369, MHS; Washington to Jay, Mt. Vernon, 10 March 1787, Johnston, ed., *Correspondence of Jay*, III, 238–40.

71. Coxe to William Tilghman, Phila., 8 Feb. 1787, William Tilghman Papers, box 2, HSP; Cadwalader to Charles Stewart, 27 March 1787, Stewart Papers, HUL.

72. Carrington to Jefferson, 9 June 1787, Boyd, ed., *Papers of Jeffer-*

son, XI, 408–9; Lincoln to George Thatcher, Boston, 9 May 1787, George Thatcher Papers, Boston Public Library; and see Wood, *Creation of the American Republic*, 483–99.

73. Boston *American Herald*, 3 Sept. 1787; "Rusticus," *New York Journal*, 13 Sept. 1787.

74. Goold to Coxe, New York, 14 June 1787, Tench Coxe Papers, Incoming Correspondence, box 27, HSP.

A Note on Primary Sources

MODERN scholarship on the Continental Congress has depended on two published collections of documents: Edmund C. Burnett, ed., *Letters of Members of the Continental Congress* (Washington, D.C., 1921–36), and Worthington C. Ford, *et al.*, eds., *Journals of the Continental Congress, 1774–1789* (Washington, D.C., 1904–37). Both were important milestones in the development of American historical editing, yet their limitations have long been apparent. Burnett did not reprint some documents that had already been published, and in excerpting letters he often omitted passages he did not consider germane to the immediate proceedings of Congress but that frequently provided revealing evidence of the delegates' political ideas and attitudes. Moreover, valuable additional materials continued to be discovered after Burnett completed his search of public archives and private holdings. Ford and his successors faced a similarly imposing task in presenting the official records of Congress. To supplement the terse entries in the daily journals, they reprinted a limited number of vital committee reports and motions that had been submitted to Congress; but these additions could hardly do justice to the massive collection of the Papers of the Continental Congress that are now on deposit at the National Archives. Although these records have been roughly indexed and microfilmed, they are organized in a way that has not encouraged their convenient use.

In conjunction with the Bicentennial, two major projects were accordingly launched to enhance our knowledge of the proceedings of Congress. The staff of the National Archives is completing a comprehensive index to the Papers of the Continental Congress that will facilitate the detailed reconstruction of many of its decisions. And a greatly expanded edition of the delegates' correspondence and other papers is now being published under the auspices of the Library of Congress: Paul

H. Smith, *et al.*, eds., *Letters of Delegates to Congress, 1774–1789* (Washington, D.C., 1976–).

Since this book was essentially completed before these projects issued their first publications, I can only look wistfully on the early results of their labors. Still, much of the most valuable material pertaining to Congress is already accessible in the printed and microfilmed editions of the papers of major Revolutionary leaders. Other important documents have been preserved in less prominent collections of personal papers and in those ever delightful (if also sometimes aggravating) autograph collections that contain everything from laundry receipts to sophisticated discussions of politics. There is an important advantage in relying on these biographical sources in addition to records organized around the proceedings of Congress, for the delegates' perceptions of issues and problems inevitably reflected their continuing experience at every level of politics as well as the information they received from correspondents at home, in the army, and in the state governments.

Anyone who undertakes serious archival research in Revolutionary history can only be staggered by the massive amount of material that has survived. Much of it will remain unpublished even after the major editorial projects now under way are completed. In the course of preparing this book, I have tried to read as widely in these sources as I possibly could and to use at least one major collection for each of the states. (Only Georgia, whose participation in national affairs was irregular, has been neglected.) The following description identifies only the most important and extensive of these sources. Other collections and publications, including contemporary pamphlets and newspaper essays that are discussed in the text, are cited in the Notes.

Among the papers of New England politicians, the most important are those of the "brace of Adamses": Samuel, who preserved too few of his own letters, and John, who I sometimes think wrote too many. Most of the extant letters written by the former are printed in Harry Alonzo Cushing, ed., *The Writings of Samuel Adams* (New York, 1904–08); others can be found (along with many John Adams letters) in Worthington C. Ford, ed., *Warren-Adams Letters* (*Collections* of the Massachusetts Historical Society, vols. LXXII–III [Boston, 1917–25]). But to reconstruct the wider range of his connections and activities, one has to turn to the Samuel Adams Papers, New York Public Library, which contain the letters he received from his numerous correspondents. For events in 1773–74, these should be supplemented by the Letters of the Boston Committee of Correspondence, in the same archive. The various letters, papers, and recollections of John Adams have long been a standard source for the history of the Continental Congress. Much of this material has already been published in L. H. Butterfield, *et al.*, eds., *Diary and Autobiography of John Adams* (Cambridge, 1961), and Butterfield and

Marc Friedlaender, eds., *Adams Family Correspondence* (Cambridge, 1963–73). But his full political correspondence is only now coming into print with the long-awaited appearance of the first two volumes of Robert Taylor, *et al.*, eds., *Papers of John Adams* (Cambridge, 1977–). Until this series is completed, historians will continue to rely on the Adams Family Papers (microfilm, Boston, 1954–59), especially Part IV, which includes the letters Adams received first as a delegate from 1774 to 1777 and then during his diplomatic career.

The Massachusetts Historical Society contains several important manuscript collections relevant to congressional politics. The Elbridge Gerry Papers and the Gerry-Russell Knight Collection cover the career of one of the longest-serving members of Congress. George Billias has recently deposited a microfilm copy of other Gerry letters he used in preparing his important biography of this major leader. Also useful were the Robert Treat Paine Papers for the 1770's and, for the 1780's, the respective papers of Samuel Holten, Henry Knox, and Theodore Sedgwick. Another collection of Samuel Holten Papers is in the Library of Congress. At the New-York Historical Society, the Samuel Osgood Papers and several sharply written letters by Stephen Higginson offer an important insight into the opposition to Robert Morris. Other valuable Higginson letters were printed in J. F. Jameson, ed., "Letters of Stephen Higginson, 1783–1804," American Historical Association, *Annual Report for the Year 1896*, I, 704–841.

However difficult they were to untangle, the affairs of Silas Deane had a major impact on congressional politics. Substantial materials on Deane have long been available in "Correspondence of Silas Deane, 1774–1776," *Collections* of the Connecticut Historical Society, vol. II (1870), and in Charles H. Isham, ed., *The Deane Papers* (*Collections* of the New-York Historical Society, vol. XIX–XXIII [New York, 1887–91]). But the Silas Deane Papers at the Connecticut Historical Society contain some unpublished material, including a lengthy manuscript history of the Revolution. At the same archive, the respective papers of Joseph Trumbull, Oliver Wolcott, Sr., William Samuel Johnson, and Jonathan Trumbull, Sr., were all useful. Much of the correspondence between Governor Trumbull and the Connecticut delegates is reprinted in *The Trumbull Papers* (*Collections* of the Massachusetts Historical Society, ser. 5, vols. IX–X, and ser. 7, vols. II–III [Boston, 1885–1902]).

For Rhode Island, a similarly valuable source is William R. Staples, *Rhode Island in the Continental Congress . . .* (Providence, 1870), which reprints the delegates' entire official correspondence. For New Hampshire, I read the Meshech Weare Papers at the Massachusetts Historical Society and a microfilm edition of the Josiah Bartlett Papers at the Dartmouth College Library. The latter collection has now been superseded by Frank Mevers, ed., The Papers of Josiah Bartlett, 1729–1795

(microfilm, Concord, N.H., 1976). The Sturgis Family Papers at Houghton Library, Harvard University, include a number of letters of William
Whipple.

Visitors to the old New York State Library at Albany who asked to
see the extant papers of George Clinton were brought folders of charred
documents, a distressing reminder of the fire of 1911. Fortunately, most
of his official correspondence as wartime governor of New York had
already been published in Hugh Hastings, *et al.*, *Public Papers of George
Clinton* . . . (New York and Albany, 1899–1914). All historians of Revolutionary and early national politics are familiar with Harold C. Syrett and
Jacob E. Cooke, eds., *The Papers of Alexander Hamilton* (New York,
1960–78), which has now reached an admirably prompt completion.
Henry P. Johnston, ed., *The Correspondence and Public Papers of John
Jay* (New York, 1890–93), is being supplanted by Richard B. Morris, ed.,
John Jay: The Making of a Revolutionary (New York, 1975–). As a
delegate, however, Jay was a very discreet correspondent; more informative sources for the ideas and politics of the New York delegation, often
the most cohesive in Congress, are to be found in the James Duane and
Robert R. Livingston Papers at the New-York Historical Society. Both
collections provide evidence of the pressures that forced reluctant moderates to commit themselves to sustained political activity. The Duane
Papers are an excellent source for the evolution of New York's boundary
policies, while the Livingston Papers have informative material on economic problems. At the same archive, the Alexander McDougall Papers
are valuable both for the course of events in New York before independence and later for relations between Congress and the army. For the
purposes of this study, the John Lamb Papers were disappointing. (All
of these collections are available on microfilm.) The Gouverneur Morris
Papers at Columbia University include revealing personal letters and
drafts of several essays evincing the keen interest in problems of finance
and supply that he shared with Hamilton and Robert Morris. The
Abraham Yates, Jr., Papers at the New York Public Library contain both
correspondence and polemical essays that trace the emergence of the
rather different views of a staunch defender of the Articles of Confederation.

The New-York Historical Society also holds the Papers of Joseph
Reed, a moderate who played a critical role in wartime politics as president of Pennsylvania. This position brought him into frequent political
contact (and sometimes conflict) with Congress, and many of Reed's
letters express sharp comments on its policies. Some of these have been
printed in William B. Reed, *Life and Correspondence of Joseph Reed*
(Philadelphia, 1847). Another candid commentator was William Livingston, the old whig, early member of Congress, and subsequently governor of New Jersey. I used the William Livingston Papers in the Massa-

chusetts Historical Society, other letters in the Henry Laurens Papers (described below), and the documents reprinted in *New Jersey Revolutionary Correspondence* (Newark, N.J., 1848), but the projected publication of a letterpress edition of his papers will be an important contribution to our knowledge of both state and national politics. Many of the logistical problems that troubled Reed and Livingston were, of course, also of critical concern to the army, as the publication of the later volumes of Richard K. Showman, *et al.*, eds., *The Papers of General Nathanael Greene* (Chapel Hill, N.C., 1976–), will certainly illustrate in detail.

The extant correspondence of John Dickinson and Charles Thomson, two major Revolutionary leaders in Pennsylvania, is disappointingly thin, but the R. R. Logan Collection and the John Dickinson Papers at the Historical Society of Pennsylvania contain several critical documents relating to the creation of a national government: Dickinson's original draft of the Articles of Confederation, an unpublished revision of the New Jersey plan of 1787, and several characteristically thoughtful letters from Thomson. Other Thomson material is available in "The Thomson Papers, 1765–1816," *Collections* of the New-York Historical Society, vol. XI (1878), and in the Charles Thomson Papers, Library of Congress. Far more imposing are the papers of Thomson's friend, Benjamin Franklin. The most recent volumes of Leonard W. Labaree, *et al.*, eds., *The Papers of Benjamin Franklin* (New Haven, 1959–), reprint important letters concerning resistance in the early 1770's, but only with the recent publication of volume XXI has this series reached the critical year of 1774. Together with the new editions of the papers of John Adams and John Jay, the completion of this project will provide a valuable supplement to Francis Wharton, ed., *Revolutionary Diplomatic Correspondence of the United States* (Washington, D.C., 1889), a dated, though still useful, collection. These three works will also make accessible the detailed analyses of American politics that these diplomats received from domestic correspondents in the 1780's. L. H. Butterfield, ed., *Letters of Benjamin Rush* (Princeton, 1951), contains a number of letters on national politics.

By temperament and profession, Robert Morris was not given to writing lengthy discussions of politics. Some revealing letters can nevertheless be found in various collections at the Historical Society of Pennsylvania and other archives. The microfilm edition of the Robert Morris Papers at the Library of Congress includes some personal correspondence as well as his official papers as superintendent of finance. Most of the latter will be published in E. James Ferguson, *et al.*, eds., *The Papers of Robert Morris, 1781–1784* (Pittsburgh, 1973–).

Thomas McKean, who represented Delaware in Congress during most of the period from 1774 to 1781, was one of the original Revolutionaries, but the McKean Papers at the Historical Society of Pennsylvania are disappointing. George H. Ryden, ed., *Letters to and from Caesar Rodney, 1756–1784* (Philadelphia, 1933), and William T. Read, *Life and Correspondence of George Read* (Philadelphia, 1870), are somewhat more useful.

Charles Carroll of Carrollton, the wealthy Maryland moderate, was a particularly sensitive observer of American politics, and his correspondence includes excellent comments on the coming of independence, the creation of new governments, the distressing developments of 1776–77, foreign policy, confederation, and finance. The substantial Carroll holdings at the Maryland Historical Society have been reproduced in Thomas O'Brien Hanley, ed., The Charles Carroll Papers (microfilm, Wilmington, Del., 1972).

Had James Madison never lived, the Constitution would probably not have been written; had he not been so sensitive to the needs of history, we might still be groping to make sense of the 1780's. The correspondence, memoranda, and notes of debates reprinted in William T. Hutchinson, William M. E. Rachal, and Robert Rutland, eds., *The Papers of James Madison* (Chicago, 1962–), are simply indispensable. They overshadow even that other monument to Revolutionary Virginia, Julian P. Boyd, ed., *The Papers of Thomas Jefferson* (Princeton, 1950–). Both collections reprint an extensive amount of correspondence concerning the deliberations of Congress. Robert Rutland, ed., *The Papers of George Mason, 1725–1792* (Chapel Hill, N.C., 1970), traces the progress of an élitist but locally oriented politician who became a major critic of Congress in the early 1780's and later a prominent anti-Federalist. Richard Henry Lee and Arthur Lee were two of the most influential early leaders of colonial resistance and, in the 1780's, two of the most committed opponents of additional powers for Congress. James C. Ballagh, ed., *The Letters of Richard Henry Lee* (New York, 1911–14), reprints most of his surviving letters; Richard H. Lee, *The Life of Arthur Lee, LL.D.* (Boston, 1829), is less reliable. Both works have to be used in conjunction with Paul P. Hoffman, ed., Lee Family Papers, 1742–1795 (microfilm, Charlottesville, Va., 1966), which is critical for the events leading to independence, factional disputes within Congress in the late 1770's, and the reverberations these conflicts continued to have into the 1780's.

The official correspondence of the North Carolina delegates and a large number of important private letters are reprinted in William L. Saunders, ed., *Colonial Records of North Carolina* (Raleigh, N.C., 1886–95), and in Walter Clark, ed., *State Records of North Carolina* (Winston, Goldsboro, and Raleigh, N.C., 1895–1906). Much of the material in the Thomas Burke Papers, Southern Historical Collection, University of North Carolina, can be found in this series, but the Burke Papers (which are available on microfilm) contain some fascinating personal letters that remain unprinted. Also useful for North Carolina is Don Higginbotham, ed., *The Papers of James Iredell* (Raleigh, N.C., 1976–).

Next to John Adams, Henry Laurens of South Carolina was perhaps the most prolific correspondent ever to sit in Congress. His letter books and loose papers are the single most important source for congressional politics in 1777 and 1778. Most of the extant Laurens papers are available in Philip Hamer, ed., The Papers of Henry Laurens in the South Carolina Historical Society (microfilm, Charleston, S.C., 1966). Despite his early participation in resistance, the surviving papers of Christopher Gadsden proved disappointing; but there are several important letters in Richard Walsh, ed., *The Writings of Christopher Gadsden, 1746–1805* (Columbia, S.C., 1966).

Finally, it would be appropriate to mention the major autograph collections that I used. The best of these is, of course, the massive Gratz Collection at the Historical Society of Pennsylvania. The same archive also has the Connaroe, Dreer, and Etting collections. The Fogg Collection at the Maine Historical Society and the Charles Roberts Collection at Haverford College are excellent. Less useful are the Frederick Dearborn Collection at Houghton Library, Harvard University, and the Emmet Collection at the New York Public Library.

Index

Continental Army (*cont.*)
313, 317–21; and French officers,
250; internal dissension in, 120–1,
142–3, 197, 245; problem of
supplying, 276–9, 291–2; staff
departments, 203–4, 209–11, 270;
see also Revolutionary War
Continental Congress: administrative
reforms, 195–6, 199–201, 203, 238,
282–4, 297, 300–1; attendance
problems, 168, 198–9, 216, 345,
355–7, 371; committee system,
194–6, 204–5; contrasted with state
assemblies, 220–4; as diplomatic
assembly, 385; as executive body,
175, 197, 383–5; factionalism in, 55,
76, 101–6, 169, 244–9, 266–9, 324;
idea of, 12–13, 15–16, 21–3;
inadequacy of powers, 279–81,
337–42, 344–8, 353–4; inefficiency
of, 198–205, 283–4; isolation,
127–32, 355, 399; as national
government, 184–5, 193–4;
pressures toward compromise in,
74–8, 117, 119–20, 243, 269–73,
285–7; and public opinion, 33–4,
38–40, 65–9, 71, 108–9, 112–13, 131,
335, 362–5; relations with state
and local authorities, 49–52, 65–9,
128–30, 164–7, 194–5, 211–15;
residence issue and problems, 111,
128, 163, 177, 199, 231, 233, 236,
334–7, 356–7; reputation of, 270–3,
372; roll calls, 248–9, 273; secrecy
of debates in, 71, 270–1, 355;
supervision of army, 130–1, 196–7,
203–4, 209–11; *see also* Articles of
Confederation; delegates; financial
policy; First Continental Congress;
foreign relations; independence;
reconciliation; resistance; supply;
taxation; western lands
Conway, Gen. Thomas, 197
Cooper, Samuel, 265

Cornell, Ezekiel, 315
Coxe, Tench, 396–7
Cushing, Thomas, 219, 267; and
resistance, 9, 11, 12, 69

Dana, Francis, 4, 347, 356
Dane, Nathan, 375
Deane, Silas, 195, 227; as agent and
commissioner to France, 94, 113,
115, 118, 249–50; career of, 219,
249–54; and confederation, 69, 137
and *n.*, 141–5; conflict with Lee
family, 250–4, 256, 259–64, 272;
keeps diary, 55, 60, 71–2; recalled
by Congress, 116–17, 246, 249–51;
and response to Coercive Acts, 23,
24, 26, 43
Deane, Simeon, 118, 251
Deane-Lee conflict, 250–4, 256,
259–64, 272
Declaration of Independence, 80–1,
89, 107–8, 179
Declaration of Rights, 58–9
Declaration on Taking Arms, 78
Declaratory Act, 4
Delaware, 140; and confederation,
188–9; and independence, 100;
loyalist activity in, 124, 165
delegates: attitudes toward office and
politics, 168–9, 216–17, 220–39,
247, 356–7; bachelors as, 356–7;
burdens of, 195–6, 199, 221–2;
financial difficulties, 235–7;
personal concerns, 125, 199,
229–31, 234–7; political
backgrounds, 224–5;
responsibilities, 64, 79, 106, 195;
sensitivity to matters of honor,
259–62; turnover of, 218–20, 247;
working habits, 201, 224
Dick, Samuel, 356

Trumbull, Joseph, 121, 245
Tudor, William, 91

Varnum, James Mitchell: on
  amending Articles, 289–94, 378;
  and impost, 313
Vergennes, Comte de, 115, 117, 265
Vermont, 156, 245–6, 286
Virginia, 219, 262; and Annapolis
  Convention, 368–9; calls for
  provincial committees of
  correspondence, 6, 12; and
  Constitutional Convention, 376–7;
  and impost, 316, 338; and
  independence, 95, 97–8; requests
  roll calls, 273; and resistance,
  24–5, 31, 33, 66–8; and western
  lands, 155–6, 159–61, 190, 283,
  285–7, 312, 352
Virginia Plan, 389, 393–5

Wadsworth, Jeremiah, 280
Walton, George, 130, 230
Ward, Samuel, 63, 69, 71, 224
Warren, Joseph, 45, 47
Washington, George, 6, 36, 338; as
  commander-in-chief of army, 78–9,
  111, 121, 197, 203, 218, 291; and
  Constitutional Convention, 140,
  376, 380, 396; nationalism of, 295;
  and Newburgh unrest, 318; on
  proceedings of Congress, 357–8;
  and supply problems, 211, 278–9
Weare, Meshech, 129–30
Webster, Pelatiah, 385

Wendell, John, 148
Wentworth, Gov. John, 66–7
West Indies, 32, 49–50, 345, 362
western lands, 155–7, 159–61, 164, 168,
  283, 285–7, 311–13, 339–40, 352–4;
  see also Articles of Confederation;
  Maryland; Virginia
Whipple, William, 127, 176, 236,
  260–1, 310
Williams, John, 234
Williams, William, 250
Willing, Thomas, 84, 335
Wilson, James, 195, 377, 380; on
  British empire, 34–5; and
  independence, 89–90, 103; and
  Pennsylvania constitution, 122,
  245; on powers of Congress and
  states, 165–7, 170–2, 183–4; on
  representation in Congress, 158;
  and revenue plan of 1783, 319–20,
  322, 324; on western claims of
  Virginia, 161
Witherspoon, John, 113, 230, 237; on
  apportionment of expenses, 179; on
  representation in Congress, 158, 161
Wolcott, Oliver, 95, 108, 150
Wood, Gordon, 110, 365, 384
Wyoming Valley, Pa., 142
Wythe, George, 91

Yates, Abraham, Jr., 310, 363;
  opposes additional powers for
  Congress, 338, 347
York, Pa., 116, 163, 177, 236
Yorktown, Va., 291
Young, James S., 217
Young, Thomas, 15

A Note About the Author

Jack N. Rakove was born in Chicago in 1947. He was graduated from Haverford College in 1968, after having also studied at the University of Edinburgh. In 1975 he received his Ph.D. in history from Harvard University, where the dissertation on which this book is based was awarded the Delancey K. Jay Prize. He teaches history at Colgate University, and lives in Hamilton, New York, with his wife, Helen Scharf Rakove, and their son Robert.

A Note on the Type

This book was set in Gael, a computer version of Caledonia, designed by W. A. Dwiggins. It belongs to the family of printing types called "modern face" by printers—a term used to mark the change in style of type letters that occurred in about 1800. Caledonia borders on the general design of Scotch Modern, but is more freely drawn than that letter.

Composed, printed, and bound by The Haddon Craftsmen, Inc., Scranton, Pennsylvania